Global Electronic Commerce

Global Electronic Commerce
Theory and Case Studies

J. Christopher Westland
Theodore H. K. Clark

The MIT Press
Cambridge, Massachusetts
London, England

This book was set in Times New Roman by Asco Typesetters, Hong Kong.

Printed and bound in the United States of America.

Library of Congress Cataloging-in-Publication Data

Westland, J. Christopher.
  Global electronic commerce : theory and case studies / J. Christopher Westland, Theodore H. K. Clark.
      p.   cm.
  Includes bibliographical references (p.   ) and index.
  ISBN 0-262-23205-7 (hc : alk. paper)
  1. Electronic commerce. I. Clark, Theodore H. K. II. Title.
HF5548.32.W47   1999
658.8′00285—dc21   99-38199
                                                    CIP

Contents

Preface   ix

1   **Introduction to Electronic Commerce**   1
The Foundations of Electronic Commerce   4
Electronic Commerce Infrastructure   6
Electronic Markets   6
Electronic Commerce Supporting Functions   7
Electronic Commerce Opportunities: Today and Tomorrow   7
Notes   8

2   **Information Technology in the Post-Industrial Revolution**   9
Digital Railroads   12
Channels and Intermediaries   15
Electronic Channels   22
Notes   24
Case Studies
Andersen Consulting: The Asia Intranet Opportunity, *Peter Lovelock and Theodore H. Clark*   27

3   **Redefining the Geography of Space, Time, and Money**   53
The Hard Middle   62
The Problem with Innovation   63
Jobs and the Internet   64
Recommended Reading   69
Notes   69
Case Studies
Financial Times Syndication Services: Making Money on the Web, *Peter Lovelock and Theodore H. Clark*   71
Security First Network Bank: The World's First Internet Bank, *http://www.sfnb.com, Theodore H. Clark and John J. Sviokla*   91
Global Electronics Manufacturing (HK) Ltd., *Theodore H. Clark and Alvin Chu*   121

4   **Supply Chain Management and Information Alliances**   141
Transforming the Value Chain Using Information Technology   141
Strategic IT and the Value Chain beyond the Firm   145
The Beer Game and the Value of Information   146
Benefits and Challenges of Sharing Information   151
Interorganizational Systems and BPR   152

Developing and Maintaining IOS Partnerships   153
Wholesale Electronic Commerce: IOS and the Internet   154
Notes   155
Case Studies
H. E. Butt Grocery Company: A Leader in ECR Implementation,
Theodore H. Clark, David C. Croson, James L. McKenney, and
Richard L. Nolan   157
Procter & Gamble: Improving Consumer Value through Process
Redesign, *Theodore H. Clark and James L. McKenney*   197

5   Telecommunications Infrastructure in Transition   221
Telecommunications Technology   221
Communications Media and Bandwidth   222
Telecommunications for Voice and Modems   223
ISDN and Packet-Switched Services   225
Synchronous and Asynchronous Transmission   228
Declining Costs of Digital Communications   228
The Rise of Computer Networks   229
The World Wide Web   232
Notes   233
Case Studies
China's Golden Projects: Reengineering the National Economy,
Peter Lovelock, Ben A. Petrazzini, Theodore H. Clark, and
John J. Sviokla   235
Philippines Telephone and Telegraph, *J. Christopher Westland*   259

6   Access to Electronic Commerce Services   273
The Roots of Electronic Commerce   273
The Internet   275
ISP Business Models   278
Notes   280
Case Studies
Asia Online: The Online Service for Asia, *Theodore H. Clark*   281
China Internet Corporation: http://www.China.Com, *Theodore H.*
Clark and John J. Sviokla   299
Hong Kong SuperNet, *Theodore H. Clark and Sarah Cook*   315

7   Electronic Auctions and Intermediaries   343
Market Models   344

Internet Auctions   353

Notes   353

Case Studies

Experiences with Electronic Auctions in the Dutch Flower Industry,
Eric van Heck and Pieter M. Ribbers   355

E*Trade Securities, Inc., *Rajiv Lal*   367

8   Electronic Financial Markets   385

Financial Markets: First Movers in Electronic Commerce   385

Basics   387

Matching and Price Discovery   389

Notes   396

Case Studies

On-Line Trading at the Shanghai Stock Exchange, *J. Christopher
Westland*   399

The Moscow Stock Exchange, *Martin Mendelson and J. Christopher
Westland*   417

Electronic Securities Trading at the Bolsa de Comercio de Santiago,
J. Christopher Westland   429

9   Digital Storefronts   445

Digital Storefronts on the Web   447

Search Engines   449

The Web as an Advertising and Marketing Channel   452

Internet Dynamics   460

Integration   462

Notes   462

10   Secure Digital Payments   465

The Origin and Development of Cash   465

Microtransactions   470

The Resurgence of Barter   474

Authentication of E-Commerce Payments   474

Identification of Individuals   477

Privacy   479

Controls   480

Encryption and Password Controls   484

Notes   490

Case Studies
Mondex Electronic Cash in Hong Kong, *J. Christopher Westland*   493
Access Security at McDonnell Douglas Aerospace Information
Services, *J. Christopher Westland*   515

11 Logistics and Service Opportunities and Issues   529
Competitive Advantage Using Logistics and Information Technology   531
Outsourced Logistics in the Supply Chain   533
Outsourced Logistics and Electronic Commerce for Physical Goods   534
Geographic Information Services and Logistics   535
The Internet and the Future of Logistics   535
Notes   536
Case Studies
Consolidated Freightways: The On-Board Computer Project,
Theodore H. Clark and James L. McKenney   537

12 Successful E-Commerce   557
Redefining the Marginal Cost/Marginal Revenue Equation   557
Turnkey E-Commerce and Site Management   558
Digital Storefronts   560
Another Network   562
From Hobby to Business   563
Information Retailers   564
Reintermediation: Travel Agents' Revenge   565
Where Multimedia Fails   566
Personalizing the Retail Cyberstore   566
Simple Auctions with Real-Time Price Quotes   567
Double-Auction Markets for Securities   568
Infrastructure   569
Design Assistance   569
Supply Chain Management   570
Consumer Durables   570
The Font of Future Wealth   571
Notes   572

Appendix   575
References   581
Index   587

Preface

There are already good books on the technical structure of the Internet and other network architectures. There have also been a large number of books giving advice on Internet retailing: the "how to make money on the Internet" genre of trade press publications.

We have, in contrast, tried to fill a niche where the offerings are not as rich: a text on the business models that make sense in a globally networked world. We assume that our audience has a basic familiarity with Internet technologies and has spent some time surfing the Web for retailing examples. We are interested in the myriad ways that the Web's capabilities can been made to support, alter, and expand the ways we do business—the business models that underlie commerce in the late 20th century.

We have sought, in writing this book, to synthesize current thought and practice into a comprehensive review of electronic commerce. Our choice of topics, in general, reflects the economic importance of specific electronic commerce implementations, vertical markets, and core competencies in the commercial sector. Chronicles of new technology, sentiments on evolution and growth of digital technology, and advice on how to make money on the Internet provide attractive copy and have sold well. We have resisted the allure of these topics, and instead have focused our attention on the revolution in industrial organization that e-commerce has made possible.

Material in the book is presented in twelve chapters, consistent with covering a chapter per week in a typical semester-long university class, with some flexibility provided for addressing a few topics in more depth or for supplementing the text with additional materials. The chapters also include case studies to illustrate e-commerce management issues and current practices.

For all of the promise and appeal of electronic commerce in revolutionizing the way we promote, conduct business, sell, and distribute, we still chose to release this material in the time-honored format popularized five centuries ago by Aldus Manutius: the printed text. Why? We are certainly not averse to new technology. However, digital media has yet to surpass the printed book in at least three ways. First, computer screens have only around 1% of the resolution of the printed page. Thus reading requires significantly more visual effort on a computer screen. Second, the quality of computer screens tends to be proportional to their power requirements. This requirement at least intermittently tethers them to an electrical source, which is a detriment to portability. Third, computer screens, with the exception of those of extremely light laptops, are considerably heavier and bulkier than books, a further deterrent to carrying reading material around.

Of more immediate concern to us, as authors, is that the technologies of digital production and distribution have greatly outpaced the legal and economic framework in which these technologies operate. Despite years of experimentation by several large publishing houses, it is not yet clear how to package digital textbooks properly. Publishers suspect (perhaps rightly so) that digital texts are even more prone to piracy than existing paper media. Contracts and revenue streams for book publishing assume that the information for which consumers pay is indelibly inked into paper. It is the paper that is counted in determining the sales volume, and thus the book revenue. There are many ad hoc ways of modulating quality of information in a book—selection of authors and limits on length, audience, and money. Yet publishers have not fully solved the problem of charging for the utility of the information rather than the quantity of the paper.

The greatest novelty of the Web is its worldwide traffic in information unbound to any particular medium—paper, CD, or magnetic. Frictionless, spontaneous, and almost limitless flow of information on the Web can be called upon to bolster arguments, flexibly demonstrate points, and expand on issues raised in the text. For authors, there are features in the Web's hypertext medium that we wish we could incorporate into our book: hyperlinking, interactive chat and paging, colorful graphics, sound and other multimedia objects, and so forth. We will be experimenting with new formats for presentation and distribution of material over the coming years as ways of extending the utility of our text.

For now, our ideas are indelibly bound to paper, but we have provided a partial compromise in this text by referring to cases in some of the chapters that are provided in electronic format on the Web. In addition, many Web references are provided throughout the text and cases to enable the reader to explore topics presented within the world of cyberspace as well as through the printed media.

No one particular medium can convey everything we would like to present in a classroom. We have presented the material in this book over the past several years in our classes, and have found that a mixture of modes—videos, Web displays, classroom discussion, software, and corporate visits—best supports discussion of the rich set of ideas presented in electronic commerce. The reader should experiment, and definitely take time out to explore the Web sites to which we refer in the text, and then move on to the hyperlinks to broaden their horizons.

With Thanks

Finally, and with gratitude, we state our customary acknowledgments for the physical realization of this book. What was once a loose amalgam of concepts, theories, and ideas jotted down on scraps of paper has finally come together in what we hope is an interesting and informative text that goes partway to covering one of the most exciting developments of this century. Who knows what lies ahead, but this will be a consideration for the millennium and subject of further research and perhaps publication.

In these days of specialization, not even a pair of authors can hope to cover all the subjects within the book. We extend our thanks to all of those who have written and co-authored the case studies that have enabled the subject to come alive with practical examples. We must also thank all of those who have given generously of their knowledge in specific areas, and in particular, the four anonymous reviewers of this work who helped us improve the final text.

We also want to express appreciation for funding provided by the Hong Kong Government Research Grant Council for research and development of the case studies.

Lastly, enormous thanks must be given to research assistants Sarah Cook and Dee Conway, who have nursed the project from its infancy to final fruition, with much effort and through many drafts.

1 Introduction to Electronic Commerce

What's my ROI on e-commerce? Are you crazy? This is Columbus in the New World. What was his ROI?
—Andy Grove, chairman of Intel

Over the past two decades, businesses in virtually every sector of the world economy have benefited from the technologies of *electronic commerce*. However, widespread interest in electronic commerce is relatively recent. Thus any definition of what is or is not included under the rubric of e-commerce is bound to be controversial and is still evolving. Nonetheless, we have posited the following definition as an organizing framework for our material in this text: "Electronic commerce—or e-commerce—is the automation of commercial transactions using computer and communications technologies."

By *commercial*, we refer to activities that seek to create arm's-length transactions between firms and individuals and involve the exchange of money, goods, or obligations. Therefore our definition of e-commerce purposely excludes interorganizational systems such as e-mail, telephone, fax, or Internet telephone, as well as internal computing accomplished by accounting, sales, inventory, treasury, personnel, or executive information systems.

Commercial transactions can transpire from business to business. Examples appear in electronic data interchange, auction markets, and distribution logistics systems. They can also occur from business to consumers. Examples appear in World Wide Web retailing and electronic stock brokerages. Electronic commerce tries to take advantage of economies in single-point keying to reduce errors and cycle time, a high degree of customizability of product or services to meet consumer desires, and customer interaction with databases at very low marginal cost.

Electronic commerce is not new, either in concept or in implementation. There have been many launchings of electronic commerce over the past two decades. Still, the rate of diffusion and acceptance—and subsequently the actual business conducted on electronic commerce platforms—has been uninspiring. In part, this resulted from the slow development of technologies that might make electronic commerce as attractive in practice as it is in concept. The most successful of more than 2,000 electronic commerce offerings provided in the two decades preceding the birth of the World Wide Web has arguably been France's videotext system Minitel, introduced more than 20 years ago. Most others have experienced only moderate success or suffered outright failure.

Public awareness of e-commerce has exploded since introduction of World Wide Web browser technology. The Web has bypassed physical networks of distributors, publishers, salespeople, and other market intermediaries, bringing products and services directly to the consumer. Web subscribers and servers continue to increase at phenomenal rates, dominating other Internet services in the process. The challenge of transmuting Web subscribers into revenue-generating customers has fueled the imaginations of Web entrepreneurs.

Developments in three essential domains have made possible the renewed viability of e-commerce. First, e-commerce platforms[1]—television, electronic kiosks, computer networks, and microcomputers—are now affordable, accessible, and user friendly. New electronic commerce platforms are emerging with mechanisms for electronic trading, retailing, advertising, and secure payment.

Second, networks of all sorts—electronic, social, producing, consuming, designing, financing, and legal—have reduced the need for modular offices on a nine-to-five schedule. Flexibility is mandated by a world of shrinking response times and accelerating operations. Global operations spread out over many time zones lend themselves poorly to success with a nine-to-five schedule. E-commerce frees producers to concentrate on their core competencies while globally outsourcing other production to those who can produce at the highest quality and lowest price.

Finally, firms are reengineering internal production and managerial functions around the possibilities of new information technology. This internal reengineering meshes well with the technologies of electronic commerce. Efficiencies gained internally from reengineering can be extended into the marketplace, to the competitive advantage of the firm.

To date, most transactions (and profits) in electronic commerce have not been in business-to-consumer retailing, but in business-to-business commerce. This is not surprising: It mimics the physical world, where business transactions outnumber consumer sales ten to one. Moreover, most business-to-business transactions are already done at a distance, by facsimile, mail, or electronic data interchange, and are easily translated to the electronic commerce realm. Business-to-business electronic commerce is expected to outpace e-commerce retailing by a significant factor for the foreseeable future.

Nearly all Fortune 500 firms have commercial Web sites, though less than 10% conduct transactions on the Web. Public relations, customer service, and technical support were the primary reasons for setting up the Web site in 70% of these firms, whereas marketing and sales were primary reasons in less than 30% of these firms.[2]

The success of Web-initiated commerce has obscured the substantial role played by older, more prosaic technologies of e-commerce, such as electronic data interchange and securities market matching systems. The Web is not necessarily best for reaching and serving customers: Strategy, products, service, speed, content, and price need to be considered first. Real success demands rethinking the roles and goals of business, and retooling to use the new technologies at hand.

Since it diminishes the economic consequences of geographical distance virtually to zero, the Internet has opened opportunities for global business on a scale that previously would have been impossible. Global e-commerce is changing the fabric of business. Jeff Bezos, founder of the highly successful Amazon.com Internet bookstore, observed:

There are quantitative changes so profound that they become qualitative. For example, e-mail is much the same as regular mail but faster. However, it is so much faster that it has the power to reshape companies, create communities, eliminate geography and revitalize the art of letter writing in a generation which had been thought to have been rendered incapable of it by television. That is a qualitative change. Now think of Internet electronic commerce as the e-mail equivalent of traditional commerce's surface post.[3]

Automation—in retailing, supply and distribution channels, and other parts of commerce—has been a major contributor of value in the world's leading economies. This contribution, though, has been uneven. Automation has bequeathed more to purely informational industries such as banking and information services than to raw materials such as oil and steel. Nonetheless, the contribution continues to accelerate with the advent of communications technologies like the World Wide Web and electronic data interchange.

For this reason, we address computer, network, and e-commerce technologies around the globe. The Internet has become so pervasive that it is no longer wise to ignore competitors or customers simply because they are not located in the United States or other physical locale. Our global perspective also allows us to investigate emerging markets, such as the financial markets in Moscow and Shanghai, or the emerging use of digital cash in Hong Kong. Emerging markets are often simpler and less tradition-bound than old and established markets, making it easier to isolate a particular effect, investigate a given innovation or to illustrate a point. Our perspective also emphasizes how much the Internet revolution is making our world a global village. Businesses can no longer afford to ignore competition from beyond their national borders.

Internet retailing is likely to play an expanding role in the future, though in ways that are dramatically different from the virtual malls that clutter the Internet today, which have largely been mediocre failures. Many consumers use the Internet to research their purchases, but buy in some other way, for example, at their local retail store. In 1997, only 3% of business-to-business Web sites were designed for direct sales, and only 9% of retail sites could process transactions on-line.[4] More than half of surveyed Internet users browse the Internet in reaching a purchase decision, but only 15% end up purchasing on-line.[5] Yet the latter is measured in computing Internet retailing statistics. Indeed, 75% of customers who shopped on the Internet in 1996 went on to purchase their goods or services through traditional channels,[6] mainly because the Internet site did not allow transaction processing to complete the sale. Thus initial uses of the Internet in retailing have concentrated on product information, and transaction processing has remained crude and unfriendly. Nonetheless, Internet retailing continues to grow 200% annually.[7] Online revenues for retailers in 1998 were in the range of $13 billion to $15 billion in North America alone. This understates the impact on markets that have aggressively adopted Internet technologies. The top 10 publicly traded online retailers—which account for 50% of online revenue—grew 160% in 1998 and revenue per order increased from $216 in 1997 to $629.[8] Online/traditional retailers—such as Dell Computer, Charles Schwab, Eddie Bauer, and lands' End—accounted for 59% of online revenues. Several other statistics capture the present state of Internet retailing (though this is to change over the next several years):

• 5% of unique visitors to sites ultimately become customers;

• 1.6% of visits result in purchases;

• Portal sites directly drive less than 30% of online retailing revenues;

• Computer goods, entertainment, travel, and discount brokerage sales account for more than 80% of the online retail market;

• Two-thirds of shoppers who get as far as putting items in a virtual shopping cart abandon the process before checking out.[9] Consider that just a couple of abandoned carts in a Wal-Mart store would be likely to unleash the wrath of management on their own cashiers. E-commerce retailing still has a way to go.

The Internet's impact on retailing goes beyond providing just another distribution channel. More subtle and important changes have been pioneered in the relationship between vendor and customer. For example, Priceline.com lets customers suggest the price at which they would like to purchase items such as airline seats, assuming that vendors would rather clear their inventory than fight for the producer's surplus.[10] Proliferation of auction sites such as *eBay*, and best-price search engines such as *Shopper.com*, accelerate this transfer of control to the customer.

The Foundations of Electronic Commerce

Interest in the potential for Internet-enabled electronic commerce grew rapidly after Microsoft's attempted acquisition of Intuit in 1995. E-commerce technologies have fostered an unprecedented range of innovations in business structure, allocation of wealth, and indeed of the fundamental definitions of commerce. Our next three chapters after this introduction—"Information Technology in the Post-Industrial Revolution" (chapter 2), "Redefining the Geography of Space, Time, and Money" (chapter 3), and "Supply Chain Management and Information Alliances" (chapter 4)—provide a historical perspective from which to view these innovations. We hope to provide our readers with an appreciation of the extent and profundity of the changes of e-commerce—and of its untapped potential—while they read this book.

We start by exploring the pathways through which business gets done. Marketing channels direct the *commerce* in electronic commerce. They are systems of independent organizations and technology that make products and services available to the consumer in a useful and accessible form. Three major types of electronic commerce channels are investigated in this book—business to consumer, business to business, and closed-group network channels.

Electronic channels change the basis of wealth: Innovation, communication, and information increasingly substitute for tangible products. In the world's developed economies, tangible goods account for roughly 20% of gross domestic product (GDP), down from more than 50% of GDP after World War II. This trend has accelerated rapidly under the influence of commerce channel automation.

A major part of our economic activity (the informational part) can now take place instantaneously over global networks. This has warped the fabric of business time and space in managing channel relationships with business partners and in reaching out to customers. The potential consequences of such global remapping were recognized nearly 40 years ago in the "small world" phenomenon identified by Manfred Kochen. Each new technology remaps our costs and distances between people and places. This in turn demands that business restructure activities to remain competitive: Channel tasks must be assigned to the best available technology. Because space and time are constrained resources, their restructuring significantly changes the costs incurred while doing business. Prudent choice of digital technologies can dramatically lower these costs by several orders of magnitude. To realize these cost savings requires a geographical restructuring of tasks, administrative structure, and corporate expertise around the technologies of electronic commerce.

Over the past three decades, management has continually evolved the electronic linkages between businesses that connect suppliers and customers within a single industry channel or supply chain. Within the apparel industry, for example, supply chain management was first known as quick response, and was viewed as a means for U.S. apparel manufacturers to gain a competitive advantage over lower-cost overseas manufacturers by competing on time rather than simply on cost. As quick response became important for U.S. retailers to reduce costs of stockouts or to avoid obsolete inventories, overseas producers were forced to adopt similar just-in-time supply processes to compete. Increased integration of point-of-sale information and fore-casting systems throughout the supply chain have enabled retailers and their suppliers simultaneously to reduce costs and improve service levels globally. These supply chain management innovations have changed the course of manufacturing, distribu-tion, and retailing in Europe, Japan, and Australia, and throughout Asia. Supply chain management and electronic data interchange (EDI) technologies were the predecessors of Internet-based e-commerce. Updated implementations of these sys-tems on the Internet currently generate more than ten times the revenue of retail sites.

Electronic Commerce Infrastructure

The next two chapters, "Telecommunications Infrastructure in Transition" (chapter 5) and "Access to Electronic Commerce Services" (chapter 6), examine the industries that predicate the Internet's successful application to electronic commerce. The availability of a cheap, reliable, and fast Internet has moved industry toward a com-mon gateway into world markets. The Internet provides the infrastructure for the World Wide Web; the Internet, in turn, runs on various wide area networks (WANs), with the majority of bandwidth provided by global telecommunications networks. The technologies of voice and data telephony provide the essential foundation for understanding the networks that make global electronic commerce possible. Internet service providers (ISPs) offer companies one-stop shopping, value-added networking specific to Internet channels, and access to the global markets that the Internet can offer.

Electronic Markets

At the center of commerce is the market. In one way or another, markets have been automating since Thomas Edison developed a reliable stock ticker more than 100 years ago. Much of the automation centered on order processing and matching in financial markets. More recently, industries have successfully automated their par-ticular product markets through electronic auctions on proprietary networks or on the Internet. These developments are addressed in our chapters on electronic markets "Electronic Auctions and Intermediaries" (chapter 7), "Electronic Financial Mar-kets" (chapter 8), and "Digital Storefronts" (chapter 9). These chapters attempt to dispel the notion that automation will eliminate channel intermediaries as electronic commerce enables manufacturers to sell products directly to consumers. In fact, electronic commerce will expand the role of intermediaries and allow new services and more efficient intermediaries to emerge.

The automation of continuous-double-auction securities markets has accelerated since the worldwide stock market crash of 1987. Our chapter on financial market automation surveys issues and technologies required to implement an electronic market cost-effectively, using appropriate technologies, to reach the widest cross section of buyers and sellers. The chapter discusses the trade-offs between policy (e.g., fairness and transparency) and the technology offerings that make a market attractive.

The ninth chapter of this text covers the most visible aspect of electronic commerce: digital retailing. Success in retailing used to require location, location, location. However, the Internet has eroded the importance of location and made distance less of a deterrent to customer satisfaction. Our digital storefronts chapter considers what the death of distance means for retailing. The effective and ineffective implementation of traditional retailing methods as well as search and discovery in digital retailing are explored in light of some of the Web's more significant successes.

Electronic Commerce Supporting Functions

After markets have matched a buyer with a seller and helped them to negotiate a price, payment must be made, and the product or service must be delivered. These activities are the topics of our chapters 10, "Secure Digital Payments," and 11, "Logistics and Service Opportunities and Issues." Our review of payment technologies details widely used payment systems. It also discusses the decision making involved in ensuring transaction security and privacy. It indentifies where centrally administered authorization schemes and cryptography can be used effectively and where decentralized systems may offer advantages to traditional centralized market systems.

Delivery consumes 10% of GDP in developed economies and is a critical component of electronic commerce transactions. When aftermarket service is included, this figure is estimated to be as much as 20% of total GDP. The role of electronic commerce in redefining logistics and service is an important factor to consider when evaluating ways that new processes and systems can be used to improve customer satisfaction, reduce costs, and increase control.

Electronic Commerce Opportunities: Today and Tomorrow

The final chapter, "Successful E-Commerce" (chapter 12), surveys examples of businesses that have assembled the various technologies of electronic commerce into winning formulas. This concluding chapter provides an upbeat send-off for current and future entrepreneurs interested in making e-commerce technology work in their own enterprises.

Notes

1. The term *platform* refers to a combination of hardware, software, and networks that provides the environment for a particular computing application.

2. Forrester Research, 1997. Reported in Survey on Electronic Commerce, *Economist*, May 10, 1997, p. 4.

3. Reported in Survey on Electronic Commerce, *Economist*, May 10, 1997, p. 6.

4. Forrester Research, 1997, reported in Survey on Electronic Commerce, *Economist*, May 10, 1997, p. 4.

5. CommerceNet/Nielsen, March 1997, reported in Survey on Electronic Commerce, p. 4. *Economist*, May 10, 1997.

6. Survey on Electronic Commerce, *Economist*, May 10, 1997, p. 4.

7. J. Borzo, *Web Sales Grow 200 Percent Annually* (1999), quoting "The State of Online Retailing," a study by The Boston Consulting Group conducted for Shop.org, at URL: www.thestandard.com

8. J. Sanchez-Klein, *Zona Sees Online Shopping Up 191 Percent* (1999), at URL: www.thestandard.com

9. Forrester Research, 1997. Reported in Survey on Electronic Commerce, *Economist*, May 10, 1997.

10. Producer's surplus accrues to the producer, and is traditionally measured as the area above the product supply curve and below the price. The concept derives from Ricardo's concept of economic rents. When pricing is purposely made dynamic—as is the intent with Priceline.com's system—producer/vendors lose the surplus, while the customer benefits.

2 Information Technology in the Post-Industrial Revolution

Electronic commerce technologies are a subset of a growing portfolio of information technologies that together have ushered in what has been called the *post-industrial revolution*. It is post-industrial in the sense that our economic foundations, business practices, and measures of wealth are less concerned with workers sweating in the factory and have accepted knowledge and intellect as the crucial factors of production. Information technology has reduced the cost of purchasing, helped manage supplier relationships, streamlined logistics and inventory, and reached out to new and existing customers more effectively. Increased consumer choice, greater convenience, and the ability to customize are driving revenue growth in a fashion not considered possible two decades ago.

The Internet has been a major driver of new commerce, but so have been proprietary networks offering banking, securities trading, electronic data interchange, intelligence monitoring, and more. Though less visible than the Internet, these technologies at present account for a much greater portion of global revenue and growth. Statistics underline the extent to which the knowledge-based post-industrial revolution has already advanced. The information technology (IT) sector contributed 28% (making adjustments for price and performance) of the United States' real GDP growth between 1996 and 1997; it contributed a similar amount in other developed economies.

The most dramatic IT growth has been seen in communications technologies—especially the packet switching technologies of the Internet. Fewer than 40 million people around the world were connected to the Internet during 1996. By the end of 1997, more than 400 million people were using the Internet,[1] and the number of Internet domain names had more than doubled from 630,000 to 1.5 million. During that period, traffic on the Internet doubled every 100 days.[2] In the same period, businesses that successfully used the Web for marketing proliferated. By the end of 1997, Cisco Systems' Internet sales were running at a $3.2 billion annual rate. In 1997, Amazon.com, the Internet bookstore, sold $148 million worth of books. One of the nation's largest book retailers, Barnes & Noble, launched its own on-line bookstore in 1997 to defend itself against Amazon.com's juggernaut. In January 1997, Dell Computers was selling less than $1 million of computers per day on the Internet. The company reported reaching daily sales of $6 million several times during the December 1997 holiday period. Auto-by-Tel, an automotive auction on the Web, processed a total of 345,000 purchase requests for autos through its Web site in 1996, for $1.8 billion in auto sales. At the end of 1997, it was generating $500 million a month in auto sales ($6 billion annualized) and processed more than 100,000 purchase requests each month. And the list goes on and on of the many examples of electronic commerce successes.

In 1996, 7.4 million people worked in the United States in IT industries and in IT-related occupations across the country. They earned close to $46,000 per year, compared to an average of $28,000 for the private sector. In a decade, the collective stock market capitalization of five major companies contributing most to the technologies underpinning electronic commerce—Microsoft, Intel, Compaq, Dell, and Cisco—has grown to more than $588 billion in 1997 from less than $12 billion in 1987, close to a fiftyfold increase in the space of a decade.

Our perspective, from the midst of the post-industrial revolution, is a deceptive one for predicting its future path. The technologies of the 18th-century industrial revolution—the steam engine, invented in 1712 and electricity, harnessed in 1831—predated their cost-effective use by close to half a century. Though businessmen recognized their potential, substantial amounts of infrastructure needed to be developed to put them to work.

Harnessing the power of steam meant less labor was needed for manual work; it also meant that factories could locate anywhere, not just in geographical areas with firewood, strong winds, and water resources. However, systems of pulleys and belts needed to be arranged first to transmit this power around the factory.

Because it required a network to contain and transmit its power, electricity had to wait 50 years before the first power station was built in 1882. It took another 50 years before electricity powered 80% of factories and households across the United States. There was considerable experimentation with standards. Thomas Edison developed direct current systems of generators and motors, but high line losses required that generators not be more than two miles away from the lights and motors that used the power. Fires were common. George Westinghouse developed 133 cycle per second alternating current generators, transformers, and transmission systems that could transmit power over unlimited distances—but had no motors for their use. He engaged Nicola Tesla to design a motor suitable for factory use. Tesla perversely chose to design a motor that operated at 60 cycles, which Westinghouse's engineers were unable to modify to work at his equipment's standard of 133 cycles. So the generators and transformers were changed to 60 cycles, which is our standard today.

Early uses of electricity tended to substitute motors directly for steam engines. Factory power still came from line shafts and belt drives. Not until factories, after 1900, began to replace belts and pulleys with copper power lines and small electric motors did fundamental changes in production occur. Factory structures were streamlined, and key processes, such as materials handling and manufacturing flows, were built directly around small, powerful, portable electric motors.

The post-industrial, IT revolution that has made e-commerce possible is similarly constrained by inefficient infrastructure, incomplete understanding of the use and potential of technologies, and evolving standards. It is all evolving much faster than did the use of steam or electricity, however. In 1946, the world's first programmable computer, the Electronic Numerical Integrator and Computer (ENIAC), stood 10 feet tall, stretched 150 feet wide, cost millions of dollars, and could execute up to 5,000 operations per second at a cost only the military could afford. Twenty-five years later, in 1971, Intel packed 12 times ENIAC's processing power into a space of 12 millimeters for $200. Microcomputers in the late 1990s perform in excess of 1 billion instructions per second with components only a few atoms thick.

As late as 1980, telephone conversations traveled over copper wires that carried less than one page of information per second. Internet usage at that time consisted mainly of messages that were simple text and that did not require large amounts of bandwidth (bandwidth is the speed at which data can flow through computer and communications systems without interference). Bandwidth requirements have increased as people have begun to send images, sound, software, video, and voice over the Internet. Late-20th-century optical fiber can transmit in a single second the equivalent of more than 90,000 volumes of an encyclopedia, and arrays of satellites in low orbit bring high-bandwidth communications to every corner of the planet.

The Internet is the glue that binds together the computing power on desks, in factories, and in offices with a high-speed, fault-tolerant, packet switching, global telecommunications infrastructure. More than 400 million people around the earth, most of whom had never heard of the Internet four years ago, now use it to research products and prices, make requests for bids to suppliers, and order goods. The Internet's pace of adoption eclipses that of all other technologies that preceded it. Radio was in existence 38 years before 50 million people tuned in; TV took 13 years to reach that benchmark. Sixteen years after the first PC kit came out, 50 million people were using one. Once it was opened to the general public, the Internet crossed that line in less than five years.

The growth of IT in the U.S. economy has been uneven and marked by spurts of activity as technology advanced in one or another part of the infrastructure. IT investment, as a percentage of GDP, grew from 4.9% of the economy in 1985 to 6.1% by 1991 with the proliferation of graphical Macintosh-like interfaces when Wintel machines (Intel chips and Windows operating system) began to penetrate homes and offices. The next spurt was in 1993, with the burst of commercial activity driven by commercialization of the Internet. From 1993 to 1998, the IT share of the U.S. economy rose from 6.4% to 8.2%. With such rapid expansion, IT's share of total nominal GDP growth has been running almost double its share of the economy, at close to 15%. In the 1960s, business spending on IT equipment represented only 3% of total business equipment investment. In 1996, IT's share rose to 45%.

Rapid technological advance has accelerated these spurts. Computing power has been doubling every 18 months for the past 30 years, while the average price of a transistor has fallen by six orders of magnitude. No other manufactured item has decreased in cost so far, so fast. It is estimated that without the contribution of the IT sector, U.S. inflation, which was 2.0%, would have been 3.1% in 1997. Thus, in real terms, the expansion of the IT sector accounts for an even larger share of overall economic growth.

This is only the beginning of the revolution, and the full extent to which new technologies will impel us can only be conjectured. Still, by looking at developments and applications in electronic commerce over the past decade, we can surmise how the "invisible hand" will select and how electronic commerce technologies will evolve and thrive over the coming decades. We address this challenge of learning from the immediate past in the subsequent chapters.

Digital Railroads

The economic impact of the knowledge-ward paradigm shift is not unlike that of the paradigm shift in the agricultural economy at the end of the 19th century. The relevant "network" technology in those days was offered by the railroads. Railroads accounted for almost 15% of U.S. GDP at the end of the 19th century—similar to the share of IT at the end of this century. With railroads, farmers were no longer tethered to the farmers' markets of their local village. They began growing large surpluses of grains for distribution throughout the United States. Railroads had made distance irrelevant (or perhaps less relevant). Universal access was important, especially to farmers: The state of Iowa enacted legislation that required railroads to provide service to within six miles (one day's buggy ride) of any farm in the state. Trustbusters worried about unhealthy synergies among network industries—such as electricity, oil pipelines, telephone, and telegraph—which could benefit from the railroads' long, uninterrupted rights-of-way. The Texas Railroad Commissioner grew to be one of that state's power brokers when oil was discovered at Spindletop at the turn of the century: He controlled the flow of oil along the pipelines that followed the rails.

We face many of the same issues and challenges today. New information technology remaps the "distances" between people and places. Remapping demands restructuring for survival. Global reach presents promises or challenges depending on your perspective: It demands a real restructuring of the geography of space and time associated with business tasks. This restructuring of space and time changes the cost structure of business and industry, tearing down barriers to entry in some venues, erecting them in others.

Electronic commerce can span national boundaries at the speed of light, making many traditional distribution and retailing channels redundant. Purely information products can thrive in a placeless marketplace that we call a *marketspace*—one that is nowhere yet everywhere, one that can eliminate barriers to entry, allowing individuals to compete alongside global giants, creating new opportunities for distribution, growth and profit. In the short run, the tremendous uncertainties yet to be faced in standards development, technological evolution, and redistribution of wealth promise to keep business turbulent. This will provide opportunities for nimble competitors, and offer new perils for those lacking imagination.

In e-commerce's new competitive order, the scarce resource is customer attention: Businesses are competing for "eyeballs." The consumables that provide business revenue are increasingly knowledge based: They are intangible, can be shared by many without diminishing their value, and can increase in value when potential customers are excluded from using them. As intangible information products have substituted for tangible products, production of tangible goods has dropped to about 20% of developed economies' GDP, down from more than 50% of GDP in the 1950s.

The shift away from wealth creation through production of tangible goods to wealth creation by information processing has increased the volatility of the environment in which business operates. This volatility appears in at least four business dimensions —*social, political, technical,* and *economic.* Over the next two decades, the technologies available for e-commerce will dictate a significant evolution of social, political, and economic policy. Global markets can defy existing ways of regulating business and place power in the hands of customers, producers, and distributors. They also tend to redefine our concept of what constitutes *value,* moving it away from tangible possessions such as gold, and toward knowledge-based assets. If this seems difficult to believe, just compare the market performance of gold, which dropped 15% in real value during the period, to the stock market capitalizations of five major companies that dominate the U.S. IT sector—Microsoft, Intel, Compaq, Dell, and Cisco— which have seen a fifty-fold increase in the space of a decade.

These new markets will create unique opportunities for businessmen with an understanding of the technologies and a global mind-set. These businessmen will dominate the world's economy in the 21st century.

Increased competition and technological change require rapid adaptation. Information technology is in demand today, because without it business cannot react rapidly to new information about competitors and its environment. Because of technology, foreign exchange, telecommunications, consumer electronics, and everything else are moving at an accelerated pace. Electronic markets put producers directly in

touch with their consumers, changing and eliminating intermediate jobs in the process. They can accurately price products and match buyer and seller, avoiding the
whims of complex market mechanics.

Information technology is rapidly evolving to support many functions in marketing channels. This restructuring of channel functions has greatly benefited the consumer. Customers are offered more efficient channels and a richer mix of products
and services because of these new technologies. The computer has grown to great
importance in the United States and other developed economies. Computing equipment used for gathering, processing, and transmitting information in total accounts
for 12% of U.S. capital stock, exactly the same as the railways at their peak in the
late 19th century[3] when they were boosting America's economy significantly. Computer networks have become the late-20th-century counterpart to railroads in the
industrial revolution.

Web-based electronic commerce still commands less than one-third of 1% of the
US$60 billion direct mail order market, with which it is most often compared.
Nonetheless, the trends are compelling, even if credible forecasts of growth are hard
to obtain. Some experts estimate that revenue generated from Web-based e-commerce
will grow to around US$7 billion by the year 2000,[4] which is slightly more than 1%
of the approximately US$600 billion of goods and services purchased annually in the
United States. (A similar figure applies to the combined economies of Japan and the
European Community.) Still, this is only a fraction of the US$5.8 trillion spent
overall in America for all transactions, wholesale and retail. Mentis Corp. projects
that the size of the electronic commerce market in 2000 will still be slightly less than
1% of total transactions in the U.S. economy (though potentially greater than 50% of
transactions involving purely software or database sales). Regardless of the exact size
projected, all forecasts of future electronic commerce transactions project rapidly
increasing sales for at least the next decade, with the size of the market eventually
reaching 10% or more of retail sales by the year 2010.

The Web has provided opportunities for clever entrepreneurs to advertise in existing
markets with new perspectives. The most common Web advertisements are banners
across the top of commercial Web sites. Advertisers' pay is based on the number of
"impressions" an ad gets, that is, how many people see the ad (regardless of whether
they click on it). Some sites charge as much as US$120 per thousand "impressions";
others can demand only $6 for the same number. More than 900 companies com-
peted for nearly $300 million in Web ad revenues in 1996. Most of the revenue is
concentrated in a few hands: The ten largest Web publishers accounted for two-thirds
of the ad money spent last year. The importance of Web advertising and the shuffle

for niche players to be effective have generated new services. One such service is a Nielsen-like ratings system used to gauge television watching (and determine ad revenues). Another is targeted advertising that tracks who you are and what you like, enabling an advertiser to follow up with targeted ads.

Allowing customers the option of electronic payments completes electronic sales through a variety of technologies, with Web technologies playing an expanding role. The U.S. Treasury contends that it will save more than $100 million a year in processing and postage costs when it enforces the requirement that all federal payments, except tax refunds, be electronic starting in 1999. Currently 65% of U.S. social security and 56% of all Treasury payments are electronic. It costs from $3 to $6 to collect a single payment, regardless of the amount of the payment. Payment collected by electronic funds transfer costs an average of $.20 and delivers the money without mail delay.[5] This is encouraging a worldwide electronic banking market that has 5 million subscribers, and around 1.1 million transactions in 1996 were conducted via Internet and telephones. By year 2000, 16% of U.S. homes are expected to conduct banking electronically.[6] Electronic payments are being considered across a variety of public services: for tracking documents, ordering and paying for copies of documents and collecting filing fees, collecting taxes and fees, ordering licenses and paying fines, and collecting payments for water and sewer bills. These services are extending to the private sector, especially in health care.

Channels and Intermediaries

Marketing and supply channels coordinate the succession of functions required to bring a product from the factory to the customer. Where a service is being sold, the channel controls contracting and settlement. At least eight generic functions must succeed for a channel to work, regardless of who, or what, is performing that function: *physical possession, ownership, promotion, negotiation, provision of market information, financing, payment,* and *risk bearing.*

Physical possession of inventory in a warehouse or on consignment is required at one or more points in the channel. How much of this inventory is stockpiled depends on the cycle times required to produce, replenish, distribute, and sell a particular product. The warehousing and distribution management functions are dedicated to transferring physical possession between channel members, and finally off to the consumer.

Ownership is distinct from physical possession in that it is a legal concept. Ownership is a contentious issue in the information age. Laws have more or less focused on ownership of real and tangible properties. Intellectual assets have only recently received the attention they deserve. Without a clear judgment on ownership, sales involving the products of intellectual activity are difficult. Unit sales of pirated software and videos, for example, are estimated to be double that of legitimate sales. Because there is a significant price differential between pirated and legitimate copies of intellectual property (e.g., a video that sells for US$30 may sell at a tenth of that price on the black market), it is difficult for legitimate channels to maintain any sort of competitive advantage. Where ownership of property is ambiguous, legitimate channels may be able to maximize their revenues by dealing with pirates. For example, a British textbook publisher found that, for a variety of reasons, it was impossible for it to publish legitimately in Turkey's market. Yet pirates were able to obtain Xeroxed copies of nearly any British text on short notice, including the publisher's own. Publishers typically distribute textbooks at marginal cost in many developing economies to thwart pirates. In the case of Turkey, this publisher simply agreed not to prosecute the pirates in turn for the pirates' maintaining the quality of their copies. The pirates essentially acted as local printers. The pirates made a profit; the publisher found the pirates to be faster and more efficient than their legitimate channels in that area; and the publisher's texts maintained a presence in the Turkish market, which opened up future opportunities for expansion in the market.

Particularly where items are large and unique, specific channel intermediaries have arisen to facilitate ownership and title transfer of goods. For very unique transactions, this may require the services of a skilled lawyer. For less unique products, say houses, title transfer has been routinized and made considerably less expensive.

Promotion of a product often demands specific talents, in addition to a wide range of customer contacts. The use of the World Wide Web for electronic commerce has spawned high-tech cottage industry of graphic artists, multimedia and communications experts, and advertising types to construct on-line Web home pages that project the producer's corporate image, promote the producer's products, and provide feedback on customer needs.

Negotiation is required for many big-ticket products, where price, options, customization, and aftermarket service can be tailored to the needs of each individual customer. Automobile and home purchases are the most prominent examples of products in which negotiation is the central function in the channel.

The ordering function has seen the most dramatic applications of information technology over the past two decades. Electronic data interchange, electronic commerce, World Wide Web order forms, telephone direct orders, and numerous other applications of computer and communications technology now make it possible to place orders conveniently with costs savings passed on to consumers.

Market information is essential for production planning, and minimizing stockouts and other forms of risk that channel members must bear. Though existing applications in electronic commerce are only beginning to realize the potential for accumulation of market information, this has been an important application for computers over the past two decades. For example, Wal-Mart has dedicated a worldwide telecommunications network and powerful Teradata supercomputers to provide itself and its vendors statistical synopses of demand patterns on a near-real-time basis.

Financing is also required for expensive products and is likely to be a significant factor in negotiation. Automobile and home purchases demand specialized financing. Sales of less expensive products, especially impulse sales, may be facilitated through routine transactions financed with credit cards. Credit cards make the transfer of funds straightforward. They can also smooth the individual's cash inflow from income with the cash outflow from purchases.

Payment must be collected if producers and channel intermediaries are to stay in business. Payment presents an increasing problem as developed economies move away from cash transactions. Credit and debit cards have greatly facilitated this move and have standardized and routinized transaction payments. Unfortunately, the safety of their use on open networks such as the Internet is still suspect. A considerable portion of the expense passed on to consumers and producers using credit cards for payment is needed to cover criminal abuse of credit cards. It may be difficult to protect against this abuse because of restrictions on consumer credit monitoring.

Risk bearing and insurance are important where products have a long production cycle (e.g., houses), where investment in inventories is significant (e.g., jewelry), or where significant responsibilities are incurred through warranties and for aftermarket servicing. Sales contracts typically state who bears the risk for performance of a product. This influences both price and marketability. For example, an automobile sold "as is" is worth less than one sold with a three-year, 50,000 mile warranty.

Marketing channels emerge as a part of the natural evolution of hierarchies and markets in an industry. Though producers may provide many of the channel functions required to stimulate and satisfy demand for their goods and services, economies of scale and access to multiple competing products may make some channel functions better suited to outside third parties. Channel intermediaries provide value by *intermediating* between buyers and sellers. They can lower the costs of transactions and make most goods and services cheaper.[7] They may consolidate particular channel operations from a variety of producers, thus achieving economies of scale (figure 2.1). For example, few magazines actually distribute their own products or handle their own subscription services: These services are provided by one or two large

More valuable than gold

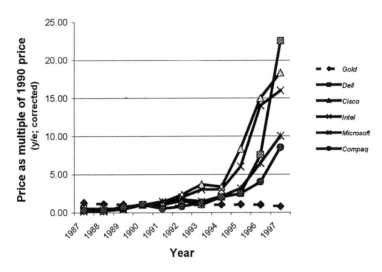

Figure 2.1
Capital appreciation in information technology

subscription processors. Consider the alternatives of magazines providing their own subscription services versus outsourcing them (figure 2.2).

It is easy to see how, as the number of producers and consumers increases, the efficiencies provided by channel service intermediaries increase. Theoretically, a single intermediary can generate the greatest efficiencies, but this carries with it the risk of monopoly control of an industry channel, with incumbent monopoly profits.

Contact lines do not tell the entire story, since different contacts require different levels of service and incur different costs. Yet at any level of support, the number of contacts required by direct channels climbs significantly faster than that required with intermediaries. Without other benefits of channel intermediaries, it might still be difficult to justify engaging their services.

Channel intermediaries smooth the flow of goods and services, helping the producer to better plan and control production, by creating possession, place, and time utilities. They do this by representing a large number of producers supplying complementary goods and services. Four benefits are realized by working through intermediaries: *breaking bulk, creating assortments, reutilization of transactions*, and *efficient search*.

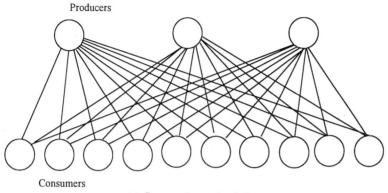

Producers

Consumers

30 Contact Lines for Subscriptions

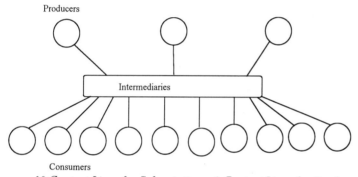

Producers

Intermediaries

Consumers

10 Contact Lines for Subscriptions; 3 Contact Lines for Producer-Service

Figure 2.2
Efficiencies from outsourced channel functions for magazine circulation

Breaking Bulk

The typical producer produces a large quantity of a limited assortment of goods; the typical consumer requires a certain quantity of a wide variety of goods. By representing a large number of both producers and consumers, an intermediary can smooth the differences in demand and supply.

Channel intermediaries break up the large quantities manufacturers produce into the smaller quantities demanded by breaking bulk. In the context of the TurboTax example broached previously, this process might begin with Intuit's factory selling a portion of its output to wholesaling and direct-mail firms such as PCWarehouse and PCConnection. Wholesalers, in turn, sell to individual stores, such as Egghead

Software. Bulk quantities are successively broken into smaller quantities throughout the channel.

Creating Assortments

In the end, the retail store selling TurboTax is likely to display it in its "Business Software" section, next to Intuit's own Quicken, Tobais's Managing Your Money, and other software. Consumers are given the freedom to choose the software that meets their specific demands. They may also be inspired to purchase complementary products that help them use TurboTax. This latter process of building up a group of products used or purchased in association with each other creates assortments.

"One size fits all" is used today only with some irony. There was a time when manufacturers had more control over their market. They used this control to establish product lines that allowed them long production runs, producing simple products that ostensibly met a broad range of consumer demands. Over the past 20 years, targeting specific customer needs has become particularly important in maintaining competitive position. Because each consumer engages in a slightly different set of business and leisure activities, a viable product typically addresses only a small subset of all the activities in which a consumer may engage—or else it risks being over-engineered and overpriced. Completely meeting the needs of consumers involves offering them a complementary set of products that can be tailored to their individual needs. Creating assortments at the retail level results in greater ability to satisfy consumer demand and encourage consumers to buy products on impulse.

Making Transactions Routine

In the days of a barter economy, exchange required at least an adequate knowledge of all products that passed through a consumer's hands. (This is still true in exchanges such as swap meets and flea markets today.) The evolution of markets has steadily eased the burden on the consumer under the presumption that consumers will buy more if the transaction is easier. Standardization of goods and services, agreement on delivery, method, and timing of payment, terms of exchange, and so forth all make it easier to conduct business. Making transactions routine is one of the major undertakings of channel management.

Intuit's TurboTax, for example, is sold on-line using a standard order form that appears on a World Wide Web page. A similar paper order form is used if one is buying Intuit's TurboTax through the mail. Payments are obtained through the same credit card procedure that customers can use to purchase thousands of other goods and services.

EDI is seldom used by individual customers but has become standard for institutional order fulfillment. Here, transactions can be routinized to the point of eliminating humans from the processing loop, effectively eliminating the labor costs associated with placing the orders. Orders for replenishment of stock are automatically made whenever stock drops below a "trigger" level. American Hospital Supply Corporation (AHSC) pioneered electronic data interchange in the medical arena with its ASAP system,[8] which originally used teletype technology to allow pharmacies and hospitals to order stock automatically. Transaction efficiencies with ASAP were improved to such a point that AHSC attained a significant competitive advantage over its competitors and a dominant position in the lucrative hospital supply industry. Rapid advancements in computer and communications technology, with the introduction of attractive, multimedia computer interfaces, have made EDI a pivotal technology in the implementation of electronic commerce channels.

Search Efficiencies

Consumers realize a significant advantage in searching for the right product to fulfill their particular needs from the channel intermediary's representation of several producers. Similarly, producers realize an advantage in searching for customers through a channel intermediary in addition to increased and more manageable demand. Channel intermediaries can provide producers with valuable feedback on customer needs that allows the producers to focus on products that target the market and production that is less subject to seasonal and regional swings in demand.

Wal-Mart provides one of the great retailing success stories of the last decade, one made possible through search efficiencies enabled by computer and communications technology. Wal-Mart has made a science of analyzing regional, product, and time-dependent sales patterns to better predict future sales patterns. Detailed sales register data is collected and funneled through a worldwide telecommunications network to powerful Teradata supercomputers on a near real-time basis. These data are subjected to powerful statistical manipulation to ascertain demand patterns that are then used to negotiate prices and order quantities from producers. The resulting market demand information is made available to producers, providing them essentially one-stop shopping for customer information. In exchange, Wal-Mart demands lower prices, and deliveries that allow them the best-managed inventories in the retail business. Some producers, such as Procter & Gamble, retain contingents near Wal-Mart's headquarters in Bentonville, Arkansas, to take advantage of this channel information to fine tune their production and better meet consumer needs.

Electronic Channels

The *commerce* in electronic commerce is provided by its own particular variety of marketing channel. The attraction of e-commerce on the Internet is the Internet's fast, accessible, widely used, and inexpensive network. If the Internet can be made to perform a useful set of channel functions, then it can potentially absorb the jobs of existing providers of those services. Global electronic commerce systems, such as those offered through the Internet, hold the potential to stimulate enormous demand and dramatically increase access.

There is current debate on the potential for global marketing on the Internet and other electronic channels eventually to relegate the channel intermediary—the middleman—to history. *Disintermediation* is the term used to describe the withering away of market intermediaries as producers use new technology to contact their customers directly.

The disintermediation of channels, it is argued, is a straightforward consequence of placing the customer directly in contact with the producer. Yet this oversimplifies the real situation. The consumer-producer relationship is complex, information intensive, and not necessarily anything that customers want to manage directly. Indeed, some intermediaries may see producers or other intermediaries usurp their jobs. However, new technology is unlikely to make a channel function disappear entirely. Rather, these functions will move forward or backward up and down the channel. Information provision and market making alone will provide many new jobs for intermediaries in a networked world. Several examples of new intermediary functions are presented in the minicases in chapter 12 (see especially "Reintermediation: Travel Agents' Revenge"). In the remainder of this section, we address specific activities that need intermediary attention even in e-commerce.

The two main services intermediaries provide—providing information and distributing goods and services—will not dissipate with electronic commerce. More likely they will expand in importance as transaction and information volume increase.

In contrast, the jobs held by the intermediaries are very likely to change. Computers can perform some skills more cheaply, better, or more quickly; new skills that previously were not valuable suddenly have value. The potential for information overload in a networked world has created a host of new channel intermediary jobs. Consider two examples of how electronic channel intermediaries can provide value to both the customer and the producer.

Travel agents intermediate between the airlines and their customers. Travel agents break bulk—for example, they can buy a block of seats or an entire airplane at bulk rates, and sell them to individuals as part of a tour. In doing so, they take on an insurance function by bearing the risk of not selling all of the seats. Because they are closer to their customers than the airlines, they have more opportunities to manage that risk. Travel agents can also create assortments—they can allow consumers to customize the hotel, car hire, and air travel components of a package to fit their own needs.

At the turn of the century, Marshall Field, the Chicago retailer, promoted the concept of retail stores as "product museums" for products that the customer insisted on inspecting personally. Products would be elaborately displayed, with the display tied to a marketing concept. Distribution still needed to be physical, and inventories of goods had to be maintained in the store. Today, informational goods such as videos, music, database searches, and magazines can theoretically be delivered through the network itself, limiting the need for on-site or mail order inventories to be kept. Even where tangible goods are sold, inventories can be consolidated at one side and the network used for order entry from a well-managed central stock.

The functions that a channel performs are largely fixed, but the institutions that perform these functions are not. In an age in which technology is rapidly and widely supplanting the traditional factors of production and distribution, competition is reshaping marketing channels at an accelerating rate. The technologies of electronic commerce have had a truly profound impact on channel structure. Electronic commerce

1. eliminates intermediary institutions by substitution or consolidation using computer and communications technology;

2. does not generally eliminate the intermediary function;

3. either automates or shifts intermediary functions forward or backward up and down the supply and marketing chains.

Electronic channels are not always justifiable. Automation of a marketing channel may have no positive effect, and perhaps even may have a negative impact on profits and operations. Many products simply are not suited for an electronic commerce channel. To better understand the way in which electronic commerce channels improve the utility of a product, consider Intuit's popular tax software TurboTax. The software production facilities of Intuit produce a U.S. federal income tax module, as well as a number of state income tax modules. These software modules must be maintained and updated continually; the majority of production costs are incurred in getting the first copy onto an internal disk inside Intuit. Intuit places this software on a floppy disk and puts it in a box with associated documentation.

The retail channel takes boxes out of the warehouse (the warehousing function) when an order is received; accounting records are created and logged (the order processing and financing functions); the firm ships a certain number of these boxes to retail stores (distribution function) where they are sold (retailing function). This channel satisfies a customer who wants to browse through a retail store, try out the software, and wants, on deciding to purchase, to walk out with the product. Retail stores are likely to stock the state tax software only for the state in which the store is located. The value-added resale channel sells site licenses and does not necessarily require that a box be shipped for every order. It satisfies customers who may be performing tax preparation as a service business, and who need several copies of the software for their operations. Customers of this channel are likely to purchase a complete set of state tax modules.

The majority of Intuit's boxes are sold through mail order. A direct sales channel responds to telephone calls from consumers who are likely to have responded to advertising (the promotional function) and who pay through credit cards (the financing function) that are processed by the sponsoring bank. This channels satisfies customers who know what they want and want to order it with minimal fuss. An electronic mail channel exists on the Internet, managed by a third party, that processes orders entered on-line through a form on Intuit's World Wide Web pages and similarly obtains financing through credit card processing. This channel satisfies a customer similar to that of the direct sales channel. The channel potentially has a greater (global) reach but may not grant as great a penetration in given markets, because more individuals have voice telephones than have computers.

Each channel provides TurboTax in a form that the consumers find desirable: the correct combination of federal and state tax modules, with or without a box. Each channel provides the product when consumers want it in a place accessible to them: immediately in their local store in the case of retail consumers, or after a short mail delay for direct-mail customers. Payment and packaging arrangements make it easy for individuals to possess the package.

Notes

1. NUA Internet Surveys estimate that there were 23–33 million Internet users in the United States in 1996, representing 83% of all Internet users. Using that calculation, 28–40 million people around the world were using the Internet in 1996. By the end of 1997, NUA estimates that 101 million people worldwide were using the Internet (see http://www.nua.ie/surveys).

2. Inktomi Corporation White Paper, 1997. Paper cites data from UUNET, one of the largest Internet backbone providers. Traffic is measured as the total amount of information going across the network (see http://www.inktomi.com/Tech/EconOfLargeScaleCache.html).

3. Productivity: Lost in Cyberspace, *Economist*, September 13, 1997, p. 80.

4. Estimated by Forrester Research for IBM Corporation, September 1996. The Internet Advertising Bureau has found that ad revenues from e-commerce have more than doubled annually since 1995.

5. U.S. Federal Reserve, 1996.

6. Lazard Frères, *Electronic Commerce Services Changing*, 1996.

7. Unfortunately, middlemen receive a great deal of unfair criticism due largely to questions about whether they are adding value or merely extracting tolls along the channel. Such animosity has deep historical roots. In medieval Europe, Aristotle's *Politics*—the standard economics text of the day—contended that "... the amount of household property which suffices for the good life is not unlimited ... there is a fixed bound." A "just price" for a commodity was fixed not by supply and demand, but by what the seller *ought* to ask. This led to widespread medieval proscription of moneylending and other intermediary functions. This moral antipathy toward intermediaries lingers on today.

8. *American Hospital Supply Corp.: The ASAP System* (A), Harvard Business School Case #9-186-005, HBS Publishing, Boston, 1986.

Andersen Consulting: The Asia Intranet Opportunity

The goal of network architecture is to have access to voice, data and images, in any combination, anywhere, at any time—and with convenience and economy.
—John Mayo, President, Bell Laboratories

Development of internal networks and networks with suppliers and vendors is strategically much more important in Asia.
—Brian Wilson, Partner, Andersen Consulting

The phrases "intracorporate networking" and "enterprise networking" first entered into common usage in the late 1980s, when corporations began to link together formerly independent and disparate local area networks (LANs). These terms enabled firms to differentiate the resulting corporate-wide network from the individual LANs of which it was formerly composed.[1] Since that early period, a considerable evolution has taken place within the intracorporate network. The former host-centric computing paradigm has been replaced by a "distributed processing" paradigm, epitomized most powerfully in the transition to client-server architecture. A key facet of this new paradigm was the need for "any-any" connectivity within the corporate network linked with increased public networking.[2]

This transition and the growth of intracorporate networks needed to be seen within the context of competitive corporate strategies. While large companies continued to make extensive use of the public telecommunications system worldwide, the strategic advantages to be gained from a firm's own intracorporate communications network were becoming increasingly appreciated. These included—most obviously—lower costs, security, and network compatibility (both hardware and software). As a result, large companies increasingly perceived their internal communications network as a central component of their competitive advantage; they had invested large sums to make the infrastructure as up-to-date as possible and to extend the geographical reach of their network.[3] Thus, through the late 1980s and 1990s, information technology consulting firms who had been able to design, implement and integrate intracorporate communications networks ("intranets") were seen to play a profound role in the global business market, and had experienced phenomenal growth.

Andersen Consulting's (Andersen) growth into Asia through the early 1990s highlighted not only the strategic importance of an integrated intracorporate communications network, but also the difficulties that existed in integrating communications within the region itself. While the demand for information, infrastructure, and services was increasing exponentially across Asia as the respective economies continued

This case was prepared by Peter Lovelock of Hong Kong University and Dr. Theodore H. Clark of The Hong Kong University of Science and Technology.

to grow, the telecommunications networks (and experience with these networks) had remained extremely basic until the mid-1990s. As a result, Andersen was able to utilize their experience with networking their own Asian operations and integrate this into their global system to provide Asian clients with the innovative solutions necessary within the emerging Asian communications market(s).

Company and Industry Background

Andersen Consulting provided management and technology consulting services and specialized in systems integration work and business (and process) reengineering. Indeed, Andersen led the world in systems integration. Its approach in assisting other companies to set up internal communications networks was focused on implementation, since "companies do not want management consultants who simply study a problem and write up a report, leaving the clients to turn theory into practical reality." In helping improve a client's business performance, Andersen would often present a series of intranet options, implement the preferred choice, and encourage optimal exploitation of the network itself. Andersen's emphasis was therefore on execution, not merely analysis; and on education, not simply consultation.

Run as a global, decentralized partnership with no central headquarters, Andersen Consulting was formed in 1989 when the consulting operation became a separate business unit within Andersen Worldwide. For all intents and purposes the two entities "operated as separate, autonomous organizations." However, from a network perspective, the two organizations operated off the same platform, that is, the Andersen Network, or ANet. While this did not compromise either organization's financial integrity in any way, it raised a series of interesting networking issues for Andersen.

It was a significant business advantage, particularly in the early days, to have a corporate communications network the size of ANet to utilize. However, an existing corporate network often raises as many problems as it solves if it is not integrated into the company's work practices and business objectives. As an example, when Andersen Consulting was formed it employed some 18,000 people. By 1996, this was approaching 45,000 people. In other words, Andersen had more than doubled in size in six years to become, quite easily, the largest of the major global consulting groups. (The industry newsletter *Management Consultant International* ranked Andersen as the world's largest consulting firm in 1995.)

All firms need to develop their own corporate culture. This was particularly so for a firm which employs a common methodology and an "intuitive" approach to work practices. Furthermore, Andersen viewed its competitive advantage as being able to "leverage its collective knowledge through replication and/or new application of knowledge." To create the required knowledge, it was essential to be able to tap into its own expertise, wherever that may reside at any given time within the company and across the world, and therefore demonstrate to clients that the group had the necessary experience and skills to tackle their problems effectively and uniquely. Thus, Andersen's strength relied on being able to bring together its own people to deal with the problem.

However, as with many large multinationals, its very size was both its strength and challenge, requiring phenomenal coordination. Thus, the organization as a whole needed to be able to respond to requests and then to quickly identify individuals with the required skills. It also needed to be able to access its own resources and database knowledge rapidly and efficiently. A further objective of Andersen's "timeliness in delivering solutions" and "dramatically shortened development time" was the ability to present clients with a précis of "best practices." Again, this required immediate access to information and knowledge.

When Andersen Consulting became a separate business unit from Arthur Andersen (AA), it became apparent that Andersen's corporate network and information objectives were substantially different from those of parent company. As a result, Andersen led the development of the communications network evolution which has subsequently taken place. In 1989, the backbone network was a Wang-based Office Automation (OA) infrastructure linking LAN servers. Communications were limited to personal contacts, telephone, videoconferencing, overnight mail, voice mail, and facsimile. Knowledge exchange was limited to in-house presentations, organized seminars, printed materials, and word of mouth.

While such a corporate communications infrastructure was not ideal, it remained fairly effective in the United States and other well-established markets such as Europe and Australia, where the communications infrastructure was good. (In the United States, the firm had a T1 connection running down the middle of the country.) However, as Andersen began to expand its global presence, areas such as Asia raised a whole new set of response-time and support problems. Clearly the provision of communications services in Asia represented a great economic opportunity for Andersen. Asia was Andersen's fastest growing region through the early 1990s and communications services was their fastest growing industry sector (table 2.1).[4] However, Andersen's ability to communicate between Asian locations using the existing networks was severely constrained.

The challenge and ultimate ambition for Andersen was to incorporate this region into their global system so that they could reach the market faster than their competitors. In some cases, this meant aiming for real-time communications access, and in Asia this posed a new set of challenges.

Table 2.1
Andersen Consulting revenue and growth by region and industry

Worldwide revenue by region, 1990–95 ($US millions)

	1995	Growth	1994	Growth	1993	Growth	1992	Growth	1991	Growth	1990
Americas	2,835	23%	1,941	23%	1,574	14%	1,383	13%	1,226	6%	1,153
EMEAI*	1,420	20%	1,181	13%	1,043	–8%	1,131	19%	950	23%	770
Asia	419	27%	330	27%	259	24%	209	27%	165	23%	134
Total	4,224	22%	3,452	20%	2,876	6%	2,723	16%	2,341	14%	2,057

Industry revenue, 1991–1995 ($US millions)

	1995	Growth	1994	Growth	1993	Growth	1992	Growth	1991	Growth
Financial services	1,125	16%	974	36%	715	6%	672	14%	590	18%
Products	1,702	23%	1,380	14%	1,212	8%	1,123	14%	986	12%
Government	396	17%	339	12%	303	5%	288	2%	281	6%
Health care	125	29%	97	18%	82	6%	77	10%	70	11%
Comms	573	57%	364	52%	239	24%	192	41%	136	39%
Utilities	282	25%	225	–3%	232	–11%	261	41%	185	7%
Others	21	–71%	73	–2%	93	–15%	110	18%	93	–8%
Total	4,224	22%	3,452	20%	2,876	6%	2,723	16%	2,341	14%

Communications industry group growth by region, 1991–95 (percent annual growth rate from prior year)

	1991	1992	1993	1994	1995
Asia	250	57	32	72	58
Americas	14	39	20	41	121
EMEAI	63	38	50	107	43
Total	39	41	24	52	57

Source: Andersen Consulting.
* EMEAI = Europe/Middle East/Africa/India.

The Asian Business Communications Market

Through the late 1980s and the early 1990s, the Asia-Pacific economic boom resulted in the increased presence of multinational corporations (MNCs) located across Asia. It also resulted in the emergence and proliferation of Asian MNCs who began to rapidly expand their operations across the region. Factors that encourageding the emergence of these regionally based MNCs included the following: the rapid rise of intra-Asian trade; growing levels of intra-Asian foreign investment; high levels of capital accumulation in Asian countries; and the rapid technical advance of the leading Asian firms. One of the key issues for emerging Asian MNCs as they expanded beyond their home base was to achieve effective communication within the corporation. This was perceived as a daunting challenge in the region where, until very recently, even the most basic of telecommunications services—let alone data services—had been very difficult to come by. In many places (e.g., Vietnam), this was still the case.

There existed, therefore, two multinational corporate markets. The first was the global MNCs who were establishing Asian operations to capitalize on the opportunities apparent in the dynamic Asian market; and the second was the emerging presence of Asian companies who were expanding their base of operations into neighboring markets. The regional MNC market was distinct from (but not divorced from) the global MNCs entering the region. A major weakness for many of the local or regionally based firms was that they were coming from highly protected national markets and were often ill-prepared to compete with the internationally competitive MNCs. Quite specifically, there was a dramatic lack of expertise throughout the region in building and managing the corporate networks required for multinational operations. Building individual local area networks (LANs) and linking these together within the confines of a single campus was difficult enough. Creating a seamless corporate-wide intranetwork that covered the region—or perhaps even reached acrosss the globe—was altogether another proposition. An additional factor which complicated the issue was the need to manage diverse (voice, LAN, and legacy) types of traffic from an ever increasing number of regional and branch offices.[5]

However, it was still predominantly local traffic which drove the data communications revolution in Asia through the mid-1990s. By the mid-1990s, the growth in LAN-related traffic in the region was enormous. Simultaneously, the increase in deployed LAN technologies and the demand for greater bandwidth began to further complicate the picture (figure 2.3). Then, in the mid-1990s, an increasing emphasis on LAN-based distributed computing, plus the sudden and dramatic growth of Internet connections, produced a rapid demand for regional corporate internetworking and

Asia Pacific Datacoms Market Growth*

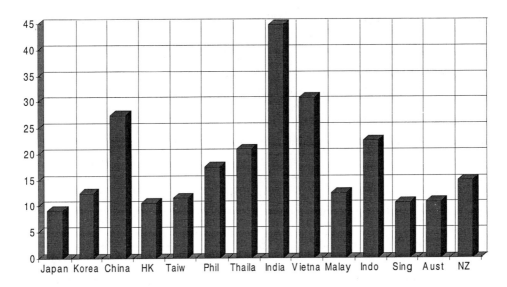

Source: East Consulting   * average percent annual growth 1994-1997

Figure 2.3
Projected annual growth in demand for data communications services, 1994–97
Source: East Consulting.

intranetworking (table 2.2). This then meant that the many offices all employing discrete local area networks subsequently and urgently required interconnection.

Andersen Consulting's Asian Networking

To the best of our knowledge, Andersen Consulting is the first business to succeed in building a global internetworked Lotus Notes environment to manage its information resources.
—Andersen Consulting Communications Industry Group

The Physical Network

By mid-1996, the "Andersen Internet" (or "Intranet") linked 95 percent of Andersen offices worldwide, connecting some 44,000 employees of which some 9,800 were based in the Asia-Pacific region (including Australia and New Zealand). Also known

Table 2.2
Asia Pacific Internet and LAN penetration, 1995

Country	Domain	Hosts	Percentage of installed PCs connected to LANs	Percentage of installed LANs connected to LANs
Australia	.au	207,426	64.4	60.2
Japan	.jp	159,776	23.5	22.4
Korea	.kr	23,791	32.9	20.6
New Zealand	.nz	43,863	44.9	54.8
Taiwan	.tw	16,166	46	28.6
Singapore	.sg	8,208	54.8	22.9
Thailand	.th	2,481	24.1	18.2
Malaysia	.my	1,087	32.8	19.5
China	.cn	1,023	13	10.7
India	.id	848	9.1	7.9
Indonesia	.in	645	20.7	10.4
Philippines	.ph	365	27.1	17

Sources: East Consulting; Mark Lotter's distribution estimates (http://www.ftp.nw.com/).

as the ANet, the Andersen Worldwide organization's infrastructure network system was predominantly a frame relay network built off a Lotus Notes platform. This hybrid Notes system had two distinct, but related, functions: first as a mail facility; and second as Andersen's proprietary Knowledge Exchange system. With the dramatic growth of intracorporate communications within and of the group itself during the early 1990s, a move was made to separate the network servers into mail servers and database servers. (In some cases the two may be in different physical locations.) While the mail and database server functions were not mutually exclusive, neither were they fully integrated.

The physical network was arranged in a hierarchy which mirrored the organizational structure of the group. This was different from the logical network, which was "hypertext," i.e., structured and emulated the matrix structure of the group's work practices. There were three distinct backbone hubs, i.e., Chicago, Sofia, and Singapore, which accordingly represented the Americas, EMEAI (Europe) and Asia.[6] Singapore was chosen as the Asian backbone hub because (1) it was "positioned nicely in the middle of Asia-Pacific"; (2) it enjoyed a "very mature infrastructure" which was highly reliable; and (3) it was cost-competitive. Initially, the Asia-Pacific backbone was distributed between Singapore, Tokyo, and Manila, but in early 1996 this was rationalized into the one central hub.

Figure 2.4 shows the basics of the ANet and Notes "network," and regions and/or countries who also had their own LANs/WANs connecting offices. The Asia Pacific network structure is demonstrated in figure 2.5, with the LAN/WAN topology for the Greater China region shown in figure 2.6. China only began introducing frame relay on a commercial basis in 1995–96. Prior to this, Andersen had connected their China offices to Hong Kong by way of a dial-up arrangement. A similar situation existed for Andersen's Bangkok office, with simple dial-in connections providing access to the ANet global network. While this meant that these "outer" offices were not on real-time access, they were connected to the worldwide network through the nearest node, which allowed interaction and the downloading of relevant information. This met with Andersen's minimum requirements of access to the Knowledge Exchange, which allowed the group to mobilize resources in these competitive emerging communications markets and "move to market" within a very short space of time. It did not, however, provide for knowledge or data replication (see below). The Beijing and Shanghai offices were connected to the Andersen network through Hong Kong.

The Notes databases worked on "both way" replication. Thus, if a change was performed to a document on a database located in Hong Kong which was a regional or area or global database, these changes were then replicated to the highest server in the ANet which would in turn then replicate those changes down the order. This was a key feature of the Notes system, which other products such as Microsoft Exchange had been unable to effect. Distinct from the database servers, the mail servers also facilitated Andersen's "resource libraries." The resource libraries held specific information, usually by industry, which could be ordered through an on-line "mail order" system. This reduced the amount of information being replicated that incurred low hits.

Changes to the mail and database servers could also be preserved locally from distributed PCs. With the vast majority of worldwide offices connected to the network by 1996, the next phase of Andersen Consulting's corporate communications network push concentrated on connecting remote users. This was done through "dial-in" or virtual LAN connections, depending on client location, length of project engagement, and number of personnel, etc. Bearing in mind the strategic importance of the network infrastructure, this organic concept of the network (it grew and shrank as employees moved from client to client, rather than being a static construct) represented a fundamental feature of the new orientation. Extending the reach of the network in this manner extended the logical network without necessarily extending the physical network. The challenge in implementing this subsequent phase was primarily a security issue, i.e., the building of secure "fire walls."

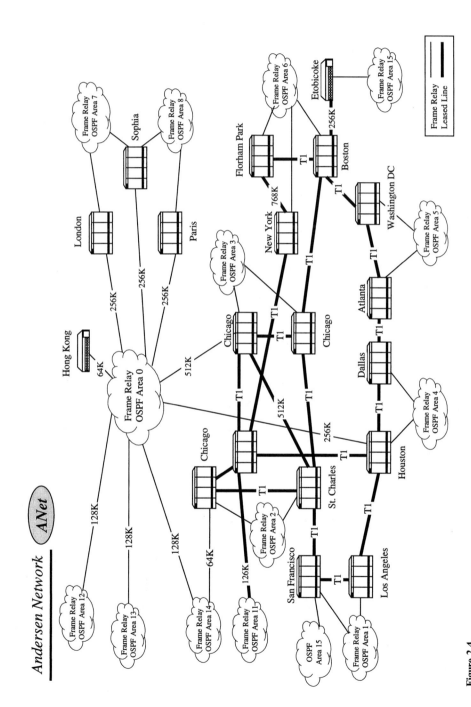

Figure 2.4
Andersen Consulting's "Anet" physical network topology and connections

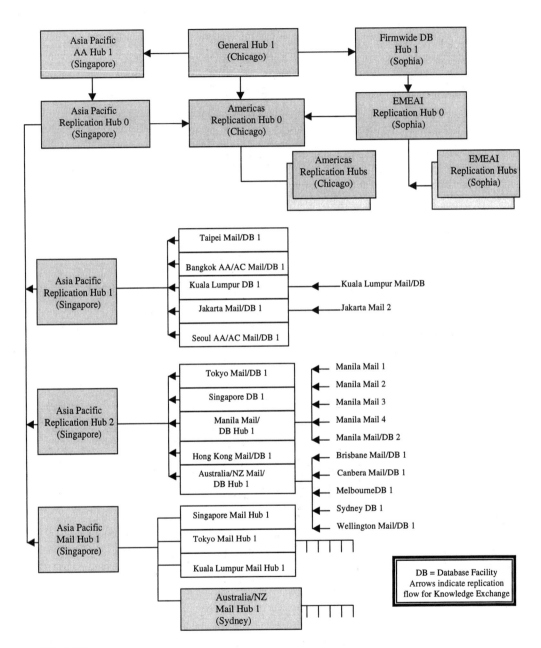

Figure 2.5
Asia-Pacific network structure and links with the global Andersen network

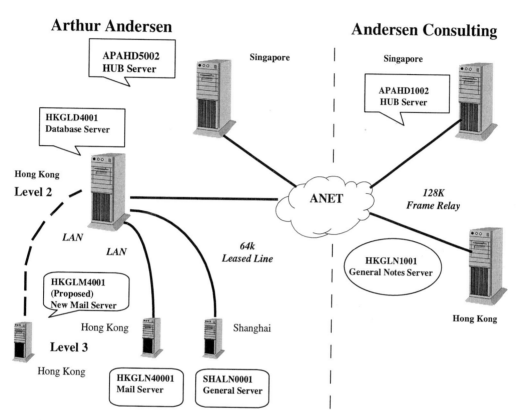

Figure 2.6
Andersen's Asia-Pacific Lotus Notes topology

The Logical Network

In the past we have concentrated on getting the basic infrastructure out there, and providing interconnectivity to all locations. We are certainly becoming more dependent on it as we and our clients become more global. It has reduced our time to market and improved quality.
—Graham Richards, Director of Information Technology, Asia Pacific

At its most basic level, the corporate system architecture provided a global communications infrastructure for the firm. It connected consultants on engagement sites with personnel in the firm's offices; it linkeds partners, managers, and staff. Less tangibly, it fostered a sense of community that was difficult to achieve in a widely dispersed organization. At the forefront of the firm's networking projects was the development and installation of the groupware link-up termed the "Knowledge Exchange." Run on the company's internal physical network, ANet, the Knowledge Exchange was an electronic platform designed to concentrate, disseminate and then replicate the firm's global information resources (figure 2.4).

The Knowledge Exchange was composed of several types of databases (figure 2.7). The majority of the firm's most valuable information (most "hits") was located in one of two types of databases, i.e., the reference databases and discussion databases. (While less commonly used, other types of databases included "tracking," "directory," "external," and "template" databases.) The objective was for the Knowledge Exchange to create a shared repository of Andersen's best industry practices (industry visions, best practices, and best process models), methods (the firm's integrated "methodology" or "building blocks," work objects, job aids, and other tools) and leading-edge technology information. It was is also set up to allow users to search external news feeds and industry analyses, and to identify consultants with particular skills. This minimized reinvention, while still allowing efficient but custom-crafted solutions, and hence the continual creation of "the firm's knowledge base."

This approach proved to be particularly applicable in Asia where both companies and the countries themselves had started from a very low technology infrastructural base and had then made rapid advances. Thus, while they may have had very little experience in communications management or in the technology itself and therefore often looked for outside advice and guidance, in many cases they also wanted to "leapfrog" intermediate technologies by applying innovative applications of advanced systems and services, such as corporate intranets and high-speed servers.

For Andersen themselves, the improved intracorporate communications network allowed a far greater degree of flexibility and appeared to improve their responsiveness and ability to innovate. It certainly resulted in an exponential growth in intraregional communications. Initially there was some doubt within the firm as to the speed of take up of the Knowledge Exchange system across Asia. As the group employed a majority of locals across a range of Asian countries that encompassed a diversity of languages, there was a fear that the predominantly English-language-based, and Western-experienced, Knowledge Exchange databases would deter Asian access. In fact, Andersen's experience was seen to be the opposite of this. With some exceptions, demand for the services was generally higher across the Asian economies where there was a need to use the firm's communications network to tap into resources from the information-rich Western countries.

As the firm grew in Asia, new offices were opened. In 1992, Andersen based 1,300 people in 9 offices around Asia. By 1996, this had grown to 19 offices with 4,300 people. In the start-up phase of a new office, MNCs tried to keep costs down as

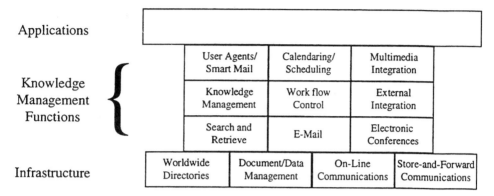

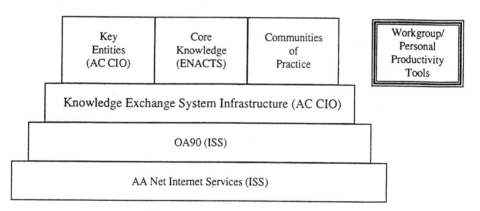

Figure 2.7
The Knowledge Exchange Model and technical architecture
Source: Andersen Consulting.

returns were minimal and essentially the office served as a coordinating point for emerging market possibilities. With little or no constant revenue generation from the new market, the MNC usually wanted to simply rent telephone and facsimile lines and perhaps network the office PCs. This was the choice open to Andersen when they opened their Taipei office in 1994. With an eye on expenses and with no dedicated communications, the firm's Taiwanese representatives attempted to minimize international calls and data requests. Reacting to the minimal communications that other Asian offices were receiving from the Taipei office, Andersen partners decided to forego an official assessment of the cost benefits of upgrading the firm's communications network in Taiwan and installed a country server, which integrated the local LAN into the firmwide resources. Anecdotal evidence suggested that intrafirm communications increased exponentially (individuals changed from saving all of their correspondence until the end of the day so they could reply with one fax, to responding to requests as they were received). As a result of this increased communication, time to market improved along with market success.

In addition to the basic communications benefits, information access also aided Andersen's market performance. In fact, easy access to information represented a fundamental cornerstone of the Andersen value proposition to clients. In tendering for a large telecommunications consultancy in Hong Kong, Andersen representatives were asked to put forward a research design for identifying similar work being carried out elsewhere. By utilizing their Knowledge Exchange database, Andersen consultants were able to extract a list and summary of industry "best practices" within 24 hours. This was of great surprise to the client, who had been struggling to design an appropriate research prospectus with their own incumbent advisors for the previous three weeks. Similarly, in tendering a bid for a new telecommunications operator in a developing country in Asia, Andersen representatives were able to include a list of industry "best practices" in the presentation. With little telecommunications expertise resident in Andersen's local office (at that time), they were able to locate and bring in the requisite experience and skills for the life of the operation (see below).

Providing Asian Intranet Services for Clients

Prior to the early 1990s, transborder private networks in Asia were a luxury. But with transport costs tumbling and data traffic to and within the region growing at 40% or more annually, developing a regional network system had emerged as a business necessity in the 1990s. Effective intracorporate communication was increasingly perceived as essential for the strategic operation of MNCs. The ability to effectively use information at an international level provided MNCs with a major advantage over national firms. This advantage for MNCs had become important in Asia during the 1990s, not only for Western multinationals, but also for their Asian counterparts. Since intra-Asian trade was growing faster than trade with the West, the competitive advantage to be gained from employing intranets had spread to the emerging Asian MNCs. But there were also a range of issues which needed to be addressed in capturing this information advantage by these Asian and Western MNCs.

The first problem firms found when seeking to construct the physical components of private networks across Asia was uncertain availability of the necessary components across the various national menus of telecommunications infrastructure choices. Across Asia, the telecommunications infrastructure was still frequently viewed as a strategic issue of national sovereignty. In contrast to the relatively deregulated markets of Europe and North America, regulatory restrictions across the state-interventionist markets of East and Southeast Asia meant that the options available for data communications were often severely limited.

Compounding the regulatory hurdles faced by network managers was the extreme range in the availability of telecommunications facilities across Asia. Markets in the region ranged in maturity from Singapore and Hong Kong, with a breadth of data services (including leased E1 and fractional E1 links, X.25 and frame relay), to countries such as Vietnam, where availability of even basic services was still extremely low. In between these extremes were scattered countries, from China—where no foreigners were allowed to manage telecommunications services and all but the most simple of value-added network services were regulated by the state—to the Philippines—where almost all value-added network services had been liberalized, but access across the island archipelago remained poor.

A further problem facing the promotion of intranet solutions was the cultural differences that exist in Asia. A much greater proportion of the market consisted of small and medium-sized enterprises or family-run businesses, as Asian management viewed a dependence on outside parties for the management of operations as hazardous for business. There was a fear that access to company information increased the risk of corporate espionage.

As a result of each of these factors, there was very little experience in building internal communications networks in Asia, and training among local IT staff had generally been low. This provided a significant opportunity for Western systems integration and networking consultants. For Andersen, intracorporate networking operations were primarily directed to being "first to market." As such, "timeliness" was measured through identifying opportunities, moving on those opportunities, and then servicing the client's needs. Given this orientation, a significant dimension of

Andersen Consulting's recent work in Asia had been in helping clients—both MNCs and local Asian firms—construct efficient intracorporate communications solutions, but with local characteristics.

The International Foods Company

The International Foods Company (IFC) was a large, European-based, multinational food processing corporation with manufacturing and sales organization in China. In many countries, such as in China, IFC's branches were rather discrete, self-contained operations, i.e., processing and distribution, which were seen as the dominant aspects of the business and were all taken care of by the local offices. As a direct result of the rapidly increasing demand for such luxuries as confectionery, competition against IFC increased dramatically as a number of other MNCs and a range of local companies entered the China market. While the company's communications network was not a large part of Andersen Consulting's initial IT planning project, it soon became clear that to address IFC's objectives—more efficient monitoring of inventory accumulation, and accurate and real-time sales information—would require a fundamental improvement in the firm's communication network across China.

IFC's China operations comprised two factories, six regional sales offices, and four depots, "all south of the Yangtze River." Prior to engaging Andersen Consulting's services, IFC's communications network in China consisted of straightforward phone and fax communications and hand-to-hand exchange of diskettes. (It should be kept in mind that until the mid-1990s, basic communications in even the major cities of China were not easy to organize.) LANs were installed in Hong Kong and its main manufacturing sites in China, but there were no standardized automation tools. IT support was extremely limited with two or three staff to assist 1,200 employees. Andersen's job was therefore to select and then implement a "comprehensive application system that integrated all business processes." This required setting-up "a cost-effective and practical network infrastructure that supported business growth" where monthly orders totaled "around 700" in an environment where the most advanced communications infrastructure was then the X.25 ChinaPac network.

In helping the client assess the problems with this environment, Andersen initially provided an assessment of the high, medium, and low-end (in terms of costs) options available—which essentially meant leased-line, X.25-based or straight dial-up phone access (table 2.3). Given the clients' requirements for security, reliability, and "timeliness," as well as for a cost-effective solution, a three-scenario cost analysis was then provided based on the X.25 and leased-line options. The suggested network strategy was to employ an X.25-based solution migrating to frame relay or "other newer but proven technology when available" (see figure 2.8). This meant employing X.25 PSN

Table 2.3
IFC's China network alternatives and Andersen Consulting's evaluation of Intranet infrastructure trade-offs

Factor	Digital leased lines	X.25PSN	Phone line
One-time cost	↓	↑	↓
Recruiting cost	↓ ↓	←	↑
Geographic coverage	↓	↑	↑
Reliability	↑	↑	←
Transmission quality	↑	←	←
Service and support	←	←	←
Installation timeframe	←	↑	←
Ease of installation	↓	←	↑
Multiuser single line	↑	↑	↓
Summary	↑ 3 ← 2 ↓ 5	↑ 5 ← 4 ↓ 0	↑ 3 ← 4 ↓ 2

(public switched network) as the corporate backbone between a data center and the processing offices, using LANs for access from all office localities, and adopting de facto LAN/WAN standards.

Asian Telecommunications Group

The Asian Telecommunications Group (ATG) was formed in 1993 to operate a national and international telecommunications wireline license. The license was awarded as part of a deregulation exercise by one of the governments of a larger Asian developing nation to promote the country as a regional telecommunications hub. The deregulation of the telecommunications industry attracted several new entrants into the marketplace. This meant that ATG needed to act quickly and effectively to establish its presence in this highly competitive market.

The challenge faced by the company was to create a competitive telecommunications company, including business processes, organizational structures, and operational support systems, all within a very short time frame in a market which lacked these skills.

In late 1993, ATG teamed up with Andersen Consulting to build the business "from a greenfield site." A joint project team was established to develop an Enterprise Business Process Architecture (EBPA), culminating in a series of workshops that "simulated Telco operations" and enabled ATG management to understand its

□ **Data Center Node** , as main corporate wide transaction processing power and data storage. It also functions as development, maintenance and operation center.

□ **Processing nodes** , as operation points such as headquarters, sales offices, factories. High-end routers will serve as entry points into the backbone.

□ **Corporate backbone network** , which comprises processing nodes linked to corporate wide application and data server via X.25 PSN. Modem for remote dial-up is recommended for backup lines.

□ **Lotus Notes Servers via corporate backbone network**, which form the corporate wide messaging and information exchange system.

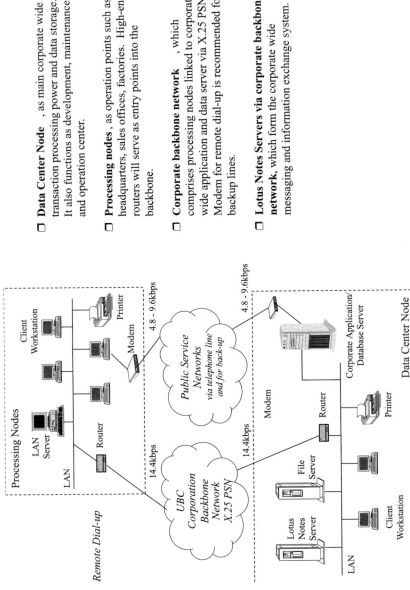

Figure 2.8
Andersen Consulting's recommendation for IFC's China network design and structure

key skill gaps and recruitment needs. Once the overall business processes had been defined and the organization structure implemented, the project team changed focus to develop the application, data, and technology architectures that were required for the communications platform to be created. The IT planning work then generated a number of key IT projects to implement the Operational Support Systems (OSS) environment as follows: network configuration system; network inventory system (AM/FM, GIS); financial management system; materials management system; alarm management system (closely integrated with the network configuration system); charging and billing system (closely integrated with the customer management system); customer management system (customer care, service orders, trouble management, task/work flow management); service activation memory administration system (enabling customer care representatives to deliver real-time service activation); and Asian Telecommunications On-Line (ATOL) services.

This final project, ATOL, was an on-line tool designed to provide point-of-need support to help users improve their work performance. Specifically, ATOL enabled the network users to gain access to task maps, deployment dependency charts, work flows, work instructions, and checklists which could support them on a daily basis in their job. The aim of the network and subsequent application was to allow for ongoing training and support in the office. The tool linked users from wherever they were in the process and then showed them where they were on the process line.

Andersen Consulting also provided preliminary assistance in the design and construction of ATG's extensive telecommunications network. This network included an advanced Fiber Optic SDH terrestrial network, an international gateway, a submarine cable, and a satellite network. By the end of 1995, ATG had more than 500 employees networked across five offices nationwide.

Japanese Manufacturing Company

Through the late 1970s and 1980s, Japanese MNCs were focused on the "triad," which consisted of Japan, the United States, and the European markets. Asian countries were seen only as a source of cheap labor for offshore manufacturing sites. By the late 1980s, the rapid sustained growth of the Asian economies was making many—including Japanese MNCs—rethink their global and regional strategies. Many Japanese companies began to focus on developing the markets in their own region and then started to integrate—or reconfigure—their Asian operations into their production and distribution networks (figure 2.9).

Thus, when Japanese Manufacturing Company (JMC) approached Andersen Consulting to provide the company with an Asian strategic evaluation, the request was motivated not by labor cost, "but by newly opened Asian domestic markets."

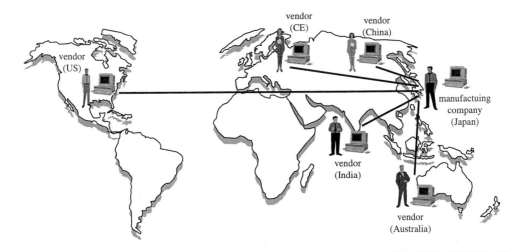

Figure 2.9
JMC's intranet strategy: Expand global sourcing opportunities and effectiveness

Three aspects were required of the networking part of this study: (1) to provide a cost-efficient, secure communications network; (2) to establish a globally optimized production-sales-logistics pipeline; and (3) to work out a new marketing strategy aimed at the Asian market (figure 2.10).

Having surveyed the possibilities, Andersen recommended that JMC divide their Asian operations into two distinct areas: the Greater China region (PRC, Hong Kong, and Taiwan), and the Indonesia-Malaysia area, centered on Singapore. The communications network was to be operated on a "hub-and-spoke" structure, deploying regional (or, "area") headquarters in each location which would replicate information "up" the network to the central headquarters in Japan. Not only did this strategy allow for greater sensitivity to local differences in marketing strategies, but also greater flexibility in communications network architecture, given the significant infrastructure differences between the northeast and southeast Asian regions, and

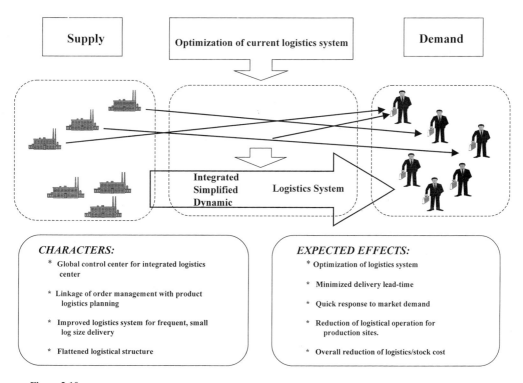

Figure 2.10
JMC's vision: Developing an integrated global logistics system

among the various countries. This recommended networking solution was also consistent with the overall networking infrastructure.

In southeast Asia the great majority of the firm's operations were centered around Singapore (northern Indonesia and southern Malaysia), which meant such that a comparatively sophisticated intranet solution could be easily and efficiently maintained. By contrast, the far greater political and infrastructure differences within the three Chinas called for far greater use of the public telecommunications systems. However, the marketing needs of the firm in southern China were seen to be less demanding, requiring less sophistication in the immediate future. Therefore, while JMC had an "Asian strategy" which they wished to pursue, Andersen Consulting was able to incorporate these different IS solutions into the client's overall business objectives. These customized IS solutions were based on different market realities and differing economic growth rates for each country in the region.

New First City Bank

The New First City Bank (NFCB) of Hong Kong was a major international bank focused upon trade finance and, in particular, international trade finance. To this extent, the bank's trade finance "mission" was to "be recognized as the leading provider of corporate and financial institution trade services to customers in their chosen markets."

Although the global trade finance business had been growing strongly, it became apparent that by the early 1990s the bank's market share was declining. In addition, processing costs per unit transaction were higher than the industry average, and productivity levels were well below global "best practice." A key reason for this, according to Andersen Consulting, was that historically, the bank's trade finance business was managed on a country-independent basis, resulting in the bank operating with inconsistent strategies, policies, and systems. This led to varying levels of service to regional and global customers. As a result, with the trend in trade finance toward global service delivery and commodity pricing, the bank was missing significant business opportunities because it was not exploiting the power of its existing global network.

A Global Trade Reengineering project was established by Andersen in association with the bank to address the operational and customer delivery aspect groupwide, identifying all reengineering opportunities and developing a fully integrated plan for the transformation of the bank's business. A key component of this was to revamp the bank's transactions systems throughout Asia.

Andersen Consulting's suggested solution was for New First City Bank to employ a "hub-and-spoke" model as a global service delivery platform. A global processing center was created in Hong Kong, utilizing imaging and workflow management technology. This network platform allowed for each country's processing functions to be removed and centralized in the processing center. The processing center could then be managed like a factory (with the goals being high productivity and quality and low costs). Documents received in the branches of each country could be scanned using image processing and transmitted to the factory for processing.

The strength of the networking strategy was to separate the transaction processing from customer service. The centralizing of document processing allowed for increased leverage on the use of the global network to capture both ends of intragroup transactions. By relieving branches of the task of transaction processing, the bank was able to employ a greater sales focus at the "front end." In addition, Andersen forecast a 40% reduction in operating cost within three years.

Intranet Issues and Opportunities

Providing networking solutions for clients in Asia was an important strategic opportunity for Andersen Consulting in Asia. Few clients had the infrastructure, scale, or skills which Andersen could offer in providing network solutions. Outsourcing of information systems was not as common in Asia as in the United States, but using a total solution provider for networking was often the only economically viable solution for companies interested in building an Asian intranet.

In contrast to the Asian environment, the U.S. and European markets for corporate networking services were much more developed and competitive. Andersen Consulting clients in the United States and Europe often had sufficient scale and expertise to set up their own internal networks. Eventually, the market for corporate network solutions in Asia would also mature, but the current environment appeared to offer Andersen an opportunity to provide a solution for client needs in Asia for which there seemed to be few economically viable alternatives.

However, one of the challenges in capturing this opportunity was the effective management of the fast-growing and fast-evolving network itself. The rapid growth in network usage required capacity to be upgraded frequently, and there were often long lead times required for adding new capacity from the few licensed telecommunications services providers within Asia. In most Asian countries telecommunication services were still a monopoly, especially for international leased-line connections. Thus order fulfillment for requested capacity upgrades was often delayed for several months. At the same time, the costs for network capacity were quite high, and Andersen needed to avoid overbuilding the network or the costs of the unused lines could become a serious financial burden.

The addition of a new client on the network presented a challenge in network management in two ways. First, Andersen might need to add new lines or upgraded capacity to manage existing client communications needs. Second, clients who had not used networking services previously often had *very* fast growth in usage of the network, requiring fast upgrades of capacity to avoid excessive network congestion. Andersen needed to improve their current systems for measuring and billing for network resources usage. The network had been growing so rapidly that measurement of usage had not been as important as simply trying to add capacity quickly enough to satisfy internal Andersen Consulting demand for data exchange (table 2.4 and figure 2.11). With new clients using the network, the growth of the network and the importance of measuring and forecasting actual usage was expected to increase.

One final issue to consider was how Andersen's intranet services should be positioned within the portfolio of all services offered by the firm. Should the Andersen

Table 2.4
Asia-Pacific "ANet" telecommunications capacity and utilization (as of September 2, 1996)

Destinations connected		Capacity	Utilization	Comments****
Chicago	Singapore	256 kbps	Moderate**	Upgraded two months ago
Sofia	Singapore	64 kbps*	Unknown**	
Australia	Singapore	128 kbps	High**	Will be upgraded to 256 kbps soon
Hong Kong	Singapore	64 kbps	Moderate to high**	
Japan	Singapore	128 kbps	Moderate to high**	
Korea	Singapore	112 kbps	Low to moderate**	Upgraded one month ago
Jakarta	Singapore	64 kbps	Unknown**	
Bangkok	Singapore	dial up line	Not applicable***	
Taipei	Singapore	64 kbps	High**	Upgrading to 128 kbps this month
Kuala Lumpur	Singapore	64 kbps*	Unknown**	
Manila	Singapore	128 kbps	Unknown**	

* This estimate is believed to be correct, but information provided has not been confirmed or there exists some uncertainty about bandwidth available.
** Precise quantitative data on utilization was not yet available, as Andersen Consulting had just begun collecting utilization statistics to assist with more effective network capacity management. However, the estimates provided were believed to accurately reflect usage. Most connections were utilized at about 45% to 60% of maximum peak capacity, with 60% utilization used as the internal threshold for upgrading network capacity. At 60% average utilization, peak network utilization would often be in excess of 80%, resulting in serious network congestion problems. Rapid growth in network usage made capacity planning and management challenging, with optimizing for both cost control and network responsiveness quite difficult.
*** Utilization is not meaningful for dial-up lines, as there is no real bandwidth constraint using these facilities. However, dial-up facilities were only cost effective when overall demand for data communications was quite limited.
**** Advance planning for upgrades was difficult due to the rapid (but not uniform) growth in network demand. However, capacity installation delays with most Asian telecommunications services providers required Andersen Consulting to plan at least two months in advance for most capacity upgrades.

network be aggressively marketed to all MNCs as the premier solution for all their networking needs? This would require aggressive marketing to provide value-added telecommunications services to all MNCs in Asia. Alternatively, should the Andersen intranet solution be a value-added resource offered only to existing Andersen clients with whom the company has had a long-term relationship? The positioning of the Andersen intranet service offerings to MNCs could also impact on other areas of the firm's consulting operations. The first strategy could provide Andersen with an entrée to new potential clients for consulting services. The second strategy could strengthen Andersen's position as a strategic partner with their core clients in helping to meet the total information systems needs of these clients within Asia as well as worldwide.

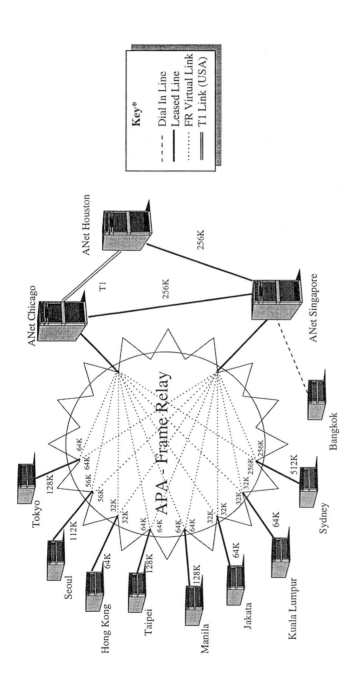

Figure 2.11
Asia-Pacific "Anet" telecommunications frame relay network infrastructure (as of December 1996)

* Dial in lines have variable capacity and usage based pricing, leased lines have fixed capacity and usage independent pricing, Frame Relay (FR) Virtual Links have fixed maximum capacity but pricing is partly fixed and partly usage based, T1 Links are high-bandwidth leased lines with discounted flat pricing.

Notes

1. Robert A. Mercer, "Overview of Enterprise Network Developments," *IEEE Communications Magazine*, January 1996, 30–37. Mercer defines enterprise networking as "a corporate-wide network that ties together the communications, processing and storage resources of the corporation by making those resources available to users distributed throughout the corporation" (p. 30). Retrospectively, he notes, the term has also been applied to "legacy" networks.

2. Heralded most forcefully by the arrival of "intranets." See, "Enter the Intranet," *Economist*, 13 January 1996, p. 68–9.

3. For an early example of an analysis of the strategic use of intracorporate networking (focused on the management and use of leased lines), see John V. Langdale, "The Geography of International Business Telecommunications: The Role of Leased Networks," *Annals of the Association of American Geographers*, 79(4), 1989, 501–522.

4. Andersen follows a matrix organizational approach, dividing itself by industry, business component, geography, and change cycle component.

5. Legacy networks are built around a host-centric computing paradigm, in which users access a few centralized mainframe computers from numerous remote "dumb" terminals that possess no computing capabilities of their own. In this model, all computing tasks are done on the mainframe, and therefore all communications are directed to and from those mainframes. Computing is oriented to activities which involve the movement of relatively modest amounts of data between the terminals and computers. As a result, the required bit rates are fairly low, and connectivity is limited to a starlike arrangement with the mainframe(s) at the center.

6. "Representing" is used here rather than "serving" because as the network progresses, traffic will be routed down the most efficient (least congested rather than the shortest geographical) route.

3 Redefining the Geography of Space, Time, and Money

More than 40 years ago, mathematicians Manfred Kochen and Ithiel de Sola Pool posed structures for "acquaintance networks" and pondered the prospect of a "world brain."[1] Although in those days they had no way of knowing what form computing platforms would ultimately take (neither the Internet nor Web had been invented yet), they saw the potential of large networks and databases on the computer.

Even without the communications networks we enjoy today, it was apparent to Kochen and de Sola Pool that the world—in a social, economic, and informational sense—was much smaller than geographic size would suggest. They called this the *small world phenomenon*: the widely held perception that the world is smaller than an actual count of individuals would suggest.

Their modeling took data from empirical studies of University of California students and from studies by New York psychologist Stanley Milgram[2] on acquaintances. Milgram studied the acquaintance networks connecting any two randomly chosen residents of New York; that is, if A and B are chosen at random, how many individuals C, D, . . . are needed to be able to say that A knows C who knows D . . . who knows B. He discovered that acquaintance chains covering New York City's population tended to be very short, two to three individuals on average.

Kochen and de Sola Poole extrapolated these findings to the global population, concluding that any individual on earth is separated from any other by an average acquaintance chain of six individuals. Kochen and de Sola Pool's *six degrees of separation* have inspired plays, movies, and a game (*The Six Degrees of Kevin Bacon*) playing on the small world phenomenon.

The small world has economic consequences as well. Computer and communication networks have nurtured two significant phenomena: the flattening of hierarchy and demise of many traditional white-collar jobs via downsizing and the development of efficient market alternatives to many internal corporate activities.

Hierarchy can be reduced and firms downsized because the speed and volume of information that can be automatically processed and shunted around the firm is several magnitudes greater than in the 1920s when Alfred Sloan implemented the philosophy of the hierarchical firm as an institution to run General Motors. Command and control was the manifesto in the early 20th century, reflecting the general economics of scarce productive resources. Late-20th-century competition focuses on time to market, innovation, and quality: These are the minimum performance requirements required to survive. Flat firms with a focus on their core competencies can experience sustainable competitive advantages.

Increased availability of efficient market alternatives to formerly internal functions means that the "make or buy" question is increasingly answered "buy." Organizations are able to develop around individual capabilities and proclivities, making efficient use of individual contributions to organizational goals in a shrinking world. Recent research has shown that simply speeding up the communications between negotiating parties eliminates many misunderstandings and dysfunctional behaviors found in group work while helping people avoid decision-making gridlock.

The bottom line: Firms must stay focused on the particular vertical market in which they compete, but are not expected to participate in or manage all of the channels in the vertical market. Conglomerates or highly vertically integrated firms may be able to compete through sheer market muscle. However, the proliferation of networked information and powerful computers makes it possible for smaller, more nimble competitors to operate more efficiently and profitably by focusing on their specific core competencies.

Information technologies and various forms of electronic commerce are redefining the nature of markets worldwide. Marketspaces—a locution for cyberspace markets that was popularized by Rayport and Sviokla—are replacing marketplaces as a preferred venue for transacting business. The shift to marketspaces for commerce is one aspect of the late-20th-century shift from an economics of physical scarcity to economics based on information processing, information content, and the emergence of information and services as primary generators of wealth.

Technology has toppled many of the old barriers of time and space, redefining the geography of commerce and profit. The impact of technology in redefining barriers of space and time is not new,[3] but the pace and extent of the changes in the global economy have accelerated dramatically with the introduction of inexpensive electronic communications capabilities such as the Internet. Companies providing the best value for customers are finding that hawking their products in marketspace is a cost-effective alternative that overcomes traditional barriers of time and space in getting goods and services to customers.

Firms' ability to transcend time and space in the global marketspace is particularly strong among firms providing intangible information products or services to their customers. Intangible information products and services are increasingly substituting for tangible products in developed economies. In the leading developed economies, the tangible goods GDP has declined from half to one-fifth of overall GDP in less than 50 years. The level of tangible production as a percentage of GDP is expected to continue declining in the future as intangible information products and services increase their share of global production value in both developed and emerging economies.

Increasing use of electronic commerce and information technology for channel automation is accelerating this trend and has enabled the emergence of the global marketspace for information-based goods and services. Improvements in communications technologies and the introduction of new technologies force companies and individuals to remap perceived distances between people and places.[4] New technological capabilities are enabling us to bridge the barriers of time and space, creating a smaller, more accessible world over times.[5] As these barriers of time and space are overcome using these new technological capabilities, innovative firms have been able to gain significant advantages in competing within this expanded global marketspace environment.

Each new technology remaps our distances between people and places and demands that we restructure the things we do to remain competitive. Competitive strategy must continually reevaluate marketing and supply channels to assure that channel tasks are assigned to the best available technology. In general, the remapping enabled by new information and communications technologies makes the world smaller. So pronounced has been the effect that it is perhaps more difficult to measure the shrinkage of the world today than it was even a decade ago. For that reason, many of the examples we use throughout this chapter are historical, taking advantage of geographical distances modern information technology is fast erasing.

For example, person-to-person selling is far too expensive in many (if not most) markets and for many (if not most) products. Still, it is the best way to nurture contacts, obtain sales, and negotiate the best price. Communication technologies can pry open previously unavailable markets and create new opportunities for previously orphaned products by lowering the cost of person-to-person selling. The growth of telephone direct selling was only the most recent great communications revolution in sales and distribution channel. The growth of Internet selling has fostered a rich, new, and exciting way to enter previously unavailable markets.

Geographical models provide a useful way to think of the transformation that communications technologies have brought about. Figures 3.1 and 3.2 illustrate the impact of increased communications capabilities and reduced logistics and barrier costs in making the world appear to be a very small place.

Prior to the massive deployment of telephone technologies in the United States, other technologies had begun the task of remapping anthropocentric perceptions of space, time, and cost. For example, the gradual replacement of footpaths with stagecoach routes for business communications and transportation was itself superseded by railroads, and then highways. Each new technology remapped the anthropocentric perception of distance.

The evolution of this remapping of distance has accelerated rapidly over the past half century (see figure 3.2). The cost structure shown in figure 3.3 is that for the United States in the 1970s. Cost structures have varied dramatically over time and across countries. Over time, costs have dropped dramatically. Where a particular

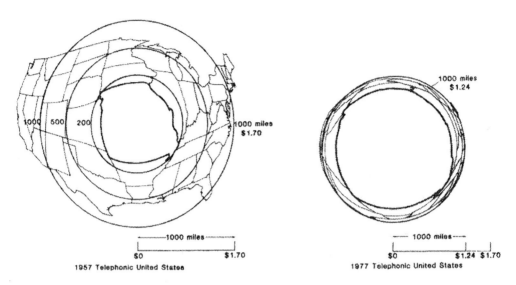

Figure 3.1
Remapping distances serviced by the telephone based on the cost of a telephone call: The evolution of cost-distance from Missouri, from 1857 to 1977
Source: Carol L. Weinhaus and Anthony G. Oettinger, *Behind the Telephone Debates* (Norwood, NJ: Ablex Publishing, 1988).

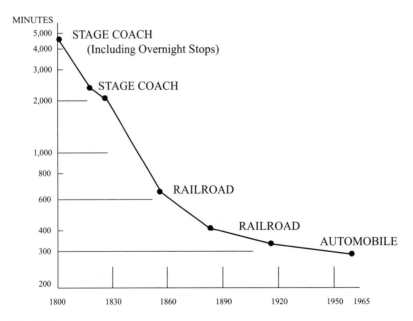

Figure 3.2
Space-time convergence for travel and communication between New York and Boston, 1800–1950

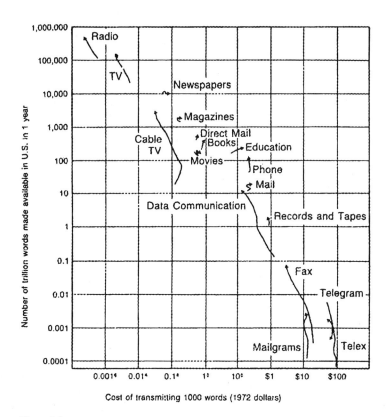

Figure 3.3
Trends in volume and cost of communication media, 1960–77
Source: Ithiel de Sola Pool, *Technologies of Freedom* (Cambridge, MA: Belknap Press, 1983), p. 610.

medium is not cost effective, it is abandoned: for example, telex, which is nearly obsolete in most parts of the world.

Table 3.1 conveys the variance in access to major channels of communication of people of various countries around the globe. Corporate communications strategy must be adjusted to each country's particular cost and availability of communications technology. The Internet, in particular, requires a fast, accessible telecommunications network. Where this has been unavailable—for example in China, India, and most of Africa—Internet based e-commerce options have been limited.

Each new technology has its own costs, often paid for in lower quality or attention. Electronic commerce is making the greatest difference in the geography of sales and

Table 3.1
Access by country to basic communication channels in 1983

	Population per post office	Population per telephone	Population per newspaper copy	Population per television	Films viewed per person per year
U.K.	2,556	2.00	2.42	2.09	1.1
Australia	2,938	1.90	2.97	2.33	1.1
Italy	3,993	2.60	12.20	2.60	2.9
India	4,815	228.50	50.00	250.00	6.6
Mexico	5,087	12.80	8.33	9.26	2.8
Belgium	5,309	2.50	4.48	3.30	2.1
U.S.	5,743	1.50	3.73	1.27	5.1
Egypt	6.696	85.60	12.82	22.73	0.9
Brazil	17,455	13.90	21.74	7.87	5.7
Ethiopia	28,860	129.00	1666.67	2000.00	0.1

Source: Encyclopedia Britannica.

distribution channels. In these channels, computer-based multimedia are replacing the sales visit, telephone call, addressing and printing costs for brochures and catalogues, and so forth. In contrast to using the post office to deliver information, the World Wide Web provides a nearly frictionless vehicle for information dissemination. In the digital converged future, cable television, expanded telephone services, and microwave and other technologies could supersede the Internet for reaching customers. Maybe we will not differentiate at all between these technologies as they migrate toward a common platform. Even electrical, gas, and water suppliers could get into the distribution market. They control long uninterrupted rights-of-way and potentially could provide high-bandwidth communications to household consumers. This may become increasingly important as more individuals choose to work at home or to operate their own businesses out of households.

The qualitative changes brought about by new telecommunications technology are transforming the way people interact in business and social settings. New telecommunications-based activities have substituted for personal activities over the past several decades. The networks of acquaintances today are more likely to based on shared interests—for example, products, hobbies, and political beliefs—than on physical proximity. Gone will be the small town, replaced by an ever expanding global village. This transition has profound implications for the quality of work.

Information and communications technologies do more than simply speed up communications and shrink space (often the extent of conventional wisdom on the benefits those technologies provide). Information in cyberspace is not constrained to one place at any time, as is document- or currency-based information. A cyber-document can be on multiple desktops at any time. This evaporation of constraints on information suggests new and innovative ways of distributing products, accomplishing work, and valuing assets. An entire range of virtual documents can be generated that serve to signal the starting or ending of tasks.

The overload of paper-based transactions in a modern corporation creates the potential for huge cost savings. Two decades ago computer databases replaced paper as the primary corporate archival record-keeping medium. Electronic communications are similarly revolutionizing interfirm transactions today. Most firms expend significant effort communication with other firms: More than 80% of transactions between firms use paper as the medium to carry information. Examples of paper-intensive transactions are requests for quotes, bids, purchase orders, order confirmations, shipping documents, invoices, and payment information. EDI replaces paper communications with electronic communications. For example, companies whose supply chains are linked through EDI can generate purchase orders directly from inventory and planning systems, send these instantaneously through the communications network to requisite suppliers, have orders processed through the suppliers' system, and have pick lists created prior to the start of the next workday. Human intervention is necessary only if there is an order to expedite, or in the case of an exception. Cost savings can be impressive. The following qualitative changes also can occur:

1. Time delays are greatly reduced. Mail and processing delays are eliminated.

2. Timing uncertainty is eliminated in some cases and reduced in others, enabling a firm to forecast cash flows more accurately, reduce lead time, and provide time-sensitive service customers demand.

3. Immediate acknowledgments provided in an EDI system mean that the buyer knows that a purchase order was received, enhancing the relationship between buyer and seller.

4. A content acknowledgment provides the buyer with fast feedback on whether the order will be filled or whether the buyer must look elsewhere, thus lowering the need for safety stock.

5. One-time keying reduces labor costs. Because data is always in computer-readable form, matching, filing, retrieving, sorting, reporting, and auditing can be completed with fewer people and at much faster rates. One consulting study estimated that more than 3% of all invoices contained errors that were the result of miskeying.

6. Paper and mail costs can be reduced.

7. Payment can be processed through bank run settlement systems the day after initiation.

8. The danger that paper will be lost, damaged, or misplaced (a large problem with archived and completed transactions) is eliminated.

RJR Nabisco estimated in 1995 that processing a paper purchase order cost the company $70; processing the same order through EDI reduced the cost to a mere 93 cents.[6]

Global reach is more than an aphorism: It represents a real restructuring of the geography of space and time associated with business tasks. Space and time are constrained resources, so their restructuring results in significant changes in the costs incurred while doing business.

An example of rethinking business structure and operations to take advantage of this global marketspace is provided in the Financial Times (FT) case study included at the end of this chapter. The FT is one of the leading business newspapers in the world, with physical distribution of this daily newspaper provided in most of the developed and emerging economies of the world. The FT has been active in many forms of electronic commerce and information service provision, and has one of the most informative and useful Web sites available today. The FT has also found that, in addition to providing FT with a new advertising and communications medium for reaching its marketspace subscribers, the Web can be used to restructure its distribution of syndicated news and management articles to its affiliated new customers. As well as reducing costs, the on-line syndication of news and management articles has enabled the FT to reach more customers globally and to improve coverage by shifting from a physical marketplace distribution process to a globally accessible and individually customizable marketspace distribution process. This shift in management processes, however, does raise a number of strategic and operational issues and concerns, which are introduced in the FT case. These issues regarding product pricing, information distribution and control, information and site security, and interface design are representative of issues that many companies will have to address in shifting from the marketplace to the marketspace for sales and distribution of their products and services.

In the world of banking, electronic communications and information technologies have long played an important role as processes have shifted from manual to automated and as information has become an increasing important component of the value-added services banks worldwide provide. Security First Network Bank (SFNB) is extending this usage of communications and information technology to the customer interface, and is the first bank in the world approved by the FDIC and U.S. regulators to offer all of its banking products and services entirely via the Web. Within the first year after receiving its federal charter to offer Internet banking services to consumers, SFNB had more than 1,000 customers from all 50 states in the United States using its Internet has banking services. In addition, the global nature of the Internet has allowed SFNB to add customers from many other countries in the world, even though regulatory restrictions allowed SFNB to offer only U.S. dollars accounts and services at the time of the case study.

For SFNB, the marketspace is much more than a theoretical concept: It is their entire business. Even so, the firm faces a number of interesting and important business issues as it attempts to manage trade-offs between the enormous challenges and opportunities it faces in this new business. For example, the most attractive opportunity for the bank to make money from this rapidly expanding marketspace may be to provide on-line software, services, and support to other established banks interested in providing Internet banking services. At the same time, SFNB also has the opportunity to use the marketspace to build its retail bank into one of the most profitable banks in the world using its radically reduced cost structure, which results from its on-line customer interface and lack of investment in physical infrastructure. SFNB must consider as well the potential need, in order to become a major competitor in the traditionally location-oriented retail banking business, for a marketspace services provider also to have a limited physical marketplace presence to be able to meet all of its customer needs.

The global marketspace is not exclusively the domain of larger firms, as the case study on Global Electronics Manufacturing (GEM) demonstrates. This eight-employee firm, with offices in Southern California and Hong Kong, manages an outsourced global manufacturing and distribution network of relationships that has enabled it to become one of the world's leading providers of private-label computer game accessories. Through its contracted factory operations in China, GEM produces (under an exclusive production outsourcing contract) computer game accessory products for many of the largest retail chain stores in the United States and Europe. Although the firm has been able to overcome barriers of time and space effectively in producing and distributing its products, it has only begun to leverage the potential of these new technologies in its global business. GEM management at the time of the case study was considering ways in which expanding the use of information technology might enable it to improve its global operations and reduce the need for managers to travel extensively to manage this global network of business relationships and activities.

Each of these three firms has been able to overcome barriers of time and space to reduce costs and increase market penetration in the global marketspace. The case studies involving them illustrate the potential for firms to leverage information technology and gain competitive advantage in an increasingly small world. These firms have been able to rethink their competitive and business environment using new technologies to redesign business processes and marketing strategies using cost-based and time-based rather than space-based maps of the world.

The Hard Middle

Jeff Bezos, founder of Amazon.com, emphasizes that the Internet, unlike any advertising medium in the past, is interactive. It responds in a unique way to each customer and is one of the few ways to reach what he calls the "hard middle" cost effectively: "If you want to reach 12 people, then the telephone, or perhaps a personal call, is the obvious choice. If you want to reach 12 million people, then take a out an advertisement on prime time television. If you want to pitch something to 12,000 people—that's the hard middle."[7]

The conventional answer to the hard middle is direct mail, an expensive and inefficient medium (see figure 3.3). The Internet's interactivity makes it easier to target customers. Most search engines—where one-third of the clicks on the Internet take place—can respond to users' queries by displaying banner ads that are likely to be of interest. The distinction between advertising and direct marketing is blurring as a result of this interactivity. Banner ads are interactive: Clicking on them opens up a new Web page, with interactivity, forms for purchasing, and so forth. The response is immediate (rather than suffering the mail delay of direct mail) and has the customer's attention (whereas many direct-mail flyers fly immediately to the wastebasket).

The Web browser has become a tool of corporate democratization. Every industry has suddenly (like it or not) become part of a global network in which all companies are equally easy to reach and corporate offices, personnel, and other physical characteristics of the firm have little bearing on their public image. Information once closely hoarded in many industries has become a commodity. The most radical change is the shift in power from the producer and merchant to the consumer. The Internet amplifies word of mouth tremendously. Corporations now carefully monitor newsgroups, mailing lists, and chat sites to find out what customers like and dislike about their company.

Merchants and producers get more feedback more quickly as a result of Internet commerce. Bezos comments: "When you go to a restaurant and the food isn't good, you rarely send it back or tell the chef he shouldn't be cooking. Online, people will do it in a heartbeat. It's not personally embarrassing."[8]

The Web has offered business an entirely new paradigm for connecting with the customer, and along with it a new look for existing applications. The major software companies have committed themselves to creating a completely consistent experience for a user who wants everything to work like the Web. The Web and its search engines offer the promise of putting products and services at the service of customers. It frees the customer from the tyranny of marketing, advertising, and sales intermediaries who control information for the benefit of producers and channel intermediaries and to the disadvantage of consumers.

It is not possible to understand fully the impact of the Web on the customer by simply looking at traditional marketing techniques. Electronic commerce on the Web reengineers the customer's role in the producer-consumer relationship. The Internet could potentially reach 320 million people in 1998, and Web based e-commerce is available to all 320 million of these individuals. However, server-resident electronic commerce information is fundamentally passive; it is up to the search engines and the customer to identify products and services of interest. Rating agencies such as Consumer Reports, search engines, and institutions with captive transaction flows such as utilities and banks are natural nexuses for electronic commerce. We address these issues further in chapter 9.

The Problem with Innovation

The laser, at 40 years of age, is a young technology. Nevertheless, it has found widespread application: in measurement, chemistry, navigation, surgery, cutting of materials, and fiber optic communication for telephones. Yet lawyers at Bell Labs, where the laser was invented, were unwilling even to apply for a patent on the invention, because it had no relevance to the telephone industry. Thomas Watson, whose aggressive leadership built IBM Corporation from a struggling firm of 4,000 employees to the industry leader with 72,000, commented in 1949 that the firm should have nothing to do with computers because the world demand would never exceed five computers.

It is not so much that these business leaders were wrong or shortsighted; rather, the original inventions (which eventually grew to be important) were very primitive by later standards. The first electronic digital computer was a hopelessly unreliable mass of 18,000 vacuum tubes, miles of wires, and associated hardware, without even a basic concept of programmed software. Only with innovation toward smaller, faster, and cheaper models and John von Neumann's invention of programmable software did the computer thrive. Successful innovation had more to do with improvement than with invention.

Computers and communications contribute to the economy in complex ways. For example, Intel's computing price/performance dropped from around US$300 per MIPS (million instructions per second) in 1990 to around US$3 per MIPS in 1998. Yet this cannot be naively translated directly into efficiency improvements, because software has used this computing power differently over time. Intel PC CPUs ran Microsoft's text-based DOS in 1990; in 1998 they run graphics-intensive Windows. The U.S. Department of Commerce estimated that declining prices in IT industries lowered overall inflation by one full percentage point in 1997 and were responsible for more than 25% of real economic growth.[9]

It is not unusual for radically new inventions to have few direct applications. Each innovation requires the subsequent invention of uses and complementary technologies (as fiber optics is to lasers; as programmed software is to computers). The steam engine was invented in the 18th century to pump water out of mines and was nothing more for decades. Then it became a source of power that allowed factories to consolidate and move away from streams and other natural power sources. Subsequently, it became a source of transportation power to bring laborers to the newly relocated factories. Finally, it provided a way to generate electricity, which allowed portable electric motors to replace steam engines, and so forth.

The Internet was for many years an invention with limited uses. E-mail provided a useful form of auxiliary communication but not much opportunity for commerce. That changed with the complementary technology of the Web browser, which opened the Internet up to a much richer world of information. With the development of secure transaction processing, the Web has been opened to electronic commerce (albeit still limited when compared to traditional retail channels). Convergence in the future with television, game software, robotics, and other technologies will expand its usefulness perhaps to a greater extent than any technology that man has seen in his history.

Jobs and the Internet

By radically changing marginal cost structure and economies of scale, commerce on the Internet offers the prospect of huge leaps in creativity and productivity. We provide many examples, in this text, of new work e-commerce has created. In the future, though, work is unlikely to be parceled in the familiar envelopes we call "jobs." The job is a recent social artifact in human history, emerging in the late 18th century. It packaged the work that needed doing in the factories of the industrial revolution. Power was not portable, and factories were set up next to the streams or woods that fueled their production. People were expected to show up for their jobs when the machines required it. The job was a controversial idea in its time. Critics claimed it was an inhumane way to work, and that most individuals would not be able to live with its demands.

Electronic commerce is changing work again, with mass production and large organizations disappearing and with place once again unimportant in getting the work done. Instead of long production runs in which the same thing has to be done again and again, production is increasingly customized, activities unbundled and farmed out to nimble smaller firms, wherever they can be done at lowest cost and highest quality. Today's organization is rapidly being transformed from a structure built around jobs into a field of work needing to be done. Patches of responsibility, in combination, are supposed to get the job done. The tasks that need to be done are increasingly transitory, requiring creativity and ad hoc response to one-time circumstances. This 18th-century vestige, the job, seems artificial when superimposed on a field of work needing to be done in the 21st century.

Just as the products of labor can be bought and sold on e-commerce networks, traffic in labor and services can be conducted as well. Electronic commerce allows us to create virtual labor markets of contingent workers, who can be called in on demand to do a given task, then sent on their way. It is a world without any place for the time clock, office, or hierarchy. Only the work to be done is important.

Figure 3.4 illustrates how far the revolution in jobs has progressed. In the 1850s, the argument was made, America would always need farmers to feed the growing ranks of factory workers who were boosting the nation's economy. During those

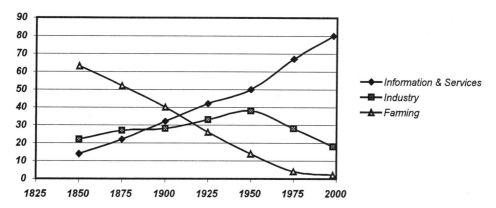

Figure 3.4
Share of U.S. employment in various sectors
Source: U.S. Labor Statistics Bureau, OECD national statistics, U.S. Commerce Department.

years, agriculture employed more than half the nation's labor force. By 1945, the agricultural labor force had dwindled to only a few percent of the total, whereas industry had grown to employ over half of the nation's labor force. As the turn of the century approaches, industry employs less than one-fifth of the labor force and accounts for around 20% of GDP, with the remaining GDP contributed by the information and service industries.

Every past revolution in industry and commerce has witnessed some key factor of production being drastically reduced in cost. From a production standpoint, relative to the previous cost, the new factor is virtually free. Over the past century, U.S. farming has steadily automated, consolidated plots of land, developed new hybrids and new techniques, and realized economies of scale. With each new innovation, the need for farming jobs declined, while productivity increased. The United States of the 1990s can easily afford to squander food: More than half the population is clinically overweight. Over the last 30 years, switching power has moved from expensive, crafted vacuum tubes to integrated circuit transistors, which are virtually free (less than $10 each).[10] Business today throws transistors at every problem conceivable, including correcting our spelling or adding up columns of numbers. To stay competitive, we "squander" transistors wherever customers appreciate the additional functionality provided.

When information was indelibly inked to paper, it was a scarce resource. With the trend toward archiving corporate transactions on computer media, firms have recorded more and more of their operations for future reference. Cheap, intangible bits and bytes have supplanted tangible and limited paper media for archival recording. With the evolution of computer displays and Internet browsers, computer screens are supplanting paper for display. This trend has accelerated in the early 1990s with the rapid commercialization of the Internet, resulting in an information glut: There is too much information for individuals to process effectively. Web-based e-commerce has pushed information technology's contribution to U.S. gross domestic product from 6.4% to 8.2% in less than five years. IT's share of total nominal GDP growth is around 15%, and IT is the single largest contributor to the robust performance of U.S. equity markets in the late 1990s. The Internet's commercialization outpaces that of any automation or communication technology in history. Radio was in existence for 38 years before it reached 50 million people; television took 13 years to reach that milestone; cable TV took 10 years; the PC took 16 years; the Internet took only four years after its commercialization in 1991, and the Web took less than five years after its introduction in 1993.

The Internet has contributed greatly in shifting business from the factory to the digital workplace. Figure 3.5 shows the dramatic growth in information technology's

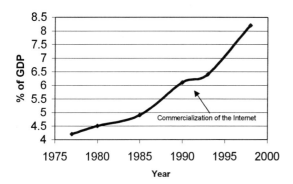

Figure 3.5
Information technology's share of U.S. GDP
Source: U.S. Department of Commerce, Economics and Statistics Administration, based on Bureau of Economic Analysis and Census data.

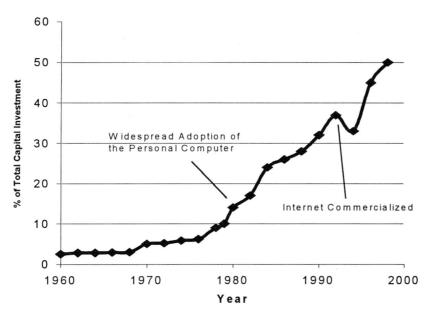

Figure 3.6
Business information technology investment as a percentage of total capital investment
Source: U.S. Department of Commerce, based on Bureau of Economic Analysis and Census data.

Table 3.2
Asian economies, 1994

	GDP (US$ billion)	% GDP by sector			Labor force (millions)	% Employment by sector		
		Agriculture	Information and services	Industry		Agriculture	Information and services	Industry
China	509.6	20.97	38.06	40.79	614.2	54.30	23.00	22.70
Hong Kong	132.0	0.20	91.50	9.30	3.0	0.05	81.30	18.70
Indonesia	174.0	16.71	50.84	32.45	79.2	50.50	38.40	11.10
Japan	4682.0	2.23	67.14	30.63	66.5	5.20	72.30	22.50
Malaysia	70.7	15.94	43.23	40.83	7.8	19.00	55.50	25.50
Philippines	62.8	22.30	52.40	26.30	25.6	46.00	43.50	10.50
Singapore	69.0	0.21	71.51	28.28	1.7	0.03	74.40	25.60
South Korea	380.0	6.91	63.24	29.85	19.8	13.00	53.70	23.70
Taiwan	241.0	3.60	67.40	29.00	8.9	11.00	61.00	28.00
Thailand	144.0	11.90	58.30	29.80	30.3	59.00	29.00	12.00

Source: Hong Kong Trade Development Council.

share of the U.S. economy. These figures are conservative, because there is no accounting for the massive investments made in databases and software customization, most of which is expensed immediately. Figure 3.6 shows the "kick" to corporate investment from commercialization of the Internet and the rush to conduct at least a portion of corporate business electronically.

By many assessments, the degree of economic activity in the information and services sector is a measure of the country's economic development. From this perspective the United States has excelled, both in developing new communications and information technology and in putting it to work. However, these trends are in no way unique to America, as table 3.2 shows for Asian economies in the mid-1990s.

Recommended Reading

Rayport, J. F., and J. J. Sviokla. (1994). Managing in the Marketspace. *Harvard Business Review*, November/December. This classic *HBR* article provides a detailed explanation of the marketspace concept, including brief case study examples and illustrations. Rather than reproduce the substance of this article in this text, we recommend it as additional reading material that can provide more insight for the student of electronic commerce regarding this revolutionary concept in marketing in a world without boundaries.

Notes

1. Their work was popularized in Ted Newcomb's 1961 book *The Acquaintance Process*. (New York: Holt Rinehart and Winston).

2. Milgram is perhaps best remembered for his experiments that demonstrated the conditions under which ordinary Americans would administer an unbearably painful electrical shock to a screaming (but otherwise inoffensive) subject. These experiments motivated the stringent controls that laboratories now impose on any tests involving human subjects. Milgram, Kochen, and de Sola Pool (along with mathematician Benoit Mandelbrot) either worked or studied at the University of Paris in the early 1950s and grew to know one another during that period.

3. J. R. Beniger provides, in *The Control Revolution* (Cambridge: Harvard University Press, 1990), an insightful study of the control and market structure implications of advances in technology during the 19th and 20th century.

4. Indeed, P. M. Senge and J. D. Sterman argued ("Systems Thinking and Organizational Learning: Acting Locally and Thinking Globally in the Organization of the Future," in Kochan and Useem (eds.), *Transforming Organizations*, New York: Oxford University Press, 1992) that local decision-making responsibility and individual autonomy lead to anarchy unless managers account for the interconnections and long-term effects of local decisions. Laudable goals such as empowering and enabling individuals often prove counterproductive unless managers act locally and think globally. T. W. Malone and J. F. Rockart ("How Will Information Technology Reshape Organizations? Computers as Coordination Technology," in Bradley, Hausman, and Nolan (eds.), *Globalization, Technology, and Competition*, Boston: Harvard Business School Press, 1993) offer suggestions for using IT to help meet the challenge of thinking globally while implementing effectively on a local basis.

5. J. C. Westland ("Bayesian Alternatives to Neural Computing," *IEEE Transactions on Systems, Man, and Cybernetics*, November 1994) describes a framework of security risks in a placeless market, and W. K. Knoke (*Bold New World* [New York: Kodansha, 1996]) offers an entertaining speculation on future life in a placeless society. The essential guide to surviving and prospering in the 21st century.

6. RJR Nabisco and the IRS are just a few. Nabisco estimates that processing a paper purchase order costs the company $70, while processing an EDI purchase order reduces the cost to a mere $0.93. Quoted on Callero Management Information Services, Inc. Web site, http://www.cmisltd.com/edi_benefits.htm

7. "Survey of Electronic Commerce," the Economist, May 10, 1997, p. 14.

8. Survey of Electric Commerce, *Economist*, May 10, 1997, p. 6.

9. *Source:* U.S. Department of Commerce, Economics and Statistics Administration, based on Bureau of Economic Analysis and Census data. http://www.ecommerce.gov/emerging.htm

10. "Gilder meets his critics," Feb. 1995, originally printed in *Forbes*. http://www.discovery.org/Gilder/critics.html

Financial Times Syndication Services: Making Money on the Web

The Financial Times online is one of the most comprehensive and readable sister sites to newspapers on the Internet. Instead of regurgitating the news and layouts of its printed parent, the FT site is fast, efficient and more importantly readable on screen. Superbly illustrated and effectively laid out, the reader sees it is more than a print duplication.
—Asian Advertising and Marketing, May 2, 1997

In May 1995, the *Financial Times* (*FT*) made a tentative entry into "cyberspace" establishing a presence on the Internet. They limited their site to the top five daily news stories, following a host of commercial and entrepreneurial organizations keen to establish themselves on the new publishing and communications medium. Operations were maintained inside the Syndication Department and the exercise was seen to be merely one (minor) aspect of marketing. The budget for the early *FT* Web site was minimal and running cost was zero. However, perceiving a greater commercial opportunity, the newspaper's Web site was relaunched in March 1996 by a specially designated "Net team" of designers, programmers, journalists, administrative staff and managers, creating a new FT department.

Worldwide, what *Wired* magazine had termed the "Great Web Expansion" was underway with a new Web page "published" for global consumption, on average, every 30 seconds. Along with the frenzy and the hype, however, the pervasive influence of the Internet and, in particular, the World Wide Web (WWW), began to spread to the more traditional medium companies. The question they were faced with was how to use this new communications tool? Was it an administrative or a mass media tool? Did it in fact represent a genuine new medium or was it more simply "old wine in a new bottle"? Did its global potential indicate the possibility of a whole new class of customers? Or was it simply a more focused version of the same demographics? In short, did the advent of the Web offer a potential new profit stream to the traditional mass media conglomerate or not?

For most large media organizations, their early attempts through the mid-1990s to exploit the new media opportunity proved fruitless. Limited bandwidth, leading to severe congestion, and disenchanted advertisers meant that the traditional economics for mass commercial communication were ineffective. By July 1996, more than 70% of the commercial providers of original content on the World Wide Web—including virtually all of the large high-profile mass media sites—had disappeared or radically scaled back their operations. This prompted Don Logan, President of Time, Inc., to retitle the World Wide Web, "The Great Black Hole." For the *FT*, Web success proved equally problematic, with the "Net team" relying on advertising alone to provide a modest return on their investment.

This case was prepared by Peter Lovelock of Hong Kong University and Dr. Theodore H. Clark of The Hong Kong University of Science and Technology.

In late 1995, however, the *Financial Times* had begun publication of a special 20-part "Mastering Management" series. By December it had become apparent that the series was a significant boost to the FT's circulation. Subsequently, the Syndication Department found itself approached by clients and customers seeking republication rights. In order to address this opportunity, the Syndication Department began to look for a logistical solution since distribution of the Mastering Management text required the storage and staggered transfer to clients worldwide of some 250,000 words of text in 20 installments over a period of many months with different publication starting dates for each new client. With their earlier Web site experience, the new project appeared to the Syndication Department to be ideally suited to the Internet. As such, the solution that they arrived at was simplistically elegant: transfer all the data onto a secure web site, set up a credit facility, and then allow customers to access the material when and as they needed.

For the Syndication Department, use of the Internet meant that the Mastering Management series—and for that matter any similar series—could be simply loaded up week by week and then stored indefinitely. No further work would be required outside of a manual registration process. Security was not a significant issue at this stage as the text had already been published. Moreover, since republication fees would be paid in advance, customers would not even be required to pay via the Internet. The beauty of the proposal was that it reduced transmission costs to a minimum through the use of the Internet to transfer text. This became the *FT*'s first genuine attempt at using the Internet to make money.

The success of the Mastering Management series led the *Financial Times* to develop an efficient method of distributing *FT* syndicated material using the Internet as the delivery medium. The reduction in transmission cost and labor time encouraged the newspaper to expand the material it offered through this mechanism, so that all of the *FT*'s syndicated services (its worldwide distribution) were centralized around the process. In addition to significant cost savings, the change had two immediate impacts. First, there was an attraction of new customers, particularly from developing countries who had access to the Internet and were able to benefit from the reduced access costs. Second, expansion of the distribution process to the *FT*'s general news service required a reevaluation of security and management issues since this material had *not already* been published.

Company Backgroud

The *Financial Times* is widely regarded as one of the world's great newspapers and a journal of record for the business community. Its reputation has been earned by

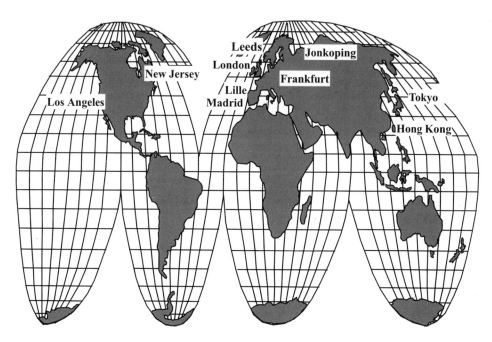

Figure 3.7
Financial Times worldwide printing locations

providing accurate reporting, market-moving analysis and consistently reliable business and financial statistics. By 1996, the *Financial Times* had a daily readership of over a million in 160 countries throughout the world, with a worldwide circulation in excess of 300,000. A 1994 survey of the European Business Readership group showed that in Europe the *Financial Times* enjoyed almost twice the readership of the *Economist* and nearly five times the readership of the *Wall Street Journal*. At that time, the *FT* was printed in a total of 10 centers across Europe, North America, and Asia (figure 3.7).

The Financial Times Group, publisher of the *Financial Times*, also provided many other international business and financial information services (figure 3.8). The Financial Times Group comprises the *Financial Times* newspaper; FT Information (various business and financial information services); Les Echos Group (publisher of France's *Les Echos*); and shareholdings which include 57% of Recoletos (Spain's leading newspaper and magazine publisher) and 50% of *The Economist*. Other electronic publishing services provided by the Financial Times Group included the *FT* website (www.ft.com) and FT Syndication.

The Financial Times is the leading global English language newspaper and has a variety of international publishing interests mainly in France, Spain and Canada. Financial Times Information provides a range of business and financial information services including on-line databases, news and research services.

FT Newspaper
Printed in UK, France, Germany, USA, Japan, Sweden, Spain and Hong Kong

FT Electronic Publishing
FT.com, FT Cityline, FT Syndication, Veritas, FT Pictures, Voice Publishing

FT Diaries

FT Information

FT Extel
Extel Market Data, Extel Exshare, Extel Real-time Data Services, Extel News, Extel Research Products, Extel Taxation Services, Extel Publications

FTEBI
FT Profile, FT McCarthy, Discovery
Business Research Centre

Broadcast Monitoring Company/Lincoln Hannah

Les Echos Group
Les Echos (Newspaper), Enjeux-Les Echos (Magazine),
J.B.Bailliere, Panorama du Medecin

FT Shareholdings and Joint Ventures:

Recoletos Group (Spain) - 97% owned by FT
Expansion, Actualidad Economica, Marca, Telva,
Diario Medico, Pool de Medios, Newsletters

The Economist - 50% owned by FT
Financial Post (Canada) - 19.9% owned by FT
AFP-Extel News Ltd. - 50% owned by FT
AFX/Asia - 30% owned by FT
Financial Izvestia - minority investment by FT
Strategic Research Group - minority investment by FT

The Financial Times is part of the Pearson group

Figure 3.8
Financial Times Group's Newspaper and Information Companies

The Financial Times Group was part of the Pearson Group, a UK-listed company with a variety of information, education, and entertainment businesses (figure 3.9). Pearson Group companies and investments included Addison Wesley Longman—the educational publisher; Mindscape—a publisher of consumer software; a 50% take in Lazard Brothers, one of London's leading merchant banks; Pearson New Entertainment—a consumer magazine publisher; Pearson Professional—a publisher of books, periodicals, and newsletters under brand names including Pitman, and Churchill Livingstone; Pearson Television—the holding company for the group's television interests, including Thames Television and Grundy Worldwide; Penguin—the book publisher; the Tussauds Group—the leading European operator of paid-for visitor attractions, including Madame Tussaud's waxworks; and the Financial Times Group. In their 1996 group annual report, Pearson stated that: "Our triple objective is to establish the *Financial Times* as the world's most authoritative business newspaper, to provide other business and professional information for a number of key sectors and to build our capacity to deliver this electronically. In information we [have] pushed through easily the largest expansion of the *FT* newspaper's overseas distribution network since the launch of its international edition in 1979."

- See http:///www.pearson-plc.com/finance/pearson.html for detailed financials.
- See http://www.pearson-plc.com/global/index.htm to view global operations.

Financial Times Syndication

Financial Times Syndication was responsible for both guarding and marketing the *FT*'s intellectual copyright. To this end a range of services was made available to users outside the FT Group; these services could be taken individually or packaged together to meet the customers' needs. As of mid-1997, services available included:

- *Daily News*—leading news and business stories from the *Financial Times*. It included an *FT* editorial and news and business summaries. Updated each evening (Sunday–Friday) with stories from the following day's newspaper.
- *Features*—a variety of background features which examine, analyze, and evaluate the people, policies, and trends in the news. Updated daily (Monday–Friday).
- *Arts & Leisure*—a variety of lifestyle features from the Weekend *FT*, including travel, sport, book reviews, and personality profiles. Updated on Friday evening each week.
- *Surveys*—in-depth reports on a specific country, industry, region, or area of business. Updated on request.
- *Information Technology*—reports on information technology developments around the world. Updated monthly.

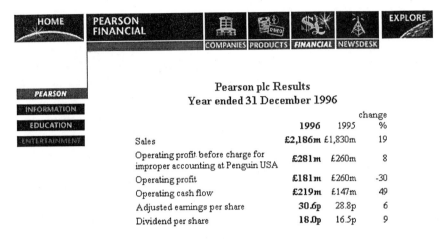

Pearson plc Results
Year ended 31 December 1996

	1996	1995	change %
Sales	£2,186m	£1,830m	19
Operating profit before charge for improper accounting at Penguin USA	£281m	£260m	8
Operating profit	£181m	£260m	-30
Operating cash flow	£219m	£147m	49
Adjusted earnings per share	30.6p	28.8p	6
Dividend per share	18.0p	16.5p	9

Detailed Reports

- Consolidated Profit and Loss Account
- Consolidated Balance Sheet
- Operating Cash Flow, Net Movement of Funds from Operations and Change in Net Debt
- Notes to 1996 Results
- Statement of Total Recognised Gains and Losses
- Reconciliation of Movements in Equity Shareholders' Funds
- Financial Ratios
- Sector and Geographic Analysis
- Investment Banking

Key Points

- HarperCollins Educational integration successfully completed.
- Pearson now second largest trade book publisher in the world.
- Strong improvement in cash generation.
- Entertainment results hit by Penguin and Mindscape.
- Substantial investment in Financial Times brand.

Figure 3.9
Pearson PLC 1996 financial information summary
Source: http://www.pearson-plc.com/finance/pearson.html

- *Mastering Management*—a special 20-part management series.
- *Mastering Enterprise*—a special 12-part series which takes an in-depth look at specific management and business topics.

News and features published in the *Financial Times* were used in a variety of ways, after agreement was made with the Syndication Department. For example, clients of FT Syndication have used features in annual reports and in promotional material as well as republishing stories in their newsletters, magazines, and newspapers. However, the *FT* retained copyright to all material. The Syndication Department was also responsible for ensuring the transmission of the *FT*'s material to its worldwide customers. In 1997, the department comprised a managing editor, a deputy managing editor, two secretaries, and two journalists.

Syndication and Worldwide Distribution: The Old Process

The bulk of the Syndication Department's revenues came from republication agreements with newspapers around the world, and by late 1995 FT Syndication served approximately 100 contracts in some 50 countries. However, the costs of establishing and maintaining a worldwide distribution (and syndication) infrastructure were substantial. In September 1995, the *Financial Times* began publication of a special 20-part series entitled "Mastering Management." The series, produced in conjunction with business schools from the United States (Wharton), the United Kingdom (London Business School) and Switzerland (IMD), aimed to introduce readers to the main concepts of modern general management.

In originally proposing the republication sales of the Mastering Management series, management assumed that distribution would simply be handled via the existing Syndication processes. This meant storing the installments (approximately 12,500 words each) on the *FT*'s specially adapted computer editorial system (known as "Edwin"). There would eventually be 20 such files. Clients would contact the Syndication Department with their requests and, as it was foreseen by management, Syndication would then distribute the series over time by simply addressing each story and transmitting it to its destination.

For the *Financial Times*, at that point in time (1995), the options for the delivery of text to clients around the world consisted of:

- hard copy (ordinary mail),
- facsimile,
- telex,

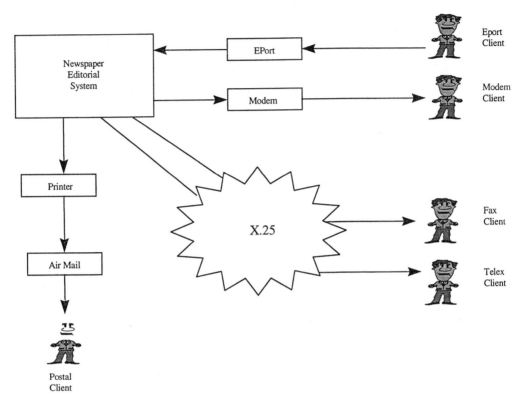

Figure 3.10
Financial Times syndication delivery: The old model

- dial-up modem, and
- X.25 (uncorrupted packets) (figure 3.10).

While this was a simple enough process, it remained labour intensive and time consuming. Syndication operated on a skeleton staff and, as already indicated, the problem with the republication sales of the "Mastering Management" series was that there was a continuing stream of customers who wished to receive the series incrementally, all with different publication starting dates. With the series paid for up front, the Syndication staff knew that downstream, management would potentially wonder why there was so much continuous effort for no incoming revenue. The challenge therefore was to find a way of centralizing and automating the distribution process.

The only alternative means for information access by clients was to collect the text files themselves. Clients with privileged access to the *FT*'s network were able to dial in and download the files. This was not feasible for all of the new customers attracted by the "Mastering Management" series. It also meant that the clients shouldered the transmission cost themselves—which was not perceived to be a strong selling point.

The Web as a Distribution Tool: The New Process

"This could be the FT's first genuine attempt at using the Internet to make money—through transmission cost savings."
—James Hook, News Editor, Syndication Department

Phase I: "Mastering Management"

One of the two journalists in the Syndication Department, James Hook, had been responsible for selecting and transferring editorial content to the earlier ill-fated *FT* Web site. It was this experience with the Web that made him think that the Internet was the ideal solution for the FT's "Mastering Management" distribution purposes and so the alternative suggestion was put to management. Hook's suggestion was to employ the spatial dynamics of the Internet and essentially bypass the issue of distribution altogether. Instead of paying to transfer the text (or paying to have the text transferred), the *FT* could simply post the text in cyberspace and allow customers to wander in and download the material themselves. There were no real security issues at this stage, since republication fees were paid in advance. A "hidden page" could be set up on the *FT*'s Internet server. This was to be given an address (http://www.ft.com/mm) which would be given only to clients; other individuals who accessed the *FT*'s home page (http://www.ft.com) would find no reference to the hidden page. The "Mastering Management" installments would be stored as ASCII files on the site. There would therefore eventually be 20 files, each containing some 12,500 words. Clients would simply access http://www.ft.com/mm, then download whichever files they wanted.

Hook mapped out the process required for management:

1. The existing "Mastering Management" series, stored on tape, would be returned to the *FT*'s editorial computer system.

2. Twenty individual files would be set up on the system, and labeled "MM1," "MM2," "MM3," etc. The files would have no expiry time.

3. The text would be subedited for past perfect tense and stored in the relevant files, with each file then containing the full set of stories from the relevant "Mastering Management" issue.

At this stage, the "Mastering Management" text would be ready to be delivered to, or collected by, clients using the old distribution process.

4. Text from the "Mastering Management" series would be transferred to the Syndication PC, and each "Mastering Management" issue would be stored in a separate hard-disk file. "Mastering Management" would then be ready for delivery to clients using e-mail.

5. A "hidden page" (address www.ft.com/mm) would be set up on the *FT*'s Internet server. Text files would be saved from the Syndication PC on floppy disks and stored on the *FT*'s Internet server. The "Mastering Management" text would then be ready to be collected by clients using the Internet.

At the time, management raised certain objections to the "hidden page" concept for distribution of FT syndication materials:

1. The new process could affect *FT* database sales. (This was considered unlikely, but the solution decided upon was to install password protection.)

2. The *FT* had a corporate image to maintain and raw ASCII files were considered unsightly and unprofessional. (The solution decided upon was to give customers only the ability to download attractively presented files, instead of allowing them to read the plain text version of the same files.)

3. The *FT*'s web server had been designed for specific read-only access. (Thus the establishment of a protocol for transferring files from the *FT* web server to the user's PC was required.)

   Each of these issues proved to be addressable and the proposal was given the go-ahead in January 1996. The site was developed and clients throughout the world were able to begin downloading the "Mastering Management" series (figure 3.11). News organizations which initially accessed the "Mastering Management" series via the Internet included: *Financial Post* (Canada), *El Cronista* (Argentina), *Business Standard* (India), *Business Day* (South Africa), and *Business Review Weekly* (Australia).

   Issue 20 of the "Mastering Management" series was installed on the site on March 22, 1996, by which time the "Net team" had redesigned and relaunched the *Financial Times* www.ft.com site. As with many other traditional media Web ventures, the

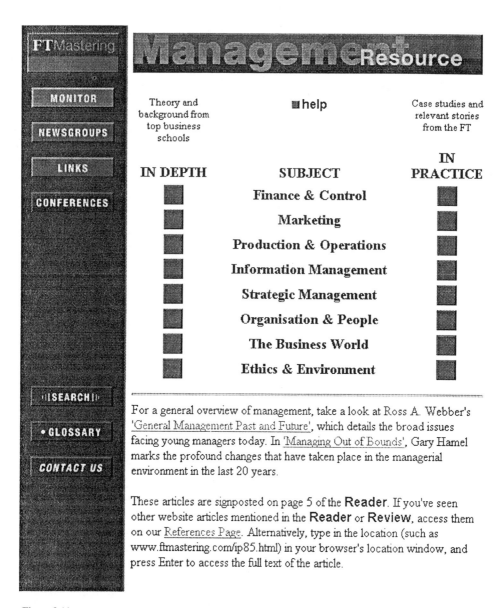

Figure 3.11
Financial Times "Mastering Management" series on the WWW
Source: http://www.ftmastering.com/resource.html

Financial Times' Web site was designed as an advertising presence or point of reference. It exploited the new medium by being linked in to the search engines and
interconnected nature of the Internet and thus advertising the *FT*'s existence, along
with services information and highlights from the news media.

However, the success of the "Mastering Management" republication venture suggested something else to the Syndication Department. Instead of merely posting an
advertisement and thus attempting to adopt the traditional mass media broadcast
model (one-to-many) to the new medium, why not use the Internet's focused architecture (one-to-one) to eliminate *all* of their distribution costs? More specifically, if the
entire contents of the Syndication Department's output were posted in cyberspace,
then instead of concentrating on serving a specific group of franchise-like clients, the
FT could open the equivalent of a virtual storefront where anyone anywhere could
wander in and choose the services they liked. These services could be either for individual purchase or for republication.

With continuing requests for republication access along with the compliments from
users of the new Internet-based distribution service (happy with the ease of access and
increased control the service allowed them), Hook approached management with the
suggestion that *all* Syndication services be made available on the Internet. A secure
Syndication Website could be designed and built for access by both browser and
FTP, with an integrated facility for transmitting material by e-mail. Hook believed
this new process could transform Syndication from an inward-oriented requests
department to an outward-oriented virtual store, thus making the most of the *FT*'s
commitment to the Web and virtually eliminating Syndication's transmission costs.

Phase II: All Syndication

By mid-1996 the Syndication Department had automated transmission of its Daily
News Service (DNS) to the Website each night. As before, DNS material was
transmitted from the *FT*'s central editorial computer system between 5:30 P.M. and
9:00 P.M. each day to a destination group DAILYNEWS, comprising several dozen
client newspapers worldwide. Now a new client—the Website—had been added.
Each story was automatically copied and directed into its slot on the browser pages
or the FTP files. Browser customers could call up the site synd.ft.com, click on the
DNS button, type in user name and password, and be greeted by the headlines of the
DNS stories. At this point stories could be downloaded. Similarly, FTP customers
could call up the relevant page, type in user name and password, and then download
the files. Hook also suggested a design dividing the Syndication Website into two
areas: administration and services (figure 3.12).

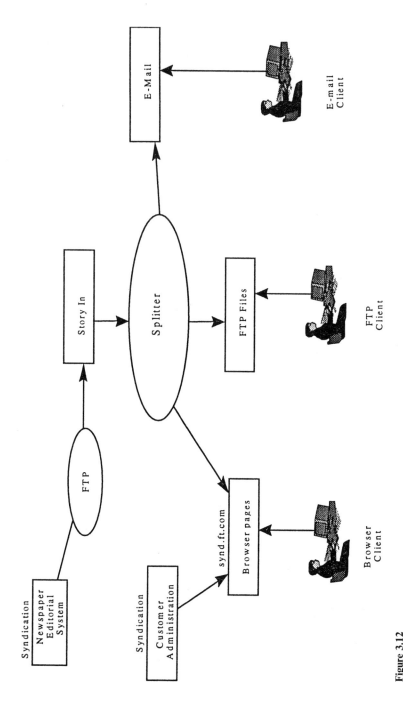

Figure 3.12
Financial Times syndication Website: The new model

■Pen Wars
Bic's acquisition plan

■Middle East
Crackdown demanded

■Earnings doubled
Weak yen a factor

■BT and MCI re-examine merger contract

British Telecommunications and MCI, the US telecoms operator BT has agreed to acquire for $23bn, are conducting a far more wide-reaching review of their businesses than was previously suggested. Sir Peter Bonfield, BT's chief executive, said yesterday the review - initiated after the US carrier's surprise profits warning last month - was "a broad, overall examination of the whole situation" and likely to last several more weeks.

■Bank of England
Insider is elevated

■Volvo/Renault
Unloading baggage

■FT in Brief
The newspaper at a glance

FROM £99 A MONTH 12.3% APR

Figure 3.13
Financial Times "Daily News"
Source: http://www.ft.com/hippocampus/contents.html

Administration. The Administration area would consist of a list of customers in alphabetical order. When a customer was "clicked" on, the customer's individual form would appear. For example:

> CUSTOMER: China Gazette
> PASSWORD: tiger
> CONTACT: Larry Ma—001-852-2632-1000
> ADDRESS: 13 Bowling St, Beijing
> NOTES: trial period only—disconnect 30/12
> SERVICES—
> NEWS: on
> FEATURES: off
> ARTS: on
> MM: off

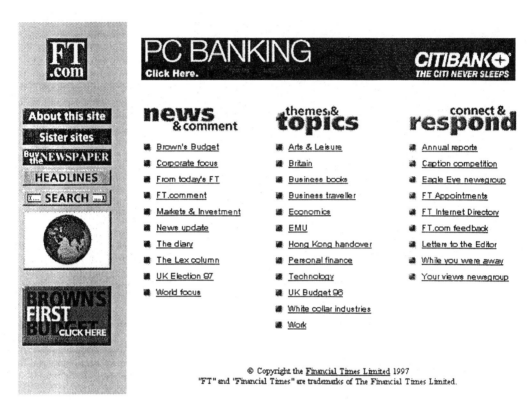

Figure 3.13 (continued)

Thus *China Gazette* would have access to NEWS and ARTS services only. Both areas would be switched off on December 30. The Syndication Department would have control of customer access.

Services. Initially there were to be four services on the site with provision made for expansion. The initial services were:

1. NEWS–The top 20 stories of the day. Copy purged automatically after 24 hours (figure 3.13).

2. FEATURES–The *FT* syndicated features. Copy purged automatically after 30 days.

3. MASTERING MANAGEMENT–The special 20-part series. Copy not purged.

4. ARTS–The weekly Arts and Leisure service. Copy purged automatically after 30 days.

Figure 3.14
Pearson Group's Information Division
Sources: http://www.pearson-plc.com/company/info.html and
http://www.pearson-plc.com/finance/info.html

Stories would be filed in chronological order, with the most recent material being at the top of the index. Stories would be named automatically, lifting the "slug" names from fields originally filled in on the newspaper's editorial computer system. The Syndication Department would have editing access to all services stored on the Website. Thus, they would be able to instantly "spike/kill items containing errors, items sent to an incorrect area, items withdrawn for legal reasons, items which are time-expired, etc." On accessing the FTP menu page, the customer would see the standard *FT* copyright information:

The customer would be asked for a user name and passwork each time he/she attempted to access a service. Each service would have a protection program which would only allow access to stipulated users, and there would be a mechanism to reveal how many times a customer had accessed the site over the previous five to seven days. If this number were to increase from, say, 20 to more than 50, the presumption would

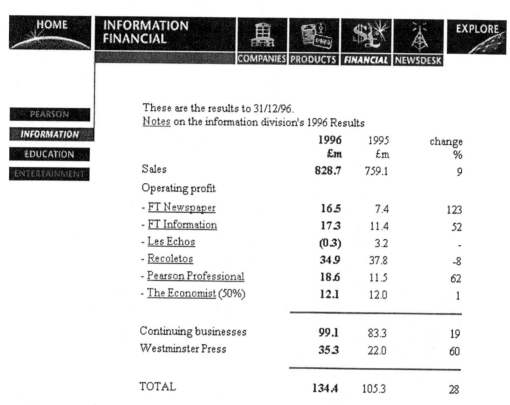

These are the results to 31/12/96.
Notes on the information division's 1996 Results

	1996 £m	1995 £m	change %
Sales	828.7	759.1	9
Operating profit			
- FT Newspaper	16.5	7.4	123
- FT Information	17.3	11.4	52
- Les Echos	(0.3)	3.2	-
- Recoletos	34.9	37.8	-8
- Pearson Professional	18.6	11.5	62
- The Economist (50%)	12.1	12.0	1
Continuing businesses	99.1	83.3	19
Westminster Press	35.3	22.0	60
TOTAL	134.4	105.3	28

Figure 3.14 (continued)

be that access security had been compromised. There would also be a PROBLEMS key on the FTP menu page, directing customers to the Syndication or Systems department for assistance.

In December 1996 the proposal was given the go-ahead, and at the end of the following month the Syndication site was launched. With the success of the site, eight further services were added in March 1997 to the original menu (figure 3.14). These were:

5. SURVEYS–Selected FT surveys. Copy purged automatically after 30 days.

6. I.T.–The monthly Information Technology issue. Copy purged annually.

7. SPORT–Articles on the finances, structure and politics of sports. Copy purged each week.

8. COMMODITIES–Stories and features from the commodities pages of the *Financial Times*. Copy purged each week.

9. REVIEW–Brief summary of the important news and business stories from the previous week. Copy updated daily.

10. PHOTOS–*FT* pictures. Material purged manually and selectively after 48 hours.

11. GRAPHICS–*FT* daily graphics. Material purged manually and selectively after 48 hours.

12. ARTWORK–*FT* drawings/diagrams/cartoons. Material purged manually and selectively after 48 hours.

Changing the Economics of Distribution and Nature of the Business

By focusing on a specific problem—distribution of text (and graphics) to multiple clients at different times—the *FT*'s Syndication Department was able to employ the Internet as a specific cost-saving solution. By the mid-1990s this was an innovative IT solution to a standard distribution problem, but it was not necessarily unique. Numerous listserv groups were employing the Net as a distribution mechanism and many intranet facilities were built on the basis of data cost minimization. However, among traditional media groups, the concept of using the World Wide Web as a means of facilitating republication distribution and sales certainly was unique.

Until this point most media groups had viewed the Web through their own mass-media lens, i.e., one-to-many. Hence they attempted to employ the Web as an advertising or marketing solution, soliciting subscriptions and/or registration. For the *FT*'s Syndication Department, the bulk of revenues was generated by republication rights sold through client media relationships around the world. This was a direct (one-to-one) relationship, with a distribution arrangement to match. Use of the Web meant that the Syndication Department was able to maintain a one-to-one relationship with its customers (the sale of republication rights), but it was also able to facilitate access to its services, more broadly advertise its availability, and completely remove transmission costs. The costs for maintenance of the Website replaced the transmission costs, but FT had already established the Website anyway, so additional costs were minimal. These Website costs could also be ameliorated among all clients, replacing the one-to-one transmission costs incurred previously. In so doing, the Syndication Department was able to attract new classes of customers, including both individuals and smaller, financially poorer media groups, such as newspapers in Eastern Europe and Africa. These groups had limited cash, but had access to the latest communications technologies, enabling them to exploit the opportunity offered by the *FT*'s Website.

At once, then, the *FT*'s Syndication Department had transformed from an inward-focused and controlled registration and transmission department to an outward-focused service department sharing both control and responsibility with the clients for access. In effect, it had been transformed from an internal media administration organ to a virtual store of information on the Web.

Management Issues and Concerns

While it represented an innovative adoption of Web technology, the Finanical Times Syndication site also raised a host of potential management dilemmas. For example, while the number of clients increased (thus increasing revenue) and data transmission was all but eliminated (thus reducing costs), management was concerned that individuals might be accessing and downloading the *FT*'s information without paying for the service. They were similarly concerned that individuals and corporations could download *and use* (publish) the *FT*'s syndicated material *without attribution.*

The previous model of distribution for the *FT* was based upon exclusive republication rights. The new model of distribution, however, meant that a vendor could pay for access to the *FT* site and then simply rebroadcast the information at no charge. Further recipients could then republish the information without attribution and the end user would be none the wiser as to where the information came from. This not only would reduce *FT*'s sales revenues, it could also reduce the brand integrity of the *Financial Times.*

To be sure, these challenges were not necessarily a product of the technology. In some senses, it was equally true that the same breaches could have occurred under the old model of distribution. Under the old system, when republication rights holders received the distributed information, they could have reentered the data and then could have rebroadcasted the information. However, this was less likely to occur under the former distribution system because of the exclusive arrangement with *FT* clients and due to the prestigious name of the *Financial Times.* The new distribution model meant that *re*distribution was significantly faster and cheaper, making it significantly easier for, say, a newspaper to contemplate redistributing the *FT* information to more financially strapped publications in the Argentine interior. Furthermore, where previously distribution had been based upon one-to-one "exclusive" republication arrangements, the new model encouraged potential customers to wander into the virtual shopfront and purchase whichever selection of services best suited their needs. This made it much more difficult for the *FT* to monitor where the information was eventually used, in much the same way that it was difficult to enforce intellectual property rights (IPR) restrictions upon a purchased book or magazine.

The central issue for management was whether an increase in revenue compensated for a reduction in (or perhaps, abrogation of) exclusivity. And, more particularly, how great an increase in revenue was required to compensate for such a reduction. Mirroring the architecture of the Internet, use of the Web reflected a shift to an open distribution platform and away from exclusive country representation. General management issues related to this specific situation included a reassessment of pricing structures (attracting the individual subscriber rather than the franchisee) and consideration of the security issues facing firms adopting an open platform architecture.

Security First Network Bank: The World's First Internet Bank
(http://www.sfnb.com)

The virtual financial institution of the future can be as small as a ten-man shop if it cuts the right deals for back-end providers. Security First Network Bank is one of the smaller banks in America, but with an electronic front-end interface to various partners, we're going to have every product that Fidelity and Schwab have and have it at better prices within six months.
—Michael McChesney, Chairman, December 1995

Michael Karlin, President of Security First Network Bank (SFNB), was considering the impressive list of successes achieved during the first year of the bank's operation. With the official opening of the bank on October 18, 1995, SFNB became the first bank to offer checking account services over the Internet. SFNB was also the first Internet bank to be federally insured by the FDIC, and the first bank to receive approval to offer all banking services over the World Wide Web (WWW). Within the first eight weeks of operations, SFNB opened nearly 1,000 on-line checking accounts, and by the end of its first year of operation, the bank had reached $41 million in deposits from Internet customers with more than 10,000 accounts from all 50 states of the United States using the Internet for their banking transactions. The products and services offered by the bank had also expanded dramatically during the first year of operations from a single basic checking account to a broad array of financial services now available. The company had also successfully completed an initial public offering (IPO) of its stock during the year, and had completed a strategic merger with Secure Ware, Inc. All things considered, the year had been a good one for both Karlin and SFNB.

However, there were still some real challenges and difficult issues ahead. One issue that still had not been clearly resolved was what the real core business for SFNB was. Should the firm focus primarily on expanding its retail banking operations or should it focus instead on selling software to other banks to enable them to provide similar services to SFNB over the Internet? For the retail banking business, there was also uncertainty about whether providing all banking services over the Internet alone was sufficient to capture the primary banking position with SFNB customers. Some customers had expressed concerns about the lack of physical banking locations where they could get cashier's checks, traveler's checks, deposit cash or coins, or maintain a safety deposit box. Perhaps a modified strategy of providing most services via the Internet but also offering a few traditional banking locations in major cities would allow SFNB to more effectively address the needs of a large segment of the consumer banking market. On the other hand, a key factor in SFNB's strategy for success in banking was operating at costs that were less than one-third of traditional banks due

This case was prepared by Dr. Theodore H. Clark of The Hong Kong University of Science and Technology and Dr. John J. Sviokla of the Harvard Business School.

to providing all services electronically without the overhead associated with traditional branch operations. It was unclear that a hybrid strategy of limited branch banking would be as effective as an extremely efficient but all electronic banking service portfolio.

Another issue associated with product offering was determining the appropriate level of risk and degree of market aggressiveness which the bank should assume in extending credit to current or potential SFNB customers. Thus far, the low operating costs of the bank have enabled SFNB to invest in very low risk assets (e.g., U.S. treasury bills) and still achieve attractive profit margins. However, some managers believed that this focus on investing only in very low risk assets was an inefficient use of the SFNB assets and needlessly limited SFNB customer service offerings. In an effort to improve both customer service and operating profits, SFNB introduced credit cards in November 1996 as the first consumer-based credit services available. The initial level of risk accepted by the bank on these first credit card customers was quite limited, but expanded credit card availability and offering of other credit services (e.g., auto loans and home mortgages) could be eventually added to the SFNB portfolio of services. For Karlin and James "Chip" Mahan, CEO of SFNB, the key issue to address was: How much financial risk should SFNB accept on its asset investments?

The future looked promising for SFNB. There were many opportunities ahead, but the problem was that the bank's management team did not have either the management or financial resources to pursue all of these opportunities simultaneously. There was some risk that if the SFNB management team did not come to a consensus and focus on selected opportunities identified as strategic for the future of the firm, the opportunities created by the first-mover advantage now possessed by SFNB could be dissipated by competitors with greater resources and established market positions. The main advantage for SFNB was time: It was clearly the leader in the industry in a number of key areas. However, this time advantage could be lost if not quickly capitalized upon and used as leverage to build additional competitive advantages in the marketplace and with the technologies involved.

· Try out SFNB's services at http://www.sfnb.com/demos/bankdemos.html.

· See http://www.sfnb.com/infodesk for a broad array of information about SFNB.

The U.S. Banking Industry and the On-Line Revolution

In 1995, the number of banks in the United States totaled 10,793 with over 59,000 branches and deposits worth in the region of $3,162,550 million. The top ten banks had average assets of $166,764 million and pretax profit of $2,756 million. A wave of mega-mergers in the industry had resulted in shifts among the rankings of the largest banks and reflected the increasing advantages of scale in banking which had been enabled by the reduction of barriers to interstate banking during the 1980s and 1990s.

As recently as 1980, as much as 70% of all U.S. individuals' financial assets were kept in banks. By 1995, that figure had dropped to 25% and the banking industry was being challenged on all fronts by eroding market share, shrinking profit margins, and unrelenting competition from nonbanks (see figure 3.15). Consumers were demanding banking services but not necessarily from traditional banks. The huge increase in choice for financial services from a wide array of competitors has lowered prices for

Branchless U.S. 'Banks' Attract Savers

By VANESSA O'CONNELL
Staff Reporter

NEW YORK — Forget the perky tellers, the marble-floors and back room with a giant vault.

A growing number of companies catering to U.S. savers coast-to-coast pay fatter interest rates and charge fewer fees than do many local banks. Because the companies typically have no branches, you must bank long-distance by phone and mail, sometimes using debit cards, ATMs and direct-deposit services.

Their pitch: We pay higher interest on your savings than you'll find offered by the bank branches in your neighborhood.

Last month, American Express Co. launched U.S.-wide a one-year certificate of deposit that always pays three-quarters of a percentage point more than an average rate as compiled by Bank Rate Monitor newsletter in North Palm Beach, Florida. The new CD recently yielded 5.85%.

In July, Cross Country Bank in Newcastle, Delaware, opened doors to savers everywhere. Several of its CDs are now the highest-yielding of any available nationwide, according to the newsletter. For example, savers can earn 6.25% on its one-year CD.

Here are a few other long-distance deals to note:

CDs by mail. Everyone knows that credit-card issuers charge the steepest loan rates around. But when *you* lend *them* cash, they often pay handsome yields. Dangling high interest rates as a carrot, they hope depositors will give them more cash to fund credit-card loans.

High-yielding CDs and savings accounts are now available from a slew of card issuers, including the new Cross Country Bank, which specializes in plastic for people with bad credit histories, and American Express Centurion Bank, the Midvale, Utah, issuer of Optima cards and other personal credit lines. A one-year CD from MBNA Corp., of Wilmington, Delaware, recently offered a 6.07% annual yield; its five-year CD paid 6.75%. A six-month CD from Advanta Corp., of Springhouse, Pennsylvania, paid 5.7%. A money-market savings account from Cleveland-based KeyCorp paid 5.25%.

But card issuers aren't the only ones casting wide nets when fishing for deposits. There's also TeleBank Financial Corp., an Arlington, Virginia, savings and loan with nearly $800 million in assets that typically pays higher-than-average yields on accounts because it doesn't have to maintain costly branch offices, a spokesman says. Its one-year CD recently yielded 5.5%.

Telebank depositor Margaret Pflug, who is 71 years old, describes herself as a "wheeler-dealer" when it comes to earning high yields on savings, adding: "I know the game backwards and forwards, and this is a great deal."

High-interest checking with a debit card. Plain-vanilla money-market mutual funds almost always pay more interest than do bank accounts. But most limit check-writing to large sums, or only a few checks a month. One exception: Investors with a brokerage account often have access to special money-market funds with unlimited checking, and sometimes even a debit card.

Now there's a second option. The 15-month-old E-Fund from Citizens Trust, of Portsmouth, New Hampshire, was de-signed to serve as a stand-in for bank accounts. It gained slightly more than 6% for the 12 months through Oct. 31, taking first place among more than 280 money funds tracked by Lipper Analytical Services Inc. Its yield was 5.28%.

Money funds keep a steady net asset value of $1 per share. So why is the fund's total return so much higher than its yield? It comes with a MasterCard debit card, and to encourage its use E-Fund puts 1% of all card-based purchases back into the $15.3 million fund. (The U.S. Internal Revenue Service limits the rebate to no more than 9.75% of the fund's investment income.)

E-Fund has a $35 annual fee, and some restrictions. You pay 65 cents per withdrawal at most ATMs, but there normally is no fee when using the card to make purchases. And there is no minimum balance, though you can't keep more than $15,000 in your account.

Still, it often beats the price of checking accounts available from local banks. On a $5,000 balance, E-Fund would yield roughly $140 in a year, assuming you made four ATM withdrawals a month and paid federal income taxes at a 31% rate. With the same balance in a checking account paying 2% interest, you would pocket $60 after taxes, assuming you pay 75 cents per ATM withdrawal.

E-Fund doesn't come with the Federal Deposit Insurance Corp. protection banks offer. But so far, it hasn't veered from its $1 a share price. Roughly 94% of the fund's investments are rated "first-tier" quality by IBC Financial Data's Money Fund Report, an Ashland, Massachusetts, newsletter. The remaining 6% is invested in floating-rate notes backed by the Small Business Administration.

Figure 3.15
Branchless banking opportunities
Source: Asian *Wall Street Journal*, November 15–16, 1996.

those services and made it difficult for banks to fight back against mutual fund companies and stock brokerages firms. With this in mind, the industry has cast a wary eye at the phenomenon of the Internet, a vast emporium where banking products could be marketed and sold.

Some senior banking industry analysts have commented that the market for Internet banking is still small and probably confined to those people who are familiar with the system and very heavy users of the Internet. SFNB have indicated that their success depends largely on two factors: first, the development and expansion of the market for on-line based financial services, and second, market acceptance of the company's products and services. With the former, doubt prevails as the market is still young and therefore acceptance of SFNB's products and services is uncertain.

· See http://www.webfinance.net/current/monroe23.html.

In contrast to the skeptical who doubted that Internet banking would emerge as a significant force in banking in the near future, Mahan believed that:

A virtual bank doing business with dramatically low operating costs will be in a position to rapidly gain market share in an industry which has already begun to shift away from traditional banking services.... The day will soon come when banks will become "electronic financial institutions."

Computer Penetration and Software Development

An important factor driving change in personal banking has been the growth in use of the personal computer (PC). In the 1980s, personal finance programs were introduced to provide graphical analyses and more convenient tracking of spending patterns, taxes, and investments. Meca was first with Managing Your Money, but Intuit's Quicken eventually captured 80% of the market. Microsoft was a late entry with Money, but is working hard to try and penetrate this market (a proposed merger between Microsoft and Intuit was rejected by the Justice Department). Until 1995, customers still had to enter their own personal financial information, but in that year, some banks began offering on-line banking via interfaces with either industry standard software (e.g., Quicken) or using their own proprietary software.

Some banking industry analysts and consultants view on-line banking as a continuation of the shift away from face-to-face transactions that began with the rapid expansion of ATM (automatic teller machine) networks. Enormous advances in computer and related communications technology are enabling a revolution in personal banking, and the new forms of on-line banking appear to be gaining momentum. Several industry surveys have indicated that there will be a vast migration to on-line banking by both the bank and consumers. By 1998, North American banks are planning to offer more than 600 Internet sites capable of services such as transferring funds between accounts and paying bills electronically, compared with only three such sites available as of January 1996. Some industry experts project that 15% of all banking customers will be using personal computers to do their banking on-line by the year 2000. Earlier efforts to promote home banking failed to catch on because the appropriate technology was not in place, but this was no longer expected to be a barrier with more than one-third of all homes owning PCs by 1996.

Increased Competition within the Industry

Another reason for the growth of electronic banking was the increasingly competitive pressures in the financial services industry during the mid- to late 1990s. Objectives for the industry included reduction of expenses, increased efficiency, and strengthening customer relationships. Electronic banking provided assistance with all three goals, especially given estimates that operating expenses of electronic banking services were only 25–30% of the cost of providing traditional banking services through existing bank branch offices. With lower costs and added services for customers, Internet banking and other forms of on-line banking appeared to be innovations no banks could afford to ignore.

Thus, "cyberbanks," unhampered by huge overhead branch "bricks and mortar" costs, could pay more for deposits, invest in safe low-yielding assets, and still earn healthy returns. With this futuristic scenario, the traditional local bank branch could easily disappear. Banking services such as ATMs, debit cards, stored valued cards, and home banking via the PC were much less expensive than the traditional bricks and mortar local branch. The saving available through nonbranch banking could become of significant advantage given the narrowing margins in the banking industry in the 1990s.

Most industry analysts expected banking expansion to be in the direction of electronic services rather than traditional bricks and mortar branches. However, there was huge uncertainty about the pace with which the industry would be transformed. In addition, achieving the cost reductions available through electronic banking services required large investments in information technology to support these new services. For example, one analyst estimated that the cost of developing the required customer interface and internal systems for on-line banking exceeded US$150 million in 1994. Investments to support on-line banking were increased at a rate of 150% per year during the mid-1990s, as banks tried to capture the opportunities enabled by these new on-line banking systems.

Efforts to Create Alliances and Industry Standards

Since only large banks could afford to develop their own on-line banking applications, most community banks would be unable to benefit from these new innovations that both improve service and reduce costs. The economies of scale in development of these services limit the number of banks that can participate in the on-line revolution without some form of collective or cooperative action by the industry. The joint venture between Visa and Mastercard to develop on-line banking standards and software was an example of one cooperative effort designed to meet the needs of small and medium-sized banks. Although initially focused on credit card transactions, some participants favored extending the development to include multiple forms of on-line banking. Microsoft was also interested in developing standards for electronic on-line banking which would utilize Microsoft software or services. Thus, the battle for developing on-line banking standards had just begun in the mid-1990s, with banks, other financial services firms, and software companies all striving to become the preferred on-line standard for consumer banking by the turn of the century.

Intuit Corp's. recent announcement that 19 of the largest financial firms in the United States are joining it to enable their customers to conduct financial business using the Internet had far-reaching implications. For the first time, consumers will make the quantum leap between banking and securities brokerage services by using appropriate software. One effect on the banking and brokerage business could be a dramatic reduction of staff and indeed buildings. Increased consolidations among banks could also result, with these mega-banks then able to offer an expand range of services to their customers.

Most of the major players at the forefront of the on-line banking revolution were not banks, but were services providers (Visa and MasterCard) or software developers (Microsoft and Intuit). They recognize that the banks were in the unique position of having access to large customer bases, mailing lists, banking relationships, and well-developed ATM and credit/debit card infrastructures. An important issue for banks in introducing on-line banking services was determining which firm in the "partnership" would be able to control the ongoing relationship with the customer. Bankers might find that customer loyalty could be higher to their on-line software provider (e.g., Intuit) than to their bank.

On-Line Banking Issues and Concerns

Internet banking was still viewed as vulnerable in several important areas, with issues related to security most important to both customers and bankers. For sound reasons, the Internet was perceived as an unsafe medium for valuable and sensitive information contained in business transactions. SFNB, working with SecureWare, claims to have developed methods which they insist have solved the security problem, but many in the industry remain skeptical.

The second important serious area of concern for Internet banking has been the lack of organization and control over the Internet itself. No one owns the Internet; therefore no one controlled it and ultimately, no one was responsible for making sure it does not fail or become congested. Would a tax payment that absolutely had to get there on time, in fact get there on time? Would customers eventually find service responsiveness degrading to the point where Internet banking was painfully slow, making alternative access technologies (e.g., telephone banking or ATMs) more attractive even if less flexible than using the Internet.

SFNB: A Virtual Bank Is Born

The concept for developing a bank on the Internet initially grew out of a discussion at a family gathering between two brothers-in-law. In July 1994, Michael McChesney (CEO of SecureWare, Inc.) talked with James "Chip" Mahan (then CEO of Cardinal Bancshares, Inc.) about an article he had recently read about two attorneys who had put up an advertisement on the Internet for U.S. green card services and had received more than 30,000 responses. Mahan asked, "Can we put up a bank on the Internet?" McChesney had been thinking about potential areas for expansion of his secure operating system and environment, and offering Internet-based banking services seemed to be a good fit with the capabilities his firm had to offer in the area of networking security. This initial information discussion eventually resulted in the creation of SFNB, with McChesney and the Cardinal Bancshares team providing the banking industry expertise and SecureWare providing the technical expertise.

Obtaining the necessary regulatory approvals for opening a bank focused entirely on providing services using the WWW was not easy, but SFNB and SecureWare management were able to demonstrate to the satisfaction of the banking regulators and the FDIC that the information infrastructure used by the bank provided greater security than the systems in use by most existing banks for providing traditional services. Most banking security problems involve insider access, and the most important issues related to security actually are within the bank rather than relating to the means of accessing the bank by customers. Even so, the security provided by SFNB and SecureWare protected customer and bank funds and data from penetration from both external and internal individuals. The SecureWare operating system used by SFNB was designed for highly secure military and national security operations, and is considered to be one of the most secure operating systems in the world. Since bankers, customers, and regulators were all concerned about security issues associated with Internet banking, SFNB selected its name to emphasis its focus on providing extremely high levels of security in its Internet banking operations. Thus, *security* of the network and customer information was truly the *first* concern at *Security First* Network Bank.

• See http:\\www.sfnb.com\infodesk\security_menu.htm for security information.

The bank received approval to offer banking services using the WWW interface jointly developed by Cardinal Bancshares and SecureWare on October 18, 1995. Within one month, the bank had almost 1,000 customers, even with little paid advertising. The best source of advertising for SFNB during the past year has been articles written about the bank in computer and electronics journals. Paid advertising by SFNB was minimal during the first year of operations, but the company was considering using more advertising in 1997 to accelerate the growth of its customer base.

• Access http:\\www.sfnb.com\newscenter for articles published about SFNB, and the video vault at this location also offers interesting interviews with SFNB executives.

While many companies have already offered banking by a personal computer for many years before SFNB opened its doors, those transactions were done by a customer linking directly to a bank using a modem and dial-up lines. Special software was required, and the services were often difficult to set up and use. Security First offered customers with Internet browser software the ability to begin banking on-line with no software and through an easy to use customer interface. Customers were able to access their SFNB account from any computer anywhere in the world via a WWW interface, with no additional software of any kind required.

• See http://www.sfnb.com/infodesk/tales.html # lessons for reflections on first year.

The Merger, Spin-off, and IPO

SFNB introduced its Virtual Vault Internet access software at the Montgomery Securities banking conference in March 1995 to an audience of bankers and investors in the banking industry. The "10-minute" presentation followed a presentation by Intuit and quickly became the highlight of the conference. After more than 30 minutes of questions and answers, the conference organizers had to terminate the discussion to move on with other events that had been planned. For three days following this presentation, the SFNB suite at the conference hotel was virtually mobbed by bankers and investors who wanted to learn more about the software, including many who wanted to find out how they could purchase rights to use the applications developed by SFNB. Karlin, McChesney, and Mahan immediately realized that the real value of what they were doing was in development of banking software, not simply in offering banking services via the Internet. In addition, Mahan realized that building a successful software company to serve the banking industry would require more capital (and management commitment) to the new venture than the directors of Cardinal Bancshares would be willing to invest in the new start-up venture.

Timing was critical for success of the new venture, and additional capital was needed in order to accelerate the development of expanded Internet banking capabilities. Both McChesney and Mahen believed they were at a critical stage in the development of Internet banking where SFNB and SecureWare would have an opportunity to lead the industry into a new era of banking services. However, if SFNB did not take the lead, then the company could quickly be overshadowed by larger banks developing their own Internet banking solutions. In addition, the synergy between SFNB and SecureWare in the development and expansion of the Internet banking software and services business made it attractive to consider merging these two separate firms to eliminate potential incentive conflicts.

On May 24, 1995, Cardinal stockholders approved a complex transaction which involved merging SFNB, SecureWare, and Five Paces Software (the company which developed the SecureWare software) and then the establishment of the new SFNB combined firm as a completely separate entity from Cardinal. Ownership of the merged company was distributed as follows:

· 25% to the *stockholders* of Cardinal Bancshares, Inc. (former parent of SFNB, Inc.);

· 20% to the *stockholders* of Five Paces Software (to become a subsidiary of SFNB);

· 25% to three new banking partners investing $3 million in the merged company; and

· 30% to the management and directors of the new merged company (held as options).

The three new banking company investors in SFNB were Huntington Bancshares, Wachovia Corp., and Area Bancshares. Huntington and Wachovia were viewed as strategic partners which would assist SFNB in gaining access to other banks in offering software to enable Internet banking. Huntington (see http://www.better-investing.org/codata/hban.html) was considered to be one of the technology leaders in the banking industry and was very enthusiastic about the opportunities created by Internet banking for the industry. Wachovia was viewed in the industry as a very conservative and well-run bank holding company. Including Wachovia in the list of initial investors in SFNB provided an important credibility for the banking industry and suggested that Internet banking could be seriously considered by even conservative banks (see http://www2.interpath.net/hpe/tbn/banking67.html). The investment by Area Bancshares, a small bank holding company in Kentucky, was beneficial in facilitating the merger with SecureWare and divestiture from Cardinal. The largest shareholder of this smaller bank was also the largest shareholder of Cardinal, and he was a strong believer in the potential of the Internet banking services to transform the industry.

Although this agreement was entered into on March 24, 1995, by Cardinal, Five Paces Software, and the three banks investing additional capital in the firm, the final merger and divestiture was sealed until approval was issued by the Federal Reserved Board (FRB) for acquisition of a software company by a bank (see http://www.ffhsj.com/bancmail/21starch/960611.htm). Banks had formerly not been allowed to own firms which supplied software to other banks, so this decision by the FRB on May 21, 1996, was needed before the merger could be completed. On May 23, 1996, the agreement entered into a year earlier was implemented and SFNB with the SecureWare subsidiary was spun off to Cardinal shareholders and the other investors in the newly merged company.

On the same day as the spin-off from Cardinal Bancshares to stockholders and investors, SFNB also issued its initial public offering (IPO) of stocks to individual investors. The IPO was priced at $20 per share and the stock price immediately rocketed to $45 per share in the first day of trading (see figures 3.16 through 3.19 for selected information from the IPO offering document). The three banks that had agreed to invest $30 million in SFNB initially in May 1995 found that their initial investments of $1.25 per share had increased in value by 3,600% in one year, and many of the managers who founded the firm became millionaires (at least on paper) overnight. (However, the management options only vested at 25% per year, so this "wealth" could not be converted to cash immediately.)

· See http://www.webfinance.net/financing/bankhl21.html for IPO information.

In connection with obtaining regulatory approvals of the merger and spin-off, Cardinal and SFNB agreed to terminate director and management overlaps between the two firms. (See figure 3.17 for information on overlaps in ownership and management between Cardinal, SFNB, and Five Paces at the time of the IPO.) Mahan agreed to resign as CEO of Cardinal and became CEO of SFNB after the divestiture.

McChesney became Chairman of the Board of SFNB and CEO of the Five Paces subsidiary of SFNB. Robert Stockwell resigned his position as Treasurer of Cardinal to become the CFO of both SFNB and Five Paces. Michael Karlin had also resigned his position with Cardinal prior to the divestiture to become President of SFNB.

SFNB Operations and Strategy

Karlin was committed to a dual strategy at SFNB of simultaneously operating a successful bank using the Internet and selling Internet software to other banks. There was obvious synergy between being able to demonstrate that Internet banking was both economically attractive and secure and being active in marketing Internet banking software solutions to other banks. However, there were also some conflicts of interest between selling Internet banking software and competing with other banks that offer Internet checking solutions.

Retail Banking Services

Most SFNB customers were professionals between the ages of 26 and 55, with 54% of customers reporting annual household incomes in excess of US$50,000. Average account balances were approximately $1,000 for non-interest-bearing checking accounts as of September 1996. (Interest-bearing checking accounts were not available until October 1996; some larger non-interest-bearing accounts were expected to switch to the new money market products which had been introduced then.) SFNB also offered one of the highest rates on CDs (certificates of deposit) in the nation, which had attracted some customers, but the primary attraction of the bank to its customers was the provision of free Internet checking with no service charges (for normal usage levels) and no required minimum balance.

The SFNB banking services offerings were highly attractive to consumers, as SFNB charged no fees for its basic checking account services or for its credit cards. The number of services had expanded greatly over time and by early 1997 included money market accounts and interest-bearing checking, savings accounts, certificates of deposit, debit cards, and credit cards. Mortgage loans, other consumer loans, business checking, and brokerage account services were expected to be introduced during 1997 to further augment the SFNB portfolio of services available on over the Internet.

• See http://www.sfnb.com/infodesk/products.html for a list of available products.

During SFNB's first year of services, the bank did very little advertising and promotion of its services. Customers found out about SFNB through articles about the

OFFERING CIRCULAR SUMMARY

The following summary is qualified in its entirety by, and should be read in conjunction with, the more detailed information and financial statements appearing elsewhere in this Offering Circular. Unless otherwise indicated, the information in this Offering Circular assumes (1) that the "Spin-Off" (defined below) and the sale of Common Stock to the Strategic Investors (defined below), both as described herein under the caption "The Spin-Off and Related Transactions," including the acquisition of Five Paces, has been consummated prior to the closing of the sale of the Common Stock offered hereby, (2) that the preferred stock to be issued in the Spin-Off is not converted into Common Stock and (3) that the Underwriters' over-allotment option is not exercised. The sale of Common Stock in the Offering is conditioned upon the consummation of the Spin-Off (as defined below).

Immediately following the Spin-Off, and in connection with the Offering, the SFNB Board of Directors has approved a 4 for 1 stock split of all of the to-be-issued and outstanding shares of Common Stock, which will become effective upon the consummation of the Spin-Off. Accordingly, all of the Common Stock information set forth in this Offering Circular, including information related to the Offering and the Spin-Off, gives effect to such stock split. Unless the context otherwise requires, all references to the "Company" refer to SFNB and Five Paces, giving effect to the consummation of the Spin-Off. For the definition of certain terms used herein, see the Glossary at the back of this Offering Circular.

The Company

Security First Network Bank is a federal savings bank and is the first FDIC-insured financial institution to execute traditional banking services over the Internet. In the Spin-Off, SFNB is acquiring Five Paces, a provider of Internet financial services delivery systems. Additionally, SFNB has entered into an agreement to acquire SecureWare, Inc. ("SecureWare") as promptly as possible following the Offering, subject to various conditions. SecureWare, an affiliate of Five Paces, is a provider of computer network security solutions.

Five Paces is the software company that developed the "Virtual Bank Manager" software used by SFNB to offer its Internet banking services. Virtual Bank Manager is the first product in the "Virtual Financial Manager" suite of software products which operate on the "Secure Web Platform" originally developed by SecureWare for the U.S. Department of Defense. In the first quarter of 1996, Hewlett-Packard Company ("Hewlett-Packard") purchased the Secure Web Platform from SecureWare. Five Paces has the right to use and resell the Secure Web Platform in its marketing of Virtual Financial Manager.

Virtual Financial Manager is being designed to allow consumers remote access to all aspects of their balance sheet via the Internet or a dial-up connection to their financial institution. The Company defines this concept as a "virtual net worth" solution, whereby consumers can have access to all of their financial asset and liability information, on a current market valuation basis, even though the information is maintained on separate computer systems operated by banks, brokerage firms, insurance companies, credit card processors, etc. The Company's initial product in the suite, Virtual Bank Manager, executes banking transactions over the Internet. Future products in the suite under development include a virtual brokerage manager, a virtual insurance manager and a virtual credit card manager.

Five Paces is marketing Virtual Financial Manager to domestic and international financial institutions. To facilitate rapid distribution and market penetration, the Company is entering into strategic alliances with systems integrators, data processors and financial institutions with strong domestic and international sales and integration operations. To date, the Company's strategic alliances include agreements with Hewlett-Packard, Unisys Corporation ("Unisys"), ALLTEL Financial Services, Inc. ("ALLTEL") and M&I Data Services ("M&I"), National Commerce Bancorporation ("NCB") and Synovus Financial Corp. ("Synovus"). Hewlett-Packard and Unisys provide products and system integration services to financial institutions worldwide, and

Figure 3.16
Offering circular summary
Source: SFNB Offering Circular (IPO) Document dated May 23, 1996.

ALLTEL and M&I provide data processing services to financial institutions. Pursuant to Five Paces' agreements with ALLTEL and M&I, Virtual Financial Manager will be the exclusive Internet banking solution offered by these organizations to their customers. In addition. the Company has entered into a non-binding letter of intent with Visa Interactive, Inc. ("Visa Interactive") for certain joint marketing efforts.

Five Paces offers three revenue models for installation and integration of Virtual Financial Manager. Under each model, the Company charges a monthly fee based upon usage. Under the first model, Five Paces offers the installation and integration of Virtual Financial Manager through its Atlanta data processing center, the operation of which is outsourced to ALLTEL. Under the second model, Five Paces offers Virtual Financial Manager directly to data processing companies, such as M&I. which will install and integrate Virtual Financial Manager as a product to be offered to their financial institution clients. Under the third model, financial institutions which operate their own data center can license Virtual Financial Manager. The Company also expects to generate one-time revenues from software installation. integration and consulting activities.

As the first financial institution to use Virtual Financial Manager and the Five Paces data center, SFNB has offered banking services over the Internet since October 1995. The Internet banking activities of SFNB presently include checking, money market and certificate of deposit accounts. electronic bill payment services, and account data and reconciliation services. It is SFNB's intention. subject to applicable regulatory approvals and business considerations. to expand its activities consistent with the development of the Virtual Financial Manager suite to include credit card lending, securities brokerage and other financial services.

SecureWare provides computer network security solutions for the U.S. government and commercial applications. The Company's strategy in acquiring SecureWare is to combine SecureWare's management expertise which led to the development of a comprehensive suite of security products with Five Paces' Virtual Financial Manager solution. The principal stockholders of SecureWare are presently the principal stockholders of Five Paces and, after the Spin-Off, will be controlling stockholders of SFNB. The acquisition of SecureWare is subject to various conditions, including applicable regulatory approvals and receipt by SFNB of a fairness opinion as to the consideration to be paid. SFNB expects to apply for such approvals and obtain such fairness opinion promptly following the Spin-Off. Accordingly. the acquisition of SecureWare is not a condition to the sale of Common Stock in the Offering. and there can be no assurance that such acquisition will be consummated.

As part of the Spin-Off, two of the nation's larger bank holding companies which SFNB believes are recognized bank technology and data processing leaders. Huntington Bancshares, Incorporated ("Huntington") and Wachovia Corporation ("Wachovia"). as well as Area Bancshares Corporation ("Area Bancshares"), have agreed to purchase common and convertible preferred stock of the Company for an aggregate of $3.0 million and licenses for use of the Five Paces technology for an aggregate of $2.0 million. The Company also has entered into other strategic alliances, selling 68.572 shares of Common Stock to NCB for $1.0 million and 137,144 shares of Common Stock to Synovus for $2.0 million. (NCB and Synovus are referred to collectively in this Offering Circular as the "Strategic Investors.")

SFNB, Five Paces and SecureWare can be found on the World Wide Web at http://www.sfnb.com, http://www.fivepaces.com and http://www.secureware.com, respectively. The Bank's headquarters is located at 300 Virginia Avenue, Pineville, Kentucky 40977 and its telephone number is (606) 337-7011. The Bank also maintains executive offices at 2957 Clairmont Road, Suite 280, Atlanta, Georgia 30329, which is where the Bank's Internet banking operations are located. The telephone number of the Bank's Atlanta office is (404) 679-3200. The executive offices of Five Paces and SecureWare are also located at 2957 Clairmont Road, Atlanta, Georgia.

Figure 3.16 (continued)

The Spin-Off and Related Transactions

The Spin-Off

Prior to consummation of the Offering, Cardinal will effect the Spin-Off of SFNB pursuant to the Cardinal Bancshares, Inc. Amended and Restated Plan of Distribution (the "Plan of Distribution"). Under the Plan of Distribution, Cardinal will distribute, pro rata to each Cardinal stockholder (the "Distribution"), 2,398,908 shares of Common Stock (the "Distributed Shares"). In addition, cash will be paid in lieu of fractional shares in the Distribution. In connection with the Distribution, SFNB has adopted an Amended and Restated Plan of Recapitalization (the "Plan of Recapitalization") pursuant to which, among other things, SFNB will (i) dividend $3.0 million to Cardinal from cash on hand, (ii) sell a combination of 2,400,000 shares of Common Stock and SFNB Class A Convertible Preferred Stock, no par value per share ("Preferred Stock"), to Area Bancshares, Huntington and Wachovia for $3.0 million, (iii) issue an additional 1,920,000 shares of Common Stock in the acquisition of Five Paces and (iv) grant options to officers, other employees and non-employee directors for up to 2,880,000 shares of Common Stock. Also as part of the foregoing transactions, Area Bancshares, Huntington and Wachovia have agreed to license Virtual Bank Manager for an aggregate of $2.0 million.

The foregoing transactions and agreements, including the Distribution, the sale of Common and Preferred Stock to Area Bancshares, Huntington and Wachovia, and the acquisition of Five Paces are together referred to as the "Spin-Off."

The Spin-Off is designed to separate SFNB's computer banking operations from Cardinal's traditional banking business, to facilitate the recapitalization of SFNB, and to provide SFNB with the requisite managerial expertise and capital structure to pursue its business plan. Although Cardinal and SFNB will share certain directors and officers, the separation of these businesses, which have distinct financial, investment and operating characteristics, is expected to permit each business to more effectively pursue its own business plan.

Stock Sale to Strategic Investors

Immediately upon the Spin-Off, SFNB also will sell for $2.0 million (or $14.58 per share) 137,144 shares of Common Stock to Synovus, and for $1.0 million (or $14.58 per share) 68,572 shares of Common Stock to NCB. The sale of Common Stock to the Strategic Investors is part of the Company's strategy to align itself with organizations which the Company believes will facilitate rapid distribution and market penetration of the Company's products and services.

Ownership of Common Stock

Following the Spin-Off and the Offering, directors and executive officers of the Company will beneficially own 20.10% of the outstanding Common Stock (without giving effect to the conversion of any Preferred Stock).

The SecureWare Acquisition

The Company entered into an Agreement of Merger with SecureWare and its stockholders dated as of April 30, 1996 (the "SecureWare Acquisition Agreement") pursuant to which SecureWare will be acquired by merging a to-be-organized wholly owned subsidiary of the Company with and into SecureWare. Under the

Figure 3.16 (continued)

SecureWare Acquisition Agreement, the Company will acquire all of the capital stock of SecureWare for aggregate cash consideration of $5.0 million and $713,000 of non-cash consideration related to the conversion of presently outstanding SecureWare options. The presently outstanding options of SecureWare will be converted into options for an aggregate of 70,400 shares of SFNB Common Stock at a per share exercise price of $4.46. Also under the SecureWare Acquisition Agreement, at the effective time of the acquisition, options to purchase an aggregate of up to 560,000 shares of Common Stock will be granted, of which 400,000 will have a per share exercise price of $12.92 and 160,000 will have a per share exercise price of $6.67. The Company will recognize over a four year period from the SecureWare acquisition additional compensation expense of $1.0 million upon the grant of the options with an exercise price of $6.67. All of the foregoing options, which will be granted to certain employees of SecureWare, other than the principal stockholders of SecureWare referred to below, will become exercisable in equal installments over a four-year period, subject to the optionee continuing to be employed by SFNB or any subsidiary thereof.

Consummation of the acquisition of SecureWare is subject to the completion of the Spin-Off, the delivery of a fairness opinion, as described below, and other conditions. The acquisition of SecureWare also is subject to applicable regulatory approvals and notices.

Because of the aforementioned conditions to the acquisition of SecureWare, there can be no assurance that such acquisition will take place. The acquisition of SecureWare is not a condition to the Spin-Off or the Offering.

The Offering

Common Stock offered by the Company	2,440,000 shares
Capital Stock to be outstanding after the Offering (1)	7,726,792 shares of Common Stock 1,637,832 shares of Preferred Stock (2)
Use of proceeds	The Company intends to use the estimated net proceeds from the Offering for general corporate purposes, including working capital. Initially, approximately $5.0 million will be invested in Five Paces for further development, marketing and support of the Virtual Financial Manager suite. Also, the SecureWare Acquisition, if consummated, will cost approximately $5.2 million, including related expenses. An additional $2.0 million is expected to be invested in SecureWare for working capital and other corporate purposes. The balance of net proceeds will remain in SFNB and will be used as working capital and to support the expansion of its Internet banking activities. Pending such uses, the Company may invest the net proceeds in short-term interest-bearing securities and accounts.
	Subject to regulatory considerations, SFNB also may consider acquisitions complementary to its business. Other than in connection with the acquisition of SecureWare, SFNB has not entered into any agreements regarding an acquisition.
Nasdaq National Market Symbol	SFNB

Figure 3.16 (continued)

(1) Based on the consummation of the Offering and the number of shares of Common Stock to be issued in connection with the Spin-Off and the Common Stock to be sold to the Strategic Investors. Excludes (a) 2,880,000 shares of Common Stock issuable upon exercise of stock options granted to directors, officers and employees of the Company at prices ranging from $0.625 to $1.25 per share (see "Management—Directors Option Plan" and "—Employee Stock Option Plan") and (b) 366,000 shares of Common Stock issuable upon exercise of the Underwriters' over-allotment option. Also does not include additional options to purchase 400,000 shares of Common Stock at an exercise price of $12.92 per share, 160,000 shares at $6.67 per share and 70,400 shares at $4.46 per share, to be outstanding upon the acquisition of SecureWare. See "The SecureWare Acquisition."

(2) The Bank's Preferred Stock, which will be issued to Huntington, Wachovia and Area Bancshares in the Spin-Off, is convertible into Common Stock on an equivalent share basis, subject to certain conditions. See "The Spin-Off and Related Transactions—Stock Sale."

Risk Factors

For a discussion of considerations relevant to an investment in the Common Stock and the Company's ability to develop and market its products and achieve its objectives, see "Risk Factors."

Figure 3.16 (continued)

Selected Financial and Operating Data

The following table sets forth certain financial and other information for the Bank. Since June 1995, the Bank has materially changed its operations and, following the Offering, the operations of Five Paces are expected to have a material effect on the financial results of the Company. Accordingly, past operations should not be considered indicative of current or future operations. The summary financial and operating data set forth below should be read in conjunction with "Management's Discussion and Analysis of Financial Condition and Results of Operations" and the Bank's consolidated financial statements and the notes thereto, which are included elsewhere in this Offering Circular. The financial information of the Bank, except for ratios, presented as of and for each of the years ended December 31, 1995, 1994 and 1993 has been derived from the consolidated financial statements of the Bank, which have been audited by KPMG Peat Marwick LLP, independent public accountants, whose report with respect to 1995 and 1994 is included elsewhere in this Offering Circular. Financial information for the Bank for the year ended December 31, 1992 has been derived from the consolidated financial statements for Cardinal Bancshares, Inc. Financial information for the year ended December 31, 1991 is not readily available because at such time the Bank had a June 30 fiscal year-end and such information is not considered meaningful. The financial and operating data for the three months ended March 31, 1996 and 1995 have been derived from the unaudited consolidated financial statements of the Bank and, in the opinion of management, include all adjustments (consisting only of normal recurring adjustments) necessary to present fairly the information set forth therein. The results of operations for the interim period ended March 31, 1996 are not necessarily indicative of the results to be obtained for the full fiscal year.

	At or for the three months ended March 31.		At or for the year ended December 31.				
	1996	1995	1995	1994	1993	1992
			(Dollars in thousands)			
Operating Data:						
Net interest income	$ 237	$ 758	$ 2,028	$ 2,829	$ 2,358	$ 2,098
Provision for loan losses	—	—	—	55	36	332
Net interest income after provision for loan losses	237	758	2,028	2,774	2,322	1,766
Non-interest income, excluding gains and losses on the sale of investment securities	52	66	246	304	260	195
Gains (losses) on the sale of investment securities	—	(50)	(50)	(168)	—	—
Non-interest expenses	1,320	686	4,207	2,451	1,564	1,831
Income tax expense (benefit)	(348)	26	(503)	156	347	195
Net income (loss)	$ (683)	$ 62	$ (1,480)	$ 303	$ 671	$ (65)
Net income (loss) per share	$ (0.07)	$ 0.01	$ (0.16)	$ 0.03	$ 0.07	$ (0.01)
Balance Sheet Data:						
Total assets(1)	$ 44,590	$ 79,922	$ 40,519	$ 77,690	$ 67,940	$68,274
Total loans, net of unearned interest income and unamortized fees(1)	20,741	61,620	21,109	59,884	49,369	43,425
Total deposits(1)(2)	39,937	71,552	34,812	70,397	61,809	61,945
Total borrowed funds	1,251	2,364	1,282	1,394	—	748
Total equity capital	2,746	5,138	3,464	5,075	5,244	4,974
Allowance for loan losses	298	558	293	556	480	510
Selected Ratios:						
Return on average assets	(6.51)%	0.32%	(2.60)%	0.40%	0.98%	(0.10)%
Return on average equity capital	(88.33)	4.92	(31.20)	5.86	13.04	(1.98)
Average equity capital to average total assets	7.37	6.44	8.33	6.82	7.52	5.13
Allowance for loan losses as a percentage of average net loans	1.43	0.91	0.79	0.97	1.05	1.13
Nonperforming loans as a percentage of year-end net loans	0.52	0.50	0.61	0.22	—	0.46
Net charge-offs (recoveries) as a percentage of average net loans	(0.02)	(0.01)	0.17	(0.04)	0.14	0.45
Net interest margin	2.55	4.08	3.84	3.87	3.58	3.20
Capital Ratios:						
Tangible	6.03%	6.38%	8.35%	6.53%	7.70%	7.28%
Core	6.03	6.38	8.35	6.53	7.70	7.28
Risk-based	14.99	14.11	19.34	14.39	17.40	17.70

(1) Reflects the reduction of loans, deposits and other assets resulting from the sale in 1995 of all of SFNB's banking offices other than its home office in Pineville, Kentucky.

(2) Includes deposits in accounts opened over the Internet of $6.2 million in 1,753 accounts as of March 31, 1996 and $433,000 in 612 accounts as of December 31, 1995.

Figure 3.16 (continued)

Name	Position at Cardinal	Cardinal Common Stock Beneficially Owned	Percent Ownership of Cardinal	Position At SFNB After Spin-Off	Distributed Shares in SFNB as a Result of Ownership of Cardinal Common Stock	SFNB Common Stock as a Result of Ownership in Five Paces	SFNB Common Stock Owned after Offering(a)	Percent Ownership SFNB(a)	Options for SFNB Common Stock	Total SFNB Common Stock and Options Held in SFNB	Percent Ownership of SFNB, Fully Diluted and Converted(b)
Directors of Cardinal											
James S. Mahan, III	COB and CEO	50,729	3.20%	Director and CEO	76,836		76,836	0.99%	929,200	1,006,036	8.22%
Howard J. Runnion, Jr.	Director	15,518	0.98	Director	23,504		23,504	0.30	92,920	116,424	0.95
Robert W. Copelan	Director	33,432	2.11	Director	50,632		50,632	0.66	92,920	143,552	1.17
Vernon J. Cole	Director	70,130	4.43		106,232		106,232	1.38		106,232	0.87
Dean Grimm	Director	7,500	0.47		11,360		11,360	0.15		11,360	0.09
Loyd G. Jasper	Director	10,037	0.63		15,204		15,204	0.21		15,204	0.12
Ryan R. Mahan	Director	34,363	2.17		52,052		52,052	0.67		52,052	0.42
John S. Penn	Director, Pres. and COO	21,707	1.37		32,880		32,880	0.43		32,880	0.27
Ronald C. Switzer	Director	46,047	2.91		69,748		69,748	0.90		69,748	0.57
Officers of Cardinal											
James S. Mahan, III*											
John S. Penn*											
Directors of SfNB											
Jack H. Brown	CFO	30,287	1.91	Treasurer and CFO	45,876		45,876	0.59		45,876	0.37
Robert F. Stockwell	Treasurer	7,227	0.46		10,944		10,944	0.14	92,920	103,864	0.85
Scot Cvengros	Sr. Credit Officer	1,756	0.11		2,656		2,656	0.03		2,656	0.02
Directors of SfNB											
Michael C. McChesney		11,410	0.72	COB	17,280	807,438	824,718	10.67	464,400	1,289,118	10.53
James S. Mahan, III*											
Howard J. Runnion, Jr.*											
Robert W. Copelan*											
Carol M. Gatton (c)		123,954	7.82	Director	187,760		187,760	2.43	92,920	280,680	2.29
Officers of SFNB											
James S. Mahan, III*											
Michael Karlin		4,849	0.31	Pres. and COO	7,336		7,336	0.09	278,760	286,096	2.34
Robert F. Stockwell*											
Steve Dubois		100	0.01	Dir. of Operations	148		148	0.00	46,460	46,460	0.38
Eric W. Hartz				VP					92,920	93,068	0.76
Officers of Five Paces											
James S. Mahan, III*											
Michael C. McChesney*											
Charles W. Ogilvie, III									185,840	185,840	1.52
David Zygmont									92,920	92,920	0.76
Robert F. Stockwell*											
Total		469,046	29.61%		710,448	807,438	1,517,886	19.64%	2,462,180	3,980,066	32.50%

*   See listing above.

(a) Represents ownership of Common Stock after giving effect to the Spin-Off and related transactions and the Offering. Does not give effect to options or conversion of Preferred Stock.

(b) Gives effect to exercise of options (excluding options to be granted in the acquisition of SecureWare) and conversion of Preferred Stock, and assumes that none of the listed persons purchase Common Stock in the Offering.

(c) As of March 31, 1995, Mr. Gatton owned 2,267,513 shares, or 29.755% of Area Bancshares. Under applicable director interlocks laws, Mr. Gatton resigned from the boards of both Cardinal and SFNB as of March 31, 1996. Upon the Spin-Off, he will be a director of SFNB.

Figure 3.17
Relationships between Cardinal and SFNB after the spin-off (and IPO)
Source: SFNB Offering Circular (IPO) Document dated May 23, 1996.

CAPITALIZATION

The following table presents the consolidated capitalization of the Bank as of March 31, 1996 and on a pro forma basis to give effect to (1) the Spin-Off (including the issuance of shares of Common Stock in the acquisition of Five Paces) and the sale of stock to the Strategic Investors and (2) the issuance and sale by the Company of 2,440,000 shares of Common Stock offered hereby at $20.00 per share. The SecureWare acquisition is not a condition to the Offering and is itself subject to various conditions; therefore, the table does not reflect such acquisition. This table should be read in conjunction with the Pro Forma Financial Information and the consolidated financial statements and notes thereto included elsewhere in this Offering Circular.

	Historical	Pro Forma
	(In thousands)	
Borrowings:		
Deposits (1)	$39,937	$39,937
Advances from FHLB (2)	1,251	1,251
Other borrowings	—	—
Total borrowings	41,188	41,188
Stockholders' Equity:		
Class A Convertible Preferred Stock, no par value:		
no shares authorized, issued and outstanding, actual; 2,500,000 shares authorized, 1,637,832 shares issued and outstanding, pro forma	—	2,047
Common Stock, no par value:		
12,500,000 shares authorized, 2,400,000 issued and outstanding, actual; 25,000,000 shares authorized, 7,726,792 shares issued and outstanding, pro forma (3)	2,002	51,790
Paid-in capital	350	350
Retained earnings:		
Restricted	—	(1,449)
Unrestricted	332	—
Total retained earnings	332	(1,449)
Net unrealized gain on securities available for sale, net of tax	62	62
Total stockholders' equity	2,746	52,800
Total capitalization	$43,934	$93,988

(1) See Note 8 to Consolidated Financial Statements as to maturities of deposits.

(2) See Note 14 to Consolidated Financial Statements for rates and maturities of borrowings.

(3) Does not include 1,637,832 shares of Common Stock reserved for issuance upon conversion of the Preferred Stock and approximately 2,689,500 shares of Common Stock reserved for issuance pursuant to stock options granted as of March 31, 1996. Also does not include options to purchase 630,400 shares of Common Stock which will be outstanding upon the SecureWare acquisition.

Figure 3.18
Capitalization of SFNB as of March 31, 1996, and after the IPO
Source: SFNB Offering Circular (IPO) Document dated May 23, 1996.

DILUTION

The pro forma net tangible book value of the Company at March 31, 1996 was approximately $4.7 million, or $0.89 per share of Common Stock after giving effect to the Spin-Off and the sale of stock to the Strategic Investors. Net tangible book value per share represents the amount of total tangible assets of the Company reduced by the amount of its total liabilities, divided by the total number of shares of Common Stock outstanding. After giving effect to the net proceeds from the sale by the Company of the 2,440,000 shares of Common Stock offered hereby at the $20.00 per share Offering price, the pro forma net tangible book value of the Company as of March 31, 1996 would have been $50.9 million, or $6.59 per share of Common Stock. This represents an immediate increase in pro forma net tangible book value of $5.70 per share to the holders of Common Stock to be issued in connection with the Spin-Off and an immediate dilution of $7.99 per share to the Strategic Investors and $13.41 per share to purchasers of Common Stock in the Offering. The following table illustrates this per share dilution.

Offering price per share..		$20.00
Pro forma net tangible book value prior to the Offering (1)	$0.89	
Increase attributable to purchasers in the Offering	5.70	
Pro forma net tangible book value after the Offering................................		6.59
Dilution to purchasers in the Offering (2)		$13.41

(1) Based on 5,286,792 shares of Common Stock outstanding as of March 31, 1996 after giving effect to the Spin-Off and the sale of stock to the Strategic Investors.

(2) Assuming the exercise of the options to purchase 2,689,500 shares of Common Stock outstanding at March 31, 1996, the immediate dilution to purchasers in the Offering would be $14.90 per share.

Assuming the Underwriters' over-allotment option is exercised in full, pro forma net tangible book value upon completion of the Offering would be $7.50 per share, the immediate increase in pro forma net tangible book value of shares owned by the holders of Common Stock to be issued in connection with the Spin-Off would be $6.61 per share and the immediate dilution would be $7.08 per share to the Strategic Investors and $12.50 per share to purchasers of Common Stock in the Offering. In addition, assuming the exercise of the options to purchase 2,689,500 shares of Common Stock outstanding at March 31, 1996 and assuming the Underwriters' over-allotment option is exercised in full, the immediate dilution to purchasers in the Offering would be $14.22 per share.

The following table sets forth the differences between the holders of Common Stock to be issued in connection with the Spin-Off and the sale of stock to the Strategic Investors and purchasers of Common Stock in the Offering (at the Offering price of $20.00 per share and before deducting underwriting discounts and commissions and estimated Offering expenses) with respect to the number of shares of Common Stock purchased from the Company, the total consideration paid and the average price per share paid:

	Shares Purchased		Total Consideration		Average Price
	Number	Percent	Amount	Percent	Paid Per Share
Stockholders after the Spin-Off (1)	5,081,076	65.7%	$ 3,697,000(2)	6.7%	$ 0.73
Strategic Investors	205,716	2.7	3,000,000(3)	5.4	14.58
Purchasers in the Offering................	2,440,000	31.6	48,800,000(3)	87.9	20.00
Total	7,726,792	100.0%	$55,497,000	100.0%	

(1) Assumes no exercise of options or conversion of Preferred Stock.

(2) Gives effect to the Spin-Off and anticipated adjustments in connection therewith.

(3) Does not give effect to expenses of $100,000 in the sale of Common Stock to the Strategic Investors, or the estimated $2.6 million of expenses in the Offering, including the Underwriting Discount, based on an Offering price of $20.00 per share.

The foregoing tables assume no exercise of stock options prior to the Offering. As of March 31, 1996, there were options outstanding to purchase an aggregate of 2,689,500 shares of Common Stock at exercise prices ranging from $0.625 to $1.25 per share, with a weighted average exercise price of approximately $0.829 per share, and 190,500 shares were reserved for grant of future options under the Employee Stock Option Plan and the Directors Option Plan. See "Management—Employee Stock Option Plan," "—Directors Option Plan." In addition, the foregoing tables do not include the 1,637,832 shares of Preferred Stock, which will be issued to Huntington, Wachovia and Area Bancshares as part of the Spin-Off but, because of regulatory ownership limits and other restrictions, are not expected to be converted immediately following the Offering. See "The Spin-Off and Related Transactions—Stock Sale." The foregoing tables also do not assume the exercise of any of the additional options to purchase 630,400 shares of Common Stock which will be outstanding after the acquisition of SecureWare. Such options consist of options to purchase 400,000 shares of Common Stock at an exercise price of $12.92 per share, options to purchase 160,000 shares at an exercise price of $6.67 per share and options to purchase 70,400 shares at an exercise price of $4.46 per share. To the extent that any of these options are exercised or any shares of Preferred Stock are converted, there will be further dilution to new investors.

PRO FORMA FINANCIAL INFORMATION

Set forth below are (i) pro forma consolidated balance sheet of SFNB at March 31, 1996, giving effect to the Spin-Off (including the issuance of shares of Common Stock in the acquisition of Five Paces), the purchase of SFNB Common Stock by the Strategic Investors and the Offering as of such date and, in a separate column, giving effect to the acquisition of SecureWare; and (ii) pro forma consolidated statement of operations of SFNB for the three months ended March 31, 1996 and the year ended December 31, 1995, in each case giving effect to the Spin-Off, the purchase of Common Stock by the Strategic Investors and the Offering, assuming that each of the Spin-Off, the sale of stock to the Strategic Investors and the Offering had been consummated at the beginning of the respective periods. For information regarding the Spin-Off, the sale of Common Stock to the Strategic Investors and the acquisition of SecureWare, see "The Spin-Off and Related Transactions" and "The SecureWare Acquisition."

The following pro forma financial data of SFNB have been derived from and should be read in conjunction with SFNB's consolidated financial statements included elsewhere herein. The pro forma information is presented for illustrative purposes only and is not necessarily indicative of the financial position that would have occurred had the Spin-Off, the sale of Common Stock to the Strategic Investors and the Offering been effected on the date assumed nor is the pro forma financial information intended to be indicative of SFNB's future financial position or results of operations. The pro forma consolidated statements of operations for the three months ended March 31, 1996 and the year ended December 31, 1995 do not reflect one-time non-recurring expenses for in-process research and development costs of $1.3 million and $3.3 million, respectively, related to the acquisition of Five Paces and SecureWare. These expenses will be recognized by the Bank in the period in which the acquisitions are consummated.

Figure 3.19
Cost basis of various shareholder groups and pro forma financial information
Source: SFNB Offering Circular (IPO) Document dated May 23, 1996.

Pro Forma Consolidated Balance Sheet

At March 31, 1996

	SFNB (historical)	Five Paces (historical)	Adjustments(1)	Company, as adjusted	SecureWare Acquisition	Adjustments	Company, as adjusted (2)
				(Dollars in thousands)			
Assets							
Cash and due from banks	$ 840	$ —	$ —	$ 840	$ 9	$ —	$ 849
Interest bearing deposits with banks	2,923	—	(3,000)(3)	52,026	380	(5,200)(6)	47,206
		—	5,900 (4)		—	—	
		—	46,203 (8)		—	—	
Investment securities available for sale ..	5,881	—	—	5,881	—	—	5,881
Mortgage-backed securites available for sale	9,739	—	—	9,739	—	—	9,739
Loans receivable	20,741	—	—	20,741	—	—	20,741
Less: Allowance for loan losses ...	(298)	—	—	(298)	—	—	(298)
Net loans	20,443	—	—	20,443	—	—	20,443
Premises and equipment	3,916	355	—	4,271	225	—	4,496
Excess of purchase price over net assets acquired	—	1,994	(108)(5)	1,886	1,534	644 (6)	4,064
Accrued interest receivable and other assets	848	911	—	1,759	300	—	2,059
Total assets....................	$44,590	$ 3,260	$48,995	$96,845	$2,448	$(4,556)	$94,737
Liabilities and Stockholders' Equity							
Liabilities:							
Deposits:							
Non-interest bearing	$ 1,806	$ —	$ —	$ 1,806	$ —	$ —	$ 1,806
Interest bearing	38,131	—	—	38,131	—	—	38,131
Advances from FHLB............	1,251	—	—	1,251	—	—	1,251
Notes payable	—	—	—	—	389	—	389
Accrued interest payable and other liabilities....................	656	4,138	(2,128)(5)	2,857	57	63 (10)	2,977
		—	(163)(9)		—	—	
		—	354 (7)		—	—	
Total liabilities................	41,844	4,138	(1,937)	44,045	446	63	44,554
Stockholders' equity:							
Common stock.................	2,002	297	2,103 (5)	51,790	52	(52)(6)	51,790
		—	3,853 (4)		—	—	
		—	(2,668)(3)		—	—	
		—	46,203 (8)		—	—	
Preferred stock.................	—	—	2,047 (4)	2,047	—	—	2,047
Additional paid-in capital	350	—	—	350	—	713 (6)	1,063
Retained earnings	332	(1,175)	(332)(3)	(1,449)	1,950	(63)(9)	(4,779)
		—	(354)(7)		—	(3,267)(6)	—
		—	(1,258)(5)		—	(1,950)(6)	
		—	163 (9)		—	—	
		—	1,175 (5)				
Net unrealized gain (loss) on securities available for sale, net of tax	62	—	—	62	—	—	62
Total stockholders' equity	2,746	(878)	50,932	52,800	2,002	(4,619)	50,183
Total liabilities and stockholders' equity	$44,590	$ 3,260	$48,995	$96,845	$2,448	$(4,556)	$94,737
Capital ratios:							
Tangible	6.03%			53.59%			50.83%
Core	6.03			53.59			50.83
Risk-based	14.99			155.64			133.96

Figure 3.19 (continued)

(1) Represents adjustments giving effect to the Spin-Off, the sale of Common Stock to the Strategic Investors and the Offering. No effect has been given to the conversion of Preferred Stock, the exercise of stock options or the Underwriters' over-allotment option.

(2) Represents the Company as adjusted for the SecureWare acquisition. Also does not give effect to exercise of any of the 630,400 additional options to be outstanding following the SecureWare acquisition.

(3) Gives effect to a $3.0 million cash dividend to be paid from SFNB to Cardinal as part of the Spin-Off. The dividend will be funded from cash on hand.

(4) Represents the equity investments by Wachovia, Huntington, Area Bancshares, Synovus and NCB, net of expenses.

(5) Reflects adjustments for the acquisition of Five Paces, including the elimination of the historical equity accounts of Five Paces at March 31, 1996. The purchase price of Five Paces includes the issuance of 1,920,000 shares of the Bank's Common Stock with a value of $2.4 million as of May 24, 1995, the date of the agreement between the Bank and Five Paces. The purchase price allocation includes: (i) a $1.9 million increase in excess of purchase price over net assets acquired and (ii) a $1.3 million decrease in retained earnings resulting from the estimated valuation of in-process research and development. A final allocation of the purchase price and valuation of in-process research and development related to the acquisition of Five Paces will be made as of the purchase date based upon the fair value of the assets acquired and an evaluation of software projects in process.

(6) Reflects adjustments for the acquisition of SecureWare, including the elimination of the historical equity accounts of SecureWare at March 31, 1996. The purchase price of SecureWare includes the payment of $5.2 million in cash and the conversion of existing options to purchase SecureWare common stock with an estimated value of $713,000 into options to purchase the Bank's Common Stock. The purchase price allocation includes: (i) a $2.2 million increase in excess of purchase price over net assets acquired and (ii) a $3.3 million decrease in retained earnings resulting from the estimated valuation of in-process research and development. A final allocation of the purchase price and valuation of in-process research and development related to the acquisition of SecureWare will be made as of the purchase date based upon the fair value of the assets acquired and an evaluation of software projects in process.

(7) Represents accrued compensation expense applicable to stock options.

(8) Represents estimated net proceeds from the Offering.

(9) Represents the tax benefit from valuation of in-process research and development and compensation expense applicable to stock options.

(10) Represents accrued compensation expense applicable to options granted to SecureWare employees.

Figure 3.19 (continued)

bank or by searching on the WWW themselves to find a bank that could provide Internet banking services. The growth in customer base during the first year was impressive in spite of the lack of advertising, but Karlin felt that continuing this growth in the future would likely require more advertising support to continue to attract new customers. Even so, word-of-mouth advertising was still one of the most important sources of new customers for the bank, and SFNB had begun to offer promotions to existing customers for new customer referrals as well as using traditional advertising to generate new leads.

One issue for SFNB management to consider was the option of expanding services beyond the exclusive base of Internet customers to include all forms of telephone or nonbranch banking. The fastest growth in the banking industry overall during the

Pro Forma Consolidated Statements of Operations

	SFNB (historical)	Five Paces (historical)	Adjust-ments	Company, as adjusted	Secure-Ware (historical)	Adjust-ments	Company, as adjusted
				Three months ended March 31, 1996			
				(Dollars in thousands)			
Interest income:							
Loans including fees	$ 459	$ —	$ —	$ 459	$ —	$ —	$ 459
Investment securities	73	—	—	73	—	—	73
Mortgage-backed securities	105	—	—	105	—	—	105
Deposits in banks	63	—	—	63	7	—	70
Total interest income	700	—	—	700	7	—	707
Interest expense:							
Deposits	446	—	—	446	—	—	446
Advances from FHLB	17			17	—	—	17
Total interest expense	463	—	—	463	—	—	463
Net interest income	237	—	—	237	7	—	244
Provision for loan losses	—	—	—	—	—	—	—
Net interest income after provision for loan losses	237	—	—	237	7	—	244
Non-interest income:							
Service charges on deposits	27	—	—	27	—	—	27
Data center operations	—	45	(45)(1)	—	—	—	—
Software development and consulting fees	—	—	—	—	377	(120)(1)	257
Securities gains (losses), net	—	—	—	—	(38)	—	(38)
Other	25	—	—	25	—	—	25
Total non-interest income	52	45	(45)	52	339	(120)	271
Non-interest expenses:							
Salaries and employee benefits	460	274	354 (2)	1,088	424	(30)(1) 63 (2)	1,545
Net occupancy expense	33	38	—	71	25	(26)(1)	70
Furniture and equipment expense	253	37	—	290	104	(57)(1)	337
Data processing	96	—	(45)(1)	51	—	—	51
Professional fees	67	16	—	83	4	—	87
FDIC insurance	19	—	—	19	—	—	19
Amortization of excess of purchase price over net assets acquired	—	—	79 (3)	79	—	91 (3)	170
Other	392	274	—	666	45	(7)(1)	704
Total non-interest expenses	1,320	639	388	2,347	602	34	2,983
Loss before taxes	(1,031)	(594)	(433)	(2,058)	(256)	(154)	(2,468)
Income tax expense (benefit)	(348)	—	185 (4)	(163)	—	—	(163)
Net loss	$ (683)	$(594)	$(618)	$ (1,895)	$(256)	$ (154)	$ (2,305)
Net loss per common share	$ (0.07)			$ (0.20)			$ (0.24)
Average common shares outstanding	9,450,964			9,450,964			9,450,964

(1) Eliminates inter-company transactions.
(2) Represents accrued compensation expense applicable to stock options.
(3) Represents the amortization of excess of purchase price over net assets acquired resulting from the acquisition of Five Paces and SecureWare based upon a six-year life.
(4) The Bank's income tax benefit is determined based upon its tax attributes subsequent to the Spin-Off. Since the Bank has no prior taxable income available for a carryback of its operating loss, the pro forma income tax benefit is limited to the deferred income tax liability at March 31, 1996.

Figure 3.19 (continued)

	SFNB (historical)	Five Paces (historical)	Adjust-ments	Company, as adjusted	Secure-Ware (historical)	Adjust-ments	Company, as adjusted
				(Dollars in thousands)			
Interest income:							
Loans including fees	$ 3,444	$ —	$(1,514)(1)	$ 1,930	$ —	$ —	$ 1,930
Investment securities	501	—	—	501	—	—	501
Mortgage-backed securities	312	—	—	312	—	—	312
Deposits in banks	138	—	—	138	50	—	188
Total interest income	4,395	—	(1,514)	2,881	50	—	2,931
Interest expense:							
Deposits...................	2,290	—	(833)(1)	1,457	—	—	1,457
Advances from FHLB	77	—	—	77	—	—	77
Total interest expense	2,367	—	(833)	1,534	—	—	1,534
Net interest income	2,028	—	(681)	1,347	50	—	1,397
Provision for loan losses	—	—	—	—	—	—	—
Net interest income after provision for loan losses	2,028	—	(681)	1,347	50	—	1,397
Non-interest income:							
Service charges on deposits ...	129	—	(53)(1)	76	—	—	76
Software development and consulting fees	—	143	(143)(2)	—	1,641	(642)(2)	999
Securities gains (losses), net ...	(50)	—	—	(50)	(29)	—	(79)
Other	117	—	(31)(1)	86	—	—	86
Total non-interest income	196	143	(227)	112	1,612	(642)	1,082
Non-interest expenses:							
Salaries and employee benefits	1,305	263	(290)(1) 283 (3)	1,561	1,053	(248)(2) 250 (3)	2,616 —
Net occupancy expense	95	6	(44)(1)	57	154	(116)(2)	95
Furniture and equipment expense	273	3	(30)(1)	246	423	(263)(2)	406
Data processing	270	—	(88)(1)	182	—	—	182
Professional fees	796	20	(26)(1)	790	9	—	799
FDIC insurance.............	139	—	(43)(1)	96	—	—	96
Amortization of excess of purchase price over net assets acquired	—	—	314 (4)	314	—	363 (4)	677
Other	1,329	136	(190)(1) (143)(2)	1,132	37	(15)(2)	1,154
Total non-interest expenses	4,207	428	(257)	4,378	1,676	(29)	6,025
Loss before taxes	(1,983)	(285)	(651)	(2,919)	(14)	(613)	(3,546)
Income tax benefit.............	(503)	—	(167)(5)	(670)	—	—	(670)
Net loss	$ (1,480)	$ (285)	$ (484)	$ (2,249)	$ (14)	$(613)	$ (2,876)
Net loss per common share	$ (0.16)			$ (0.24)			$ (0.30)
Average common shares outstanding	9,450,964			9,450,964			9,450,964

(1) Represents the Bank's results of operations eliminated as a result of the Branch Sale on June 12, 1995. See ''Management's Discussion and Analysis of Financial Condition and Results of Operations.''

(2) Eliminates inter-company transactions.

(3) Represents accrued compensation expense applicable to stock options.

(4) Represents the amortization of excess of purchase price over net assets acquired resulting from the acquisition of Five Paces and SecureWare based upon a six-year life.

(5) Represents additional income tax benefit which is limited to the Bank's deferred income tax liability at December 31, 1995.

Figure 3.19 (continued)

1990s had occurred in the nonbranch banking services sector, which included mort-gages and credit card services. SFNB was well positioned to offer a wide range of banking services to customers nationally using toll-free customer phone support, Internet banking, bank-by-mail services, and other forms of nonbranch customer support. Although SFNB offered all of these forms of customer interface for its Internet banking customers, the firm had not been willing to expand its marketing efforts to attract customers who were not primarily interested in the Internet banking features offered. As long as the retail banking operations were viewed as primarily a showcase for the development and sale of Internet banking software to other banks, this focus only on Internet customers was appropriate. However, if SFNB intended to operate a retail bank as an independent, profit-maximizing entity, then there were important customer segments which had not been adequately targeted by the firm's existing marketing policy which at that point in time focused on Internet customers only. (For example, retired investors with large CD investments might find SFNB rates attractive even if they had no interest in using the Internet for banking.)

Another important question that Karlin and his management team had been discussing was whether SFNB needed to have physical banking branch locations to support and complement the Internet banking service offerings. Some customers were concerned that they would be unable to get a cashier's check or wire transfer funds if needed without having a physical bank branch located somewhere in their general area. SFNB's growth during the first year had been impressive without having any physical branch locations for customers, but some members of the SFNB manage-ment team believed that the lack of physical locations would artificially constrain the growth of the bank in the future. Thus, SFNB had decided to open branch locations in three major metropolitan areas with high concentrations of existing and potential customers: Atlanta, Boston, and San Francisco.

• See http://www.webfinance.net/current/sfnbbr36.html regarding branch banking.

One bank branch location would be opened in each city, with the branch uniquely designed to fit with the SFNB Internet banking services capabilities. Customer ser-vice specialists would be available in the branch office in each city to assist customers with any needs that could not be done via the Internet interface (e.g., providing a cashier's check or traveler's checks). The bank branches could also assist customers with cash deposits, coin deposits and withdrawals, and other services typical required by business banking customers.

Business banking services had not yet been introduced in late 1996, but were under development and would be available in early 1997. Some smaller businesses would find branchless Internet banking attractive due to the lower costs and added conveniences available, but many companies would require branch banking services to be available before they would consider shifting to SFNB for their primary banking relationship. Although providing business checking accounts and other banking services was often more profitable than providing personal banking services, the Internet was not as well suited for serving the needs of these customers. At the same time, many smaller business users would be likely to find the convenience and flexibility of on-line banking very attractive. Thus, the move toward offering limited branch banking facilities might enable SFNB to more effectively service the needs of these potential customers for business banking services. In addition, it was important for SFNB to provide Internet-based business banking services to demonstrate to potential banking industry clients that the SFNB software could meet the banking needs of all the important customers of these potential clients.

Providing Software and Services to Other Banks

One important reason for expanding the SFNB services offerings, in addition to providing better services to retail customers, was being able to offer a full range of products and services to banking clients interested in the SFNB Internet banking software and services. Sales of software (and the associated annual licensing fees and services based fees) to other banks using the Virtual Vault software represented a large portion of total income for SFNB. Fee-based income for providing check clearing and other services could be much larger than the income from providing retail banking services over time. The key to success in the software and services business was to establish the SFNB offering as the de facto standard in the industry before competitors could develop equally attractive alternative solutions. Thus, the software and services opportunity was a race against time versus others in the industry. SFNB management believed that they had a clear lead relative to the other potential players in the Internet banking services industry, but also recognized that their competitors were investing substantial resources in trying to overcome the SFNB lead. Many potential competitors had started with a larger asset base and more staff than SFNB, and could easily subjugate this lead position so it was vital that SFNB concentrate on improving and expanding its range of Internet banking services.

• See http://www.webfinance.net/current/02brsfnb.html about banking services.

The demand for SFNB services from U.S. banks was quite large, but only a few banks had fully deployed the Virtual Vault software and related applications by the end of 1996. Between 10 and 20 banks were expected to have SFNB software installed and then be able to provide complete Internet banking services by the end of 1997. Most of the large U.S. banks had expressed interest in SFNB's software, but few had committed to adoption by early 1997. One important goal for 1997 was to add several of the large U.S. banks as confirmed clients for SFNB's Internet banking services.

In addition to licensing Internet banking software to other banks, SFNB was also offering a virtual banking presence on the Internet using the SFNB systems for smaller banks or credit unions. These virtual banking services could appear to the customer to be offered only by their local bank (with the client bank or credit union providing check-clearing services) or could be offered as a banking affiliate of SFNB (with SFNB providing check-clearing services). Most larger banks were expected to license the software for use on their own systems, while smaller banks would benefit from being able to use the SFNB virtual banking facilities to offer Internet services without requiring a substantial investment in capital or systems development or support. Although few banks were willing to outsource the check-clearing and other banking services provided to their customers, there were a large number of very small credit unions that might find complete outsourcing of banking operations to SFNB for Internet and other banking services an attractive option. Many of these very small banks and credit unions already outsourced their check clearing to larger banks or services bureaus, and many of these smaller institutions might find that offering Internet banking options through SFNB to their customers could actually improve customer service and reduce costs simultaneously.

This virtual banking service could even be offered to affinity groups, enabling organizations or large groups to open their own "virtual banking presence" on the Internet. Although the initial screens for these SFNB affiliates would be customized to the needs of their closed user group, all banking services would be provided by SFNB. Affinity banking had proven successful in the credit card market, and was a potentially large market for expanding SFNB's banking services.

Global banking was also an important opportunity for SFNB. Several clients interested in purchasing SFNB software and services were among the largest non-U.S. banks in the world. SFNB had established positive contacts and relationships with banks in nearly a dozen different countries or separate economic zones, including Australia, Japan, the United Kingdom, and Hong Kong. However, opportunities for selling SFNB banking software and services overseas had not been pursued aggressively, as resources were still too limited within the firm to invest heavily in expanding overseas. There was too much demand for providing services to U.S. banks to focus significant resources on the global market yet.

Resource Constraints and Resulting Implications for Strategy

Although Karlin would like to be able to take advantage of all the opportunities available for expanding both the retail banking and the industry software and services markets, the SFNB organization was simply not large enough to be able to capture all the opportunities available to the firm. The limited number of skilled managers and staff available was the most critical constraint for the organization, as traditional capital-intensive limits to growth simply did not apply in this people and information-intensive business. Thus, a large portion of the already limited management time and energy was focused on recruiting highly talented staff who could help the company grow more quickly in the future. However, even hiring new staff involved a trade-off of foregoing immediate opportunities to develop and harvest new revenue streams immediately using scarce management time and talent in order to use this scarce resource for recruiting and training new members of the SFNB team.

The company was cautious about adding too many people too quickly, especially in the software development teams. The developers working on Internet banking applications and other related services were experienced and very productive, and adding lots of new programmers to these software development projects could potentially even slow down development by forcing the most productive programmers to become managers and trainers of less-experienced staff. Thus, there were very real limits on the effective rate at which the programming staff of the organization could economically expand. Even so, David Zygmont, Vice President of Development, noted that the software development team working on Internet banking and related applications had expanded from 3 people in January, 1995, to 15 people by summer of 1995 and then to more than 50 people by the summer of 1996.

Zygmont recognized the need to continue to expand the programming staff over time, but did not necessarily view larger software development groups as being able to produce new innovations faster than smaller teams. In fact, many of the additions to the group were working on applications that were individual components that would be added into the core Internet banking applications portfolio over time. The massive resources available with some of the software companies (e.g., Microsoft, Intuit) were also viewed as less of a threat than might be suggested when comparing relative size of the software development teams, since much of the core development still needed to be done by a small group of experts who understood both the banking and the technological requirements of the new systems and processes. Building a new system with a large team was not necessarily an advantage, as most new software innovations had been developed by relatively small core development teams.

Even though he did not necessarily view the large scale of the major software companies as a significant threat the future of SFNB, Zygmont recognized that continued growth in staff was needed to meet the challenges of maintaining market leadership in the increasingly competitive on-line banking services market. Zygmont explained:

Continuous hiring is a challenge and we must manage our growth rate so we do not spend all our time in hiring and training instead of developing software. Finding the top people who can work effectively with our current team is difficult. We have to interview at least 100 people to hire 20. It is also difficult to go from a small team to a big organization. We need to develop more formalized project management team roles.

Part of the growth in programming staff requirements was driven by the development of new applications, and part of the growth was needed to customize or modify applications and interfaces to work with new banking industry customers for the SFNB software and services. Thus, too rapid growth in expanding the customer base could place strains on the ability of the organization to continually improve the product offering. However, most of the customization work could be performed by individual customer service teams, and thus, availability of staffing was the only real issue limiting the ability of the firm to expand its customer base. For development of the core applications, increasing the scale of development without losing control continued to be an issue as the size of the development group expanded and project management became an increasingly important role which needed to be institutionally formalized.

For Karlin, the constraints on growth and limited existing resources meant that it was important for SFNB to focus its efforts on the most important strategic issues and opportunities that would enable the firm to capture a strong position as the leader in Internet banking. Given the many opportunities available for SFNB and the need to focus the limited resources of the firm on the most important areas, one of the key challenges for the SFNB senior management team was to decide how the organization should allocate its resources to maximize the long-term strength and value of the firm. In addition, there was a related issue regarding how much of the firm's scarce management and programming talent should be invested in hiring and training new people in the short term to increase the capabilities of the firm in the long term to capture more of the opportunities available in the market.

Increasing staff too quickly could enable other firms to catch up to SFNB's leadership position in the industry by delaying either market expansion of new clients or new applications development in order to spend key resources in hiring and training of the new people. Growing too slowly could slow the growth of the firm in the future and might allow larger firms to capture strong positions in segments of the market that SFNB was not able to adequately service with its more limited staff. Thus, the issue of growth and focus were both difficult and challenging issues that made life interesting and exciting for Karlin and the rest of SFNB's senior management team.

Global Electronics Manufacturing (HK) Ltd.

John Carson, president of Global Electronics Manufacturing (GEM), a small manufacturing company with offices in the United States and Hong Kong, had been contemplating the company's expanding business operations and opportunities in Hong Kong and China. By outsourcing much of its production but coordinating and managing the entire production processes, GEM had been able to build a highly competitive and successful business.

However, there were several issues and challenges that Carson had to deal with to enable the firm to continue to grow and prosper. For example, GEM was highly dependent on a single large U.S. retailer for most of its sales revenues, and the company needed to consider whether it should pursue opportunities to develop other markets globally or to develop branded products that would be sold through multiple distribution channels. GEM was also tightly linked with a limited number of suppliers, and Carson was considering the trade-offs involved in developing alternative supply relationships versus strengthening existing supplier interdependencies through long-term contracts.

Carson was also interested in exploring opportunities for using information technology capabilities more effectively in the company and with customers or suppliers to reduce production cycle time and cost while simultaneously improving quality. Finally, Carson and his management team were interested in new growth opportunities within related markets using either capabilities and connections with people in the Greater China region or by leveraging existing customer relationships to expand the range of products supplied to these customers.

Company and Industry Background

From 1987 to 1993, the global video game industry averaged 40% growth annually and reached more than US$12 billion in worldwide retail sales by 1994, with sales approximately evenly divided between the U.S. and non-U.S. markets worldwide. Wholesale U.S. videogame revenues reached US$3.8 billion in 1994 (figure 3.20). The video game market was in a transition period during 1995 and 1996, as the next generation of hardware platforms loomed on the horizon and new players were entering the market. The 16-bit home video game platform had dominated the market since 1989, but had given way to advanced 32-bit platforms during 1995 which helped to shake up the market during the Christmas holiday season. During 1996,

This case was prepared by Dr. Theodore H. Clark and Alvin Chu of The Hong Kong University of Science and Technology. The names of the company and the key managers involved have been changed at the request of the company to maintain confidentiality and privacy.

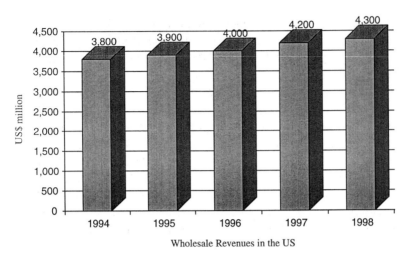

Figure 3.20
Video game market projection
Source: *Advertising Age*, 1995.

several vendors were expected to introduce even faster and more expensive 64-bit videogames that would further fragment and expand the market for these video game players and the other products associated with these machines, such as joysticks and other control devices.

Surveys of the market in the mid-1990s indicated that 42% of American households owned a video game system, with 70% of these homes having preteenage children. The survey also indicated that there was an adult player in 62% of homes with a video game system, and the adult player was said to be the major player in 27% of video game homes. As video game systems increased in sophistication, the percentage of adult players increased. The largest group of adult video game players were single males between the ages of 18 and 35, who had first started playing video games on simple arcade-type systems during the 1980s. This segment of video game consumers had been the largest purchasers of the new 32-bit high-performance systems introduced in 1995.

GEM primarily designed, manufactured, and distributed joysticks and other peripheral hardware equipment associated with the home video game market. The company, founded by Carson in 1985, maintained its headquarters location in southern California and had an office in Hong Kong which coordinated production and logistics for its China suppliers. Virtually all products were produced in China and were then exported to either the United States or Europe. In addition to videogame joysticks, the company also supplied other peripheral accessories for videogame products.

GEM had captured a significant share (almost 20%) of the video game accessory market despite its small size by providing high-quality private-label products at very low costs and supplying these products to some of the largest retailers of video game systems and accessories in the United States and Europe. By 1996, GEM had become the primary supplier of joysticks and other accessories to one of the largest U.S. retail chains. GEM had been able to expand its market share with this important U.S. customer by providing innovative products to support newly introduced video game systems and by proving that it could consistently and reliably supply products at low cost through its supplier network in China.

Carson started the business by distributing/manufacturing electronic toys and gifts, and as an agent/manufacturer of electronic products for other product suppliers. Sales of these items and of videogame supplies were highly influenced by consumer spending trends and overall economic conditions. During the 1980s, the home video game market boomed, and GEM dropped most of its other product lines to meet the rapidly expanding demand for joysticks and other video game peripheral products. Carson's contacts and experience in producing electronic products enabled him to capitalize on this fast-growing market opportunity and provided the opportunity for the company to expand both revenues and profits dramatically.

The decision to move to the video game accessory segment was a bold one at that time, as there were existing competitors with production capabilities in place that GEM had to battle to acquire market share in the business. In addition, capital was limited for the small company, so extensive investments in factories or inventories were difficult to finance. Thus, Carson focused on developing relationships with reliable overseas manufacturers that could supply components and provide product assembly with consistent quality standards. Using his extensive contacts with manufacturers in China and with component suppliers, he was able to produce joysticks at competitive costs compared with existing products, and was able to negotiate a large volume contract for private-label supply with the large U.S. retail chain store which still provided most of the company's sales in 1996. Prior to developing this strong relationship for private-label product supply, GEM had provided products to smaller retailers under its own name brand, but most of this branded product market had been neglected during the past few years as the relationship with this large U.S. retail chain store had expanded to include new products and larger production volumes.

As a small company, GEM had an advantage in adapting quickly to change and responding to customers' needs for flexibility by readjusting its production lines with minimal overhead costs. All of GEM suppliers produced products on demand with short-term contracts, and they were also small firms capable of responding quickly to changes in demand or product design. GEM produced products compatible with almost all videogame systems, with each system requiring slight differences in joystick controls or appearance to meet physical requirements and target market demands. Thus, the company produced many varieties of joysticks using similar production processes in the China factories.

None of GEM's products were licensed by the video game manufacturers, but GEM had recently approached a new manufacturer of high-performance video game systems to discuss the possibility of obtaining a license to become an officially approved vendor of add-on equipment for this fast-selling product line. Licensing could increase costs by requiring payment of a fee for each product produced, but also could provide opportunities to expand market share because unlicensed competitors would be restricted from offering products which utilized the proprietary interface patented by this new player.

Product design and marketing at GEM largely responded to the development of new video game platforms, and product performance and features were designed to match capabilities of these new and upgraded video game systems. Both GEM and the large retail customers participated in the design process, with GEM generally playing a leading role in suggesting new product introductions. The company did not emphasize marketing strategy and advertising, as products were distributed primarily through the major U.S. and European chain stores for which GEM was the private label supplier. However, they did have some retail sales under the GEM name, and were considering expanding the company's focus on this alternative branded product channel. One issue that Carson was considering was how much management focus should be given to expanding sales of the GEM branded products to new customers. In considering this issue, Carson also wondered what impact any shift in management focus toward branded product sales might have on its existing customer relationships.

Products and Operations

GEM produced multiple video game accessories, but the primary product line was joysticks and other similar game control devices that were substitutes for joysticks, such as a recently introduced "steering wheel" controller. These joysticks were not simply copies of the original joysticks provided with the videogame systems, but included value-added features that enhanced the gaming experience for most players. Videogame buyers often purchased additional controllers to allow multiple players to participate in the game or to gain these value-added control features.

GEM invested significant management time and effort in the design of high-performance joysticks and other control devices to provide the customer with a superior gaming experience versus using the standard controllers supplied with the video game system. Since joysticks and other control devices represented the primary focus of management attention in the mid-1990s and contributed most of the company's revenues and profits, this description of products and operations will focus exclusively on joysticks and related video game controller products.

Joysticks, like the systems they supported, had relatively short life cycles, so responsive product development was crucial to keeping up with market trends and remaining competitive in product offerings. Product designs were not copyrighted or patented; if a design was successful for an extended period, it could easily be imitated by others. Thus, flexibility and responsiveness to market changes were more important than developing the ultimate product that would dominate the market.

Joystick design and production involved three different types of components, all of which were important for success in the market. Plastic components influenced the appearance and feel of the joystick or controller, and were vital for consumer satisfaction. Electronics components provided most of the value-added functionality in the joystick and represented a major part of the cost of the completed product. Packaging was important as it was often the only thing that the customer could see before purchasing the product. Thus, packaging had to be attractively designed to communicate the value of the product to the consumer, especially since joysticks and related control devices were often purchased on impulse at the time that the initial video game system was purchased.

The design, marketing, and production process are described for the product overall, then for each of these components, and the final assembly process is then described. A summary overview of the entire production and design process is provided in figure 3.21.

Plastics

The design layouts and specifications of the plastic component parts of the joystick were initially conceptualized and drafted out by GEM's U.S. office staff. These design drafts generally described the look and feel of the system without explicit details of each plastic component. The designs were sent to the Hong Kong office via fax or courier, where they were converted into AutoCad detailed drawings with the assistance of local CAD subcontractors. During this stage, full-scale plaster models of the casing were made as reference samples to test the feel of the design and provide assistance for finalizing the product specifications. These design updates were transferred back to the drawings and a new prototype plaster sample was produced to test

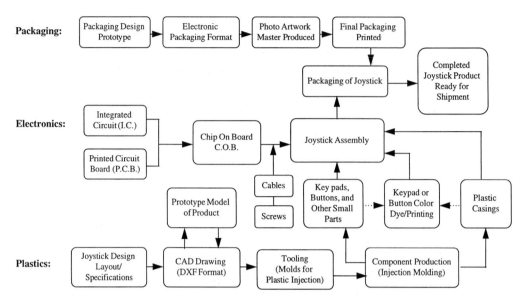

Figure 3.21
Joystick production process flowchart

the design again for comfort and appearance. Once the joystick design was finally approved, a digital file of the design layouts and detail production specifications were submitted to the mold tooling producer (the tooler) to make the master molds required for mass production. The entire design and prototyping process could take as long as six weeks, but was often completed with three weeks or less when time was critical.

The tooler used CNC (computerized numeric control) equipment to cut cast steel materials into the negative shapes of the casing and components needed. The making of the master mold usually required one to two months of time, with consecutive test runs of the injection mold conducted before the mold was accepted as completed. Adjustments could be made to the mold during development and even after completion. However, adjustments usually involved cutting away additional metal rather than adding metal, requiring additional plastic to be used in the production operation. Since use of additional plastic in production increased costs, it was important to provide a very detailed and accurate initial design to minimize both model development time and variable production costs.

Maintaining frequent contacts with the tooler was crucial to provide feedback early in the process and to monitoring the quality and progress of the mold forms. In some cases, molds might have to be completely redone if the designs were not sufficiently detailed and problems surfaced, or if the tooler did not maintain adequate quality standards. Some mold manufacturers were located in Hong Kong, but many had relocated operations to China to reduce costs. Unfortunately, relocation to China also made communications more difficult and quality controls were not as strong, resulting in more problems in the mold development process and greater demands on GEM management's time.

Mold production represented a significant cost for most products, and it was a fixed cost that had to be incurred regardless of how many or few final products were eventually sold. Each model produced cost US$10,000–$25,000 and could produce between 1,000 and 2,500 units of output from each mold per day. Most plastic components were produced in a single mold for an individual product, but some larger or more complex products required multiple molds for a single product. The mold design and development processes generally represented the longest time constraints for new product development. Nevertheless, GEM had insufficient scale of mold production to provide these services in house.

Occasionally, problems with a new product mold required that a complete new mold be produced by the tooler in an emergency. If the mold could not be finished on time, the whole production schedule would lag behind and the shipments could not reach the customers during the high season on time. GEM had recently terminated its relationship with a tooler because problems with their mold required substantial rework of the plastic components during production, which resulted in the company losing sales of a recently introduced controller for a new video game system. This problem occurred during the peak Christmas season, and the tooler was not able to solve the problem in a timely manner. A new tooler was contacted that could provide a new mold to meet GEM's production requirements, and additional business had later been shifted to this new tooler. The previous mold producer might be used again in an emergency, but had lost its preferred status due to its inability to respond quickly.

Manufacturing of these plastic components using the molds produced either in Hong Kong or China was outsourced to independent factories in China, with GEM representing one of the largest customers for most of these plastic component producers. Most of the plastic component suppliers also provided assembly services. Scale economies for both plastic component production and assembly were not large, and GEM had sufficient volume to insource this production operation. In fact, the company had at one time owned its factories, but had found that outsourcing production was more cost effective and had actually provided increased control relative to ownership of production in China.

Ownership of production had involved significant "unofficial" expenses for operating in China or transporting products to or from China. Frequent payments were required to government officials for which no receipts were provided. A manager operating a small factory for a foreign corporation had limited power to negotiate the level of payments required from customs or other government officials. In addition, it was difficult to determine if fees "required" for unofficial payments were actually paid in the amounts stated, or whether these fees were inflated to provide an unofficial bonus for the manager.

This "agency problem" and the lack of negotiating or bargaining power for a manager of a foreign factory were overcome when GEM outsourced all production in China to small factories that were locally owned and managed. Although the source of savings was not transparent, it was clear that local factory managers were able to reduce this overhead cost of unofficial payments, and aggressively competed with other factories to provide the lowest cost and highest quality products and assembly services as they tried to expand their businesses. GEM had several suppliers in China for plastic component production and assembly, and had been able to maintain attractive prices and excellent service quality over long periods of time by carefully managing these supplier relationships. GEM succeeded partly by using short-term contracts with flexible production terms combined with long-term relationships with open communications and trust in a stable relationship based on mutual benefits.

Electronics

Inside the joystick are electronic components and interconnected mechanisms that are customized and programmed to control the game playing features. These value-added functions include continuous firing, bombing, and rapid direction changes. Electronic components consist of integrated circuit (IC) chips acquired from various vendors, printed circuit boards (PCBs), and other electromechanical parts. Some IC manufacturers developed standardized chips for use in joysticks or other controllers, but creating standardized IC components for recently introduced videogame systems usually required at least four to six months. Thus, GEM had to custom design components for new video game systems until the vendors had developed standard chips for the new systems. Standardized IC chips developed specifically for a video game were generally less expensive than custom-designed components, so having strong relationships with innovative suppliers could provide a cost advantage for new products.

Sales of accessories for new video games were often substantial, as the videogame systems and accessories market was essentially a fast-moving "fashion business" within the electronics industry. New products and services were the primary drivers of new sales, and "quick responsive" in product design and innovation were essential for success. At the same time, since joysticks became commodity products within a few months following introduction, low-cost designs and production were also critical for success. Maintaining strong relationships with leading specialized IC vendors enabled joystick manufacturers to have the "latest fashions" at lower total system costs. Thus, selection of the right partners was a critical factor for success in this fast-moving business.

Several vendors were able to supply complete electronic systems including the IC and other components already installed on the PCB. This complete system was referred to as a "Chip on Board" (COB). These COB electronics systems were ready for final product assembly. Since vendors of these systems sold their COB products to multiple firms, it was unlikely that any joystick manufacturer would gain a significant competitive advantage through use of these standardized systems. However, some COB systems provided increased flexibility or functionality or lower costs than other COBs.

GEM had a strong relationship with a small specialized semiconductor manufacturer in Taiwan that was one of the leaders in producing COBs for the joystick manufacturing industry. For this supplier, GEM was one of their largest customers for standard joystick IC chips, although the vendor also sold the same products to other firms. When standardized ICs and COBs had not yet been developed, GEM had to develop custom IC chips and PCB designs. This involved additional costs, but was necessary to capture early sales for a new video game system. GEM relied on outside vendors to provide this specialized electronics design. Most of these electronic designers were affiliated with specialized IC vendors or with PCB producers and assemblers who competed with the COB vendors.

When custom-designed IC chips were used in the COB, one vendor would often supply the components and a different vendor would supply the PCB and assemble the COB. Sometimes the PCB vendor and the assembly factory were even different firms. Thus, production management for these nonintegrated operations was more complex than purchasing a completed COB system.

The decision of which vendor to choose for PCB and components assembly was often based on the production capability and schedule of the vendor, which changed over time and depended on the level of volume GEM had ordered and on the overall conditions within the electronics industry. The time required for product assembly was often as important as the cost quoted for providing services, and so maintaining good relationships and flexibility with vendors was important.

Printing and Packaging

The staff handled packaging design by themselves using standard desktop publishing software, which reduced both the cost and the time required for product packaging development. This also allowed the company to involve the customer and various members of the production and design staff in the process, building on the strengths of multiple members of the team. However, when management time was tight, this function could be outsourced to publishing design vendors who used the same software. The packaging design represented the first impression of the product for consumers in a retail store, and GEM was largely responsible for producing an effective advertising image, even for most of their private-label products. However, the largest chain store customers also wanted to be involved in packaging design to maintain consistency across products produced by multiple vendors. The design had to deliver a clear and attractive message regarding the unique features of the product.

Once the packaging design was completed, the electronic data of the design was submitted on a Syquest removable hard disk to the printer along with the product packaging specifications. The printer generally used the digital design submitted to produce the printing plates in Hong Kong, and produced the final printed packaging in China using these plates. The printed boxes were then shipped directly to GEM subcontractors in China. The printing factory had to maintain either capacity or inventory to be able to respond quickly to demand. Neither GEM nor its assembly factories carried more than one-week production requirements of the final packaging materials in inventory.

Assembly and Inventory Management

The finished plastic, electronics, and product packaging materials were delivered to an assembly plant in China to complete the last production stage. GEM contracted most of its assembly and packaging to two different factories in Shenzhen, China (about a two-hour drive from Hong Kong). All work-in-process inventory was stored at the factories or in several other locations in China, with no inventory stored in Hong Kong. The factories received the COB and product packaging materials as needed, with all requests for materials for production going through GEM and no orders allowed directly to the component or materials suppliers. The assembly factories were responsible for maintaining sufficient capacity or inventory to meet peaks in demand, but GEM management worked closely with the factories to help them manage inventory and production levels to be able to meet expected demand while avoiding excess inventory costs.

Maintaining efficient inventory management was important to control costs and minimize stockouts of components or final products. GEM provided the COB and packaging materials to the plastics production and assembly factory, so much of the inventory carrying and financing cost was actually provided by GEM, even though the inventory was physically stored at the final assembly location. However, since inventory was stocked at several different locations which were several hours' drive apart from each other, there was inconsistent information about the availability of products and components stocked in each of these warehouses. Thus, one important concern of the Hong Kong office manager was the need to find a better way to track and manage inventories within China.

Assembly was a labor-intensive process that did not require a high degree of workforce skills. Quality control was important and was one of the key management challenges for GEM associated with production and assembly within China. GEM management had been reasonably successful in educating their key assembly suppliers on the standards of quality that were acceptable for the U.S. and European markets. Albert Walter, the Hong Kong office manager, generally visited the China factories several times per week, as quality inspections and troubleshooting assistance were needed on a regular basis. It was essential to have staff located in Hong Kong that could visit the factories frequently to be sure that quality standards were maintained and that any problems were quickly resolved.

Channel Relationships and Virtual Integration

GEM's relationship with its channel partners could be described as virtual integration, with channel functions tightly linked operationally but with independent ownership of each stage of production. Thus, the channel functioned as if it were vertically integrated, with tight controls and fast feedback throughout the entire production process, but it was also able to overcome the management disincentives (i.e., agency costs) that were often associated with vertical integration.

For example, the factories in China coordinated activities closely with Hong Kong and U.S. office staff for production of GEM products, but also acted independently to fill slack capacity with products from other companies. Getting a factory manager to hustle and get outside business would have been more difficult for a company-owned factory, but in this case, the factory manager knew that his personal income and net worth were dependent upon marketing his services to others and providing responsive and high-quality services to GEM. In addition, the local factory owner fully understood that his personal income *and entire investment* in the factory would both be threatened if he lost the GEM contract due to quality problems, poor service, or inflexibility. Thus, GEM was able to "staff" the factory with a highly motivated local Chinese manager by allowing him or her to own the factory and profit from improving its operations. At the same time, GEM worked closely with the China factory managers to help them find ways to reduce cost or improve quality so that the entire channel benefited.

From the customer perspective, GEM also acted as a virtually integrated channel, especially for its large U.S. retail chain customers. This large chain provided all marketing and distribution for the private-label products provided by GEM once the products had reached the United States. The retailer frequently provided product packaging designs as well, although GEM would often suggest packaging designs for the retailer to consider. The retailer and GEM negotiated product wholesale costs (prices to the chain) and specifications. However, since GEM had a thin margin on products sold to this large chain, these price/cost negotiations were generally discussions of trade-offs or options for consideration, rather than adversarial pricing negotiations. GEM had gradually become the major supplier of private-label video game accessories for this large chain, as the firm repeatedly demonstrated its ability to deliver high-quality products at costs low enough to allow the retailer to charge very competitive retail prices.

The relationship between GEM and this large U.S. retailer had evolved to become more of an interdependent relationship between firms with closely aligned objectives rather than an independent relationship. The retail chain obviously had significant bargaining power in the relationship, but it would not be able to supply products less expensively by owning the production operations than it could by purchasing products from GEM, so vertical integration was not a viable alternative for the retailer. Thus, either GEM or a similar firm was needed to act as production coordinator and supplier for this retailer. Since GEM had proven its ability to reliably deliver high-quality products at attractive prices, the retailer had become almost as dependent on GEM as GEM was on this single large customer.

Maintaining long-term relationships with suppliers and buyers was crucial for GEM's success in the highly unstable world of video game accessory manufacturing. A stable relationship with material suppliers enabled GEM to obtain early access to key components and to gain access to extra supplies and production capacity to respond quickly to highly variable consumer demand. It was impractical to purchase inventory buffers in sufficient quantity to smooth out demand fluctuations, as obsolescence was rapid in this business and the costs of many components declined rapidly over time. At the same time, it was important to accurately forecast and respond to demand changes as quickly as possible, as customer purchases of these accessory products were often made on impulse at the time the original video game system was purchased. By maintaining strong relationships with key suppliers, GEM management was able to leverage these long-term relationships to coordinate and adapt to the specific product design, development, and changes in the electronics market when needs arose. All suppliers with whom GEM had developed these long-term relationship had proven their ability to provide reliable parts and components to match with the production schedules.

By sourcing most products from a few key vendors, GEM had been able to reduce the costs involved in searching for the best price every time from a large number of vendors. However, the company generally tried to have at least two vendors for all key components whenever possible. GEM had been able to improve operating efficiency and product sourcing reliability through streamlined purchasing relationships, which was important for successfully meeting market demand for their products. GEM could therefore guarantee reliable delivery of finished goods that were of consistent quality to its customers. This, in turn, reduced the cost of monitoring and inspection for the retailers, and enabled them to reduce costs by using GEM as a sole supplier of many of their key products.

Even with these advantages of close relationships, GEM was concerned that they might not always receive the best prices available in the market for some products. Thus, they often tested new suppliers for small volumes of components or services to determine if less expensive alternatives or improved services might be available. New suppliers were often used during periods of peak demand, and were then able to retain a portion of GEM components business long-term if they were able to provide competitive services and pricing during the most difficult supply periods. However, some parts, such as molds, were purchased only occasionally or were difficult to source from multiple vendors, so developing relationships with more than a single firm was not viable for these areas.

Organizational Structure

GEM's organizational structure (figure 3.22) consisted of a small team of managers and staff involved in administration, marketing, and operations management. Although the GEM organization had several hundred employees working in component production and product assembly in China, the company had only eight full-time employees. The company used a combination of Western and Asian management styles within its team of local Chinese and expatriate staff, and had adjusted effectively to cultural differences involved in operating within a business community that was primarily Chinese.

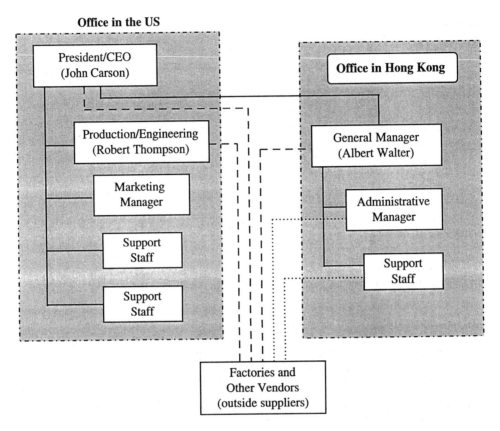

Figure 3.22
GEM organizational structure and staffing

Carson and his brother-in-law, Robert Thompson, managed the U.S. operations, assisted by a marketing manager and two clerical employees. Walter managed the Hong Kong offices with the assistance of two local Hong Kong employees who handled most of the administrative and accounting details. Since Walter was unable to speak Chinese, the local staff members often provided liaison services with the China operations, although the China factory owners were generally adequate in their use of English. Carson maintained close relationships with customers and did much of the marketing for the company, while Thompson supervised product development and operations management. Both Carson and Thompson traveled to Hong Kong frequently to oversee the Asian operations, and were involved in decisions regarding component sourcing and in the entire new product introduction process.

The company's success was largely based on Carson's experience in the industry and personal business judgment and contacts. GEM responded quickly to changes in technology and to product trends. In addition, Carson kept tight controls on costs and overheads. Thus, the office in Hong Kong was quite modest, with basic furniture and simple layout in less than 600 square feet of space, which included space used for on-site accommodation for the office manager. On the frequent visits to Hong Kong by Carson and Thompson, they also used the office as their motel accommodations to minimize costs. Thus, although the company had been quite successful in expanding both revenues and profits, they operated on very tight margins and were obsessed with cost control in all areas of the business.

By coordinating and outsourcing various production activities for design, manufacturing, and distribution, GEM had essentially developed a form of virtual integration of the entire supply chain involving many companies where each added value to different parts of the value chain. Carson's primary concern was developing ways to further simplify and reduce costs across the entire value chain, with particular focus on the operations and the manufacturing process managed by GEM. In the fast-moving and highly competitive electronics industry, reducing lead time and increasing channel responsiveness to changing demand for new and existing consumer products was crucial for success.

Walter described the need for flexibility and responsiveness by noting that "one day is a long time in this business." Thus, GEM was continuously striving to find ways to remove days or hours from the new product development cycle and to improve efficiency and effectiveness in the production process. By finding ways to save time, the firm would be able to build and maintain competitive advantage relative to competitors. It was easy for competitors to copy GEM product designs. Thus, the key to differentiating the company in the market was to be able to deliver products that the consumer wanted faster and more reliably than any other firm in the industry.

Role of Information Technology

Information technology had not been a critical factor in GEM's success, but was becoming increasingly important as the company attempted to streamline the new product introduction process and develop better systems for responding quickly to changes in demand. In addition, information technology was becoming an important tool for supporting core business processes in multiple areas of the business. GEM's management team believed that more effective use of information technology would enable the company to shorten the product development cycle, improve responsiveness, increase control over inventories and costs, and reduce costs of the development and production processes.

Information technology applications were used by many of GEM vendors, in virtually all areas of the business except assembly. For example, the electronics firms used computer aided design (CAD) tools for developing custom IC chips used in the COBs for new products, and some circuit designers also used computer applications for design of the PCB layout and associated standard component circuits. The mold designer used CAD for drawing the design specification schematics, and the mold tooler used CNC machines in creating the mold for the plastic component production. The art work for the packaging was completed using a PC software application that produced camera-ready copy that was sent to the printer and used for direct production of the printed packaging for the products.

With the retail customer, GEM had been required to adopt EDI for order receipt, and had developed a relatively simple but low cost process for accepting these orders and translating them into information that was useful for their internal management processes. This process involved receiving the orders from the U.S.-based EDI service provider network, stripping off all the details and other information from the message that were not needed for ordering by using a PC text editor or word processor, and then faxing the essential information to the Hong Kong office for entry into the ordering systems.

Although this manual system for receiving EDI orders appeared inefficient, for the limited number of orders received by GEM from this single large customer via the EDI, this seemed to be the most cost-effective solution available. Carson was not convinced that the company needed to invest in any more-sophisticated EDI software, and the retailer was satisfied with this process for accepting EDI orders, as it was relatively easy for GEM to implement and allowed the retailer to use their standard EDI ordering processes. Although there was no real benefit of EDI for GEM, the cost of receiving orders via EDI in this way was minimal, and the retailer had required all vendors to become EDI compatible.

Although Carson did not see EDI as a big opportunity, he felt that using the Internet could offer some significant opportunities for improving efficiency and redesigning existing business processes. The Internet might be able to reduce time delays in new product introduction, in particular. For example, the current production process involved sending artwork sketches for the product packaging via express courier (e.g., Federal Express) to Hong Kong, where they were translated into final camera-ready artwork using a standard PC application. The computer files or prints made from these files were then sent via express courier to the retail customer for final approval (for private-label products).

The cost of producing this artwork in Hong Kong was less than in the United States, but sending physical pictures and diskettes through the mail slowed this process significantly, especially when there were several rounds of changes by the customer. By using FTP (file transfer protocol) for transferring these large files (several megabytes for the final printing graphics files) electronically, the company would be able to take advantage of the most cost-effective production capabilities in either the United States or Hong Kong while eliminating the cost and time involved in using international courier services for data and image transmissions. FTP could also be used for sending CAD drawings back and forth between the United States and Hong Kong to allow Thompson to work more closely with the local prototype and plastic component mold designers without physically being in Hong Kong. Some of Thompson's trips to Hong Kong could be avoided if they could learn to use the Internet effectively for transfer of CAD drawings and for e-mail discussions of the drawings.

In time, Carson believed that the Internet could become an important tool for saving cost and time. However, few of GEM's vendors were current users of the Internet, which limited GEM's ability to use some applications. In addition, the limited resources of the firm and extensive opportunities being pursued limited the amount of time that anyone in the company had to develop the needed skills and interfaces to use these capabilities. Although he could see that this was an area that needed to be developed, he was not sure how high a priority the development of alternative business processes that used these new capabilities should have relative to the needs of running the business to deliver products today and spending time to develop the products to provide sales for next year. GEM had just recently connected to the internet for both its U.S. and Hong Kong offices, but still used fax and phone for most information transmission and communications. In time, Carson expected that more communications within the firm would use the more cost-effective e-mail alternative to fax and phone, but changing established patterns of communications even within a small firm was difficult.

Another area where information technology would be of benefit for the business was in inventory management and improved control procedures. Carson and Walter had a reasonable estimate of how much inventory was in the pipeline and where it was, but the current methods of tracking inventories were not very precise or detailed. In effect, they knew what components they had paid for, and what had been shipped, and were able to determine inventory from this data. However, since the data was not computerized, small quantities of inventory could be lost or forgotten.

Since some of the factories might also use some components for other customers (there were no exclusive contracts with vendors or assembly providers), Walter was concerned that there was some risk that inventory might be stolen or lost if more formal methods of tracking products and components were not developed. This had not been a major concern in the past, as the company had been managed on an almost zero inventory basis, but was becoming a more important issue as the company continued to expand and add more products. Inventory management would become even more important if the company began to expand its branded product marketing efforts.

To address this inventory management need, Walter had contracted with a local Hong Kong vendor to develop a simple but integrated inventory management and production accounting system. This system was also expected to be useful in tracking costs by product line. Cost accounting for production had not been needed in the past, when there were only a few products, but was becoming more of a concern as the number of products increased. Even so, most of the costs were still relatively easy to identify with a single product, so the production accounting and inventory management systems would be able to run on standard PC applications with some relatively modest customization for the GEM requirements to simplify the user interface for the system.

GEM's management team realized that there were many areas where information technology might be able to help improve operations, but the real challenge was finding management time to address these opportunities while still making money today by managing the business effectively. Carson was also reluctant to add additional staff to the payroll to address these opportunities, as one of the keys to the success of his firm had been tight management of overhead costs, and he was not convinced that the cost of an IT specialist could be justified based on the potential savings available. Thus, subcontracted vendors would be used to develop any needed applications, and any new systems or processes introduced would need to be simple enough to be used by the existing management team.

Management Issues and Concerns

Production and new product design troubleshooting required a lot of management attention, especially for the Hong Kong operations that interfaced with the China factories. Each staff member had to understand the manufacturing procedures and operations and all employees worked closely with the factories to get shipment out on schedule during high demand seasons (e.g., for Christmas sales). The local Chinese office staff were more than simply clerks or secretaries, and provided a vital facilitating role to ensure that products were provided to the factories as needed and that shipments were sent to the United States on time. With several 40-foot containers of products being shipped to the United States or Europe each week, the office staff was quite involved in making sure that the entire production and shipment process functioned smoothly. Unfortunately, this also meant that there was little slack time for detailed accounting support or inventory management. Thus, office support tools would be helpful in enabling the staff to perform their existing functions more effectively and expanding their abilities to provide better inventory tracking and management.

Improved productivity was also needed simply to manage the increasing volume being produced and shipped from the China factories over time. Carson wanted to avoid adding additional staff, if possible, but clearly needed to increase the capabilities of the Hong Kong office for dealing with increasing product variety and complexity. The U.S. office capabilities would also need to be expanded to handle the increased complexity and demands of branded product sales to new customers and to expand private-label sales to additional retail chains. This increased capacity could be created either by adding more staff or by leveraging technology to increase the productivity of the existing staff. Carson believed that both would be required, but the use of Internet and other technological support tools could allow key managers to utilize their time more effectively to facilitate growth in the business.

Inventory management had not been much of a concern for GEM in the past, as products were preordered by the major retail chains several months in advance so that the company could accurately estimate production requirements. However, many private-label customers were reducing product-ordering lead times, and branded product sales to smaller customers often involved highly uncertain demand with short order fulfillment lead times. Thus, demand forecasting and inventory management was becoming more important over time. GEM also might need to increase its limited U.S. warehouse space if sales of branded products continued to expand and private-label lead times decreased further. However, Carson wanted to avoid this expense if possible, as costs of U.S. warehouse operations were much greater than the costs of product storage and handling within China. He was interested in developing systems that would allow him to maintain low inventory storage costs and overheads.

4 Supply Chain Management and Information Alliances

Supply chain management (SCM) involves the adoption of electronic linkages between two business that are related as suppliers and customers within a single industry channel or supply chain. Within the apparel industry, SCM was first known as quick response (QR), and was viewed as a means for U.S. apparel manufacturers to gain a competitive advantage over lower-cost overseas manufacturers by competing on time rather than simply cost. As QR became important for U.S. retailers in reducing costs of stockouts and obsolete inventories, overseas producers were forced to adopt similar just-in-time (JIT) supply processes to compete with the U.S. apparel manufacturers. Increased integration of point-of-sale (POS) information and forecasting systems throughout the supply chain has enabled retailers and their suppliers to reduce costs dramatically and improve service levels globally. Within the grocery industry, the implementation of SCM innovations was introduced under the banner of efficient consumer response (ECR). ECR was viewed as a way for grocery chains to compete with the lower-cost mass merchandisers and club store chains that had grown rapidly during the 1980s. These SCM innovations have dramatically restructured the U.S. consumer goods channel and are in the process of changing the nature of manufacturing, distribution, and retailing in Europe, Japan, and Australia, as well as throughout Asia.

Transforming the Value Chain Using Information Technology

The processes or activities by which a firm delivers value to its customers can be referred to as the firm's internal value chain (see figure 4.1). Business process reengineering (BPR) involves examining this internal value chain to understand how processes can be changed or augmented using information technology to improve efficiency, reduce cycle time, and improve services provided to customers. The value chain can also be viewed from the perspective of the entire flow of goods and services used to transform raw materials into products or services consumed by end users of these goods. This external or industry value chain often includes multiple firms linked together as suppliers and customers in a single value chain flow of goods and information.

Both company and industry value chains are unique to a particular industry or company context. For example, in figure 4.2, the company value chain for a bank is shown to contrast with the value chain shown in figure 4.1, which is more typical of a manufacturing company. The industry value chain for a grocery retailer or manufacturer is shown in figure 4.3, with the industry flows of goods, cash (payments), and information all identified.

Secondary or Support Functions

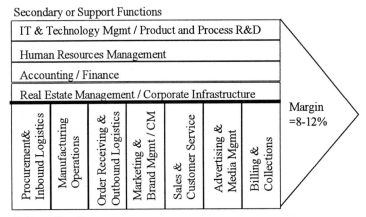

Primary Functions

Figure 4.1
Internal value chain for a consumer goods manufacturer

Support Functions

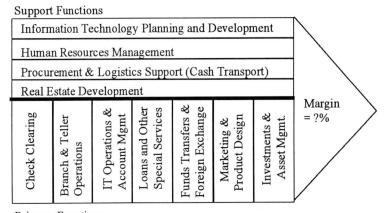

Primary Functions

Figure 4.2
The value chain for a large retail bank

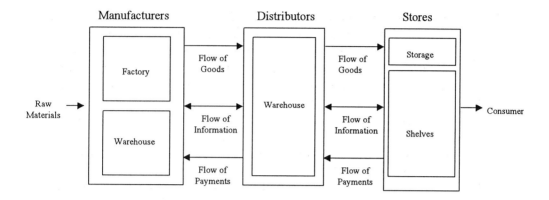

Flow of goods is frequent and high volume, and may be provided by trucks owned by one of the channel members or by a third party.

Flow of information was minimal for most channel members in the early 1990s, mostly conducted via voice telephone, paper mail, and face-to-face communications.

Figure 4.3
Simplified grocery industry value chain

One of the most important advances in retail logistics and operations in the past 20 years has been the development and introduction of automated store ordering systems using POS data from the checkout registers. Store managers and staff are busy and often do not have time to check the inventory of each item on the shelf each day. This can become a problem when unusually high demand for an item should trigger an immediate order or a larger order quantity than normal. Automated ordering systems can be designed to forecast demand patterns based on historical and seasonal demand data and then use this data to develop orders based on actual daily (or even hourly) demand from the POS data collected at the checkout registers in each store. Grocery and general merchandise retailers who have adopted these systems have been able to improve store shelf management sufficiently to stock more products in the same amount of space while simultaneously reducing the number of times that stockouts occur in the stores. These systems can be developed to support either warehouse delivery items or items vendors provide directly to the store (e.g., fresh milk is delivered directly to avoid spoilage).

Marketing opportunities available through using the POS data from each customer's purchases are just beginning to be realized. Some leading grocery chains are providing customers with frequent shopper cards that can be used to track individual customer purchases. Targeted promotions can be provided to customers individually, with mass media advertising replaced by specific promotions targeted at each customer based on prior purchases. Vendors are often willing to offer extremely attractive promotions to targeted customer segments (e.g., free trial product for a customer who has not purchased any of the firm's product in the past year but who regularly purchases a competitor's product). Thus, some leading retailers have begun to market cooperatively with vendors for specific targeted customer segment promotions that tend to increase customer loyalty without significantly increasing cost for the grocery chain. In many cases, targeted promotions can actually increase average effective margins realized by the chain while also increasing customer loyalty by shifting more of the cost of the promotions to vendors. The vendors, however, are quite willing to pay higher costs for these targeted promotions because they are actually able to reach their priority target market for promotions without having to offer these same discounts to their entire customer base.

Cashier operations were automated via the use of bar code scanning systems years ago, and are clearly dependent upon IT for effective operations. However, grocery stores have simply discarded these POS data for many years as an unimportant by-product of the improved checkout process. Now, many leading retailers have begun to recognize that these POS data represent a potential gold mine of information if they can learn to use them more effectively in their operations. In addition to using frequent shopper cards, some chains have started accepting credit cards for payment, which can then be linked to information from the POS scanning system regarding individual shoppers' purchases. Although most grocery chains worldwide have yet adopted these systems, the potential benefits enabled by these customer-specific innovations could provide retailers willing to take the lead in developing and deploying these systems with a significant competitive advantage in the market.

Electronic commerce can take advantage of opportunities to automate processes within the firm that permit faster or lower-cost marketing and delivery of goods and services to consumers. However, one of the most significant areas of opportunities in sharing electronic information and leveraging the value of information is through linking businesses within a single industry supply chain using electronic commerce capabilities. These applications are often described as interorganizational systems (IOSs) and represent an area of IT investment that has been considered strategic in the IT field for more than 30 years. In fact, you could describe some of these early strategic IOSs in the banking and airline industries as among the earliest examples of successful electronic commerce applications.

Strategic IT and the Value Chain beyond the Firm

To evaluate the IT applications' potential to affect a company's or industry's value chain, we need to understand the value chain both within a firm and outside its boundaries. Many strategic information systems cross the boundaries of the firm in some way and provide IT connections to suppliers, customers, or competitors. Systems developed and deployed only within a single firm have often proven relatively easy to duplicate over time and have generally only provided temporary advantages to adopting firms. However, systems that create linkages and interdependencies outside of a single organization can often shift the balance of power in an industry in ways that can become difficult for competitors to duplicate or overcome. These interorganizational systems, which extend beyond a single firm's boundaries, involve applications that affect the value chain of a firm or industry.

Before examining such interorganizational systems, it is important to clarify what we mean by an industry value chain. Michael Porter[1] describes an industry value chain as the value system that links multiple value chains together for firms within an industry. A firm that operates in multiple industries has value chains for each industry in which the firm competes. These business unit value chains then link into the value system for that industry and may also have linkages with other business unit value chains that can, in some cases, provide the firm with advantages of scope in operations or scale management of support functions.

Information systems have the potential for dramatically improving channel efficiency by sharing information between suppliers and customers. This shared information has obvious marketing advantages, as has already been illustrated in the example of vendors using POS data in grocery stores to target specific consumer groups for promotions. Information sharing with other firms can also dramatically reduce inventory levels and total production costs throughout the entire industry value chain.

The industry value chain is often referred to as the supply chain, the demand chain, the distribution channel, or simply the channel. Interest in SCM has increased dramatically since Procter and Gamble (P&G) and Wal-Mart demonstrated the potential for innovative SCM approaches using IT and process innovations to dramatically reduce inventories, stockouts, and costs within the U.S. consumer goods manufacturing and retailing industries. These innovations and other similar supply chain management innovations are described in the case studies included at the end of this chapter.

Although sharing of information in the supply chain or channel provides participating firms with enormous benefits, it also involves considerable risks. One of the most valuable aspects of IOSs is their potential for reducing customer or supplier power by increasing switching costs. Interestingly, IOSs can often increase switching costs and commitment for both customers and suppliers in a channel relationship, reducing the bargaining power of both parties at the same time. When this reduction of channel power occurs simultaneously over partners, it can result in a virtual channel alliance, with long-term relationships based on mutual trust replacing market-based short-term contracts. Alternatively, when power reduction in the relationship occurs only in one direction, then customers or suppliers locked into a weaker relationship with a more powerful channel partner may find themselves unable to realize any significant benefits from the IOS innovation.

Many suppliers of the U.S. auto industry have found that their large auto manufacturer customers have captured all of the benefits of IT innovations such as EDI.[2] Smaller firms have been forced to adopt these innovations to maintain supplier relationships with these large customers, but realize none of the savings from these innovations. Many smaller firms in other industries have experienced similar outcomes, and have been reluctant to adopt these IT innovations under the assumption that their larger channel partners would retain the savings while the costs of adoption remain with the smaller firms. At the same time, these smaller firms are finding that as large firms continue to invest in IOSs and channel partnership relationships, the smaller firms must adopt these IT innovations eventually as a requirement to survive in the increasingly competitive global economy.

The power of shared information within a channel in reducing costs and improving efficiency can be quite dramatic (Fig. 4.4). Many clothing, food, and general merchandise retailers and manufacturers have invested substantial resources in IT and process innovations designed to improve supply chain efficiency. Using this supply chain model, we can examine the effect of information systems innovations on the entire industry. In industries that have high demand uncertainty, providing information faster throughout the value chain can dramatically reduce total industry costs and inventory levels.

The Beer Game and the Value of Information

A common business school game, the beer game, is used to illustrate the value of information in a common business situation. In the beer game, there are four firms (which could represent groups of firms): a retailer, a distributor, a wholesaler, and a manufacturer. The retailer sells beer to consumers from inventory on the shelf. The distributor ships beer to the retailer from warehouse inventory. The wholesaler ships

Connectivity
Established

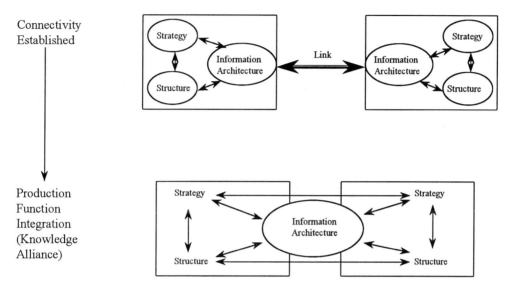

Production
Function
Integration
(Knowledge
Alliance)

Figure 4.4
Interdependencies resulting from shared information

beer to the distributor from warehouse inventory. The manufacturer also has warehouse inventory, as beer production can be increased only gradually when market
demand shifts occur.

When demand for beer is relatively constant, each firm is able to manage inventory
levels quite well and the entire supply chain is in balance. However, when retail
demand increases quickly, there is an interest effect on the rest of the channel. Inventories for firms later in the channel information flow increase dramatically, which
decreases overall channel efficiency. Lets examine a simple illustration of this effect.

Assume demand for beer at a retailer suddenly increases from 100 cases to 150
cases per day during a one-week period when colleges in the area go on spring break.
(These are no classes during this period, so the students can drink more beer.) Also
assume that the retailer has sufficient inventory to meet this new demand level, but
only for one day before stocking out of beer (average inventory is thus set at 150% of
daily average demand).[3] The retailer quickly realizes that he needs to order more
inventory quickly to be able to meet this much higher level of sales. He does not
know how long this higher sales demand will last or if sales might even be higher
tomorrow, so he decides to order enough product to meet this new demand and
provide his normal inventory buffer (50% of sales) at this higher level of demand.
Because both the amount of the demand and his new inventory requirement to meet

demand uncertainties at this higher demand level have increased, instead of his usual order of 100 cases, the retailer needs to order 225 cases: 150 cases because of the higher beer demand, 50 cases to replace his depleted inventory, and 25 more cases to increase his inventory to 150% of this new higher level of sales (so he will have sufficient inventory to react to any future variations in demand).

Assume that the distributor maintain a 100% inventory buffer to serve his retail customers (e.g., 200 cases to service the typical order of 100 cases per day from his retailer). He now has a problem, as demand from his customer has increased by much more than the 50% increase in consumer demand, as he has received an order for 225 cases of beer instead of the normal 100 cases. Unfortunately, he is simply not able to meet this new demand. The best he can do is to ship 200 cases of beer, which completely uses up the 100% inventory buffer. However, he is determined that he will not be caught short of products again, so he increases his target inventory level from 200% of prior demand levels to be 200% of this new demand level. This will enable him to provide better service to his customer if demand surges again. To reach this new inventory target and replenish his now empty warehouse, the distributor places an order not for his usual 100 cases, but for 475 cases: 450 cases (225 cases times 200%) to meet his new inventory requirement plus an additional 25 cases for his back order (ordered by the retailer but not shipped).

The wholesaler receives an order for 475 cases of beer, instead of the usual 100 cases, and is amazed at how quickly demand for beer seems to be increasing. Assume that he has stocked sufficient inventory to be able to meet three times the average demand. Thus, he can only ship 300 cases to the distributor, and must place the additional 175 cases on back order. However, to be sure that he can meet any further demand increases, he also increases his inventory buffer. Because he is a very smart wholesaler, he decides to increase his inventory level to only twice the level of this new demand just in case this is a temporary demand increase. Thus, he orders 1,125 cases from the manufacturer to meet this new level of demand (475 cases) plus enough to increase his inventory to twice this new level of demand (and 475 cases), plus the 175 cases he still has on back order for the distributor after shipping all of his inventory.

The manufacturer now is completely baffled by this sudden increase in demand. The order from his wholesaler is now 1,125 cases, instead of the typical 100 cases shipped previously. Although he has 500 cases in inventory, this is clearly insufficient to meet this new surge in demand. Thus, he immediately goes from one shift to three shifts at the factory and hires hundreds of workers overnight to meet this new demand. Overtime productions by all workers and the use of some of the newly hired workers allows the plant to double production for the day (not triple, as the new workers are still learning). This 200% of average production (normally 100 cases per day which equals his standard daily order) plus his entire inventory of 500 cases enables the manufacturer to ship out 700 cases of beer, with the remaining 425 cases ordered by the wholesaler placed on back order.

The next day, the retailer demand is still 50% higher than normal, but he has ordered enough product to meet this higher demand level and his inventory has been replenished overnight by his distributor to a level that is sufficient for this new demand level. He orders the exact amount of this new demand to replace the beer that had been sold that day, or 150 cases. This order of 150 cases plus the 25 cases still on back order will replenish his sold stock and increase total inventory to the 225 case new target level (150% of sales).

The distributor is relieved that the order is not as high as it had been the previous day. The dramatic increase in demand the prior day was apparently an isolated incident, so he adjusts his new inventory targets to this more reasonable level of demand. He ships 175 cases (150 cases ordered and 25 cases back order) to his retailer customer from the existing inventory of 300 cases received from his wholesaler the prior day. He also adjusts his inventory target to 300 cases of average demand, or twice the level of the retailer's new order. He then calculates that the 175 cases already on back order from the wholesaler will be sufficient to replenish his inventory to this 300 case level so finds that no additional order is needed.

The wholesaler is relieved that the distributor appears to have overestimated the actual demand so revises his own inventory targets back to a more moderate level of 500 cases. Since he received 700 cases from the manufacturer and only needs to ship the 175 cases on back order to the distributor, he does not need to place any additional order. In fact, with the 425 cases still on back order from the manufacturer, he has more than enough inventory in stock now (525 cases) and already on back order. The manufacturer produces and ships 200 cases to the wholesaler, reducing his back orders due to 225 cases, but maintains the higher production level to try to rebuild inventory buffers, which are still zero.

The third day of the higher demand, the retailer sells and orders 150 cases. The distributor inventory target remains at 300 cases, and he orders 150 cases from the wholesaler. The wholesaler adjusts his inventory target to 450 cases (300% of the new demand level) but already has 575 cases in inventory and 225 cases on back order still from the manufacturer. Thus, he again places no order with the manufacturer. The manufacturer, concerned that orders are not coming in now, decides to layoff all temporary workers and eliminate overtime staffing after the completion of the production schedule for that day since the demand does not appear to be as large as initially indicated. After shipping an additional 200 cases from the production for that day, there will be only 25 cases in back orders remaining, which the normal production schedule of 100 cases per day appears likely to be able to accommodate given the lack of new orders.

The fourth day, the retailer and distributor both sell and orders 150 cases. The wholesaler still has 625 cases in inventory plus 25 cases still coming on back order, so is able to fill his current 150 case order from the distributor without placing any new order with the manufacturer. The manufacturer produces 100 cases and ships the last 25 cases back ordered four days earlier to the wholesaler, and starts to rebuild inventory with the remaining 75 cases produced.

The fifth day, the retailer sells and orders 150 cases, as does the distributor also. The wholesaler still has 500 cases of inventory on hand after receiving his 25 cases back order and shipping 150 cases to the distributor. Since only 450 cases are needed in inventory, the wholesaler places no new order the manufacturer to replenish his inventory to the target level of three times his average daily sales.

The sixth day, the retailer and distributor both sell and order 150 cases. The wholesaler ships 150 cases and orders 100 cases to bring inventory back up to the target level of 450 cases. The manufacturer is relieved to see that demand has returned to normal at last, and ships the 100 cases from current production. As manufacturer inventory is still low at only 175 cases, a modest amount of overtime work is added to increase production to 150 cases to be able to rebuild inventory since demand appears to be stable again.

The seventh day, the retailer, distributor, and wholesaler all sell and order 150 cases. The manufacturer produces and ships 150 cases. Demand has finally reached steady-state for the entire system. Of course, this occurs just as the students are now returning from break, so the next day, retail demand for beer declines back to the 100 case per day level that was typical prior to the vacation week. Fortunately, in the scenario described, the manufacturer still was below his target inventory level when this second shift in demand occurred, so the shock to the production system is not as large as it was when demand increased. However, it still takes five days at normal production for the system to reach a stable equilibrium with all firms maintaining stable inventory levels.

This simple example illustrates the shock that a single unexpected event can have on demand across the channel. In the actual game used in the classroom, the demand is not so stable, and firms have to try to minimize inventory costs, production costs, and lost sales.

When this beer game is introduced to business school students, they are allowed to act in the role of one of the companies in this supply chain. Their challenge is to minimize inventories and stockouts (backorders) given uncertainty about potential changes in demand. The game includes both increases and decreases in demand of varying duration, which are not known in advance to the students. The students try to develop algorithms that will result in lower inventories and lower variations in production than occurred in the above scenario.

Although business school students are generally able to better manage production than the firms in the example provided above, the variations in inventory and production are always large. In some cases, they even run out of available products at the retail store to serve increased demand (which results in costly lost sales to consumers).

After playing the game (with different demand shifts than used in the introduction of the game), the students are then provided with an additional source of information to use in capacity and inventory planning. All firms in the channel are provided with the data from the retailer on actual daily sales. Thus, the manufacturer knows exactly when sales have increased or decreased and by how much on the same day as it happens.

This new information allows the students to dramatically improve inventory and production capacity management in their firms. Average inventory levels decline dramatically, and production shifts are much more modest, resulting in significant cost savings for the entire channel. Although this game and the suggested demand shifts are much simpler than real life, the potential for shared information to reduce inventories and production costs in the channel is very real.

Benefits and Challenges of Sharing Information

The actual savings in many industries may only be moderate compared to the savings for students in the beer game example, but these savings often represent a return of more than 10 times the cost of developing and implementing the systems required to enable these savings. The real challenge in implementing these shared IOS applications is not developing the technology. The IT components of many of these systems are quite well understood. The real challenge is developing the environment of organizational trust and sharing that can enable introduction of these capabilities within the supply chain.

For vertically integrated firms, introduction of such systems is relatively simple. For most firms, establishing trust is not easy. Firms must learn to share both channel information and the savings resulting from the use of that shared information. Introduction of IOS innovations often requires a high degree of support and financial commitment from upstream channel suppliers to encourage adoption by downstream channel distributors and retailers. However, some visionary retailers have been able to see the potential benefits of such systems across the entire channel and for their firms and have strongly encouraged their vendors to adopt (and pay for) these systems. Generally the benefits for these leading retailers are provided in terms of faster response times and lower retailer inventory levels.

Because the most expensive inventory storage in the entire channel is in the retail store, a reduction of retailer inventory requirements in the store offers substantial cost savings. The vendor is willing to absorb the increased costs of providing a higher service level and more frequent distribution in return for lower production and storage costs that result from faster information flows with the new shared information systems.

The development and introduction of IOS applications can be difficult, but can also provide attractive benefits across the entire channel. Many firms in the 1990s are learning that they must cooperate using IOS to be able to compete effectively in an increasingly global and intense business environment. Learning to develop successful relationships based on trust is becoming vital for firms in many industries globally as they begin to cooperate to compete.

Interorganizational Systems and BPR

The introduction of virtually all IOSs has required redesign of existing processes across the channel. However, many of the early IOS innovations resulted in unintentional process redesigns by those who adopted them. In many cases, these unintentional process changes resulted in substantially lower power for the firms that accepted these IOS innovations from their developers. Although these early IOSs did provide benefits for both innovation champions and followers that later adopted these systems, the IOS champions that developed the systems were often able to capture a large portion of their entire value.

Most firms today recognize that IOS implementations can dramatically shift the balance of power within an industry and are reluctant to adopt proprietary systems that could lock the firm into a long-term relationship with a single firm. However, not all such relationships are bad. As long as firms recognize that the nature of the interorganizational relationship is changing as firms implement new IOS applications, the balance of power within an industry can be maintained regardless of who actually develops or manages the physical IOS infrastructure. The implementation of an IOS, however, does tend to increase interdependence within the channel across all relationships affected by the new IT and process innovations introduced with the IOS application.

Effective utilization of IOS can enable firms to effectively integrate their operations vertically without the need to own their channel partners. This can be a concern for some firms that find that the more vertically integrated IOS relationship reduces their control and power. However, many small firms have found new opportunities for providing value-added services to larger companies that could have only been sourced internally without the development of these IOSs, which enable organizational control to extend beyond the boundaries of the firm. Thus, one implication of the expanding use of IOSs to enable virtual integration of an entire supply chain is that many more firms are finding attractive options for outsourcing their operations.

The potential for IOS to redefine entire business systems can provide leading innovators with powerful competitive advantages. In fact, it is possible now to create entirely new ways of competing in the market through IT-enabled alliances. The creation of new forms of IT-enabled alliances can transform companies and even reengineer the scope of the businesses in which they compete.

Of course, opportunities for transforming industry relationships also can be viewed as alarming risks for some firms that are not beneficiaries of these new IOS innovations. Few firms can afford to ignore the potential of IT and particularly IOS in transforming industry structure and relationships. Some firms may even find that adoption of an IOS can reduce their power in their channel relationships, as the IOS innovation leader seeks to maximize the potential benefits through shifting power within the channel. Other firms may find that failure to join an IOS could leave them at a serious competitive disadvantage that becomes increasingly difficult to overcome.

Developing and Maintaining IOS Partnerships

In general, IOS innovations increase interorganizational interdependency, as linkages between information systems eventually lead to increased linkages between organizational strategy and structure as well. Firms that develop or adopt IOS applications need to consider the long-term strategic implications of these systems on organizational power and dependence within their channel relationships. In most cases, if these issues are considered and addressed during the early stages of an IOS relationship, firms with a reasonable balance of power in an existing relationship can establish policies and guidelines in an atmosphere of mutual trust that can resolve most concerns in order to provide mutual benefits from the IOS implementation and adoption.

Smaller firms probably have no choice but to accept the terms and conditions the IOS leaders offer in order to gain the potential benefits of these innovations. Where possible, these smaller firms should seek to adopt IOS applications that provide them with as much independence as possible, such as an open IOS network that is owned not by a single firm but by an independent third party or by an industry cooperative.

Alternatively, these firms can establish themselves as virtually integrated business units of the IOS business network that is linked with a single firm. These virtual integration relationships, which involve high degrees of organizational dependence, can be attractive if the firm has key skills or resources that other firms cannot easily provide or if switching costs for both parties in the IOS are large. In this situation, the high dependence may be mutual interdependence, which can provide a solid basis for a long-term and mutually attractive relationship.

Establishment of IT-enabled alliances involving mutual dependence is becoming more common. Although there are clearly risks involved in entering into these information partnerships, the benefits that result from these new business networks can be quite attractive. When these information partnerships create new business opportunities or offer dramatic cost reductions in existing businesses, they have the potential to transform both businesses and industries.

Wholesale Electronic Commerce: IOS and the Internet

Although establishment of long-term relationships based on trust can enable firms to adopt proprietary IOS applications without necessarily increasing risk, most firms prefer to shift to more open platforms shared by multiple firms. They perceive that these open platforms reduce the risks of being locked into a single customer or vendor relationship that can result from organizational costs of switching to a new system. These shared systems have evolved in many industries as common shared platforms used by multiple customers and vendors for electronic commerce applications. Although all IOS applications could be considered a form of electronic commerce, this term is generally restricted to describing IOSs that are shared by a large number of firms over a common platform. Early examples of electronic commerce generally used infrastructures developed and managed by an independent third party for the industry (such as IBM or GE) or by an industry association. Since the mid-1990s, many shared applications have been introduced that utilize the Internet and its associated Web capabilities.

There is a strong trend in business toward using the Internet as a backbone for many forms of business-to-business electronic commerce to replace proprietary communications channels, and the Internet can enable many new forms of electronic commerce. However, it is important also to realize that the Internet by itself is simply a communications infrastructure that can facilitate development of shared electronic commerce applications. Proprietary IOS applications can also be developed on the Internet. These proprietary applications are often referred to as intranets and have gained a lot of attention in the past few years.

Companies adopting any form of electronic commerce, with or without the Internet, should consider the implications of these new systems on internal organizational processes, on relationships and bargaining positions within the channel, and on relative competitive advantage of the firm relative to its competitors. Although the adoption of IOS often can provide important cost savings and competitive advantages, it is important to consider how a different form of IOS might create advantages or disadvantages for your firm in the market. In some cases, your firm may be able to influence the evolution of electronic commerce infrastructures and applications within your industry by your choices regarding IOS adoption or development.

The Internet's potential to transform business relationships and establish new forms of business networks is only just beginning to be realized. Many firms are experimenting with the Internet to try to understand how it can be used to improve business operations, but few firms have created new business opportunities at this time. From an electronic commerce perspective, some of the most powerful examples of success and profitable implementation of electronic commerce applications have been within the business-to-business area of IOS linkages. These strategic IOS systems have provided firms with ability to reduce costs and improve services dramatically, and are some of the earliest and most notable successes of IT investments over the past 30 years. The area of supply chain management using IT networks in IOS applications has become increasingly important over the past 10 years, and has provided firms in industries as dull as trucking or retailing with competitive advantages relative to less innovative firms in their industries.

Notes

1. Michael E. Porter, *Competitive Advantage* (New York: The Free Press, 1985), pp. 33–59.

2. T. S. Mukhopadhyay, S. Kekre, and S. Kalathur, "Business Value of Information Technology: A Study of Electronic Data Interchange," *MIS Quarterly*, vol 19, no. 2, p. 137–155, 1995.

3. This assumption is not critical for the beer game model. Any reasonable assumption in which the increase in demand is much larger than average daily demand variations produces similar results. The assumption made here simply makes the demand behavior in the channel easier to illustrate for students.

H. E. Butt Grocery Company: A Leader in ECR Implementation

Fully Clingman, COO of the H. E. Butt Grocery Company (HEB), was pleased with the progress the company had made in implementing category management (CM) and continuous replenishment (CRP). These programs had enabled the company to reduce prices to strengthen customer loyalty and increase sales while maintaining or improving profit margins. Despite the success of these programs, Clingman was concerned about the planned expansion of several mass-merchandise chains into the south Texas market with superstores that combined grocery and general merchandise formats. HEB's market position was strong, but these low-cost nationwide chains represented a serious threat.

The Efficient Consumer Response (ECR) vision for improving grocery channel performance was developed by a joint industry project team that included manufacturers, retailers (including HEB), and wholesalers. The ECR vision suggested multiple new programs, including CRP and CM, that would improve total channel efficiency and allow grocery retailers to compete more effectively with mass merchandisers (e.g., Wal-Mart) and club stores (e.g., Sam's Club) for sales of traditional supermarket products. HEB was a leader in CM and CRP implementation, but Clingman wondered whether all the ECR ideas made sense for HEB. If so, which aspects of ECR should be implemented next, and how quickly should implementation proceed? In addition, how should HEB respond to the introduction of mass-merchandise chain superstores? Finally, should HEB continue to contribute time and knowledge to industry efforts to improve grocery channel efficiency, or should all management attention be focused on the immediate threat of the new superstores and other alternative retail formats expanding in traditional HEB markets?

Company and Industry Background

H. E. Butt Grocery Company was the 13th largest grocery retailer in the US, with 1992 sales of approximately $3.2 billion (table 4.1). US retail grocery sales in 1992 totaled $376 billion, with the top five national retailers representing about 21% of total sales. The grocery channel consisted of companies in three major subcategories: retailers,[1] distributors, and manufacturers (figure 4.5). Retail grocery competition was regional in scope, with the largest chains operating in multiple regions but without any truly national competitors.

This case was prepared by Theodore H. Clark and David C. Croson under supervision of Professors James L. McKenney and Richard L. Nolan.

Table 4.1
Leading U.S. retail grocery chains—Comparison of total sales and number of stores

Sales rank	Company name	Number of stores	1992 sales ($ millions)
1	Kroger Co.	2,215	22,145
2	American Stores Company	925	19,051
3	Safeway Inc.	1,105	15,152
4	Great Atlantic & Pacific Tea Co.	1,202	10,499
5	Winn-Dixie Stores, Inc.	1,166	10,337
6	Albertson's, Inc.	651	10,174
7	Food Lion, Inc.	1,012	7,196
8	Publix Super Markets, Inc.	416	6,305
9	Vons Companies, Inc.	346	5,596
10	Pathmarks Stores, Inc.	147	4,340
11	Giant Food, Inc.	156	3,473
12	Stop & Shop Supermarket Co.	120	3,352
13	H. E. Butt Grocery Company	213	3,204
14	Fred Meyer, Inc.	72	2,854
15	Ralphs Grocery Company	160	2,841
16	Grand Union Company	252	2,800
17	Bruno's, Inc.	256	2,658
18	Smith's Food & Drug Centers, Inc.	121	2,650
19	Food 4 Less Supermarkets, Inc.	249	2,475
20	Meijer, Inc.	80	2,300
21	Hy-Vee Food Stores, Inc.	160	2,250
22	Hannaford Bros. Co.	95	2,066
23	Giant Eagle, Inc.	134	2,060
24	Dominick's Finer Foods, Inc.	101	2,000
25	Stater Bros. Markets	108	1,821

Source: Progressive Grocer Marketing Guidebook, 1993.

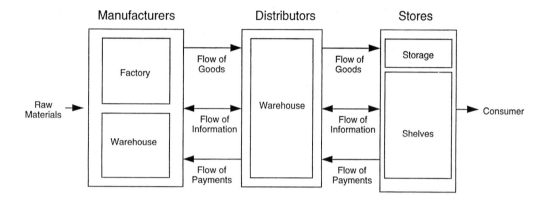

Flow of goods is frequent and high volume, and may be provided by trucks owned by one of the channel members or by a third party.

Flow of information was minimal for most channel members in the early 1990s, mostly conducted via voice telephone, paper mail, and face-to-face communications.

Figure 4.5
Simplified grocery industry functional value chain

Distributors supplied retailers with goods in case quantities and could be (1) independent, (2) owned by a group of retailers called a *cooperative*, or (3) owned by a retail chain (a *captive distributor*). Most retail chains used captive distributors, vertically integrating to combine retail stores and distribution. Vertical integration was not limited to retailer/distributor combinations; some manufacturers also vertical integrated into distribution by providing direct store delivery (DSD) for their products. Manufacturer DSD was common for (1) branded products where freshness was critical (e.g., dairy products, snack foods, and breads), (2) branded products with large movement volumes (e.g., soda and beer), and (3) products that required extensive instore inventory management (e.g., greeting cards and panty hose).

Manufacturing and retailing were each highly concentrated in horizontally differentiated segments of the overall grocery channel. Retailers were highly *geographically* focused, with the top three retail chains in a geographic market (e.g., city) generally controlling 70% or more of sales. Manufacturers were focused on *product categories*, with a single manufacturer often controlling 40% or more of a single branded product category (such as salty snacks or soap). Both methods of dominance offered significant scale economies, leading to structural concentration and focused strategies. Although both manufacturers and retailers had integrated into the distribution role, goods supplied by independent wholesale distributors accounted for approximately 50% of grocery product sales, mostly through small chains and independent retailers.

Channel pricing policies encouraged retailers and distributors alike to purchase significant quantities of goods far in advance of demand at reduced promotional prices, to be offered later to customers at the standard retail price, a practice known as "forward buying." As much as a whole year of product volume would be purchased during a single promotion. Manufacturers typically offered retailers a wide variety of promotional allowances and rebates, whose complexity, combined with forward buying, made it difficult to determine the actual net cost of a product on the shelf.

Periodic price promotions to consumers were useful in increasing total product consumption but caused systematic forward buying as an unintended consequence. In addition to the incentive to make arbitrage profits on merchandise, forward buying on promotions also gave retailers an incentive to push the over-inventoried product through to consumers in the place of products not promoted, purchased, or warehoused in large quantities. Large purchases at the tail end of promotions also allowed manufacturers to sell product in advance of consumer demand, resulting in higher short-term accounting profits. Thus, the practice of forward buying provided manufacturers with some long-term product push, and changes in the level of forward buying affected short-term profits.

By 1990, large inefficiencies across the channel motivated retailers and manufacturers to begin investigating alternative channel-supply approaches that eliminated or discouraged forward buying and dramatically reduced inventory levels across the channel. The *Efficient Consumer Response* (ECR) report, published in 1993 by Kurt Salmon Associates under the auspices of the Food Marketing Institute (FMI), proposed a number of technological and managerial changes that promised total annual savings of approximately $30 billion if implemented completely. Initial reactions to this dramatic proposal were mixed, but many retailers and manufacturers believed they would be forced to implement ECR to remain competitive over the coming decade.

An important driver of the ECR project and other efforts to improve efficiency and change channel policies was the growth of alternative store formats competing with supermarkets for consumer dollars. Discount drugstores (e.g., Walgreens), discount department stores (e.g., Wal-Mart), and wholesale-club stores (e.g., Sam's Club) had all gained market share in products frequently purchased in supermarkets. Wal-Mart had been particularly effective at negotiating mutually attractive supply agreements with manufacturers that reduced costs and inventory for both partners.

The combination of technological and managerial innovations, developed and refined in cooperation with vendors, enabled Wal-Mart to sell products profitably at prices lower than most grocery retailers could maintain. The new channel design pioneered by Wal-Mart was copied by other discount retailers and, by 1993, had become the dominant channel design for discount merchandisers and warehouse-club stores. The ECR proposal recommended that similar changes be pursued in the retail grocery channel to reduce total channel cost, allowing the grocery channel to compete more effectively with these alternative formats.

An important unresolved issue impeding ECR implementation was the planned distribution of benefits and costs between manufacturers, wholesalers, and retailers. Since manufacturers' after-tax returns on sales were frequently 5–10 times those of retailers or wholesalers, some retailers expressed concern that manufacturers would capture most of the benefits of ECR while leaving retailers with most of the costs. Other retailers believed that ECR would shift power from manufacturers to retailers, enabling retailers to capture most of the ECR benefits. Pre-tax profit margins for retailers were generally 1%–2% of sales. The ECR study suggested that consumers would eventually capture all benefits of ECR via falling prices (up to 11% savings) as implementation became a competitive necessity for manufacturers and retailers.

Changing channel policies and behavior, as suggested by the ECR proposal, required the emergence of a new attitude of trust and cooperation between retailers and manufacturers. Such trust was difficult for many managers, who had learned to negotiate in a "win-lose" environment and had problems believing the ECR "win-win" promise. Negotiations were complicated by the fact that either win-win or win-lose outcomes were possible, so cooperation and self-interest needed to be pursued simultaneously as channel relationships evolved.

Retail Store Operations

HEB operated over 200 full-service supermarkets throughout central and south Texas, with average sales per store of approximately $300,00 per week. Information technology had long been an important part of the company's strategy to control costs and keep prices low. A compulsive focus on improving efficiency, supported by technology and systems, enabled HEB to offer very low prices while still achieving attractive profits for the chain. In 1989, the drive to reduce costs and prices led HEB to adopt an Every Day Low Price (EDLP) strategy. Charles Butt, chairman and CEO of HEB, was active in the chain's management and strongly believed that maintaining low prices was critical for the company's long-term strength.

Technology and Systems to Support Retailing

A leader in POS (point of sale) scanning adoption in the 1970s, HEB had implemented scanner systems in all of its stores during the 1980s. Store operation was
supported by other systems, including automated time and attendance reporting,
DSD receiving and invoicing, and electronic mail (e-mail). Introduced in the MIS
group, e-mail usage gradually expanded throughout the company, providing instantaneous on-line communications between stores, warehouses, and headquarters
locations. By 1990, e-mail was considered a key operational system and accounted
for as much traffic as all other on-line data systems combined.

With the introduction of POS scanners and the data they provided, the use of
information systems had become integral to store operations. Early scanner problems
increased management awareness of dependence on these systems, which had initially
been justified on the basis of reductions in direct cost through improved speed and
accuracy of checkout. As customers came to appreciate their increased convenience
and accuracy, scanners eventually became a competitive requirement in HEB's
region. Equipment reliability was of major concern because scanner malfunctions
caused customer delay and lost sales. Dedicated minicomputer systems, designed
specifically for POS scanning, provided acceptable reliability but limited flexibility for
integrating the systems with other applications.

HEB has installed UNIX-based minicomputers in all stores during the early 1990s.
These in-store processors were linked to the headquarters (HQ) mainframe and to all
other systems within the stores, including the POS scanners. Much of the dialogue
between the stores and headquarters used this computer-to-computer link in an
ongoing exchange of information on sales, orders, and personnel.

To strengthen this network, HEB installed a VSAT-based communications system
linking all stores to the HQ computers during the early 1990s. This system enabled
a major increase in the flow of internal communications at minimal cost and facilitated the development of software applications linking stores and HQ systems tightly
together. HEB justified the VSAT investment through communications cost savings
and improvements in both marketing effectiveness and operational efficiency.

Communication infrastructure was an important element of retail store operations.
A store manager at one of HEB's larger stores used his e-mail system extensively
both from home and at the office. He also relied heavily on the Motorola hand-held
radios carried by all managers and assistant managers in the store. During a one-
hour interview, the store manager handled five requests for information or advice
without significantly interrupting the interview.

Store managers relied heavily on technology support since the volume of sales had
increased dramatically during the previous decade, with no increase in management

staff or selling floor space. Shifting store-to-HQ communications to the asynchronous e-mail link enabled HEB to "keep managers on the floor, not in the office." Since a store manager's typical schedule required him to work 60 hours or more per week, the ability to handle many e-mail communications from home in the evenings was helpful.

E-mail links to all stores allowed store managers to communicate useful ideas and innovations to other store managers directly. HEB's culture limited most communications to a hierarchical store-to-HQ or HQ-to-store flow, but lateral communication was possible and occasionally helpful. For example, one store manager developed a solution to a back-room stacking problem in pallet storage, using a new type of pallet in the lower storage racks. He thought this solution would be useful for other store managers but noted that sharing solutions to common problems was not a typical application of e-mail despite its apparent effectiveness.

Retail Pricing and Merchandising Strategy

Bob Chapman, VP of procurement, carefully examined successful retail strategies and future trends in the industry during the late 1980s. Wal-Mart and Food Lion were shifting to EDLP and away from traditional promotion-oriented pricing (high-low). HEB in the 1980s was departmentally organized, with the grocery department responsible for procuring all grocery products.

Beginning in 1989, HEB shifted to a mixed EDLP and promotional-pricing strategy. This combination of EDLP and limited promotions had been very effective in stimulating sales. EDLP was the primary pricing policy for the chain but was supplemented with specials that focused on perishables and snack-food items. The move to EDLP reduced average prices to customers, requiring HEB to find cost savings in order to maintain company profitability.

One challenge for retail managers at HEB was improving pricing accuracy. Each store's scanning system operated independently; centrally generated price changes were not always updated correctly at the store level. In addition, some stores failed to update shelf pricing labels on time, resulting in customer complaints that items were not scanned correctly even when the scanned price was correct. The failure to implement pricing changes at the store level was a serious concern for HEB management. Store managers did not intentionally fail to change shelf prices, but they sometimes neglected to follow through on labeling due to lack of staff, time, or attention.

Checkers also occasionally undercharged customers for products, such as produce, that were not scanned. For example, some checkers were unable to accurately differentiate between the various types of apples. Rather than asking the customer, checkers would simply charge the lower price of two similar items, providing a large but inconsistent discount for some customers. With over 800 produce items, checkers were often uncertain. In an effort to improve pricing accuracy, HEB tested installing self-service produce weighing and labeling systems. One store manager noted:

We will make more money if we let the customer weigh and label fruit and bulk goods themselves. Our customers are more honest than our checkers are accurate.

The Customer Select Circle Card

In the late 1980s, HEB led the industry in developing a system to use POS data to create useful customer information for improved marketing. Customers were invited to apply for a free "Select Circle" card that would provide discounts when used at checkout. A direct mail campaign announced monthly specials for Select Circle members, and scanning systems in stores were programmed to discount these items upon presentation of a Select Circle card. Although only 28 HEB stores in two cities offered this program by early 1990, a significant portion of sales in these stores was to customers using these cards.

The Select Circle program allowed HEB to gather information about individual customers' purchases over time which could then be used in marketing and planning. The POS scanning systems transcended their original cost-reduction role, becoming an important information-gathering tool. Early uses of customer purchase data were simple but effective, indicating the strategic value of the information if effectively harnessed. For example, after several weeks of store remodeling, customer purchase records were analyzed to determine who had stopped shopping at HEB during the construction. Special mailings to these customers announcing remodeling completion and offering a special discount on their next visit to their local HEB store generated a very positive response, and customer loyalty was quickly regained.

However, the targeted promotions offered by the Select Circle program were viewed as inconsistent with the overall move to EDLP in the early 1990s. The customer POS card was discontinued until the company was able to determine how to use the generated information more effectively. Early experiments with using the data demonstrated that the idea had great potential for targeted marketing, but the cost of gathering and analyzing the data seemed to be higher than could be justified by the marketing benefits alone.

Dick Silvers, VP of MIS, described a similar frequent-shopper program implemented during his tenure at Vons previous to joining HEB. By offering a free turkey to card-carrying customers spending more than $400, Vons added more than 1.2 million frequent shoppers to the system during the promotional period. Silvers believed that the customer POS cards had the potential to increase customer loyalty, but he also realized that the strategy conflicted with EDLP by offering preferential discounts to some customers while implicitly raising prices to others.

Store Ordering and Inventory

Each HEB store had a limited storage space for inventory. This storage area, located in the rear of the store, was primarily used for bulky items sold in large quantities (e.g., soft drinks and diapers) and for promotional items experiencing a temporary surge in demand. On-shelf inventory for most items was sufficient to cover sales for several days. This inventory buffer enabled the store to miss a product shipment if the store made a mistake in ordering, or if the warehouse was out of stock, without stocking out on the shelf.

Ordering was still largely a manual process of inspecting shelf stock and back-room inventory levels to determine what product order quantities were needed. A store employee entered orders into a hand-held computer terminal while walking up and down the aisles looking for items requiring replenishment. The employee scanned the store shelf tag of an item to be ordered and manually entered the quantity requested. After verifying that these items were not in the store's back room, the employee transmitted the order to the HQ mainframe using the satellite network. The mainframe computer then routed the order to one or more of the seven HEB product warehouses for selection, loading, and delivery to the store.

Some managers at HEB believed that POS data could be used to automate this ordering process. However, Silvers pointed out that scanning accuracy was not yet sufficient to support computer-assisted ordering (CAO). Accuracy was only about 90–95% for scanning items, and at least 97% accuracy would be needed to make a CAO system cost-effective. Increasing store POS accuracy to take this step in improving operating efficiency had thus become a critical issue for store managers during 1993.

Store Manager Concerns

One of the biggest frustrations for HEB store managers was store maintenance. For example, the store manager had no autonomy to hire local plumbers because HEB contracted centrally for plumbing repairs. This meant that HEB saved money by contracting in quantity but occasionally received poor service. If a store freezer went down on the weekend, there was no one at HQ to coordinate or help with the problem. Store managers wanted to be able to hire outside service providers if needed in an emergency and suggested creating an allowance for this purpose. One store manager described the current situation: "The bigger we get, the worse the bureaucracy gets. Getting something fixed is pure hell."

Managers were also concerned about the existing stores' ability to cope with the increased sales volume as HEB's success in cost reduction and marketing resulted in market share gains. Traditional rules of thumb for safety stock no longer applied, and the risk of stockouts was increasing. Merely providing enough products on the shelf for peak shopping times was a challenge. Shelves could not be restocked from 4 p.m. to 7 p.m. in many stores due to the sheer number of customers in the aisles, and some high-volume items would stock out if not replenished within this period. Store managers wanted product variety reduced to provide additional depth to handle the increased volume. On the other hand, product merchandisers wanted to increase the product variety offered, enabling the chain to meet differentiated customer needs. Generally, the store manager was faced with the combination of increasing SKUs and sales volume.

Warehouse Operations and Logistics

HEB operated an extensive warehousing and transportation system to service its more than 200 retail stores. Information technology, an important element of its distribution system, had enabled HEB to dramatically reduce logistics costs over a ten-year period. While the logistics system had changed significantly over time, Ed Clark, senior VP of distribution, described past and projected future changes in logistics and distribution as "evolutionary, not revolutionary."

In the late 1970s, HEB had installed a computerized warehouse management and inventory control system to reduce costs and improve delivery response times. Using this automated system, the time between store ordering and delivery decreased from more than 24 hours to less than 12 hours, which in turn reduced store stockouts and allowed stores to keep lower inventory levels on hand. Of course, with lower costs of supply and storage came an increased dependence by the company on the information systems supporting the new process.

Expanding product offerings through the 1980s complicated the store supply problem and further increased demands on the logistics system. The number of separate items, or SKUs, offered in an average HEB store increased from around 30,000 in 1980 to 55,000 in 1900. Also, average revenue per store tripled as store size increased dramatically during this decade. The average number of truck deliveries from the warehouse to the store increased from about 18 per week in the early 1980s to 29 per week in 1990, and warehousing and transportation costs as a percentage of sales were reduced by more than 30%. Although information systems were an important driver of this improvement, equally important were close attention to details and a culture obsessed with reducing costs.

Joe Lutton, manager of warehouse receiving, described HEB's distribution system as "procurement driven" with the primary focus on serving the needs of retail stores and customers, not minimizing distribution costs. Reduced distribution costs during the 1980s had been achieved without making significant changes in the way the procurement process worked. Although improvements in logistics had substantially reduced costs, even larger gains were promised from changing the entire procurement process and policies, as proposed by the ECR study.

Over 1,300 vendors supplied products to the chain, but the top 100 represented 65% of HEB's total volume. If these larger vendors converted to an ECR approach, the performance of the entire logistics and warehousing system could dramatically improve. The ECR report suggested retailers and manufacturers could reduce total channel inventory levels from 104 days to 61 days for dry-grocery products[2] by combining information technology innovations with organizational and process changes. Distribution warehouses were projected to experience the greatest reduction in inventory levels, from 40 days under traditional processes to 12 days using ECR, and most of these warehouse inventory savings resulted from the effective use of CRP.

Improving logistics involved many trade-offs. For example, a larger pallet size meant more inventory but less handling. Since stockouts were unacceptable, larger pallets meant larger average deliveries, especially for slower-moving items. Smaller case sizes required more handling but could reduce retail store shelf space and inventory requirements, allowing expansion of store SKUs in some situations. As the number of product SKUs increased, smaller pallets and cases made increasing sense for some products. However, changing pallet or case sizes involved complex cost trade-offs for both retailers and manufacturers since larger pallets and cases were less expensive to pack and handle.

HEB's internal analysis confirmed the industry's informal rule of thumb that items with less than one pallet per week of sales were not worth warehousing. These items went through jobbers, independent distributors that delivered small quantities of products directly to the stores. When volume increased, HEB would try to switch the products to the warehouse logistics system, since using a jobber added about approximately 20% to product costs.

Transportation and Warehouse Receiving

HEB-owned transportation handled 40–50% of inbound[3] product shipments and all store shipments, except DSD products. Transporting manufacturer products to the retailer's warehouse on retailer-owned or -contracted trucks was referred to as *backhauling* (even if the trucks were sent empty to the product vendor to pick up a load). HEB handled about 28,000 backhaul loads annually via a fully owned subsidiary, Parkway Trucking. A separate group of local drivers, employed directly by HEB, provided product delivery from warehouse to store.

During an average week, the major constraint on inventory storage capacity occurred on Thursday evening, the peak inventory day of the week, as inventory was received for the weekend store demand. Since Thursday evening was the point of maximum warehouse use, it mattered little which day of the week products were received, and weekly turns formed a more useful measure of warehouse demand than daily turns. However, from a cost of capital perspective, daily turns were the key driver of inventory carrying costs. Management frequently focused on minimizing the costs of inventory financing and assumed that the handling and storage costs for inventory would also be reduced by reducing average daily inventory levels.

Efforts to minimize the number of days of inventory on hand could lead to artificial peaks in the warehouse operation and the total supply chain. Fox example, inventory received on Thursday and sold on Friday constituted only one day of inventory but required the same warehouse capacity as product received six days earlier. Since inventory carrying costs drove replenishment behavior, product deliveries were artificially crowded into inventory warehousing times, making the system more difficult to manage for both HEB and vendors.

Policies for common-carrier deliveries were established to be convenient for HEB warehouse operations and to minimize storage for HEB but were not necessarily convenient for vendors or shippers. Early deliveries were discouraged, and vendors were sometimes charged storage fees for delivery before the contract date. This fee for early delivery encouraged manufacturers to ship exactly to order dates, even if the actual range of acceptable delivery dates could be considerably broadened with little real cost for HEB.

Understanding the physical constraints and trade-offs in the distribution system was important once inventory buffers were reduced. Management performance-measurement and incentive systems required careful design to encourage behavior that improved overall channel efficiency rather than maximizing a single local measure of efficiency.

An example of improved efficiency that had occasionally created problems for the overall channel was the process used for receiving backhauled products. Non-backhaul drivers were required to schedule an arrival time for deliveries. Upon arrival, the truck was unloaded by either the driver, HEB employees, or third-party workers, with the costs of unloading paid by the manufacturer. HEB employees then verified that the shipment paperwork was accurate. The unloading and verification process often took several hours, during which the truck was idle. For backhauls, HEB allowed the drivers (HEB employees) simply to drop the trailer in the receiving terminal yard. Since the driver was not required to unload, the trailer was moved to the dock later and unloaded at the convenience of the warehouse staff. A "mule" driver at the warehouse yard moved the trailers to and from the loading docks to unload products.

This backhaul process saved time for drivers, saving HEB money on payroll, but occasionally resulted in stockouts at the warehouse when the product needed was actually on a trailer somewhere in the yard but for some reason could not be located. Because the final location was not recorded when a trailer was dropped, locating a particular shipment could be extremely difficult. With forward-buying inventory buffers before CRP and other efforts to reduce inventories, a trailer could be misplaced for a week or two and not be missed. The focus on reducing inventory and costs had exposed problems in the backhaul trailer drop-off process for managing in a CRP environment.

Several technical solutions were being evaluated in 1993 to address this trailer drop-off problem. One option was to have each driver check in upon arrival and be assigned a numbered parking space for the trailer. The entire parking area could be number and a database system used to track merchandise location until unloaded. An alternative more convenient for the drivers was to issue each driver a radio transmitter to attach to the trailer which would uniquely identify the load. The driver could then drop the trailer anywhere in the yard to be located later using an electronic triangulation device. This method would conserve driver time but would require investments in hardware that might not be justified by the cost savings generated. A final alternative was to drop trailers at unloading docks immediately upon arrival, thus eliminating the entire yard storage buffer. This real-time unloading would require better coordination of delivery schedules and could increase the cost of HEB backhaul logistics. However, improved scheduling and direct unloading would improve warehouse operations, generating offsetting cost reductions.

Category Management Background and Strategy

HEB management was intensely focused on driving costs out of the grocery retailing and distribution process and experimented with a new organizational structure during 1988 to try to reduce resistance to change and develop cross-functional skills and understanding throughout the company. This major restructuring combined logistics and procurement into a single functional area known as prolistics, and store operations and marketing into a single unit known as retailing. The vision of this new structure was that prolistics would be responsible for delivering products to the store at the lowest possible cost, and retailing would focus on selling the products to the customer effectively and efficiently.

After several years, the company moved away from this innovative structure when HEB restructured to integrate marketing and procurement under category management responsibility and separated the distribution and purchasing. Although the prolistics structure was short-lived, the change enabled the chain to more clearly see the benefits of CRP and other innovations. Organizational changes at HEB also dramatically reduced vertical thinking in the organization, and cross-functional awareness and relationships created during the prolistics era continued to benefit the company long after it had shifted away from that structure. The shift to category management,[4] beginning in late 1989, was facilitated by the early organizational changes and by HEB's increased focus on managing total channel costs.

Clingman asked Chapman to lead the transition to a CM structure and philosophy. Chapman had planned to retire early in 1991 but agreed to remain with HEB until late 1993 to manage the CM transition. He was given responsibility for establishing CM across all procurement departments, beginning with grocery procurement.

The conversion from buyers to category managers required new skills and capabilities, resulting in the need to replace many of HEB's experienced buyers. Before the change to CM, four buyers and four assistant buyers handled all grocery product procurement at HEB; only one grocery buyer made the transition to category manager. By 1993, there were 15 category managers for grocery products, including 3 handling only DSD products. Each of these category managers had much greater total responsibility but managed a narrower set of products than the buyers they replaced.

Chapman received approval from Clingman to hire anyone lower than a VP in HEB's hierarchy as a category manager. To obtain the skills needed for the category manager roles, Chapman was also authorized to look outside the company and outside the industry, if necessary. For a culture that emphasized promotion from within and the value of industry experience, hiring outside the company and industry was quite unusual. Chapman recognized that an MBA and strong analytic skills were very valuable in a CM position and frequently offset the lack of specific grocery experience.

Chapman and Clingman encouraged category managers to gain field experience in operations. Although Chapman hated to lose these people from their CM roles, he recognized the value of having strong analytical leaders out in the field. One way to ensure a steady flow of analytical skills into critical positions throughout HEB was to designate several CM positions as training positions to move on to other functional areas within the company. However, for most of the category manager positions, Chapman wanted to keep the same individual on the job for a long time to develop deep experience and encourage investment in learning on the job.

This conversion to a new organizational procurement and merchandising structure and philosophy also involved implementing a new category manager incentive program. The new program was particularly lucrative for high performers, providing

50% of salary as a bonus for reaching 100% of targets and an additional 2% of salary bonus for every 1% achieved over the goal.

CM had proven quite effective for HEB. Clingman noted that the company's operating profits increased significantly with each category manager added. These profit improvements helped fund the shelf-level price reductions of the EDLP strategy, which was implemented at the same time as the shift to CM. Over the five years from 1989 to 1994, category managers had greatly expanded their role and influence, assuming responsibility for store display management and several other tasks formerly handled in marketing or other functional areas.

CM evolved as new responsibilities were added over time, with the category manager effectively acting as a general manager for the categories under his or her responsibility. Tim Flannigan, director of category planning and analysis, described CM as more than a program or initiative at HEB; it had become the philosophy around which the company operated by 1993. Category managers were HEB's primary profit centers, with almost complete responsibility and authority for all decisions affecting their categories.

Clingman viewed the category manager role as an intermediate stage in the transition within HEB from buyers to general mangers of space, time, and cost, which were the key elements influencing customer satisfaction and financial success. Clingman expected this transition to take several more years to complete, for substantial changes in organization culture and structure were required.

An important issue, as yet unresolved in 1993, concerned the problem of allocating category mangers' scarce time to the most productive tasks. They were expected to spend at least 35% of their time performing category analysis of product and promotion profitability, with the straightforward mechanics of daily or weekly buying only a small part of the overall position requirements. One HEB manager expressed concern with the shift in responsibilities given the resources and time available:

The category manager job is changing, and I'm not sure the changes are consistent with the original CM vision. Should we have category managers doing analysis or administration? If analysis, shouldn't we provide more support to do some of the number-crunching and administration? Category managers need better tools or more resources to allow them to get everything done given the new reponsibilities that have been added to this position. Expecting them to carry a significant administrative responsibility as general managers of the business, without providing the system and tools needed to manage this expanded role efficiently, does not allow them to use their time optimally and limits their effectiveness.

Profile of a Category Manager

Chapman received many referrals from within HEB for candidates desiring to move into CM jobs, one of the organization's most visible positions in the early 1990s.

Category managers enjoyed the high-impact position and tolerated long work hours but were eventually able to take some time for personal activities after a few months of learning how to perform in their new roles. The category manager role was still evolving, with the scope of the job increasing in depth but narrowing in breadth of focus. Chapman wanted to flatten HEB's organization by pushing more responsibilities to highly capable category managers. Combining merchandising and procurement in one position, for example, facilitated workiing more cooperatively in strategic relationships with vendors.

Category Manager Mike Robinson had a systems background, coming from 13 years of accounting and finance at HEB. Analytical capability and an ability to learn merchandising were critical skills for category managers to be successful. They also had to feel comfortable with information systems. Although he had worked in HEB stores during college, he had never before held a merchandising position. In his first 18 months as category manager, Robinson had worked 55–65 hours during a standard week and 80–90 hours during peak weeks. He held responsibility for all candy and dairy items in HEB's channel, from checkout-counter displays to warehousing specifications.

Robinson believed that ideally category managers should spend half of their time on proactive analysis. He felt that 80% of his activities during 1993 were reactive, responding to manufacturer initiatives or crises at the warehouse or store. Robinson looked forward to having better tools for routine tasks to free up more time for proactive analysis. Eventually, category managers would have decision-support systems available to aid in analysis, but these systems had not yet been completed. Information systems lagged somewhat behind the evolution of the category manager's role. Flannigan was working with the Information Systems group to develop systems to facilitate the category managers' routine tasks as well as "informate" their decision-making for non-routine tasks.

A Commitment Not to Divert

Diverting referred to the practice of a wholesaler or retailer buying products using manufacturers' promotional or volume discounts, only to resell the product to another retailer or wholesaler at a price below list but above the promotional price. From the manufacturers' perspective, this activity offered quick profits to wholesalers and retailers at the manufacturers' expense. Manufacturers who suffered from diverting spent significant amounts of time and money verifying orders to protect the integrity of their complex pricing structures. HEB had not practiced diverting to other retailers since starting CM in 1989, and Clingman viewed this commitment not to divert as part of an overall commitment to improving channel cooperation:

We view the decision (to refrain from diverting) as a relationship builder to put on the table. This decision may have cost us significant money, but it's impossible to quantify how much it has helped in relationship building.

Although no product shipped to HEB was diverted elsewhere, category managers might occasionally still *buy* from a diverter. Robinson received offers of extraordinary prices on diverted candy, but these "deep deals" were rarely accepted due to the concern that quality and freshness might be inferior in diverted product. Such considerations were especially strong with products whose interim storage conditions significantly affected their final quality. Robinson noted:

Grocery warehouses can get very hot, so all candy must be kept in refrigerated storage to maintain its quality. When you buy diverted candy, you never know whether it's been refrigerated all the way down the line. And take a chance on buying diverted dairy? Forget it!

An Example of CM Decision Marking

The process of making the decision to put Altoids™, a premium mint offered by Callard & Bowser, at the checkout stand provided an interesting example of CM activities. The category manager drew upon multiple data sources in his analysis this decision:

· Sales of mints were flat despite growing candy sales, and thus the mint subcategory was considered to be dying. This fact was confirmed by both HEB data and external literature sources.

· Mints occupied $1\frac{1}{2}$ rows in the current checkstand configuration, which was a lot of prime sales area to be used for an item with flat sales.

· Scanning data indicated that some mints were much better performers at the checkstand than others, so elimination of several weak products could be entertained without significant fear of loss in sales.

· Altoids™, a premium imported product, was the most profitable DSD product in the store in sales per unit of shelf space. This excellent performer was buried in the candy section; as $1.99, its price point was considered too high for the checkstand. Moving this item to the checkstand and eliminating slower-moving mints could potentially simultaneously increase checkstand contribution and free up space for other new checkstand products.

The decision to review mint performance and the Altoids™ product was primarily reactive, not proactive, since it came in response to a broker's request that HEB consider reslotting the product. However, Robinson's analysis of the proposed new slotting demonstrated the category manager's ability to use multiple sources of data quickly to make an important product-location decision. With more time freed from routine tasks, category managers would be able to make decisions like this one with increased frequency, taking the initiative instead of waiting for vendors' suggestions.

As of 1993, most category managers were still too overwhelmed with information and daily crisis resolution to be able to devote substantial time to proactive management. A troubling issue was whether, in being more proactive in merchandising the stores, they might unintentionally dilute or remove vendors' incentives to provide fees for new product introductions or product repositioning. Since moving to a more proactive mode was obviously costly in manager time and information requirements, the potential for losing this source of revenues was doubly troubling. It was an open question whether category managers could effectively use this proactive approach to aggressively seek repositioning money for opportunities that made strong sense for both HEB and the vendors.

Continuous Replenishment and Electronic Data Interchange

HEB was one of the first companies to team up with Procter & Gamble in a CRP relationship. In November 1989, Chapman introduced the concept of CRP in an HEB operating committee meeting based on news that P&G had formed an alliance with Wal-Mart to reduce inventory and product supply cost for both partners. Fully Clingman asked HEB senior managers to set up a similar arrangement with P&G before the first of the year. Chapman observed:

Fully's concern was that he didn't want to be at a competitive disadvantage to Wal-Mart. I was tickled to death that Fully made that demand. The deadline itself was silly, but it threw down the gauntlet to the rest of the executive team that this was something to pay attention to.

P&G agreed to discuss the benefits and requirements of the CRP program with HEB senior management. P&G presentations about CRP helped Chapman sell the rest of the organization on the benefits of the new program. The prospect of greatly increased inventory turns was exciting for warehouse managers, and store managers were interested in the promise of increased service levels engendered by reduced stockouts.

The underlying logic of CRP was that P&G would supply HEB with products based directly upon warehouse shipment and inventory data rather than upon receipt of HEB-generated purchase orders. Using HEB-provided warehouse and inventory data, P&G would determine the order quantity needed, assemble the delivery, and notify HEB electronically that the shipment was coming. The information on retail store demand for products on CRP was electronically transmitted to the manufacturer daily. This continuous demand information provided much quicker and more accurate feedback on consumer demand behavior to P&G than the traditional ordering process.

Although HEB was the second grocery retailer to adopt the new CRP system with P&G, the time between the introduction of the first and the second grocery-chain CRP linkages with P&G was so short that the two retailers were essentially both first movers in the adoption of CRP and developing the systems and processes needed to support it. Together, P&G and HEB worked to develop the policies and process changes needed to implement CRP in a grocery channel context, and both companies learned from each other. The relationship the two companies established through CRP also extended into other areas of channel cooperation as the "channel partners" worked together to eliminate non-value-added costs throughout the channel.

By directly coupling their information systems, HEB and P&G eliminated six to ten days from the previous order cycle. In addition, P&G agreed to give HEB the average deal price paid during the prior year for *all* products, recognizing that HEB purchased almost the entire annual requirements for all P&G products at deal prices by forward buying. This long-term, net-price deal eliminated the incentive to forward buy and facilitated adoption of the CRP innovation.

The major benefits of CRP for HEB were a dramatic reduction in inventory levels and reduced ordering and logistics costs in routinely supplying its warehouses. The benefits for P&G included more predictable demand and commensurately smoother manufacturing processes, as well as reduced logistics costs. The success of the CRP trial with P&G encouraged HEB to expand the relationship to other vendors. Key vendors began to adopt CRP with HEB as Chapman and Clingman emphasized its win-win potential.

The CRP program initially used a single personal computer to handle communications with vendors. It required an Electronic Data Interchange (EDI) link to transmit warehouse movement data at high speeds; EDI links could be established using either a PC program or a mainframe application. The use of a PC system for initial EDI transmission provided HEB with minimal development cost in a flexible implementation that could evolve as needed. However, the PC system was not tightly linked with the mainframe ordering system, required a lot of manual support, and was limited in capacity to only a few vendors.

EDI was essential for CRP since the volume of data transmitted and the frequency of transmission both increased dramatically in comparison with the traditional ordering process. Traditional ordering systems involve the transmission of purchase orders for a limited subset of a vendor's product line. CRP required daily transmission of data on store orders and warehouse inventory levels for all of the vendor's

SKUs; it increased the total data transmitted between companies by at least 100 times the level of information shared under the traditional ordering systems. In addition, data quality and timeliness became more important with lower inventory levels since any errors could lead to retail-store stockouts. HEB management believed that providing the quantity and quality of data needed to support CRP without using EDI would be economically and operationally impossible.

Using a PC for EDI transmission enabled HEB to implement the new ordering process quickly without relying on expensive, time-consuming mainframe software development. This allowed HEB to gain experience in implementing the new process and to begin adapting the organization to take advantage of CRP capabilities quickly. However, once the processes and policies had been developed to support CRP, it was time to develop the systems needed to expand the innovation more broadly.

The success of the CRP trial and other cooperative efforts to improve channel efficiency encouraged HEB to expand the channel partnership relationship to other vendors. In early 1991, Clingman and Chapman visited top executives at General Mills, Quaker, Pillsbury, Campbell Soup, and other large food manufacturers among HEB's major suppliers. For each vendor, Chapman supervised the creation of a presentation booklet describing the joint benefits of working together in a more cooperative relationship, along with the importance of HEB to the vendor. The top-to-top management visits outlined the overall benefits of working together, with CRP cited as one way to cooperate to improve channel efficiency and effectiveness. Joint planning and merchandising were also emphasized as opportunities for improving channel effectiveness through cooperation.

Expanding the CRP Program

Béa Weicker Irvin shifted from her position as category manager to become the manager of procurement systems in September 1991. Her first responsibility in the position was to evaluate the total costs and benefits of CRP pilot tests from both HEB and vendor perspectives to determine if this new innovation was sustainable and as attractive as it appeared to be initially. In October, Irvin presented her findings that the savings from CRP were real and substantial, that opportunities to improve total channel efficiency were substantial, and that a cost-effective project should be initiated to develop mainframe capabilities at HEB to support CRP. She was asked to spearhead the development of the CRP systems and business processes and to manage their deployment at HEB.

Irvin worked together with a cross-functional team to develop and implement the CRP program, including Tony Casas, MIS systems analyst; Tom Baldwin, warehouse systems manager; Mark Lewis, traffic operations manager; and several category managers responsible for the primary relationships with vendors involved in CRP and related efforts to improve channel performance. Irvin was responsible for (1) leading systems design and development from the business side, (2) formalizing the business processes involved in implementing CRP, (3) coordinating HEB cross-functional and interorganizational operations, and (4) marketing the CRP program to build a critical mass of vendor partners.

To assist vendors and facilitate CRP marketing efforts, Irvin produced a booklet explaining CRP to potential partners and describing the requirements to become one of HEB's CRP partners. This booklet became a "how-to manual" for CRP implementation, essentially explaining HEB's policies and processes for CRP that had been developed by Irvin. The manual described a step-by-step approach to going on-line with HEB and established the terms under which CRP partners would be accepted. To Irvin's surprise, this manual was greeted with enthusiasm outside HEB, becoming an industry standard and important benchmarking document quoted and cited by other firms in their own documentation. Since part of HEB's strategy as a leader in CRP was to set the standards for how CRP was to be implemented, this industry reaction to the guidelines was gratifying.

By the end of 1991, HEB had implemented CRP with four vendors and was working with others to begin using the new process. None of the vendors cared whether HEB used mainframe- or PC-based EDI, since the retailer hardware was transparent to vendors provided that EDI standards were in place. Although using a PC minimized initial cost, the processes within HEB for using PC-based EDI links were manually very intensive. In addition, the limitations of the existing PC application would clearly limit the expansion of CRP. Therefore, in late 1991 HEB began developing a mainframe system to replace the PC system used for the pilot CRP implementations.

Jack Brouillard, newly appointed CAO and CFO in 1991, was a strong supporter of EDI. Having come from an apparel-retailing background, he had seen the benefits of EDI and Quick Response. He supported expansion of CRP in the context of a larger EDI development project, and championed the development of a flexible EDI mainframe capability for the company. Brouillard's vision was that HEB would cost-justify the development of EDI systems to support CRP and would then leverage that investment by converting other paper processes across the channel to EDI linkages, including purchase orders, invoices, funds transfer, pricing information, and other forms of data transmission.

The mainframe system to implement EDI and support CRP was developed during the fall of 1991 and spring of 1992 and was ready for CRP implementation in May

1992. In early 1992, Lynn Johnson joined the CRP team as the second MIS systems analyst assigned to help develop the EDI and CRP systems. To prepare for the systems transition and because Irvin's maternity leave overlapped the system cutover time, Agnes Moody also joined the CRP/EDI implementation team in April 1992.

Irvin was out on maternity leave during May through June 1992 but kept in touch with Moody, the rest of the HEB cross-functional team, and vendors' CRP teams via e-mail, phone, and voice mail during this period. As soon as the mainframe system became operational, new vendors were added to the CRP program, with Moody handling many of the details of bringing the new vendors up "live" on the CRP system. Irvin also provided support during the process from home during her leave.

Irvin and Moody worked together during 1993 to expand HEB's electronic relationships with vendors. Irvin contacted potential CRP partners and explained the potential benefits, costs, and business process requirements involved in a CRP relationship. Moody got involved once vendors had committed to CRP, working with them to make the decision to link a reality.

Besides managing ongoing, developing, and potential CRP relationships, Irvin was also involved in a number of special projects for senior management at HEB. This required that Moody provide support for ongoing vendor discussions to ensure a smooth process even if Irvin was unavailable. Baldwin and Lewis also worked closely with vendors involved in CRP relationships to improve total channel efficiency and overcome any startup problems during the transition to CRP.

The transition to the mainframe eliminated capacity limitations for EDI and CRP, and opened a new era of expansion for HEB in the development of electronic trading relationships. By the end of 1992 there were 10 active CRP vendors and a large pent-up supply of vendors interested in joining the program. During 1993, 26 new vendors were added to the CRP program, and EDI was introduced as an alternative for ordering with vendors. Although the productivity benefits of using EDI for purchase order transmission were still viewed as limited, the data quality benefits (e.g., integrity and speed) were both notable and important. In addition, the costs of implementing EDI ordering with vendors were minimal since the system was required anyway to support CRP.

EDI ordering expanded during 1993 to represent 43% of total product volume by the end of the year, and CRP represented an additional 31% of volume, for a total of 74% of vendors using direct EDI linkages for ordering. Savings for EDI became more important as the percentage of electronic ordering approached 100% of all ordering transactions. Even so, the benefits of CRP implementation greatly exceeded the benefits of using EDI for ordering. CRP involved restructuring existing policies and processes but EDI ordering was simply an automated systems implementation.

However, EDI used for invoicing, pricing notification, and payments, with a completely reengineered ordering, invoicing, and payment process, could offer dramatic improvements in productivity; these integrated EDI processes were being tested and developed with several vendors during 1994.

CRP vendors' assumption of responsibility for ordering reduced the time category managers required for buying administration, thus freeing more time for real CM. Tony Merta, one of HEB's veteran category mangers, had been an early advocate of CRP and encouraged many of his vendors to adopt the new approach. By eliminating replenishment purchasing from his job for these vendors, he was able to spend more time on proactive analysis. In his view, CRP enabled category managers to shift from reactive to proactive management of the category. He attributed his success in CM in part to his early recognition of CRP's benefits in leveraging his scarce time and attention. Unlike many category managers, he was able to maintain a schedule of 50–55 hours per week while effectively managing his categories, due partly to the high level of CRP usage for his vendors.

A new purchasing system installed in August 1990 also reduced required buying time and improved overall inventory management. CRP's improvements helped category managers see the potential for reducing inventory levels with vendors not yet on CRP. One manager noted that HEB never realized how poorly inventory levels had been managed until CRP demonstrated the dramatic improvements that were possible with better inventory management and new channel systems and processes.

By improving ordering and inventory-management sytems, processes, and policies (e.g., EDLP to replace promotional pricing) with vendors not yet on CRP, HEB was able to improve inventory turns for all vendors by mid-1994. The entire system had become more efficient for all vendors and there was less opportunity for incremental improvement through CRP adoption. Even so, HEB was still able to reduce inventory levels by implementing CRP with vendors, though the gains were far less dramatic than those of the first few years of CRP implementation.

EDLP agreements with vendors also helped reduce the workload for category managers by eliminating the need to negotiate and administer high-low promotional pricing, allowing them to focus on product selection and merchandising to improve overall category profitability. EDLP also reduced the incidence of invoice deductions, which were often caused by complex and frequently changing vendor pricing, thus reducing the number of HEB and manufacturer employees required to verify invoices in the respective accounting areas, previously an expense borne by both sides without benefit for either. Negotiations with vendors over deductions that the chain took but that were not on the vendor invoice were generally conducted between the category manager and the manufacturer's sales representative. These negotiations frequently consumed considerable time and resulted in zero net benefits for the channel overall, so the shift to EDLP or net-pricing, as required for CRP, provided immediate overall channel benefits through eliminating this source of inefficiency in the channel. Removal of this negotiation over deductions also allowed retailers and manufacturers so focus more time and energy on better serving consumer needs and increasing overall profits from the joint relationship.

CRP and Improved Channel Coordination

In contrast to the image of two computers talking with one another via EDI and eliminating the need for human interaction, CRP implementation encouraged extensive interpersonal contact between HEB and its CRP partners. Essentially, the use of CRP provided a parallel channel for communication of detailed information about product demand and replenishment needs, allowing the existing communications channel to be used more effectively for discussing new opportunities to improve product merchandising and further improve total channel logistics.

The process of implementing CRP provided an opportunity for establishing effective, manager-level, cross-functional teams involving both vendors and HEB, without the formal trappings and organizational hierarchies involved in traditional vendor-customer relationships. These teams were initiated and run at the front-line manager level and established lasting organizational relationships that intersected both organizations at multiple points. Harvey McCoy, VP of grocery category management, illustrated the change in channel structure and relationships using the comparison shown in figure 4.6. From an intersection of two pyramids linked only at the sales representative and category manager point of interface, the communications and coordination between the two organizations had been flattened and extended to a network or web of relationships across both companies. Distribution, information services, finance, and other functional areas were not entirely dependent upon the sales-to-CM communications channel, although the relationship between sales representatives and category managers remained the primary relationship between the two companies.

Cross-functional teams had few formal meetings but extensive communications, working at a functional level to improve joint processes across the companies. In some cases, the communication was so extensive that friendly relationships developed across organizational lines, and teams exchanged résumés, jokes, and pictures of their families. A typical CRP vendor implementation team involved representatives from sales, distribution, information systems, and marketing, with some vendors including a representative from finance as well.

BEFORE PROCESS CHANGE   AFTER PROCESS CHANGE

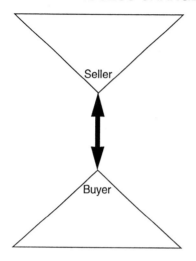
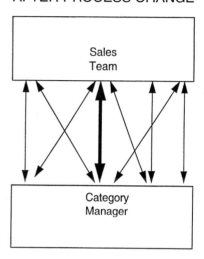

Figure 4.6
Interorganizational communications linkages

HEB was not concerned about the prospect of other retailers investing in CRP to erode its first-mover advantage, but rather was concerned that other retailers were not investing in CRP quickly enough to encourage manufacturers to take the plunge. Vendors incurred initial investments and up-front costs to start CRP and needed a sufficiently broad core of retailer partners to reach a minimum efficient scale. Chapman elaborated:

Many of our current [CRP] vendors can see the incremental savings potential of CRP and believe that they are close to reaching the scale necessary to justify the investments. But net costs of CRP investments are still larger for most new vendors than the early implementation savings. If we asked most vendors to share their net savings during the first year or two of implementing CRP, they'd end up sending us a bill! CRP's benefits vary for each vendor, and depend on both speed of implementation and ability to eliminate product flow inefficiencies within the vendor's organization.

CRP implementation was clearly a process facilitated by cumulative learning, with vendors experienced with other partners able to move quickly once the initial negotiations were completed. Experienced partners that were new to HEB came on line very quickly. Most vendors, however, were inexperienced with CRP and required several months to shift to the CRP ordering process. At the other end of the spectrum, Mead Johnson, which had CRP relationships with other retailers, was able to reach an agreement and "go live" with CRP within two weeks of its first contact with HEB's CRP team.

HEB's relationship management approach implemented by category managers helped overcome resistance from those vendors still skeptical about CRP's benefits, shifting their perspective from a short-term "win-lose" view to a long-term potential "win-win" view. The requirement of a nonantagonistic mindset was one reason few buyers were able to make the shift to the new category manager role. Implementing CRP with manufacturers required a similar shift in attitude to make the program work effectively. Cooperation and mutual trust were essential for enabling these more efficient channel logistics approaches to be implemented.

The creation of stronger interorganizational relationships was one of the most important benefits of CRP implementation and provided a model for developing more effective relationships with non-CRP vendors as well. Ideas developed with CRP partners to improve channel operations could often be expanded to all vendors to reduce HEB's and vendors' total costs. Not all gains from cooperation with vendors were transferable to other relationships, but new opportunities for "win-win" process improvements were continually being discovered with CRP partners, some of which could be then expanded to reduce total costs for HEB and vendors for all products.

Managing CRP and EDI Implementation

Once the new CRP relationship was operational, Irvin evaluated vendors' progress, comparing existing service and iventory levels to the goals laid out in the previous negotiations. Overall productivity benefits of CRP were impressive, with average warehouse inventory turns two to three times the average level experienced before CRP adoption. Besides reducing inventory, CRP also reduced warehouse stockouts and transportation costs for both vendors and HEB. Inventory levels, transportation costs, and stockout levels had previously been viewed as conflicting constraints, such that reductions in one area resulted in increases in one of the other two areas. With CRP, simultaneous reductions were possible in all three areas.

Negotiating and establishing CRP relationships with new vendors required as long as one year for vendors without prior CRP experience and less than two months for vendors with prior CRP experience. Vendors would run CRP in parallel with the traditional paper-based purchase-order-driven system for several weeks to test the all-electronic program before making a final commitment to CRP. Moody checked the electronic version for bad UPC codes, ensured that orders met HEB standards, and communicated to vendors precisely the steps required to correct errors and ensure long-term accuracy. Although she was not directly involved in the initial negotiations with vendors, she often entered the evaluation and implementation process early on to aid vendors with technical issues and address their concerns regarding EDI and CRP implementation. Both Irvin and Moody provided coaching and hand-holding to ease the transition for new CRP vendors to the new systems and processes. This often involved helping vendors through the installation of new software ordering programs or forecasting tools.

Electronic Data Interchange: From 10 to 500 Partners in Eight Months

Initially, the EDI system was developed only for CRP partners to link with HEB. However, using the mainframe system, HEB was able to expand EDI for purchae order transmission to over 500 non-CRP vendors within eight months at little additional systems cost. This shift to EDI represented about 80% of purchase orders issued by the company and simplified the ordering process for most of HEB's products. All of HEB's large grocery-product vendors were linked via EDI systems by mid-1994, with 96% of grocery purchase orders transmitted via EDI or generated via EDI-enabled CRP linkages. HEB was using EDI mainly for purchase orders (POs) but was in the process in 1994 of extending EDI capabilities to encompass invoicing, warehouse receiving, and other information linkages.

During 1993, Moody allocated about half of her time to the support of new and existing CRP vendors and half to developing EDI linkages with new vendors. She handled the entire EDI relationship-building process for POs. Irvin was not involved in these EDI discussions because the decision to link electronically for PO transmission was mostly an administrative and technical issue rather than a negotiated relationship-based arrangement. Category managers sometimes suggested vendors that might be interested in EDI ordering. Moody would cold-call these vendors to explain the benefits of EDI and to inquire whether they would be interested in becoming an EDI vendor. She initiated contact with about 90% of the EDI relationships that had been established with HEB.

Moody first went after vendors that sold products through one of the nine major brokers that worked with HEB. In the first four months, HEB added 300 EDI vendors on a pass-through basis through brokers. The rest of the vendors were added as direct EDI relationships. Most of the large brokers were already using EDI in their relationships with their larger vendors, but still used paper- or fax-based orders for small vendors. Moody approached these brokers with an EDI proposal, and later established direct EDI links with some brokered vendors.

HEB's success rate in getting vendors to use EDI was very high: 90% of the vendors contacted agreed immediately to use EDI; a few said they would have to wait several months for the required systems to be developed; and only 1% of vendors contacted claimed to be totally EDI incapable. However, the paper process within most vendors was difficult to change. Even though HEB had successfully established EDI links with most vendors by late 1993, some vendors were still printing out and rekeying POs received through EDI into the same order-entry systems they had used before the EDI linkage.

Generally vendors had been open and honest about their capabilities, but some suffered under resource constraints and multiple priorities. Few had enough staff to handle all the requests they received for EDI linkages. Moody had to push these vendors to make any progress at all, spending 90% of her time on the phone generating support for these projects within the vendor organization. Her biggest frustration was that vendors could not reach her since she was always on the phone, leading to protracted phone tag episodes. This situation was addressed in late 1993 when an assistant was added to the department to help Moody with her EDI responsibilities.

The Transition to a New CRP Management Team

In August 1993, Sue Kehoe took over the primary responsibility of managing the CRP process, replacing Irvin as manager of procurement logistics. The title of the position was changed from manager of procurement systems to manager of procurement logistics to reflect the increased focus on the overall logistics process, and not merely procurement information systems. Similarly, Baldwin's position was relabeled manager of distribution logistics. Irvin and Baldwin had worked together as a team to improve HEB's logistics process. Process improvements were facilitated by CRP, but extended far beyond the product ordering process.

CRP's initial success was due largely to the joint leadership and intense efforts of Irvin and Baldwin, combined with the consistent support of category managers and procurement management. HEB senior management provided the necessary environment for innovation and process improvements by supporting Irvin and Baldwin throughout the change process and by encouraging the entire organization to seek out and embrace opportunities to improve existing processes. The CRP program was clearly established by mid-1993, and Clingman wanted to shift Irvin and Baldwin to new challenges and opportunities and turn over responsibility for operating and expanding CRP to new managers. Irvin was assigned to lead a systems development team working on improving product-supply logistics between HEB's warehouse and the stores, referred to as computerized store ordering. The objective of the computerized store ordering project team was to establish the systems and business process foundation to enable a fundamental redesign of the entire product-supply logistics processes, beginning within HEB but then expanding to all value-chain relationships.

By mid-1994, this project was well underway, but the new store ordering processes had not yet been implemented.

Mike DeNisio took over the position of manager of distribution logistics from Baldwin in 1993. Baldwin was transferred to a new retail distribution support center developed to support an alternative store format that HEB was operating in the Houston area. The new format provided limited product selection combined with very low operating costs, profit margins, and retail prices. This new retail format had proven effective in expanding market penetration and discouraging new competitors like Food Lion from entering the region with a similar strategy. Some of HEB's most talented managers had been sent to Houston to operate and support the new stores, which provided a new model for potential expansion of the chain to extended market areas outside the existing HEB markets.

Kehoe and DeNisio continued working together to improve vendor relationships, to expand new vendors' use of the CRP approach to product replenishment, and to raise the overall quality of logistics execution with vendors and within HEB. By the end of 1993, 34 vendors were on CRP and over 30% of HEB's grocery product purchases (in dollars) used CRP for replenishment orders. Overall warehouse inventory turns for grocery products went from 11.3 to 23.4 between 1991 and 1993. This increase in inventory turns was caused by increased numbers of CRP relationships, by the new purchasing system, and by increased shifting from promotional pricing and forward buying to long-term pricing agreements (e.g., EDLP) with vendors. With CRP vendors, overall inventory turns had increased even more dramatically. Part of this improvement in inventory turns with CRP was caused by the adoption of long-term pricing agreements required to implement CRP. The logistics efficiencies enabled by implementing CRP provided further inventory reductions beyond the benefits of EDLP pricing.

During the first half of 1994, HEB increased the number of vendors on CRP to more than 60 and significantly expanded the use of CRP with existing vendors. By August 1994, HEB had reached 96% penetration of grocery ordering generated via EDI or CRP, with almost 60% of all grocery replenishment volume using CRP. By almost completely eliminating manual ordering, the internal processes used for ordering had been redesigned to take advantage of the electronic ordering capabilities. CRP had become the standard in the organization, with category managers encouraging non-CRP vendors to get on the program.

In spite of this rapid expansion of vendors using CRP, HEB intentionally limited CRP use to only those customers willing to cooperate with it to reduce total channel costs. An example of HEB's intentionally limiting CRP adoption was its decision not to allow a vendor to become a CRP partner until problems with damaged products through improper pallet loading were resolved. Although HEB deducted for all damaged products, the handling of the damaged goods and the paperwork required for deductions increased total costs in the channel.

HEB worked hard to help trading partners understand that CRP was not just an ordering routine supported by new technology, but rather a new approach to the business which had as its goal the most efficient and effective management of information and product movement possible. It was imperative that vendors work with HEB to resolve as many logistics inefficiencies as feasible before taking over responsibility for ordering and inventory management.

Improved Operating Performance through CRP Relationships

Warehouse stockout levels for non-CRP products averaged about 6% overall in 1991, and stockout levels with CRP were less than 1%. During the early period of CRP implementation, Irvin was concerned that service levels (percent of orders filled, or the opposite of stockout levels) were too high with many CRP vendors, indicating that inventory could be reduced further without reducing service levels below acceptable levels. A target service level of 97% (or 3% stockout level) seemed to be about the right level from Irvin's perspective, since the retail stores had enough inventory on the shelf for most products to be able to miss a distribution-center shipment without experiencing product stockouts on the retail shelf. Irvin worked with vendors to increase stockouts to the target level, and by 1994 Kehoe noted that CRP and non-CRP services levels were both almost exactly at 97%, with category managers and vendors both targeting and meeting the same overall performance standards.

Although reducing service levels to reduce inventory levels seemed like an attractive tradeoff for HEB, vendors were reluctant to do so since they had no incentive to reduce service levels in order to reduce inventory and no measurement tools to confirm that retail sales were not lost at a 97% service level. Aggressive targets for inventory reduction needed to be established and tracked to be sure the maximum benefits from CRP were realized for the retailer.

Better logistics management through CRP also enabled optimizing both cube and weight loading of trucks, resulting in substantial savings in transportation cost. For example, with one CRP vendor, transportation costs as a percentage of product-shipment volume were reduced by almost 20% during 1992, benefiting both HEB and the vendor.

Some vendors were more aggressive than others in managing inventory, and not all products benefited equally from the shift to CRP. Large bulk products that were relatively stable in demand, such as pet food, were extremely well suited for CRP. Fresh products like orange juice benefited less from CRP since inventories were already low due to the need to maintain freshness and limit spoilage. However, CRP did provide vendors of fresh products with a more efficient distribution system to get products on the shelf more quickly and to increase their freshness.

The dramatic improvements realized for some products surprised some HEB managers who had not realized that such service levels and inventory turns were possible. For example, one beverage product had inventory turns of over 25 per year before CRP, which was respectable for even CRP products. After several months of CRP operation, the vendor was able to increase product turns to more than 100 per year! This provided only a few days' warehouse inventory for a high-volume product, a situation that would have been considered unreasonable in a pre-CRP environment. The vendor worked with HEB to provide excellent service with minimal safety stock levels. In fact, there was often more inventory in transit to HEB warehouses than was in the warehouse for this fast-moving product.

Efficient Consumer Response

Efficient Consumer Response (ECR) was introduced by David Jenkins, former chairman of Shaw's Supermarkets, at the Food Marketing Institute convention during January 1993. ECR was a broad term covering multiple technological and managerial innovations and was described as a new channel paradigm that would transform retailers, distributors, and manufacturers into more efficient and interlinked organizations (figure 4.7).

Many within the grocery industry viewed ECR as necessary to allow grocery retailers to compete with alternative-format retailers like Wal-Mart. However, ECR's potential benefits were at least as large for manufacturers as for retailers, for improved logistics, reduced promotion inefficiencies, and more predictable damand promised to reduce operating costs for both ends of the channel. The ECR concept evolved through a cross-industry committee structure with representatives from a variety of grocery channel participants. The ECR committee structure offered the potential to improve relationships between vendors and retailers, but the committees and subcommittees were difficult to manage given their large size.

HEB had been intensely involved with the ECR committee from the beginning, but in late 1993 it withdrew from all ECR task forces to focus on meeting the new threat created by the entry of mass-merchandiser superstores in the HEB region. Management resources were limited, and even though ECR was viewed as an important effort for the industry, focusing management attention on competing aggressively and effectively with these new entrants was more important for HEB's survival.

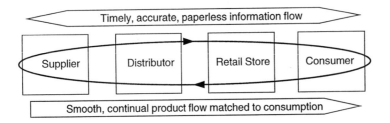

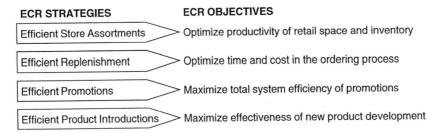

Figure 4.7
The ECR vision—A continuous channel process
Source: Adapted from Kurt Salmon Associates, Inc., *Efficient Consumer Response: Enhancing Consumer Value in the Grocery Industry* (Washington, DC: Food Marketing Institute, 1993).

Clingman and Silvers recognized the benefits CM and CRP created but they also believed that not everything in ECR was necessarily right to implement in 1994; there were parts of ECR that did not promise adequate return for the cost of implementation and others that were not even feasible yet.

An attractive aspect of ECR in the early implementation process at HEB was computer-assisted ordering (CAO). This was an implementation of CRP principles *within* the firm for automated ordering, based on POS data, from the store to the warehouse. Combining CAO with CRP would enable the development of a fully linked channel, with vendor shipments driven by individual stores' POS data. Wal-Mart had shifted to this completely integrated approach to channel inventory management, and HEB management believed that automated ordering using POS data would eventually become a requirement to remain competitive in the grocery channel. However, Clingman wanted more than CAO, as traditionally defined; computerized store ordering (CSO) with manual assistance was the real goal, not manual ordering with computer assistance. Irvin was given the challenge of implementing this new CSO vision within the company.

Unfortunately, scanning integrity in 1993 was inadequate to support a CSO process. Silvers believed that HEB needed to improve scanning accuracy from 95% to

98% to support CSO, marking scanning accuracy a major priority of the retail store operations group over the next year. HEB also needed to develop the ability to forecast store demand more accurately to facilitate CSO development once scanning accuracy was adequate to support such system. Little historical data had been saved on daily item movements by store, making preliminary analysis of demand patterns difficult without a history upon which to base initial predictions. Improving the capability to forecast store demand using daily scanner movement would significantly reduce uncertainty in ordering. This movement toward a more sophisticated planning and tracking system for store ordering could enable HEB to increase product variety in the stores without increasing the risk of stockouts. Using technology to improve store operations was hardly new to HEB, but the level of information intensity in the new technology-enabled applications was increasing dramatically.

Using POS data in an integrated channel CSO and CRP process could also enable HEB to cross-dock product shipments from vendors directly to stores. Wal-Mart's distribution cost for most products was about 2.6% of sales, similar to HEB's cost. But for cross-dock shipments, Wal-Mart's distribution cost was only 1.3%, representing an enormous advantage. J. C. Penney had experienced similar savings using cross-docking. HEB experimented with cross-dosking for some fast-moving products during 1993 and 1994 (e.g., private-label sodas). However, the point of ordering needed to shift from the store to the warehouse (via CSO) or to the manufacturer (via POS-driven CRP) for cross-docking to be practical for more than a few product categories.

The real challenge for HEB and others in implementing ECR was not technological innovation or adaptation but changing the organizational processes and structure to facilitate the new capabilities enabled by technological innovations. ECR was not a technology solution; it was a paradigm for organizational change. Many companies saw ECR as a large investment in technology, but Silvers believed that what HEB really needed was better organizational communications and coordination, not just more technology. He commented:

CRP is not a technology; it is the way we do business. It is our vision. We've just written the steps for implementation of our vision. In the same way, ECR is about a vision for the future, not about technology.

Clingman was concerned that the core assets on which HEB depended were rapidly becoming obsolete. Supermarkets and distribution centers in good locations were not sufficient to compete with the new breed of national superstore competitors, who used information and responsiveness to drive costs out of every stage of the channel. Even though HEB had removed millions of dollars in costs from the chain over the past year, this was not enough. Capabilities and flexibility were becoming more important than asset-based investments in gaining competitive advantage in the 1990s, and Clingman wanted to be sure that HEB was well positioned to survive and grow in this new era.

Clark described the positive cycle of improvement created by focused efforts to eliminate inefficiencies:

As [inventory] slack is removed from the system, the system needs to perform better. Removal of slack puts pressure on performance. Pressure to perform better leads to removal of slack. As performance pressure continues, new forms of slack are exposed.... As the industry moves toward an integrated information channel for ordering and logistics, the distribution center may eventually be eliminated or greatly reduced in size. Eventually, warehouses could become cross-dock terminals, or products may even be delivered directly to the store via intermediary shipping providers.

The Evolution of Information Technology at HEB

HEB initially used information system to automate clerical tasks and then to automate customer checkout using POS scanners in the late 1970s. Operational support expanded during the 1980s with the introduction of warehouse management systems, time and attendance reporting systems, DSD receiving and store ordering systems, and extensive communications systems.

Information technology applications had enabled HEB to reduce costs through improved operating efficiency, but these systems were not considered key elements of the overall organizational strategy until the 1990s. However, it had been long clear to Clingman and other senior managers that HEB was becoming more dependent on information technology for effective operations, and that investments in these systems would be increasingly important in the future.

Embracing CRP as part of the organizational vision demonstrated the potential for information technology combined with organizational change to dramatically improve performance. The potential of CSO, cross-docking, and other elements of the ECR program suggested that information technology was becoming an even more important component of the future infrastructure of the company. Electronic shelf tags were one technology that Silvers was considering a shaving a potentially major impact on store operations and capabilities. Such tags could increase price credibility with consumers when the store promised immediate matching of any lower price in the market, providing the customer with a real low-price guarantee.

HEB required four to five days to change prices using printed shelf tags, and even then store personnel did not always change prices correctly on the shelf. In-store printing could speed up the process of changing shelf prices and could be implemented independently or in parallel with a phase-in of electronic shelf tags. In-store printing would overcome one of the problems of the current price changing process, wherein price tags shipped with products in advance were sometimes lost or misplaced before the new prices went into effect.

Silvers thought HEB might be able to justify using electronic shelf tags on the highest-volume items, but having electronic tags for all 35,000 items in the store would be economically impractical. Since the top 14,000 items represented about 80% of sales, installing electronic tags on these items would probably be sufficient to generate a consumer perception of instantaneous price reponse. The cost of 14,000 tags came to about $120,000 total at 1993 prices, but the price per tag was expected to decline significantly over time. The payback on electronic shelf tags was hard to estimate, since it depended on customer perception and competitor reactions. HEB planned to test the systems in Victoria, Texas, where both Wal-Mart and Kmart were opening superstores. This trial by fire would provide a test of the capabilities of the new shelf tags and a test of rapid pricing changes and responses in competing with the new stores.

HEB was also investing in many other technological capabilities that could be useful for future ECR applications. For example, a new software package for the in-store processors would improve DSD tracking and efficiency and also reduce shrink on DSD products.[5] The new application would also eliminate substitution of unapproved products by DSD vendors for standard items, a practice common with the manual system used through mid-1994. Item substitution created problems in scanning, for the new item codes were not programmed into the system, which often resulted in checkout delays (to find the price for an item) or shrinkage (the checkout clerk sometimes giving an item to the customer free to avoid delay when lines were long). The new DSD system would require vendors so scan all products in the receiving area of the store. The system could also be expanded to allow store receiving to scan all products received to track shrinkage in the warehouse-to-store logistics process. Many store managers claimed that shrinkage in the chain was due largely to incorrect deliveries, but warehouse managers claimed that all of the shrinkage had to be due to losses at the store level, for the distribution shrinkage allowance given to all stores was greater than the actual level of shrinkage in distribution.

HEB clearly recognized that POS data were important to improve the store ordering process and move from a reactionary mode of operations to a forecasting and planning model. In spite of lower accuracy than desired, many vendors found HEB's and other retailers' POS data to be of great value in planning and analysis. Some vendors valued grocery retailers' POS data sufficiently to provide partial funding for a new startup firm called Efficient Marketing Service (EMS), which offered free expert "data scrubbing" services to supermarket chains, providing cleaned-up data that were more useful for planning and analysis. HEB did not have the capability to "scrub" its own POS data and was pleased to have EMS provide the service for them. EMS not only provided these services for free to retailers, they also paid the supermarkets for the right to sell the data to vendors.

Silvers described long-range planning for information systems at HEB as starting and ending with "tomorrow." Clingman didn't care for a lot of long-range planning, since "the future is easy to describe: nobody knows what will happen." Instead of planning extensively, Clingman and Butt believed in reacting immediately and building flexible capabilities. Silvers described one benefit of working in a closely held private company: budgets and plans were not viewed as major constraints when a promising new idea needed funding. Even if MIS didn't have sufficient funds in its budget, Clingman would still fund an idea that made sense. This was a significant change for Silvers, who had previously worked for a publicly traded retailer with tight budget controls and rigid planning processes for funding new ideas. The flexibility of working for a private company, especially one committed to being an industry leader, was one reason Silvers joined the HEB management team.

One area of focus of the MIS group was augmenting the category mangers' roles and responsibilities. Category managers used data to support analysis of product placement, introduction, and profitability but were not yet using the available data completely and systematically. They were still learning how to do this and did not yet have tools developed to automate the analysis process.

Flannigan was responsible for designing tools to deliver information quickly and flexibly to category managers. It was easy to store and provide data by category but not so easy to determine what tools were needed to be able to manipulate the data effectively. In the system design process, the first question to be addressed was who would develop the applications, for HEB did not have the skills in-house to do so. The MIS staff, although capable, knew that their inexperience with client-server applications or object-oriented systems would hurt their ability to develop effective CM tools. HEB could outsource the development of these tools, or seek to develop the necessary skills, or limit systems development to applications that could be developed with in-house skills. Neither of the alternatives to outsourcing seemed particularly attractive given the intensifying and urgent competitive environment.

The logistics and warehouse operations area viewed information technology as critical for operations and a substitute for inventory in the channel. As information replaced inventory, it also replaced skills required under the old inventory-based processes with new information-based skill requirements. An early example of the impact of information technology on the organization was the 1978 implementation of computer-controlled warehouse inventory. Complexity increased by a quantum leap with the new system, and inventory was indeed dramatically reduced. As an unpleasant side effect, however, almost half of the skilled managers in the warehouse were replaced because they were unable to adapt to the new systems. Innovations in information technology have repeatedly resulted in dramatic change for the people and organization. Efforts to use information reduce inventory and cost in the channel were beneficial for HEB overall but created problems for employees skilled in the old processes.

Periodic organizational restructuring at HEB had reduced resistance to change at the senior management level, where managers viewed themselves as cross-functional in skills and interest. Clark observed that the shift to prolistics and then to CM "reduced the need to defend old methods and procedures and solved some [territorial] issues." Clingman expected to see even greater changes in the future: "What we've seen in the last 20 years is nothing compared to [changes during] the next 20 year."

In spite of the benefits of the organizational restructuring in facilitating intra-organizational coordination, several managers were concerned that HEB still had too many vertical walls between functions with too much empire building. "We're all organized vertically, and the work flows horizontally," observed Clark, who was concerned about the inefficiencies still in the company due to vertical specialization and "report card" management. The "report card" referred to management performance evaluation criteria, which affected individual and group bonuses; criteria in the "report card" clearly influenced behavior, but not always in constructive ways. Aligning incentives correctly was essential for creating a cross-functional working environment, but determining the proper incentives in a complex and multi-functional world was difficult. Shifting incentives could discourage workers, who might view the changes as designed to decrease payments for performance, but job requirements were increasingly fluid, making determination of clear and consistent performance objectives difficult. Clark believed that HEB was managing the "report card" tradeoffs and challenges fairly well, but he also thought that the existing system (which used as many as 20 criteria with complex weighting factors) to evaluate performance still needed to be improved and frequently reviewed.

Clingman recognized the need to overcome organizational barriers and was determined to bring young managers with innovative ideas quickly into the senior management group to help design the store and the company of the future. HEB needed to build a second level of management expertise that would strengthen and challenge the senior management group. Younger managers with excellent track records were being rotated into several functional positions as part of a long-term strategy for developing cross-functional management teams.

Future Issues and Challenges

Chapman was concerned about the rapid pace of change at HEB. He believed the company learned by doing but was worried that too many initiatives begun at the same time might lead to confusion instead of learning. An important issue for Chapman was "how much change should the company try to manage at one time?" In particular, he believed that HEB would benefit more by continuing to improve, support, and expand the role of the category managers than by investing limited resources in new technological innovations with less immediate payoffs.

Clark was concerned about CRP's effectiveness during times of high inflation, when HEB could profit from purchasing more inventory than is required to satisfy immediate customer demand. Forward buying provided a good inflation hedge during the 1970s and cost the company little compared to the gains on the short-term investment, especially while interest rates were lower than inflation. If high inflation levels returned, HEB and vendors would need to deal with the challenge of finding creative alternatives to forward buying to avoid disrupting the efficient product flow and retain the benefits of CRP.

Silvers wanted to see HEB move more quickly in expanding EDI capabilities such as invoicing, receiving, and payment. He was also interested in exploring other ways that HEB could use technology to improve operations, such as electronic shelf tags. He was interested in the potential for joint ventures, partnerships, and alliances with other firms to improve HEB efficiency or operations. For example, several major trucking firms had computerized all of their trucks to improve distribution and tracking. A partnership with one of these companies might offer HEB an opportunity to either outsource trucking transport to a company able to use technology to improve its own operations, or to copy innovations by a transportation leader that HEB could benefit from via its trucking subsidiary.

Notes

1. Retailers with 10 or more stores were generally described as *chains*, and smaller retailers were called *independents*; chains provided more than 70% of total US retail grocery sales.

2. Dry-grocery products excluded produce, frozen, dairy, bakery, meat, deli, pharmacy, photo, video, and floral. The focus of the ECR report was improving channel efficiency for dry-grocery products, which

represent about one-quarter of total channel sales volume. The ECR savings and principles are also projected to apply within other product segments in the channel, but to a more limited extent. The benefits of ECR for produce products are expected to be quite limited.

3. Inbound shipments were products transported from the manufacturer to the retailer warehouse. Inbound transport could be provided by the retailer, the manufacturer, or by an independent trucking company. When the retailer provided transportation, the manufacturer paid an allowance to reimburse for the cost of this service.

4. Categories were products from multiple vendors with similar characteristics (e.g. pickles, candy, or soups). Prior to CM, procurement was often structured around vendors, rather than product categories.

5. Shrink was a term used to describe any loss in inventory versus what was theoretically in the store. Sources of shrink included shoplifting, employee theft, vendor overstating actual delivery quantities, losses of product from warehouse to store in transportation, product damage at the store, receipt of damaged products not credited for replacement, and errors in scanning that provided free products or excessive discount to consumers.

Procter & Gamble Worldwide (P&G) is one of the largest manufacturers supplying grocery retailers and wholesalers and a leader in designing how branded consumer-goods manufacturers go to market. P&G's process innovations are driven by its focus on improving consumer value by eliminating nonvalue-added processes in the channel. Changes at P&G in organization, systems, procedures, and policies affected both the company and the entire channel. These changes were governed by the recognition that manufacturers, distributors, and retailers have to cooperate in creating industrywide approaches to drive inefficiency out of the grocery distribution system.

Many changes leading to organizational and channel transformation were initially viewed as information systems innovations (e.g., developing systems to automate existing practices). Breakthrough change came with the realization that the success of P&G brands depended on eliminating all processes that didn't deliver value to brand-loyal consumers. The promotional frenzy of the late 1970s and 1980s that characterized the retail industry had produced a backlash among brand-loyal consumers, who felt they weren't getting fair value day-in, day-out. P&G studies showed that less than half of their promotional dollars were passing through to the consumer and that swings in price were creating variability and massive inefficiency, not only in P&G's manufacturing and distribution systems but throughout the entire grocery supply chain.

As a result, P&G redesigned how it went to market as a branded consumer-goods maker. Its actions fell into two broad categories: participation in industrywide efficiency improvements, and pricing policy changes, both necessary to improve the value of its brands. As its new pricing strategy was implemented, P&G also took a leadership role in working with the grocery industry—including other manufacturers—to significantly accelerate the adoption of more efficient systems, policies, and practices in the grocery channel (figure 4.8). These industrywide changes resulted in dramatic improvements in P&G's and retailers' effectiveness in delivering value to the consumer.

Company and Industry Background

P&G's sales of $30 billion in 1993 were evenly divided between the United States and the rest of the world. P&G had developed a reputation for aggressive and successful

This case was prepared by Theodore H. Clark under the supervision of Professor James L. McKenney.
© 1995 by the President and Fellows of Harvard College.
Harvard Business School case 9-195-126.

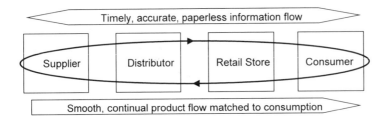

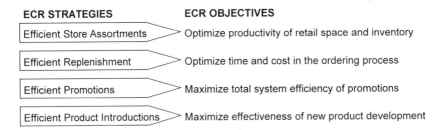

Figure 4.8
The ECR vision—A continuous channel process

"world-class" development and marketing of high-quality consumer goods over more than 150 years of operations. Throughout its history, the company focused on providing superior performing brands that gave consumers good value.

P&G's post–World War II growth came from three sources: acquisitions, development and marketing of new brands, and international expansion. Its acquisitions included: Duncan Hines and Hines-Park Foods (food products), W. T. Young Foods (peanut butter and nuts), J. A. Folger (coffee), and Clorox Chemical Co. (bleach). In 1957, the U.S. Federal Trade Commission (FTC) sued P&G to force the divestiture of its Clorox subsidiary. This effectively terminated the growth by acquisition strategy for two decades, forcing P&G management to grow through new-product development and international expansion.

P&G's international strategy was to take core U.S. businesses—soap, toothpaste, diapers, and shampoo—and replicate them to the rest of the world. International sales increased from virtually zero in 1953 to $4 billion in 1985. During this expansion period, new geography was conquered for existing brands, and P&G rotated managers to different locations between the U.S., Europe, and Asia. During the 1980s, P&G international shifted to developing and marketing products tailored to the needs of each market. This increased focus on understanding and meeting consumer needs worldwide enabled P&G to expand international from about $4 billion (31% of sales) in 1985 to $15 billion (50% of sales) in 1993. Ed Artzt, president of P&G International from 1983 to 1990, was appointed CEO of the company in 1990.

By 1993, P&G's product lines included a wide assortment of products, with the company organized into five product sectors: Health/Beauty; Food/Beverage; Paper; Soap; and Special Products (e.g., chemicals). Each sector was organized into product categories, and each category was responsible for a group of brands. Most new-brand introductions were based on improvements or extensions of existing products. Several new products, such as Pampers disposable diapers and Pringles potato chips, were developed to meet basic consumer needs not yet served by existing products. Extensive market research, low-cost and effective advertising, and aggressive R&D investments enabled P&G to increase sales in the U.S. market from $1 billion in 1955 to almost $9 billion by 1985.

Competition for most of P&G product categories was concentrated, with two or three branded product producers controlling more than 50% of total branded product sales in each category. This concentration for the top three brands in any product category was typical for other manufacturers as well, although increasing sales of private-label products were eroding market share for the major brands in some categories. For some products, such as soaps or diapers, P&G and one competitor controlled more than 70% of the market. The strong consumer pull for P&G products provided the company with an advantage in dealing with retailers and wholesalers.

P&G products were sold through multiple channels, with grocery retailers, wholesalers, mass merchandisers, and club stores the most important in product sales volume. While relationships with retailers and wholesalers had not always been harmonious, P&G management recognized the need to serve the needs of both the consumer and the channel in order to be successful in the market. Demand for P&G products was primarily driven by pull through the channel by end consumers, rather than by trade push, with the trade frequently carrying P&G products because of consumer demand and competitive necessity rather than due to the trade's strong loyalty to P&G as a channel partner. Relationships between P&G and the trade through 1980 had primarily been based on negotiations over short term initiatives and promotions. Increased use of promotions was part of the trend during this period, with P&G competing with other manufacturers for retail shelf space and promotional displays through various types of periodic promotions. Forward buying of promoted merchandise by 1985 had become the norm of the industry, with many brands stocked with over three-months' supply.

Pricing and Promotions

Product promotions had existed to a limited extent for decades but expanded dramatically during the 1970s, partly due to President Nixon's imposition of price controls in 1971 as part of an attempt to reduce inflation. The combination of high inflation, relatively low interest costs, and large promotional discounts made the economics of forward buying very attractive for chains. Product procurement cost depended upon so many different allowances and other incentives provided by manufacturers that the actual cost of a single product at any one time on the shelf was impossible to determine. Inability to understand costs and the discounts and allowances available from aggressive purchasing resulted in a focus in the channel on "buying for profit" rather than "selling for profit."

This reliance on a multitude of promotional programs coupled with forward buying increased retailer inventories and required manufacturers to also maintain large inventories in order to be able to meet the high demand artificially created by forward buying during these promotional periods. Variation in consumer demand was increased by store promotions, and variation in manufacturer demand was further increased by retailer forward buying activities, making changes in demand difficult to forecast accurately for manufacturers. This uncertainty about total demand and large fluctuations in periodic demand not only increased manufacturer inventory requirements but also resulted in higher manufacturing costs than would have been possible in a direct pull through demand environment.

One of the objectives of channel-transforming innovations in the 1990s was to develop more collaborative and mutually productive relationships with channel partners, replacing negotiations with cooperative efforts to better serve consumer needs efficiently. By combining consumer loyalty with improved channel efficiency and relationships, P&G believed that market share for P&G products would increase and the cost to serve the channel and the end consumer would decline, enabling all members of the channel to benefit.

Retail Distribution Channels

Retail grocery was the most important channel for the sale of P&G products and consisted of manufacturers, distributors, and retail stores (figure 4.9). Approximately half of all retail grocery sales volume went through chains of stores which provided their own distribution and warehousing of products, and half through wholesalers who primarily served small chains and independent retail stores.

Profit margins for grocery retailers were low, typically 1–3% of gross sales before tax. With low unit prices and high volumes, store operating profits were highly

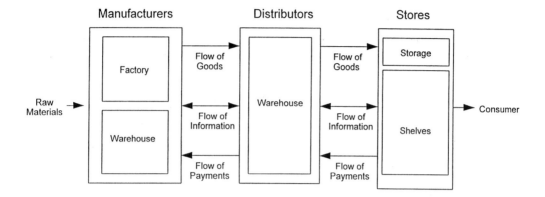

Flow of goods is frequent and high-volume and may be provided by trucks owned by one of the channel members or by a third party.

Flow of information was minimal for most channel members in the early 1990s, mostly conducted via voice telephone, paper mail, and face-to-face communications.

Figure 4.9
Simplified grocery industry functional value chain

dependent on providing efficient operations. Total sales volume per store and per square foot of retail space were critical factors influencing retailer profitability. Since advertising was a significant cost for most retailers, regional market share was a critical factor influencing retailer profitability by leveraging the fixed costs of regional (e.g., newspaper) advertising.

Mass-merchandise (e.g., Wal-Mart) and club-store (e.g., Sam's Club) retailers supplied a limited assortment of P&G and other grocery-channel products at low margins, enabling them to offer attractive prices to consumers. These formats grew rapidly during the 1980s. Even though club stores offered a limited product selection and provided less service than traditional grocery retailers, a significant segment of consumers was willing to replace grocery-store shopping with club-store purchases, with the attraction of lower prices at the club stores more than offsetting the inconveniences involved. A McKinsey study of alternative distribution channels for grocery products, published by the Food Marketing Institute in 1992, demonstrated that the more efficient distribution and merchandising of these alternative formats enabled them to offer lower prices to consumers than traditional grocery retailers. This study served as a wake-up call to the grocery industry, suggesting that existing processes needed to be improved to enable it to meet the challenge of these rapidly growing alternative formats.

Improving Channel Efficiency and Service

In the mid-1980s, P&G management launched several projects to improve service and reduce costs across the channel. The first effort focused on improving supply logistics and reducing channel inventory via a process that eventually was called continuous replenishment (CRP). The second was a project to revise the ordering and billing system to improve total ordering and service quality for channel customers.

The Early Logistics Improvement Trials

In 1985, P&G tested a new approach to channel logistics for replenishment ordering with a moderate-sized grocery chain. This test involved using electronic data interchange (EDI) to transmit data daily from the retailer to P&G on warehouse product shipments to each store. P&G then determined the quantity of products to be shipped to the retailer's warehouse by using shipment information rather than shipping based on retailer-generated orders. Product order quantities were computed by P&G with the objectives of providing sufficient safety stock, minimizing total logistics costs, and eliminating excess inventory in the retailer's warehouse.

The results of this initial trial were impressive in inventory reductions, service level improvements (e.g., fewer stockouts), and labor savings for the retailer. Besides other savings, the retailer was able to eliminate several buyer positions through this process restructuring. However, the benefits for P&G were unclear, and the new ordering process was more costly for P&G than the old one where the retailer determined order quantities.

The second test of the new ordering process was with a large mass merchandiser. In 1986, P&G approached this retailer's management with a proposal to dramatically change the way diapers were ordered and distributed in an effort to reduce retail store stockouts, lower product acquisition costs, and minimize total inventories. Limited warehouse capacity forced the retailer to purchase P&G diaper products in small quantities to be delivered directly to each retail store. Retail stores had frequent stockout problems, and the cost of these small orders delivered directly to the store was high for both P&G and the retail chain. Diapers were an important product category for this retailer, and it wanted to price diapers lower than other retailers in their markets. Unfortunately, the distribution system used for procurement resulted in higher acquisition cost for diaper products than many of its competitors (e.g., supermarkets), who were able to order in truckload quantities.

P&G proposed that the retailer inventory diaper products in the chain's distribution warehouse, provide P&G with daily data on warehouse orders received from the stores, and allow P&G to use the daily warehouse shipment data to determine warehouse replenishment volumes needed. This new replenishment process would limit the retailer's warehouse inventory to acceptable levels, eliminate costly LTL (less-than-truckload) shipments, and reduce stockouts for retail stores. Both P&G and the retailer would benefit by reducing costs and increasing sales. Sales increases would result from lower retail prices enabled by lower costs and from providing better service to consumers through greater product availability.

The new replenishment process resulted in substantially lower product acquisition costs through truckload volume purchases, enabling lower retail pricing. Without increasing inventory levels or stockouts, the retail chain was able to expand P&G's diaper SKUs in the stores. The combination of lower prices, reduced stockouts, and expanded SKUs in the stores dramatically increased P&G's diaper sales through this retailer's stores. This new process represented a major change in channel ordering and logistics and established the basic principles of what eventually became known as CRP (continuous replenishment program). This second trial demonstrated the potential for logistics innovations to offer mutual benefits to retailers and manufacturers by reducing channel costs and increasing consumer sales.

In early 1988, top executives from P&G and another mass-merchandise chain met to discuss ways to improve logistics in the channel. The retailer was warehouse constrained due to rapid growth and was relying heavily on costly LTL shipments to meet demand. LTL shipments were expensive for both partners, and made it difficult for the retailer to increase diaper sales. During the meeting, the CEO of the mass-merchandise chain suggested the P&G simply ship products on a just-in-time basis when needed using the retailer's actual sales data. Deals and promotions would be replaced by a constant allowance that resulted in an equivalent net-price for the retailer to remove forward-buy incentives.

A multifunctional team worked together for the rest of the conference to work out many of the details of implementing the new process. With top executives from both companies committed to rapid adoption, and building on P&G's experience with two other retailers, implementation of CRP took less than two months in total. In April 1988, P&G began shipping products based on retail demand data, placing orders automatically for the retailer. Information on demand was transmitted via fax and phone until EDI links were established.

Expanding the CRP Innovation

The success of the CRP program with leading mass-merchandisers generated interest from other retailers in the new process. By 1990, most large mass-merchandisers had fully implemented CRP. In 1990 and 1991, three grocery chains adopted CRP with

P&G, and the innovation proved highly successful in reducing inventory and stock-out levels for these early grocery pioneers. CRP adoption started with diapers and then expanded rapidly to other products as the potential for mutual cost reduction was demonstrated across the channel. CRP's success with early partners led the head of the diaper product group to commit $1.5 million in development funding during 1991 to expand the initial CRP system into a more robust production system that could be expanded to as many customers as needed. The increased sales and profits from the initial adopters of CRP were enough to justify the entire development cost being funded by this single product category!

The diaper product group then used CRP as a tool in selling an expanded diaper product line (boy and girl diapers) to retail chains. The new product line doubled the total number of SKUs in an already crowded product category but was needed to better respond to customer needs and meet competitive pressures. CRP enabled the diaper product sales force to offer customers a solution that managed the increased number of SKUs while reducing both inventory levels and stockouts for the retailer. Since a barrier to expanding product SKUs was the resulting increase in inventory required, CRP proved helpful in marketing the new diaper product line.

During 1992, 14 additional grocery chains implemented CRP with P&G, and existing CRP customers continued to expand CRP usage to new product lines. During 1993, an additional 15 new grocery chains or divisions of grocery chains adopted CRP. By July of 1994, a total of 47 channel customers had adopted CRP with P&G, and more than 26% of P&G sales volume was ordered via CRP. As these customers expanded use of CRP to new product lines and across multiple distribution centers, total CRP demand from these customers alone was expected to increase to 35% of P&G sales by the end of 1994. Ralph Drayer, VP of customer services, expected use of CRP to reach 50% or more of total US product shipment volume by the end of 1995.

Increased retail sales were an important benefit of the CRP program of P&G and its distributors. Sales of P&G products through CRP retailers increased 4% more on average during 1993 than sales through non-CRP retailers. Although some of this difference could be attributed to faster-growing retailers adopting CRP, Drayer believed that some of the gain was due to sales gained from competing products due to reduced stockouts, lower retail pricing, and expanded product selection in the store. However, even if only 1% of the 4% sales increase was due to competitive share gains, this represented a huge competitive and economic gain for P&G. One food division manager said he would "gain more market share by expanding CRP than through [product] line extensions."

The Role of EDI

When P&G began expanding the use of EDI with retailers to improve ordering efficiency, problems with order quality increased significantly. The sales representative or customer service representative in the manual process was often able to catch some of the problems and manually adjust retailers' orders to work in the P&G systems. Some of these adjustments later resulted in errors in the collections phase, but at least the order was entered and shipped. Removal of this human buffer created problems for most EDI orders could not be processed without manual intervention. These early EDI trials with customers increased costs for P&G instead of providing savings since most orders had to be manually reworked and rekeyed into the OSB system. Without process redesign, using EDI for ordering offered little benefit for P&G or customers, although it did highlight problems and misunderstandings.

EDI represented an important part of P&G's strategy to improve the efficiency of the ordering process and was essential for CRP implementation, but EDI alone was not viewed as particularly important in the effort to improve efficiency and order quality. One P&G manager described EDI as "an enabling technology" that, if implemented without changes in interorganizational processes and policies, represented little more than "a fancy electronic fax." Another manager explained: "EDI is simply an electronic envelope, not a system. It does not fix anything and, by itself, is not a solution. However, when implemented in parallel with process and systems reengineering, it can become a powerful tool."

An important role for EDI at P&G was to provide an essential platform for CRP operations. One manager described CRP as "two-way EDI with tight links into the systems of both companies." Of course, CRP required more than system changes, but the degree of interconnection with the systems of each organization was much tighter with CRP than was required for EDI with non-CRP customers. This linkage between systems across the two companies, enabled by the EDI link, resulted in error-free interchange of large amounts of data automatically between the companies. CRP dramatically increased the amount of data shared by companies in the channel, which made EDI essential for effective operations. Although early CRP trials had used fax and phone for data transmission, several P&G managers expressed the view that CRP without EDI was not viable:

The problem [with manual entry of data] is that any error would probably result in an out-of-stock condition. The risk of [data entry] keying errors in an non-EDI environment is just too great. You also have a lot of data that need to be entered, which would require extensive manual support. CRP without EDI is just not viable.

EDI offered companies economic benefits by reducing transaction costs, which encouraged EDI adoption, even without making the commitment to CRP. Although the potential benefits from CRP were much larger than the benefits from EDI ordering alone, the challenges in shifting to CRP were greater than many retailers were willing to face. EDI provided an easy first step for companies that wanted to be technologically prepared for the new era without committing to the management and policy changes required to implement CRP.

Drayer observed that successful implementation of CRP required both senior management commitment to the innovation and a relationship of trust between management at the two organizations linking their systems:

Companies that have made the choice to be interdependent will move to CRP. You can't remain independent with CRP.... This is not something you can just connect between customers and suppliers. You need to understand the management changes required.

The Ordering, Shipping, and Billing Systems

In 1987, P&G management approved a major rewrite of the entire ordering, shipping, and billing (OSB) system, which took several years and cost tens of millions of dollars to complete. The systems in use at the time had been developed during the 1960s and had been upgraded many times. The batch processing system was both inefficient and ineffective; upgrading it was considered a competitive requirement for P&G to be able to provide the level of service required by customers. The OSB system supported all P&G activities in serving channel customers, including pricing, ordering, shipping, invoicing, and separate credit systems. The OSB project integrated many separate systems that did not work well together across functions and product sectors, enabling P&G to improve consistency and overall service levels.

The charter of the OSB development team was to understand how the business worked and then to automate the existing processes with sufficient flexibility to meet the various needs of the different sectors and functions. In some cases, standardization was allowed to simplify design and improve practices to a common level across the organization. The system absorbed a lot of the complexity of the existing processes which contributed to the cost of development, and was designed to eliminate manual processing steps but not to redesign the existing processes.

The rewrite of the system and the simultaneous upgrade of the hardware infrastructure were necessary but significant additional performance improvement opportunities remained because of complex pricing and promotion practices. The process and performance levels in 1988 (prior to OSB rewrite) are shown in figure 4.10, with comparable data for 1992 (after OSB rewrite) shown in figure 4.11. Invoice deductions by customers were still quite large in 1992, although the new system had helped some in this area. Although the new system did improve order shipment quality, problems with the existing pricing and promotion policies and processes still created deductions. It was clear that the front end of the OSB system, which involved pricing and promotions policies, needed to be revised.

Redesigning the Complete Ordering Process

P&G managers realized they needed to improve the total ordering process, starting with pricing policies and practices. Improving ordering quality required a simpler pricing structure that customers could both understand and track in their systems. A new pricing structure, introduced by Durk Jager, EVP responsible for all U.S. operations, dramatically simplified expansion of the new OSB system capabilities and represented a significant change in corporate strategy and policies. Pricing policy changes were critical for improving consumer value and building brand loyalty and facilitated expansion of the OSB systems to allow improvements in billing accuracy and reductions in invoice deductions. The combination of pricing policy changes and systems improvements benefited both P&G and channel customers.

The standardization and simplification of processes and policies across the organization accelerated under the leadership of Artzt and Jager. Challenging traditional practices and policies became acceptable and welcome, as long as suggested changes could be shown to improve consumer value by eliminating processes or costs that did not add value to the channel or products. One manager observed:

Jager made it okay to make change happen faster. The ideas were bubbling in the organization and the pace of change accelerated dramatically.

Redesigning the ordering process involved a combination of systems and business process changes which had to be carefully integrated. A key element of the new ordering process was the development of common databases for product pricing and product specifications. This shared vision of business simplification and a common database was solidly grounded in the philosophy of "simplify, standardize, then mechanize." The common databases developed to support simplified pricing were designed to provide data directly to the customer's own system electronically. This resulted in dramatic reductions in invoice deductions for retailers using the new pricing database to verify or confirm purchase order information.

The combined changes in systems, strategy, organization, and policies resulted in a dramatic improvement in total order quality at P&G (figure 4.12). Billing errors

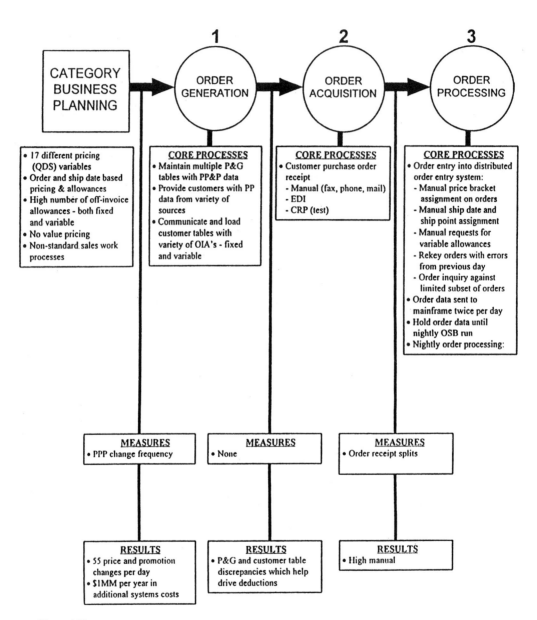

Figure 4.10
Total order management process before new OSB (1988)

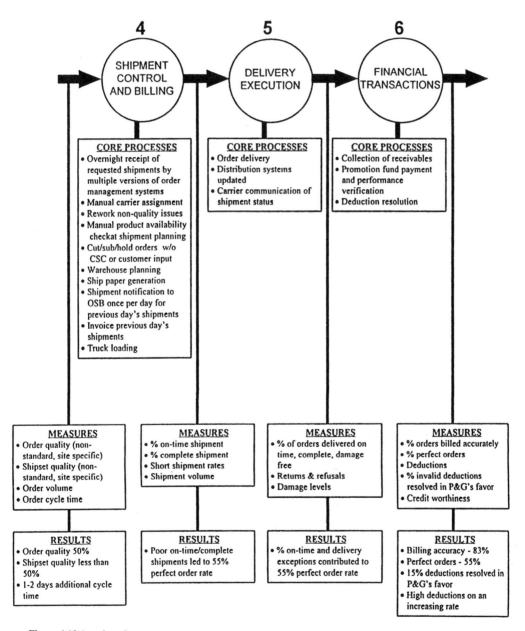

Figure 4.10 (continued)

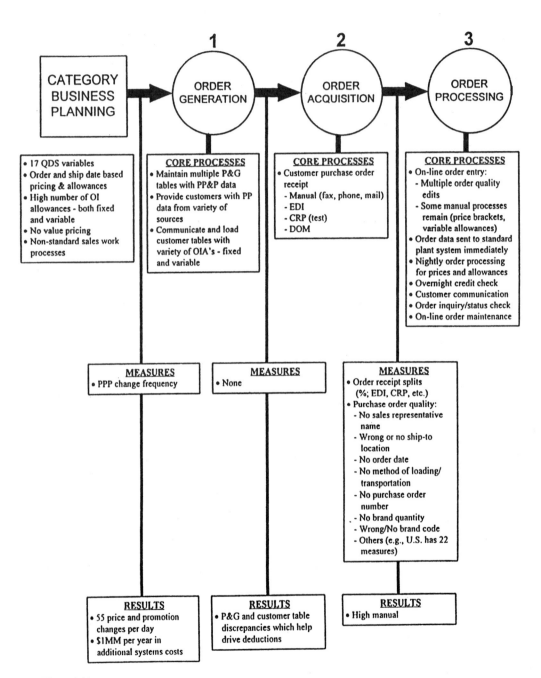

Figure 4.11
Total order management process after new OSB (1992)

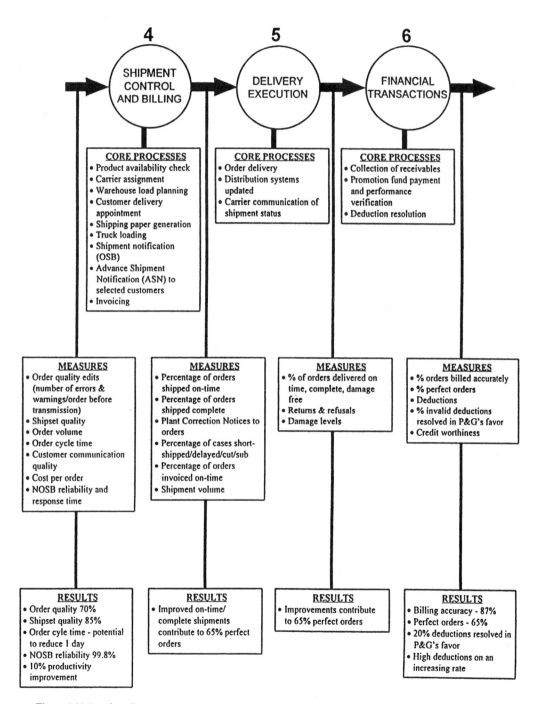

Figure 4.11 (continued)

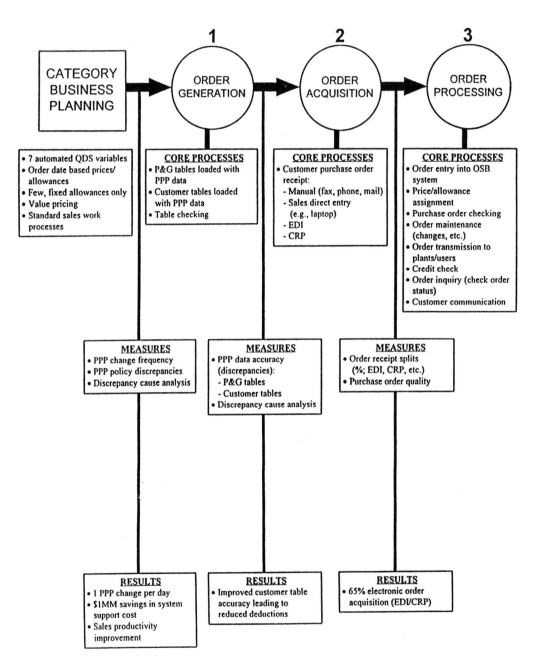

Figure 4.12
Total order management process after redesign (1994)

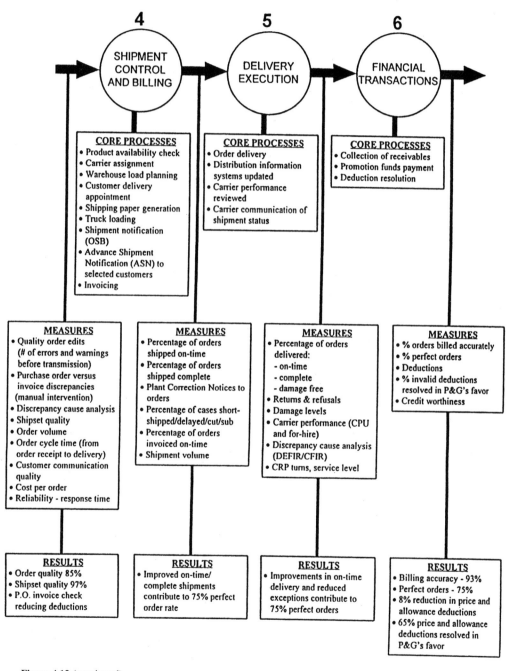

4 SHIPMENT CONTROL AND BILLING

CORE PROCESSES
- Product availability check
- Carrier assignment
- Warehouse load planning
- Customer delivery appointment
- Shipping paper generation
- Truck loading
- Shipment notification (OSB)
- Advance Shipment Notification (ASN) to selected customers
- Invoicing

MEASURES
- Quality order edits (# of errors and warnings before transmission)
- Purchase order versus invoice discrepancies (manual intervention)
- Discrepancy cause analysis
- Shipset quality
- Order volume
- Order cycle time (from order receipt to delivery)
- Customer communication quality
- Cost per order
- Reliability - response time

RESULTS
- Order quality 85%
- Shipset quality 97%
- P.O. invoice check reducing deductions

5 DELIVERY EXECUTION

CORE PROCESSES
- Order delivery
- Distribution information systems updated
- Carrier performance reviewed
- Carrier communication of shipment status

MEASURES
- Percentage of orders shipped on-time
- Percentage of orders shipped complete
- Plant Correction Notices to orders
- Percentage of cases short-shipped/delayed/cut/sub
- Percentage of orders invoiced on-time
- Shipment volume

RESULTS
- Improved on-time/complete shipments contribute to 75% perfect order rate

6 FINANCIAL TRANSACTIONS

CORE PROCESSES
- Collection of receivables
- Promotion funds payment
- Deduction resolution

MEASURES
- Percentage of orders delivered:
  - on-time
  - complete
  - damage free
- Returns & refusals
- Damage levels
- Carrier performance (CPU and for-hire)
- Discrepancy cause analysis (DEFIR/CFIR)
- CRP turns, service level

RESULTS
- Improvements in on-time delivery and reduced exceptions contribute to 75% perfect orders

MEASURES
- % orders billed accurately
- % perfect orders
- Deductions
- % invalid deductions resolved in P&G's favor
- Credit worthiness

RESULTS
- Billing accuracy - 93%
- Perfect orders - 75%
- 8% reduction in price and allowance deductions
- 65% price and allowance deductions resolved in P&G's favor

Figure 4.12 (continued)

decreased by more than 50% from 1992 to 1994, and the percentage of billing disputes resolved in P&G's favor increased by more than 300% during the same period. The first-year savings from increased collections on invoices alone were enough to pay for the entire cost of development of the new pricing systems. P&G's customer teams were also able to concentrate on providing better service and marketing new products instead of spending time resolving billing problems. P&G's redesign of the total ordering process required fundamental changes in its structure, policies, and systems but yielded dramatic benefits in cost reduction and quality improvement. In addition to reducing invoice deductions, the redesigned business process allowed P&G to reduce costs throughout the entire ordering process.

Radical Restructuring of Pricing

The long-term strategic goal of increasing consumer value and brand loyalty, CRP's need for simple and stable pricing, and the need to reduce pricing complexity to improve quality in the ordering process all supported the decision to replace existing pricing structures with a simplified "value-pricing" program. This new pricing program was introduced initially for dishwashing liquids, where this new pricing approach was accepted, generally without much resistance. As the pricing change became accepted generally, although not universally, value pricing was gradually implemented for more products (table 4.2). By late 1993, almost all P&G products were on some form of value-pricing plan.

The shift to value pricing represented a radical change in policies and was driven mostly by concern that frequent and complex promotions were eroding the value of P&G's brands. Brand loyalty declined in the United States during the 1970s and 1980s, due to the wild price swings that came with constant promotional activity. Frequent promotions rewarded only those consumers most sensitive to price and acted as a disincentive to brand-loyal consumers. Value pricing eliminated incentives for retailer forward buying and essentially offered constant procurement costs combined with some flexible allowances or funds provided for retail store promotions.

Value pricing offered important benefits for CRP customers, encouraging increased CRP adoption. Implementation of CRP with the first few customers required prototyping new net-pricing terms that eliminated variable discounts and promotions in order to remove incentives for forward buying. There was little benefit in trying to improve channel logistics efficiency while using a pricing structure that encouraged inefficient purchasing practices (e.g., forward buying). Until P&G restructured pricing, efforts to extend CRP were constrained because it lacked a standardized pricing structure that would eliminate forward-buying incentives.

Table 4.2
Value pricing timing and product volume

Value pricing initial date	Product brands or categories	Percentage of total P&G shipment volume
July 1991	All liquid dishwashing products, some bar soap products, some Duncan Hines products	8.2
August 1991	Metamucil	0.6
November 1991	Bold, Liquid Bold, Solo, Cascade, Liquid Cascade, all Bounce products, Downy Sheets, all Comet products, Mr. Clean, all Spic and Span products, Top Job, Lestoil, Gain, Ivory Snow, Dash, Dreft, Oxydol	11.3
February 1992	Pantene, Liquid Safeguard	1.0
April 1992	Luvs, Pampers	7.0
July 1992	Old Spice Deodorant, Downy Ultra and Regular, Secret, Sure, Bounty	12.8
October 1992	Always, Attends (retail)	2.0
November 1992	Liquid Cheer, Liquid Tide	4.3
January 1993	Prell, Cinch	0.5
March 1993	Tide Powder, Cheer Powder, Era	10.2
May 1993	Puffs	1.0
July 1993	Head & Shoulders, Charmin/White Cloud, Scope	8.9
August 1993	Hawaiian Punch	1.3
Total product volume with no off-invoice allowances in August 1993		69.1

Implementation of value pricing reduced the number of pricing changes at P&G from 55 per day in 1992 to less than 1 per day in early 1994. In July 1994, all remaining variable promotional allowances were eliminated for the last few product categories using these incentives, and geographic pricing differences were eliminated as well. Temporary price reductions or special promotions were allowed only to meet significant competitive threats to P&G brands, and they had to be approved by Jager.

There was considerable resistance to the change in pricing philosophy from some P&G senior managers, in spite of the obvious advantages, since this was completely the opposite of the high-low pricing strategies many executives had used to create new brands and strengthen P&G product market throughout their careers. Jager noted that the new pricing did cost P&G sales over the period, but that this incremental revenue actually cost P&G more to generate than the income created by the promotions. Thus, while sales were lower than would have been possible using promotional pricing, profits were stronger, and the company was better positioned to build a future based on value-priced products for brand-loyal consumers.

Leading the Grocery Channel Transformation

Working with retailers, wholesalers, other manufacturers, industry trade associations, and consulting firms, P&G participated in the development of the Efficient Consumer Response (ECR) vision of channel innovations that would enable grocery chains to compete effectively with low-cost alternative retail formats. ECR became a banner for a wide variety of innovations in the grocery channel that would improve efficiency (figure 4.8). Various joint industry ECR committees were established in a coordinated effort to explore opportunities for channel process improvement.

CRP was an important element of the ECR vision. The ECR report by Kurt Salmon Associates, published in January 1993, suggested that 38% of the $30 billion in savings projected from implementing ECR in the grocery industry could be realized through more efficient replenishment ordering. Many grocery channel members were able to realize significant savings immediately by adopting CRP without waiting for the remainder of the ECR proposals to be fully developed. P&G was a clear leader in the implementation of CRP and other ECR programs and wanted to increase the pace of ECR and CRP adoption in the industry overall.

The Change from Brand to Category Management

In the late 1980s, P&G management made a significant change in its brand management structure to improve coordination and efficiency. Multiple brands were combined into product categories, under the responsibility of a category manager, who managed individual brands as part of the overall category portfolio. For more than 50 years, the brand management approach had served P&G well, and the company had been recognized as the benchmark for excellence in brand management. The introduction of category management was a dramatic shift for a company that had pioneered brand management in the 1930s.

The category management approach provided more flexibility in restructuring the P&G product line. Brand restructuring or consolidation would have been more difficult to achieve under the prior structure. Brand managers maintained responsibility for advertising and limited promotional programs, but category managers established overall pricing and product policies, which enabled P&G to eliminate weaker brands. For example, the elimination of the White Cloud brand by merging the product into the Charmin line would have been resisted by a White Cloud brand manager but was strongly supported by the toilet-tissue category manager, who reported to the paper products sector manager. Category management also avoided conflicts between similar branded products in the same channel for advertising and distribution resources.

The shift to category management was consistent with the company's efforts to simplify and standardize operations and product lines. Many unnecessary SKUs were eliminated when SKU differences did not provide significant incremental value to the consumer. At the same time, new SKUs were added as new products and innovative extensions of existing product lines were developed. In total, the number of SKUs P&G offered remained about the same during the early 1990s, but the restructuring of SKUs provided consumers with greater choice of products that were specifically tailored to their needs, and eliminated a proliferation of product variety that was based simply on labeling or packaging differences.

Manufacturing and Planning Improvements

Although the initial benefits of CRP were reductions in inventory, stockouts, and handling and transportation costs, increased adoption of CRP by P&G customers offered dramatic cost saving opportunities for production and raw-material purchasing. P&G managers estimated that at least 10% of the cost of production for paper products was the cost of excess capacity required to handle product demand variations. Value pricing reduced demand uncertainty by eliminating forward-buy distortions, and CRP further reduced demand uncertainty and allowed almost instant feedback on demand resulting from product innovations or pricing changes.

The potential benefits of CRP for production cost and inventory savings were quite large. Savings in inventory or production were not automatic, but the shift to a more stable environment enabled P&G to negotiate more attractive pricing with suppliers and to use internal production capacity more efficiently. In some cases, the efficiency gains from value pricing, rationalized product lines, CRP ordering, and dramatic improvements in process reliability resulted in sufficient excess production capacity to eliminate entire production plants. During the 1990s, many P&G plants were expected to close as a result of improved operations due to the new policies and processes. In 1993, P&G took an extraordinary charge of almost an entire year's profits to reflect the actual and expected costs of closing unneeded plants and reducing total employment levels for the company (table 4.3).

The CRP savings for diaper production were estimated based on experiences of multiple plants with different levels of CRP ordering by customers. The results of this analysis are shown in figure 4.13 and represent the early results of CRP adoption on the production process. Paper product managers believed that further costs savings could be realized as P&G teamed to better use the improved information about demand that was available through CRP ordering data. Through more effective negotiating with vendors and better use of actual demand data for planning and scheduling, additional savings could be realized in production.

Table 4.3
Selected P&G financial statistics

	1987	1988	1989	1990	1991	1992	1993
Net sales	$17,000	$19,336	$21,398	$24,081	$27,026	$29,362	$30,433
Net earnings	$786	$1,020	$1,206	$1,602	$1,773	$1,872	$2,015
Net earnings per share	$1.13	$1.49	$1.78	$2.25	$2.46	$2.62	$1.87
Net earnings as % of sales	4.6%	5.3%	5.6%	6.7%	6.6%	6.4%	6.6%
Dividends per common share	$0.68	$0.69	$0.75	$0.88	$0.98	$1.03	$1.10

Note: These numbers exclude extraordinary charges of $459 in 1987 and $1,746 in 1993 for costs of restructuring (plant closings and staff reductions), and a charge of $925 to reflect accounting changes in 1993.

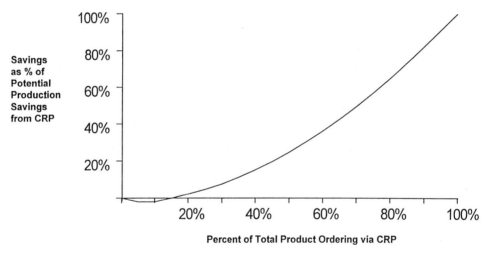

Figure 4.13
Projected manufacturing cost savings using CRP ordering
Source: Estimates based on interviews with P&G manufacturing and product category executives.

Customers and Category Management

The second most important aspect of the joint industry ECR vision was the retailers' shift from buyers to category managers that was taking place among leaders in the industry during the early 1990s. Although the cost savings from this shift were not as dramatic or easily quantified as the savings from CRP adoption, the potential profit improvement of the shift to category management could easily exceed the cost savings from CRP. Category managers in retail chains were ideally responsible for the entire profit of a product category across all stores. Replacing buyers, who were primarily focused on cost or promotional deals, with category managers responsible for both profits and meeting consumer needs required new skills and capabilities. The shift from buyer to category manager represented a new mindset, for both the individuals in the role and the overall organization. Few buyers were able to make the transition to the new role, and few organizations could make the shift in procurement and merchandising strategy without a strong CEO vision and mandate for change.

The shift to category management benefited both retailers and P&G category managers were better positioned to understand the true costs and profits generated from each product in their category. P&G customer teams were able to use solid economic analysis with category managers to demonstrate that their brands should be given additional shelf space or variety because the retail profit per unit of shelf space for P&G brands was higher than most other products in the category. In addition, category managers were able to appreciate the storage and handling savings provided by P&G's simplified pricing policies and logistics programs.

Sale of the CRP System to IBM

In late 1993, P&G announced the sale of their CRP system to IBM's Integrated Systems Solutions Corporation (ISSC) subsidiary. The P&G CRP system was to be offered by IBM to all manufacturers as a service provided by IBM, with P&G out-sourcing support and operations of their CRP systems to ISSC. Within two weeks, Ralston Purina signed up as IBM's first customer, and five other manufacturers had become IBM CRP clients by mid-1994. Many other large manufacturers had expressed interest in the IBM service offering, which offered manufacturers CRP systems capabilities quickly, at low cost, and with experienced operating personnel. This IBM CRP service offering allowed retailers to interact with multiple vendors in a common format, creating a powerful force in the industry for standardization. The availability of the IBM CRP service also increased the attractiveness of CRP for manufacturers and retailers by reducing barriers to CRP adoption.

The decision to sell the CRP system to IBM was primarily based on strategic, not economic, justification. The net benefits to P&G and its customers of implementing CRP increased as the total number of customers and other manufacturers using CRP increased. Therefore, it was more important for P&G to be sure this innovation was rapidly adopted by the industry overall than to try to gain advantage from being the technological leader of the innovation. The sale to IBM increased the probability of other manufacturers adopting CRP by providing them access to a complete CRP service offering with quick start-up capability.

In addition, the agreement with IBM reduced P&G's cost of operating the CRP system, since the IBM service contract cost was less than the cost of operating the system using P&G's internal staff and systems. IBM planned to run the applications using excess capacity at the Kodak operations center that IBM was managing under an IT service contract. Thus, IBM was able to operate the outsourced CRP operations on capacity that would otherwise be underutilized from another outsourced MIS operations client. The outsourcing of CRP services to large manufacturers also gave IBM an opportunity to demonstrate the potential benefits of MIS services outsourcing to multiple potential clients, who might be interested in further outsourcing services that could be linked with the CRP applications over time. In summary, P&G's sale of CRP systems to IBM offered important strategic and operational benefits for both companies and provided the credibility of a third-party platform offering to increase the attractiveness of CRP for the industry.

Jager believed that any technological advantage P&G lost by selling the proprietary CRP system to IBM would be more than offset by the benefits for consumers and for the company of having the grocery industry fully embrace CRP. Increased adoption of CRP by P&G's customers would allow the company and its customers to improve internal processes and reduce costs. Jager explained:

By eliminating nonvalue-added processes, we will ultimately win in the market by providing the best product to the consumer at the lowest cost through the channel.

5 Telecommunications Infrastructure in Transition

The Internet and other networks on which we conduct electronic commerce are for the most part built around the existing global telecommunications infrastructure. As a foundation for deploying the opportunities provided by global electronic commerce, it is important to understand the underlying telecommunications infrastructure. Modern telecommunications infrastructure allows firms to expand their markets, manage channel relationships with business partners, and serve customer needs, while redefining the structure of cost, time, and space within their business operations.

In recent years, the price/performance ratio of communications technologies has dropped even faster than that of computing chips. Gordon Moore's famous law predicts a doubling of chip processing speed every 18 months; a similar calculation for communications switching technologies would double switching speed every nine months.[1]

Telecommunications Technology

Telecommunications technology has dramatically changed the way computers are designed and managed, enabling vast networks of interlinked terminals to operate as a collective system. Of course, advances in communications technologies have also enabled low-cost mobile voice (and data) cellular phone networks to be developed and will in time lead to the deployment of broadband-switched networks to the home that will bring a variety of entertainment and communications services to consumers. However, our focus in this book is on the advances in telecommunications that have already taken place to enable more efficient and higher-speed exchange of digital information between computer systems in different locations. These advances in digital communications capabilities have enabled the development of the Web and the dramatic growth of electronic commerce applications, both using the Web and using other communications standards and transmission media.

This chapter provides an introduction to this critical enabling technology and a discussion of the potential for further improvements in telecommunications technologies that will change the way we take advantage of electronic commerce opportunities. However, this text provides only a very limited discussion of voice communications technologies and issues, as voice telecommunications is not as essential part of electronic commerce. Although voice communication is often important for companies to manage effectively and can be critical for effective operations of the company, the technological issues involved in data communications are generally more complex than those for voice communications. Management of data communications is sufficiently important for effective computer networking that many companies with extensive data networks have merged the management of voice and data networks within the IT functional area. At the same time, computers often use telecommunications facilities initially designed for voice transmission, so it is important also to understand how basic voice telecommunications facilities can be effectively used within computer communications systems.

Communications Media and Bandwidth

Communications involves the transmission of information across some form of electrical conducting medium. Communications media include telephone wires, other types of wire, coax cables (similar to those often used for TV antennas), and fiber optic cables. Some communications are even transmitted using the air as a conductor (e.g., cellular phones), but this consumes bandwidth or spectrum frequency in the region where the information is being broadcast. *Bandwidth* refers to the amount of capacity used in a transmission medium. If transmission of information is very efficient, a lot of data or voice traffic can be sent in a limited amount of bandwidth. Some forms of communications are more efficient than others, so the amount of bandwidth used for a specific quantity of voice or data traffic is not constant across all media or technologies.

Air and space (e.g., satellites) are good media for transmitting a lot of data to many customers at the same time, as wires are not required to connect to each recipient. However, since there is a finite amount of bandwidth available in the air within a specific area, there must be some form of management of this bandwidth to prevent overcrowding of the *frequency spectrum*, the range of bandwidths available to allocate to different users for communications applications. This spectrum allocation is almost always performed by a government or regulatory agency, and generally involves issuing licenses allowing companies to use portions of the frequency spectrum for specific applications. Thus only a few cellular phone licenses can be provided since the amount of bandwidth available to allocate to these applications is limited. In addition, companies must efficiently utilize the bandwidth received or they may find that they are unable to provide the quality of service desired as the number of users on that fixed bandwidth increases.

An unlimited number of users can access a broadcast form of communications, such as television or radio, but a point-to-point service consumes more bandwidth as the number of users of the service or the amount of information transmitted increases. Thus, air and space are generally effective communications media only for use in wideband[2] broadcast services (e.g., television or radio) or for very narrowband services (e.g., cellular phones used for voice or limited data traffic). Although new communications technology is continually enabling more efficient use of fixed bandwidth resources, the amount of data transmitted in computer applications is generally too large to permit usage of air for transmission except in limited applications. However, tightly focused microwave system transmissions are often allowed for both voice and data communications, because these systems are designed to avoid congestion of the airwaves except in the direction in which they are pointed. Satellite systems are a type of microwave system that is pointed to a receiver in space and can also be useful as part of data communications networks. Even so, most communications networking of computer systems is designed to utilize high-bandwidth-cable-based media.

The most common forms of computer network connections within businesses are coax cable and twisted-pair wires[3] (similar to telephone wires). Coax cables provide very high bandwidth and have been the preferred connection for computer networks for many years. However, they are harder to install and modify than twisted wires. Thus many companies have begun to adopt twisted wires as the media for their communications networks. Twisted wires can also transmit and receive highbandwidth information, but only over relatively short distances (a few hundred meters or less) unless special electronic repeaters (similar to amplifiers) are installed.

Communications bandwidth in computer communications often refers to the maximum amount of information that can be transmitted over a particular medium or communications system. This bandwidth is generally measured in terms of bits per second (bps), or in other words, the maximum number of computer bits (*0 or 1* signals) that can be transmitted in a single second. Typical computer networks within the office use media that allow 10 million bits per second (10 Mbps) or greater bandwidth. Typical international linkages between computers use media that allow transmission rates between 2 and 64 thousand bits per second (2–64 kbps).

Telecommunications for Voice and Modems

Voice communications services are designed to transmit human speech and generally have relatively limited bandwidth capacity. Standard voice services provided by most telecommunications firms are limited to about 3000 to 7000 hertz of bandwidth. Hertz is a measure of analog bandwidth, whereas bps is a measure of digital bandwidth. Although translation between the two measures of bandwidth is not exact as it depends on the technology and some other key assumptions about type of usage for each, voice traffic is generally transmitted without compression over digital media at 64 kbps, and data traffic over analog voice lines generally can be transmitted (without compression) at speeds of up to 10 kbps (and sometimes even up to 20 kbps with extremely high-quality connections). Analog transmission refers to voice type service, where the information has both volume and pitch (frequency) and is continuously variable (e.g., not digital). Digital transmission uses only discrete transmission signals, generally limited simply to transmitting many bits of *0* or *1* information very quickly. Analog transmission sends a wide range of information rather slowly. Digital transmission sends lots of small bits of data very quickly.

There is some loss of efficiency in transmitting digital information over analog phone lines or analog information over digital transmission lines and equipment. Even so, most voice traffic is now converted to digital signals at some point in the telephone network, because high-capacity digital communication media cost much less than analog transmission media of similar capacity. Unfortunately, most telecommunications services still use analog consumer interfaces that require digital information transmitted over the voice network to be converted into analog signals and then reconverted to digital upon receipt at the final location. During transmission, these analog signals containing digital information may then themselves be converted to digital signals, but each conversion process results in inefficiencies in the usage of the available bandwidth. One type of telephone service developed in the 1980s, ISDN (integrated services digital network), allows both voice and data to use the phone network with maximum efficiency.

When the volume of data communications to a single location is not large enough to justify the fixed monthly cost of a leased line (generally priced at the equivalent of between 20 and 100 hours per month of voice telephone traffic), then standard voice lines must generally be used for transmission of digital information. To use this analog voice network, digital information must be converted to sounds using a modem. Since few people can justify the connection of a leased line into their home, most residential users of networks use the standard voice telephone network to connect to computer networks. Most businesses use the voice network only for connections where the total traffic between two locations is not sufficient to justify a leased-line connection.

Modems take digital information and convert it into sound for transmission over the voice telephone network. This process is similar to what a CD-ROM player does with music that is digitally recorded on the CD but transmitted in analog format to your stereo amplifier so that your ears can hear and enjoy the information that was stored digitally. Modems also convert these sounds that have been encoded by another modem back into digital information so that the receiving computer can use the data. (Computers can't process sounds directly, so this reconversion to digital is essential.) Sometimes computers using modem communications have problems at high speeds because of noise on the voice telephone line. Humans are quite good at filtering out noise when we listen to speech over a phone line, but this noise can result in errors in reconverting information transmitted as sound to another computer via a modem. Digital transmission media are much more resistant to noise interference than are those for analog communication, so modems may operate at speeds much lower than the theoretical ideal speed for data transmission to reduce errors resulting from noise.

Transmitting and receiving modems must also use the same standards for converting data to and from analog or the information they exchange will not be interpreted correctly. For example, most modems for personal computers use a Hayes-compatible standard for modem commands and communications to avoid problems with both software interfaces and communications protocols. In addition to converting information to analog sounds, most modems used today also use digital data compression to reduce the bandwidth required for transmitting data. Data compression involves recoding the data to remove repetitive patterns and using a complex translation that allows information to be transmitted (or stored) using fewer bits. Data compression can dramatically reduce (often by a factor of five or more) the size of data actually transmitted. This allows modem manufacturers to claim transmission speeds over a single phone line of 33 kpbs or even 56 kbps, even though the actual speed of transmission over the telephone line of digital bits is only one-third of these speeds. For the computer user, the transmitting modem appears to send and receive information at the stated (compressed) speeds as long as the receiving computer modem is equipped with the same data compression software.

ISDN and Packet-Switched Services

Key technologies are rapidly improving switching speed (the speed at which data can be transmitted by the network switching equipment) on existing infrastructure, especially copper lines installed over the past century. One hundred years of voice telephone network development have left a legacy of broad penetration into nearly every household that affects current capabilities significantly. It might be cost effective to install high-bandwidth alternatives such as optical fiber cabling in place of copper, but the time and legal expense required to procure rights of way into these households is often prohibitive. So in the near term, a very large part of any consumer-oriented communications network needs to run on copper.

Telephone companies offer several types of copper-based digital data transmission alternatives, including packet-switched services, several varieties of ADSL, and ISDN (the first commercially available version of ADSL services). ISDN provides two voice channels or a 128 kbps data channel, whereas ADSL is predominantly a data pipe providing an asymmetrical bandwidth of up to 10 Mbps downstream (from switch to customer) and 800 kbps upstream. However, an ADSL access network is an overlay network and therefore does not require the expensive and time-consuming switch upgrades (which are expensive and difficult investments for telephone companies to justify economically) that slowed the adoption of ISDN.

These services offer the customer digital transmission over the telephone network, although access to the packet-switched services is often available only via either a leased-line connection or a modem connection over a standard voice line. However, the leased-line connection for a packet-switched network service may be much more affordable for connecting a number of locations than leased-line connections between each of the individual locations, because a single line from each building to the network can connect all locations in an integrated digital network. Thus, a packet-switched network can be much less expensive than leasing facilities between each location to carry traffic.

Packet switching refers to a process of dividing a message into many small messages referred to as packets. Each packet is transmitted independently over the network through intermediary computer nodes until it reaches its final destination. Within each packet is information on the destination computer, source computer, and sequence of this packet in the order of the total message. The packets sent over the network are reassembled in order at the receiving computer after all packets have been received.

Packet switching is efficient for data transmission because small packets can be more densely packed on the network than large messages. In addition, individual packets can take alternative routes to reach the final destination if one path is overly congested. Thus, packet switching is commonly used in computer networks to increase effective capacity of the network and reduce traffic congestion.

Public packet-switched services are a type of low-cost data network service local telephone companies or other service providers offer to take advantage of the increased efficiency of packet switching and provide a lower-cost alternative to using standard telephone lines for data transmission. For high volumes of data transmission, leased lines may still be less expensive than these public packet-switched services, but for locations with moderate to low volumes, these packet-switched networks can provide a very cost-effective solution.

With the ISDN service, all information is transmitted over the telephone network digitally with no conversion to analog occurring anywhere in the network. Voice calls are converted to digital format within special ISDN telephones. (Standard phones cannot be used with ISDN service unless a converter similar to a modem is attached to the phone to convert voice to data.) For voice phone calls, ISDN provides a higher quality connection than is possible using standard telephone service. With compression, ISDN lines can be used for video conference calls, though the transmissions suffer from rough quality. ISDN provides a high-speed and relatively low-cost means of transmitting data over the telephone network.

The developers of the ISDN standard envisioned that this single service would be able to integrate all voice and data services into a single connection from the telephone company into the home or office. ISDN has proven to be a popular service among high-bandwidth users of network services, such as heavy users of the Internet from home or small office locations. The transmission speed of ISDN is insufficiently fast, however, for multimedia-intensive tasks, such as video on demand and video conferencing.

Higher bandwidths, up to around 10 Mbps in 1998, are being sent across copper cable through asymmetric digital subscriber line (ADSL) services. The name was coined by Bellcore in 1989 and refers to the two-way capability of a twisted copper pair with analog-to-digital conversion at the subscriber end and an advanced transmission technology. ADSL uses the frequency spectrum between 0 khz and 4 khz for voice and between 4 khz and 2.2 mhz for data over a twisted-pair copper line, usually a telephone line. This line then provides asymmetric transmission of data, up to 10 mbps downstream (to the customer) and up to 800 kbps upstream, depending upon line length and line and loop conditions.

A rough idea of the advantages of each technology can be identified by considering the minimum time required to download a three-and-one-half minute video clip: Over a 28.8 kbps modem this takes 50 minutes; over a 128 kbps ISDN line, 10 minutes; over a 10 Mbps ADSL line, 10 seconds. ADSL services should be widely available in the near future because they can be implemented over existing twisted pair copper networks, with the capacity to deliver the communications speeds required of advanced Internet-based electronic commerce.

ADSL allows telephone companies to invest in hardware terminals at the ends of a short length of copper wire to multiply the wire's data transmission capacity by more than 1,000 times. Individual homes could therefore have a moderately low-cost means of receiving fast images and data from the Internet and Web a reasonable cost. ADSL equipment is still expensive in 1998, but is expected to cost less than a typical home computer by the end of the century, which will dramatically increase the potential bandwidth that can be used for electronic commerce applications. New capabilities will emerge that will take advantage of this higher bandwidth to the consumer, and the power of electronic commerce will increase as an attractive alternative to traditional retail channels.

Synchronous and Asynchronous Transmission

Transmission of digital or analog information can be either *synchronous* (at the same time) or *asynchronous* (not at the same time). Most voice traffic is synchronous (for two parties to talk to one another, they must be linked simultaneously), but voice mail is asynchronous voice communications (the sender and receiver are not required to be in communications at exactly the same time).

Synchronous data transmission is ideal for applications that require a lot of data to be transmitted at one time. Data can be transmitted very quickly using synchronous transmission, with a fixed number of characters grouped together for transmission as a single block of data without any breaks between characters. Synchronous communications require special characters or flags to be inserted at regular intervals into the data transmitted at regular intervals to ensure that both systems are using the same timing. Special data characters are also inserted in front of blocks of data to signal the receiving computer that a new block of data is being sent. The data plus the header information is called a frame, but the exact format of the frame varies among the different communications standards in common usage today. With synchronous data transmission, terminals generally require storage or buffer areas, because the terminal may not always be able to process or display the information as quickly as it is received.

Asynchronous data communications is simple and cheap, but requires an overhead of two to three bits per character. Each character requires a start bit (and a stop bit) to signal the receiving computer that a character is being sent. A parity bit is often sent as well to enable the receiving computer to determine if there was an error in transmission or receipt of data (If there is an error, the sum of bits is not correct as parity bit is used to make sum even or odd for all characters transmitted.) Most personal computer modems use asynchronous transmission, but this form of communications requires 20% or more overhead burden relative to synchronous transmission when large blocks of data are being transmitted frequently. Asynchronous communications is more efficient when the amount of data in each transmission is small.

Declining Costs of Digital Communications

Digital communications costs are declining much faster than those of voice communications as new technologies and standards are enabling faster data transmission with lower bandwidth and as the costs of the bandwidth itself decline. Since the mid-1970s, the cost of data communications the United States has declined even faster than that of computing, providing companies with significant incentives to take advantage of these lower costs in redesigning computer systems. In addition to these declines in costs, the reliability and quality of digital communications media available have improved. The same dramatic improvements in electronic and optical technologies are powering the computer and digital communications revolutions and are bringing similar new and affordable capabilities into the business world.

Affordable data communications are driving new network architectures and new forms of distance-interdependent organizational design. For example, companies are able to integrate teams in different locations into flexible and temporary virtual departments to work on specific problems. Hospitals are able to share data with doctors in other parts of the country or even the world. Video conferencing has become an affordable reality for many firms, enabling experts to increase their leverage across the firm while simultaneously reducing travel expenses and burdens. Telecommuting is being introduced in many firms to allow employees to work from home in the evenings or weekends, and in some cases, to shift the workplace entirely from office to home.

The rapid decline in the costs of both computing and communications technologies implies that computers and computer networks are becoming more cost-effective and powerful tools in businesses every year. Over the past 20 years, information technology costs have declined by a factor of 10 or more for large systems and by more than a factor of 100 for smaller systems. Thus applications that were only silly dreams 10 or 20 years ago are now common reality. The difference in cost performance between the systems of 20 years ago and the systems available today for the same task is greater than the difference in labor costs between the United States and China. Thus even within China and other countries where labor costs are low, information technology is becoming an important and necessary tool both to reduce costs and to improve quality of production. In addition, information technologies are able to perform many tasks today that are not possible using human labor, especially when these tasks involve storage and dissemination of structured information at a national or global level.

The Rise of Computer Networks

Dramatically lower costs of microcomputer networks relative to the larger minicomputer and mainframe systems has resulted in a shift toward networks of smaller systems to perform tasks formerly possible only with large, centralized information systems. This has shifted the control of information technology away from the central

MIS group in many companies and into the firm's operating departments. Thus even general managers who have no real interest in information technology as a field of study may find that information technology expenses are consuming an increasing portion of their budget. In addition, information technology is becoming more strategic and vital to firms at the same time as these technological capabilities, infrastructure, and expenses are becoming increasingly difficult to manage and control.

A computer network can be viewed as the result of any linkage between two or more computer systems. Temporary connections (such as dialing up another computer via modem for a brief connection) are generally not considered to be sufficient to call this linkage a network, although the connection is often made by a PC calling into a network of computers or by one network calling another. Thus, a *network* generally is defined as two or more computers linked together with communications hardware and software on a permanent or semipermanent basis. Networks can be used for sharing resources, such as printers and data storage (memory), sharing programs and other software capabilities (often with site licenses), sharing data files across different individuals or departments on a common system, enabling specialized processing and centralized data to be available for many users, providing access to specific information internally or outside the organization, integrating or coordinating information and processes across business units, coordination or management of scarce non-IT resources (e.g., airline reservations), connecting with customer or suppliers to manage channel operations jointly, and many other useful applications within and outside the firm.

Many networks in use today are designed around the Ethernet network model. *Ethernet* is a broadcast bus-type network (meaning lots of connections onto a shared transmission cable or bus) initially designed to provide a suitable communications systems for building distributed computer systems. To reduce the number of collisions on this bus-type network, Ethernet networks use a special type of communications software to detect multiple accesses of the network. This collision avoidance and detection system is known as CSMA/CD (which stands for collision sense multiple access with collision detection). Although this does help manage the problem of collisions with large networks, Ethernet networks can still become congested when usage levels are high. Bus-type networks can quickly go from acceptable performance to almost complete failure due to excessive congestion when usage increases gradually over time (and gradually increasing usage is common on networks). In other words, Ethernet systems do not fail gracefully; little time elapses between the onset of problems and serious network congestion. On the other hand, as long as usage levels are within the acceptable range for the network design, Ethernet communications provides an inexpensive and relatively fast-response network connection for use with distributed computing networks.

The Internet is itself a network of networks, using a standard protocol known as TCP/IP. The development of common standards is very important for networking computer systems, as without common standards it is not possible to share information among different systems or across different but connected networks. Thus, the Internet is less a physical entity than a set of standards that different firms agree to follow for connecting their physical telecommunications capacity to enable global sharing of information across these interconnected networks. Similarly, the Web is also simply a set of standards for sharing information between separate computer systems and physical transmission networks.

As communications technologies continue to advance in providing faster speeds and lower costs for transmitting large amounts of data, new standards that take advantage of these capabilities are likely to emerge over time. These standards may be absorbed into the Internet and Web standards, or may emerge as a competing standard. The most powerful challenge to the Internet standards may come from telecommunications firms as they eventually deploy switched broadband video networks to individual homes using a combination of fiber, coax, and ADSL over copper wire technologies. In the short to medium term, the technology most likely to be rapidly integrated into Web will be the ADSL protocol for transmitting high bandwidth data over traditional copper wires into the home.

Telecommunication and computing technology is advancing to enable a wide range of new high-bandwidth services to be delivered to the home. Today, businesses can easily afford the bandwidth and systems required to change processes to use the new media and computing power to change the way they are managing their businesses and relationships with customers and suppliers. However, for the consumer, the Internet and Web have only begun to tap into the potential for delivering large amounts of information into the home. Though it is impossible to predict accurately when consumers will be ready to adopt and pay for these high-bandwidth communications capabilities to expand information delivery into the home, few industry experts or students of history in our modern times doubt that the home of the future will have much greater information processing and communications capabilities and technologies than we have available today. The standards and technologies used to connect residential consumers in the future could differ greatly from the Web as we know it today. However, the increased capabilities and lower costs of networked communications and computing in the future are certain to make electronic commerce increasingly attractive in the future.

The World Wide Web

E-commerce got its boost from the technologies of the World Wide Web. Originally a system for communicating the equations, charts, and discoveries of high energy physics, the Web was pushed into the mainstream of computing in 1993 by Mosaic, a software package designed by a resourceful physicist at the National Center for Supercomputing Applications, Marc Andreessen (later the founder of Netscape). Mosaic was a Web browser, that is, a computer program that allows its user to "browse" around a network in search of nuggets of information. Mosaic combined physicist Tim Berners Lee's 1980 idea of a World Wide Web with the underlying hypertext organization of the Web. As an organizing concept for information, hypertext had been around since the 1940s, predating modern data-centered computing. In the 1960s and 1970s, an eccentric dyslexic named Ted Nelson publicized hypertext through his Xanadu project. The Web, following in the footsteps of the highly successful Gopher system for text-based retrieval of Internet information, brought hypertext to the Internet.

Mosaic benefited from being introduced during the early period of rapid growth following Internet commercialization. Not only did Mosaic benefit from the commercialization of the Internet, but its graphical user interface helped facilitate the rapid growth in commercial use of the Web and marked the birth of electronic commerce as we know it today. Although electronic commerce had existed on the Internet in limited forms prior to the introduction of the Web protocols (e.g., as USENET posted messages and e-mail-based transactions), the use of the Internet for commercial purposes was insignificant prior to the introduction of Mosaic.

Conceived originally as a military communications system,[4] the Internet relied on fail-safe packet switching, which allowed message encryption, tracking, and efficient use of networks of widely varying speed and reliability. The Web, built on the battle-tested infrastructure of the Internet, proved an almost instant success. In May 1993, when Mosaic was released, there were approximately 50 Web sites worldwide; there were in excess of 50 million sites at the beginning of 1998.

The attractiveness of the Internet system for the military is obvious: There is no central command and control point, allowing any surviving points to reestablish contact in the event of an attack on any one point. These same features make the Internet *scalable*; that is, growth and congestion in one part of the network have minimal impact on other parts of the network. This feature has become far more important than the original military fail-safe objectives of a redundant network of networks.

The World Wide Web used the Internet infrastructure and software standards to provide computer users with easy display and navigation with interactive multimedia content based on a global hypertext system for linking any multimedia resource: pictures, video, sound, downloadable files, and so forth. Linked documents can refer to other linked documents, which in turn can refer to other linked documents, indefinitely in a "web" of links. Several concepts and terms are key to understanding the Web:

1. *URLs* (Unified Resource Locators) are just documents in hypertext.

2. The Web's retrieval mechanism is called *HTTP* (Hypertext Transfer Protocol)—thus the *http://* preceding a Web address. A *communications technology protocol* is a set of guidelines for the way in which programs at either end of a communications link can talk with each other.

3. The logical structure of a hypertext document is described in a language called *HTML* (Hypertext Markup Language). The *markup language* part of this term refers to the language in which Web pages are programmed. HTML is, unfortunately, a user-hostile throwback to the era of early word processors, when edit marks were explicitly depicted in arcane codes, and native HTML is in the process of being phased out.

The mechanisms, protocols, procedures, hyper-linkages and so forth of the Web have expanded telecommunications networks into a much richer form than any in which they have ever existed in the past. We now think of the network not just as a way to get information from one place to another, but as a structure that adds value by distilling and associating information with a worldwide repository of knowledge along the way. We address value-added Internet processes and access to the Internet's global knowledge repository in the next chapter.

Notes

1. G. Gilder, *Microcosm: The Quantum Revolution in Economics and Technology* (New York: Simon and Schuster, 1989).

2. Wideband services can transfer a great deal of information, whereas narrowband services have less capacity. Television is a wideband service, partly because of some inefficiencies in the standard modes of transmission used and partly because of the large amount of information transmitted in a video signal. Radio transmissions are moderately information intensive, but are still generally considered wideband relative to the current utilization of bandwidth of cellular services today. Cellular systems are designed to use very little bandwidth for each voice transmission to allow the cellular service provider to use a fixed amount of bandwidth for many service subscribers.

3. Wires used for high-bandwidth data transmission are always twisted to prevent them from acting as an antenna and receiving interference from broadcast transmissions in the air. A long, untwisted wire makes a

very good antenna and would act as both a receiver of and broadcaster of information for the general public, neither of which is particularly desirable for a computer communications media. Twisting the wires can eliminate this undesirable antenna characteristic of long wires.

4. Internet development followed in the footsteps of several successful packet switching networks operated by IBM, Federal Express, GE, and Tymeshare in the 1960s that allowed remote dial-in access to computers. The first Internet (called then the ARPANET Information Message Processor) was installed at the University of California at Los Angeles on September 1, 1969, on a Honeywell 516 with 12 K of memory (considered a powerful minicomputer at that time). Additional nodes were soon added at Stanford Research Institute, the University of California at Santa Barbara, and the University of Utah. Almost immediately, this technology was transferred to the U.S. Defense Department's Advanced Research Projects Agency.

China's Golden Projects: Reengineering the National Economy

Developing the information industry, establishing a national economic information network and promoting information services for the economy and society are badly needed for China's modernization drive.... Promoting information services and integrating them with industrialization will greatly enhance the quality of China's national economy and will help change the economy from an extensive one to an efficient one.
—Hu Qili, Electronics Minister, June 17, 1994

Comprising 31 provincial-style entities (including Taiwan) and 517 cities, China is one of the world's largest countries; although its land mass is only slightly larger than that of the United States, its population is more than four times greater. As the country has begun to "open up" to the outside world, its economy has been growing quickly. According to International Monetary Fund data, China's domestic economy in 1995 was more than four times larger than it was in 1978, becoming roughly 50% the size of the U.S. economy. In other words, the country had met Premier Deng Xiaoping's stated economic reform objectives: to double, then redouble the size of the domestic economy in little more than 15 years.

Politically, the economic reforms introduced in China have been explained and rationalized as market socialism. By this is meant an economy in which a basically socialistic system (i.e., state planning and public ownership) is retained, but market system elements are incorporated so as to improve economic performance and increase social welfare. However, a decade and a half of piecemeal efforts have created a morass of half-reformed enterprises and multilayered government authority, which the government appears to believe can be rectified by information systems. In particular, "informatization" has been put forward as a substitute for legal and institutional reforms. While privatization, price rationalization, and other more difficult structural reforms have been stalled or shelved, informatization is promoted as the tool for macroeconomic control.

Reform and Growth in China

Before economic reform began in 1978, China pursued a policy of self-reliance. Its economy was one of the world's most isolated and represented a tiny share of world trade. Domestic industry was protected from foreign competition by direct controls on imports and investment. Foreign trade and currency exchange were under the monopolistic control of a central government ministry, which used an overvalued

This case was prepared by Peter Lovelock and Ben A. Petrazzini under the supervision of Dr. Theodore H. Clark and Professor John J. Sviokla.
© 1996 by the President and Fellows of Harvard College.
Harvard Business School case N9-396-283.

currency to support the import-substitution policies of the central plan. Only the central foreign trade ministry and its 12 trade corporations were permitted to engage in international trading activities.

In December 1978, the Central Committee of the Communist Party accepted Deng Xiaoping's proposals for reforming China's economic structure. The objectives of the reform were to improve economic performance and raise people's living standards. Among Deng's policies were two key reforms. One freed farmers from the constraints of the commune system by allowing them to farm on a family basis. The other was the initiation of the "Open-Door Policy," which aimed to attract foreign investment and trade and to begin to modernize China's economic industrial structure through the importation of Western science and technology.

Six months later, the first special economic zones (SEZs) were created and a joint-venture law implemented. The SEZs were to attract foreign investment by offering concessionary terms and an attractive business climate. Four trial zones were established: three in the southern Chinese province of Guangdong (Shenzhen, Zhuhai, and Shantou) and one in neighboring Fujian province (Xiamen). Other zones gradually were established to broaden support for the reform drive. Economic policies in these SEZ cities were substantially more flexible. According to Deng, the SEZs were to act as windows to the world for technology, management, knowledge and foreign policy, to better serve China's modernization programs.

As a result, foreign direct investment (FDI) played an important role in China's contemporary economic development. Since the reform, China's exports increased at an average of 16% and imports at more than 15% a year. In Shenzhen, the industrial output value in 1985 was about US$800 million, an increase of 53.5% over 1984, or up by 40 times on the pre-SEZ, 1979 figure. By 1994, Shenzhen's industrial output was up to US$12.2 billion. Annual growth rates for China's total trade were more than three times the world rates between 1978 and 1990. Real GNP grew by an average of almost 9% a year.

By 1988, however, inflation was running at 24%. The government had no effective macroeconomic means for controlling an overheated economy, and the years between 1987 and 1993 became a rollercoaster ride of boom and bust cycles. Moreover, the economic reforms were seen to have affected the political process in several potentially destabilizing ways. First, economic diversification increased the number of social and institutional interests in society, thereby making the political process more complex and difficult to manage. Second, the decentralization of economic power threatened to reduce the authority of existing political institutions. This in turn demonstrated the increasing tension between emerging new political processes and the old political institutions.

It was within this environment that China's leadership began to see the possibilities in applying information technology to bring the economy under some kind of systematic central control. The initiation of Deng's economic reform and open-door policies had also created the environment for the rapid expansion of China's telecommunications capacity. As early as 1980 network expansion was considered necessary for promoting a more vigorous domestic economy. By 1985 telecommunications investment exceeded 1% of GNP for the first time. Although China still trailed many other nations in this regard, investment levels continued to rise and, progressively, infrastructure deployment began to be funded from a diversity of new sources such as private companies and individuals.

Telecommunications Infrastructure in China

China's telecommunications network consisted of public and private networks. "Public" and "private" conveyed different meanings in China, however. Public and private networks alike were owned by neither the State nor the public. Rather, the public networks were those run by the Ministry of Posts and Telecommunications, while private networks were simply those *not* operated under the MPT. Further, the Chinese divided telecoms networks into three somewhat distinct systems: telephone, data/computer (or value-added), and cable networks—representing the telecom, electronics/computer, and cable TV industries respectively. This division resulted from a distinct vertical and hierarchical administrative system.

From the founding of the People's Republic of China (PRC) in 1949 to the initiation of reform in 1978, telecommunications was used primarily for connection between the central government and its local branches, to strengthen central government control over local authorities. By 1980, China lagged well behind international standards. Public telephone service was almost nonexistent. Practically no telephone service was provided to households except for high-ranking government officials. In a country with approximately 250 million households, only about 1,000 urban households had their own telephone. Many small towns had no phone service at all.

Through the reform era, however, China's senior leaders, including Premier Deng Xiaoping and President Jiang Zemin, repeatedly pointed to the role of information sciences and technology in modernization. As aspects of the domestic economy, particularly along China's coastal regions, became progressively integrated into the international trading economy, the emphasis on IT increased (see table 5.1).

Foreigners in China attempting business were consistently frustrated by the difficulty of making a telephone call. In the early 1980s, more than one-third of all calls never got through because the ancient telephone exchanges were overloaded. Yet

Table 5.1
Telecommunications infrastructure statistics

	Unit	1980	1985	1990	1995
Switch capacity	(million lines)	4.43	6.14	12.32	58.00
Toll circuits	(thousand circuits)	22	38	112	1,050
Main lines	(million lines)	2.14	3.12	6.87	37.00
Phone density	(percentage of population)	0.22	0.3	0.6	3.02
Mobile phones	(thousands of phones)	0	0	18	3,200

international connections were often far easier to get than domestic ones. The situation did not really begin to improve until well into the early 1990s. By 1993, with reliability in the network as a target for improvement, provincial capitals and large cities were registering call success rates in excess of 70%—including peak hours. In 1987, AT&T customers placing calls to Shanghai had to dial an average of five times to complete one call. By 1995, most callers were reported to be getting through on the first try.

Even so, networking in China was still quite limited in the mid-1990s. Computer penetration was less than 1 per every 400 people, and telephone penetration was still only 3 per 100 residents. Most businesses in the major cities did have telephones by 1995, but outside the largest cities even basic telecommunications facilities were generally unavailable. By 1995, more than 500,000 of the 800,000 villages in China still did not have access to a single telephone. In the banking industry, inter-provincial networking had just begun in 1995. Even then, checks written on a branch of the same bank often could not be deposited in a different province for that same bank, as there was no arrangement established for inter-provincial clearing of checks for most banks across China. Business travelers frequently carried large sums of cash to complete business transactions and to pay for hotel and food expenses, as credit cards were uncommon; even if available, they were only accepted for payment if the card had been issued on a local provincial bank.

The Political Economy of China's Telecommunications

Since the late 1980s, the Ministry of Electronics Industry (MEI) had been trying to break the communications monopoly held by the MPT, unsuccessfully arguing in favor of competition. If the 30 or so private telecom networks around the country could be grouped together, asserted MEI, they could provide a second public network, at once increasing China's telecommunications facilities and creating a competitor to the conservative MPT. This argument was consistently defeated on the basis of the State's universal service obligation: competition would result in remote areas not receiving telecommunications service. In the highly demarcated world of Chinese administration, MEI was told to stay on its side of the technological divide.

However, by the early 1990s MEI had changed tack: data communications—information—was the new crucial ingredient to being internationally competitive, and the data communication demands, both for international and domestic business, were going to grow exponentially as China reintegrated into the international economic community. With the public telephone network already painfully overloaded, waiting lists for a household telephone exceeding 12 million, and the MPT already committed to ambitious growth targets, it was suggested that a second network was required to facilitate the growth of data communications. Thus, in 1993, Hu Qili, Minister for the Electronics Industry, went before the State Council to sell them the idea of the "Three Golden" projects—China's version of the information superhighway. Crucially, he did so on the basis of data communications, not competition or liberalization. Moreover, while telephones involved a demarcation dispute with the MPT, computers were traditionally the preserve of MEI.

In late 1994, the State Council formally approved the creation of two new telecom entities. One of the entrants, Ji Tong Communications Co., was a corporate arm of MEI. Licensed in 1994, Ji Tong was seen as the "builder" or integrator of the new network. The other, China United Telecommunications (known also as Unicom, or Liantong in Chinese), was set up in July 1994 with the intention of offering long-distance data communications to compete with the MPT. The distinction between voice and date was not articulated.

Unicom began operation in July 1995 with four mobile GSM in Beijing, Shanghai, Guangzhou, and Tianjin. Unicom's initial ambition was to link some of the 30 or so national private communications networks and 3,000 local private networks into a domestic competitor to the MPT. Combined, the private networks could have provided transmission lines two to three times longer than the MPT's with greater data transmission capacity, but with only about 3.5 million telephone lines in total—approximately 10% of the MPT's public switched telephone network (PSTN) in 1994. The basis of this operation was Unicom's shareholders, which include MEI, the Ministry of Railways, the Ministry of Electric Power, and several large state companies (see table 5.2). In 1995 Unicom's stated plans were to be carrying 10% of China's long-distance calls and 30% of mobile calls by the year 2000.

In selling the Golden Projects to the State Council, Minister Hu provided a further incentive: the fact that computer information systems tended to be centralized, allowing for greater administrative control. Thus, Zhu Rongji's call for a national public economic information network later became the Golden Bridge Project; Chairman Jiang Zemin's call to facilitate a genuine Central Bank in China became

Table 5.2
Ownership of the new telecommunications providers

List of LianTong's shareholders	List of JiTong's shareholders
Ministry of Electronics Industry (MEI)	China Electronic Leasing Co., Ltd.
Ministry of Electric Power (MEP)	Beijing Economic Development & Investment Co.
Ministry of Railways (MOR)	Shenzhen Guoye Trade Co., Ltd.
China International Trust and Investment Corporation (CITIC)	Dongguan Tongpai Telecommunication Industry Co.
China Everbright International Trust and Investment Corporation (Everbright)	Nanjing Radio Factory
China Resources Group Co., Ltd.	Tianjin Optical and Electronic Communications Co.
China Huaneng Group Co.	China Electronic Appliance Corp.
China Merchants Holding Co., Ltd.	Beijing Wire Communications Factory
China National Chemicals Import and Export Corporation	Guangzhou United Communications Corp.
China National Technology Import and Export Corporation	China National Electronic Import and Export Corp.
China Trust and Investment Corporation for Foreign Economic Relations	China National Electronic Device Industry Corp.
Beijing CATCH Communications Group Co. (on behalf of Beijing municipal government)	China Zhenhua Electronic Industry Corp.
Shanghai Science and Technology Investment Co., Ltd.	Zhuhai Dongda Stockholding Group, Ltd.
Guangzhou South China Telecommunications Investment Corporation	Changzhou Electronics Development Corp.
China (Fujian) Foreign Trade Center Group	Shenzhen Sangda Communications United Corp.
Dalian Vastone Telecommunications and Cables Co., Ltd.	Beijing Kangxun Electronics Corp.
	The 54th Research Institute of the MEI
	China International Trust and Investment Corp.
	Tianjin Communications & Broadcast Corp.
	The 7th Research Institute of the MEI
	The 34th Research Institute of the MEI
	The 1st Research Institute of the MEI
	Wuhan Zhongyuan Radio Factory
	China Electronic System Engineering Corp.
	China Tong Guang Electronics Corp.

Table 5.3
Golden Projects "milestones"

March 1993	Initiative to build a national public economic information network by Zhu Rongji launched. Afterward named the "Golden Bridge Project."
June 1993	Chairman Jiang Zemin calls for speeding up project of electronic credit card in major cities, referred to as the "Golden Card Project."
June 1993	Vice Premier Li Lanqing's initiative to set up a foreign trade information network for improving import-export trade management referred to as the "Golden Gate Project."
December 1993	High-level leading committee under the State Council formed, under the title of the "Joint Committee of National Economic Informatization," responsible for promoting and coordinating Golden Projects activities.

the Golden Card Project; and Vice Premier Li Lanqing's initiative to link the Ministry of Foreign Trade and the Ministry of Custom's import/export trade management system, so as to reduce smuggling and regain some administrative control over the coastal ports, became the Golden Customs Project (see table 5.3).

Responding to the threat of foreign competition, the MPT rapidly began to upgrade its services. In October 1994, it launched a high-quality, dedicated-line communications service, ChinaDDN, for transmitting digital data at high speeds. It also upgraded its existing packetswitched data network, Chinapac. Thus, by 1995, with Ji Tong and Unicom together committed to building the Golden Bridge, China was suddenly constructing three national information backbones.

The Golden Projects

China's Golden Projects represented an ambitious telecommunications and information infrastructure initiative aimed at developing an information economy and building an administrative infrastructure. Since the initial Three Goldens were proposed by Minister Hu, a series of other Golden projects were proposed for development (see table 5.4). Once built, they would provide value-added voice, data, and video communications as well as the delivery mechanism for a range of other information services—from cable television to home banking to trade facilitation (see table 5.5).

In Chinese, "golden" (jin) gives the expectation of expensive, important, and valuable. The Golden projects were thus perceived as a significant strategic initiative. When proposed, the agenda, or objective, of the projects was threefold:

1. To build a national information highway as a path to national modernization and economic development. To the Government this was attractive because it provided the fundamental link between information and economic development.

Table 5.4
Summary list of the Golden Projects

	Name	Full title	Major ministries, departments and enterprises
Tier One	Golden Bridge (*Jin Qiao*)	National Public Economic Information Communication Net.	Ministry, of Electronics, State Information Center, Ji Tong Co.
	Golden Customs (*Jin Guan*)	National Foreign Economic Trade Information Network Project	Ministry of Foreign Trade, Customs Department, Ji Tong Co.
	Golden Card (*Jin Ka*)	Electronic Money Project	PBoC, Ministry of Electronics, Ministry of Internal Trade, Great Wall Computer Co.
	Golden Sea (*Jin Hai*)		State Statistical Bureau, PBoC, State Information Center.
Tier Two	Golden Macro (*Jin Hong*)	National Economic Macro-Policy Technology System	China Exlm Bank, Ministry of Finance, State Information Center
	Golden Tax (*Jin Shui*)	Computerized Tax Return & Invoice System Project	Ministry of Finance, Ministry of Electronics, National Taxation Bureau, Great Wall Computer Co.
	Golden Intelligence (*Jin Zhi*)	China Education & Research Network (CERnet) (and talented personnel network)	State Education Commission
Tier Three	Golden Enterprise (*Jin Qi*)	Industrial Production and Information Distribution System	State Economic and Trade Commission
	Golden Agriculture (*Jin Nong*)	Overall Agricultural Admin. & Information Service System	Ministry of Agriculture
	Golden Health (*Jin Wei*)	National Health Information Network	Ministry of Health
	Golden Info. (*Jin Xin*)	State Statistical Information Project	State Statistical Bureau
	Golden Housing (*Jin Jia*)		
Tier Four	Golden Cellular (*Jin Feng*)	Mobile Communications Production & Marketing Project	Ministry of Electronics Industry
	Golden Switch (*Jin Kai*)	Digital 2000 Switch Systems Production Project	Ministry of Electronics Industry, Ministry of Posts & Telecoms

Table 5.5
Brief description of the Golden Projects

	Main objective	Role
Golden Bridge	The key to society's informatization, and the platform for China's information superhighway. A public network backbone and international network interface. Transmission of data, voice, and image and, eventually, multimedia information.	Connect all ministries at provincial, city and district level with 500 city administrations, more than 1000 large- and medium-sized enterprises, and 100 focal enterprise groups and national key projects.
Golden Customs	Construct the foreign trade tax network, the foreign currency settlement, domestic returns, and quota management systems. Build and EDI platform and an import/export statistical database.	Realize an internationally accepted trade accounting practice. Implement a paperless trade system.
Golden Card	Build and electronic-based financial transaction system and information service; and, consequently have 200 million credit cards being used by 300 million people across 400 cities within 10 years.	Realize a unified credit card system to promote finance and commerce.
Golden Sea	Build a data network with N-ISDN capability, linking China's top government leaders with other institutions, organizations and offices under the direct jurisdiction of the Communist Party Central Committee.	Set up an information system that will provide reference data for internal Party use.
Golden Macro	Build a state economic and policy support system through the construction of a synthesized statistical, industrial economic, income tax, commodity price, investment, natural resource, capital, energy, and transport and communication database.	Supply information to—and, hence speed-up—national economic policy modeling; to therefore advance the Open Door program.
Golden Tax	Make use of computerized *danwei* tax receipts and direct bank connections to facilitate the flow and use of funds across the country.	Introduce smart cards and develop a "Golden Tax Card" so as to reduce incoming tax receipts and increase paperless accounting.
Golden Intelligence	Enable teachers and research professionals to have timely an precise information and enable international and local communication and cooperation.	Link most of the country's higher institutes of learning within this century, and thus enable the education community's horizons to expand from the local to the international.
Golden Enterprise	Design and build an integrated enterprise target (quota) and distribution system; build a countrywide enterprise and product database.	Disseminate macro-economic information, and supply and demand market trends.

Table 5.5 (continued)

	Main objective	Role
Golden Agriculture	Develop an agricultural supervisory, calculation and forecasting system.	Develop the agricultural industry's production, marketing, and village economic situations; hence develop a synthesized trends database.
Golden Health	Develop and apply computer technology, communications technology and scientific information distribution to the medical sector.	Network 500 of the largest hospitals across the country.
Golden Information	Develop real-time information flows.	Complete a statistical target system.
Golden Housing	Create a real estate information network.	Build an information bridge for real estate management, coordinating government, banks, developers, and real estate agents.
Golden Cellular	Provide the basis for a coordinated mobile communications strategy, and develop national roaming standards and systems.	Develop a strong, competitive and unified domestic industry.
Golden Switch	Build China's domestic digital switch manufacturing industry.	China was to be producing the switches and lines needed for its basic telecommunications objectives by 1997.

2. To drive the development of information technology in China. In the early stages of industrial development, the Government had consistently taken a very active role in promoting "strategic" industries. Companies associated with the Golden Projects also benefited from a determination to protect infant industries and develop strong domestic markets.

3. To serve as a tool of unification, of the country (from the center to the provinces), and of the Government (across ministerial and industrial demarcation lines). The Central Government perceived the ability to act as an information gatekeeper, thus re-developing administrative centralization.

Tier One: The Three Goldens

The Three Goldens actually encompassed four projects, as they included the "secret" Golden Sea project—a security and administration network for the leadership. It was on the basis of this first set of programs that the new information technology push was given State Council sponsorship. It was also as a result of the political weight given to these projects that others were later launched.

Golden Bridge   Golden Bridge was the infrastructure for the informatization of the national economy; that is, the backbone off which everything else was to be run. This was also known as the China National Economic Information Network. It adopted a hybrid network architecture incorporating both satellite and landline networks. Initially, the Golden Bridge network was constructed as a medium-speed "information highway" (at a transmission speed of 2Mbps) throughout the country. Even so, this allowed 220,000 characters of text (800 pages) to be transferred across the country, from Shanghai to Chongqing, in five minutes. Previously, this would have taken two hours.

While construction of the backbone was of fundamental importance and the subject of much debate within the engineering community in China, it was not the focus of the Golden Projects. The Golden Projects package was an applications-driven initiative whose political support resulted from a perception of how what was being offered would refocus the economy and reassert administrative control. Hence, Golden Bridge as the platform was only the means to an end—with the various applications representing the realization.

Golden Gate (aka Golden Customs) Golden Gate was a foreign trade information network linking the Ministry of Foreign Trade and Economic Cooperation (MOFTEC) and the Customs Bureau. Before 1978 only the central foreign trade ministry and its 12 trade corporations were permitted to engage in international trading activities. By the early 1990s the Open Door Policy had opened the door so widely that there were over 9,000 "representative" organizations providing international trade services. As a result, the purpose of the Golden Gate Project was to construct an information and communications network to re-centralize effective administration of China's foreign trade business.

The initial goal was to interconnect the different networks of China's foreign trade organizations, including the systems for export tax returns, foreign exchange settlement, quota and license administration, and import/export statistics collection. Following this, foreign trade private networks and value-added services were made to conform to the X.400 standards to pave the way for the implementation of electronic data interchange (EDI). The EDI focus of the project meant that paperless trade in the future would be in line with international foreign trade.

Golden Card Golden Card was an electronic money project. First, it was a credit card verification scheme designed to promote the use and dissemination of credit cards. It was intended to provide an interbank, inter-region clearing process, allowing traveling business people to use credit cards of checks to make payments in areas of the country other than where the issuing regional bank was located. Second, the project was to provide a computerization and clearing facilitation so that a genuine Central Bank could be established. This intention was part of larger bank reforms in China.

The first step of the project was to put into practice one card that could be used throughout the country, and to have 200 million credit cards in use by 300 million individuals across 400 cities by the turn of the century. According to banking authorities, this would "reduce the amount of cash in circulation, strengthen the control of money supply and modernize the financial system."

Parallel with the card project, a national clearing system, the Centralized National Automated Payments System (CNAPS), was established. To strengthen the role of the central bank, the Government used its IT restructuring program to replace provincial branches of the People's Bank of China (PBoC) with regional offices. Thus the administrative structure of the banking system paralleled the network architecture. These steps served to centralize decisionmaking and minimize administrative interference from local authorities. As a result, central bank headquarters would have a much greater control over monetary policy.

Because banking and consumption habits would take time to develop, an integrated financial market, akin to developed Western markets, would also take time to emerge. However, in contrast to the West, credit cards in China were initially used in the role of cash cards, reducing the circulation of cash and strengthening financial management. Users of the cards were required to have bank deposits verified before they could use the cards to draw on those deposits. Thus, the cards acted much more like debit cards than credit cards.

Given the size of the task, the Golden Card project was being approached in phases (see table 5.6). The first stage was for the banks within each of 12 major cities to be linked by an ATM switching network. These cities then become hubs that gradually spread the electronic banking network through the smaller cities of China's provinces. Following this, nearly 500 secondary cities would be added by the turn of the century, when minor cities and townships would be patched in.

MEI outlined the implementation of the card project in September 1993, and a Golden Card Project Office was opened in October. The office comprised representatives from the People's Bank of China, MPT, MEI, the Ministry of Internal Trade, and the National Tourism Administration. To strengthen the unity of the project, a Golden Project Committee was formed in June 1994, headed by Minister Hu Qili and Deputy Manager Chen Yuan.

Golden Sea   This was an information system interconnecting China's top government leaders and providing them with immediate access to reference data from other institutions, organizations, and offices under the direct jurisdiction of the Communist Party Central Committee. The system was set up and piloted in October 1994; by 1995, it was operational—the first Golden Project to begin. Linked to the State

Table 5.6
Golden Card project stages and objectives

1. The Trial Stage (1994–96) objectives are to:
- set out plans for developing the bank card market and to establish the bank card service management system with financial institutions as the dominant participants;
- build a complete set of regulations to unify bank card standards and service procedures, allowing market mechanisms to operate, "raising the social economic effect";
- work on the 12 trial cities and districts, with the emphasis on setting up networks and bank card information exchange centers at the same time, and networking them to the specialized bank service processing centers and People's Bank of China's (PBoC's) city processing centers in these cities, so that special users, machines and networks can be shared, business cards can be mutually accepted, and resource sharing and parallel services can be fulfilled;
- unify and organize trial IC cards in several cities and districts where magnetic cards are being developed to encourage use of "smart" IC cards as "IC cards are safe, difficult to fake, have low requirements on telecommunication networks, and can be processed off-line";
- establish nationwide bank card information exchange service centers, networked with the bank card information exchange centers and PBoC's national processing centers in the trial cities and districts, so as to allow simultaneous transfers and timely payments on receiving information from authorization made in other cities.
- issue 30 million bank cards (of which 10 million will be credit cards) in the nation by the end of 1995.

2. The Promotion Stage (1996–99) objectives are to:
- improve the environment for issuing cards, networking, applications and services in the trial cities;
- select 30 to 50 cities to set up bank card information centers to accept inter-city and district bank card usage and allow simultaneous authorization and timely settlements;
- establish a second nationwide bank card information exchange service center to supplement and complement the first center;
- have 60 million cards issued by 1999;

3. The Popularization Stage (2000–03) objective are to:
- complete the laws, regulations, systems and monitoring mechanism related to bank card services;
- complete the networking of 400 cities in the country, as well as allow simultaneous authorization and timely settlements;
- in a number of cities, to promote bank card services to the economically advanced county capitals and towns in the periphery of these cities;
- to issue 200 million cards in 400 cities covering 300 million people in China by 2003.

Statistical Bureau, the PBoC, and the State Information Center (SIC), it was a data network with N-ISDN capability.

Tier Two: Information Management

The projects in tiers two and three were developed following the political backing given to the Three Goldens. Whereas the agenda of the first tier projects was the rollout of the information network(s), the objective of the tier two projects was to exploit the applications-oriented nature of the program. Each project was designed to apply information networks to economic reform.

Golden Macro   This was to serve the Government's Central Economic and Financial Leading Group for macro-control over national economic activities. The network linked seven key government institutions including the State Planning Commission, State Statistical Bureau, the PBoC, and the State Information Center. One of the Project's first applications was to carry out research on China's pricing policy. Officials justified this user-based project at the information centers as a way to build the bridge between the market and the planned economy—i.e., the adoption of new information technologies to develop the so-called market-socialist economy.

Golden Tax   Golden Tax was a data network designed for the State Tax Administration (STA) to piggyback onto the satellite network of the People's Bank of China (PBoC); the aim was to link STA's auditing center in Beijing with its 50 regional offices and 800 bureaus to facilitate better collection of income and value-added taxes and to eliminate tax evasion. As with a number of the other Golden Projects, it was centered on the technology of the intelligent (IC chip) card.

China's new taxation system had been in place since the beginning of 1995. Through the new system, the administration set up a collection and management system for value-added tax. (China's taxation bureaus handled about 10 billion invoices each year.) The State's tax revenue would come mainly from enterprises' turnover tax. And the value-added tax was the core of turnover tax, bringing in about 50% of the country's tax revenue. Although the whole management system for value-added tax would be established by the year 2000, it was estimated that China would need 10 years to establish an advanced taxation management system matching those in Western countries.

According to government officials, fake invoices designed to help enterprises and individuals dodge China's taxes had become widely available; both government and commercial enterprises adopted various methods to create false bills to help reduce taxes. As a result, an estimated US$1.2 billion to $3.6 billion (Rmb10 billion to Rmb30 billion) of taxes were lost each year in China because of such fraud. Thus, an effort to crack down on tax evasion and increase government tax revenues provided justification for the Golden Tax Project network.

The Golden Tax Project attempted to let the Tax Bureau directly know the sales volume of companies. Phase One, completed in the latter half of 1994, connected 50 cities. Phase Two interconnected the networks in nearly 400 cities through 1995 and 1996.

Golden Intelligence and China's Internet Service   One of the drivers for introducing Internet connectivity into China was the demand from foreign businesses to have

E-mail access, both for convenience and as a way of cutting down on communications costs. Until the China service was finally commercialized in June 1995, however, E-mail did not tend to reduce a company's bills significantly, since foreigners were essentially making long-distance international calls to one of the world's 2 million host computers where they could then send and receive their daily E-mail in bulk packets. This approach had the benefit of allowing for at least 14,400 baud as long as the foreign provider (CompuServe or America Online) offered it. Until Chinpac (see table 5.7) was truly dependable, this would be the option chosen by many foreigners living and working in Beijing.

The public (or commercial) Internet service provided through the MPT's cooperation with U.S. long-distance operator Sprint was, by 1996, available only in Beijing and Shanghai, with the MPT planning to link a further six cities—Shenyang, Guangzhou, Xian, Wuhan, Chengdu, and Nanjing. As of 1996 the MPT, through its Data Communications Bureau (DCB), was the only legitimate provider of Internet service, and was doing so through two distinct service providers: its newly established ChinaNet service, and as the largest investor in a semi-private subsidiary, International United OnLine (IUOL). There was, however, a certain expectation by 1996 that private Chinese companies would begin to offer commercial Internet alternatives given the proliferation of networks, information, and on-line systems (see table 5.8).

Excluding the commercial providers in China, the major Internet developments were within the academic community. The Golden Intelligence Project—another name for CERNET (China's Education and Research network)—would connect regional computer networks with university campuses. The CERNET project, funded with Chinese government seed money of US$9.6 million (Rmb80 million), was the first major Internet development project across China and was placed under the direct management of the Chinese State Education Commission. Ultimately, all campus networks across China would be interconnected—with each other and then into the Internet. The CERNET center was in Beijing's Qinghua University.

Interestingly, while the academic community was the first to develop Internet usage in China, it was the commercial world that spurred the Government to act. Indeed, the start up of the commercial Internet venture enabled the MPT to regain control of a telecommunications service it had missed. For the first Internet connection was established by the Chinese Academy of Science (CAS), which registered the "CN" domain name, exclusively used for all of China's Internet access, with the Internet Society in 1990. An associated reason for commercializing the service was that, after its establishment in May 1994, the CAS network was often overloaded. A new system, charging access at market rates, was seen as a way of relieving congestion on the single existing connection.

Table 5.7
Data transmission pricing in China

Commercial dial-up rates

	ChinaNet		IUOL		China-On-Line*	
	A	B	A	B	Individual	Corporate
Connection fee	$37.50	$37.50	$180***	$180***	$81.25*	$250.00
Monthly fee	$75.00**	$12.50**	$60.00	$18.00	$25**	$125
Time duration	40 hours	6 hours	25 hours	6 hours	na	na
Storage incl	1.5 MB	1.5 MB	1.5 MB	1.5 MB	na	na
Extra time	$2.50/hr	$2.50/hr	$3.50/hr	$3.50/hr		
Extra storage	$25.00/MB	$25.00/MB	$25.00/MB	$25.00/MB		
Private IP user	$6.25/month	$6.25/month				
Public IP user	$1.25/month	$1.25/month				
Services	full Internet via "Chance" software		full Internet via "Internet-in-a-Box" software		E-mail only	

Note: There are a number of large companies, like Motorola and Boeing, that have Internet E-mail gateways.
* China-On-Line is a Canadian company providing E-mail service only.
** ChinaNet chargeable duration doubled on public holidays, weekends, and off peak periods (21:00–07:00).
*** This includes software installation + training; if you already have software, the connection fee is $37.50, which includes software installation + training; if you already have software, the connection fee is $62.50 less for the individual subscriber the service can only be used from 18:00 to 08:00 during the week.

ChinaNet's dedicated connection mode****

	19.2 kbps (and less)	64 kbps	> 64 kbps
Monthly rate**	$200	$600	$600 × 0.8 × (speed/64)
Traffic included	25 MB	100 MB	100 MB × (speed/64)
Rate per end user	$37.50	$37.50	$37.50
Extra traffic	$10/MB	$10/MB	$10/MB

** Chargeable duration doubled on public holidays, weekends, and off peak periods (21:00–07:00).
**** Via frame relay, 80% discount will be given for monthly fee; for IP address users who access via Chinapac, $200 monthly fee will be paid as 19.2kbps dedicated connection mode temporarily but no volume limitation.

Table 5.8
Major internet services networks in China

Network	Full title	Main users	International connection
CASnet	China Academy of Sciences Network (NCFC Network)	links 30+ research institutes	One 64 kpbs line
Tunet	Qinghua University Campus Network	lecturers, students	through CASnet
Punet	Beijing University Campus Network	lecturers, students	through CASnet
BUPTnet	Beijing University of Posts and Telecoms Network	lecturers, students	through CASnet
Canet	China Academic Network	scientists	through CASnet
Crnet	China Research Network	scientists	through CASnet
CERnet	China Educational and Research Network	lecturers, students and scientists	through CASnet
CASSBnet	China Academy of Science Shanghai Branch Network	scientists	through CASnet
CASWBnet	China Academy of Science Wuhan Branch Network	scientists	through CASnet
CASNBnet	China Academy of Science Nanjing Branch Network	scientists	through CASnet
IHEPnet	China Institute of High Energy Physics Network	scientists	One 64 kbps line
SSTCnet	State Science & Technology Center Network	researchers, government	through IHEPnet
SICnet	State Information Center Network	government depts, enterprises	through ChinaNet
ChinaNet	China Public Internet Network	public network	Two 64 kbps lines
Bcnet	Beijing Chemical Industry Network	lecturers, students	One 64 kbps line

Initially, the two commercial providers, ChinaNet and IUOL, used the Chinapac national X.25 network; then, through the MPT's two international gateways, in Beijing and Shanghai, users accessed the Internet via U.S. carrier Sprint's SprintLink service, which provided an international line at 64 Kbps, nowhere near enough for those in government debating China's Information Superhighway, who pointed out that the Hong Kong academic network connected to the United States at 2Mbps. Moreover, for the dial-up user, although the access they paid for was set at an official 9,600 bps, this regularly dipped to a mere 2,400 bps.

Resolving these issues, however, involved far more than technical questions. In China, where the SEZs and the Open Port Cities provided the first significant degree of access to the world as part of the Open Door policy, the importance of business communication provided the impetus for the rapid growth of a national communications infrastructure. International data communications were becoming recognized as fundamental for everything from real-time financial information to market competitiveness, technology transfer, and academic and scientific excellence.

Tier Three: Golden Sectors

The third tier of Golden Projects represented sector-specific applications of the new information technology program. Three of the outlined projects, Golden Enterprise, Agriculture, and Health, applied to the most problematic and fundamental spheres of the Chinese economy. The fourth project, Golden Information, was an attempt to address democratic centralism's greatest administrative problem: national statistical collation and accounting. By contrast, Golden Housing was an attempt by Central authorities to address the problem of property speculation.

Golden Enterprise   Golden Enterprise applied to the construction of internal networks in China's 12,000 large- and medium-sized enterprises, and their interconnection according to different circles of business. The economic information from this system was collected for the State Council, and used to make macro-control and scientific decisions. The computerized national data network was for information on products, sales, and marketing of commercial and industrial enterprises. The whole implementation of Golden Enterprise engineering was expected to take 10 to 15 years, beginning in 1995.

The Golden Enterprise Project would offer on-line services, and assist commercial and industrial firms in their efforts to make efficient use of personnel, capital, and natural resources. One of the objectives of the project was to promote optimal allocation and appropriate use of various resources so as to reduce personnel, material, and capital waste in businesses.

Golden Agriculture   Golden Agriculture was a databank service network providing agricultural information, weather reports, and market information. Also known as the "China Rural Satellite Communications Network," the project was under the jurisdiction of the Ministry of Agriculture. With an eye to both domestic and foreign markets, the ministry set up the nationwide information network to help farmers manage their production, sales, and use of technology. The plans were for a nation-wide free market system built around several agricultural wholesale markets.

While central authorities originally planned to extend public telephone service to all villages by the year 2000, doing so meant physically installing almost a million kilometers of cable and raising huge amounts of capital. Given this task, the Government lowered its goal to providing phone service in 70% of villages by the year 2000. The China Rural Development Trust and Investment Co. (affiliated with the Ministry of Agriculture) planned to launch a geo-synchronousorbit satellite to provide low-cost communications for more then 500,000 villages within phone service. Connected with the MPT's public networks, each village would have a small portable satellite earth terminal costing around US$1,000. Based on a seven-year operational period, cost-per-minute would equal US$0.06–0.08, regardless of distance.

One specific objective of the Golden Agriculture project was curbing localities' reporting of false economic data. Between 1985 and 1995, Chinese courts prosecuted more than 20,000 cases of local officials forging statistics to impress their superiors or to earn more Central Government funding. Thus, this IT project became a part of the inspection campaign targeting local statistics on industrial and agricultural output, farm income, investment, and prices.

Golden Health   The Ministry of Public Health's high-speed information exchange system for hospitals would eventually include a medical health card policy, remote diagnostics, and remote education to link China's 14,713 hospitals beyond the county level. The first phase of Golden Health identified 500 of the country's largest hospitals for linkage.

The network, centered in the Medical University of Beijing, would link the LANs of 11 medical universities with hospitals nationwide. This hospital network would also be interlinked with CERNET and the Internet. The telemedicine project would link the hospitals, outpatient clinics, and diagnostic centers, and supply patients with an electronic health card. Golden Health would provide laser cards able to contain up to 1,000 pages in Chinese characters covering the patient's medical history, medical treatment, and images. Since China's hospitals used about 22% of their space for storage of files, the Health Card would free space for more beneficial medical use.

Golden Information Golden Information, or the State Statistical Information Project, was administered by the State Statistical Bureau to network the various statistical collection departments across the country, so as to provide basic statistical and demographic information in a more efficient and timely manner. Single workstations sent the latest statistics to central data banks, where the information was processed for network users. The commercial aspect of this information resource allowed the Bureau to compile and sell various sector-specific information profiles, as well as access to various government databases.

Golden Housing Property speculation and associated corruption represented a significant problem facing authorities since the beginning of the reform era. Money intended for large-scale infrastructural or development projects was often siphoned off into property deals, as these were seen as having a greater potential for high returns. The Golden Housing project was initiated to address this problem through a nationwide sharing of information of real estate—i.e., through the centralization and coordination of information. The aim was to create a network serving as an information bridge for real estate management departments of the Government, banking institutions, real estate developers and agents, as well as customers.

The Golden Housing network was divided into a central network, provincial network, and municipal network. The municipal networks in various cities were connected to real estate development companies and real estate trading information companies in the nearby city. The national real estate trading center lay in the central China city of Wuhan. The number of cities connected to the network reached 30 in 1995 and 50 in 1996.

Tier Four: Golden Industries

While the fourth tier of projects did not specifically represent networking or IT-based efforts, they were no less strategically important to the Government's program. China very consciously followed a policy of import-substitution and domestic dominance of "key and strategic industries." For that reason the following projects were given the "golden" imprimatur; moreover, their inclusion in the Golden program (along with administration under the Joint Committee for National Economic Informatization) demonstrated the approach was all-encompassing, not that of a series of ad hoc projects.

Golden Cellular Golden Cellular was formalized in August 1994 by bringing eight of the largest domestic mobile communications manufacturers together to form Jinfeng Communications. Jinfeng's initial focus was twofold: to tackle Motorola and

Ericsson's domination of China's mobile communications market; and, to provide the platform for developing a national mobile standard. Authorities believed that standardizing the industry was one way of providing the basis for a coordinated mobile communications strategy, and developing a "national champion" in what emerged as a very lucrative market sector. By 1995, China had the third largest mobile communications market in the world.

Golden Switch   Golden Switch aimed to build China's domestic digital switch manufacturing industry. Again, to tackle foreign domination, China set up a single large domestic telephone exchange producer by grouping eight State-owned enterprises. Begun in 1995, the objective was to be domestically producing the switches and lines necessary for its telecommunications program by 1997, including more than 13 million lines per annum.

The Golden Projects as an Example of National Reengineering

Business reengineering can be defined as the merger of process innovation and information technology innovations to achieve significant improvements in performance. Using these criteria, China's Golden Projects can be viewed as an example of process reengineering at the national level.

China's telecommunications sector comprised five administrative levels—national, provincial, municipal, prefectural, and country—each of which was relevant in terms of finance, management, personnel, etc. This sectorial breakdown mirrored the administrative structure of the Government and of the Communist Party. However, each level of the telecommunications structure was relatively autonomous. Planning represented a process of negotiation among all levels, with the most important and intense level being that between the provincial authorities (PTA) and the central ministry (MPT). At each stage, the MPT set the Plan and handed it down. The PTA added the detail and in turn handed it down. The PTB (the country level) added a greater degree of detail (e.g., locality, penetration rate), at which point the Plan was passed back up the chain. Students of modern China will recognize this mass line concept of administration, which has been employed by the Communists since pre-Liberation days. Students of socialist development more generally will recognize the essence of democratic centralism. And, as students of China's IT roll-out (i.e., the Three Goldens), we can begin to better understand the justification and rationale for the huge State expenditure being deployed.

It could certainly be argued that for the Chinese leadership, IT represented a new solution to an old problem. The objectives and the processes remained what they had been since imperial times, but now IT seemed to allow for a crucial tightening of the administrative process—increased efficiency of an old system. In other words, at a time of threateningly high inflation, institutionalized corruption, and multilayered bureaucracy, IT innovations were seen by the leaders in Beijing as a way of combating a potentially desegregating economy. Suddenly, the age-old fear of China's central leaders—"the mountains are high, the emperor lives a long way away"—could be addressed. The introduction of distance-insensitive technology meant that Beijing could effectively "look over the shoulder" of Guangzho—the farthest province in the south—as policies were administered.

The Golden Projects could thus be viewed either as a major thrust forward to develop an information highway in China to improve the efficiency of the economy; or as an effort to use IT to centralize information and control over the business activities within the nation.

In fact, what the corporate reengineering literature may allow us to do is to reconceptualize the old "Nation, Inc." model of national economic administration (e.g., Japan, Inc. or Singapore, Inc.). It is well accepted that China should be considered not as one integrated market but rather as a composite of quite different markets: from the freewheeling, resource-rich South, to the industrial-heavy North, to the desert hinterlands of Xinjiang and Gansu, and on to the Tibetan plateau. As the above analysis suggests, while the Government does not want to stifle competition, it is attempting to oversee the direction along which competition develops.

It is also true that in China, different branches of government can focus their efforts and cooperate on tasks only when someone above them in the hierarchy takes the initiative. When there is no such authority figure, different branches will fight rather than cooperate, even if they agree on a common goal. The Joint Committee of National Economic Information has provided the authority and the Golden Projects have provided the coordination in the use of IT in national economic administration.

Thus, China's Golden Projects can be seen from multiple perspectives and offer different benefits to various sectors of China's economy and government. As an example of a program of major investment and change, the Goldens are an interesting and provocative illustration of reengineering at a national scale in a country of more than 1 billion people. As such, it surely represents one of the most ambitious reengineering projects ever undertaken. Even so, the Government of China is determined to move cautiously and carefully into this new area of opportunity as it struggles to capture the benefits of radical performance improvements without losing control of the pace and nature of the changes involved. The Chinese describe their view of revolutionary change in economic structure and national infrastructure as attempting to cross a rapidly flowing river to reach a great objective, but moving carefully and gradually in the process while "walking barefoot and feeling the stones beneath our feet." The challenges for China in implementing this major investment in information infrastructure may prove educational not only for China's national policies but also for multinational firms that are also struggling with implementing large-scale change without losing control of a decentralized organization.

References

"A. S. Watson to Supply First Secure Cable TV System," *Telenews Asia*, July 14, 1994, p. 7–8.

"Capitalism with Chinese Characteristics," *Economist*, November 28, 1992, p. 6–8.

"China's Ji Tong Company and Bellsouth Establish Joint Venture," *PR Newswire Atlanta*, January 27, 1994.

"City of the Plain," *Economist*, March 18, 1995, p. 18–19.

Curry, L. "Out of Line," *Far Eastern Economic Review*, December 1, 1994, p. 64–66.

Davidson, W. H., Wang, D. M. and Hom, S. C. "Telecommunications Policy and Economic Development: Models for the People's Republic of China," *China Economic Review* (1:1), 1989, p. 93–108.

"Electronics Minister Hu Qili on the Development of Information Services," BBC Summary of World Broadcasts, July 5, 1994.

Fung, N. "Snags Plague Card Industry: Lack of Clear Authority Causes Market Uncertainty," *South China Morning Post*, January 11, 1995, p. 5.

"Golden Projects," CTC News, China Telecommunications Construction (1:9), May 20, 1995, p. 9–10.

"Government, Business Linked by Computer," *Beijing Review*, May 1–7, 1995, p. 7.

"Highlights," *China Telecommunications Construction* (7:3), April 1995, p. 58–64.

Jiang, L. T. "Information Highways and the 'Golden Projects,'" Data Communications Technology Research Institute, Ministry of Posts and Telecommunications, p. 1–17.

Kao, J. "Phoning Home," *The China Business Review*, July–August 1992, p. 6–10.

Li, N. "Minister Hu Calls for Modern Electronic Information Processing Industry," *Beijing Review*, February 20–26, 1995, p. 12–17.

Li, X., Wu, J. and Liang, Y. "Connecting China Education Community to the Global Internet—The China Education and Research Network Project," *Connecting China*.

Liang, X. J. "Information Industry in China," *Beijing University of Posts & Telecommunications*, May 1995, p. 1–17.

Lohr, S., "China Endorses PowerPC Chip by IBM," *The New York Times*, May 4, 1994.

Murray, G. "China Sets Priorities for Massive Telecom Investment," *Japan Economic Newswire*, March 31, 1995.

"Net Assets," *China Economic Review*, May 1995, p. 14–15.

Ping, Z. S. "A Brief Introduction to the 'Golden Card Project,'" Bank of China Headquarters, p. 1–10.

Qian, Z. J. "The Necessity and Feasibility of Constructing the National High-Speed Information Infrastructure in China (CNSII)," China Telecommunications Construction (7:3), April 1995, p. 19–20.

Rajendran, J., "AST and Compaq Battling for Burgeoning China Market," *Business Times*, May 23, 1994, p. 13.

Ramsay, L. "China Sees Great Leap Forward in Telecommunication Ability," *The Financial Post*, April 1, 1995, p. 30.

Riley, J. "Intel Agrees to Key China Deal," *South China Morning Post*, March 7, 1995, p. 1.

Segal, G. "China's Changing Shape," *Foreign Affairs* (73:3), May/June 1994, p. 43–58.

Shirk, S. L. "How China Opened Its Door," Brookings Institution, Washington, DC, 1994.

"The People's Republic of China Is One of the Fastest Growing Economies in the World," *Business America*, February 1994, p. 14–15.

Ure, J. "Telecommunications, with Chinese Characteristics," *Telecommunications Policy*, April 1994, p. 182–194.

Vines, S. "Peking's Gag Artists Eye the Internet," *The Independent*, June 22, 1995, p. 14.

Xiong, B. Q. "Information Superhighway and Telecommunications in China," *China Academy of Telecommunications Technology*, May 1995, p. 1–8.

Philippines Telephone and Telegraph

Marilyn Santiago, CEO of Philippines Telephone & Telegraph (PT&T), read the securities analyst's report.

RECOMMENDATION ... SPECULATIVE HOLD
PT&T is a long-distance toll provider with an extensive national digital network. The company's financials have been burdened by high interest charges. The company aggressively invested in diversified products and services to counteract the adverse effects of the declining popularity of telex and telegraph (PT&T controls 95% of this market in the Philippines). Telex and telegraph revenues have been declining about 15% annually, giving way to increased fax communications. The diversification moves were also designed to keep pace with the expected rise in competition in the industry. However, earnings are expected to recover this year (first quarter 1994 earnings are up 125%).

The report's conclusion accurately reflected her own concerns regarding the ambitious upgrades undertaken in PT&T's telecommunications networks over the prior two years. It was now August 1994, and investors had become concerned with the return on their investments in PT&T's telecommucnations infrastructure.

PT&T was a public utility company that operated and leased telecommunications systems for domestic and international public communications services. The services that the company provided included telegraph, telex, leased voice/telegraph channel, high-speed data channel, facsimile, and point-to-point telephone on a nationwide basis.

PT&T had the second largest and most extensive national telecommunications "backbone" system in the country (after Philippines Long Distance Telephone). Its long-distance network consisted of

1. a microwave backbone system from the north (Baguio) to the south (Cagayan de Oro) via Manila and Cebu,

2. a very high/ultra high frequency radio system for the peripheral and lateral stations, and

3. an integrated digital network for major cities such as Metro Manila, Metro Cebu, Metro Davao, and Metro Cagayan de Oro.

If the firm were to realize the potential competitive gains offered in the Philippines' newly liberalized telecommunications market, it would have to strategically expand the use of its newly installed bandwidth. Now that PT&T's investment in new switching and information technology was complete, Marilyn Santiago was prepared to explore economically viable markets for PT&T's telecommunications services.

This case was prepared under a grant from the University of Southern California Center for International Business Education and Research by Associate Professor J. Christopher Westland.

Table 5.9
Comparison of technology dispersion, 1994

	Telephone density index (telephones/100)	Television density index (televisions/100)
U.S.	76.9	83.3
Brunei	26.3	38.5
Indonesia	0.9	5.5
Malaysia	11.3	14.5
Philippines	1.4	4.1
Singapore	50.0	37.0
Thailand	3.5	10.7

Recent History of Telecommunications in the Philippines

The Philippines archipelago was experiencing somewhat of an economic resurgence, after the doldrums of the Marcos years. Foreign direct investment was up 30%, inflation was relatively stable at 10%, and GDP was increasing at roughly 5% (though industrial output did not keep pace, remaining at under 1% growth).

The Medium-Term Philippine Development Plan aimed to·raise the telephone density index (TDI) from its current 1.4 telephone lines per 100 population, to 4 telephone lines per 100 population by 1998 (see table 5.9). This would require the installation of about 1.32 million additional telephone lines (about a 40% increase over current levels) and $2.5 billion worth of new investment (the Philippines GDP is around $40 billion). Much of this was targeted toward rural areas, where about 60% of the populace lives. By 2010, the government hoped to have a TDI approaching 10, at a total cost of $14 billion.

The ultimate dream of the Philippine government was to interconnect all islands of the archipelago by an extensive state-of-the-art digital backbone—a high-capacity information highway designed to blanket the country with phone, fax, and potentially video·services. At present, only PLDT, Radio Communications Philippines, Inc. (RCPI), and Philippines Telephone and Telegraph (PT&T) had digital lines in place. The government proposed to build the backbone for the entire country itself, and then privatize it.

The Ferdinand Ramos government's goal was to provide universal access to telephone service across the Philippine archipelago. Questions remained concerning who would be responsible for providing universal access (especially since rural lines were expensive as a result of the challenging terrain). Even the concept of universal service was debated. Walk-in telecommunications services such as telex and telegraph had provided effective communication to the rural populace for decades.[1]

Antonio Samson of Philippine Long Distance Telephone Company (PLDT) estimated that the average capital cost of PLDT's lines was $2,000/line allocating all costs, or $1,400/line allocating only equipment costs, with a marginal cost of around $400 for the local connection. This is one of the highest costs per line in the world (the United States' figure is about one-tenth that at $200/line). Rural service could cost as much as $4,000/line, and DIGITEL, in its bid for the Luzon system, set a price of $12,000/line.

This high cost reflects the difficulties in setting up microwave towers or running cable under the ocean in attempts to connect rural island populations. There was considerable debate concerning the importance of linking peripatetic fishermen (who might often be on their boats) or farmers (who spent most of their time in the fields). Acceptable alternatives, it was argued, could be provided by linking the general store in a village, and allowing all of the villagers access; or alternatively through cheap, mobile, single side band (SSB) radios all operating on the same frequency, providing a party line service through a single line.

The Department of Transportation and Communications had recently enacted Executive Order 109 which mandated several changes. There had been more than 50 independent telephone companies, long distance operators, and domestic record carriers in the Philippines in 1994 (see figure 5.1). The government, through an aggressive reallocation of franchises (licenses which allow telephone operators to operate in an area with a given service), planned to drop this to 11, eliminating most of the smallest village "mom & pop" operators in the process (see table 5.10).

Operators of the profitable international long-distance gateways were required, also, to provide domestic service of at least 300,000 lines (this applied to PLDT and PT&T). This service was allocated among the 11 areas shown in table 5.10 and among 7 operators. This promised to effectively close down most of the "mom & pop" operators.

The moves were intended to eliminate a backlog of service orders, which until recently had totaled 600,000 lines, resulting in an average three-year wait for service. This tended to make cellular service very popular with businessmen. Though it was considerably more expensive, it could be switched on in one day.

The government had yet to address the "gray area" between cable television operation and telecommunications transmission. Legally, cable television operators were "broadcasters" (one-way communication) and were not allowed to participate in the market for two-way communications. Technologically, this made little sense. Britain had operated for nearly a decade allowing cable television companies to

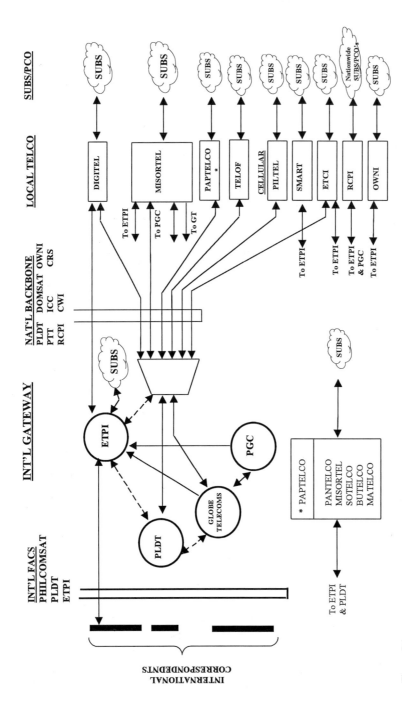

Figure 5.1
Philippine telephone infrastructure

Table 5.10

Comparative highlights *(in thousand pesos; fiscal years ended June 30, 1989–1993)*

	1989	1990	1991	1992	1993
Revenues					
Telegraph	102,590	118,619	132,516	133,979	129,331
Telex	79,325	65,901	72,203	70,053	53,939
Leased channels	47,710	54,772	74,818	69,938	77,027
Data communications	28,532	38,489	58,400	69,067	74,740
Facsimile	303	1,057	2,061	3,725	6,112
VODEX (long distance)	45,489	56,737	76,247	100,204	121,518
Others	10,637	12,844	11,571	11,525	8,794
Subtotal	314,586	348,419	427,816	458,491	471,461
Expenses					
Salaries and wages	85,881	110,731	133,339	152,065	160,742
Depreciation and amortization	58,897	79,085	75,773	88,202	89,367
All other expenses/deductions	140,455	129,455	188,443	193,982	199,799
Subtotal	285,685	319,271	397,555	434,249	449,908
Net income	28,901	29,148	30,261	24,242	21,553
Dividends paid	26,353	20,138	18,000	4,000	
Retained earnings	15,811	30,149	43,476	64,783	87,403
Property, plant, and equipment, net	787,250	941,977	1,149,863	1,478,386	1,744,248
Stockholders' equity	365,802	514,052	525,946	545,103	566,656
Total assets	950,702	1,139,347	1,405,300	1,849,700	2,083,109

Statements of income and retained earnings

	1993	1992
Operating revenue, net of provision for doubtful accounts of P2,634,874 in 1993 and P2,908,493 in 1992	468,826,261	455,582,680
Operating expenses		
Operations	240,692,541	227,378,659
Depreciation and amortization	89,366,907	88,202,253
Supplies, rent, and power	51,574,134	45,350,647
Taxes, licenses, and fees	14,727,992	15,107,140
	396,361,574	376,038,699
Operating income	72,464,686	79,543,981
Other charges, net	(47,744,269)	(53,336,056)
Income before income tax	24,720,417	26,207,925
Provision for income tax (note 9)	(3,166,930)	(1,966,370)
Net income	21,553,487	24,241,555
Retained earnings, beginning	64,783,274	43,475,953
Dividends to common stock *(note 8)*		(3,999,987)
Revaluation increment absorbed through depreciation *(note 1)*	1,065,751	1,065,753

Table 5.10 (continued)

Statements of income and retained earnings

	1993	1992
Retained earnings, end	87,402,512	64,783,274
Earnings per common share (note 1)	0.05	0.06
Assets *(in Philippine pesos)*		
Property, plant and equipment (notes 1, 2, and 4)	1,744,247,645	1,478,385,969
Investments (note 1)	5,246,437	5,277,024
Current assets		
Cash (including deposit substitute of P110.8 million in 1993 and P100 million in 1992)	151,250,549	137,263,468
Trade accounts receivable, net of allowance for doubtful accounts of P5,426,169 in 1993 and P2,791,295 in 1992 *(note 6)*	65,991,697	62,362,993
Other accounts receivable	41,297,696	37,062,478
Advances on purchases *(note 6)*	19,398,859	11,839,455
Materials and supplies *(note 1)*	24,644,533	85,587,858
Prepayments	4,987,589	7,938,460
	307,570,923	342,054,712
Other assets (notes 7 and 10)	26,044,227	23,981,967
Total assets	2,083,109,232	1,849,699,672
Stockholders' equity and liabilities		
Stockholders' equity		
Capital stock *(note 3)*	479,253,736	479,253,736
Revaluation increment in property, net of portion absorbed through additional depreciation charges *(note 2)*		1,065,751
Retained earnings *(notes 2 and 8)*	87,402,512	64,783,274
	566,656,248	545,102,761
Long-term debt (note 4)	952,276,870	811,504,406
Current liabilities		
Notes payable *(note 5)*	400,250,954	320,256,031
Trade accounts payable	8,683,598	21,234,700
Accrued expenses	7,274,974	7,968,967
Other accounts payable	19,458,745	14,609,284
Accrued interest payable	17,347,693	8,856,086
Current maturities on long-term debt *(note 4)*	43,803,189	42,746,836
	496,819,153	415,671,904
Due to affiliates, net (note 6)	944,565	14,086,926
Other liabilities and deferred credits (note 7)	66,412,396	63,333,675
Total stockholders' equity and liabilities	2,083,109,232	1,849,699,672

Table 5.10 (continued)

Statements of cash flows *(in Philippine pesos)*

	1993	1992
Cash flows from operating activities		
Net income	21,553,486	24,241,555
Add (deduct): Noncash charges to operations		
Depreciation and amortization	89,366,907	88,202,253
Allowance for doubtful accounts	2,634,874	2,908,493
Gain on sale of property	(741,266)	
(Increase) in trade accounts receivable	(6,263,578)	(12,020,992)
(Increase) in other accounts receivable	(4,235,218)	(25,089,522)
(Increase) decrease in advances on purchases	(7,559,404)	31,267,516
(Increase) decrease in materials and supplies	60,943,325	(57,852,449)
(Increase) decrease in prepayments	2,950,871	(1,467,120)
(Increase) in other assets	(2,062,260)	(4,621,389)
Increase (decrease) in trade accounts payable	(12,551,102)	528,345
(Decrease) in accrued expenses	(693,993)	(1,742,429)
Increase (decrease) in other accounts payable	4,849,461	(9,239,591)
Increase in accrued interest payable	8,491,607	302,565
(Decrease) in due to affiliates	(13,142,361)	(587,276)
(Increase) in other liabilities and deferred credits	3,078,721	2,524,186
(Decrease) in premium on common stock		(1,085,026)
Dividends paid		(3,999,987)
Net cash provided by operating activities	146,620,070	36,269,119
Cash flows from investing activities		
Proceeds from sale of property	834,655	
Additions to property, plant, and equipment	(355,321,971)	(416,725,645)
(Increase) decrease in investments	30,587	(53,597)
Net cash used in investing activities	(354,456,729)	(416,779,242)
Cash flows from financing activities		
Additional long-term borrowing	181,509,732	547,051,324
Debt servicing-long term	(39,680,915)	(190,508,056)
Increase in notes payable—short term	79,994,923	76,913,759
Dividends paid		3,999,987
Net cash provided by financing activities	221,823,740	429,457,040
Net increase in cash	13,987,081	48,946,917
Cash—beginning of the year	137,263,468	88,316,551
Cash—end of the year	151,250,549	137,263,468

Table 5.11
Key industry players

Players	Foreign partner	IGF	CMTS	LEC
Capitol Wireless	Korea Telecom	×		×
Digital Telecommunications, Inc.	Jasmine (Thailand)			×
Express Telecommunications, Inc.	MILLICOM		×	
Eastern Telecommunications Phils. Inc.	Cable & Wireless	×		×
Globe Telecom, Inc.	Singapore Telecom	×	×	×
International Communications Corp. (ICC)	TELSTRA	×		×
ISLA Communications	SHINAWATRA (Thailand)	×	×	×
Philippine Long Distance Telephone Co. (PLDT)		×	×	×
Philippine Global Communications (PGC)	COMSAT	×		×
Pilipino Telephone PILTEL	PLDT		×	×
SMART Communications, Inc.	FIRST PACIFIC	×	×	×
BELLTEL	BELL SOUTH			

provide basic telephone service; the United States was poised similarly to open its markets.

The DOTC's Executive Order 109 reflected the government's increasing criticism of PLDT's de facto monopoly, which controlled 94% of the industry, and maintained de facto control over long distance access. PLDT, with net assets of $1.2 billion, controlled the most extensive public-switched telephone network (PSTN) and subscriber base in the country. Interconnection with PLDT's PSTN was a must for all other telecommunications operators to survive and maintain their international or domestic operations. PLDT planned to add over one million lines to its own network by 1998.

The small telephone operators (through their umbrella lobbying organization) complained about the rigidly detailed regulation and low rate of return on telecommunications investments (mandated by DOTC at 12%, regulated through the rates charged to customers).

Revenue sharing was also faulted. For international calls, PLDT, which controlled international access, gave local operators only 12% of gross international revenues on

Table 5.12
Corporate milestones

1880	Eastern Extension lays first international submarine cable between the Philippines and Hong Kong.
1897	An inter-island cable was laid to connect Manila to the Islands of Cebu, Panay, and Negros.
1928	Eastern Extension becomes part of Imperial and International Communications, Ltd (IICC).
1934	IICC becomes Cable and Wireless Ltd.
1951	Eastern Extension granted a new franchise.
1969	First international tropospheric scatter link to Taiwan.
1974	Constitutional changes required Eastern Extension to be 60% Filipino; Cable and Wireless retains 40%. Venture resulted in Eastern Telecoms/ETPI.
1977	Okinawa-Luzon-Hongkong (OLUHO) cable system established; Eastern Telecoms is the Terminal Operator of the Philippine end, and Currimao Cable Landing Station is constructed.
1978	Philippine-Singapore (PHILSIN) cable completed; first leg of the ASEAN Cable System.
1980	Taiwan-Luzon (TAILU) cable completed; Currimao Cable Landing Station is considered the largest cable head operations in the world.
1985	First to introduce enhanced packet switching technology.
1986	Incorporation of Asean Cableship Private Ltd.; Eastern Telecoms is designated as the Philippine representative.
1987	Eastern Telecoms files application to become the country's second International Gateway operator; challenges the PLDT monopoly.
1989	Awarded license for international gateway operations.
1990	Start of commercial operations of International Gateway Facility; direct dial and home country direct service introduced.
1991	Managed Fax Service—SUREFAX and intelligent prepay card phones introduced.

outgoing international calls, and none on incoming messages. For Philippines long distance, revenue sharing was 30% for the local operator and 70% for the toll operator. Because of low capacity utilization, and high cost of local lines, the local operators often incurred higher costs than the toll or international carriers.

PLDT had successfully fended off challenges in the courts in the past, but Cable & Wireless, with proposed investments of close to $220 million in the Philippines, was threatening a more aggressive stance in the future.

The Department of Transportation and Communications (DOTC) was the main policy-making body for telecommunications, reporting directly to the Congress of the Philippines (see figure 5.2). Its current secretary, Jesus V. Garcia, Jr., was a lawyer by profession. Prior to accepting his post under the Ramos government, he was head of the Conference of Inter-island Shipowners and Operators, in addition to managing a publishing empire.

Garcia was committed to implementing the Ramos government's program of "decentralization, devolution, deregulation and democratization." His policy-making

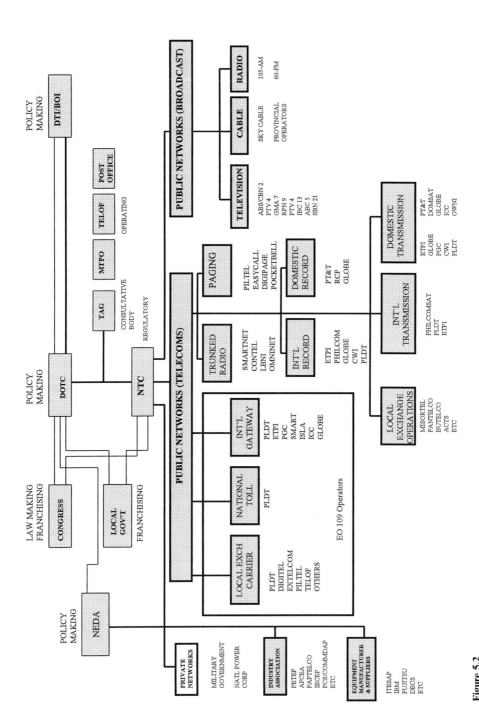

Figure 5.2
Telecommunications industry structure

priority was universal access, expanding communications facilities to rural areas and urban centers outside of Metro Manila. This was dearly needed considering that the Philippines suffered one of the lowest telephone density indexes.

Several programs were placed in effect to streamline policy formulation and implementation, in addition to rationalizing and trimming the workforce. Franchise grants (licenses to provide telecommunications services) were provided to cellular phone networks offering competitive rates, or to those expressing willingness to finance fiber optics technology. Garcia was particularly interested in encouraging investments which would break the monopoly of the Philippines Long Distance Telephone Co.

The Ramos government had floated a National Telecommunications Development Plan (NTDP) in 1991 that detailed implementation strategies to the year 2010. The main thrust of the plan was to liberalize service provision, while keeping control within the sphere of Filipino companies (no external multinational could own more than 40% of the equity of a telecommunications provider). Garcia stated that "from now on, the private sector will be the engine of growth of telecommunications with the Government acting only as a regulator, and regulating only as minimal an aspect as possible, leaving free enterprise to work and run its course."

PT&T's Choices

PT&T faced the daunting prospect of being a small player in a game dominated by PLDT. With deft and clever management, lobbying, and investment decisions, Marilyn Santiago knew that there were substantial opportunities to expand the scope of PT&T's operations. The time was opportune, given the current administration's stated penchant for deregulation and open markets. Yet even with a government that openly favored smaller operators, PLDT's substantial asset base and de facto control of country-wide toll service and long distance access presented substantial barriers to entry for PT&T. Several issues were of concern.

1. PT&T's toll lines provided it considerable revenue, given government-mandated revenue sharing of 30%/70% for the local operator versus the toll operator. Local service providers were lobbying to adjust this to 5%/50% to reflect the much higher capital costs of the local operator. Because of low capacity utilization, and high cost of local lines, the local operators often incurred higher costs than the toll or international carriers. Preferring to focus on PLDT, PT&T, to this date, had avoided conflicts with other operators.

2. PT&T sought to expand its role as a toll service provider, by forming a consortium with Philippine Global Communications that would build a $100 million nationwide fiber-optic telecommunication backbone network. Others were still being invited to join the consortium. Despite arrangements already made, Santiago had misgivings. A nationwide fiber-optic telecommunications network would benefit data intensive industries such as banking and insurance, but would not necessarily provide a wider scope of services. The Philippines, with a telephone density index of just 1.4, might not be ready for a "high-fiber" diet.

3. PT&T planned to bid aggressively for new customers by offering new services and value-added features (computer-to-computer data transmission, leased telegraph and data channels, call forwarding, etc.). Aggressive marketing of value-added services seemed almost necessary. Plain-old telephone service (POTS) pricing was regulated to 12% ROI (mandated by the DOTC), while debt issues covering capital costs for PT&T's new digital network were between 15.7% and 18.7% for various debt instruments, with PT&T's debt-to-equity ratio currently at 267%. PT&T felt that the allowed ROI should be raised to 20% to cover capital costs for network expansion.

4. PT&T needed to retain its existing customer base for telex and telegraph, whose revenues were declining at 15% annually. This customer base was mainly walk-in business to small message accepting counters.

Telex service offered interactive communication between teleprinters nationwide and worldwide through circuit switching systems (the service is no longer offered in the United States; in the Philippines, PT&T had 95% of the market). PT&T's telex machines had direct access to the international trunks through its affiliate Capitol Wireless, Inc.

Telegraph service was provided through the company's nationwide network of 601 branches and message accepting counters. These remained the country's basic record mass-based communications, especially in the countryside where telephone services covered only about 20% of the archipelago. PT&T had 70% of the market, mainly through walk-in customers, though 30% of this was accounted for by institutions.

To provide an alternative to these declining revenue sources, the company became the major provider (with PLDT) of Vodex services. Vodex was a low-cost direct-dial facility for local long distance calls and facsimile transmissions offered through public calling booths in areas not served by local telephone companies for long-distance service. The company also was aggressively promoting its Faxgram and Megafax products (e.g., enticing telegraph users with gift items) for walk-in fax service.

Presenting a greater challenge to PT&T retaining telex and telegraph customers was the government's plan to provide universal telephone service. This threatened to undermine any walk-in service, since universal access aimed to make it convenient to call from home.

5. PT&T wanted to install about 300,000 land lines to provide greater local coverage and service provision. This was almost necessary in light of the decline of walk-in business in fax, telex, and telegraph. Unfortunately, this expansion would require over $1 billion capital investment over a three-year period, and the company was not in a position to incur any additional debt. The other alternative was to reorganize, giving a larger equity interest to outside investors. Telectronic Systems, Capitol Wireless, Excel, and Societe Italiana Telecommunique all had been suggested as partners in this expansion.

Marilyn Santiago contemplated the decisions that lay ahead. There was a need to move quickly, and many options appeared attractive. The ultimate test of prudence in this choice would be long-run profitability to the company. As she pondered, the telephone rang.

Should she answer it? It had been a long day. Marilyn closed her briefcase, and let the telephone switch over to her voice mail. She would return the call tomorrow morning.

Note

1. For a discussion of the merits of universal service, see J. Browning (1994), "Universal Service," *Wired*, September 1994 (also available on-line at http://www.wired.com/wired/archive/3.01/glaser.if.html; http://www.wired.con/wired/archive/2.09/universal.access.html).

6 Access to Electronic Commerce Services

In today's world of ubiquitous computing on the desktop or laptop, where nearly everyone in business uses computers in some way or another, it is easy to forget how alien and strange the corporate computing landscape was only some 20 years ago. In those days, mainframe and network expertise were typically gained through apprenticeship at a vendor such as IBM, AT&T, or DEC. Journeyman programmers were scarce, and held considerable power in corporations simply through their understanding of the arcane code that implemented a firm's accounting and commerce systems. Not only were systems poorly documented but also descriptive manuals were badly organized. Much of a firm's institutional knowledge was held captive to the whims and peccadilloes of lowly programmers and clerks. Service bureaus gave management an opportunity to wrest control from these tyrannical technocrats, and subject computer and network operations to greater scrutiny—but at a high cost.

However, the computing universe had changed by 1990. Maturation of the networked microcomputer, the ubiquity of packaged solutions for nearly any software application, the deregulation of telephone services, and the rise of the Internet with its flat pricing structure made it possible for businesses to carry out a thorough examination of their deployment of technologies for electronic commerce. New business models emerged that reduced barriers to entering a product or service market. In many cases, these business models obviated economies of scale in networks and computing, and that intensified competition for customer attention in the marketplace.

The Roots of Electronic Commerce

The earliest forms of computer-based electronic commerce date from the late 1960s. In those days, they served a variety of purposes, that is, time sharing of mainframe computing CPU cycles, for example, by GE Information Services; packet-switched express mail delivery, for example, by Federal Express; business-to-business facsimile transmission; and data transfer delivery, for example, by AT&T. Businesses could acquire early e-commerce services by leasing the value-added networking services of international telephone companies, and by acquiring leased computer time and network access offered by the large in-house shops of GE, IBM, McDonnell Douglas, and EDS. (See, e.g., the case study "Access Security at *MDAIS* McDonnell Douglas Aerospace Information Services in chapter 10).

In the 1970s and 1980s, businesses extended their networks to reach out to customers and business partners by electronically sending and receiving purchase orders, invoices, and shipping notifications. The result of this was a proliferation of

EDI transmitted over value-added networks (VANs). In the 1980s, vendors such as McDonnell Douglas and General Motors introduced computer-aided design, engineering, and manufacturing over these communications networks, which allowed managers, engineers, and users to collaborate on design and production.

The consequences of this laissez-faire development of electronic commerce were felt throughout the 1970s and 1980s. Bewildering arrays of proprietary network architectures, computer architectures, and clumsy text-based computer interfaces of proprietary software were haphazardly grouped together with vendor hardware, making electronic commerce and computing both labor and capital intensive. None of this came cheaply. All but the largest firms were locked out of e-commerce technologies by their sheer cost and scale. In response, service bureaus grew out of the internal corporate computing operations of larger firms. They used their already substantial economies of scale to offer network and computing services of greater reliability and lower cost than even large firms could develop internally.

The traditional market for electronic commerce services, over these three decades, from 1960 to 1990, can be encapsulated into five divisions:

1. *Electronic mail*, providing store-and-forward services for the business-to-business exchange of information. *Mailbox* services transferred information directly from the sender to the receiver; *gateway* services transferred information only as far as a corporate server.

2. *Enhanced fax*, providing point-to-point delivery of documents encoded as fax rather than e-mail, which usually implied that there was nontext information that needed to be encoded.

3. *Electronic data interchange*, providing computer-to-computer exchange of information using standardized transaction formats. These transactions typically involved purchase or sales functions.

4. *Transaction processing*, supporting credit, claims, payment authorization, and settlement of transactions. Transaction processing services often involved collaboration between an information transport service and an authorization provider, such as a bank.

5. *Groupware*, employed within a secure, managed environment, which supported e-mail, calendaring, scheduling, real-time conferencing, information sharing, and workflow management.

These five electronic commerce services defined the distinct networks and protocols by which information to, from, and about electronic markets was transported.

The Internet

The Internet was created in 1969 as a scalable (i.e., offering users the same performance regardless of size), fault-tolerant (i.e., able to recover and operate despite damage to one or more components,) proprietary military-university packet switching network (refer to the Internet timeline given in the appendix). In 1991, the Internet was opened for commercial use, initially dominated by commercial activities of military aerospace contractors.

No technology, no matter how clever or seductive, can survive without a compelling reason to use it, the so-called killer application. The popularity of electronic mail on the early Internet was completely unanticipated by its designers and became the accidental killer application. In general, e-mail took on a less formal tone than typewritten correspondence, so the formality and perfection that most people expected in a typed letter did not become associated with network messages, probably because the network was so much faster and so much more like the telephone. This did much to advance the quantity of content communicated by e-mail. To this day, those attempting to depict the Internet have trouble drawing parallels with familiar media. The debate continues: Is the Internet more like a telephone, or a television, or a backyard fence, or some mutant hybrid of all of these? The usefulness of the Web for e-commerce depends on the answer to this question.

Since its commercialization in 1991, the Internet has grown into a common, though not yet universal, transport for all five types of e-commerce. With its low cost and flat rate structure, it is steadily narrowing the commercial niches available to competing technologies. The Internet has evolved beyond its initial e-mail transport function with an expanding set of Web-based multimedia capabilities. Customer service, advertising, infomercials, and collaborative workgroups are thriving on the commerce-enabled Internet. Beyond its global breadth of coverage, specific aspects of the Internet's historical development have made it well suited for commercial applications. They have contributed some weaknesses as well.

The introduction of Web browser software in 1993, originally as a vehicle for high-energy physicists to exchange research data, brought a wide range of multimedia transport capabilities to the Internet—pictures, text, video, and audio. Marc Andreessen of the National Center for Supercomputing Applications, and inventor of Mosaic, the first Web browser, went on to cofound Netscape Communications Corporation, thereby expanding the Internet's commercial capabilities through continual development of browser and Internet server software.

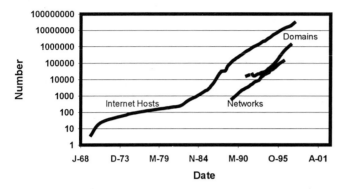

Figure 6.1
Growth of the Internet

The number of Internet hosts (i.e., uniquely addressable sets of Internet databases residing on one or more machines, defined as domain names with a unique IP address) in 1998 is somewhere in the region of 30 to 40 million, doubling annually (figure 6.1).[1] This probably understates the real number of Internet hosts by a factor of three to four. Most Internet hosts are hidden behind corporate firewalls, serving as intranets. So sophisticated and pervasive has Internet technology become that it broadly substitutes for other vehicles inside the firm for disseminating information concerning policy and procedures, collaborative work, meetings, technical manuals, and history.

Electronic commerce service provision on the Internet has matured in three distinct stages. In the first stage, the Internet was primarily a transport mechanism for e-mail, static information, and Web-based ad copy. File downloads were not widely used (many sites did not allow file transfer areas because of their common use to exchange pirated software), and transfer of information lacked security, integrity, performance, and predictability.

The second stage of electronic commerce growth began in 1995, initiated by a variety of secure transaction processing services that made purchases and transaction completion over the Internet a reality. The added security and privacy of transaction processing opened up the Internet to a variety of commercial and corporate uses. This stage has also seen the rapid evolution of help desk and technical support technologies for the Web, and the use of the Web on a broad scale for collaborative work, idea exchange, and chat. More than three-quarters of Internet users have downloaded software and information through file transfer protocol (FTP); and more than half have used newsgroups. The emergence of powerful Web search engines superseded traditional Internet search tools such as Gopher, Archie, and WAIS, and col-

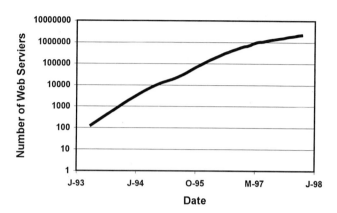

Figure 6.2
Number of Web servers worldwide

laborative software by Netscape, Lotus, and Microsoft has been used by more than half of Internet users.[2]

We are entering a third—though certainly not final—stage of Internet maturation. In this stage, electronic commerce is experimenting with new interfaces, business models, and technologies—for example, interactive television, Web TV, and push technologies—that will make transaction-based Internet access available to a broad base of consumers. Internet-based electronic commerce should accelerate with the emergence of more engaging machines and interfaces than those of the desktop computer. Both business-to-business and customer-directed commerce will benefit. Equally important will be the integration of legacy databases, for example, for sales, credit, customers, and so forth, into the corporate intranet for mission-critical applications. Collaborative processing is evolving with greater reality and immediacy because of the incorporation of dataconferencing and videoconference capabilities onto intranet/Internet platforms.

As vendors compress more functionality into their Internet servers, implementation of Web service has surged at medium and large firms. Firms may feel more comfortable running their own operations in situations where intranets contain proprietary or sensitive information. Many also feel that they need to nurture in-house expertise in Web design and operation as Internet technologies grow all the more pervasive. By 1998, more than 80% of firms in the United States had deployed Web servers, with the number expected to reach 100% by 2000 (see figure 6.2). Netscape Enterprise Server on Unix is currently the dominant server software. Microsoft has successfully leveraged the growth of Windows NT to promote a suite of Internet information servers drawing on SQL server database engines with Access forms, queries, and reports for commercial transaction processing. Microsoft provides a compelling out-of-the-box platform for Internet-based electronic commerce.

Firewalls are Internet servers through which all transactions coming from the Internet need to pass prior to entering a particular firm's intranet. The firewall server—one or more computers with firewall software installed—tightly monitors incoming transactions for content and identity in order to avoid viruses, spoofing, and other "hacking" threats from outside the firm. Despite widespread public concern about Internet security, firewalls are implemented in only about half of U.S. firms, and an even lower percentage internationally. Industry's relatively low level of firewall implementation reflects the fact that the greatest barrier a firm has to external hackers is the hacker's limited knowledge of the architecture and operations of the firm's systems.

ISP Business Models

The labyrinth of software, hardware, and networking required of Internet/intranet systems created a robust market for Internet service providers (ISPs). These ISPs profit from economies of scale in the application of software, hardware, and network access across customers. They may offer Web site design, transaction processing, help desk support, and other services as well. One-stop shopping is attractive to new users and small firms. Yet there is a strong trend toward firms purchasing their own Web server installations (more than 80% of firms now purchase) and away from rental of external services (less than 20% acquire the services of an ISP). This trend will accelerate with wider adoption of transaction-based electronic commerce applications, in which the firm will have a desire for greater control over data and operations.

Rapid advancements in technology and the swift convergence toward common information transfer protocols (typically TCP/IP based) have condemned many previously viable business models for e-commerce and Internet service provision to obsolescence, or at least substantial disadvantage in long term. Time sharing in the 1970s gave way to smaller midrange computers; on-line information services such as Prodigy, America Online, and Compuserve, found it difficult to compete on access alone against the free World Wide Web information content provided by cheap, unbundled Internet access. (For example, see the Asia Online case study included in this chapter). In light of these trends, ISPs will need to rethink their fundamental business model in the near future. ISPs are likely to specialize in profitable niches— credit and transaction processing, file transfer, help desk, video rental and so forth— or as intermediaries in particular vertical markets.

The Internet is only partially displacing the traditional providers of electronic commerce services. More importantly, it is enabling providers and users to extend their reach into previously impenetrable markets. Small firms have not traditionally conducted electronic commerce because of high costs and complexity. These firms are benefiting most dramatically from cheap, reliable access to Internet-based electronic commerce services.

In a world without clear advantages of economies of scale, electronic commerce service providers are obsessed with value added: How do they restructure service pricing to rationalize the value of services as opposed to the cost of the network transporting the information? Strategies that address this question require nimble competition, customization, and sensitivity to user demand and market trends.

E-commerce service providers are increasingly focusing on sculpting distinct niches in vertical markets where they can customize and streamline their offerings. The emphasis is on taking advantage of core competencies to service a particular cross section of customers better. Traditionally, EDI services providers have concentrated on markets such as transportation, manufacturing, mass merchandisers, apparel retailers, and grocery retailers (e.g., see the Procter & Gamble case study in chapter 4).

Another trend is the growing importance of standards and their adoption by a larger community (again illustrated in the P&G case, when the company sold its proprietary CRP software to IBM's ISSC). A market leader has the potential to impose its own standards on a market through the implementation of its own technology (e.g., Microsoft with some of its technologies).

One of the biggest challenges for ISPs is what services to offer and how to differentiate their product from those of competitors. For example, in the highly competitive Hong Kong business market, Asia Online is finding it difficult to achieve any significant profit margin in the Internet access business. Thus, it has decided to target value-added Internet content aggressively and to provide an attractive bundle of services that will attract both customers accessing the Internet from other providers and advertisers and retailers interesting in reaching these customers. America Online in the United States has transitioned through the same processes, but has also found providing value-added services and user interface context more attractive than simply providing basic Internet access. However, the challenges of providing attractive content are even more difficult across Asia than in the United States owing to the wide range of cultures and languages that make the Asian "market" far from homogeneous.

In comparison to Asia Online, China Internet is struggling with the challenges and opportunities of bringing the Internet to the most populated nation in the world. The China Internet Corporation case illustrates some of the challenges and opportunities facing firms trying to bring electronic commerce into developing nations. The Internet and electronic commerce are definitely global and reach virtually every nation of the world, but there are still some unique challenges associated with bringing these capabilities into some parts of the world where telephone penetration is still less than 1% of the population. In developing countries, services taken for granted in the United States or Europe (e.g., automated interbank check clearing) may well be defined as electronic commerce capabilities enabled by an emerging information and communications infrastructure.

Notes

1. Mark Lotter, *Network Wizards,* 1997. http://www.nw.com
2. Business Research Group, "Commercial Uses of the Internet," Newton, MA., July 1997.

Asia Online: The Online Service for Asia

Wai-yee Lam, newly appointed Chief Operating Officer of Asia Communications Global Limited (ACGL), could finally settle in her new office after a long week of orientation with the senior staff. As a 12-year Telecom veteran with the recent career achievement in international market development for Hongkong Telecom, she considered taking the new assignment in ACGL most exciting and challenging. The most apparent challenge was to build an attractive and easy-to-use service that would enable ACGL to stand out in the crowded and anonymous Internet market in Asia, but more importantly to lead the team to achieve the company's mission in becoming the leader in providing advanced on-line services and quality Asian content to individuals and companies around the world.

The most imminent priority for Wai-yee Lam was to develop an overall business model for ACGL to encompass all the business elements (access, content, commerce and cost) and determine the geographic on which the company was to focus. Lam was also eager to identify new product and revenue streams for ACGL to stay ahead of competition as well as to ensure a piece of the Internet market for the future.

Company Background

Asia Communications Global Limited was the holding company of Asia Online Limited and AsiaTech Publications Limited. Asia Online Limited was restructured into an Internet service provider from a small local bulletin board service in May 1995, with the intent to package and distribute on-line information on Asian business and culture. AsiaTech Publications, sister company and strategic partner of Asia Online, was involved with publishing of information in the technology and on-line services industries.

ACGL was cofounded by four well-regarded businessmen, Thomas Yuen, Philip Wong, Sam Lim, and Michael Ng, all of whom have been very successful in their careers. Thomas Yuen, one of the cofounders of AST, a Fortune 500 company, was a well-known Silicon Valley entrepreneur and is the Chairman of ACGL. Philip Wong, the Deputy Chairman and CEO of ACGL, became popularly known for turning AST into one of the leading PC companies in the Asia/Pacific region for over eight years. Michael Ng was the Executive Director of Legend Holdings Limited, the largest computer distributor in China. Sam Lim was a wealth and very successful investor in Hong Kong. Having strong technical and business background in the IT industry, these gentlemen shared a common interest and common vision in

This case was prepared by Dr. Theodore H. Clark and a team of MBA students from The Hong Kong University of Science and Technology (including Vicky Au, Michael Chang, Jimmy Cheurn, Albert Ho, Margaret Leung, Sandra Leung, Henry Pau, and Jimmy Ying).

the emerging Internet market and decided to invest in the start-up Internet company with a view to participating in the developing Internet industry. ACGL is financially backed by several strong investors: Peregrine Direct Investment Limited, Japanese-capital SOFTBANK Holdings Inc., and California-based venture capital partnership The Cutler Group. ACGL received from these investors US$20 million capital toward the middle of 1996.

Asia Online started as a company of five and had expanded by mid-1997 to over 100 staff in Hong Kong and offices in Taiwan and the Philippines. Asia Online has been aggressive in recruiting highly talented professionals in the industry to join its management team. The recruitment of Wai-yee Lam, who earned a strong reputation in the telecommunications industry and in developing international markets, was a good example showing their commitment in bringing expertise into the development of its business. In September 1996, Jonathan Leung, who has had extensive experiences in the IT industry, was appointed General Manager of Asia Online (Hong Kong) responsible for the overall management and strategic planning of the Hong Kong operation.

The structure and organization of the company was still fluid and dynamic. Apart from the few administrative staff and the management team, the majority of the existing staff belonged to the technical support team and customer service team. There was also a small product development team responsible for the creation of applications and services for Asia Online. As the strategic focus of the company was still evolving along with the development of the Internet industry, it was expected that the organization structure of the company would continue to be defined.

Asia Online's Products and Services

Asia Online was an Asian-content-driven on-line service provider utilizing the Internet as an access platform. It offered a wide array of business and consumer information databases, on-line travel and financial services, on-line shopping, entertainment center, and more. The content business was seen as a major revenue stream for the future, even though it was in a business development stage being subsidized by the access business.

High-speed access to the Internet was a major service offering to both individuals and businesses. Asia Online had about 15,000 access subscribers in August 1996 and the number had increased to 25,000 within six months (table 6.1). This growth rate was maintained and Asia Online had around 30,000 subscribers by mid-1997. According to a SRH study in early 1997, Asia Online was the third-largest ISP in Hong Kong, with market share exceeding 11%.

Table 6.1
Hong Kong Internet users

		1996	1997	1998
Internet user	HK	0.47 M	0.70 M	0.96 M
	Global	45 M	90 M	150 M
PC penetration (household)	HK	0.57 M (34%)	0.63 M (38%)	0.66 M (40%)
	U.S.	37.1 M (38%)	41.2 M (40%)	47.5 M (45%)

Source: Various statistical journals.

Asia Online Network Services also offered leased-line connections and full Web design services and marketing consultancy on an ad hoc and retainer basis. Strategic relationships with third parties such as EUnet, Datacraft, and Cisco had been established on a regional basis to provide customers with immediate access to high-quality products and services in each market. Asia Online also maintained full sales technical support and customer service capabilities to build and service a portfolio of corporate leased-line customers among Asia's growing list of multinational corporations.

The Development of the U.S. Internet Industry

The Internet was seen as a hype by some and as the future by others. Started as a military project in the United States with the primary function of electronic mails and file transfers, the Internet was popularized by the World Wide Web around 1990. Termination of government subsidy had pushed the Internet one step further in its commercialization in 1993. By 1997, it was an industry on its own as well as an embedded part of every business. Newly created business segments such as Internet access providers, Web hosting, Website creation, Web-enabling software, and high-speed access equipment were then all multimillion-dollar industries. The phenomenon brought about by the Internet was fast becoming an essential element of the information age that was revolutionizing the way we worked, lived, and played.

For businesses, the Internet represented a new medium, a new way of reaching customers. Companies realized the growth of their business would be linked to the growth of the Internet. Virtually every corporation and organization, regardless of size and scope, had set up Websites as vehicles for information distribution and self-promotion. Internally, companies were also utilizing intranets as means of communications and implementing corporate information technology strategies.

For consumers, the Web was very appealing, with all the multimedia elements and the myriad of information. Search engines and Web directories were all-encompassing to bring desired information to users' browsers. Special interest groups from across the world could meet in virtual space to discuss the latest in topics of interest. Communications was made easier with electronic mail, not only for businesses, but for personal and social purposes.

Many forms of entertainment could be found on the Web, ranging from the very controversial pornographic materials to various Websites pertaining to music, movies, fun, and games. Also as an alternate source of entertainment, the Internet had information on leisure and travel about any special interest and any travel destination. It was estimated that about 25% of time spent on the Web was entertainment related, with activities such as casual surfing, chats, bulletin boards, playing games, and shopping.

In a report released in October 1996, U.S.-based Forrester Research estimated that by year 2000, one third of businesses and 25% of households in the United States would have Internet connections and that businesses would set up half a million publicly hosted Web sites. Besides the much sought after Internet access market for connectivity to the Web, there was tremendous expectation for electronic commerce in the realm of the Internet. The research company estimated that electronic commerce would represent US$66 billion in U.S.-related Internet revenue by year 2000. Forrester reckons that the three nontechnology segments that would generate significant revenue from the Internet in 2000 are content providers, financial services, and consumer retailers.

At the end of 1996, it was estimated that there were approximately 45 million people using the Internet, with roughly 30 million of those in North America, 9 million in Europe, and 6 million in Asia Pacific. Even though there was a lag in Asia, the growth rate of Internet users was the fastest. A survey done in April 1996 suggested that about 100,000 people in Hong Kong regularly use the Internet. Japan was estimated to have about 500,000 regular Internet users, with more than 1,000 ISPs. Other Internet markets in Asia that are growing, albeit at a slower pace, included Taiwan, Singapore, Korea and Australia. So the question for the untapped, yet fast developing Asia market was: Who would be best positioned to capitalize on this tremendous opportunity and how might they do it?

Different Business Sectors of ISPs

The core business of ISPs has traditionally been Internet access provision. This was often bundled with Web hosting services as well as various kinds of on-line services. Under close examination and unbundling the products and services provided, every ISP business could be segmented into one or more of the following business activity categories.

Table 6.2
Hong Kong ISPs' traffic capacity

	Asia Online	HKT IMS	HKT NETPlus	Star Internet	SuperNet	AT&T
HKIX	2 × T1	T3	T1 + T3	T1 + E1	T1	T1
Other local	T1	E1			T1	T1 + 256 kbps
U.S. backbone	T1	2 × E1	T1	2 × T1	T1 + 768 kbps	
Asian network	64 kbps	64 kbps	960 kbps			

Source: Various Hong Kong ISPs.
Note: E1 = 2.048 Mbps. T1 = 1.544 Mbps. T3 = 45 Mbps.

Internet Access

Based on monthly subscription fees of around US$20, regular dial-up services were provided to allow individuals and businesses to have Internet connections. The Internet access provider would generally have established a dial-up modem pools and points of presence for users to have local dial-up facilities. High-speed access services such as ISDN and dedicated leased line were also offered for the more demanding users and corporate customers. Ease of access and quality and speed of the connection were points of comparison between different ISPs (table 6.2). ISPs' traffic capacity to the Internet backbone, an essential element of an ISP infrastructure, was also an important consideration for potential subscribers. Since the access business involved a good amount of fixed cost, there were generally economies of scale in operation and volume was a key factor. However, Internet access providers later found that customer service, another highly considered factor when choosing among access providers, grew in proportion to the subscriber base, generating another operational concern for expanding access businesses.

Web Hosting

The appeal of being able to access millions of new customers as well as supporting existing customers had lured companies to establish a Web presence. Companies' Websites were highly publicized and had increased visibility of companies. Having had a Website on the WWW was already a business norm. Large corporations generally have their own hardware and software facilities to maintain their Websites. Even with the new generation of tools which make it possible for companies to build and maintain their own Websites, companies were finding it beneficial to seek external expertise in application creation and hosting. Essential to this business would be graphical expertise and experience with the latest in Internet software programming.

Electronic Commerce

Electronic commerce via the WWW was a segment that was generating high expectations. It could be separated into two categories: business-to-business commerce and retail commerce. EDI (electronic data interchange) on the Internet platform would create a standard for documentation exchange between businesses, resulting in efficiency and accuracy. On the retail front, companies were building electronic commerce applications which allowed customers to directly order goods and services from their own computers. The term "electronic commerce" encompassed many of the additional processes which support these transactions. These included electronic delivery of the product, order processing, billing, credit card payment, credit check, electronic cash transactions, and customer support. A major hurdle that was still being overcome was the issue of security in on-line transaction, which was more a social acceptability issue than a technological one.

Content Provider

The WWW was a means of searching for various kinds of information. If such information, or content, could be found at a centralized and convenient location, the potential to attract heavy traffic presented a great opportunity for advertisers and marketers. This was the aim of many content providers who seek to reap advertising revenue. Information and content would generally be provided free of charge to attract a larger base of readership, adding more value to the advertisers. Other content providers chose to charge usage of content on subscription or membership basis. Such content would generally appeal to specific audiences valuing the information provided. While some content providers were themselves creators of the content, others were packagers of content, much like content resellers. Content packagers usually use partnership and alliances as a strategy for content acquisition.

While some ISPs provided end-to-end offers to their customers by packaging Internet access, Web development tools, training, Web hosting, and on-line services, there were other small niche players with very focused target customer segments. As with any other business, the Internet services business involved a significant amount of market segmentation and product differentiation. There were the higher-end services geared toward business customers and individuals with quality concerns, while there were also basic cost-effective services for the price-conscious users who were less sensitive to quality issues such as congestion, system stability, and support.

The Hong Kong Internet Market

Just as ARPANET was the original seed of the Internet in the United States, the HARNET (Hongkong Academic and Research NETwork) was the very first form of interconnection of networks in Hong Kong. HARNET started as a network platform to be shared by all Hong Kong higher educational institutions in 1992. The 64 kbps link to the United States was upgraded to 128 kbps in September 1993. Before then there were very little commercial elements within the Hong Kong Internet community. In late 1993, a small commercial Internet service provider (Hong Kong Super-Net Ltd.) set up its own 64 kbps link to the United States, which began to spark commercial interest in Internet in Hong Kong. In 1994, Internet on the nonacademic side continued to grow, albeit at a very slow rate. It was not until 1995 that the general public awakened to the Internet phenomenon in the United States and business potential for access provision to the Internet was realized. In that year, more than 50 Internet service provider licenses were issued. This growth in the Internet access business continued. By the end of 1996, there were over 90 licensed Internet service providers for the Hong Kong market.

Varying in both size and scope, among the ISPs with larger subscriber base that have sprung up in Hong Kong were Hongkong Telecom IMS Netvigator, Hong Kong Star Internet, Asia Online, and Hong Kong SuperNet (table 6.3). Each of these major ISPs tried to leverage its core competencies, vying for a share of the subscriber base of less than 200,000. Netvigator and Star Internet, the top two ISPs in Hong

Table 6.3
Pricing scheme for individual users

	Unlimited usage				Per usage			
	Asia Online	Star Internet	HKT IMS	AT&T	Asia Online	Star Internet	HKT IMS	AT&T
Join	$88	$98	$50	—	$88	$98	$50	$100
Annual fee	—	—	—	—	$188	$50	$280	$68
Monthly fee	$108	$108	$108	$128	—	$20+	—	—
Usage								
Free	—	—	—	—	—	—	—	$18
Additional	—	—	—	—	$8/hr	$10/hr	$10/hr	$12/hr
Storage								
Free	5 MB	5 MB	5 MB	—	5 MB	5/MB	5/MB	2.5 MB
Additional	$10/MB	$20/MB	$20/MB	—	$10/MB	R20/MB/m	R20/MB/m	$8/MB/m

Source: Various Hong Kong ISPs.

Kong, had the advantages of their existing telecommunications business, capitalizing on network connectivity, customer care, and billing, which allowed them to quickly grow their subscriber base.

As the ISP business took shape and began to develop, the Internet access business started to have a more clear distinction from the on-line services business. ISPs have traditionally been engaged in access provision and various hosting/Web development services. Competition has been intense due to low barriers to entry: Information was easily available at very low cost, and access was universal and nonexclusive. Technologies were available to all with low setup costs. Anyone could start up an ISP with phone lines and a high-end server. On the customer front, switching costs were low as most software has built in compatibility to competitors' products.

By 1997, despite the highest level of ISP licenses issued, the number of active ISPs had converged somewhat to a more sustainable number and companies were finding their niche market segments. The market trend was for the players to specialize in one layer of business or sector with narrow focus and grow their consumer base over time. Some companies saw opportunities in providing content and facilitating electronic commerce. Being in a technology-driven industry with a pool of Internet-related expertise, ISPs were in a good position to provide commerce-related services bundled with traditional access services.

Asia Online's Competitive Position and Its Strategic Direction

The business vision of Asia Online was in fact beyond its home base in Hong Kong. Asia Online saw the lack of a comprehensive source of socioeconomic data on the Asia Pacific region, home to more than half the world's population, as an untapped business opportunity in the Internet business. The mission for Asia Online was to stand out in the Internet industry as an Asian content provider, i.e., a provider of contents with major emphasis on Asian issues. The company has therefore embarked on an aggressive growth plan that called for linking the currently fragmented on-line Asian communities into a single, powerful regional "network." Asia Online was also in a very unique position to merge the East with the West. Ties in the Asian communities could be leveraged with the business connections with the United States. Even the board of the company had a balanced composition of East and West, with representation from Peregrine and SOFTBANK.

As described by Steve Case, President and CEO of America Online, the guiding principles for the success of an Internet business can be expressed by eight Cs: content, context, community, connectivity, commerce, cost, control, and customer service. Asia Online realized the importance of encompassing these eight Cs of the Internet business into their business platform. The essence of the Internet was the dissemination and sharing of information. On the Web, content is king. Asia Online realized that in order to provide customers a wide array of information, alliance with other overseas content providers was important. Asia Online had established agreements with local and U.S. partners to provide a variety of news and information on entertainment, travel, and tourism.

However, as the content available on the Internet continued to expand, customers would need guidance on the Net when faced with the ocean of information. The context of how information is gathered and presented has become increasingly important. This was also where Asia Online focused its product differentiation efforts. It revamped its on-line services in early 1997 to provide a more user-friendly home page for its current and new customers. In order to allow for more customer flexibility, Asia Online redesigned its on-line services, which were originally tailored for one browser, Microsoft's Internet Explorer, to also accommodate other popular browsers, such as Netscape Navigator. It had also started to offer different information in the context of channels—entertainment, travel, and sport—to suit special interests of different individuals.

Connectivity and cost would be the two factors in fostering the dynamism of the Internet growth (table 6.4). These included ease of access and stability. Users wanted to be able to get connected at first dial-up attempt and stay connected at minimum cost. Asia Online has spent a lot of effort in finding ways to allow customers easy access in terms of use of browser and overseas access. It had a relatively large bandwidth in Hong Kong with separate T1 lines to Hong Kong Internet Exchange, the Hong Kong gateway for international Internet traffic, and to the U.S. Internet backbone. It also offered roaming services by joining GRIC, Global Reach Internet Connection, an alliance of global ISPs and telephone companies (figure 6.3).

In view of the intensity of existing competition, customer service has become a focal point in terms of competitive advantage (table 6.5). Not all customers had a good understanding of IT issues and concepts. An average customer might find the whole process of connecting to the Internet rather complicated: installation of the dial-up kit, installing browser software, and setting up the various log-in parameters. Asia Online's original on-line service registration process was commented to be user unfriendly by most average users. To improve its level of service, Asia Online increased its staffing in the customer service department from 10 to over 20 by early 1997. It also invested in an interactive voice response system to automate and better manage the more common queries. It had also offered 24-hour round-the-clock customer service hotlines.

Table 6.4
Pricing scheme for corporate users

	20 users	10 users		20 users		30 users		>30 users		Per user	
	Asia Online	Star Internet	HKT IMS	Star Internet	HKT IMS	Star Internet	HKT IMS	Star Internet	HKT IMS	AT&T	SuperNet
Join	$88	—	$50	—	—	—	—	—	—	$150/ID	$170/ID
Monthly fee	$350	$350	$350	$500	$500	$650	$650	—	—	$250	$175
Usage											
Free	50 hr	50 hr	50 hr	70 hr	70 hr	100 hr	100 hr	125 hr	150 hr	30 hr	25 hr
Additional	$6/hr	$6/hr	$6/hr	$6/hr	$6/hr	$6/hr	$6/hr	$6/hr	$6/hr	$10/hr	$22/hr (peak) $7/hr (non-peak)
Storage											
Free	50 MB	30 MB	30 MB	60 MB	60 MB	90 MB	90 MB	100 MB	120 MB	—	2.5 MB
Additional	$10/ MB/m	$20/ MB/m	$20/ MB/m	$20/ MB/m	$20/ MB/m	$20/ MB/m	$20/ MB/m	$20/ MB/m	$20/ MB/m	—	$8/MB

Source: Various Hong Kong ISPs.

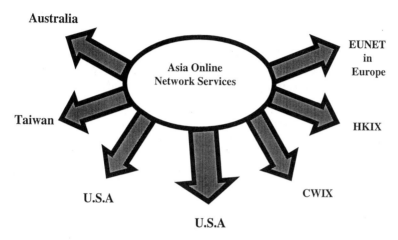

Figure 6.3
Asia Online's Network Capacity
Source: Asia Online Limited, January 1997.

Table 6.5
Hong Kong ISP service comparison

Product/services	Asia Online	HKT IMS	Star Internet	AT&T	SuperNet
Access	Π	Π	Π	Π	Π
E-mail	Π	Π	Π	Π	Π
E-mail to fax	Π				Π
Hosting	Π		Π	Π	Π
On-line shop	Π	Π	Π		
Video conference			Π		
Roaming	Π	Π	Π		Π
MAC compatible	Π		Π		
Newsgroup	Π		Π		
Advertising	Π	Π	Π		Π

Source: Internet Age, January 1997.

Strategically, Asia Online reckoned the need to build an Asian community in the Internet to be key. To be able to empower customers to take control of the medium for their own household needs was vital to its future success. Through early entries into the developing markets, Asia Online would stay ahead of competition. It has already opened offices in Taiwan, the Philippines, and China, and has set plans to move into the rest of the Asian countries in a very aggressive manner (figure 6.4).

Key Operating Issues

As the organization and the size of the business continued to expand, human resources management became a major concern for the company. In a new and highly competitive industry, Asia Online found it a constant challenge to find the right level of experienced technical staff and at the same time to retain them. The high staff turnover became a hidden cost to the existing operation of the company. The problem intensified as the expansion called for setting up more effective and efficient operations in selected countries within Asia. Putting together a long-term staff development program and an attractive reward system became a priority for the senior management.

The expansion of the business also called for a change of company culture and management system. ACGL had to be transformed from a small entrepreneur type of company into a world class corporation competing in the Asia region. Not only did the company have to support such growth with a lot of capital and human resources investment, management also saw the importance of building more systemization and control into the once very organic organization. A more structured organization with well-defined division of responsibilities had to be incorporated, while at the same time not stifling creativity and entrepreneurism. A set of consistent operational guidelines also needed to be developed and explicitly communicated throughout the organization. The success of such transition would be crucial to the future expansion of the company.

More importantly, the increasing operation cost that resulted from the expansion of business would put a burden on Asia Online's asset management. It became an imminent priority to pay attention to operational cost and cash flow of the company.

Key Management Issues

According to its top management, the biggest challenge for Asia Online was to develop an overall business model for the company to synergize across all products

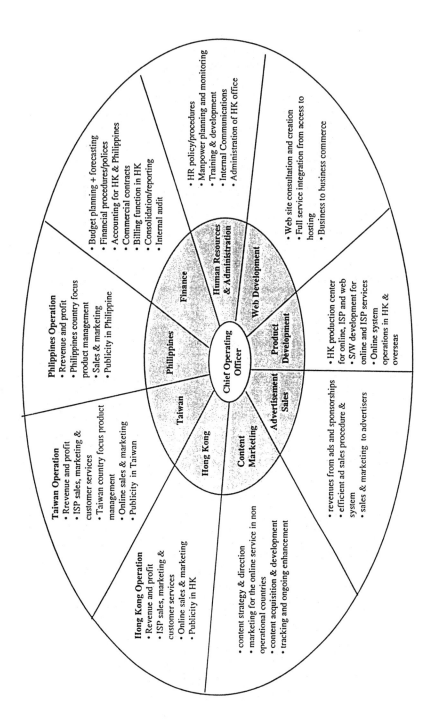

Figure 6.4
Asia Online's teaming chart
Source: Asia Communications Global Limited.

that Asia Online offered and extend that operation into other key Asian markets. It was even more important for the management to understand how the development of the Internet would impact the revenue stream and cost structure of the different products in the future. In early 1997, the revenue stream of the company came primarily from the Internet access services.

The Highly Competitive Access Business

One of the key management issues for Asia Online was to determine how much focus should be put on the access business. The Internet access business was fairly homogeneous. It was very difficult to build brand and product differentiation as the level of technology was very standard throughout the industry. It was also a highly competitive sector: There were low barriers to entry (start-up cost can be as low as HK$1.2M), and most ISPs operated at a very low profit margin. The cost structure of access business in the consumer market depended largely on the number of subscribers. Reaching a critical mass was important in determining the economics of operation, and that is all tied into competitive pricing, volume, and margins. Building brand visibility and gaining market share therefore became critical in maintaining a competitive advantage in the industry. Major players, like Hongkong Telecom IMS, with its inherent high brand recognition and investment, had been focusing their efforts on advertising and promotion campaigns in expanding consumer base ever since their launch, which has proven to be a very successful strategy. By mid-1997, Hongkong Telecom IMS had about 40% share of the total Internet access market in Hong Kong (figures 6.5 and 6.6).

In Hong Kong, retail outlets could be much more powerful as compared to other cities in the world. The highly concentrated retail environment in Hong Kong made shopping very convenient and a part of everyday life for most people. Widely distributed products at retail could usually generate higher brand awareness in the market. Both Hongkong Telecom IMS and Hong Kong Star Internet had a broad reach of retail shops to sell their telecom products. Such retail setups could allow them to run consumer promotion in high visibility and also made the account sign-up process much more convenient for most first-time Internet users. In addition, they also used cross promotional schemes with their other telecommunication products. Asia Online, on the other hand, was relatively less visible in the mass consumer market with only one office location, in Causeway Bay.

Management of Asia Online, however, was questioning the use of mass consumer marketing techniques to gain market share and to manage loyalty. They believed that with the scale of the current Internet business, perhaps none of the ISPs were making

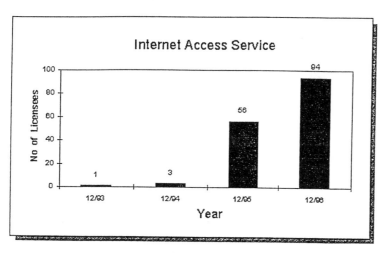

Figure 6.5
Number of ISP licensees in Hong Kong
Source: Office of Telecommunications Authority, April 1997.

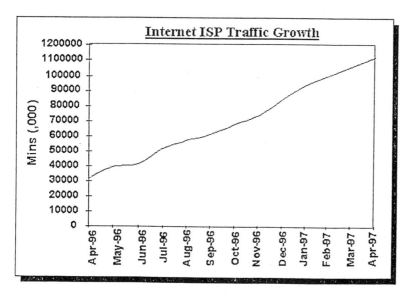

Figure 6.6
Internet traffic growth rate in Hong Kong
Source: OFTA, April 1997.

any profit from the access market alone. Instead, Asia Online was deploying a more targeted strategy in reaching a group of higher-end customers. By mid-1997, Asia Online launched a member-get-member program to encourage referrals from existing users. Incentives such as free service would be given to members who successfully introduced new members. For the long term, Asia Online also aimed to focus on providing access service to corporate customers which would be less sensitive to cost but more quality and service oriented as compared to the mass consumer market.

While it took time for the response of the member-get-member program to mobilize, Asia Online found itself lagging further behind on its subscriber growth when compared to its major competitors. It therefore became a strategic decision for Asia Online to reconsider if it should increase its marketing investment in the access sector to build the critical mass that could enable it to be competitive and profitable.

Opportunity in the Content Business

Management of Asia Online firmly believed that the future of Asia Online's business lay primarily in the development of its content business. The key issue here was to determine what should be obtained through alliances and partnerships and what should be created in house considering time to market and capability. As for the content sector, differentiation of products was more visible. Industry players could use variety, context, language, or even organization and presentation of information to compete for and appeal to specific targeted audiences. Asia Online had chosen to concentrate on the context and language elements by repackaging Asian content supplemented by Asian languages. Moreover, content ownership has become an emerging concern in the industry with regard to intellectual property rights over information, which may jeopardize Asia Online's position as a content packager. A "make-or-buy" decision had to be made with certain contents, with the use of content acquisition as a possible strategy.

The competition in this sector was also getting intense. Not only did Asia Online have to face keen competition from existing publishers and newspapers which were well-established media, but it also had to compete with overseas content packagers like Pointcast, which used an innovative information delivery system known as the "push technology." Local players like Hongkong Telecom IMS and Hong Kong Star Internet also became increasingly aggressive within this sector and achieved growing popularity through the publishing of their Internet magazines. There was immediate need for Asia Online to partner with information providers to ensure supply of quality contents for its exclusive use.

Business Potential in Electronic Commerce

The major issues that have hindered the growth of electronic commerce have been Web security and consumer behavior. There were two common phenomena in Web security. Psychologically, consumers would feel uncomfortable conducting transactions in cyberspace through the Internet with a retailer or service provider that had no prior reputation. This would limit business opportunities for companies that operated business only on the Internet. In addition, even for the companies that had earned strong reputations, consumers were concerned about data security on the Internet during the actual data transmission process. This was a perception that most consumers had, even though data security was no worse via Internet than by phone or walk-in transactions. There has been a lot of development in the United States to change the people's perception on Web security and to provide ways to enable electronic commerce to become more viable and acceptable to consumers.

Electronic commerce remained a controversy in Hong Kong. Both successful and unsuccessful cases were seen. Hongkong Telecom has been quite active in pursuing such business opportunities and has partnered with aggressive local companies. Asia Online, on the other hand, held a rather realistic opinion on the growth potential of electronic commerce in the coming one or two years in Asia. The management of Asia Online believed that electronic commerce in Asia will grow but will involve changing people's perceptions about security on the Web and their shopping habits.

Web Hosting and Web Marketing Consulting Services

Given its acquired skills and expertise in utilizing the Internet for communications and commerce, Asia Online has also expanded into Web hosting and Web marketing consultancy services. It perceived itself as an end-to-end solution provider for businesses wanting to establish a Web presence. By offering its services to enable companies to adopt quickly to cyberspace, it also hoped to encourage the growth of the Asian community on the Internet.

Future Challenges

Asian Diversity

The unique thing about Asia is that it comprises so many different cultures and different languages. There is also a whole new generation of young Asians who have very different value systems from the traditional Asians. As a content provider to this diverse group of consumers, Asia Online faced a challenge of a fragmented market.

Asia Online has been working very hard to identify the right context to appeal to all of the Asians across the region. The real challenge for Asia Online was to repackage and translate the common elements of Asian culture as well as to seek out specific uniqueness and presenting in a captivating manner.

Paying for Content

The issue of paying for content was one of the biggest challenge facing the industry. The challenge was to be able to create unique and innovative products and services that consumers will value and pay for. Asia Online was keen to differentiate itself from the mass market, as it believed there existed a premium market where customers would pay for high quality and a valuable source of content. It is faced with a very promising future in the Internet age, and the Internet may change the economics of distribution.

The challenge to be taken up by Wai-yee Lam was the need to define the appropriate strategic direction and steer ACGL on course both operationally and financially.

China Internet Corporation (http://www.China.Com)

China Internet Corporation (CIC), founded to serve both businesses wishing to conduct electronic commerce within China and those intending to trade with companies within China, provided Internet access and advertising; it did not offer Internet services to the public. James Chu, CIC's Chief Executive Officer, explained:

> We are a "business-only" organization. By keeping it so, we eliminate people who take up valuable resources doing "Web cruising" or "world chat" or "Internet phone." We specialize in advertising and communications services, enabling manufacturers, trading companies, and service providers, such as attorneys, to attract overseas customers over the Net.

CIC staff sales representatives were directly marketing this service to companies in Hong Kong either trading with China or interested in participating in CIC's global World Wide Web (WWW) advertising and communications services in that country. Although CIC had been successful in attracting Hong Kong corporate customers, Chu felt that hiring sufficient staff for marketing the company's services across China would be impractical. Instead, CIC was considering an agency relationship with other firms to help secure the pace of growth desired.

The structure, compensation, training, and management of this agency sales force were important issues Chu was pondering in late 1995, in preparation for expanding services into mainland China. The unique conditions within China and the nature of the business services CIC offered made these marketing strategy issues particularly challenging.

Chu also had to develop a formal business plan for the CIC organization in order to raise capital from potential investors. This plan, which would be based on data from this case, would also be used in a prospectus accompanying a possible public stock offering.

Industry and Company Background

The rapid growth of the Internet globally (see figure 6.7) was partly driven by the introduction of business applications on the network in the early 1990s. In 1995, business and commercial users exceeded academic subscribers for the first time. Many Internet business applications focused on providing electronic commerce alternatives to traditional consumer retail and mail order shopping. However, Internet use for business-to-business electronic commerce was also growing and offered substantial benefits for firms able to harness the power of this new tool.

This case was prepared by Theodore H. Clark under the supervision of Professor John J. Sviokla.
© 1996 by the President and Fellows of Harvard College.
Harvard Business School case 9-396-299.

Millions of Internet Host Computers

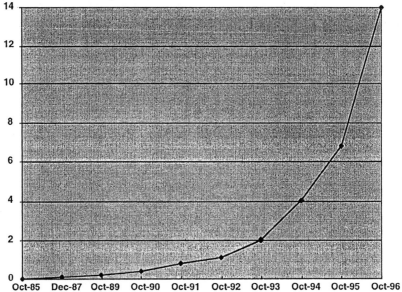

hosts doubling each year
users growing at 10%/month, and is estimated to be approximately ten times the number of hosts indicated in this chart.
total traffic packets growing faster than number of hosts or users

Figure 6.7
Growth of the Internet worldwide

Several large Internet-service providers (ISPs) had emerged to provide on-line access for individual users, offering a new marketing platform for companies selling goods and services to these consumers. These ISPs (e.g., America Online and CompuServe) were mainly focused on serving the US consumer market, though some business customers also used them for business-to-business commerce applications. At the same time, many smaller ISPs addressed market niches in the growing information industry. Proactively responding to market trends and changes, these entrepreneurs offered a range of services including full Internet access, remote disk space, business information services, multimedia advertising, custom WWW home page design, order transaction processing, and payment verification and processing services.

By early 1995, the global expansion of the "information society" had reached the territory of Hong Kong, although there were only six ISPs, and only one of these was officially licensed. By late 1995, however, more than 40 licensed ISPs existed, plus a steadily increasing number of firms seeking to enter the market. Each ISP was trying to position itself quickly to expand market share and reach a minimum level of profitability. Since there were virtually no"rules of the game" or well-defined regulations governing Internet operations, it was entirely up to the market and the players themselves to set and adjust to price and other business standards.

Among the many ISPs in Hong Kong, China Internet Corporation (CIC) had a unique background and strategy, facilitated by close linkages to its parent company's core businesses. Founded in 1994, CIC was a partially owned subsidiary of the Xinhua News Agency, the official news media agency of China throughout the world. CIC's other (minority) shareholders included several prominent Hong Kong companies and families, and several wealthy overseas investors.

CIC referred to itself as the "Virtual Gateway Into China". It hoped to provide companies and enterprises in mainland China with business promotion opportunities by taking advantage of the existing global information network. CIC was founded to provide Internet services to mainland companies and state-owned enterprises for business-only purposes.

CEO Chu viewed the company as more than another ISP, for CIC did not simply provide direct Internet access for clients. Indeed, CIC planned to limit clients' access within China to only the information contained within the CIC network, providing no access to non-CIC WWW sites. Thus, CIC offered a user-friendly, Chinese language-based graphical WWW interface within China for clients to view home page information provided by other CIC clients.

By following this approach, CIC avoided direct competition with China Telecom's basic Internet service—and did not need a special license to operate in China. CIC was not considered an open communications network; it was instead a value-added data service provided to a "closed" user group. At the same time, the CIC network offered unrestricted global email access within and outside China to and from all Internet subscribers. CIC also would provide unlimited access outside of China to all of its clients' English WWW home pages. However, within China, CIC clients were only allowed to access WWW information stored within the CIC network.

Some international journalists claimed that this restricted access to the global WWW from within China represented censorship. According to Chu, however, it was not information censorship but simply a business decision to limit access and usage on the network to information that facilitated the commercial goals of the network while eliminating potentially wasteful non-commercial uses. Without this limitation, the costs of non-productive network usage would burden all users by increasing the costs of providing services. In addition, CIC wanted to avoid any government concerns over potential abuses of the network.

Xinhua News Agency had many years of experience in facilitating economic and trade development between the US and China, and CIC was viewed as an extension of these efforts. This use of the Internet to facilitate commerce and business development was considered a strategic move to deploy a new business channel. Thus Xinhua could expand beyond its traditional role of providing print media, offering new services in a format that was attractive for both browsers and advertisers and providing many exporters and importers with viable alternatives to existing trade journals and exhibitions.

Moreover, introducing electronic commerce capabilities could dramatically affect productivity and effectiveness for both government and commercial operations. In larger cities like Beijing or Shanghai, telephones were commonly available for even residential users, and many businesses used fax machines for communications. Some government agencies also used the packet switched service the Ministry of Posts and Telecommunications (MPT) introduced during 1994 for data transmission. Nevertheless, most information was still transmitted by voice telephone or fax between major cities, and via postal services for the less developed areas of the country. By using satellite antennas for access, the CIC network could bypass existing infrastructure limitations and would even be able to reach the villages and towns that had no telephone access.

Becoming the "Virtual Gateway" into China

Hong Kong was traditionally viewed as the commercial gateway to China. CIC's mission was to create an alternative "Virtual Gateway" for firms conducting business with companies in China based on electronic commerce. James Chu projected that CIC's subscriber base would grow by more than 20,000 members by the end of 1997, and would reach more than 50,000 subscribers by the year 2000, with most of this growth coming from the mainland.

CIC members outside of China paid an initial lifetime membership fee of $6,000 (HKD) and an additional average fee of approximately $2,000 (HKD) to cover the cost of creating Chinese and English home pages. These members also paid a $388 (HKD) monthly fee for unlimited usage of the CIC network in Hong Kong to access members' home pages and global email; the first six months' monthly fee was paid in advance along with the fees for membership and home page development. Each member received a customized home page on which to display information (in Chinese and English) for other members and for WWW browsers globally (English only). The home page included full-color catalogue photographs of products or services offered. Although this $388 (HKD) monthly fee offered unlimited WWW access worldwide, it covered neither the cost of translation into Chinese nor the offering of this same information within China. That required an additional fee, which by late 1995 had not been determined. However, the fee would probably be similar to that charged in the Hong Kong CIC service.

CIC planned to open offices and Web sites during 1996 in Beijing, Shanghai, and Guangzhou through Xinhua News Agency's existing offices. In addition, "stations" or WWW sites would be built overseas, leveraging Xinhua's existing infrastructure and business connections. This would offer an additional business channel for international firms and would allow China's companies to link electronically with the rest of the world. The network would also facilitate commerce within China between firms that might otherwise be forced to seek international sources for products because they were unaware of local alternatives.

Additional Value-Added Services

CIC's service package allowed clients not comfortable with computers to market their products and services through WWW home pages. CIC members did not even need a computer to offer products through the Web globally: they could use fax transmission and receipt interfaces for sending and receiving messages translated to and from English. CIC members could also design and create Web pages in Chinese or bilingually (Chinese/English) without owning a computer—which represented an important value-added service differentiating CIC from its competitors.

In addition to providing direct access to email globally, CIC also planned to offer translation services for clients using the CIC network. This email translation service would allow mainland China executives with limited foreign language abilities to participate in foreign commerce transactions, with each trading partner communicating in his or her own language. For example, when overseas Web users browsed through the "http://www.China.com/" site and identified products they were interested in, they could email the advertiser through the CIC address displayed. Once received by CIC, this English email message would be translated into Chinese and either emailed or faxed to the client in mainland China.

These email translation and fax interface services would allow CIC members to save money on international calls by using the Internet for commercial transactions. Although the charges for these services were extra, they would be much lower than the costs of using traditional fax via telephony or of obtaining equivalent English/Chinese translation services from independent providers. Moreover, the Xinhua News Agency's offices throughout China could send and receive faxes and already had a large team of expert translators to support the firm's publishing operations.

Other Internet Service Providers in China

By late 1995, other ISPs in China included ChinaNet, CERNET, the High Energy Physics Lab, and an announced but not yet approved service to be offered by the Ministry of Electronic Industries (MEI). The number of Internet users in China had increased from 3,000 in March 1995 to 40,000 in July, a growth largely fueled by the access these new ISPs opened up. In addition, several other companies expressed interest in offering Internet services, although none had yet been licensed by the central government.

ChinaNet, a public Internet service offered by China Telecom, a subsidiary of the MPT, was introduced in mid-1995. Despite high interest in the service, its penetration had been slower than anticipated. ChinaNet provided full global Internet access for all subscribers, although high usage fees for international data transmission (send or receive) limited usage to email only for most subscribers; businesses generally limited usage to domestic data transmissions and brief international messages. Nevertheless, multinational firms found the ChinaNet service extremely valuable, for it bypassed difficulties with the local phone network and offered consistent access in and out of the country.

CERNET, established by the Chinese government, offered full Internet access to selected faculty members at a variety of universities and research institutes throughout the country. There were no usage or connection fees but access was limited to email for most users due to bandwidth constraints. Researchers or faculty requiring WWW interface capabilities had to justify their need, and abusing the service through excessive non-research activities (e.g., for pornography or games) could result in privileges' being terminated. Commercial enterprises were not officially allowed to use the network, but some businesses did obtain access by using accounts of faculty or research staff affiliated with commercial businesses. Since many faculty pursued outside business opportunities to supplement their limited academic salaries, commercial usage of the CERNET was more common than officially acknowledged.

The High Energy Physics Lab (HEPL), the first Internet site in China, still maintained a dedicated link with Stanford University even though HEPL had formally joined the CERNET group as well. Although the number of users was relatively small, the amount of data transmitted between China and the US was relatively large, justifying this dedicated line. Commercial usage of the link was not officially allowed, and any transactions that did exist were confined to a relatively narrow area of expertise and applications.

The Golden Internet service had been announced, by the MEI, in mid-1995, as part of the so-called Golden Projects, but as of late 1995 the State Council had not yet approved it. (The Golden Projects represented efforts to revitalize the economy by developing an information infrastructure throughout China; MEI sponsored or promoted many of these infrastructure projects.) Although approval of MEI's service was uncertain, the State Council had already authorized a partially owned subsidiary of MEI in the local and long distance (domestic) telecommunications market to compete with China Telecom and the MPT. Thus, the State Council might also approve MEI's offering an Internet service in competition with the MPT service.

Overall, while several Internet services were available in China, only ChinaNet was officially approved for business subscribers. (Table 6.6 compares CIC's offerings to those of alternative providers.) CIC did not wish to compete with MPT's ChinaNet for Internet access, but it did wish to establish itself as the dominant Internet service company for business transactions within China and between China and the world.

Table 6.6
Differences between China Internet Corporation and Other ISPs

1. We are a "business only" organization—by keeping it "business only" we eliminate people doing "web cruising" or "world chat" or "Internet phone," etc. All these activities take up valuable resources and could interfere with others who want to conduct business on the Internet.

2. We offer "total service"—we do not just provide Internet access. Instead, we will do anything that is necessary so that our members can concentrate on doing business instead of becoming a computer expert. For example, will do research for them, translate for them, and help them with the computer if they have problems with it.

3. We offer specifically "advertising and communication" services—we automatically will set up colorful web pages for our members and provide email accounts that are easy to use without charging extra for these services.

4. We offer "flat fee" service—we only charge $388 per month instead of charging our members by the hour. (Not including the HK Telecom PNET surcharge.)

5. We will have "mirror sites" around the world—if more and more people from foreign countries look at our data, we will set up mirror sites near our users so that they can access our information much faster than trying to get it from Hong Kong every time.

6. We will have a private email network in China—our members can send emails to their companies or factories in China using email, thus saving a lot of money in IDD calls.

7. We have an easy to remember name—China.com—by reserving this name exclusively to CIC, users of our database can easily remember our name and will be able to enter it correctly by memory into their computer.

8. We will do a lot of publicity abroad—CIC will be doing a series of publicity, advertising, and news releases abroad so that more and more people will notice our existence. Since the press release of the launching of CIC, the news has been carried by *Wall Street Journal, Financial Times, Bloomberg, Reuters, Asian Wall Street Journal, SCMP*, and various foreign newspapers.

9. We are a subsidiary of Xinhua News Agency of China—CIC has strong backing from China and will be here to stay for a long time, even after 1997. Xinhua is also the clearing house for international financial and economic information in China.

10. We are a world-class company—by making use of Xinhua News Agency's resources and offices worldwide, CIC can function as a world-class company easily.

Marketing CIC Services in China

The biggest challenge CIC faced was dramatically expanding the number of subscribers, particularly within China. While a direct sales force had been effective in marketing services to potential members in Hong Kong, Chu was concerned that this method could not accommodate his ambitious growth objectives. He thus considered using agents. But he also had to keep in mind the costs of this expansion in order to determine how much equity capital would be needed.

Marketing Alternatives and Compensation Issues

Of the several alternatives for using an agent's network for rapid expansion, one involved contracting with individual agents who would represent the company on an exclusive territory basis, thereby effectively becoming an outside sales force. Another option was granting broad but nonexclusive agency rights to a number of companies throughout China that would sell the CIC services to their existing customers and affiliated companies. A third option was establishing a multi-level marketing program. Here, companies would sign up other companies and individuals to sell CIC services through broad networks of contacts throughout China.

Chu was concerned that insufficient resources for training and managing individual agents might constrain growth. In addition, marketing skills were scarce in China, so finding suitable individuals could be difficult. It would, therefore, be more effective to work with existing companies that could add the CIC Internet service to their existing portfolio of offerings. However, he also recognized that the sales force within these agent companies might also have to be trained in order to effectively present the benefits of joining the CIC network to their customers. The multi-level marketing approach, too, was appealing, as it offered the ability to expand rapidly. But it also risked some loss of control. Chu felt that maintaining a closer link with the selling agents was important, and preferred to build his own staff to supervise and support local sales agents throughout China, rather than relying on others.

By the end of 1995, Chu had the capabilities and systems required for rapidly expanding the number of CIC network customers, and he needed, therefore, to decide which marketing structure to adopt as well as how future agents would be compensated. Agents had to ramp up quickly to the point of selling at least eight new memberships per month (after a one-week training period). Based on salary and commission levels in Hong Kong, this suggested that an agency commission of 50% of the lifetime membership fee alone should be adequate to pay a sales representative's monthly salary in Hong Kong—and would be more than adequate for China. Since total labor costs in China (including all benefits) were less than half the compensation levels required in Hong Kong, an individual agent in China working on a similar commission structure could earn a very attractive wage, or a company agent could earn an attractive profit for their firm.

Even so, Chu wondered if a 50% commission of the initial membership fee was adequate. Hong Kong agents earned a 10% commission on the initial membership fee, the home page development fee, and the first year of monthly fees, and Chu was uncertain whether commissions in China should also be paid for these other revenue sources. Commission on monthly fees could be provided for a limited period (e.g., six to twelve months), or on a longer-term basis, if needed to provide sufficient incentive for agents to aggressively market CIC's services. No commissions were being considered for additional fee-based services, such as email translation, as they would be priced close to cost and thus not generate sufficient margin to support additional marketing expenditures.

Assumptions for Projecting Revenues

The most critical uncertainty in developing the business plan was the projection for revenue growth based on subscriber volumes achieved. Since net revenue growth was a function of sales force structure and compensation as well as market size, estimating the economic trade-offs of these marketing alternatives was crucial. In addition, it was important to project the size of the total potential market to provide reasonable penetration estimates. Unfortunately, determining the size of the market in China for CIC services was difficult, as data were limited. For example, one State agency officially estimated an excess of 300 million businesses in China. This implied one business for every four residents!

Using secondary information, Chu estimated that about 70% of the Chinese population (of about 1.3 billion) was employed in very small family businesses, with the remaining 30% working in businesses of more than 20 employees. With an average size of the latter businesses estimated at 200 employees, the result was about 2 million businesses within China of a size and scope that could benefit from the CIC network services (1.3 billion × 30%/200 = 2 million). Of these 2 million businesses, Chu projected that about 50% were focused on export and import opportunities, but only about 10% of those would have either the sophistication to understand the potential benefits of CIC services or would be interested in adopting Internet-based commerce over the next five years. This reduced the total market size within China to approximately 100,000 firms, with Chu projecting that CIC would be in a strong position to capture at least 50% of this target market. These estimates were based on conservative assumptions, and Chu believed that the actual market opportunity could be much larger as China's economy continued to grow.

Estimating the size of the Hong Kong market was easier. Slightly more than 100,000 companies were registered in Hong Kong, a territory of 6 million residents (one company per each 60 residents). However, many businesses were small firms focused on serving the domestic market. Potential CIC clients were companies involved in international or inter-provincial commerce. Based on data from market analysts and other Hong Kong sources, Chu estimated the total size of the potential market of medium to large companies at between 10,000 and 15,000 firms. Of these companies, only 3,000 were actively promoting products through trade shows, trade journals, or other forms of international advertising. These 3,000 firms were the most likely prospects for adopting the CIC commercial Internet service, and Chu believed he could capture about 60% of this market.

Pricing and commission structure would have significant impact on the pace of network expansion, the level of costs incurred, and the amount of net revenues generated by the expanding subscriber base. Chu needed to make decisions on these key issues in order to project future costs and revenues for the China market opportunity. (Additional key assumptions and costs for expanding within Hong Kong and China markets are included in tables 6.7 and 6.8.)

Network Costs for Expanding Services

CIC's strategy for the Chinese market involved opening operations in the three largest cities in 1996, and expanding to include other large cities during the next several years. The Xinhua News Agency satellite network would provide backbone service facilities for interconnecting locations across China, using an existing network that was connected to 30 of the largest commercial districts and provinces. Customers could use regular telephone lines, provided by China Telecom, to dial up and access the network via modems, or could gain direct access via dedicated lines from China Telecom or via satellite services for larger customers. Within four years, CIC expected to offer services to all 30 of these large commercial districts across China.

Special business lines were required for CIC to receive calls over China Telecom's network; they had to offer "call hunting" and other features so the network would function properly for CIC dial-up services. These lines were significantly more expensive than standard business lines. (Estimated costs of installation and monthly service per phone line are shown in tables 6.7 and 6.8.) Each dial-up line could handle between 15 and 20 subscribers, depending on their level of average usage. Commercial rack-mounted modem banks were needed to support the level of reliability customers required, and could support up to 16 phone lines per modem bank using a transmission rate of up to 56 kbps (with compression). Long distance leased lines would be made available by Xinhua News Agency's corporate network using a combination of

Table 6.7
Business plan assumptions for CIC in Hong Kong (HKD)

Revenues:	
Initial membership fee:	$6,000 per new account
Content development fee:	$2,000 per new account average, but varies
Monthly fee for network usage:	$388 per account per month (first 6 months in advance)
plus	$0.09 per minute for connection charge from phone company billed through to users.

(This fee is included in monthly line rental costs below but is billed through to customers.)

Telephone line costs (approximate monthly costs):	
Line installation cost:	$500 per phone line
Line rental and usage costs:	$1,500 per phone line (1 line per 15 customers)

(including a $1,340 monthly usage fee billed at $0.09 per minute for average estimated usage)

International leased line costs:	$15,000 monthly per circuit (one per 300 customers)
plus	$15,000 total initial connection cost for both ends

Total hardware costs (modems, computers, routers, installation, a/c, etc.):	
Purchase costs	$95,000 for each 16 dial-up phone lines connected
Computer hardware	$960,000 per each 1,500 customers,
plus	$480,000 per each 5,000 customers,
Maintenance	5% of total installed (undepreciated) cost of hardware

Total software costs:	
Software purchase	$50,000 one time fee for misc. software,
plus	$75,000 for each 1,500 customers,
plus	$360,000 for each 5,000 customers
Software license	$80,000 per year for each 5,000 customers
Software upgrades	$6,000 per year for each 1,500 customers

Staff costs and requirements (approximate estimates):	
Marketing staff:	$8,000 per month plus 10% commission; 8 new accounts/month per person
Marketing training:	$20,000 per month with no commission; 4 new market staff trained/month
Network staff:	$25,000 per month; 1 person for 6 new accounts/ month or 1,000 existing accounts
Content development:	$20,000 per month; 1 person for 7 new accounts/ month
Support staff:	$15,000 per month; 1 person per 3 other staff members plus 1 receptionist

Office expenses:	
Renovation costs for space for 20 employees:	$300,000
Monthly rental costs for space for 20 employees:	$40,000
Travel, supplies, etc. for 20 employees per month:	$250,000 (includes all non-rent expenses)

Advertising:	
Annual promotion projected:	$2,000,000 to generate leads resulting in up to 3,000 new accounts

However, only 60% of these leads would be realized as sales during the first year of promotion.

Table 6.8
Business plan assumptions for CIC in China (HKD)

Revenues (per customer):	
Initial membership fee:	TBD (Make recommendation or use HK prices)
Content development fee:	TBD (Make recommendation or use HK prices)
Monthly fee for network usage:	TBD (Make recommendation or use HK prices)
Telephone line costs (approximate, per location):	
Line installation cost:	$11,000 per phone line (special business terminal line)
Line rental and usage costs:	$2,500 per phone line (1 line per 20 customers)
Interprovincial leased line costs:	$30,000 monthly per circuit (one per 400 customers)
plus	$100,000 total initial connection cost for both ends
International leased line costs:	$120,000 monthly per circuit (one per 1,000 customers)
plus	$200,000 total initial connection cost for both ends
Total hardware costs (including facilities and installation, for each location in China):	
Purchase costs	$120,000 for each 16 dial-up phone lines connected
Computer hardware	$1,240,000 per each 1,500 customers,
plus	$760,000 per each 5,000 customers
Maintenance	5% of total installed (undepreciated) cost of hardware
Total software costs (for each location in China):	
Software purchase	$50,000 one time fee for misc. software,
plus	$75,000 for each 1,500 customers,
plus	$360,000 for each 5,000 customers
Software license	$80,000 per year for each 5,000 customers
Software upgrades	$6,000 per year for each 1,500 customers
Staff costs and requirements (approximate estimates, per location):	
Marketing staff:	$5,000 per month plus 10% commission; 8 new accounts/month per person
Marketing training:	$30,000 per month with no commission, 4 new market staff trained/month
Network staff:	$10,000 per month, 1 person for 6 new accounts/month or 1,000 existing accounts
Content development:	$10,000 per month, 1 person for 7 new accounts/month
Support staff:	$6,000 per month, 1 person per 3 other staff members plus 1 receptionist
Office expenses (per location):	
Renovation costs for space for 20 employees:	$300,000
Monthly rental costs for space for 20 employees:	$40,000
Travel, supplies, etc. for 20 employees per month:	$250,000 (includes all non-rent expenses)
Advertising (per location):	
Annual promotion projected:	$2,000,000 to generate leads resulting in up to 3,000 new accounts

However, only 60% of these leads would be realized as sales during the first year of promotion.

satellite links and land lines, but CIC's business plan needed to provide for compensation for the use of these facilities at a rate comparable to the cost of leasing long distance circuits from China Telecom. A cost of $200,000 (HKD) was projected for each leased circuit, and Chu estimated that at least one 64 kbps long-distance circuit would be needed to support each 20 telephone dial-up access lines in the network.

Each city or network service location also required hardware and software to operate the Internet services. The hardware and software could support a very large number of customers, but service might degrade if more than 5,000 customers used a single server in one location. Finally, software licenses were needed for each location, with both initial costs and annual license fees plus upgrade costs required for the software used at each site. Less expensive equipment configurations might be possible, but Chu felt that this level of minimum scale investment would offer the speed of access and services business customers in an all-commercial network would demand.

Staffing Requirements for Growth

A sales agent in Hong Kong could close 8 to 10 sales per month, but selling in China might be more difficult given a greater area to cover and less user sophistication. At the same time, there was less competition in China, which might simplify the selling process. All told, Chu figured that each sales representative might be able to generate no more than an average of eight new accounts per month, and agents might generate slightly fewer sales per employee if they offered other products or services. Sales managers would have to train and lead these sales efforts. While a single manager could coordinate the activities of up to 30 sales reps or agents, that person could train only about four new people a month, Salary and benefits costs for company sales employees were expected to be approximately $3,000 (HKD) per month in China plus a 10% commission on sales revenues, including the first year of monthly fees plus fees for lifetime membership and customer home page development. Sales agent coordinators (and trainers) would cost at least $30,000 (HKD) per month, including benefits, as most coordinators would come from outside China and would have living costs covered in their monthly compensation levels. Supervision and coordination requirements were expected to be similar for either internal sales representatives or external agents.

CIC would also need additional staff for content development and network support. Content development staff created the WWW pages for new clients, being able to work with up to seven new customers per month. Network support staff, who assisted customers with new services connections and maintained the existing network, could support up to six new customers per month and service up to 100 existing customers. Consistent with the "living corporation model" described below, the leaders of these staffs would come from within the groups, so no additional costs were projected for any management staff for these functional areas.

Additional personnel would be required to assist other employees with administrative activities, and would be shared and allocated as needed. One person would be required for every three employees in an office, plus a receptionist for the office. Each office would have its own sales representatives, content developers, network staff, and administrative staff, with at least four employees in each of these areas for even a very small operation. Xinhua News Agency would generally provide office space, but it would cost CIC approximately $40,000 (HKD) per unit per month, in addition to $300,000 in renovation costs for each unit added per location. Each unit of space could support approximately 20 employees in total (including sales employees, but excluding external sales agents, who would have their own offices).

Managing the CIC Organization: The Living Corporation Philosophy

CIC's success and adaptability in the market was in part due to its unique structure and policies. Chu described CIC as a "living" corporation or organization. Living corporations evolved naturally as business needs and requirements emerged. Chu compared a living corporation to a group of cells within an organism, in which individual cells divide, expand, or are replaced naturally as environmental conditions change. The living organization was not based on hierarchy, position, or authority, but rather on individuals' ability to serve the group most effectively. Individuals that did so would expand in their influence and importance, and clone themselves by attracting or hiring followers to assist them in serving the whole.

Leadership in the living corporation evolved from within the groups of individuals in the organization; each division or team developed its own leaders in an atmosphere of harmony and without interpersonal conflicts. Chu advocated this model as the ideal structure for a firm facing an uncertain environment, and explained such a fluid organization worked particularly well in a high tech society where a flat, flexible company structure was preferable to a more rigid hierarchy.

One important management concept that Chu taught his staff was "the finger principle." Whenever members of the company noticed a problem, they were asked to point their finger at its source. As long as the finger pointed away from themselves, however, the individuals failed to fully understand the problem and were powerless to fix it, thereby becoming frustrated and feeling powerless. Only when the finger pointed towards the individual seeing the problem could that person find a way to fix it. Chu illustrated this power of this approach:

One of the systems engineers recently told me we had a serious problem. I asked him to point at the problem. He said that sales were the problem. I asked what he could do about it, and he said he could do nothing, as the problem was in sales. (The implication was that the engineer wanted me, the CEO, to solve this problem for him, since it was not within his power to solve it by himself.) I then asked the engineer to reflect on the problem again *and to choose to make it his own problem*. I then asked what the engineer could do now about his problem. Once his perspective had changed, he realized that the problem was his, so it was up to him to do something to solve it.

So he called a meeting with the sales staff and the engineers and explained WHY actions in sales were creating problems for him and for the other engineers. The issue was then resolved directly between the meeting participants via discussion and negotiation. Management intervention was unnecessary once the individual seeing the problem *chose to make the problem his own*, rather than pointing at some other department or manager. With this understanding, he was able to find a way to solve the problem himself.

Other Challenges

In addition to expansion and compensation issues, CIC faced other concerns, some of the toughest being how to develop the right skills, attitudes, and enthusiasm among the staff. Human resources management was a key issue in a living corporation. Chu was especially aware of the need to push his people to continually hone new skills and abilities to adapt quickly to changes in the environment.

Further, several CIC shareholders were interested in issuing a public offering of stock so as to benefit from the market's high valuation of both ISPs and Asian stocks in general. It was unclear how an offering would be received since CIC was a young company without an established customer base; however, the investment for expanding throughout China was greater than the amount of funding that Xinhua and other current investors could provide, so some form of additional outside financing was necessary. If optimistic growth projections were realized, up to US $50 million could be required during the next two years.

This level of funding would be difficult to obtain without going public, but both within the firm and among the board of directors there were questions about the optimal timing of such a move. It was also unclear whether the offer should be issued on the US stock exchange or through the Hong Kong financial markets. In any event, Chu would have to provide investors with a business plan including financial projections that were neither too optimistic to be believable nor too pessimistic to be attractive. In one month, a meeting was scheduled with current and potential investors, who would discuss the public offering issue; Chu's plan (based on data drawn from tables 6.7 and 6.8) would have to be ready by then.

The CIC service sat at the intersection of advertising and publishing on one side, and electronic commerce and data transmission on the other, functioning as a toll booth for access to the information highway of China. The close relationship between CIC and Xinhua News Agency was a competitive advantage, as the State Council had recently declared that all economic information and international news would have to be cleared through Xinhua before release within China. CIC had to go through the same clearance process as other information services providers, but it had closer relationships with Xinhua. Thus, CIC expected to receive faster responses or be granted more flexibility and autonomy than many other firms operating within China.

Chu also wanted to develop some product and service bundles that could more effectively market CIC and capture more of the value of its services for customers. He wondered what alternative pricing packages should be part of the CIC offering, and what information services could or should be bundled with CIC basic access. Chu was also interested in learning how the firm could more effectively capture advertising funds from network services providers and how this advertising could be more effectively packaged to reach the users of information. For example, he had recently reached an agreement with a transportation information publisher to maintain a site on the CIC network for shippers and freight forwarders in Hong Kong. The information would be provided and maintained for free, but member firms would pay to have on-line rate quotation and shipment tracking services for their clients using the CIC network. In addition, the free service had been helpful in marketing CIC to a new group of customers, who were now CIC members.

Finally, CIC had entered into agreements with Oracle, Sun, and other firms to develop products or provide services jointly. These opportunities created a platform for future growth and services expansion—but also required resources that might otherwise be available for marketing services directly or through agents. The company was fully committed to supporting all existing partnerships, but Chu was uncertain how much of the firm's limited resources should be invested in developing additional relationships and in creating new services and capabilities versus in marketing existing service offerings.

Thus, as he began to formulate a plan for CIC's future, Chu realized that his company faced interesting challenges in its attempts to become the Virtual Gateway to China. Given limited resources, his living corporation's efforts had to focus on both the greatest opportunities and the greatest obstacles if it was to achieve the critical mass needed to preempt the competition as well as provide the services needed by businesses across China and their trading partners worldwide.

Hong Kong SuperNet

The Internet can be thought of as the great public highway for computer communication. It is the largest non-private computer network in the world and is growing at a rate of nearly 100% per year.
—Bob Coggeshall, Project Manager for Hong Kong SuperNet

The Hong Kong SuperNet was an applied research and development project set up by the Hong Kong University of Science & Technology (HKUST) in July 1993. The service was launched in October 1993 and provided users with dial-up access to the Internet. Direct competition came from Hong Kong Internet and Gateway Services (HKIGS), which provided similar services and was set up in August 1993. The launch of SuperNet and HKIGS gave local computer users access to the Internet's vast information warehouses on a casual basis for the first time and enabled them to send and receive files and e-mail around the world at a fraction of the cost of telephone and fax. As the first licensed Internet service provider (ISP) in Hong Kong, SuperNet generated a lot of interest within the community.

After 18 months of rapid growth, 1995 was a year of uncertainty for SuperNet. On a positive note, the business side continued to grow, so that the existing core of staff was expanded and some new systems were implemented. Because of this expansion, priority was given to the critical business functions, such as customer billing and financial accounting. However, SuperNet had reached a period in its development where it could no longer be managed effectively as a project. Several different approaches to management by the university were tried, but none of these proved particularly effective. Professor Eugene Wong agreed to assume full responsibility for the executive management of SuperNet, in addition to his regular duties as Vice President for Research and Development. Under the circumstances, he was the most qualified person for the job, as his earlier experience had included being the founder, President, and CEO of the Ingres Corporation in the United States prior to joining the faculty at HKUST.

SuperNet continued to expand during 1995, and it became apparent that HKUST did not have the resources or commitment to manage the company effectively. During 1995, there were serious discussions within the faculty on the future of SuperNet and whether the company should be sold. If the rationale for that decision could be justified, then one of the key issues to be considered was what factors should be considered in choosing a suitable buyer. During late 1995 and early 1996, serious discussions were conducted with several potential buyers or partners. The process and results of these meetings then redefined the precise reasons for selling this suc-

This case was prepared by Dr. Theodore H. Clark and Sarah Cook of The Hong Kong University of Science and Technology with the assistance of Professor Vincent Shen.

cessful start-up company and the evaluation criteria that would be used for selecting potential buyers.

Background and Setting

The Internet had rapidly evolved from a U.S.-based academic and research project in the 1970s to become a global information superhighway in the 1990s. Until 1991, the Internet was still sponsored by the U.S. government, and users of the Internet were required to follow an "acceptable use policy" (AUP), which prohibited commercial traffic through the network. Although many companies had access, the Internet was primarily available only to their research and development departments, which used the service for research only and not for commercial purposes. However, it was clear by 1992 that the U.S. government could not afford to continue funding expansion of the Internet. Therefore the National Science Foundation (NSF) encouraged the formation of a nonprofit company called Advanced Networks and Services (ANS) by three private companies: IBM, a computer manufacturer; MCI, a long-distance telephone company; and MERIT, a computer networking company. As a private company, ANS accepted connections from commercial companies to the Internet for a fee.

Like ripples on a pond, the addition of commercial users to the Internet expanded services available and demand for the Internet exploded. Resources such as library catalogues, journal and software archives, financial news, and many other services became available. A number of entrepreneurs in the United States saw that they could advertise and market their goods using the global network and formed companies that provided U.S. customers with easy access to the Internet. These companies that provided consumers and businesses with connections to the Internet were known as Internet service providers (ISPs). There were about 30 ISP companies formed in the United States by the end of 1992.

The Internet in Hong Kong in 1992

Although Hong Kong was fairly advanced in telecommunications, the Internet did not come to Hong Kong until early 1992, when a connection was made through a leased 64K line to NASA Ames by the University and Polytechnic Computing Centre (UPCC). At that time, Internet access was restricted to staff and students associated with the tertiary institutions, who made use of the connection to exchange messages and research data with other colleagues worldwide. Since companies did not have access to the Internet at that time, telephone and fax were still the primary mode for fast communication in Hong Kong.

Hong Kong in the late 1980s and early 1990s had become an attractive place for a large number of professional people to come to live and work. Many of these professionals were familiar with the Internet and found lack of access in Hong Kong very frustrating. The availability of Internet services even influenced career decisions for some overseas professionals in Hong Kong. For example, the Computer Science (CS) Department at the university received an inordinate number of job applications from people who were attracted by the advertisement of "unlimited access to the Internet." Some unsuccessful applicants for these posts had requested guest accounts so that they could have some access to the Internet. However, the AUP in operation at that time effectively prevented the university from providing computer accounts to these outside individuals. Researchers at the university who had collaborative projects with government agencies and commercial companies found it difficult to exchange data and documents with their collaborators using only fax and diskettes.

Hong Kong SuperNet

Being aware of the accelerating pace of development in the United States, CS Department faculty members began to discuss the possibility of forming an ISP in Hong Kong. They knew that the technology was available, clearly the need was there, and they believed there was great potential for such a company within Asia. The market opportunities for an ISP were particularly strong in Hong Kong, as there was a broad base of sophisticated personal computer (PC) users ready to adopt the Internet. A successful venture in this area would not only contribute to the university's task of serving the community, but could also provide employment opportunities for HKUST graduates.

Public (government provided) funds could not be committed to support such a venture, but a donation could be used to fund such a venture. In November 1991, Sino Land Company gave the university $20 million to establish the Sino Service Research Centre (SSRC). This provided the university with the flexibility needed to be able to fund an ISP start-up in Hong Kong.

Sino Service Research Centre

Professor Vincent Shen was appointed the Interim Director and the SSRC began operations on July 1, 1992. The SSRC was committed to supporting two kinds of activities: "applied research," which would demonstrate the viability of research ideas by building software prototypes, and "business development," which would commercialize the successful prototypes for eventual profit. The hope was that some of the business development projects would generate enough returns to keep the

SSRC going indefinitely, even if the donor could not provide additional funding in the future.

As interest grew within the university for providing a public ISP service, it became clear that a project to form an ISP for Hong Kong could be funded through this development program. Although the funding was available, there were still insufficient staff within the CS Department. The university in 1992 was still in an early and rapid growth phase, as it had commenced official operation in 1991 and was intensively recruiting new faculty members from top U.S. and international universities. To ensure success, the university had to find someone with the time and energy required to take care of the project and commence the initial start-up process.

It was very important to preserve the momentum of the project, so Professor Shen appointed Bob Coggeshall as a consultant for the SSRC in October 1992. Coggeshall's initial assignment was to study the feasibility of starting an ISP in Hong Kong and to compare the HKUST proposal with similar operations in the United States. His report formed the basis of the Hong Kong Supernet proposal (figure 6.8), which was submitted to the SSRC board for funding in November 1992. Coggeshall was then appointed Project Manager of Hong Kong SuperNet in March 1993. His background as an independent software consultant was ideal and his experience seen as very relevant to the project, as he had participated in the founding of Colorado SuperNet, an ISP based in Denver (table 6.9).

The SSRC Advisory Board met in February 1993 to consider the proposals received in 1992. The proposal for Hong Kong SuperNet was discussed at length, and it was unanimously agreed to provide funding of HK$1.5 million. Within the document, there was a detailed first-year budget (table 6.10). Hong Kong SuperNet was expected to recover its entire cost of operation within the first three years.

The proposal recommended that the fee structure be made as simple as possible, as this would reduce overhead in billing subscribers. The fee would be made up of an initial sign-on fee, a monthly subscription fee for a limited duration of free connection, and an hourly usage fee for excess usage. The only potential refinements might be a discount during off-peak hours to reduce demand on the modem pool.

Two major factors accelerated the board's decision on funding SuperNet. First, a potential competitor, Hong Kong Internet and Gateway Services (HKIGS), had been identified. Second, a potential customer in the form of the university's Centre of Computing Sciences and Telecommunications (CCST) was interested in using some bandwidth of the leased line in order to improve Internet services to the university community. It was agreed that CCST would be considered as a special customer in exchange for some temporary personnel and a loan of some start-up equipment.

Sino Software Research Center

Project Abstract
Title: *Hong Kong Supernet*
Principle Investigator: Dr. Vincent Shen

Vincent Y. Shen

Date: November 1992

New ☒
Renewal ☐
Progress Report ☐

DESCRIPTION
This is a proposal to establish Hong Kong Supernet (HKS) - the first commercial internet-work access facility in Hong Kong. HKS will promote technological advancement by delivering a variety of electronic communications services to individuals and businesses at an affordable cost.

RELATED WORK ELSEWHERE	HOW OURS IS DIFFERENT
Commercial Internetwork Providers (CIPs) are being established worldwide. A survey of existing internetwork providers is included in the appendices	HKS would be the first Commercial Internetwork Provider in Hong Kong

RELATED WORK IN SSRC	MILESTONES
None.	Month 0: Approval, Initiate recruitment of staff. Equipment Proposals, Acquire space, place orders for communications links. Issue press releases. Months 1-2: Arrival of staff. Finalize equip. selection. Order equipment. Develop ad materials. Months 3-4: Complete staffing. Complete equip acquisitions. Setup equipment. Develop billing system. First day of service.

DELIVERABLES	BUDGET SUMMARY
Quarterly Progress Reports. Functional subscriber services within 4 months of funding approval.	First year: Operating Expenses: $2,339,000 Projected Income: $119,000 TOTAL REQUEST: $2,220,000

POTENTIAL BENEFITS TO HONG KONG
Hong Kong Supernet (HKS) will open up the vast resources of the global internetwork beyond the existing confines of the large universities. This will benefit the community through education and communication. HKS will also serve to increase the community's technological literacy, thus increasing the value of Hong Kong labor and its future global competitiveness.

Figure 6.8
The Hong Kong SuperNet proposal

Table 6.9
Using Colorado SuperNet growth to estimate growth of Hong Kong SuperNet

Colorado SuperNet	
Service area population:	3.3 million
Number of subscribers:	800
Resultant subscribers per 100,000 population:	24
Years of operation:	2
Hong Kong SuperNet	
Service area population:	5.8 million
Estimated subscribers per 100,000 population:	24
Resultant number of subscribers:	1,406

Source: The Hong Kong SuperNet proposal.

The university also decided that the scheme should be partly funded by the newly formed RandD Corporation, which was the commercial arm at HKUST set up to market any technologies developed there. A presentation was made to the RandD Corporation board in February 1993. Further interest in the project came from the Chairman of the Board, Michael Gale, who was also Chief Executive Officer of Hong Kong Telecom. At that time, Hong Kong Telecom was considering a move into the computer networking area and collaboration with SuperNet was seen as mutually beneficial. Two staff were assigned from Hong Kong Telecom to assist with both the business and technical plans. RandD Corporation decided to commit $1.5 million to the scheme, which then made SuperNet a joint project funded by the SSRC and the RandD Corporation.

Becoming Operational

In order to protect the trade name, Hong Kong SuperNet had to be registered as a company. Coggeshall and Shen were not sure as to strength of the partnership with the RandD Corporation, so they jointly registered the company using their own funds in March 1993. This shell company was kept active until April 1995, when it was transferred to RandD Corporation, which subsequently transferred the SuperNet operations to the Hong Kong SuperNet Limited Company.

As soon as Bob Coggeshall took up his appointment, a range of activities were undertaken that would eventually lead to the deployment of the services provided by SuperNet. These included setting up a business organization, establishing advertising procedures and pricing, recruiting personnel, and setting up accounting and billing systems. Bob Coggeshall's enthusiastic approach generated the momentum and drive of the project. Staff who were busy setting up the new organization were affected by this approach and so were very willing to consider and support new initiatives at the time. With his previous experience, Bob Coggeshall wondered about the future of the project. He had seen that when an organization became mature, it had a tendency to split into several groups. New initiatives were not received with the same open minds within these older organizations, as they tended not to satisfy all parties.

Malcolm Brown from Hong Kong Telecom was also a key facilitator of the project and provided valuable assistance with the business plan. A large number of pricing and subscription models were examined before the plan was approved by the board of the RandD Corporation. Personnel from Hong Kong Telecom CSL helped during this planning stage, and a proposal was looked at carefully as to whether the Super-Net service could be included in part with the existing CSL Spectrum service.

When it came to advertising SuperNet, the staff considered different account options to determine the most effective approach. It was important to encourage corporate clients, as their income was viewed as fairly stable, but equal consideration had to be given to individual clients, as their value lay in passing on valuable recommendations to their colleagues. A press release in October 1993 announced "low cost access to the . . . Internet," ensuring that the package appeared attractive to both individual and corporate customers.

Coggeshall saw the billing strategy as a key component to the success of SuperNet. With this in mind, he personally designed the system so that it was consistent with the advertised billing strategy. With frequent enhancements, the system became such a good advertisement that a new ISP in Japan expressed interest in licensing the software. However, the opportunity to capitalize on the sale of the billing software was never finalized, as further work would have been required to "harden" the system, and the possible maintenance obligations in the future were a concern to HKUST managers. Unfortunately, the billing system eventually became a problem area for SuperNet because of human operating errors combined with software errors. In hindsight, it might have been more cost-effective to have purchased a commercial accounting package initially.

From the time of Coggeshall's appointment in March 1993, it soon became clear that there were huge demands on his time in setting up all the activities needed to make SuperNet operational and ultimately a successful venture. His time was very limited when it came to the training of other personnel, so it was decided that consultants would be hired and appointed to get on with the day-to-day running of the project. They would be assisted by specifically appointed students who might, one day, want to join the organization officially. Coggeshall knew that the group working on SuperNet comprised some very talented people. In his experience, he knew that talented people could often be difficult to work with; it was the responsibility of management to provide some sort of scheme to keep them interested and dedicated.

Table 6.10
Hong Kong SuperNet estimated budget year 1

Month	1	2	3	4	5
Personnel					
Manager	47,500	47,500	47,500	47,500	47,500
Technician			15,000	15,000	15,000
Administration assistant	2,500	5,000	10,000	10,000	10,000
Student assistant 1		5,000	5,000	5,000	5,000
Student assistant 2			5,000	5,000	5,000
Miscellaneous					
Advertising/promotion	2,000	3,000	3,000	3,000	3,000
Office expenses	1,950	1,950	1,950	1,950	1,950
Travel					
Clarinet news subscription			1,560	1,560	1,560
Equipment					
Initial equipment		278,000			
Telco lines					
16 standard lines		3,744	3,744	3,744	3,744
Circuit to U.S.		89,700	89,700	89,700	89,700
Installation costs		10,200			
Monthly total exp.	53,950	444,094	182,454	182,454	182,454
Total annual exp.					
Subscriber income					
Current subscribers				0	50
New subscribers				50	50
Total subscribers	0	0	0	50	100
Est. monthly subscriber income	175			8,750	17,500
Monthly loss	−53,950	−444,094	−182,454	−173,704	−164,954
Accumulated loss	−53,590	−498,044	−680,498	−854,202	−1,019,156

He hoped that, in this case, future opportunities with the company would inspire the students and staff to work together as a cohesive group with the dedication required to make the project a success.

Competition

Interest in using the new on-line information services expanded rapidly and, by early 1995, there were six ISPs in Hong Kong. SuperNet was the only ISP to hold an official license and one of only two carriers that provided a direct overseas link for their customers to the U.S. Internet. Smaller providers, such as Internet On-line Hong Kong (IOHK) and XXact Information Services (now Asia Online) were among a handful of smaller ISPs that were set up in 1994. These smaller ISPs piggybacked off

Table 6.10
(continued)

6	7	8	9	10	11	12
47,500	47,500	47,500	47,500	47,500	47,500	47,500
15,000	15,000	15,000	15,000	15,000	15,000	15,000
10,000	10,000	10,000	10,000	10,000	10,000	10,000
5,000	5,000	5,000	5,000	5,000	5,000	5,000
5,000	5,000	5,000	5,000	5,000	5,000	5,000
3,000	3,000	3,000	3,000	3,000	3,000	3,000
1,950	1,950	1,950	1,950	1,950	1,950	1,950
						15,600
1,560	1,560	1,560	1,560	1,560	1,560	1,560
3,744	3,744	3,744	3,744	3,744	3,744	3,744
89,700	89,700	89,700	89,700	89,700	89,700	89,700
182,454	182,454	182,454	182,454	182,454	182,454	198,054
						2,338,184
100	150	200	250	300	350	400
50	50	50	50	50	50	50
150	200	250	300	350	400	450
26,250	35,000	43,750	52,500	61,250	70,000	78,750
−156,204	−147,454	−138,704	−129,954	−121,204	−112,454	−119,304
−1,175,360	−1,322,814	−1,461,518	−1,591,472	−1,712,676	−1,825,130	−1,944,434

one of the two bigger providers, primarily HKIGS. They were connected to the Internet through local leased lines linked to another provider, which had a leased line to the United States. The cost of the local leased line was only a fraction of the cost of a leased line to an overseas connection, and so these piggybackers were able to offer much cheaper services than the two larger companies.

At the time of the first press release in October 1993, SuperNet stressed the differences between the services it was offering and those of its competitors (figure 6.9). Other companies offered databases, shareware, libraries, and other information services, but the main advantage of SuperNet lay in direct access to the vast global Internet, which included thousands of information services plus access to the millions of direct e-mail users. The service also offered access to business news wire information and to Nexus and Lexus, the newspaper and legal database services. Coggeshall

For immediate release
26 October 1993

HKUST Offers Advanced Computer Networking Services to Public

Low cost access to the world-wide computer network known as 'Internet is now being offered to the public, the Hong Kong University of Science and Technology announced today.

Internet, which can be accessed with a personal computer and a modem (a device which connects computers to telephone lines), enables its users to reach the tens of thousands of information services offered by more than 12 thousand organizations in over 45 countries.

Access to the Internet will be offered by Hong Kong Supernet for prices starting at HK$140 per month.

Internet users are able to send and receive electronic mail with any of the estimated 20 million other users; 'chat' by keyboard in real-time global conversations; read newspaper wire reports as they are sent; get and give advice on any number of special interest topics (there are thousands) and share computer software.

"The Internet can be thought of as the great public highway for computer communication," said Bob Coggeshall, Project Manager for Hong Kong Supernet. "It is the largest non-private computer network in the world and it is growing at a rate of nearly 100% per year."

Although the Internet had its beginnings more than 20 years ago as a US academic and government research project, private businesses have recently taken the lead in Internet membership as companies have realized its strategic importance. Companies use it to communicate with their customers and employees, and even to advertise products world-wide at very low cost.

"Cost is not the problem, its know how," said Coggeshall, "and HK Supernet will address that problem by offering tutorials, help documents, and discounted books."

Hong Kong Supernet is the result of a research project funded initially by the Sino Software Research Center of HKUST. It is now being made available to the Hong Kong community through the HKUST RandD Corporation Ltd., an independent business unit of the University whose mission is to facilitate the commercialization of the University's research results.

Hong Kong Supernet will hold a press conference and demonstration on Wednesday, October 27, 4-5pm in Lecture Theatre A of the HKUST Campus. For information, please call the Office of Public Affairs at 2358-6307.

Figure 6.9
HKUST press release announcing SuperNet's services to the public

explained that he had been contacted by lawyers interested in Lexus who were paying thousands of dollars to access the service in the United States, compared to the $175 it would cost them for SuperNet in Hong Kong on a monthly basis. Some on-line service providers advertised that they had access to the Internet, but it was not entirely clear the type of access and what services they provided to their users. Some services were limited to only electronic mail and Usenet News, and did not allow the posting of the customer's own news articles, transfer of files at high speed with FTP, making interactive connections anywhere on the Internet with Telnet, or allowing real-time worldwide group conversations with IRC chat. SuperNet went to great lengths to stress that all the above services were provided to its customers.

Other consumer-oriented services on the Internet at that time included the book-store and citation catalogues, which enabled users to order books or hard copies of academic articles over the network and pay for them by credit card. However, with all of this, Coggeshall realized that only a very small proportion of lawyers and consumers were likely to invest the time necessary to familiarize themselves with the Internet (figure 6.10). Potential customers would be attracted to an ISP that provided basic education to local users; SuperNet provided customers with tools like the menu-driven front-end Gopher to help them use the service.

Coggeshall noted that the response to the service launch had been excellent and felt that this demonstrated the pent-up demand in Hong Kong for inexpensive data communication services. He saw the huge opportunity for SuperNet, stating "(the Internet) is really starting to snowball now. People are realising that they can build a virtual private network over the Internet at a fraction of the cost (of traditional tele-communications carriers)." He added that "SuperNet's primary market consisted of small companies and individuals who have at least a partial notion of what the Internet is, as they are the easiest sell." A long-term aim of the company was to encourage local people and companies to use the Internet as a medium to access their customers or specific business information.

Anyone examining the commercial potential of the Internet realized that it offered a very cheap alternative to standard IDD (international direct dial telephone call) communications. Coggeshall explained: "If you used Internet e-mail you got much cheaper communications . . . to send a one-page fax will take up about one minute of IDD, which costs around HK$20. Over SuperNet, if you prepare an e-mail message, then it will take just a few seconds to send and the charge is HK$25.00 per hour."

SuperNet celebrated its first year in business by announcing that it would have an additional 256-kilobytes-per-second link to the U.S. Internet. Until recently, Super-Net and HKIGS had both offered a single 64 kbps leased-line connection to the Internet; the new circuit was twice as fast as the fastest circuit into Hong Kong. With

SuperNet rated as Asia's leading Internet access provider-An educated service

Education is the key to the efficient use of the Internet.

This is according to Pindar Wong, the project manager of Hong Kong SuperNet, which was recently named Asia's top Internet access provider by the Singapore-based *Asia Internet Report.*

The Internet (the Net) just in case you haven't heard about it, is the on-line telecommunications services network which boasts more than 20 million "club" members around the world.

SuperNet is a service that has crossed the research frontier to give business users a taste of the Net in the territory. Its move has been so popular that its subscriber base is growing at 15 per cent every month.

SuperNet is run by RandD Corporation, a wholly owned subsidiary of the Hong Kong University of Science and Technology.

It was formed as part of the Sino Software Research Centre at the University but it is not only this background that makes education vital to its progress, says Mr Wong.

"Its easy enough for people to connect to the Internet," he said. "But is they don't know how to use it there is no benefit."

To allow its members to make the most of their connect time, SuperNet offers free training seminars. This strategy helps satisfy one of the two aims of SuperNet:

    a) to introduce the Internet as a means of communications and technology transfer in Hong Kong; and

    b) to provide a commercial service

Last week it had 2,100bill-paying accounts and 4,495individual log-ins-ins. A total of 50 per cent of its subscribers use the Net as a business tool. It also has several customers with dedicated leased lines, such as Macao Telecom or CTM (Companhia de Telccomicacoes de Macao).

SuperNet was the brainchild of Professor Vincent Shen, the head of the department of Computer Science at the fledgling HKUST. "The idea was that the University had used the Internet for sometime and there was no commercial service provider in Hong Kong," Pindar Wong said.

The university aimed to promote the Internet beyond the academic community and fill that gap.

Previously, Internet access was provided in Hong Kong by HARNET (Hong Kong Academic Research Network), which is managed by a syndicate of educational institutions and still serves many thousands of students and researchers in the territory.

Mr Wong said SuperNet had been successful in its aims with a strong emphasis on customer service.

It was officially launched in November, 1993. Mr Wong remembers the launch day well because SuperNet received more than 300 phone calls from potential subscribers.

However, the date was preceded by many months of wading through red tape, purchase orders and other paperwork.

Company hardware and software was not the only major investment. A trains-Pacific communications line from Hong Kong to the backbone of the Internet in the United States does not come cheaply and not every streetmarket operator can expect to operate one.

"I spent about six to eight months working ahead of the launch," Pindar Wong said. "It was certainly a non-trivial exercise."

The first hurdle was to obtain a license to operate a telecommunications line from Hong Kong to the U.S.

The PNETS (Public Non-Exclusive Telecommunications Services) licence was granted through OFTA, Hong Kong's Office of the Telecommunications Authority.

(This is the body that ordered a switch to eight-digit telephone numbers for Hong Kong subscribers and has set a timetable for the downgrading of Hongkong Telecom's monopoly in Hong Kong).

"To obtain a licence, we had to demonstrate that we were a long-term operation," Mr Wong said. "Certainly, being associated with the university helped out application."

SuperNet's subscriber growth rate required quick responses from his hardware suppliers, according to Mr Wong.

"We cannot order equipment fast enough," he said. "Some components are ordered in advance from the United States and it takes up to five or six weeks to deliver. By the time they arrive we need to order even more hardware. This is a truly astonishing period of growth."

SuperNet, which is a member of the Commercial Internext Exchange (CIX), is connected to the backbone of the Internet in the U.S. by two fibre-optic trans-Pacific circuits (256kbps and 64kbps). It boasts different levels of Internet service - dial-up, premium and dedicated access.

The dial-up access is aimed at individuals and small businesses seeking a low-cost ramp to the Internet. There is a sign-up fee of HK$175 and a minimum monthly charge of $175.

There are off-peak and peak time charges for connect time beyond the $175 value.

On-line data storage is available, with the first 2.5Mb free with the monthly billing. Subsequent storage is charged at $20 a month per megabyte.

Premium access is for networked customers to access through a special reserved telephone line.

Dedicated access means the user has an exclusive line to the SuperNet and the Internet provided by Hongkong Telecom to allow high data transfer rates.

Contact the Hong Kong SuperNet by E-mail on INTERNET: infor@hk.super.net, by telephone on 2358 7924 or fax 2358 7925.

Source: Hong Kong Standard (February 16 1995)

Figure 6.10
Article on the background and strategy of Hong Kong SuperNet
Source: *Hong Kong Standard*, February 16, 1995.

the total bandwidth available at 320 kbps between the United States and Hong Kong, SuperNet had five times the bandwidth commercially available in the Hong Kong market available from the rest of the ISPs combined. SuperNet was the first commercial (ISP) to have broken the 64 kbps barrier. When potential customers considered which ISP to choose, the bandwidth of the connection to the Internet used by the provider was an important factor.

The License

This is a prerequisite for operating. It's like any other business; if you are going to do business, then do it correctly.
—Dave Curado, Network Manager, Hong Kong SuperNet

Advisors to SuperNet emphasized the importance of having a public non-exclusive telecommunication service (PNETS) license before offering Internet services. This PNETS license was required by law to operate any public telecommunications-based value-added service, which included operating as an ISP. The cost was generally passed through to users as a connection time fee. SuperNet made an application for the license in June 1993 and received it from OFTA (Office of Telecommunications Authority) in July of the same year.

Hong Kong Telecom informed SuperNet more than a year later (late 1994) that as a PNETS license holder, it was required to use modem lines that began with the "300" prefix. All PNETS license holders would be required to pay Hong Kong Telecom $5.40 an hour in usage fees for these PNETS lines calls. Although this would cut into profit margins (SuperNet was charging $25 per hour connection fee for peak-time and $10 per hour for off-peak usage), charges would be applied to all PNETS carriers.

It was assumed by everyone working on the SuperNet project that other ISPs had applied for and received the PNETS license, as this was required by law. The PNETS fee scheme was expected to end the disparity between the smaller ISPs, who were offering cheaper services using leased local lines, and the other larger ISPs, who were using more expensive leased lines to an overseas location. However, the issue appeared to fall into a grey area legally. Some ISPs argued that browsing the World Wide Web (WWW) and downloading vast amounts of information did not constitute a telecommunications service and therefore should not attract the PNETS levy.

After some investigation, the SuperNet team found that none of their competitors at that time held the required PNETS license and therefore held a cost advantage over SuperNet. It appeared that these other Internet providers had received advice from industry experts who claimed that the PNETS fees did not apply to ISPs (figure

6.11). SuperNet had directly contacted the government and had complied with the official government policies requiring payment of PNETS fees as a licensed PNETS provider.

According to some sources, Hong Kong Telecom was alleged to have informed the providers without the PNETS license in early 1995 that if they did not increase the number of lines their services used, they would not be charged the PNETS fee. If they wanted new lines, all existing and new lines would be changed to "300" numbers, which would allow Telecom to bill them for the PNETS fees.

Action and Reaction

Action was taken by the Commercial Crime Bureau (CCB) after a complaint, supposedly made by OFTA, that these service providers were running telecommunications networks without the required license. Raids were carried out in March 1995, when all offices of ISPs who did not hold the required license were closed, thus affecting an estimated 10,000 Internet users in Hong Kong who were unable to access the network for weeks (figure 6.12). In the ensuing media coverage, OFTA denied that it instigated the CCB raids; OFTA stated that it had been conducting its own investigation into the telecommunications licensing issue with relation to ISPs. At the time, it looked as if the CCB had usurped the role of OFTA, which was the official authority responsible for licensing telecommunications operators.

It was subsequently confirmed that many ISPs had been working with OFTA and were never given any reason to believe that there was any threat to their "unlicensed" businesses. However, the sudden raid cut off all Internet access in Hong Kong except for SuperNet. The fact that many of the users affected by the CCB's action—some large corporations, foreign consulates and even police officers—were using the Internet for day-to-day communications, research, and business activities was apparently ignored by the bureau.

In the ensuing publicity, one reason given for the raid by the CCB was that the unlicensed ISPs had been involved in computer hacking. However, the search warrants used by the police stated that the ISPs were suspected of "maintaining any means of telecommunications without a license."

The CCB seemed to have adopted a wider interpretation of the Telecommunications Ordinance than had OFTA itself. The telecommunications ordinance did state that it was illegal to maintain any means of telecommunication without a license. There were two possible interpretations of this provision in relation to Internet providers. One is that the "means of telecommunications" was provided by the fixed-line network and not by computers, modems, fax machines, telephone handsets, or television receivers that were or may be connected to it. So, it was argued, ISPs were within the law, as they all used regular telephone lines provided by Hong Kong Telecom. Under this narrow interpretation, only Hong Kong Telecom was required to be licensed, not the ISPs, as they merely use the "means of telecommunication" provided by Hong Kong Telecom.

However, the CCB stated that computers, modems, and any commercial services that used them were "means of telecommunication" and, as such, required a license. If they did not possess a license, the service providers were in breach of the law.

Even if this interpretation was legally correct, the unlicensed ISPs argued in their defense that they were all using regular telephone lines provided to them by Hong Kong Telecom and were subscription customers. The CCB's actions were viewed as an excessive and unnecessary use of police power with no thought for the interests of the end users. It was agreed, in May 1995, that the seven ISPs who were raided by the police would not be prosecuted.

The action had severe consequences for both individual users and businesses. Most companies connected to the Internet in Hong Kong at that time registered domain names as virtual sites on the Internet. (Domain names are the addresses of sites that can point to physical computers connected to the Internet, such as Hong Kong SuperNet, or virtual sites, such as that maintained by the South China Morning Post under the name "scmp.com"). However, companies with virtual sites on service providers were badly affected by the government's action and it took several weeks to sort out their communication problems. Any organization that wanted to switch its virtual domain from one of the affected service providers to Hong Kong SuperNet faced complex technical problems. According to Aaron Cheung, Managing Director of Hong Kong Link, one of the ISPs whose operations had been suspended, the normal turnaround time for changing domain names to a new ISP was 14 days. Even after name changes have been registered, technical difficulties exist that require computers on the Internet to be informed electronically of the change of domain addresses.

With most of the competition (all but CompuServe) removed at a single stroke, SuperNet was able to dominate the field. However, Internet users affected by the government's crackdown on unlicensed ISPs were not able to switch to SuperNet easily. It was possible to get a new account with SuperNet, but organizations with domain names on the Internet had some difficulties switching to SuperNet. Cheung noted that "even if the changes can be made fast with exceptional handling, mail (to these domains) may not be received correctly."

The average user was also left in the position of being a little confused as to how much he/she was actually being charged for the Internet. Many users were very

Internet service providers in licensing snarl
Government acknowledges 'grey area' as it sets out to investigate unlicensed operators
by Anna Foley

Only one of Hong Kong's eight-plus commercial Internet service providers appears to have secured a Public Non-Exclusive Telecommunications Service (PNETS) licence, which is a requirement by law for operating public Internet gateway services in the territory.   But authorities concede that the issue falls into a grey area.

Confusion over the specific conditions under which Hong Kong-based commercial Internet service providers *must* obtain a PNETS licence to operate highlights the inherently ambiguous nature of some telecommunications regulations.

While the founders of HKUST RandD Corp. administered Hong Kong Supernet contacted the government and were informed of the need to apply for a PNETS licence, other Internet providers such as Asia On-line sought advice from experts within the telecoms industry and concluded that no licence was necessary.

"We applied for PNETS when we first set up. It was a neophyte move - we were only the second (independent) Internet provider in Hong Kong and we didn't know what the licensing requirements were, so we called the government and asked them. They responded by saying we needed a PNETS licence," explained Dave Curado, network manager at Hong Kong Supernet.

While applying for the licence "took some doing and was a red-tape-type affair," according to Curado, he believes it was a worthwhile process. "This is a prerequisite for operating," he said. "It's like any other business - if you're going to do business, then do it correctly."

Criminal Offense
Eric Lam, director of telecommunications at the government's Office of the Telecommunications Authority (OFTA), confirmed that a service provider must "first obtain a PNETS licence for establishing and maintaining a telecommunications installation for value-added services in Hong Kong."

As to how this rule should be applied to local Internet service providers, Lam explained that the main criteria for requiring a PNETS licence are for the company to have its own physical telecommunications set-up, such as a computer routing Internet traffic, and be offering that service commercially to third parties.

"This is a grey area," Lam conceded. "But according to the law, they should take out a licence." He cited Section 8.1 of the telecommunications Ordinance as stating that a company will require a licence to establish or maintain any means of telecommunications in Hong Kong which is being offered as a public service. "Contravention of Section 8.1 is an offence and the defendant is liable, on conviction, to a fine of HK$15,000 and imprisonment for two years," Lam added.

Lam stressed that applying for a PNETS licence should not be considered a hurdle to operation by Internet providers. However, applicants are required to supply details of their telecommunications equipment, technical support facilities, the service to be provided and corporate financial information.

What's more, aside from an annual HK$750 PNETS licence charge, Lam confirmed that PNETS licensees are charged a 9-cents-per-minute-on-line usage charge in addition to the monthly flat-rate line paid by standard business users.

According to Lam's records, Hong Kong Supernet is the only Internet service provider in Hong Kong to have a PNETS licence. Even Hong Kong Internet and Gateway services (HKIGS) - the first company to offer independent commercial Internet services in Hong Kong - does not have one. Aaron Cheung, founder of HKIGS and recent Internet start-up HongKongLink Communications, was unavailable for comment.

While HKIGS, HongKongLink and Hong Kong Supernet are the only independent Internet providers in Hong Kong to operate their own international leased-line connections to the United States, a plethora of other commercial providers have sprung up who "piggy-back" onto one of the international gateways by running their own local leased-line links to it.

Newly-established HongKongLink feeds five such resellers, at least three of whom offer their own commercial services - InfoLink Company, Internet Connections and Asia On-line. HKIGS, meanwhile, services a further three of whom two - Internet Online and CyberNet HongKong - operate commercial Internet services for the public. While none of these providers maintains its own international telecommunications connection, the fact that they have a physical telecommunications set-up and market the Internet connection as their own commercial service is enough to qualify them for PNETS licence, in Lam's view.

However, Dion Wiggins, CEO of Asia On-line, maintains that he talked to Hongkong Telecom about the need for a licence when he was first considering establishing the service, "and they said we didn't need one because we weren't providing international services." Wiggins' contact in Hongkong Telecom, who described himself as just a friend giving advice, and who preferred not to be named, explained that he had merely set out the options. He echoed the general view that value-added telecoms licensing is a grey area. "Put it this way - the answer is not that simple," he said. "I said that if they were transferring a call from Point A to Point B, connecting to another database, and if they did not own that information source, then they did need to apply for a PNETS licence."

Action Soon

Pindar Wong, project manager at Hong Kong Supernet, says he is outraged by the licensing issue because other Internet providers are able to avoid the 9-cents-per-minute PNETS leased-line charge and so can undercut Supernet's rates. And he is adamant the licensing requirements should be upheld to protect consumers. "Licences are there to protect the customer. I'm all for the free market but it's in consumers' interests to only go with people who are licensed," he said.

Wong stressed that a number of could-be Internet start-ups had approached his company in the past asking to resell its Internet connection, but he had rejected them all for not having a PNETS licence.

While OFTA's Lam maintains that he cannot see any good reason for local Internet providers not to want to apply for a PNETS licence, he has revealed plans to check out the situation. "I will send out an inspections team to ask questions and to see if there are any problems and if companies are aware of the need for a licence," he said. "I will be happy if they (the unlicensed Internet providers) to opt to take up a licence now."

Figure 6.11
Articles about the ISP licensing issue and CCB raid
Source: *Computerworld Hong Kong*, January 19, 1995.

DATELINE ASIA - PULLED OVER ON THE SUPERHIGHWAY

The Internet is not a global resource for the exchange of information. It is a hotbed of crime. It must be true. No less an authority than the computer crimes division of Hong Kong's Commercial Crimes Bureau (CCB) say so.

Which is why early in March, armed only with warrants, screwdrivers and an uncomfortable-looking gaggles of officers from the Office of the Telecommunications Authority (OFTA), the CCB raided seven of Hong Kong's nine Internet service providers and carted away van-loads of electronics and staff.

The CCB produced warrants saying the seven had been operating for many months without a HK$750 (US$96) licence from OFTA. The raided companies produced letters from OFTA which said that licensing requirements were currently under review.

The companies suggested that the law was particularly vague when it came to any telecommunications service more advanced than two tine cans connected with string. The OFTA officials discovered they had urgent business elsewhere and left, pausing only long enough to say their presence at the raids was at the request of the CCB, which wanted their technical assistance in a computer hacking investigation.

In pained tones (presumably because of the OFTA dagger stuck in its back), the CCB told reporters that, yes, it was conducting a hacking investigation and that the seven companies were suspected of being used by criminals for unauthorized use of the Internet. They had to be closed down and their equipment seized for the gathering of evidence.

The estimated 10,000 disconnected Internet customers were livid that their personal property stored on the host computers was now open to scrutiny by the police. They were also puzzled as to how anyone could make unauthorized use of something that is owned by nobody and needs no authorization to use in the first place.

There was also a severe problem in the CCB logic circuits regarding the closures. Would the CCB next start closing down supermarkets because it suspected shoplifters were at work? How about closing all Hong Kong roads to traffic to deter speeding or illegal parking?

The backlash to what the CCB had presumably seen as a straightforward operation to stomp on a few undesirables - real or

imagined - must have come as quite a shock. It certainly lit a fire beneath the government's Information Policy Panel. The panel is an otherwise unremarkable talking shop that most people didn't even know existed until it invited all concerned parties, including a loudly disgruntled bunch of Internet users, to explain what all the fuss was about.

Blinking in the unaccustomed daylight and visibly straining to de-tune their massive processing power down to the level of government bureaucrats and policemen, the Internet's explained a few simple Net facts. Such as how cutting 10,000 individuals and businesses off from the rest of the world and seizing their personal property could cause just a little resentment.

The CCB replied that its investigators didn't read the contents of private messages, only the headers saying who the message was to and from.

Local legislator James To, never one to mince his words, told the Information Policy Panel that it looked to him as if the police had obtained warrants under false pretenses and that the Internet providers had a clear case for suing the CCB's blue serge pants off. James To is, after all, a lawyer.

CCB chief superintendent Neil McCabe took all this in his stride. He didn't flinch when it was pointed out that an Internet operator with a licence was just as open to people using his system for illegal purposes as one without a licence.

OFTA, clearly relieved that all the mud was being lobbied in the direction of the CCB, was the voice of reasonable and caring bureaucracy. Its officers told the panel they had since gone to extraordinary lengths to help the seven Internet companies over their licensing problem and were happy to report that all were now operating legally.

Neither the seven companies nor OFTA were prepared to jeopardize their newly consummated relationship with revelations about who might have been stalling on that particular issue.

Nigel Armstrong

Figure 6.12
Article about the ISP licensing issue and CCB raid
Source: *Asian Business*, June 1995.

worried that they would receive a large bill for retroactive payments. As a result, many disenchanted clients switched to SuperNet. In addition, the publicity and media coverage resulting from this event led many people who had never had access to the Internet to decide to subscribe. Whereas 10 applications a day was the norm prior to the CCB raids, during the six weeks following the CCB raids, SuperNet experienced a surge of business, with up to 100 applications per day being processed. This one incident proved to be the lucky break that put SuperNet far ahead of all other ISPs at that time.

Challenge and Opportunities for Hong Kong SuperNet in 1995

The Internet had become a massive informal network of computers spread across more than 45 countries by early 1996, connecting tens of thousands of databases and boasting of more than 20 million registered users (figure 6.13). Internet users were

Millions of Internet Host Computers

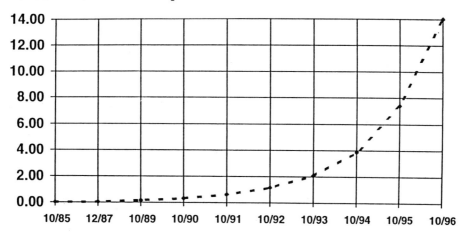

hosts doubling each year

users growing at 10%/month, and is estimated to be approximately ten times the number of hosts indicated in this chart.

total traffic packets growing faster than number of hosts or users

Figure 6.13
Growth of the Internet worldwide

able to send electronic mail to and receive electronic mail from any other network user, "chat" with each other via computer in real time, read news reports as they were being sent, discuss thousands of special interest topics, and share computer software. Industry experts believed that the Internet was growing by one million subscribers per month in early 1996.

However, far from being a seamless and easy-to-use connection, driving along the information superhighway was compared to starting on a journey on a road with no signposts and many potholes on the way. Lack of knowledge coupled with human error were seen as factors that inhibited growth and acceptance of the Internet within the Hong Kong business community at this time.

By the beginning of 1996, there were more than 40 licensed ISPs in Hong Kong, and new ISPs were being licensed at a rate of five per month (table 6.11). Each ISP wanted to take advantage of an expanding market share and reach a minimum scale required to achieve profitable operations.

Enhanced Personal and Business Communications

Personal communications services were close to the hearts of many Hong Kong people. Portable telephones, pagers, and fax machines all managed to reach very high levels of penetration in Hong Kong. The latest entrant to this market was electronic mail, which appealed to the group labeled "young professionals," aged between early 20s and late 30s. SuperNet's clientele was evenly divided between individuals and businesses at this time, partly driven by the low cost of using the Internet. "Even compared to fax, there are economic advantages; you can send the same amount of information over the Internet as on a single fax page for about a tenth of the cost," Coggeshall observed.

Coggeshall said that offices in Hong Kong needed a cost-effective way to communicate with their head offices overseas, and electronic mail was the easiest, most cost-effective way of doing this. Two advantages of e-mail lay in confidentiality and convenience. A fax could be read by anyone, and a telephone required the recipient to receive the call simultaneously. E-mail offered confidentiality without requiring simultaneous connection, which was a huge bonus when time differences often made it inconvenient to place a business call.

Security Issues

At the start of 1995, SuperNet acted as a gateway for about 2,000 people in Hong Kong. Customers could gain access to the Internet for as little as $4 per hour, reinforcing Hong Kong's position as the least expensive point in Asia for accessing the network. However, there were still security concerns regarding using the Internet that

Table 6.11
Pricing for four major ISPs in January 1996

Comparison of four major ISPS				
Vendors	Backbone	Dial-up charges ($)	Leased line charges ($)	Value-added services
Asia On-line	256 kbps to the U.S.	Sign up: $88 Monthly fee: $120/10 hours Additional: $11.4/hour	1.64 kpbs Set-up and connection: $7,000 Monthly fee: $3,800 2.128 kpbs Set-up and connection: $10,000 Monthly fee $7,200	Web page design & hosting, LAN to Internet consultancy
LinkAge On Line	64 kbps, 256 kbps, T1 to U.S.	Sign-up: $98 Monthly fee: $98/5 hours Additional: $15/hour	1.64 kbps Set-up: $15,000 Month: $12,000 2.128 kbps Set up: $15,000 Month: $16,000 3.256 kbps Set-up: $15,000 Month: $28,000 4.512 kbps Set-up: $15,000 Month: $48,000	Web site design & set up & hosting, LAN to Internet integration training
HK Star Internet	768 kbps to U.S.	Plan A- Sign-up: $98 Monthly fee: $168/12 hours Additional: $10/hour Plan B- Sign-up: $98 Fee: $50 year Hourly fee: $20/hour	1.192 kbps Set-up: $4,700 Month: $3,720 2.64 kbps Set-up: $8,000 Month: $9,200 3.128 kbps Set-up: $12,000 Month: $20,900	Web site design and set-up; Web page design & hosting, LAN to Internet integration consultancy
Supernet	64 kbps & 256 kbps to U.S.	Sign-up: $175 Monthly fee: $175 Additional hourly charge: 9am–6pm: $25 6pm–9pm: $10	19.2 kbps Set-up: $5,000 Month: $5,000	Lan to Internet integration consultancy

Source: Comparison of charges in cyber wars (*Hong Kong Business*, January 1996).

posed a barrier to widespread acceptance, especially when it came to conducting business transactions. Two major dangers lay in existing flaws in the operating system software (which drove the computers on the Internet) and human error. The latter was thought to have been responsible for a security lapse at SuperNet in January 1995, which exposed private information about its customers. Confidential billing information about several thousand users was available to anyone using the system for a short period of time until the gap in security was plugged (figure 6.14).

SuperNet at that time was used by the Hong Kong government, the Royal Hong Kong Jockey Club, and the Hong Kong Productivity Council. Confidential information including names, addresses, and telephone and fax numbers, along with the number of hours logged into the system and related charges, were stored in computer files normally unreadable by users. However, the files on SuperNet were accidentally stored in a way that temporarily made them accessible to all system users. Pindar Wong, SuperNet's project manager responsible for maintaining such data, acknowledged that the lapse could have been damaging to his customers. He said that he did not know how the SuperNet files had become available to all users and added that the billing software was designed to ensure private information was protected from unauthorized access.

Setting the Boundaries

The Internet has no boundaries, so we have to define our own limits.
—Pindar Wong, Project Manager, SuperNet

We should all fight to stop any kind of censorship, on the Net and elsewhere. How long before information about China and Taiwan is banned? How about roller-blading being a subversive activity in Singapore? The Internet was set up to overcome censorship.
—Letter to *Eastern Express*, February 1992

Another important issue was Internet access to pornographic files. In April 1995, SuperNet willingly cooperated with the government to voluntarily end access to this material, earning itself the name "Hong Kong CensorNet." Pindar Wong felt strongly about the rights of people on the Internet, but knew that it was in the company's interest to comply with local laws and industry practices, particularly given the affiliation with HKUST. This action would set an example to other ISPs in what otherwise was an anarchic culture. With the many issues needing to be addressed in areas covering equal access, libel and defamation, freedom of expression, and intellectual property rights, he knew that it was important for users and service providers to reach solutions that were fair to all.

Oversight exposes confidential data

by ARMAN DANESH

A Security lapse at Hong Kong's largest commercial provider of access to the Internet global computer network has exposed private information about its users.

Confidential billing information about several thousand users was available to anyone using the system until the gap in security was plugged by the operators, acting on information revealed by the *South China Morning Post*.

The system, Hong Kong SuperNet, is used by the Hong Kong Government and major organizations including Hongkong Telecom, the Royal Hong Kong Jockey Club and the Hongkong Productivity Council.

The confidential information - including names, addresses, telephone and fax number, along with the number of hours logged into the system and related charges - is stored in computer-generated files normally unreadable by users.

But the files on SuperNet, which is based at the Hong Kong University of Science and Technology, were stored in a manner that made them accessible to all system users.

The breach was brought to the *Post's* attention by a computer expert who said at least 10 other users had gained access to the information, some for business purposes. It is unclear how long the files remained unprotected.

Such information may fall under legislation being drafted for consideration by the Legislative Council. Under the proposed bill, which is a response to a report by the Law Reform Commission's privacy committee, operators of information systems containing private data would be required to ensure privacy.

Any person who maintained such systems would be required to register with an information commissioner and make a declaration of purpose, Secretary for Home Affairs Michael Suen Ming-yeung said.

When made aware of the security lapse, SuperNet's project manager, Pindar Wong said SuperNet was responsible for safeguarding such data.

"This is unacceptable," he said. "This is proprietary information. It is a private thing between the customer and the supplier."Mr Wong acknowledged the lapse could be damaging to his customers.

SuperNet user Apple Computer International has expressed concern that private information about the company was so easily accessible.

The managing director of Asia Concepts, James Henry, said "I do not expect that information to be available without my consent." The local computer company uses SuperNet to access Internet.

Mr Wong said he did not know how the SuperNet files had become available to all users. He said when the software that generated the monthly billing files on his system was developed it was designed to ensure private information was protected from unauthorized access.

"We should have a very strict security policy as far as files like these," he said. "We're not all perfect. I intend to fix this."

According to an Internet security expert, a mistake of this sort was likely to have been caused by human error. Office of the Telecommunications Authority head Alex Arena said there was no privacy code in Hong Kong to help guarantee the confidentiality of such information He said privacy and security issues were not taken into account when licences were issued.

"Up until now, there have been no laws that cover it. We will be considering privacy in the future," he said. "As we move into a competitive environment, we will be looking at it more seriously."

Source: **South China Morning Post**
(January 30th, 1995)

Figure 6.14

Article concerning exposure of confidential information by Hong Kong SuperNet
Source: *South China Morning Post*, January 30, 1995.

The Price War

Competition has heated up, but we continue to grow and are still the leading ISP in Hong Kong. Competition is not a threat. It is, only when you're unable to respond. We differentiate ourselves from competitors by quality, reliability and regional presence.
—Professor Eugene Wong, Chief Executive for SuperNet

Internet charges varied wildly in Hong Kong in early 1995, as competition between the ISPs increased. SuperNet charged users $25 per hour, HKIGS and Hong Kong Link both charged $20 per hour, whereas IOHK charged $8 per hour. Further escalation of price competition occurred at the beginning of the year, when Asia Online slashed its connection charges by almost 75% to $4 per hour. Dion Wiggins, Chief Executive Officer for Asia Online, justified the action by saying that now, many people who previously could not afford access to the Internet, could do so. In announcing the price cuts, Wiggins indicated "there were companies making a lot of money in Hong Kong through unreasonable access charges and only offering Internet." In response, Pindar Wong noted that if Asia Online were providing international value-added networking services, there should be a 9 cents per minute local telephone charge, which was a $5.40 per hour additional cost.

This cost excluded other substantial costs of providing Internet services, such as the leased line from Hong Kong Telecom, expensive routers, and advanced Sun Sparc-Stations. SuperNet at the time had kept its dial-up price the same for more than a year, during which time business had grown by about 15%. SuperNet managers did not consider Asia Online a threat at all, in spite of its aggressive pricing policies. "Threatening on price alone, with an unestablished user based and unestablished service quality, is suicidal," said Pindar Wong.

The Window of Opportunity

We have a simple and elegant architecture. The timing is right and the technology is ready. What we are seeing is the timely convergence of technology.... The logical layer will be there forever. The Internet was designed with democracy and it has empowered the masses to develop content and technology.
—Professor Eugene Wong, Vice-President for Research and Development (HKUST), Vice-Chairman of Asia Internet Holdings (AIH)

One of the challenges for HKUST to consider when evaluating options for selling SuperNet was determining the market value of the company if sold. Determining a fair market value for SuperNet was difficult. Although the business was growing at an accelerating rate, there were many companies entering the market, so competition provided an impetus for a decision on SuperNet's future. Looking at the competition, Professor Wong began to get a feel for what SuperNet was probably worth but wondered how he could give a further value to the company and ultimately to his customers. One factor he realized was that there was no dedicated high-speed Internet backbone network for the region of Asia. With the growing volume of Internet business in Asia, this was a gap in the market that needed to be filled. Despite the high volume of Internet traffic within Asia, most Asian countries were connected to the Internet via the United States, and this U.S.-centric topology was not conductive to development of networking within the region.

Initially, HKUST management discussed selling SuperNet to the highest bidder. After much discussion, this simple objective was redefined and examined and financial gain gave way to other considerations. As the issues were discussed, it became more important to find potential buyers who were willing to develop what the university had nurtured. It was considered important, first, that buyers should exhibit long-term vision and be committed to taking SuperNet into the 21st century. Second, they should have an excellent grasp of the technological aspect of the business together with the vision to predict where the Internet, and SuperNet's competitors, might jump next. Third, they should be the sort of people that the university would wish to maintain a relationship with, as the future might bring some sort of further collaboration. This personal aspect of a potential buyer was seen to be very important in the negotiation process. HKUST Professor Eugene Wong knew from past experience that private companies would always strive to achieve the best deal for themselves. He hoped that any negotiations would be conducted in an honest and trustworthy atmosphere. A final consideration would be the current staff working at SuperNet together with the existing customer base, both of whom would want a buyer who could carry on the present excellent relationships.

Asia Internet Holding (AIH)

In October 1995, Eugene Wong initiated discussions with companies in Japan and Singapore that led to the formation of Asia Internet Holding (AIH) (figure 6.15). AIH consisted of Hong Kong SuperNet, Internet Initiative Japan (IIJ), the Sumitomo Group of Japan, and Sembawang Corporation of Singapore. One of the immediate objectives was seen as allowing intra-Asian traffic to be routed within Asia rather than having to go overseas. A secondary, but no less important, objective was to provide a common medium for linkage to the Internet for all ISPs, especially for ISPs in countries that at that time did not have any service.

PRESS RELEASE FOR 16 OCTOBER 1995

PAN ASIA CONSORTIUM TO BUILD INTERNET BACKBONE NETWORK

The three leading Internet service providers in Asia - Internet Initiative Japan (IIJ), Pacific Internet of Singapore and Hong Kong SuperNet - have joined forces with Sumitomo Corporation to build a high speed Internet backbone network for Asia.

The Internet has rapidly evolved from a U.S.-based research network to become the de facto global information infrastructure. The expansion of commercial services on Internet has been rapid, and nowhere more so than in Asia. Despite the high volume of Internet traffic within Asia, today, most Asian countries connect to the Internet via the U.S. This U.S.-centric network topology is not conducive to the development of the Internet in Asia. Internet communication between Asian countries now has to routed via the U.S., thus incurring unnecessary cost and congestion in the trans-Pacific links. A high speed Internet backbone for Asia is overdue.

The new joint venture, Asia Internet Holding (AIH), will have a "distributed hub" system, with Tokyo as the main network hub having very high speed T3 links to the U.S., and Singapore and Hong Kong as regional hubs. This network topology will evolve as appropriate in accordance with traffic demand and the tariff schedules for international leased circuits.

Asia Internet Holding will be established in Japan next month. With an initial paid up capital of U.S.$6 million in equal contributions from the four founding general partners, it will build and operate a backbone Internet network for Asia. The backbone will provide a common interface for all Internet service providers in Asian countries to link into Internet, in place of individual connections to the U.S.

Many multinational corporations operating in Asia are looking upon the Internet as a platform on which to build their own private networks linking offices, factories and staff all over Asia and the world. Asia Internet Holding will work with Internet service providers in Asian countries to serve this market by providing reliable and secured communication via the Internet.

Asia Internet Holding will invite those multinational corporations and Internet service providers making use of its service to invest in the company so as to evolve it into a broadly owned Asian company. International information service providers will also be encouraged to use AIH infrastructure to reach out to clients throughout Asia.

Figure 6.15
Press release announcing the formation of AIH

AIH would be seen to offer economies of scale, uniform standards, and flexible bandwidth choice. For the ISPs, the main advantage would be the ability to piggy-back on a set of high-speed lines without the need to negotiate links. AIH offered a simple alternative for a country joining the Internet for the first time in that it could simply connect to the nearest AIH touchdown point. In the past it would have had to arrange for a circuit to the United States, as well as organizing for a local ISP in the United States through which to route its traffic.

Tokyo was to be the main network hub and would have high speed links to the U.S. Internet backbone network. Singapore and Hong Kong would act as regional hubs within this network, and would evolve in accordance with traffic demand and tariff schedules for international leased circuits. The AIH partners hoped that the new backbone would "expand the commercial uses of the Internet tremendously in the region and be a one-stop-shop for companies seeking to set up virtual private networks linking all their Asian manufacturing bases." AIH hoped that many man-ufacturers in Japan, Hong Kong, and Singapore who had widely distributed manu-facturing facilities in Asia would see the importance of going to one ISP for a turnkey solution as opposed to different ISPs in each location.

With regard to the optimum network, AIH looked at the tariffs among the various telecoms providers involved. At that time it was admitted that there was a lot of artificiality in the structure that could not be changed, but the aim was to concentrate on the natural clusters of countries around Singapore, Japan, and Hong Kong. It was felt that it would be advantageous for SuperNet to continue its role as an ISP in Hong Kong and that would encourage other ISPs to join the Asian backbone. The four partners put an equal investment into the US$6 million venture, but customers were encouraged to sign up early with the promise of a share in the business.

The timing of this investment in AIH was believed to have increased the market value of SuperNet. By being a full partner in AIH, SuperNet provided far greater value to its customers by giving them immediate access to a large portion of the rapidly growing Asian market. This strategic move was believed to be a major factor that contributed to the final successful sale of SuperNet. Some felt that without being a member of AIH, SuperNet might not have been able to find any potential buyer.

7 Electronic Auctions and Intermediaries

Many situations arise in both commercial and personal ventures in which a buyer or seller of a commodity or service does not know precisely how much it is worth. This is especially true with unique or rare commodities, or where there is little information about the cost to contractors who could produce the services. In this situation, it is better to buy or sell at an auction than to post a price. In fact if there is a capacity constraint, posting a price fails to exploit the fact that some buyers might be willing to pay more before the seller hits the capacity constraint (or vice versa for the seller).

Consumers are supposed to maximize their consumer surplus. *Consumer surplus* is the difference between the *reservation price*, that is, the price of a purchased commodity expressed in monetary units, and its selling price. The reservation price can also be defined as the highest price that a buyer would be willing to pay and the lowest price that a seller would be willing to accept. As long as the buyer's reservation price is higher than the seller's reservation price, an exchange of goods is possible that will increase the consumer surplus of both buyer and seller. The challenge for both is to reach the best possible price for the goods being sold, which often means finding out as much as possible about the reservation prices of potential buyers and sellers.

Auctions are a way for buyers and sellers to get information about the reservation prices of potential buyers in the market for a particular product. Obtaining this information usually involves *search costs*—for example, visiting showrooms, researching journals, and asking associates. Auctions are one way of obtaining this information from a large number of buyers at relatively low cost. Information technology has provided other means of acquiring information, which are still evolving with the development of the Web as a worldwide information base.

In an efficient world, the consumer would continually compare the marginal surplus associated with an additional piece of information with the marginal search cost associated with obtaining that extra information. In practice, it is difficult to impose this discipline on consumers. Auctions provide consumers some assurance of efficiency in price search and in matching buyers and sellers.

There are numerous steps involved in selling a product or service:

1. Target the market for potential buyers.

2. Create an awareness of the company's product and the market as a whole (i.e., the substitutes that exist in the market).

3. Develop potential buyers' interest in the product (or service) and identify the specific needs that will motivate sales, define the product, and instigate purchases.

4. Educate the market about the product, how it is used, and how the customer will benefit.

5. Find a price at which both buyer and seller are satisfied.

6. Close the sale.

7. Deliver the product.

8. Service, technical support, warranty service and follow-up: Support customers after the sale.

Items 1 through 5 are essentially search costs and can amount to a substantial portion of the product's delivered cost. A number of market models minimized these search costs as a primary objective. The evolution of new information technology for search has provided new avenues for reducing these search costs.

Market Models

The basic search question an auction market seeks to answer is: What is the price of a good or a service? This question can be expressed in one of two ways for a *simple auction*—that is, one in which there is one seller and many buyers, or vice versa. In the first case, each buyer knows his or her own precise, personal assessment of the worth of the product, but not the value the other potential buyers assign to it. Each of the values is independent of other bidders' reservation prices and thus conveys no information about the value that any other buyer assigns. In the second case, the item to be auctioned has a single objective value, which none of the buyers knows. Auctions allow buyers to share their information about the common value.

Real auctions are likely to have elements of both *private-value* and *common-value pricing*. Goods such as oil field drilling rights definitely have a value in common to all oil companies (the potential buyers). On the other hand, goods such as consumer electronics fit the private-value model, in which each buyer holds it to have some intrinsic value independent of the value assessed by other buyers. Electronic auctions have so far found in moderately valued consumer goods their widest applications outside of securities markets (discussed in chapter 8).

Vickrey[1] presented four models of private-value simple auctions given the assumption that buyers hold independent, private assessments of the value of the good. Since this assumption addresses the sorts of markets that exist for consumer goods, Vickrey's auction models establish the de facto standard for the simple auction forms that have grown to importance in e-commerce.

Without an auction to search for the price at which a buyer and seller are willing to trade, buyers are forced to be price takers. *Price taking* is common practice with low-valued retail goods: Grocery stores and discount chains mark nonnegotiable prices on the goods for sale, and consumers have the option of either taking this price or not buying the product. Obviously, these prices cannot be set at random, because customers often have the choice of buying the same or similar products at a competitor's store. However, neither can buyer and seller easily engage in the sort of exchange of information required to maximize the utility (i.e., well being) of both parties to the transaction.

The most common and widely recognized auction format is that of the *English* (or *progressive*) *auction*. In the English auction, bids are freely made and announced publicly until no purchaser wishes to make any further bid. A utility-maximizing bidder participates if, and only if, he can win the auction with a bid that is less than his reservation value for the product and drops out only if the bid "on the floor" equals or exceeds his reservation value.

The *Dutch auction*, so named because it is used in Dutch flower markets, and in fish and fruit markets in Belgium and Holland, starts the offer price at an amount believed to be higher than any bidder is willing to pay; an auctioneer or clock device lowers the price until one of the bidders accepts the last price offer. The first and only bid is the sales price in this type of auction, which provides a fast way to sell perishable goods.

The Dutch and English auctions are unrestricted auctions in which where buyers (or bidders) openly acknowledge their choices by calling out a price. *Sealed-bid auctions* exist where bids are not public, but sealed in an envelope. In a *second-price sealed-bid auction* the sale is awarded to the highest bidder at the price set by the second highest bidder. In a *first-price sealed-bid auction*, sale is awarded to the highest bidder at the highest bid price.

Both the English (or progressive) auction and the second-price sealed-bid auction result in identical prices in a given situation. They are *demand revealing*, as they correctly price the goods or services sold, and only their implementation differs. Both the first-price sealed-bid auction and the Dutch auction result in identical prices in a given situation. They do not necessarily price the goods or services correctly, because bidders' high bids depend on their preference or aversion to risk.

In addition to these simple auctions, buyers and sellers may also engage in double auction markets. A *double auction* assumes that several market participants on both sides of the market publicly announce their demand and supply prices. The market price (publicly announced) is the one that equates supply and demand (i.e., clears). Securities exchanges tend to be double auctions, if the volume and liquidity of traded assets is significant. Though more complex, double auction markets are arguably efficient; that is, their prices reflect all available (price-relevant) information, and their current prices transmit the private information of the better-informed dealers to the less-informed, and these prices correctly aggregate the possibly conflicting information available to the individual buyers and sellers.

Latency

Where auctions provide the primary vehicle for exchange of information about the personal and public values of a commodity or service, the speed at which that information is transmitted among buyers is paramount. The time required for a signal to travel from one point on a network to another is called *latency*. In traditional public auctions, where bids are submitted by open outcry, all bidders receive information about other bids at the moment they are shouted out.

In contrast, network latencies in securities markets and auctions inject into the public broadcast of each bid a delay that is likely to vary from bidder to bidder. Latency may put some bidders at a disadvantage, because buyers who receive information first may use it to *front-run*—that is, to place new bids that take advantage of supply-demand imbalances, to the disadvantage of buyers who receive information later. The growth of program trading, which allows trading computers to buy and sell directly with an exchange based on real-time investment algorithms, exacerbates latency's impact. If certain groups of buyers know they are at a disadvantage because of latencies in a market's network, they may refuse to trade in that market, lowering its liquidity, profits, and efficiency.

Latency is a critical factor in the design and implementation of electronic markets. Markets spend exceptional amounts of money to assure that all market participants receive their information at exactly the same time. For example, Aucnet, the first electronic automobile auction set up in Japan, was able to promote its electronic auction successfully to dealers only after investing in a communications satellite to ensure that all bids were transmitted around Japan with bid-processing latencies of no more than 0.2 seconds.

The speed and frequency of bids has a great deal of bearing on the acceptable network latency allowed in any given market. Aucnet runs a dealer auction for used cars in which a sale is made on average every 20 seconds. Bids are made in fixed, 3000-yen increments by pressing a button on a computer console. Immediately before a sale, dealers may make several bids a second. In this environment, a 0.2 second latency was the maximum that the dealers would allow, and to minimize delay and cost, a combination of dial-up telephone lines and satellite transmission of images and data was connected.

The fixed and variable delays in information transmission with different media need to be carefully considered in design of any electronic commerce system. Markets do not always have the luxury of restricting the geographical area over which they can allow traders to participate, or of choosing the fastest transmission technology. In addition, alterations in the speed of communications in an electronic commerce network can be even more onerous for participants to accept than absolute delays in information transmission. The discrepancies in latency rates among market participants can be especially hard to accept when the delay variations may systematically disadvantage some firms for reasons beyond their control.

Chile's stock exchange, The Bolsa de Comercio de Santiago, faced such a problem within the confines of Santiago. Many of the member brokerage firms had offices inside the exchange building, where the exchange was running its administrative systems on a 10 Mbps Ethernet backbone. Yet the exchange forced brokers inside the building to connect to the market data feeds at the same speed as brokers who would dial in from outside the building; in 1995 this was 9600 bps. In this means, the exchange artificially multiplied the latency 1,000 times to ensure that brokers with offices inside its building did not front-run brokers outside the exchange building.

The ill-fated Globex—the $100 million, first-ever round-the-clock electronic trading system developed by Reuters and the Chicago Mercantile Exchange (CME)—faced an even more daunting challenge. Globex was designed to trade CME contracts around the globe. Even under the best of conditions, the latency between Hong Kong and Chicago nodes of a satellite link is two to three seconds. Two to three seconds' systematic delay in information delivery and trade execution translates to a minimum five seconds for execution. Where stakes are high and bidding is intense, traders need a continual flow of the latest bid-ask prices or risk being systematically outmaneuvered. Five-seconds-per-transmission-cycle delays can, for an institutional trader, translate into millions or billions of dollars of losses. Needless to say, traders who were serious about trading stayed in Chicago, where they could participate directly in the CME.

The situation becomes even more serious on the Internet, which by its architecture cannot make guarantees about latency. Auction sites such as OnSale solve the problem by setting a fixed length of time that an auction is open, typically several days. Bids accumulate in a heap, which is displayed on the specific auction page of the OnSale Website. Winning bids are chosen only at the close of the auction. Though there is the possibility of a rush of bids near the closing time, this has not generally been a problem for the auction. Leaving auctions open for several days can also increase global participation, because bidders are not forced to be awake and logged in at odd hours.

The previous examples lend some intuition to the role that network latencies play in setting up electronic auction markets. This is by no means exhaustive. With the evolution of networks, auction formats, and intelligent agents for bidding and product search and purchase, latency can be expected to impact buyers' and sellers' trading behavior in ever more subtle and complex ways. Successful electronic auctions need to consider how to address the impact of latency for each particular electronic auction market.

Sticky Prices

In liquid markets for *fungibles*—that is, goods whose individual units can be exchanged with each other—prices fluctuate to reflect imbalances of supply and demand. If they do not (for example, if market makers fail to raise prices when they are too low) then suppliers lose money by having to sell substantial quantities at too low a price. Where goods are perishable, too high a price can leave the seller (for example, the produce counter of a grocery store) with moldering and unsold goods at the end of the day.

The reach and liquidity provided by a global network, instantaneous response, intelligent agents for search and price discovery, and legions of buyers and sellers should sufficiently lubricate the price-setting machinery to assure that neither of these situations occurs under normal circumstances. However, in many situations, factors other than supply and demand systematically determine prices. One case discussed earlier occurs when (for example, in the petroleum industry) buyers place a common value on a commodity, and demand-revealing auction mechanisms may reveal this value but do not necessarily clear demand and supply imbalances. Prices may be sticky for at least three other reasons and thus may not reflect supply-demand imbalance:

1. The quality of a product is hard to assess.

2. Consumers dislike frequent price changes.

3. The market is dominated by a few firms that might fear price wars if prices are allowed to move too freely.

Commodities such as used automobiles have a quality that is difficult to assess. Consumers and dealers find it difficult to determine how good the product is, and making a mistake can be time consuming and costly. Dealers therefore specialize in automobiles of a few companies, because they are familiar with their idiosyncrasies, and have the repair personnel to deal with problems.

Customers also generally buy the same brand again, despite the fact that competitors may offer the same features at a lower price. However, if prices rise too much, customers may reconsider their loyalty to a logo. Auto manufacturers therefore set dealer prices, even though a popular model may be in short supply. If manufacturers raise prices opportunistically, customers are likely to grumble and go elsewhere for their next purchase. By the same token, if demand is slack, they are unlikely to lower prices too much, because raising them again would be likely to drive away repeat customers as well as bargain hunters.

Markets can lubricate prices in quality-sensitive markets by making more quality information available to purchasers. Every major on-line used-automobile market reports the results of an extensive quality check and offers aftersale warranties as well to minimize the impact of quality effects on market price. For example, Auto-By-Tel also offers used cars available at their 2,700 associated dealers. A digital photo of the vehicle, and the quality audit report accompanies vehicle listings, along with a stringent 135-point certification quality check. Auto-By-Tel offers used car customers a 72-hour money-back guarantee and a 3-month/3,000-mile warranty. It covers the added cost of the warranty and quality check through the resulting higher margins that derive from more flexible pricing.

Consumers dislike price changes on goods or services that must be consumed over a substantial time or at some time in the future. Subscription to Internet services is one such example. Consumers prefer a monthly subscription charge and dislike per-usage charges. Most consumers would be particularly unwilling to pay additional charges based on the total usage of the ISP's service, that is, charges that go up when *other* users use the service. Yet service quality depends on the total level of usage over all users. So service is typically rationed through congestion, that is, slowing down response times during peak hours.

Finally, the threat of a price war may make competitors wary about adjusting prices in response to supply and demand. The service department of a particular automobile dealer may be overstaffed and overworked. However, it is more likely to try to attract customers by diversifying its service, for example, through expertise in particular models, customer perquisites such as shuttle services, and so forth, rather than adjusting prices.

In all three of these circumstances, more efficient auction markets are unlikely to make prices more flexible. It can be seen that when prices are fixed for too long, substantial supply-demand imbalances may arise. Under these circumstances, the availability of global networks is likely to "correct" prices very quickly once any particular suppler decides to reassess their rates.

Intermediaries

New technology does not remove channel functions, but the intermediaries may be moved forward or backward within the channel. However, the functions these intermediaries (or middlemen) perform are likely to change significantly. Some skills are no longer needed in an electronic commerce world, and other previously important skills may suddenly have additional value. Channel intermediaries provide value by interposing between buyers and sellers as they lower the costs of transactions and make most goods and services cheaper.

Examples throughout history have labeled middlemen with an unsavory reputation. Ostensibly, they are begrudged their "unearned cut" of the proceeds of a sale, and such animosity has deep roots. Aristotle's *Politics*—the standard economics text in medieval Europe—stated that "the amount of household property which suffices for the good life is not unlimited ... there is a fixed bound." This bound was called "wealth." A "just price" for a commodity was fixed not by supply and demand, but by what the seller ought to ask. Adam Smith, in *The Wealth of Nations*,[2] forever changed this perception by introducing the twin concepts of the "invisible hand" (pricing to clear), and "perfect liberty" (a free and competitive market).

Some "experts" make claims that global marketing on the Internet will soon relegate the middleman to history, as global communications can allow consumers to bypass intermediaries by making their own product choices and obtaining, as they perceive it, better value. However, a modem in every living room will not necessarily remove the need for retail stores or intermediaries, as the two main functions of providing information and distributing goods and services will not cease with the advent of electronic commerce. Intermediaries are valuable in collecting and retaining information concerning price and quality, and whether computer mediated or not, it is a time-consuming, labor-intensive process that can be subject to many errors. Information the intermediaries obtain may then be used by many customers with similar needs. Intermediaries can also provide customers with collective bargaining discounts that arise from their repeated and predictable use of producers' goods and services. Travel agents are examples of intermediaries who specialize in finding the most convenient flights, car rentals, and hotels, often packaged and at a better price, than consumers acting on their own. They use their knowledge to book better trips for their clients and can therefore charge a premium for this service.

Travel agents' activities have information counterparts in the channels for real and tangible goods. As a group, travel agents can break bulk; for example, they can buy a block of seats or all seats on an entire airplane at bulk rates, and sell them to individuals as part of a tour. They can also create assortments by allowing consumers to customize the hotel, auto, and air components of a package to fit their own needs.

Distribution and E-commerce

Electronic commerce can coordinate distribution, transport, and buying in bulk, which has the effect of lowering total distribution costs. In a futuristic scenario, retailers would be put out of business, because customers would no longer be motivated to visit their stores. Excess stocks and declining sales would then burden retailers, and cheaper and more efficient electronic services would force them out of business. Informational goods such as videos and magazines might be delivered through the network itself, and retailers would be relegated to the role of product museums for those products that the customer insisted on inspecting personally, a concept promoted originally at Marshall Field's in Chicago in the 1930s.

Even with the advent of new technologies, the functions of intermediaries will not change, because collecting information is a labor- and time-intensive task. However, this group can exploit new opportunities and challenges. As barries to entry are lowered, for example, for jobs such as travel agents, a wider range of individuals may position themselves as intermediaries in this market. Instead of competing on private information, these agents will compete on value-added knowledge advantageous for all sides. Some may excel at packaging combinations of rental cars, flights, and hotels; others may excel at qualitative judgments about hotels or air service.

The corresponding fall in the cost of and time required to collect this information will increase productivity, and customers will respond accordingly by asking for more services from intermediaries. Within this activity, intermediaries will contribute in a positive manner to the value of the product and to their customers and, as purchasing costs are lowered, they will generate more demand for their services.

EDI

One of the earliest applications of electronic commerce was electronic data interchange applications with the explicit goal of lowering purchasing costs. Purchasing materials and services is a complex process with many intermediate steps and parties. Traditional Purchasing required at least a minimal set of paper documents to come together to make a purchase voucher: a purchase order, shippers from the vendor, bills of lading from the transit company, invoices from the vendor, receivers from the warehouse, disbursements from the cashier, and sundry debit and credit memos reflecting disputes or discounts. The process of matching all of these documents to a voucher (and there might be hundreds in a single voucher) was a time-consuming, error-prone sequence of communications, arithmetic, and sorting functions. Michael Hammer[3] recounted the situation at Ford Motor Co. in the 1980s, where over 500 clerks handled accounts payable and purchasing. Consolidation of the paper documents in digital form on a central server lowered the number of clerks required for the process to around 125—a 75% reduction in labor costs.

This led to better inventory control (fewer stockouts, lower stock levels, shorter lead times) and lower production and development cycle times. Customer service became more efficient and effective with lower sales and marketing cost. The search was then for serendipitous identification of new markets (new sales opportunities) using new sources of product development intelligence.

New Technologies in the Quest for Competitive Advantage

Electronic commerce may not be new. Nevertheless, implemented with the latest powerful technologies that were not available with previous incarnations, it provides a renewed channel for marketing goods and services with exciting possibilities, one that may be used in conjunction with other channels, and one that may or may not be available to some producers (especially small producers) who have been cut off from other channels. It opens vast new opportunities for the producer, and at the same time, it threatens traditional patterns of commerce and division of labor. It offers the potential for anyone, no matter how big or small, to open virtual storefronts and offer a wide variety of products and services that can be ordered and paid for electronically through the network. This allows more products and services to be sold to a wider audience at lower operating costs. Reaping the benefits of electronic commerce requires a revision of current channel management knowledge. It changes the nature of the game, lowering monetary and size barriers to entry that firms face, but raising new barriers contingent on technical acumen and nimble response. This involves rethinking customers, reengineering marketing and distribution operations, and retooling to meet the demands of competition engendered by a technology that dramatically lowers barriers to market entry. Used prudently, electronic commerce can promise new sources of revenue generation over the next decade. Firms that are complacent—that do not rethink, reengineer and retool for these new competitive dictates—will find it difficult to maintain a competitive edge.

Bill Gates, in *The Road Ahead*,[4] predicted:

Often the only humans involved in a transaction will be the actual buyer and seller.... This will carry us into a new world of low-friction, low-overhead capitalism, in which market information will be plentiful and transaction costs low. It will be a shopper's heaven.

Yet experience leads us to believe that middlemen are not that easily stymied. Often the biggest retail sites simply block the queries of intelligent agents. Where they do not, pricing tends to become uniform, often with hidden warranty, shipping, and accessory charges that agents overlook. A more likely scenario is that the advanced capabilities of search engines and agents will open up new opportunities and challenges for intermediaries while they close old ones.

Internet Auctions

The nature of the product and potential volume of transactions determine the format chosen for selling it. Price taking is adequate for catalog merchandise, which tends to involve small transactions. Simple auctions are appropriate when there is one seller and many customers, as is the case in normal circumstances for goods in retail stores. They are also appropriate when there is one customer and several suppliers, which may be the case for big-ticket items such as houses and automobiles.

Double auctions require relatively high transaction volumes and the continuous presence of buyers and sellers in the market. If the volume is too low, buyers and sellers do not post orders often enough to make the market very liquid. There are probably few goods or services with sufficient exchange volume to justify a double auction.

Although Internet auction transactions are small relative to the total volume of transactions completed via auctions worldwide in 1998, the number of auction markets on the Internet and the volume of transactions at these auction markets is increasing at a rapid pace. For goods that are not time sensitive in their transactions or delivery, the Internet provides a low-cost communications medium that is ideally suited for electronic auction markets and will facilitate increased use of electronic auctions as an efficient search and price discovery mechanism for commerce.

Notes

1. W. Vickrey, "Counterspeculation, auctions and competitive sealed tenders," *Journal of Finance* 16 (1961), p. 8–37.

2. A. Smith, (1723–1790). *An Inquiry into the Nature and Causes of the Wealth of Nations* (New York: Random House, 1985).

3. M. Hammer and J. Champy, *Reengineering the Corporation: A Manifesto for Business Revolution* (New York: Harper Business, 1993), p. 39–42.

4. B. Gates, N. Myhrvold, and Peter Rinearson, *The Road Ahead* (Viking Penguin, 1995), p. 163.

Experiences with Electronic Auctions in the Dutch Flower Industry

Introduction

Since the end of the nineteenth century flower products have been marketed with the help of the Dutch auction mechanism. In those days flower growers formed a cooperative and developed their own local marketplace. In the last decades these local cooperatives have merged into larger organizations, like, for example, Flower Auction Aalsmeer (VBA) and Flower Auction Holland (BVH), each with an annual turnover in 1996 of approximate U.S. $1 billion. More recently, there has been an ongoing debate in the Dutch flower industry about (1) the decoupling of price discovery and logistical processes in the Dutch flower auctions; (2) the increasing imports of foreign flower products at the Dutch flower auctions; and (3) the use of new information technology (IT) in this industry. VBA and BVH were close to their limits in terms of complexity, capacity, and room to expand. One of the answers to these limits was the introduction of electronic auctioning. In this article we will present and investigate four electronic auction initiatives: (1) the Vidifleur Auction (VA); (2) the Sample Based Auction (SBA); (3) the Tele Flower Auction (TFA); and (4) the Buying at Distance Auction (BADA). This article aims

- to describe the development, implementation, and effects of four different electronic auction system initiatives in the Dutch flower industry;
- to explain through an in-depth analysis a better understanding of the reasons for the failures of the VA and the SBA, and the successes of the TFA and the BADA.

Analyzing Exchange Organizations

Due to the convergence of IT and telecommunication and the proliferation and availability of bandwidth, the impact of electronic markets is expected to grow rapidly. Their effectiveness, however, is dependent on their design. Existing research in this new area provides examples of relevant issues supporting an effective design. What is lacking, however, is a systematic classification of various complex issues that arise when designing and implementing electronic markets. Prior research on the effects on exchange organizations and processes typically applied transaction costs and agency theory to predict shifts from hierarchies toward market or other intermediate forms of organization (Malone et al., 1987; Hess and Kemerer, 1994). A central argument of these articles was that IT would improve communication searches, monitoring,

This case was prepared by Eric van Heck, Erasmus University Rotterdam, and Pieter M. Ribbers, Tilburg University, The Netherlands.

and information-sorting capabilities, to reduce transaction costs and allow purchasers to take advantage of production economics available in markets. A critical drawback of this analysis was the definition of markets in abstract economic terms (i.e., markets coordinate economic activity through a price mechanism) without consideration for differences in market organization. For example, some different market types include direct search markets, brokered markets, dealer markets, and auction markets. Auction markets were critically analyzed from an economic point of view by Davis and Holt (1993), Hendricks and Porter (1988), and Rothkopf and Harstad (1994). More recently, the flower auction markets were investigated in more detail. Ajit Kambil and Eric van Heck (1996) specified a generalizable model of exchange processes and developed a process-stakeholder analysis framework to evaluate alternative market designs. In this framework (see figure 7.1), five trade processes (search, valuation, logistics, payments and settlements, and authentication) and five trade context processes (communications and computing, product representation, legitimation, influence, and dispute resolution) are distinguished.

   This framework is applied to analyze a number of IT initiatives in the Dutch flower markets. Van Heck et al. (1997) investigated the Tele Flower Auction and the competitive advantage of new entrants, as was suggested in Clemons et al. (1996). Van Heck and Ribbers (1997) compared the Tele Flower Auction with the Sample Based Auction initiative. In this article we will combine the different results from these studies and we will present an overview of the past and current experiences of electronic auctions in the Dutch flower industry.

The Dutch Flower Industry

Industry Background

The Netherlands is the world's leading producer and distributor of cut flowers. The Dutch dominated the world export market for cut flowers in 1996 with a 59% share and for potted plants with a 48% share. The world's two biggest flower auctions are in Aalsmeer (VBA) and Naaldwijk/Bleiswijk (BVH); every day on average 30 million flowers—originating not only from the Netherlands but also from countries such as Israel, Kenya, and Zimbabwe—are traded in 100,000 transactions. The Dutch flower auctions play a vital role in Holland's leadership of this industry, by providing efficient centers for price discovery and transactions of flowers between buyers and sellers. These auctions traditionally use the "Dutch auction" as the mechanism for price discovery. They are established as cooperatives by the Dutch growers.

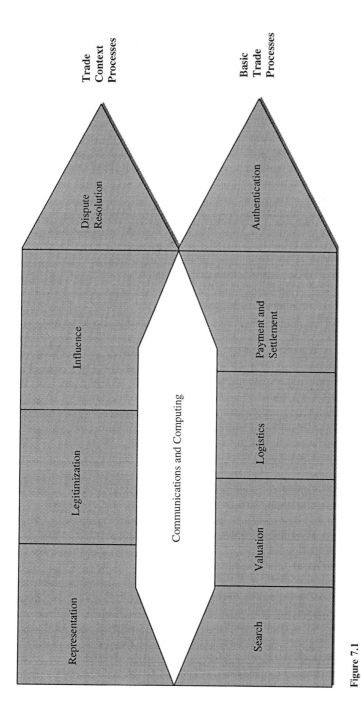

Figure 7.1
Generalized model of exchange processes
Source: A. Kambil and E. van Heck, "Re-engineering the Dutch flower auctions: A framework for analyzing exchange operations," New York University, Department of Information Systems, Working Paper Series, Stern IS-96-24, New York, 1996.

The Dutch Flower Auction Concept

The following auction rules characterize the Dutch flower auction concept (see also Van Heck et al. 1997). Dutch flower auctions use a clock for price discovery, as follows. The computerized auction clock in the room provides the buyers with information on producer, product, unit of currency, quality, and minimum purchase quantity. The flowers are transported through the auction room, and are shown to the buyers. The clock hand starts at a high price determined by the auctioneer, and drops until a buyer stops the clock by pushing a button. The auctioneer asks the buyer, by intercom, how many units of the lot he or she will buy. The buyer provides the number of units. The clock is then reset, and the process begins for the leftover flowers, sometimes introducing a new minimum purchase quantity, until all units of the lot are sold. In the traditional way buyers must be present in the auction room. In practice, it turns out that the Dutch flower auction is an extremely efficient auction mechanism: It can handle a transaction every four seconds.

Four Electronic Auction Initiatives

In this section we will discuss the characteristics of four electronic auction initiatives in the Dutch flower industry. Table 7.1 describes the main characteristics of the electronic auction initiatives and their processes.

The Vidifleur Auction

Vidifleur intended to use video auctioning to decouple price determination and logistics, and to allow buyers to trade from outside the auction hall. When the product arrived at the auction, a picture was taken, digitized, and stored in auction computers. These computers transferred the picture for display to a screen in the auction hall, where buyers could bid for the product based on the image of the product. Buyers were also able to bid for and look at the potted plants on computer screens in their private auction offices. The computers in the private office provided a screen-based representation of the clock which was synchronized with the clock in the auction hall.

Buyer reaction to screen-based trading was negative and led to the termination of the experiment in late 1991. Buyers cited three main reasons for not adopting the new system. First, the clock-based trading system provided no new efficiencies for the buyer. Second, the quality of the auction hall video display was perceived as poor, and trading from outside the auction hall created an informational disadvantage. In floor-based trading the buyers could observe each other and the reactions of other

Table 7.1

Characteristics of four electronic auctions in the Dutch flower industry

Focus theme					
Variables	Indicators	Vidifleur auction (VA)	Sample-based auction (SBA)	Tele flower auction (TFA)	Buying at distance auction (BADA)
General parameters	Intermediary	Flower Auction Holland (BVH)	Flower Auction Aalsmeer (VBA)	East African Flowers (EAF)	Flower Auction Holland (BVH)
	Sellers	Dutch growers as member of cooperative	Dutch growers as member of cooperative	Non-dutch growers	Dutch growers as member of cooperative
	Buyers	Wholesalers	Wholesalers	Wholesalers	Wholesalers
	Products	Potted plants	Potted plants	Flowers	Flowers
	Start (End) Year	1991 (1991)	1994 (1994)	1995	1996
Basic trade processes	Search	Buyers can have a look in the storage rooms	Buyers can have a look in the storage rooms	Buyers can search supply data base	Buyers can search supply data base
	Valuation	Dutch auction clock	Dutch auction clock	Dutch auction clock	Dutch auction clock
	Logistics	Via auction room to buyer's place	Directly from grower's to buyer's place	Directly from storage room to buyer's place	Via auction room to buyer's place
	Payments and settlements	Within 24 hours; guaranteed by intermediary	Within 24 hours; guaranteed by intermediary	Within 24 hours; guaranteed by intermediary	Within 24 hours; guaranteed by intermediary
	Authentication	Quality grading on lot	Quality grading on sample	Quality grading on lot	Quality grading on lot
Trade context processes	Communication and computing	Computerized clock in room and on PC screen, video image on screen in room	Computerized clock, EDI with growers and buyers	Computerized clock on PC screen, 2 digital images on PC screen, EDI with growers and buyers	Computerized clock in room and on PC screen, 1 digital image on PC screen, EDI with growers and buyers
	Product representation	Real lot on site; video image on screen	Sample of lot	2 digital images on PC screen	Real lot on site; digital image on screen
	Legitimation	By intermediary	By intermediary	By intermediary	By intermediary
	Influence	Growers are owner of intermediary	Growers are owner of intermediary	Intermediary is importer of foreign flowers	Growers are owner of intermediary
	Dispute resolution	By intermediary	By intermediary	By intermediary	By intermediary
	Overall result	Failure	Failure	Success	Success

major buyers to specific bids. Third, at the back of each auction hall is a coffee shop where buyers interact informally and share information about the market. Again, access to the social interaction and information was more difficult through screen-based trading.

The Sample-Based Auction

Flower Auction Aalsmeer began a sample-based auction for trading potted plants in 1994. In this concept, growers send a sample of the product to the auction house along with information on available inventory. During the auction the sample represents the entire inventory available to buyers who can bid for the product and specify product packaging and delivery requirements. Growers then package the product as specified and deliver it the next day to the buyer location in the auction complex or to other buyer warehouses. Buyers have to be physically present in an auction room. Growers, buyers, and the auction used electronic data interchange (EDI) to share all information required in this process. This trading model reduces the number of times a product is handled, reducing overall packaging costs and damage.

The different actors, the growers, the buyers, and the auction expected a number of different benefits. First, by uncoupling logistics and price determination, the auction and growers expected the number of transactions per hour to increase. In reality the number of transactions per hour decreased as buyers had to specify terms of delivery. Second, while the auction expected 45% of the supply of potted plants to be transacted in the sample-based auction, only 10% of the product was transacted this way. Thus, SBA also did not effectively reduce storage requirements at the auction. After numerous attempts to increase the volume of sample-based auctions they were discontinued in late 1994. The system had a negative effect on the functioning of growers, the auction house, and buyers. The sample-based auction system ended up a complete failure.

The Tele Flower Auction

An important effect of the import restrictions imposed by the Dutch flower auctions was the creation of TFA by East African Flowers (EAF) (Van Heck et al, 1997). EAF is one of the biggest importers of cut flowers; they specialize in supply from East Africa (Kenya, Tanzania, and Uganda). For EAF, the effect of the import restrictions was that 30% of their imports could no longer be traded via the Dutch auction clocks during the traditional import season; in the summer season 100% of their imports could not be traded at all. EAF announced the creation of TFA in December

1994. On March 24, 1995, TFA was launched with 2 growers and 70 buyers. After some months, EAF decided that growers from other countries (for example, Spain, Colombia, France, India, and Israel) were allowed to use TFA. After one year, approximately 35 growers and 150 buyers were connected to TFA.

In TFA, buyers can bid via their personal computer (PC) screens. Each PC is connected to a fully computerized auction clock. Logistics and price discovery are uncoupled. Flowers are no longer visible for buyers, and buyers are no longer physical in an auction room. The PC provides the buyer with information on the next flower lots. On his PC the buyer can earmark interesting lots, so at the time those lots will be auctioned, the PC will warn the buyer. The PC provides information on the producer, product, unit of currency, quality, and minimum purchase quantity. For each lot two images are presented on the PC screen. The underlying auction concept remains the same: Dutch flower auction. On the PC screen the buyer sees the Dutch auction clock. The clock hand starts at a high price, and drops until a buyer stops the clock by pushing the space bar at the keyboard of the PC. The auctioneer asks the buyer, via an open telephone connection, how many flowers of the lot he or she will buy. The buyer provides the amount. The clock is then reset, and the process begins for the next units, until the remainder of the lot is sold.

Growers send the flowers to EAF, and EAF stores these flowers in Amstelveen. Logistics and price discovery are uncoupled within the auction hall. The distribution of the flowers from the Amstelveen area to the buyer's addresses (nearby the traditional auctions of Aalsmeer, Naaldwijk, and Rijnsburg) is done by transporters of EAF. Transport costs are paid by EAF.

Compared with SBA, buyers can trade at a distance. TFA provides better and more frequently updated supply information. The speed of the TFA system is amazing. Not only the auctioning process, but also the after-sales process is very fast; sometimes within half an hour products are delivered at the buyer's address. It soon became clear that one of the main propositions of TFA was that the quality of the flowers determines the buyers' trust in the TFA concept. TFA's motto is: "Buyers have to trust the quality blindfold" because buyers cannot physically see the product anymore. Still, buyers who are nearby TFA can inspect the imported flowers; 30% of the buyers do so regularly. Reliable product information and stable quality control are essential. Quality control is done by TFA's quality inspectors at the grower's place, at the distribution point in Nairobi (Africa), and at TFA in Amstelveen. Buyers also trust the IT innovations. One of the reasons seems to be that the Dutch auction clock is still the price discovery mechanism; buyers are used to that mechanism. Buyers were enthusiastic about the quality and the delivery time of the auctioned products, and about the service level of TFA. The prices were on average not higher or lower than in the traditional Dutch flower auctions. TFA expects a turnover of 50 million for the growing season 1995–1996. Among the seven Dutch flower auction, TFA ranks fourth.

The Buying at Distance Auction

Flower Auction Holland started in June 1996 with the concept of "buying at distance" elaborating on their previous experiences with the Vidifleur project. The concept is that buyers can connect via a modem their PC with several auction clocks in the auction rooms. On their PC screen they can click on an icon and open up a window for every clock available. The "buying at distance" project started with 6 clocks and 16 buyers. In 1997 already 60 buyers are on the waiting list. Buyers can search in the supply database for certain products or growers. Buyers like the better communication through this system between the purchase people and the sales people within the buyers' firm. Also lower travel costs were reported. On the other hand the auction house mentions that the amount of buyers (physically or electronically connected) in one marketplace will be stable or increase, and that will increase the auction prices.

Some Lessons Learned

The following lessons are learned from the experiences with electronic auctions in the Dutch flower industry.

Lesson 1

The application of information technologies to trading can enable increased efficiencies and separation of informational and physical trading processes. This in turn will permit more varied forms of trading customized to different user requirements (Kambil and van Heck, 1996).

The four cases illustrate the use of IT to separate the informational and physical trading processes. In all cases the valuation and logistical processes are increasingly decoupled from one another in time and space. TFA uncouples logistics and price discovery in the auction hall. Therefore, the internal logistics of the auction hall are much simpler, compared with the traditional auction system. This fact explains why TFA has a much better logistical performance and service level, in the opinion of the buyers. EAF paid much attention to the after-sales program (providing transport to the buyers).

Lesson 2

Conformance of the actual and the perceived quality of the product, logistical performance, and IT performance result in high trust contributes to a successful electronic auction system (Van Heck et al., 1997).

In the SBA the buyers chose to discount the prices bid for nonsample lots by nearly 10% because they could no longer authenticate quality by visual inspection. Logistical performance was questioned by growers, and buyers. No problems were reported about the IT performance as such.

In the TFA case, sellers and buyers find that TFA keeps their promises concerning quality of products, delivery time of products, and reliability of IT performance. Buyers trust the TFA products. Usually, they get better products than expected from the data and images provided on the PC screen, due to a centralized quality control program. Buyers also trust TFA, because the underlying auction concept is the same: Dutch flower auction. Buyers trust the IT innovation: If a buyer is the first buyer to push the space bar at the keyboard of the PC, he or she is certain that the computer network transfers this signal fast and reliably, independent of the distance between the buyer's computer and the auction computer.

Lesson 3

Market organizations are the meeting point for multiple stakeholders: buyers, sellers, and intermediaries with conflicting incentives. Given existing or competing market alternatives, no new IT-based initiative is likely to succeed if any key stakeholder is worse off after the IT enabled innovation (Kambil and Van Heck, 1996).

In the two cases of failure, the application of the process-stakeholder framework clearly identified that either the grower or the buyer was worse off from the innovation. For example, the SBA failed to meet expectations for many reasons. First, the incentives and benefits to buyers and growers (in particular) did not change substantially to encourage their participation in this market. Specifically, growers received no extra compensation for modifying packaging and delivery practices to suit the customer. Second, the growers perceived that they got lower prices in a slower auction. To overcome this disadvantage growers would break the same product into different sample lots so that it would be priced multiple times during the auction, hoping it would lead to higher prices. Third, the auction rules initially did not provide incentives to buyers by supporting transactions on large lots. Instead, the auction maintained rules to favor transactions in small lots. Thus, an insufficient number of buyers and sellers initially adopted this new form of trading. In the Vidifleur auction, the buyers did not perceive a new benefit from the system. The video quality was poor, authentication of quality less convenient, and trading on-line did not provide all the information available in the auction hall.

Lesson 4

New entrants, facing established dominant players, can quickly build competitive advantage with an innovative auction system concept (Van Heck et al., 1997).

The TFA case demonstrates the way a new entrant may use IT in an innovative way, in order to enter a market and compete with dominant players in that market. The efforts to reduce foreign access to the traditional Dutch auctions led buyer organizations and foreign growers to announce the creation of competing auctions. Indeed, EAF's development and introduction of TFA is one of the initiatives in response to these import restrictions by the traditional Dutch flower auctions. It is the first time in Dutch history that an importer organization has performed this function. Traditionally, the Dutch flower auctions are established as cooperatives by the Dutch growers. Another interesting point was the high speed of entrance. The import restrictions took effect in October 1994; at that time EAF developed the first ideas about TFA. TFA started in March 1995. So EAF developed and implemented TFA in a few months. This case shows that new entrants can quickly build a competitive advantage. It illustrates the conclusion derived by Clemons et al. (1996) concerning the strengths of new entrants in a competitive market. Besides the strengths of TFA, the weaknesses of the traditional Dutch auctions partly explain the success of TFA. The cooperative structure of the Dutch auctions (every single grower has one vote), the complexity of the after-sale logistics (due to the coupling of the logistics with the price discovery process), and their inability to implement IT innovations quickly further decreased the market share of TFA's competitors.

Conclusions

We presented current research on the Dutch flower auctions. The process-stakeholder framework, proposed by Kambil and van Heck (1996), is useful to (1) evaluate or explain the successes or failures of IT-based initiatives in markets; and (2) design new electronic market systems. In the near future we expect that more varied forms of trading will emerge. Electronic auction markets, with a Dutch auction concept, will be one of these forms. However, one of the important weaknesses of the Dutch auction concept is that it is a supply oriented trading mechanism. In the last couple of years the flower industry (and not only this industry) has become more demand oriented. Therefore, trading via brokerage systems has become more popular. On the other hand, as the Internet evolves to a powerful and reliable infrastructure for electronic commerce, electronic Dutch auctions will become a popular trading mechanism in some industries.

References

Clemons, E. K., Croson, D. C., and Weber, B. W. "Market Dominance as a Precursor of a Firm's Failure: Emerging Technologies and the Competitive Advantage of New Entrants," *Journal of Management Information System* (13:2), 1996, p. 59–75.

Davis, D. D., and Holt, C. A. *Experimental Economics.* Princeton University Press, Princeton, NJ, 1993.

Hess, C. M., and Kemerer, C. F. "Computerized Loan Origination Systems: An Industry Case Study of the Electronic Markets Hypothesis," *MIS Quarterly*, September 1994, p. 251–275.

Hendricks, K., and Porter, R. H. "An Empirical Study of an Auction with Asymmetric Information," *American Economic Review* (78), 1988, p. 865–883.

Kambil, A., and van Heck, E. *Re-Engineering the Dutch Flower Auctions: A Framework for Analyzing Exchange Organizations*, New York University, Department of Information Systems, Working Paper Series, Stern IS-96-24, New York, NY, 1996.

Malone, T. W., Yates, J., and Benjamin, R. I. "Electronic Markets and Electronic Hierarchies," *Communications of the ACM* (30:6), 1987, p. 484–497.

Rothkopf, M. H. and Harstad, R. M. "Modeling Competitive Bidding: A Critical Essay," *Management Science* (40:3), March 1994, p. 364–384.

Van Heck, E., and Ribbers, P. M. A. *Economic Effects of Electronic Markets*, Discussion Paper no. 9669, Center for Economic Research, Tilburg University, Tilburg, The Netherlands, July 1996.

Van Heck, E., and Ribbers, P. M. A. "Introducing Electronic Auction Systems in the Dutch Flower Industry: A Comparison of Two Electronic Auction System Initiatives at the Dutch Flower Auctions," submitted to *Wirtschaftsinformatik*, 1997.

Van Heck, E., van Damme, E., Kleijnen, J., and Ribbers, P. "New Entrants and the Role of Information Technology, Case-Study: The Tele Flower Auction in the Netherlands," in *Information Systems— Organizational Systems and Technology*, J. F. Nunamaker and R. H. Sprague (eds.), Proceedings of the Thirtieth Annual Hawaii International Conference on System Sciences, volume III, IEEE Computer Society Press, Los Alamitos, 1997, p. 228–237.

E*Trade Securities, Inc.

Introduction

E*Trade pioneered the electronic deep-discount brokerage business in the late 1980s and has experienced phenomenal growth since 1992. Electronic brokerage firms make extensive use of technology in most customer interactions and, as a result, can achieve significant cost advantages over traditional brokerage firms. E*Trade's strategy until now has been to continually pass these cost savings from automation on to its customers as they amortized their fixed costs over a greater number of accounts. The company charges a fixed commission rate on trade executions up to 5,000 shares ($14.95 NYSE, $19.95 NASDAQ), a 75% savings compared to the traditional discount brokers. As of the spring of 1996, E*Trade is at critical juncture in its development and faces many challenges. A flood of new competitors are establishing Internet sites and for the first time in its history, E*Trade has been dethroned as the price leader. In April 1996, a new entrant, eBroker, has introduced "no frills" trading through the Internet at a flat $12 per trade. In addition, Charles Schwab, the leading discount brokerage firm, is preparing itself for entry directly into E*Trade's domain. E*Trade is being forced to reexamine its business model and choose a strategy with which to address the changing environment. While some executives within E*Trade believe they should continue to lower prices and go head-to-head with eBroker, others believe the company faces a larger challenge from Charles Schwab's entry into the market. Defending against Schwab would require focusing resources on enhancing its product/service offering, which might jeopardize E*Trade's low-cost position.

The Company

History

Trade*Plus, the parent company of E*Trade, was founded in 1982 as a PC financial management service bureau by Bill Porter. In 1992, the visionary Porter launched E*Trade Securities, a pioneering on-line brokerage services provider based in Palo Alto, California. Initially, E*Trade generated most of its revenues by providing back-office on-line processing services to discount brokerage firms (Fidelity, Schwab, and Quick & Reilly). Although E*Trade continues to service Quick & Reilly, the company has moved away from a "private label" strategy to aggressively pursue a direct-

This case was prepared by Chuck Glew, Mark Lotke, Mario Palumbo, and Marc Schwartz, under the supervision of Rajiv Lal, Professor of Marketing and Management Science, Stanford University Graduate School of Business.

to-consumer business model. In 1995, over 80% of revenues were derived from trading commissions by E*Trade customers. Additional revenues are generated from interest on customer cash balances and margin accounts, connect-time revenue sharing with on-line service providers, and third-party processing services. As a result of the shift from full-service to discount brokerage, increased PC penetration in the home, and the explosion of the Internet, the company has experienced dramatic revenue growth ($2 million in 1993, $10 million in 1994, $22 million in 1995, and budgeting in excess of $50 million for 1996).

The company's stated internal strategy is to *become America's dominant deep-discount brokerage firm by fully automating the front- and back-office trade processing function and maintaining its position as the low-cost provider.* The company has made significant information technology investments in automating order entry, customer support, trade execution, and post-trade clearing and confirmation. In September 1995, General Atlantic Partners, a New York–based private investment firm focused on investing in high-growth information technology companies, made a significant minority equity investment in E*Trade. These funds are being used to accelerate E*Trade's transition to self-clearing (presently provided by Herzog, Heine, and Geduld), bolster E*Trade's customer support infrastructure (systems, personnel), and launch an aggressive marketing campaign (print, TV, radio). In May 1996 the company filed with the SEC for an initial public offering scheduled for that summer.

Product

E*Trade provides its 50,000 customers with trade execution on stocks and options, and by year end, is likely to offer mutual funds. In addition to trade execution, the company provides stock quotes (real-time or delayed), news services, consolidated monthly statements, and limited portfolio analytics. Customers can access E*Trade through various low-cost channels including touch-tone telephone (TeleMasters), on-line service providers (CompuServe, America Online, BOA HomeBanking), direct modem link, and most recently, the Internet. E*Trade launched its Internet home page in January 1996 and as of May 1996 over 35% of all trading is done over the Internet.

Pricing

E*Trade's brokerage services appeal to active, independent investors who routinely make their own investment decisions and do not want to pay full-service commissions. E*Trade offers this growing customer segment a compelling value proposition: a flat $14.95 commission rate on all NYSE trades up to 5,000 shares and $19.95 for all OTC trades. As seen in table 7.2, E*Trade's commissions are typically 50% to

Table 7.2
Comparison of commissions

	100 Shares @ $40		5,000 Shares @ $20	
	Fixed component	Variable component	Fixed component	Variable component
E*Trade listed	$14.95	—	$14.95	—
E*Trade OTC	$19.95	—	$19.95	—
Lombard listed	$34	—	—	$100
Lombard OTC	$34	—	—	$75
e.Schwab	$39	—	$39	$120
PCFN	$60	—	$100	$100
NDB listed*	$33	—	$33	—
NDB OTC*	$28	—	$28	—
Ceres	$18	—	$18	—
Schwab/Fidelity	$56	$26.40	$155	$110

* Includes $3 postage fee per order.

75% less expensive than traditional discount brokerage firms such as Schwab or Fidelity, particularly for larger trades.

By leveraging information technology and passing savings on to consumers, E*Trade has steadily lowered its commission rates from $24.95 to $14.95 over the past two years. The company consistently offered the industry's lowest commissions until April 1996 when a new entrant, eBroker, began offering $12 trade execution under a "no frills/no service" market positioning.

Advertising-Marketing

Advertising plays a significant role in the brokerage business not only because it creates brand awareness, but also because it is the first step in the customer acquisition process. Brand awareness is critical in the nascent electronic brokerage business because most of the competing firms are new to the business and because many customers have an aversion to depositing their money with a firm they have never heard of. These issues are especially important on the Internet, which has the perception of being unsecured. In addition to creating brand awareness, most advertising in this industry also compares the advertising firm's product-service offering to competitors.

In January 1996, E*Trade aggressively increased its advertising budget to raise awareness, generate new account inquiries, and unveil its new Internet site. The company placed weekly full-page ads in the *Wall Street Journal*, complementing its continued television (CNBC business channel), local radio, and magazines (*Individual Investor, Smart Money, Forbes*) campaign. These ads focused on E*Trade's low commission rates (with accompanying comparison tables) and featured bold tag lines such as:

E*Trade is leading the electronic trading revolution.
In fact, we started it.
How else could we charge just $14.95 per trade?
Your broker is obsolete ...
(above a picture of a young boy sitting next to his computer sticking his tongue out at a tired, paper-inundated broker).

In February 1996, E*Trade altered its advertising campaign to emphasize product/ service enhancements. The new ad states "E*Trade saves you up to 78% on broker-age commissions (bells and whistles included)" and lists 24-hour access, free quotes, on-line portfolio management, free checking, and margin and IRA accounts.

These successful campaigns have positioned E*Trade as the electronic brokerage leader in the eyes of investors and generated significant new account inquiries. Unfortunately, the company was not adequately prepared for the response as wait times for customer service surged. This upset both current customers who had ques-tions concerning their trades as well as new customers who were less than impressed with their first interaction with the company. In addition, competitors have begun to locate and publicize holes in the E*Trade service offering. For instance, Lombard, an electronic brokerage competitor, includes a column in its advertisement comparing the minimum check amount that can be written from the account. Lombard has no minimum while E*Trade will only honor checks written on the account in excess of $500.

As E*Trade and its competitors continue to advertise nationally in an attempt to build brand awareness, customer acquisition costs are rising. In addition to the adver-tising component, customer acquisition is generally a several-step process consisting of an initial inquiry, often by e-mail or telephone, and often a follow-up conversa-tion, either to answer specific questions or to check on the status of the application. These customer service-intensive interactions are quite costly for E*Trade. With low margins per trade, E*Trade's new customers must trade frequently for the company to recoup total customer acquisition costs.

The Market

Segmentation

The market for trading and brokerage services is divided between three primary segments: full-service brokers, discount brokers, and deep-discount brokers. The increasing presence and use of technology as the primary vehicle of trade execution has led to the creation of a fourth segment, the electronic deep-discount broker. This distinction is not entirely clear as a number of firms including large discount brokers like Schwab and Fidelity have introduced on-line offerings alongside and in conjunction with their traditional products and services.

Full-Service Brokers.   A full-service brokerage provides a broad range of services, from helping to develop an investment strategy through performance measurement of the executed strategy. The important distinction of this class of brokerage houses is their participation in all aspects of the investment process, from initial decision through execution and follow-up. These services may include the following: suggesting investment opportunities, providing research reports, executing the trade, offering customer-service support, and issuing monthly reporting statements. Brokers tend to be proactive, making suggestions to their clients and trying to influence their investment choices, as well as increasing their investment and trading activity. The brokerage could be a stand-alone institution or a separate department or trust division of a larger entity. Typically, these services are used by households with more than $100,000 in assets. Brokers are paid a significant percentage of their compensation through commissions (typically $150 to $300 per trade), thus they are rewarded for spurring this activity, and potentially are able to collect additional fees depending on the extent of their financial-planning advice. The broker-client relationship is often a long-standing one-on-one relationship in which word-of-mouth referral plays a large role in new-client development.

Full-service brokers tend to offer their own line of products, and when they go outside of their family of products, they will usually only sell "load" funds which generate additional commissions. Products offered include retirement accounts, credit products, insurance, and portfolio planning. Full-service brokers provide newsletters and industry-specific and company-specific research reports written by a team of in-house analysts. Full-service brokers sometimes provide access to initial public offerings (IPOs) of stock and secondary offerings that are being underwritten by the investment banking arm of the firms. Examples of full-service brokers are Merrill Lynch and Smith Barney Shearson.

Discount Brokers.   Discount brokers, such as Charles Schwab and Fidelity Investments, offer limited services for investors who do not need specialized product offerings and who do their own research. These institutions make their revenues primarily on the number of trades they execute and on margin account charges. The financial profile of a discount brokerage client is broader, ranging from minimal assets to about $250,000 in assets on average. Clients typically tend to be more active traders who do not require specialized and personalized service and are willing to make this trade-off for lower commissions (typically $80 to $100 per trade). Customers in this segment make their own trading decisions without the support and advice of the broker.

Recently, discount brokers have become closer in service to full-service institutions, with the exception of the personalized service and investment advice. They have been moving more and more to differentiating themselves through increased service offerings to the point where 800 telephone numbers, monthly account summaries, quotes, and general investment advice are the norm and not points of differentiation. However, information tends to be general in nature and is not geared toward specific investments, industries, or portfolios. In fact, even when asked directly, representatives will not lend their advice with respect to specific trades. Examples of discount brokers are Charles Schwab and Fidelity.

Deep-Discount Brokers. Deep-discount brokers take the discount concept one step further and provide even fewer service offerings and less flexibility in trading, but for a measurably lower price (typically $40 to $60 per trade). Historically, price has been the primary means of differentiation in this segment, but there is some indication that the minimum threshold level of service has been increasing lately. Original deep-discount outlets were cheap alternatives set up in the Midwest, where low-cost labor allowed even further price declines. Examples of deep-discount brokers are Quick & Reilly, Waterhouse, and Olde.

Electronic Deep-Discount Brokers. Electronic deep-discount firms include companies that were founded as electronic-only trading outfits (PC Financial Network, E*Trade), as well as discount and deep-discount brokerage firms that offered a portion of their services through the electronic medium. Initially, trading in this segment was conducted through the telephone or in PC-based on-line environments such as America Online (AOL) or CompuServe. Much of the current trading volume and expected growth, however, is coming through the Internet. Current commission levels range from E-Broker's $12 and E*Trade $14.99/$19.99 per-trade offering to the $40 range with very minimal customer-service levels. This might result in a limited number of quotes, shorter hours of operation, longer waits for making contact, potentially less advantageous trade execution, less detailed account correspondence, restrictions on margin account trading, and fewer product offerings (mutual funds, bonds, 401(k) accounts). Many deep-discount brokers conduct a large percentage of their business through means that minimize the labor component, including electronic on-line services or through automated telephone lines. Examples of electronic deep-discount brokers are Lombard, National Discount Brokers, and e.Schwab.

Value Chain

The value chain for investment services from the customer's perspective includes the following activities: investment strategy, investment decisions, trade execution, portfolio servicing, and performance measurement. As one would expect, the different brokerage firm types span various sections of this chain. The full-service broker participates in investment decisions and is more likely to offer a higher level of service at other points in the process, as well as more detailed statements. Discount brokers, on the other hand, operate in a more focused area of the chain, primarily providing trade execution with limited support, customer service, and performance measurement.

The value chain as it relates to the brokerage firms includes the following areas: marketing, research provision, investment advice, trade input, trade execution, and account servicing (see table 7.2). There are two ways in which these activities differ by firm category. First, it is possible that one aspect of the value chain is missing entirely for a particular type of firm. As mentioned earlier, this is the case with investment advice as it relates to the discount brokerage firm—it simply does not exist. The other point of differentiation is the degree to which the particular part of the chain is emphasized. For instance, full-brokerage firms are likely to spend more absolute dollars on account servicing than deep-discount brokers, although this relationship may not hold as a percentage of the trading commission.

Market Size

Brokerage firms generate their revenue from commissions, margin accounts, and auxiliary services. A significant portion is generated from commissions, and in 1991 total industry commissions were estimated to be in the neighborhood of $12 billion. Although this figure is not expected to change significantly through 1998 (slight increase in volume, slight decrease in average commission), the distribution between segments is projected to change. Full-service brokers' commissions are estimated to decline from $10 billion in 1991 to $8 billion in 1998, while discount brokers' share is expected to increase from $2 billion to roughly $4 billion over the same time period. On-line discount commissions are expected to comprise almost 10% or $400 million of the discount brokers' share by 1998.

From 1994 to 1998 the number of trades conducted is estimated to increase from 100 million to 144 million. Full-service brokers will see their trading volume hover around the 65 million mark over this period, while discount brokers' volume will increase from 30 million to 65 million, and on-line services will account from 13 million trades in 1998, up from 5 million in 1994. According to Forrester Research, growth in on-line brokerage accounts is anticipated to increase at 30%, from 550,000 in 1995 to 1.3 million in 1998. The two largest players, Schwab and PCFN, account for about 60% of the market (or 150,000 accounts each), with Fidelity controlling 13% and E*Trade with 6%. The remaining 20% of the market is divided up among a number of the smaller players.

Market Evolution

The market has evolved in a fairly straightforward manner, with the discount brokers providing an alternative to customers who did not require the level of service offered by a full-service brokerage house, and hence, did not want to pay for services that were not being utilized. Discount brokers could employ less labor (and less skilled labor) because a variety of services and hand-holding was not required of them. Although a number of players entered the market with this strategy, it was Charles Schwab that gave wide-scale credibility to the approach and institutionalized the discount broker concept. At a time when firms were offering low prices but skimping on service, Schwab's strategy and eventual scale allowed it to "gentrify" the market by providing a truly professional approach to what at one time was a "bucket shop" mentality. Its approach was to remain neutral in the investment decision and simply execute trades. Over time it sought to decrease its dependency on trading volume by offering more products and services to enable it to generate charges for "assets under management."

The increasing use of technology is rapidly transforming the security brokerage business, which was once a sleepy, relationship-based, primarily local industry. Technology has helped to increase economies of scale and to permit rationalization in the industry. Increasingly, discounters such as Fidelity and Charles Schwab have leveraged technology to substantially reduce the cost of executing a trade and per- forming account-related servicing. A major component of this cost-reduction strategy has been the severing of the personal relationship between a particular broker and a particular client. Customers of these two discounters use national toll-free numbers as their primary interface with the firm. They speak to a different representative each call. This aggregation of customer inquiries helps to reduce total variability in demand patterns, allowing far fewer customer-service representatives and brokers to be employed. However, through sophisticated uses of technology, these firms are able to maintain high customer-service levels because each representative has access to the customer's entire account history. In addition, significant economies are realized by aggregating the functions dealing with the collection and manipulation of account data.

Although Schwab and Fidelity served a specific market need, its relatively high level of customer service created the potential for another layer of firms beneath it.

Because the discounters' increasing scale enabled them to substantially enhance customer service without increasing price, the remaining firms were left with price competition as the only viable strategic alternative. As they began to compete on price, they created a third-tier price umbrella. This third tier was initially satisfied by deep-discount brokers and is increasingly served by electronic deep-discount brokerage firms.

E*Trade, and the new breed of electronic brokerage firms, have been able to dramatically reduce costs beyond the discounters by leveraging technology not only in the back office but also in the customer interface. To reduce costs, E*Trade relies upon pure electronic order intake, which results in lower compensation costs per trade. However, to make the model work, E*Trade must also attract high-volume traders who can generate high profits per account, even with low per-trade margins.

Cost Structure

The importance of leveraging technology to reduce costs cannot be overstated. The primary benefit comes in the form of labor cost savings. The average spent on employee compensation per trade executed is $40 for Schwab, and $8 for E*Trade. These dramatic cost reductions, in conjunction with a much lower commission schedule, produce an average operating income per trade of only $6.63 for E*Trade versus $11.46 for Schwab. However, in terms of operating income per account, E*Trade's more frequent traders generate an average income of $120, versus only $50 for Schwab's (table 7.3). E*Trade has much lower commissions and costs that are counterbalanced by the frequency with which its customer base executes trades.

In summary, there are major differences between the economic models employed by the various brokerage firm segments. First, E*Trade has much lower commissions that tend to attract more frequent (and, hence, more profitable) traders. Second, E*Trade has a substantially lower cost structure, primarily because of lower com-

Table 7.3
Revenues by cost type*

	Schwab	E*Trade
Compensation per trade	$39.61	$8.22
Communications/DP per trade	$8.57	$2.83
Occupancy and equipment per trade	$7.40	$1.52
Marketing and selling per trade	$3.53	$4.10
Operating income per trade	$11.46	$6.63
Average number of trades per account	4.41	18.18
Operating income per account	$50.60	$120.00

* Estimates from industry experts and company records.

pensation costs and greater use of technology. Because a lower level of support is provided, E*Trade needs far fewer employees per trade, increasing productivity. Finally, E*Trade is much more profitable on average, with twice the profitability per account of Schwab.

Customers

Segmentation

Customers can be segmented based on a number of different characteristics, each of which affects how a particular company should address the market. The following are potential criteria with which to analyze the customer pool: frequency of trading, size of trades, wealth, technology usage, time/knowledge constraints and information/service needs (hand-holding).

An investor can be judged more or less likely to utilize the services of a particular type of firm based on the degree to which he or she fits these criteria. One would suspect the full-service broker client to have low to moderate frequency of trades, a higher-than-average size of trade, significant wealth, less comfort with technology, and less available time or business knowledge. These investors are not impacted by the higher cost of the trade because they value the additional service they are receiving and because the commission will comprise a lower percentage of the actual dollars traded. Additionally, their greater wealth is likely to make it difficult for them to rely on themselves to "put their money to work."

At the other end of the spectrum, one would expect the electronic deep-discount broker client to have a higher frequency of trades, a moderate average size of trade, moderate wealth, comfort with technology, and more time and business knowledge. Although at the outset these are likely to be the pools they will attract, the challenge for each of the market segments is how to attract those customers who fit several of the categories but not all of them. For instance, how can a firm like E*Trade appeal to a customer who, based on his/her trading size and volume, will benefit from E*Trade's service offering, but may not have much comfort with technology?

The issue of customer segmentation is especially important for the trends associated with the increasing penetration of electronic trading. As more firms vie to gain share as well as capture new growth, it will be important for firms to identify which customer-segments are most valuable to them and then develop a strategy to ensure that they will gain a disproportionate share of their business.

There are certain obstacles to Internet trading that will permanently discourage a large set of potential customers (those who might otherwise be inclined to select

E*Trade's price/service offering). First, there are concerns about the security of the Internet. More technically savvy customers know that it is much easier for a thief to steal a carbon copy of a credit-card receipt than it is to intercept and decode an encrypted message on the Internet. However, the popular press has made much of the potential for hackers to intercept credit-card numbers, and by logical extension, brokerage account information, on the Internet. The electronic brokerage firms must continually fight this misperception, which will likely be fueled by mass publicity, should a break-in ever occur. Second, because the Internet is a shared network, E*Trade has no control over its speed. Often the Internet is quite slow, or demand peaks in such a way that customers get locked out of E*Trade's web site. This can create an enormous amount of frustration for investors, especially if they are intraday traders. Finally, the least tangible of these factors is the perception that electronic deep-discount brokerages provide less advantageous trade execution for customers. Discounters such as Schwab and Fidelity have been emphasizing their better trade execution through superior position, volume, and more personal approach. There is no empirical data to support the claims by the discount brokers; however, in focus groups and in Internet chat areas, customers have mentioned trade execution as a concern.

E*Trade's Customers

E*Trade customers are active, independent, empowered investors who are comfortable in the on-line services world. They are attracted to E*Trade's low commission rate for two primary reasons: These investors make their own investment decisions and resent paying high brokerage fees, and they trade frequently (five to six executions per month) so that the commission savings quickly become significant. E*Trade's high-volume customers trade in excess of 10 times a month and hold 75% of their disposable investment assets in individual equities and 25% in mutual funds, whereas E*Trade's lower-volume customers trade three to four times a month (still above average for the industry) and hold 25% of their assets in individual equities and 75% in longer-term-oriented mutual funds.

E*Trade's demographic analysis shows their typical customer household to have dual annual incomes above $75,000, professional/technical occupation(s), graduate school education(s), children, a single-family home worth in excess of $200,000, and overrepresented interests including stocks/bonds, PCs, investing, science/technology, and real estate investments. Over 75% of E*Trade's customers have been discount and deep-discount brokerage customers, and the majority of them still maintain accounts at their other brokerage firm (primarily with Schwab and Fidelity). Customers have several reasons for maintaining multiple accounts, including easy access to mutual fund investing, existing 401(k) plans established by their employers, and prior relationships (applies to full-service brokers only). Many customers establish an E*Trade account on a trial basis with the intent of gradually transferring their higher turnover stocks into the account over time.

E*Trade's customer base has roughly doubled each year over the past four years. The company expects future growth in new accounts to come from active investors who are becoming increasingly comfortable with technology, and to a lesser degree, younger technology enthusiasts who begin to fit the demographic profile of an individual investor. Because the annual commission savings increase with trading activity, it is no surprise that E*Trade's core, early-adopter customers were high-volume traders. Over time, E*Trade has established a brand image as the leader in the electronic trading segment, and once customers make the decision to switch, E*Trade appears to be one of the most respectable, reliable options. This has helped them attract medium to low-volume customers who might not benefit as greatly as the high-volume traders. It is the company's belief that as more services become available and customer service improves, price will become less of a reason for switching. Customers have, for the most part, been satisfied with their E*Trade experience. Recently, however, the flurry of new accounts generated by the national advertising campaign has created some severe customer-service problems, including excessive telephone wait times (often greater than 20 minutes per call), difficulty logging onto the web site, and sign-up delays. Customers typically keep their old account (usually with Fidelity or Schwab) open, and any major problem is likely to cause them to return to their old brokerage firm. In this sense, the electronic discount brokerage firms, as a group, get only one shot every few years at each of the discount brokerage customers. A single service gaffe can drive that customer away from the electronic brokerage sector for years.

Although it may seem that there are few switching costs in this business, barriers can actually be quite high, and E*Trade is working hard to increase them. First, reputation is critical in this business. Because most investors are quite careful with their money, they are no more likely to place their account in fly-by-night brokerage firm than they are to buy a risky penny stock. A brokerage firm must carefully cultivate its reputation. Established firms have a major advantage in the process of attracting new customers. Second, many of the electronic deep-discount firms, including E*Trade, are trying to follow the discounters' lead of building an investment "home" for their customers. The more hooks a firm gets into a customer's wallet, the more likely he is to stay. Fidelity and Schwab provide a wide enough range of services to serve as a customer's only financial-services vendor. Many customers are reluctant to leave Fidelity or Schwab because the firms provide everything from checking to tax planning. Also, the consolidation of financial information on a single statement is very important to most customers. They value the simplicity of receiving all financial information from one company. Third, switching assets in and out of a brokerage firm can be quite difficult. Some firms charge fees or otherwise try to prevent transfers out. In many cases, however, the actual barriers are much smaller than either the psychological or perceived barriers. Third, because there are significant differences between the customer bases of the firms, there are some services that are easy for one firm to provide but difficult for others to duplicate. For instance, most of E*Trade's customer base is on-line, allowing for fast and customized electronic communication. For Schwab or Fidelity to communicate with their customers in the same way requires significant manpower in the customer-service centers. Finally, because tracking customer activity is relatively easy in this business, there is also the possibility of creating loyalty-incentive programs, modeled on the airlines' frequent-flier programs. Such programs might reward frequent traders with enhanced customer service, free investment products (such as free investment research reports or a subscription to the *Wall Street Journal*) or free real-time quotes.

Potential Future E*Trade Customers

Because many high-volume traders have already joined an electronic deep-discount brokerage firm and because of national, mainstream advertising, the next wave of customers who join E*Trade are likely to have a profile very different from current customers. First of all, they are more likely to be lower-volume traders, who do not receive as large a cost savings form trading electronically. Therefore, they are probably less price sensitive. In addition, because of the proliferation of firms offering fixed commissions between $12 and $34, having the lowest commissions might not be as important as it used to be when the lowest competitive firms were priced in the high $30s or low $40s. They also tend to be less technologically savvy and feel that Internet security is not at a level sufficient for them to feel confortable. This group of customers also tends to need more hand-holding, and values greatly the ability to speak to a live person when they have a question or want to get more information. So the next wave of customers may be less profitable (because they trade less frequently) but may be more costly to serve because of the high advertising costs needed to attract them and the higher service levels required throughout the relationship.

Competition

E*Trade faces significant competition from a growing set of competitors, which come in three varieties: (1) electronic pure plays, (2) deep-discount migrators, and (3) discount migrators. The electronic pure plays (PC Financial Network and E*Trade) pioneered the industry, as these firms were incorporated as technology-focused, electronic-only brokerage firms. During the early 1990s, E*Trade and PCFN competed primarily on access through the on-line service providers. PCFN was the first to establish a presence on Prodigy, and as a result, signed up many of Prodigy's customers. Likewise, E*Trade dominated on CompuServe. E*Trade and PCFN established relationships with America Online about the same time and basically split AOL's customers 50/50.

With the explosion of the World Wide Web (Web), the graphical portion of the Internet, and easy-to-navigate Web browsers, barriers to access were virtually eliminated. Brokerage firms were no longer required to establish relationships with online service providers, as they could reach customers directly over the Internet. The deep-discount brokers embraced this paradigm shift more rapidly than the discount brokers, who were hesitant to cannibalize sales from their installed base. Drawn by the opportunity to regain their price-leadership position and lower their cost structure, deep-discount brokers established their own home pages (Aufhauser), whereas other less technologically savvy brokers (National Discount Brokers, Jack White) relied upon Security APL's Internet brokerage electronic storefront.

The discount brokers entered the electronic brokerage market gradually because they had to consider the effect of lending credibility to the emerging market, thus accelerating customer migration. Schwab and Fidelity first experimented with touch-tone trading, offering a 10% discount on commissions. This discount was then expanded to include trades that were entered via branded front-end trading software that accessed the brokerage firm by modem. Both Schwab and Fidelity have yet to offer trading over the Internet, citing security reasons. A brief description of E*Trade's leading competitors is provided below:

PC Financial Network

Founded as an electronic brokerage firm in 1988, PC Financial Network (PCFN) is jointly owned by an investment bank, Donaldson, Lufkin & Jenrette (DLJ), and Pershing & Company, a leading clearinghouse and market-maker. An on-line trading pioneer, PCFN claims to have the largest number of on-line brokerage accounts (over 300,000); however, industry insiders estimate the number of active accounts to be closer to 150,000. The company currently limits its on-line trading services to America Online and Prodigy. PCFN's commissions are toward the high end for on-line brokers. PCFN currently charges a minimum of $40 per trade up to $2,500 in principal value, with commissions rising to $100 plus 0.1% of the principal value for trades in excess of $40,000. In addition, PCFN provides its customers with 100 free real-time stock quotes for every trade execution. Initially a technological leader, the company has recently become more of a follower. PCFN's lack of Internet presence, coupled with the decline of Prodigy, has significantly reduced the company's growth rate.

National Discount Brokers

Founded as a traditional deep-discount brokerage firm, National Discount Brokers (NDB) is a wholly owned subsidiary of The Sherwood Group (NYSE: SHD). In October 1995, NDB launched its on-line services on the Web through the PAWWS Financial Network, a financial Web site established in March 1994 by Security APL, a Chicago-based portfolio accounting software and service-bureau vendor. The PAWWS home page serves as a single integrated site for financial information, real-time quotes, portfolio accounting, securities and market research tools, and on-line trading. Customers can chose among several brokerage firms besides NDB including Jack White & Company's Path On-line and Howe Barnes' The Net Investor. NDB is among the more aggressive on-line brokers with respect to low price. NDB currently charges $20 per trade for OTC stocks or up to 5,000 shares of any listed stock for $25 plus $3 postage and handling.

Lombard Institutional Brokerage

Founded as a traditional deep-discount brokerage firm in 1992, Lombard Institutional Brokerage aggressively embraced on-line brokerage services. In October 1995, Lombard began offering its customers the option of placing orders over the Internet through its own designed and managed Web site. By March 1996, on-line trades accounted for about 15% of total transaction activity. The company estimates that by 1998, 50% of Lombard's trades will be executed on-line. Lombard positions itself as a premium service provider at $34 per trade (whether placed on-line or with a live broker over the telephone). In addition to promoting its cost savings vs. traditional discount brokers, Lombard's advertisement also emphasize its investment information, charts and graphs, and accessible customer service. In April 1996, Lombard announced its intent to spin off its Advanced Technology Group (ATG) as an independent company focused on providing turnkey Internet software/transaction processing systems. These third-party solutions are designed to enable banks and brokerage firms to more easily enter the on-line brokerage business. Lombard's 1995 revenues are estimated at $24 million. The firm is privately held and is considering an IPO in early 1997.

TransTerra

TransTerra, an Omaha-based financial-services corporation, has four separate subsidiaries which target distinct price points in the on-line brokerage market, three of which offer trading services over the Internet. Only its highest-end offering, Accu-Trade, is not available over the Internet. AccuTrade charges $48 per transaction, is available over AOL and Windows direct modem link, and offers "power tools for the active investor." In September 1995, TransTerra acquired Aufhauser, the first brokerage firm to launch a stand-alone Web site (February 1995). TransTerra charges $34 per trade through Aufhauser's WealthWEB site; however, recently the company has started experimenting with a combination $800-per-year unlimited trading commission and $20-per-month for real-time quotes in targeting active traders. In February 1996, TransTerra launched Ceres Securities On-line with the help of Net-Broker's Broker On-line, an electronic toolkit for the construction of full-featured electronic brokerage services. Ceres charges $18 per trade. Finally, in April 1996, with substantial advertising in financial publications, TransTerra launched its cheapest on-line trading subsidiary, eBroker. Designed to capture the rock bottom price segment of the market, eBroker offers the lowest commission per trade of any on-line broker (including E*Trade) at $12 per trade. Advertisements feature the $12 commission and tell investors, "Don't call. Don't write," implying there is absolutely no customer service provided. Using a scaled-back version of Aufhauser's trading engine, eBroker is attempting to skim away the most valuable high-volume traders and also test the elasticity of demand for possible market expansion.

Charles Schwab

Charles Schwab, a NYSE-listed company, is the market leader in traditional, non-electronic discount brokerage services, serving slightly more than 50% of the total discount brokerage market. Schwab is known for its high levels of customer service and its reasonable prices. Schwab began testing more limited service offerings at lower prices with its touch-tone telephone trading system, TeleBroker, in 1994 and with its direct modem, on-line interface, StreetSmart, in 1995. Customers trading through either of these less-labor-intensive options received a 10% discount off Schwab's typical $60 to $80 commission rate. However, customers always had the fall-back option of speaking to the highly trained customer-service representatives. In 1996, Schwab crossed over the threshold into electronic brokerage with the launch of its e.Schwab, a premium-priced ($39 per trade) on-line brokerage option. E.Schwab advertising emphasizes the Schwab name, well-established reputation for customer support, and breadth of products and services. Its full-page ads in the *Wall Street*

Journal declared the "end of the commission compromise." Presently, e.Schwab is available only by direct modem link, but the Internet product is operational in beta release (80% of the modem functionality has been ported) with a full-scale Internet rollout scheduled for July.

Decision

E*Trade must decide how to react to the growing competitive pressure from e.Schwab on the high end and eBroker on the low end. With several competitors offering commissions below $20, E*Trade has lost its historic point of differentiation. Some executives within the senior management team argue that E*Trade should quickly and decisively regain its price-leadership position. Other managers believe that price differences at this level are indistinguishable to the customer and that E*Trade should increase its value proposition by enhancing its product and service offering while maintaining its current commission structure. The company must decide where it can create a profitable and sustainable position along the price/quality (service) trade-off.

8 Electronic Financial Markets

It is easy to get the impression that the thrust toward global electronic markets emerged with the Web. However, the revolution really started at least a century ago. The first technologies that electronically extended the reach of markets were associated with the securities markets, especially in the booming economy of 19th-century America with its premier New York Stock Exchange.

Financial Markets: First Movers in Electronic Commerce

In the 1860s, the New York Stock Exchange (NYSE) experienced an increasing demand by customers to scrutinize the skill and speed with which the exchange's floor brokers executed orders. In response, investors were allowed to witness trades from the gallery of the exchange. This solution, being limited both by the visual acuity of investors and the capacity of the gallery, proved generally unsatisfactory. Brokerage firms tried another expedient, "pad-shoving," which involved messenger boys collecting sales figures from the exchange and running from one brokerage house to the next shouting the latest prices. Only the messenger boys' speed and endurance limited communications bandwidth.

The invention of the stock ticker in 1867 by E. A. Calahan, an NYSE employee, reengineered many pad-shovers completely out of the business. Even though ticker technology was slow and crude with frequent breakdowns, the added speed and reach of the ticker changed the local geography of the New York securities community and lowered costs along the way.

One of the pivotal advancements in e-commerce technology began with a breakdown of the ticker on the Gold Exchange. Thomas Alva Edison, then a young man of 22 and recently fired from his railway job after the discovery of his homemade chemical laboratory in the baggage car, was temporarily living in the boiler room of the Gold Exchange. He was able to repair the ticker, and was immediately hired at $300 per month by the owner of the ticker service to manage the shop that made the stock tickers. This was an important first break for the inventor, who, in a short time, improved the speed and reliability of the stock ticker until it became a fixture in every brokerage office.

Tickers evolved over the next century to carry the increasing volumes of the exchanges and to satisfy investor demand for greater speed. The transparency and immediacy of information provided by the ticker was an important part of an efficient securities market. In 1952, the NYSE introduced the leased-wire system of operation of its ticker service and installed a system of tape recorders in the Quotation Department to speed up dealer quotations posted in active stocks. In 1973 the Market Data System Two went live, displaying worldwide trade and volume information. Important as these developments were, they were still only technologies for reporting trades whose source and negotiation occurred elsewhere.

That changed in 1976 with introduction of the Designated Order Turnaround System, or DOT, which processed buy and sell orders from member firms around the world. DOT was initially designed to transmit market orders for 100-share blocks of stock electronically from member firms to the trading posts on the exchange floor. By the 1980s, it was handling more than 35,000 orders per day. DOT was one of the first electronic order flow management systems. It roused intense interest in information technology for efficiently capturing and processing orders in securities markets (and of course, profiting from the commissions generated on the increased volume).

Two firms that pioneered order flow technologies were Charles Schwab & Co. and Bernard L. Madoff Investment Securities. In the 1980s, Madoff invested heavily in technology that would lower its cost of trading in New York Stock Exchange–listed securities. Rather than becoming an Exchange member, Madoff listed as a member on the Cincinnati Stock Exchange, allowing it to trade NYSE listed stocks during the time the NYSE was closed. (Members of the NYSE are not allowed to trade after hours.)

Armed with technology for lowering transaction costs and trading longer hours, Madoff went after order flow. Discount brokers such San Francisco's Schwab extended their own systems to make trading in NYSE-listed securities cheap, easy, and widely accessible to customers, which generated enormous volumes to feed Madoff's voracious matching system.[1] Today Madoff's volume in NYSE–listed stocks is approximately 10% of total trading in NYSE securities. Madoff handles this volume through 40 to 50 brokers electronically monitoring trades in real time; the NYSE employs almost 100 times that many people on its floor alone.

The consummate developments in electronic commerce often appear first in the securities markets. The reason is financial: Enough money is involved that securities markets can ill afford *not* to be pioneers in new technologies of electronic commerce. Electronic commerce has an enormous impact on the stock markets, eliminating the privileged positions of market makers and democratizing access for traders. Electronic securities markets lead electronic commerce in the design and implementation of high-volume, ultrareliable order processing and product information dissemination systems. We can learn much about the future shape of global electronic markets by investigating the tasks, policies, and operations of electronic financial market systems. E-commerce for tangible goods and services will evolve to focus on supply chain management and wholesaling and away from the retail focus we see today. As this happens, high-volume, ultrareliable systems similar to securities markets will become de rigueur for electronic commerce.

Basics

Markets exist because they solve problems facing buyers and sellers. In exchange for problem solving, buyers and sellers are willing to pay for access to and use of a market. This makes plausible the prospect of creating and operating a market for profit, generating revenues through commissions and listing fees to the market operators and dealers. Without this, markets would never be created, and there would be little incentive to own or operate one. Because market owners are often dealers in commodities, services, or securities, they are most likely to be the primary beneficiaries of such a market.

Financing usually becomes less expensive as markets become more liquid for two reasons in particular:

1. Deliveries can be more closely tailored to planned production, thus lowering inventory carrying costs and providing more of the advantages of *kanban* or just-in-time inventory management.[2]

2. Liquidity facilitates collateral lending because lenders generally consider assets that can be readily bought and sold more valuable.

Financial markets are typically continuous double-auction markets (in contrast to the "simple" auction markets delineated in the last chapter). They are double auctions in the sense that both buy and sell orders are matched against each other, as opposed to simple markets, which are only opened to buy orders. Double auctions assume there are several market participants on both sides of the market who publicly announce their prices so that the market price (publicly announced) is the one that equates supply and demand (i.e., clears). Though double auctions are more complex, three arguments favor their use when prices must be finely tuned to clear supply and demand:

1. Double-auction markets are efficient; that is, their prices reflect all available (price-relevant) information.

2. Current prices transmit private information of the better-informed dealers to less-informed dealers.

3. Prices correctly aggregate possibly conflicting information available to individual buyers and sellers.

Financial markets' continuity and liquidity are closely related. Continuity insures liquidity because a request to buy or sell a particular quantity of securities at a particular price (i.e., an *order*) can be made at any time, rather than having to wait for a specific auction date. Four aspects of market operation are necessary for liquidity:

1. Sales must occur frequently enough that buyers and sellers do not become impatient.

2. The spread between bid and ask offers must be narrow.

3. Bid and ask orders, as well as sales, must be executed quickly.

4. Price changes between transactions should be small and recover quickly.

Other desirable market characteristics are fairness, efficiency, transparency, orderly trading, and best price discovery. Markets are considered *fair* if one trader cannot systematically profit from the actions of another trader. Fairness, or at least the impression of it, is important, since it is unlikely that many would trade in a market that placed them explicitly at a disadvantage.

Markets are *efficient* when prices reflect underlying value, supply, and demand for a security. The speed and completeness with which new information is incorporated in price is one measure of a market's efficiency. Fairness and efficiency require that information about the security, as well as information about offers, sales, and the trading environment, be available to all traders in the market. The amount and timeliness with which this information is disseminated is called the market's *transparency*. The precise character and amount of transparency is often open to debate. For example, to attract order flow, a market generally must provide real-time information on orders to buy or sell shares that have been placed. Some information, such as the identity of traders, probably should not be displayed if a market wants to maintain the broadest level of participation in that market. If trader identity were displayed, then sellers might take advantage of a large buy order by raising the price. When trader identity is disguised, traders can break a large order into several small orders, leaving the price less exposed to manipulation.[3]

Traders derive considerable information from price movements in a securities market. Sometimes changes in price alone can impel dramatic increases or decreases in a security's price. To control this, markets have developed specific safeguards. For example, for a specialist to be permitted to trade on the NYSE, 75% of the specialist's trades must counter price trends in the market. Additionally, "circuit breakers" automatically stop trading if the Exchange detects an excessive drop in prices. Such subsystems promote *orderly trading* on the underlying value of securities.

The securities exchanges also discard the price-taking assumption of traditional retail markets, in which goods are given a price (e.g., on a sticker attached to the product, or in a catalog) and the customer can either take it or leave it. Instead, they support the more elaborate price search involved in matching the varying preferences of buyers and sellers (supply and demand). *Best price discovery* is the market characteristic that assures the matching of buy and sell orders so that traders realize the best price possible for both sides.

Any discussion of financial markets would be incomplete without mention of behavior explicitly prohibited in nearly every market. Wash sales, artificial market activity, matched orders and circulation of manipulative information are deceptions likely to damage market credibility.[4]

In a *wash sale*, the owner sells a quantity of product to a buyer who sells it back at a contrived (usually higher) price. A wash sale involves no real change of ownership, but attempts to manipulate price and misinform other traders. As other traders offer a higher price for the product, the owner can sell at a profit. *Artificial market activity* has the same intent as a wash sale but involves more than two traders. Groups of traders (often including management from the firms of traded securities) "churn" stocks to set price artificially, then profit from that artificial price. *Matched orders* exist when two or more traders collaborate by placing offsetting orders with two different brokers (to hide the activity); for example, one contracts to buy 1,000 shares of a stock at $35, and another to sell 1,000 shares of the same stock at $35. If the price without this trade is $30, then the effect is to misinform the market about the security's value. Certain individuals, for example, newscasters and columnists, are held in trust by the public and thus have the ability to manipulate a product's perceived value. If they do this for remuneration, to the advantage of specific traders, then they abuse that trust and misinform the trading public at large. They may be guilty of *circulation of manipulative information for remuneration.*

Matching and Price Discovery

Markets are matchmakers for buyers and sellers. The stated price at which a market sells or buys a particular commodity is typically the price at which the last trade took place.[5] Market prices may be set through two classes of mechanisms: (1) quotes of prices at which registered dealers in securities are willing to buy and trade (as is the case in the U.S. National Association of Securities Dealers Automated Quotation system, or NASDAQ), and (2) price matching of bid and ask offers (as is the case on the NYSE). The former occurs in a *quote-driven* market; the latter occurs in an *order-driven* market. Each approach has its own particular strengths and weaknesses.

Quote-driven systems are sometimes criticized as giving dealers the power to manipulate prices to their advantage. However, thinly traded securities might never clear (i.e., never be bought or sold) if dealers did not set the price. Order-driven markets generally require high volumes of trading.

The next sections look closely at specific examples of these two approaches to matching buyer and seller. The NASDAQ system is a quote-driven system of electronically linked competing market makers. The NYSE is an order-driven system with physical floor trading and monopoly market makers (specialists) who are obligated to provide liquidity. The New York Stock Exchange is the archetype for various U.S. regional exchanges on which floor trading is central to operations. In contrast, NASDAQ has no trading floor where market makers meet. NASDAQ automated a previously sluggish market in which individual dealers who kept inventories of particular securities quoted and compared bid and asked prices for securities over the telephone. Both systems handle comparable trading volumes (around 50 billion shares annually), though the majority of NASDAQ's trades tend to be dealer-to-dealer adjustments of inventory. NASDAQ share values average only about one-third of NYSE share values.

The exchanges trade in equity securities (stocks), debt securities (bonds), and derivatives contracts based on the underlying value of debt, equity, and commodities. The distinguishing feature of these "products" is that they represent uncertain claims to assets in the future. Otherwise their value depends on the ability to resell them in a secondary market. The secondary market tends to convert the security into a "summary" of rational expectation about the underlying asset value.

Traders may participate in a market for various reasons. If the market is to profit from fees based on market use (the most commonly suggested way of funding electronic commerce), then it must cater to traders who, as a group, provide the greatest potential dollar and transaction volumes of trades. Traders fall into two broad groups:

1. traders who participate in order to buy the product (*value-motivated* traders)

2. traders who buy or sell short[6] in order to make a profit on price changes motivated by imbalances in supply and demand (*speculators* and *liquidity providers*)

The traditional floor trading market system of the NYSE, which depends on the physical presence of traders at a distinct location, contrasts with the open, scalable market system of NASDAQ, which reflects more closely the features and services offered by networks such as the Internet. Each system has its advantages and disadvantages. Both the NYSE and NASDAQ are successful, global, secure, high-dollar, high-transaction-volume systems. In this regard they mirror the aspirations of an information highway.

In both the NYSE and NASDAQ, there are varying levels of participation, and varying requirements of the traders. This contrasts sharply with principles of democratic, universal access often championed in (now rather dated) references to an "information superhighway." Where money is involved, markets must be secure, and information controlled. The securities exchanges have accomplished this admirably.

The New York Stock Exchange

The New York Stock Exchange evolved over the last two centuries into its current form, incorporating both features and products as traders came to demand them. It was not the product of a central grand plan. Rather like the Internet, it expanded and changed as individuals sought to use its facilities for their specific purposes.

In its formative years[7] during the first half of the 18th century, the NYSE was an ad hoc auction market at the foot of Wall Street. The market dealt in both commodities, such as tobacco, and securities. The securities auctioneers ultimately separated and took up trading under a buttonwood tree at 68 Wall Street. The brokers who traded there ultimately tired of auctioneers' domination of the market. They instituted the formal Buttonwood Tree Agreement in 1792, which stipulated that (1) brokers were to trade only with each other, and (2) commissions were to be 0.25%. Until 1972, the NYSE was run as a "voluntary association" of brokers, who paid dues, conducted business, and agreed upon trading rules and regulations.

The NYSE's physical floor provides limited physical space for transacting business. Membership on the NYSE is therefore strictly limited and is relatively expensive. The "products" sold on the exchange are listed securities, consisting of more than 2,200 stocks of more than 1,700 companies. For a firm's stock to be listed, the exchange requires that the firm's earnings, market value of publicly held shares, and capitalization exceed specified minimum levels. Listing and membership restrictions assure control and quality of exchange transactions and that parties will be able to meet obligations contracted on the exchange floor. Exchanges that have failed to maintain this level of quality, for example, the Vancouver Stock Exchange, have lost reputation, and traders have taken their business elsewhere. As noted above, trading on an exchange must be seen above all as fair and honest.

Owing to restrictions on membership, traders wishing to buy or sell a specific security must contract with a member (for a commission) to represent them as an agent, or broker, on the trading floor. Membership itself is a commodity that may be used, sold, or leased by the member. The high cost of membership means that members are typically corporations or partnerships and may serve several functions on the floor. Three of these functions are particularly important: commission brokers, specialists, and floor brokers.

Most members are registered as *commission brokers*. These members represent securities firms (e.g., firms such as Merrill Lynch) that deal with the public at large, gathering orders off the NYSE floor. The main job of commissioned brokers is to get the best possible price for the customer. Brokers are agents who act on the behalf of their customers (traders). Because they bear the risk that a trader may not follow through on an agreement made in the market, they have evolved certain minimal controls over their customers. At a minimum they demand personal and contact information, acknowledgement that the customer is of legal age, with employer and credit references and investment objectives. For riskier investments, such as options, they require the customer to provide income and net worth statements and a statement of investment experience.

The second largest number of members are registered as *specialists*, a special group of brokers designated to maintain a fair and orderly market.[8] The specialist is a dealer (i.e., trades from his own inventory of securities) and is obligated, on 75% of transactions for his own account, to trade counter to the market trend. The specialist holds a monopoly in making a market in the securities assigned to him. (Each listed security has only one specialist, and may be traded in only one spot on the exchange floor.) In compensation for his special status, the specialist must make 75% of his trades in pursuit of an orderly market (i.e., buying on down-ticks, and selling on plus-ticks). Though this typically results in losses to the specialist, which must be made up in the remaining 25% of trades, specialist trading provides the market with continuity and liquidity.

Floor brokers are the third group of members, though their ranks have declined in number in recent years as additional functions have been automated. Floor brokers work only for other members, taking transactions which the other members are incapable of handling at the moment. They primarily provide excess capacity for overloaded brokers when order volume is high. SuperDOT (the successor to DOT, discussed above) has taken over many floor broker functions with its ability to handle high volumes of transactions. Automation of order acquisition through SuperDOT has also decreased the importance of actually being present on the floor to trade.

The great advantage of electronic trading systems over floor trading counterparts is their ability to capture orders, almost instantaneously, from potentially anywhere in the world. No longer do traders have to travel to a specific location. This opportunity, though, is only potential. Brokers cannot allow just anyone to dial up and trade on an exchange system. Rather, individuals who want to trade through a broker must set up an account, and usually must meet a minimum set of requirements that provide reasonable assurance that they will complete any trades agreed upon in the exchange.

The exchange does not maintain monopoly control over trading in listed securities. In recent years, the proportion of trades in listed securities traded on the NYSE floor has steadily declined, as large insurance firms, pension funds, and banks transact directly with each other, avoiding trading commissions. In addition, automation has allowed independent exchanges to develop—such as Bernard Madoff's brokerage—that do much of their trading in NYSE-listed securities. Firms that are not members of the NYSE are not restricted by its rules over trading. This has made it increasingly difficulty for the NYSE to impose order on the market in listed securities. It also exposes these securities to a sort of price war in which independent systems can discover and trade securities less expensively than the major exchanges.

In 1972, the NYSE reorganized as a not-for-profit corporation and adopted a board of directors (replacing a former board of governors) responsible for governing the exchange. The reorganization toward a more formal corporate structure reflected, to some extent, the greater complexity of operation undertaken by the exchange.

The National Association of Securities Dealers Automated Quotations System

The NASDAQ system was brought on-line in February 1971. It automated the work of an informal dealer network handling off-exchange trading in unlisted stocks commonly referred to as the over-the-counter (OTC) market.[9] Until 1971, trading in this market was conducted through ordinary voice telephone conversations, and it still is for U.S. securities not listed on NASDAQ (perhaps as many as 50,000 equity issues). The OTC market is the primary market for all debt trading in the United States (off-exchange trading has been uncommon outside of the United States) as well as U.S. government and agency issues, municipal bonds, and money market instruments. More than 4,000 common stock issues of publicly traded corporations are listed on NASDAQ. Traders on NASDAQ are dealers who make markets (i.e., trade out of their own securities inventories) by making a two-sided market (buy and/or sell) by quoting a price they would pay a prospective seller (bid) or a price they would charge a prospective buyer (ask). Market makers do not deal directly with the public; rather they trade with each other from their own inventories.

The NASDAQ market is a *negotiated market*, in contrast to the NYSE, which is a double-auction market. No comparable function to the specialist exists on NASDAQ. Rather, each listed security may have multiple market makers; in fact, heavily traded securities such as Microsoft and Intel might have dozens of market makers.

The NYSE assigns the specialist to make markets based on offers in the order flow. In contrast, NASDAQ provides a centralized computer database, which broadcasts firm quotations initiated by NASDAQ market makers (not by traders placing orders) to everyone on the system. Traders interested in buying or selling either must be dealers, who can trade directly with other dealers, or must hire a NASDAQ dealer as an agent.

NASDAQ displays allow three levels of dissemination of quotations. Retail brokers use *level 1*, which allows their customers to view only the high current bid price and low current asked price (i.e., the "inside market") in order to decide whether they would like to buy or sell from the dealer posting either quotation. *Levels 2* and *3* both display all firm quotations. *Level 3* also allows a dealer to adjust a quotation as the market changes, and is intended for use by NASDAQ market makers.

Though there are close to 50,000 securities traded OTC, only around 4,500 are listed on the NASDAQ system. Most of the other 45,500 companies cannot meet the listing requirements of NASDAQ; many are traded inactively, are bankrupt firms, old mining claims, start-ups, and the like. It is unlikely that anyone would actively support an organized market for such issues. In the past, when markets have been lenient with regard to these sorts of issues, the high likelihood of collapse of the market and low reputation of issues has kept traders away and made it difficult to run a profitable operation.

Prices for non-NASDAQ OTC securities can be found in a daily publication called the Pink Sheets, in which market makers post nonbinding bid and ask quotations. In June 1990, the NASD provided an automated alternative to the Pink Sheets: the OTC Bulletin Board. Other exchanges have used similar bulletin boards to provide an up-to-the-minute public listing for thinly traded securities. Securities listed on a bulletin board system lack (1) liquidity and (2) implicit assurances about quality provided by listing requirements.

Neither the NYSE nor the NASDAQ system allows the public direct access to the order flow. Instead, orders are collected, managed, and completed under the supervision of a broker or a dealer in an agency capacity. Brokers and dealers must meet stringent educational, personal, and capital requirements and be of general good character. Both exchanges monitoring operations extensively, as does the U.S. Securities and Exchange Commission.

Once a transaction has been completed on the exchange, the respective buying and selling securities firms compare their recorded details of the transaction with each other. Each produces a confirmation of the transaction to be sent to the other, generally through the mail, but also through EDI. Comparison data from each brokerage party are entered into the Securities Industry Automation Corporation's

(SIAC's) computer system, which prints out a "contract sheet" summarizing the transaction and noting any discrepancies in its recording on either the buyer's or seller's side.

Because the brokerage firms generally handle large volumes of trades, the SIAC best uses its processing capacity by offsetting sales of securities by purchases, so that only the net balances of shares are transferred between firms. This process of computing the net balances is the *clearing* process. If there were no clearing process, all transactions would have to be settled by individual share certificate delivery and payment. Clearing allows the trades occurring between customers of any particular brokerage firm to be handled by that firm. This is significantly more efficient, and less error prone, since errors can be tracked down and corrected within the firm. The clearing process eliminates 90% of potential securities transfers in U.S. exchange operations.

Clearing of securities transactions is typically outsourced to third parties. For example, the National Securities Clearing Corporation (NSCC) (which itself outsources data processing operations to the SIAC) clears most NYSE and American Stock Exchange (AMEX) trades as well as a large number of OTC stock trades. All listed options transactions flow through the Options Clearing Corporation (OCC). The NSCC nets all trades submitted to it, determining securities positions and account settlements. The NSCC then transfers securities held in participants' accounts at the Depository Trust Company (DTC), or produces "balance orders" that will direct the physical delivery of securities to firms. The DTC is responsible for safekeeping of securities certificates, a significant operation given the massive quantity of certificates issued. Both the NSCC and the DTC are funded by participants' contributions. Individual participants contribute based on volume of processing performed for that participant.

After clearing, the transfer of the stock or bond occurs. Transfer involves the change of title of ownership to a security. Today, physical transfer of certificates is kept to a minimum. Some widely traded securities, for example, T-bills, Treasury notes, and bonds, do not employ physical certificates: Transfer is solely by a book entry. Transfer completes two activities: (1) the physical certificates (if they exist) are transferred to the buyer, and (2) the transfer is recorded on the books of the issuer of the securities certificate. Firms issuing securities usually engage a bank or trust company as a transfer agent, rather than handling this activity themselves.

Delivery and transfer of securities and clearing of securities transactions, for most of the history of organized securities exchanges, have been "bottleneck" operations in the securities exchanges. Two developments have alleviated the problem significantly:

1. vastly improved, automated data processing for back-office operations, and

2. standardization of receipt and delivery terms codified in the NASDAQ's Uniform Practice Code and the rules and regulations of the NYSE and other exchanges.

Notes

1. The "Online Trading at the Shanghai Stock Exchange" case study included in this chapter shows how the Shanghai Stock Exchange used information technology to extend trading hours, bypass brokers, and make listed securities widely accessible to customers at low cost, generating enormous volumes. In 1996, the turnover in Shanghai Stock Exchange–listed securities is the highest of any securities exchange in the world—on average 2.25 transactions per share per year versus a typical 0.7 transactions per share per year for most OECD exchanges. "The Moscow Stock Exchange" case study describes another emerging market, one in which brokers and the Exchange have kept trading and settlement inaccessible to the average investor. Turnover in 1996 for Moscow Stock Exchange–listed securities is almost the lowest in the world: on average 0.10 transactions per share per year. Contrasts in the two cases illustrate the pivotal role of information and communications technologies in market efficiency and liquidity.

2. Kanban control uses the levels of buffer inventories in the system to regulate production. When a buffer reaches its preset maximum level, the upstream machine is told to stop producing that part type. This is often implemented by circulating cards—the *kanbans*—between a machine and the downstream buffer. The machine must have a card before it can start an operation. It can then pick raw materials out of its upstream (or input) buffer, perform the operation, attach the card to the finished part, and put it in the downstream (or output) buffer. The number of cards circulating determines the buffer size, since once all cards are attached to parts in the buffer, no more parts can be made. When the machine picks up raw materials to perform an operation, it also detaches the card that was attached to the material. The card is then circulated back upstream to signal the next upstream machine to do another operation. This way, a demand for a unit of finished goods percolates up the supply chain.

3. Fairness and transparency of trading are central to the information technology implementation presented in this chapter's case study on the Bolsa de Comercio de Santiago. The case focuses on the trade-offs between market policy (e.g., fairness and transparency) and the technology offerings required to make the market attractive (e.g., Ethernet communications lines and program trading). It also provides an opportunity to discuss technical considerations of fault tolerance and on-line transaction processing (both of which are essential for the order matching and recording process) and decision support systems, which provide real-time transaction and summary data. In addition to administrative aspects of designing a system for electronic commerce, the case also introduces significant concepts and terms in client-server technology, and the administrative and policy implications of what appear to be strictly technical decisions in design of a computer system.

4. Promoters of commerce on the Internet tout the open and universal access it offers. Certainly this invites a larger market for products, but it also invites manipulation, which in the long run would surely drive customers away. Any sort of commerce—electronic or otherwise—would be unlikely to thrive in an environment that fails to regulate, monitor, and control adverse manipulative behavior. Thus electronic commerce is rapidly awakening to the relevance of these proscribed activities in its bailiwick as well.

5. This fact is dictated by an accounting principle that reuires that the stated cost of an asset be valued at the historical cost of an arm's-length transaction.

6. In a *short sale*, the seller sells securities that he does not yet own, in anticipation of a future price decline. These shares are typically borrowed from owners using the same broker as the one the short seller uses. This is primarily a speculative activity, and carries with it the risk that the borrowing cannot be covered. A *stop order* to buy becomes a market order, that is, an order executed at the best possible price, when the last trade of the security sells at or above the "stop" price; a stop order to sell becomes a market order when the last trade of the security sells at or below the "stop" price. The "stop" price is a trigger that initiates an

aggressive purchase or sale of the security. Primary uses of stop orders are to prevent losses on other sorts of contracts, often speculative.

7. R. Sobel, *N.Y.S.E.: A History of the New York Stock Exchange* (New York: Weybright and Talley, 1975).

8. Oddly, this function was not legislated by the NYSE, but rather (in true Internet style) grew out of a chance event. In 1875, an NYSE member, a certain Mr. Boyd, suffered a broken leg, which restricted him to a chair on the trading floor. As a result of his limited mobility, he confined his trading to Western Union stock, which was quite active at the time. His trading was so successful that he continued to confine his trading to Western Union stock even after his leg had mended. Thus he became the first specialist member.

9. The term "over the counter" arose in the 19th century when many corporate headquarters and treasurers' offices were located on Wall Street, close to the NYSE. An investor interested in buying shares in an unlisted company would be unable to do so at the NYSE, but could walk to the nearby corporate treasurer's office, and purchase, through a barred window, *over the counter*, the shares of that company.

On-Line Trading at the Shanghai Stock Exchange

It all started in 1979 when Deng Xiaoping initiated the "responsibility system"—a capitalist innovation which abolished central quotas and allowed farmers and some township enterprises to sell their goods on the open market. Many became rich in the ensuing decade, buying cars, houses, and consumer goods. Savings grew with the growing wealth of the populace, endowing China with one of the highest savings rates in the world—between 35% and 40% of GDP over the past decade. With the introduction of economic reforms in the 1980s, average annual growth was pushed to nearly 10%. In the early 1990s, Chinese trade with the rest of the world reached 35% of its national income, compared to 6% in 1970. Industrial output grew to around 75% of GDP in the 1990s from 43% in 1949, reflecting a rapid shift out of rural agriculture as the country modernized. By 1997, China's gross domestic product reached US$3.6 trillion at purchasing power parity[1] or about half that of the United States, generated by a population of 1.25 billion people. 1996 retail price inflation was contained to around 10%, while private consumption growth accelerated to 8.5%, with gross domestic investment growth projected to average 13.8% per year.[2] This modernization required substantial amounts of investment capital.

The Shanghai Stock Exchange (SSE) plays a vital role in enabling the direct financing of the burgeoning Chinese economy. Stock markets match firm management's preference for long-term funds that minimize income risks and reduce transaction costs with investors and lenders who generally prefer to lend for short periods because of their uncertainty about future cash needs. This conflict of preferences can be resolved through the activities of a secondary market in securities.

The Shanghai Stock Exchange is a member-owned and -managed nonprofit legal entity with about two-thirds of its members located in Shanghai. The Shanghai Stock Exchange was established with five objectives in mind:

1. Provide a centralized forum for trading securities

2. Manage spot trading of listed securities

3. Provide centralized clearance and delivery

4. Provide custodial services

5. Disseminate securities market information (through the *Shanghai Security News*, which was sold to China's news agency, Xinhua, in 1995)

Shanghai established the first stock exchange in China's history in 1891, near the end of the Qing dynasty. At that time there were two markets. The most active market was in foreign shares (primarily British and U.S. firms), while the other market dealt

This case was prepared by J. Christopher Westland.

in Chinese companies. Operations ceased during the Japanese occupation. Following the war, from 1945 to 1949 the Shanghai Securities Exchange was very active, trading in foreign shares, Chinese shares, and government bonds. After 1949, trading ceased until Deng's restructuring of private enterprise in the 1980s.[3] In 1981, treasury bonds were issued for the first time; by 1987 a secondary market emerged in Shanghai with three major features:

· Enterprise bonds were issued by several big enterprises.

· The number of financial institutions buying and selling increased from one to six as enterprise bonds and stocks were increasingly traded in the secondary market.

· Securities came to be preferred to bank deposits, due to their higher yield.

By 1990, the trade network in Shanghai had expanded to include 47 counters and agents. The Far East Credit Rating Corporation, designated in 1988 to give ratings to enterprise bonds and commercial paper, provided some transparency to this informal market. That year, the Shanghai Stock Exchange moved into the PuJiang (formerly Astor House) Hotel. To this network was added another exchange in southern China across the border from Hong Kong—the Shenzhen exchange. In 1997, the Shanghai Stock Exchange consolidated its operations in its new building in PuDong.

Despite the large size of China's economy, combined market capitalization at China's exchanges in Shanghai and Shenzhen amounts to no more than US$150 billion. China's market capitalization is only 10% of nominal GDP, compared to Hong Kong's market capitalization, which is 300% of GDP. China's exchanges are less than one-fiftieth the size of the New York Stock Exchange, less than one-third the size of Hong Kong's stock exchange, and roughly at parity with regional exchanges in Seoul and Bombay.

In 1996 shares worth US$1.6 trillion traded on emerging stock markets, equivalent to 12% of the value of all shares traded worldwide. Of all of these markets, only China had turnover in excess of 200%, a remarkable testament to the success of exchange systems for trading securities.

Products Bought and Sold on the Exchange

Common Stock

The market for Chinese equities is dichotomized into A shares, which only People's Republic of China (PRC) citizens may buy, and B shares, which must be purchased with foreign funds. The majority of listed companies are state-owned enterprises

(SOEs)—defined as those fully owned by the top two tiers of China's government—accounting for 70% of listings. Joint ventures between foreign companies and SOEs account for another 20%. Township and village enterprises (TVEs), the highly successful progeny of Maoist communes, make up the remainder of issues.

B shares are quoted in *renminbi* (RMB) but must be purchased in U.S. dollars, which are exchanged at official rates (swap-in/swap-out). Share ownership is restricted because the exchange feels that unbridled foreign participation distorts the market, forecloses opportunities for Chinese investors, and is difficult to regulate.[4] Most B shares are also those of state-owned enterprises, where industrial output is growing at around one-twentieth the growth rate in the private sector. B shares tend to trade at price earnings multiples of about half those of A shares. In 1992, the China Securities Regulatory Commission (CSRC) announced the creation of H shares of Chinese companies listed on the Hong Kong exchange. The same share of a given company may sell at significantly different prices in the A, B, and H markets. In addition, Chinese corporations that have listed on the Hong Kong Stock Exchange for several years have come to be called "red chips." The number of seats has risen to as high as 6,000, but was cut to 1,600 when the Shanghai Stock Exchange moved to PuDong in August, 1997.

A shares may be traded on the floor, but more often, trading bypasses the floor completely. The Shanghai Stock Exchange issues a security card that identifies an individual as being authorized to trade in listed securities. The security card allows traders to bypass brokerage firms (and reduce brokers' commissions). This provides a more efficient use of the floor, by channeling routine trades directly to computer matching. Trades are captured at a brokerage room when traders post an order with the clerk in the brokerage room. The order is posted in the exchange's system through computer-to-computer communication. Matching takes place automatically. Security card holders still have to go through a brokerage firm to buy or sell securities and to settle and clear the transaction. Security cards make the job of the brokerage firm easier by identifying the client to the brokerage, and allowing automated management of the client's account balance. In contrast, B shares (which are designed for trading by overseas investors) are traded only through brokers and on the floor; H shares and N shares are, of course, traded in Hong Kong and New York respectively.

Liquidity is quite good in A shares, where there is widespread participation by China's populace through about 3,000 brokerage rooms around China. Turnover is around five times per year. B shares are less liquid, and there has been considerable interest in engaging more overseas investors in their purchase. Much of the current trading in B shares is done by Chinese within China, though they must pay for these shares with dollars in accounts outside of China.

One of the difficulties in fostering overseas trading in B shares arises from the still evolving state of telecommunications in China. Shanghai has a modern fiber-optic local loop. Unfortunately, laying trans-Pacific cables with anywhere near the bandwidth required for trading is still prohibitively expensive, especially for an exchange whose primary concern is efficiency (read: low cost provision of quality service).

In 1992, the Shanghai Stock Exchange started to experiment with distributing new issues by means of price auction and price determination through its trading network. The success of this approach has encouraged this to be tried in the T-bond market, and with new placement of rights issues for listed companies.

A shares can be traded by any trader with a Shanghai Stock Exchange–issued security card. These traders can trade directly with the exchange's computer system. Thus orders may come directly from trading counters—where there is a transaction-by-transaction cash settlement and exchange of securities—or through member brokers—where the exchange provides net settlement of brokers' accounts. Settlement is completed on the same day as the trade $(T + 0)$. Exchange commissions are approximately 0.65% of trades.

As in many emerging markets, price volatility can be more strongly influenced by the money coming into the market than by the business fundamentals of the traded firm. Volatility in the Shanghai market is very high by the standards of most developed economies, a situation that poses difficulties to orderly trading. This tends to compound the exchange's challenges in the face of problems inherent in securities laws that are still evolving, and in the difficulties faced by the China Securities Regulatory Commission in policing insider trading, misuse of funds, and false disclosure. Volatility is tightly monitored—important in a market where there is a rapidly expanding group of investors of varying levels of sophistication. The exchange will not allow prices for a given security to vary more than 10% from the prior day's closing price. When the 10% mark is reached, trading is not halted. Rather the settlement prices simply are not allowed to exceed 10% of the prior day's price. This limit does not apply to initial public offerings (IPOs) on the first day; it takes effect only on the second day after issue.

China shares volatility continues to abate as Chinese accounting standards are placed on the same footing as those followed in other markets. Because the listed companies are generally SOEs, their accounting practices have focused on production rather than on the consumer market, with emphasis on stewardship of state funds, costs, and cash flow. Profit, depreciation, provisions for losses, and asset valuation, especially for land, which is not tradable in China and thus cannot be assigned a secondary market price, are all poorly accounted for, yet pivotal to proper securities pricing.

B shares are traded through automated screen trading with settlement on transaction-by-transaction basis. Because these shares are intended to be traded by overseas investors, communications are important. Satellite for uplink and downlink through AsiaOne satellite are maintained. The exchange applies a flat commission schedule to transactions involving B shares. Settlement is made by the third day following the transaction $(T + 3)$ to allow for international bank clearing.

T-Bonds

Treasury bonds (T-bonds) are issued by China's Ministry of Finance, with size, interest rate, maturity, and other terms of each bond issue approved by the State Council, in consultation with the People's Bank of China (PBC). T-bonds are issued in six different maturities: 6 months, 1 year, 2 years, 3 years, 5 years, and 10 years. Starting from a 15% level in 1981, debt issuance covered more than 45% of the budget deficit by 1987, and in 1994, it entirely financed China's deficit.

Until 1991, trading in T-bonds was conducted exclusively in the OTC markets and volume was relatively small—around RMB 2.8 billion in 1988. Due to the lack of a nationwide network, this OTC market was characterized by significant price differentials across the regions. With the establishment of securities exchanges and a nationwide computerized trading network in 1991, trading became more centralized. This virtually eliminated regional price differentials. Volumes increased to over RMB 50 billion that year. From 1992, trading activities started to concentrate in the Shanghai Stock Exchange, Wuhan Securities Centre, and the Securities Trading Automatic Quotation System (STAQ). Toward the end of 1992, trading in T-bonds declined as capital was diverted to the increasingly liquid A share securities market.[5]

In October 1993, the Shanghai Stock Exchange launched a bond futures contract to increase trading volume of T-bonds. It was designed as a series of standardized forward contracts on each outstanding issue, thus providing a full set of hedging vehicles. The trading of futures contracts became very active toward the end of 1994. Monthly volume of contracts hit 50 million contracts (each contract with a face value of RMB 20,000) in January 1995. The volumes were abnormally high given the limited issue of underlying T-bonds (1992—RMB 102 billion, 1993—RMB 31 billion, 1994—RMB 102 billion). The speculative frenzy eventually forced the authority to stop T-bond futures from trading in May 1995.[6]

T-bonds, because they are traded in large blocks compared to common stocks, rely on floor trading with net settlement on the day of transaction $(T + 0)$. Commissions are approximately 0.3% of trades. Transfer has been scripless, but is going back to exchange of physical certificates during settlement. Buyers in rural areas like to hold the actual certificates, and thus certificates are being distributed to boost trading volume and liquidity. In addition, the exchange of physical certificates obviates the need for traders to register with the exchange (for a security card) before trading— important in rural areas.

Repurchase Agreements

Repurchase agreements (repos) were introduced in December 1993 to provide investors with a more complete investing vehicle, thus to boost T-bond liquidity. Bond repurchase agreements bring about a mortgage function in the T-bond market.

Government securities repurchase markets exist in both the Shanghai Stock Exchange and Securities Trading Automatic Quotation System. On the SSE, repurchase agreements are standardized one-month, three-month, and six-month contracts. On STAQ, they are typically structured to suit both buyers and sellers. Individuals are prohibited from trading T-bond repurchase agreements.

Corporate Bonds

State-owned enterprises and financial institutions are authorized to issue and sell bonds on the secondary market. As would be expected, these command generally higher interest rates than T-bonds. They are also more popular than T-bonds due to China's lack of credit history, and with no SOEs ever having gone bankrupt, the higher rates come with no apparent additional risk. Trading is light in the secondary markets, since the smaller size of this market limits liquidity, and higher interest rates encourage holding to maturity.

Future Products

The exchange has experimented in T-bond futures in an attempt to increase liquidity of that market. Currently it sells no derivatives (except a few warrants), but has plans to sell options, including index options, and futures for selected securities to meet the increasing demands for risk management tools for China's flourishing economy.

Electronic Trading

The Shanghai Stock Exchange (and its sister exchange in Shenzhen) use a continuous double-auction order-driven trading system, assisted by a computer network to transfer order information from brokers to the floor and back again. During opening hours, information on trade prices and volumes is continuously disseminated to traders, and buy and sell orders are continuously received. Both exchanges have supporting clearinghouses. Standard board trading lots are used with aggregate par value of RMB 1,000 (about US$175) in Shanghai, and 2,000 shares in Shenzhen. The two exchanges are similar in organization and systems, though Shenzhen's volume is roughly half Shanghai's.

The exchange floor opens Monday through Friday from 9:30 A.M. until 11:30 A.M. (at which time prices are frozen), and reopens after lunch from 1:00 P.M. to 3:00 P.M. Opening prices are generally set to clear the maximum number of outstanding bid and ask orders on hand at 9:15 A.M. They may be set differently if there are substantial imbalances between buying and selling and it is felt that a different price is appropriate to clear the market. For thinly traded stocks, the opening prices will be set at their closing prices from the last business day.

The trading system runs on a Hewlett-Packard HP9000-T500 computer, with peak processing of 5,000 transactions per second. This is sufficient to handle peak exchange volume of two million transactions per day, with peak periods at the beginning and end of the trading day. The HP9000 is, with the addition of processing boards, scalable to 20 million transactions per day. Cisco routers control traffic on the local and wide area networks controlling traffic to and from brokerage rooms throughout China. These rely on a fault-tolerant combination of direct digital network, satellite, and analog transmission. The exchange has been clever in applying a cost-conscious set of components for exchange automation that make effective use of both microcomputer and state-of-the-art computer and communications technology.

Trading on the Shanghai Stock Exchange is dominated by small investors—99.4% of the Shanghai Stock Exchange's clients are individuals; another 0.6% are institutions, with only a vestige of direct participation by securities houses. The Shanghai Exchange has implemented a number of innovations to bring on-line trading to the small investor. China's limited telecommunications capacity requires several levels of support to reach its desired customer base. Brokerage rooms provide the equivalent of Internet cafes for those who do not have a telephone, modem, and computer at home. In addition, real-time stock transaction quotations are provided on-line, free to subscribers of Shanghai's cable television service. A computer card can provide the same cable TV quotation service, but on a computer screen; over 50,000 were sold in their first year. Traders with a modem and computer can open a trading account with one of the local banks. The exchange then provides them free connectivity software and free real-time quotations, allowing trading in and out of that bank account. The StockStar electronic trading Internet site provides services similar to E*Trade in the United States, though the level of support provided traders directly from the exchange has provided it little latitude for profit.

Information Dissemination

China is a continent-sized country which needs sophisticated communications systems to allow access to its exchanges. Shanghai's Stock Exchange has invested in two networks: STAQ, a national-wide system for broadcasting transaction prices; and NET, an automatic security trading system for stocks as well as government bonds. Sixteen networked securities trading centers with broadcast and screen facilities have been established around China. In 1993 these received new fiber optics and satellite communication systems which replaced dedicated telephone lines. Communications are now supported by an optical fiber network throughout the city of Shanghai. A combination of local fiber loops, dedicated satellite communication systems (using the AsiaOne satellite for communications linkage) and telephone lines offers two-way communication with 3,000 trading counters in over 300 cities around China. There are roughly five million investors around China, and around half of the monetary trading volume originates outside of Shanghai.

The exchange floor has gone through substantial changes in its first decade. It has supported as many as 6,000 seats (i.e., booths with microcomputers and telephones) spread over eight trading halls, representing the 500+ authorized financial institutions who are members of the exchange. Firms must have registered capital of more than RMB 5 million to be members. The new 27-floor exchange building in the PuDong (literally: Shanghai East) area of Shanghai will dedicate all space from the ground up to the ninth floor to exchange operations. The exchange floor in PuDong holds 1,700 traders on a floor double the size of Tokyo's and triple the size of Hong Kong's floor. Most business, though, is conducted off the floor, through terminals and automated matching, and floor brokers spend a disproportionate time reading their newspapers. The floor provides no formal trading or market-making functions. It provides a focal point for market management and supervision, and for market sentiment. Li Quian, an exchange official, explains that "It is also a symbol of Shanghai's success."[7]

To facilitate transparency of market activities, the communications network automatically disseminates trading information:

1. to the Exchange's trading room display (a large digital screen on the trading floor),

2. to a telephone inquiry network for people not on the trading floor,

3. to over 20 news organizations, TV and radio stations,

4. to Reuters, Telerate, and other global financial services, and

5. publishes a newspaper, *Shanghai Security*, with a circulation of several hundred thousand.

There are 1,000 minor satellite downlink stations, and one major uplink station in PuDong. In brokerage rooms in Shanghai and other major cities in China, satellite systems typically provide backup order placement functionality in case telephone lines are not operable. In remote parts of China, such satellite systems are the sole communication channel allowing investors to participate in the trading of securities listed on the Shanghai Stock Exchange. Since 1993, the state has encouraged individuals and institutions outside of Shanghai to participate in securities listed on the Shanghai Stock Exchange, which it would like to truly be a national exchange. There are currently more transactions posted by traders outside than inside Shanghai.

The exchange actually engages two systems vendors to provide software and services for the collection and dissemination of trading information. They provide basically the same service. Since customers can choose either one, this provides considerable incentive for both vendors to maintain their quality of service and sophistication of software.

China's Securities and Exchange Commission worked to insure reliability of disseminated information. It has installed stringent controls over the information reported by companies, and has prohibited the accounting profession from certifying forecasts of corporate performance.

Information on all transactions is also transferred to the exchange's market monitoring group, which attempts to control insider trading, rumors, and collective efforts to control prices. First priority in automation of exchange functions has gone to the A shares. B shares are purchased in dollars, though denominated in *renminbi*, and information on those shares is broadcast in both English and Putonghau (literally "the common language," the standard spoken Chinese today). Thus additional systems development is required in supporting B shares.

Trading

As with other securities exchanges, many of the trading decisions take place outside of the stock exchange, in the offices of large securities firms. China's securities firms have been hard put to keep up with the demand for stocks. Volume rapidly increased after 1992, fueled by the wealth of Chinese businessmen looking for higher returns than banks were able to offer. Participation extended even to peasants from mountain areas, who were keen to purchase quick turnover of shares in the market called *zha-gu*, or "stir-fry" stocks. Connected to the markets by computer, fax, and telephone, investors outside the two exchange cities now outnumber those inside, despite the rudimentary development of China's telecommunications. The influx of new investments has caused Shanghai's volume to surge over the past three years.

Limit, buy, and sell orders are put into a database on the central data server, which is responsible for matching orders when buy and sell prices cross. The system is able to automatically distribute dividends and handle payment for subscription of new stocks of listed companies. The system transmits settlement price and volume to brokerage rooms around China via a combined digital data network (DDN), satellite (downlink for dissemination, uplink for trading information), and backed up by an analog telephone-modem system. All communication is computer-to-computer.

Chinese securities laws impose some order on the off-floor brokerage function. Brokers are required to comply with customers' explicit terms for transactions conducted on their behalf, including (1) type of security, (2) volume of trade, (3) bidding conditions and margin level, and (4) time of authorization. To prevent insider trading, employees of securities authorities, managers of the securities exchanges, employees of the broker handling the transaction, and employees of the governmental agency regulating or controlling the issuing company are prohibited from trading in its shares (Zhao and Li 1992). Compliance with these guidelines is enforced by a monitoring department and a compliance department (i.e., investigation) in the exchange organization.

Seats in the Shanghai Stock Exchange are classified as "real" and "virtual." Virtual seats are either remote terminals or handsets that are connected to the matching software through DDN, satellite uplink, or analog telephone link. There exist 1,000 low-bandwidth satellite uplinks for posting orders remotely, and one broadbank satellite uplink (in Pudong at the Shanghai Stock Exchange) to disseminate bid, ask, and settled trade prices and volumes.

Order placement security is enabled by either a touch tone or a magnetic card verification system. The touch tone system requires the cashier/broker to enter trader identification, security code, password, limit price, and quantity of the buy or sell order. The magnetic card system (i.e., a standard-sized credit card for stock transactions) enters trader identification and security code automatically, requiring keying only of password, limit price, and quantity of the buy or sell order.

A magnetic card system is provided by the Shanghai Stock Exchange and provides an additional level of security over trading. Individuals wishing to trade in the Shanghai Stock Exchange need to procure a magnetic security card from the exchange. This card uniquely identifies the trader's account with the exchange. The exchange handles its own transfer/clearing accounting. Through this account identification, traders can obtain information about their account position from the exchange.

Banks and brokerage houses issue separate debit cards which allow traders to buy and sell without exchanging cash. These reflect account balances with the bank.

Traders who do not have a security card can trade, with the broker acting on their behalf. Some banks incorporate the security card number and information into the debit card. Not all brokers have a direct connection to the exchange. Particularly in remote areas of China, brokers need to dial into their seat on the floor (or through satellite uplink) to place orders. Even in Shanghai, some brokerage firms insist on their own staff dialing for traders, even if the traders can directly place orders with the exchange. This provides an additional layer of security and control over trading.

Markets in most countries over the past decade have invested significantly in automation of various components through database and communications technologies.[8] Without automation, markets are constrained to operate at the speed of their human facilitators—frequently too slow for complex or high-volume market services, and too localized for a large country like China. In order to speed transaction processing, automated markets may be stripped of all but market-matching functions, and other functions dispersed to brokers, clearinghouses, and similar operations. In keeping with this trend, the Shanghai Stock Exchange has developed their own proprietary software for matching and price discovery, whose only function is matching and detection of price crosses.

Probably the greatest concern of Shanghai Stock Exchange management today is efficiency of operations. With some restrictions, this means providing—at the lowest possible price—a level of exchange service to investors commensurate with other bourses around the world. Many companies listed in Shanghai's A and B markets have also become interested in listing in Hong Kong's exchange (with judiciously named H shares) and in the New York Stock Exchange (extending the analogy with N shares), opening new venues for capital-hungry concerns.

Chinese exchanges are designed to provide floor trading and settlement facilities, to supervise members and listed companies, and to be sources of market information. But their power over listing selection is very limited.[9] Listing a company on the Shanghai Stock Exchange is strongly influenced by forces external to the exchange, a situation that creates some problems with responsibility and control for the Exchange. The State Council, China's most powerful political body, reigns over the entire process, through its Securities Policy Committee, chaired by vice-premier and People's Bank of China governor. Under the governor lies the China Securities Regulatory Commission. The Shanghai and Shenzhen Exchanges are subordinate to the CSRC.

Shanghai recognizes only one public market and no private placement market. The authority in charge has full discretion in granting the right to publish issuance of shares, leaving the applicant company uncertain of the outcome. Once a company obtains the right to issue, however, no restriction is placed on its listing as long as the issuer has more than RMB 1 million in registered capital, a positive book value in the previous two years, and more than 300 identifiable shareholders, with more than 10% of the shares in public hands.

Obligations for disclosure include issuance of a prospectus for securities, semiannual and annual financial reports—the basic information most investors expect to receive. Because of differences in Western and Chinese accounting practices, reporting may still be perceived as inadequate. Application for public issuance is submitted to the local branch of the People's Bank of China (the authority in charge of securities administration). False disclosure is punishable by a fine between RMB 100,000 and RMB 200,000 (US$12,000 to US$24,000) plus damages to third parties (Zhao and Li 1992).

Brokerage Rooms

A particularly exciting innovation in Chinese securities trading in recent years has been the introduction of neighborhood brokerage rooms to encourage the investment of funds by China's people, who have one of the highest savings rates in the world. The immense popularity of trading counters and brokerage rooms in China has done much to abate liquidity shortages that dogged the market until recently.[10] Until the widespread installation of trading rooms, China's securities markets suffered from a lack of capacity to absorb large buying or selling pressure without causing severe adverse price movements.

China's investment banks rely on a clever mix of appropriate technologies cost effectively delivered to bring their services to the people. Brokerage rooms provide just the right amount of technology for a country with straggling telecommunications infrastructure and few PCs. Electronic investment technology is brought close to every home, but not into it. Investors meet in a pleasant and convivial neighborhood atmosphere. In China, as elsewhere, more is not always better. Appropriate technology is intelligently embraced which fits the customer and the tasks at hand.

Small investors are served in a large hall crowned with an electronic bulletin board broadcasting the latest securities prices. In the front of the hall are windows through which clerks can process buy or sell orders for listed securities. The bank also provides software for technical analysis of securities prices on computers at the front counter. Over 50 algorithms for technical analysis may be called up in the software; moving averages and other cycle analysis can be customized by the user.

Major investors—those with over RMB 500,000 in the market—are treated to their own desks and computers (complete with technical analysis software) in one of several rooms cloistered within the maze of halls leading from the main brokerage room. Despite the greater stakes, the unique and convivial atmosphere of investing still permeates these rooms. Though orders could be posted directly to the stock exchange's electronic matching system directly by these computers, the China Commercial Bank chooses to act as an intermediary. A secretary is provided for each of the VIP rooms, and actually places buy or sell orders at the request of the investors. Besides providing a professional touch for the customer-investor, this also provides the bank with an additional modicum of control.

Trading Operations

Over their five years of operations, China's securities markets have developed a surprisingly sophisticated palette of technologies for execution, monitoring, and reporting. Order placement security is currently enabled by either a touch tone or magnetic card verification system. The touch tone system requires the cashier/broker to enter trader identification, security code, password, limit price, and quantity of the buy or sell order. An identification card system identifies a trader, and allows trades with only the input of password, limit price, and quantity of the buy or sell order.

The exchange has established a monitoring department to assure that trading remains in a "normal" range commensurate with the underlying value of the company's security, and supervises substantial market players. A compliance department is responsible for investigation of questionable activities uncovered during monitoring.

Settlement and Payments

Clearing and settlement are the responsibility of a wholly owned subsidiary of the Shanghai Stock Exchange—the Shanghai Securities Central Clearing and Registration Corporation. Central depository, trades, and clearing are all paperless. There is no need to print a physical copy of the security, as a database is maintained of ownership of all shares.

The Shanghai Stock Exchange uses a three-tiered clearing and settlement system. The first tier involves investors who have a magnetic account card to clear through their bank. The second tier handles the transactions between these banks and Shanghai Securities Central Registration and Clearing. The third tier allows securities trading centers and "registered companies" (i.e., banks) in other parts of China to clear through Shanghai Securities Central Registration and Clearing.

Along with traditional plastic and magnetic strip credit cards, Chinese banks also issued debit cards, and "smart" versions of both debit and credit cards. "Smart cards" are credit-card-sized plastic cards containing an embedded microcomputer that has been programmed to function as an "electronic purse." Card operations eschew central monitoring and control of transactions. This is very much in line with Asian business's fondness for cash. While the West gravitated toward purchases on credit, through cards or installments, most transactions in China are still handled in cash.

China Commercial Bank successfully introduced China's first smart debit card using technologies which had been introduced previously be U.S. and European banks. The combination of microcomputer chip and magnetic strip gives the card both extensive data storage capability—useful for maintaining account balances and personal information—and computational ability, which have allowed an unprecedented level of privacy and security in banking.

The bank's card has a built-in calculator, can be locked using a cryptographic key, and can be plugged into a computer terminal. The cards can be reloaded (with cash) through automated teller machines (ATMs) and, eventually, enabled telephones. A balance reader can be used to check the value remaining. Transfer between cards is enabled by an electronic wallet, transfer from a bank account to the card-chip by an ATM machine or by a specially equipped telephone.

The typical smart card payment is small, often spent at newsstands and fast food outlets, and on public transport systems. Higher-value transactions occur in supermarkets and petrol stations. Because of the low transaction costs possible with an onboard microprocessor, the smart debit card is appropriate for the more modest incomes of China. Overall, the smart cards reflect the intelligent and pragmatic application of state-of-the-art technology to meet China's unique needs.

A smart card purchase begins with placing the debit card into a terminal. A number of steps insure that the transferred value reaches the correct destination and that fraud does not take place:

1. Registration: Information from the customer's chip card is validated by the shopkeeper's card stored in the terminal, and vice versa.

2. Value transfer: The shopkeeper's terminal requests payment of a certain amount, and transmits a digital signature with the request. Each card checks the authenticity of the other's message.

3. The customer's card checks the digital signature and, if satisfied, sends the amount, with its own digital signature attached. At this point, the value is deducted from the total value on the customer's card.

4. The chip card in the shopkeeper's terminal checks the digital signature and, if satisfied, sends acknowledgment, again with a digital signature.

5. Only after the amount has been deducted from the customer's card is value added to the card in the shopkeeper's terminal. This prevents the possibility of duplication

or unauthorized creation of value. The digital signature from this card is checked by the customer's card. If valid, this ends the process.

6. If at any point a check fails, e.g., because of a power failure, the protocol is designed to continue automatically and complete the transaction if possible, e.g., once power is restored. If this is not possible it automatically records a detailed log of the failed transaction.

Security is enhanced by the use of smart cards, and this fact is not lost on bank management. Fraud involving banknotes and coins can take place through the use of adequate forgeries produced with relatively inexpensive technology. With smart card technology, a perfect forgery of the card and its resident information is required. If a forgery of the chip or the cryptography is not perfect, it will fail. China Commercial Bank's system for completing person-to-person digital cash transactions assures that it is neither necessary nor possible to track and record details of personal transactions. Users are assured a level of privacy similar to currency-based transactions because the bank does not track the movement of e-cash after it is issued to consumers. Its decentralized chip-on-card system allows essential information to be kept on the card, and out of central databases, insuring a high degree of privacy, portability, and security.

Opportunities and Challenges

The Shanghai Stock Exchange has identified seven areas as significant challenges over the next several years:

1. Transaction cost control (to blunt competition from other markets)
2. Competition from other exchanges
3. Growing volume
4. Futures products
5. International trading clients and telecommunications
6. Foreign funds management
7. Convergence of B share technology and operations with that of A shares

The first two items are crucial to success, and increasingly tied to each other. The Shanghai Stock Exchange has emphasized efficiencies and appropriate technology in its operations, because these ultimately determine the price (i.e., commissions) at which the exchange can offer its services. With relatively few issues available to foreigners, and with the potential for well-managed Chinese firms to list on larger, more liquid exchanges such as the Hong Kong or New York Stock Exchanges, the challenges to the Shanghai Stock Exchange are significant. American Depository Receipts and N shares on the New York Stock Exchange and H shares on the Hong Kong Stock Exchange both pose challenges to the exchange by allowing investors often more convenient avenues to acquiring ownership of Chinese firms.

Firms are motivated to list with Chinese exchanges both because of significant differences between Western and Chinese accounting which are expensive to reconcile, and as a way to tap into the substantial savings of local Chinese, who have one of the highest rates of personal savings in the world. Chinese companies are recognized by Chinese, who may have relatives working for the listed company or may have dealt with the company themselves. This level of brand recognition is not available to Chinese firms listing outside of China.

Accountants are the main source of quality and performance information about the products sold in securities markets. Information disclosure in China may differ substantially from comparable Western statements, because of differences between Chinese accounting principles and generally accepted accounting principles (GAAP). Reconciliation of the two standards can be daunting, as illustrated by the case of Brilliance China Automotive Holdings. Brilliance decided to list on the New York Stock Exchange in 1992. Conversion of its financial statements to GAAP required the investment of over 11,000 man hours by Arthur Andersen, Brilliance's accountants, before their statements met the requirements of the New York Stock Exchange.[11] The adoption of Western software packages for automating corporate accounting and for providing reports of financial performance would greatly improve investor's assessments of fairness and, by lowering investors' perception of market risk, could increase liquidity.

Despite the central role of computers in matching, electronic brokerage transaction systems in China are still in their infancy. This reflects the rudimentary state of telecommunications, which makes transmission of voice (let alone data and fax) difficult in much of China. Out of the 800,000 recognized villages in China, 500,000 lack even one telephone. Electronic transactions systems bring reliability, increased size of the client base, and speed of access to the market. This gives liquidity and consequently the ability to pass on risk to the market rapidly. Their ability to link into a settlement system reduces transaction costs.

In the related banking sector, banks have been undergoing a technological revolution. Electronic transfer of funds, the use of automatic tellers, the transmission of accounting records through telecommunications, and the offering of a full range of banking services are moving retail banks into the modern world. This should provide a positive impetus to the integration of China's investment banking, brokerage, and market functions into global financial networks.

Until the widespread installation of trading rooms, the Shanghai Stock Exchange's market suffered from a lack of depth—i.e., the capacity to absorb large buying or selling pressure relative to the average size of transactions without causing severe adverse price movements. Lack of depth was most apparent in the early 1990s, when demand for shares far outstripped supply and prices were highly volatile. Demand was influenced by rapid economic growth in the south and by the chance given to savers to diversify their savings away from bank accounts.

Over the coming year, the contrasts of investment technology offerings in China and other world bourses are likely to provide an interesting mix of old and new. As this technology evolves the customer will be the ultimate winner in the automation of the China's securities business.

Notes

1. Nominal GDP was US$660 billion in 1996.

2. Two-Year Economic Outlook: China. *Business Asia*, 28(17), August 26, 1996, p. 9.

3. W. A. Thomas, Emerging Securities Markets: The Case of China, *Journal of Asian Business*, 9(4), Fall 1993, p. 90–109.

4. P. B. Potter, Securities Markets Opening to Foreign Participation, *East Asian Executive Reports*, April 1992, p. 7–9.

5. *Guide to Bond Markets 1994—China*, Springfield Financial Advisory Limited.

6. *AsiaMoney*, October 1995, p. 15–20.

7. Capitals of Capital, Survey, *The Economist*, May 9, 1998.

8. Securities markets applying some level of automation have appeared in one form or another for almost 100 years, e.g., stock tickers have provided automated real-time reporting of securities prices for nearly a century. Recent developments in computer and communications technology have made plausible the complete automation of market functions. The ultimate form that these electronic markets will take is still being defined.

9. Bulls Go Wild in a China Shop, *Euromoney*, October 1994, p. 56.

10. Varying Fortunes of China Chips, *Euromoney*, March 1996, p. 15.

11. H. Sender, Pin-Striped Pioneers, *Far Eastern Economic Review*, November 12, 1992, p. 59.

References

Ametz, A. W. The Role of Financial Reform and Development in China's Economic Reform and Development, *Journal of Asian Economics*, 2(2), 1991, p. 337–371.

Bears in a China Shop, *The Economist*, May 14, 1994, p. 75.

China Stock Market Year Book, 1994, 1995.

Euromoney, Bulls Go Wild in a China Shop, October 1994, p. 56.

Euromoney, Varying Fortunes of China Chips, March 1996, p. 15.

Forresal, R. P. China's Financial Markets, *Journal of Asian Economics*, 6(2), 1995, p. 267–274.

Glorious Five Years: The Official History of the Shanghai Stock Exchange. Shanghai: Shanghai Stock Exchange, 1996.

Potter, P. B. Securities Markets Opening to Foreign Participation, *East Asian Executive Reports*, April 1992, p. 7–9.

Prystay, C. Easing off the Brakes. *Asian Business*, 32(8), August 1996, p. 24–26.

Sender, H. Pin-Striped Pioneers, *Far Eastern Economic Review*, November 12, 1992, p. 59.

Shanghai Stock Exchange Annual Report, Shanghai: Shanghai Stock Exchange, 1995.

Shanghai Stock Exchange Brochure, Shanghai: Shanghai Stock Exchange, 1996.

Thomas, W. A. Emerging Securities Markets: The Case of China, *Journal of Asian Business*, 9(4), Fall 1993, p. 90–109.

Two-Year Economic Outlook: China. *Business Asia*, 28(17), August 26, 1996, p. 9.

Xu, L. L. China's Financial Reform in the 1990s, *Journal of Asian Economics*, 2(2), 1991, p. 353–351.

Zhao, J., and Q. Li. Trading Stocks in China, *East Asian Executive Reports*, June 1992, p. 7–12.

The Moscow Stock Exchange

Russia, a vast country with a wealth of natural resources, a well-educated population, and a diverse industrial base, continues to move forward from its old centrally planned economy to a modern market economy. The breakup of the U.S.S.R into 15 successor states in late 1991 destroyed many economic links. Most are now being replaced by a variety of business relationships fostered by the growth of Russia's private sector.

The paths that Russian and China have taken in their separate transitions from command to market economies contrast starkly. Russia has accepted a "shock treatment" sanctioned by Western banks and academics. China has opted for a managed approach, which has spared its people the harsh economic realities forced on the Russian people, but has left China with an underproductive state sector. Stock markets have been pivotal in both moves from centrally planned to market economies. The Moscow Stock Exchange's role in dismantling and privatizing the state sector provides an alternate example of how privatization can be managed.

History of Equity Trading in Russia

Shares in Russian firms were traded on the St. Petersburg Stock Exchange (now a Russian Naval Museum) from the latter part of the 19th century. Trading stopped during World War I, with free markets being abolished after the Bolshevik Revolution of October 1917. Under the next seven decades of Soviet rule, all production and commerce were centrally planned by the Communist government.

The Soviet economy was founded on heavy industry—on large-scale factories, smelters, refineries, extraction and processing of raw materials and natural resources. Much of Soviet budgetary allocation through the 1950s and 1960s was directed toward infrastructure development. The country formed a national electricity grid (now a joint stock company known as "Unified Energy Systems"), a gas exploration, drilling and refining behemoth (now the joint stock company "Gazprom"), a nationwide telecommunications system ("Svyazinvest" and "Rostelecom"), oil exploration and distribution corporations ("Lukoil" and "Surgutneftegaz," inter alia), car and truck manufacturers ("Logovaz," "Zil," and "Kamaz"), diamond and gold processing organizations, and so forth.

Through early 1992, all Russian Federation industrial enterprises were 100% government financed, controlled, owned and operated. Directors of the industrial enterprises were most often ex-government officials or regional business leaders with

This case was prepared by Martin Mendelson, CEO of Kitai-Rus Securities, Moscow, and J. Christopher Westland.

intimate government sponsors. Mikhail Gorbachev, as an example, was a Communist Party member, close friend and protégé of then Soviet General Secretary Yuri Andropov, and leader of the Stavropol region, a prominent agricultural and industrial area in southern Russia. Gazprom's chief executive through the 1980s, Viktor Chernomyrdin, was appointed Prime Minister of the Russian Federation in 1992 as was Security Council Leader Boris Berezovsky, owner of newspapers, a television station, auto dealerships, and an oil company. Western privatization consultants could have neither anticipated nor appreciated the depth and importance of connections between the post-Soviet public and private sector when they entered the world's largest privatization in late 1992.

Russian president Boris Yeltsin's government has rapidly moved to open markets since its economic reform program was launched in January 1992—by freeing prices, slashing defense spending, eliminating the old centralized distribution system, completing an ambitious voucher privatization program in 1994, establishing private financial institutions, and decentralizing foreign trade. The following year, the country's leaders—a group largely unschooled in modern business and management practice—entered a crash course in privatization. The privatization effort of the early 1990s was as unprecedented in size and scope as it was in the number of insider transactions that dominated the program. Enterprise directors and government officials "privatized" entire departments and factories, taking profitable assets for themselves and leaving the scraps for "outside" investors.

Nonetheless, the privatization effort was a success. The establishment of modern financial markets and the modernization of banking helped the nonstate sector to contribute approximately 75% of official GDP by 1997, up from 62% in 1994. This contribution may understate the true contributions from privatization. By some estimates, the official GDP figure of around US$700 billion (at purchasing power parity, with a bit over 10% contributed by exports) is only 50% of the actual GDP.[1] The underreporting of economic activity to avoid an inequitable tax system obscures actual income. Russians save 32% of their income (slightly short of the Chinese savings rate) while the Russian government consumes only 15% of the official GDP (compared to 30% of GDP in the United States). These amounts are comparable to state-sector consumption in China, where official figures understate GDP, and faulty tax collection is again to blame.

Market-based privatization helps markets to communicate supply and demand information in order to efficiently coordinate production and distribution of goods. Russia's privatizations sought these efficiencies through increased ownership and accountability for productive assets by firm management.

Vouchers: The Roots of Shareholding

Russian capital markets were created to raise capital for production through open and transparent markets for debt and equity. Capital markets allow investors to participate in management through share, voucher, and other ownership instruments, letting them accurately value an enterprise's productive assets. Until the creation of capital markets, the assets of state-owned enterprises were almost impossible to value, which in part led to the necessity of voucher programs which initiated the pricing of firm assets.

Russia's voucher privatization program was begun in mid 1993, concluding on July 1, 1994. A product of the Russian Federation Government Committee on Private Property (*GosKomImushchestvo*, or *GKI*), it was the system that directly led to the creation of secondary capital markets in Russia. It was the first step in correctly valuing the remnants of the Soviet productive plant. Privatization Director Anatolii Chubais boasted that the program "would enable millions of Russian residents to own shares in Russian enterprises, and would attract investment to restructure and reconstruct Russian industrial enterprises."[2]

Each voucher specified in which enterprise the recipient "owned" a share, and each voucher had a certain nominal price (similar to a bond). Vouchers represented an ownership stake in the company and possessed intrinsic value as secondary markets for voucher trading became available (vouchers in some Russian companies, when converted into shares one year later, increased in real value 5,000–10,000 times). Just before the commencement of the voucher program, the GKI organized a promotional campaign to educate the public regarding the merits of the voucher system. Jaded by investment scandals that had proliferated after the collapse of the Soviet state, voucher holders generally perceived these promotions as attempts to swindle them. This skepticism was soon borne out.

A dearth of economic information and communications allowed voucher holders in remote regions to be easily duped by friends, colleagues, and the companies for which they worked. They would be asked to hand over vouchers in exchange for food (sausages were popular) or in certain circumstances, for the promise of future, unspecified "dividends." In one particularly egregious case, Gazprom announced to residents of the Yamal Peninsula (an area with large natural gas reserves) that their voucher investment interests would be better represented by the Yamal Investment Fund (a fund controlled indirectly by majority shareholder Gazprom).[3] The residents were all employed by Gazprom, and had little alternative but to turn in vouchers— for a minimum period of three years to the Yamal Fund.[4]

Vouchers ultimately became stock shares at a voucher auction. Due to GKI's limited resources and enormous mandate, many voucher auctions were announced just days, or even hours, before an auction was scheduled to take place.[5] Auction locations were rarely announced, and auctions were often inaccessible to potential purchasers; many auctions were held on enterprise premises accessible only through special *propuska*, or entrance passes.[6]

Local governments could also influence the rate of exchange—a particular voucher might exchange for one share of the company at the Moscow auction; the same voucher could exchange for 100 shares in Vladivostok. This made it almost impossible for individuals without travel money or government ties to participate in the voucher auctions. In response to these restrictions on voucher exchange, voucher funds and markets emerged in early 1994 with the express purpose of buying vouchers from individuals. Voucher funds had to buy ownership shares at open auctions, which, as a rule, "featured much higher share prices than the closed auctions through which insiders were able to purchase shares."[7]

Voucher funds' ability to influence enterprise performance depended on a number of factors, including management compliance with new policy, management disclosure practice, and support by local and regional government officials. Without access to financial information, voucher funds were severely restricted in their evaluative capacity—a significant liability for an instrument which was intended to value enterprise assets. Given voucher funds' relatively small ownership stakes, the funds also often required the cooperation of other shareholders in order to put forward new policies.[8]

Voucher funds' alternative to attempting to influence enterprise performance under an existing ownership arrangement was to trade the voucher/shares. Frydman, Pistor, and Rapaczynski reported that "funds reporting that they actively trade on the secondary market for enterprise shares amount to 57% of the total number of funds, and 25% of funds' companies are traded on average."[9] Most funds traded privately and through local or regional exchanges. Participants in trades were mainly other voucher funds, suggesting a limited, fairly illiquid, and controlled market. Trading among voucher funds tended to consolidate a particular fund's holdings in specific enterprises. While a consolidation of holdings may have increased a fund's ability to influence enterprise management, a fund's potential influence was ultimately limited "by the size of the stakes that the state and insiders hold and their willingness to consider divestiture."[10]

Oddly, voucher/share prices tended to be least expensive for the largest and most profitable enterprises. In an efficient and open market, one would expect the opposite

—share prices would be highest for the most sought-after enterprise shares. However, the larger the enterprise in Russia, the greater the level of control exercised by management over share prices and voucher auctions.[11] Larger enterprises often restricted employees from selling shares to outsiders, restricted reregistration (*pereregistratsiya*) of shares, and made selling shares by individuals and enterprises all but impossible by employing local tax authorities to monitor individual and bank account transactions.

These and other measures made purchase and sale of vouchers by so-called outsiders practically impossible. *Outsiders*—also known as *undesirable shareholders*—are individuals and enterprises unrelated to the given firm, such as banks, investment funds, and foreign investors.[12] Private owners of industrial enterprises in developed market economies are primarily outsiders, and insider ownership is relatively insignificant. In contrast to developed market economies and leading transition economies in Central Europe and Southeast Asia, private owners in the Russian Federation and China are generally insiders. Commercial entities in Russia and China holding majority outside ownership stakes also have on average very significant insider ownership stakes.[13]

Russian outsiders tended to favor active involvement in corporate governance and management accountability. They were likely to support the stripping and sale of unproductive assets, streamlining staff and operations, and other actions which might tend to increase their wealth. For the entrenched *apparatchiki* of former state firms, such meddling was odious.[14]

Immediately following the voucher program's conclusion in July 1994, Russia launched its controversial loans-for-shares program. The loans-for-shares program provided banks with ownership stakes in enterprises in exchange for short-term loans to the government. Russia transferred portions of enterprises which the government had already supposedly privatized into the hands of banks that were able to assist the government in paying off overdue salaries, pensions, and social subsidies. The most efficient firms came to be run by their banks as creditors became interested in direct management of the assets in which loans were invested. In some cases this was a defensive move by bankers to dismantle various social welfare obligations—e.g., schools, retirement income, and so forth—which firms incurred under the Soviet state, and were unwilling to relinquish even after de facto privatization.

Loans for shares allowed bankers to cheaply acquire control of some of the best remnants of the Soviet state plant. The banking-industrial conglomerates that ultimately resulted came to be known as financial industrial groups (FIGs). By 1997, Russia had successfully privatized 90% of its industry, and seven FIGs dominated the major industries brought forth from that privatization.

Capital Markets

In 1994, during the early days of equity trading, Russia's market consisted of brokers and dealers with stock shares, vouchers, and other privatization certificates. Price search was conducted over the telephone and fax (reminiscent of the over-the-counter market that preceded the United States' National Association of Securities Dealers Automated Quotations system) and by traveling to distant regions by plane, train, and sometimes even on foot. In 1994 and 1995, a broker's trip to a distant region where shares of Lukoil or Rostelecom were being sold at below-market prices by local residents (and, occasionally, by company officials), could net a 100% return on purchased shares merely from transporting them to Moscow. This may mark one of history's extreme cases in a liquidity-driven market. Improved market efficiency from automation dropped that geographic-liquidity-induced return to around 20% by 1997. As equity trading became more regulated, and information spread to the regions through paper and Internet information bulletins from 1995 on, brokers and traders moved to computerized trading systems such as the Russian Trading System and AK&M (similar to the NASDAQ).

Despite the large size of Russia's economy, total capitalization of shares listed on the Moscow Stock Exchange still amounts to only around US$100 billion in 1997 (up from around $20 million two years earlier). Though Russia's market capitalization is roughly that of China's stock markets, turnover is less than one-twentieth of China's.

By 1997, a host of computerized systems existed in Russia's investment houses to process trades actively and effectively. While no singular system dominated the Russian market, larger investment houses were focusing on system implementation as trading volumes doubled and tripled. At Renaissance Capital, Russia's premier investment bank (headed by former CSFB Russia Director Boris Jordan), for example, ten Sun Microsystems servers running proprietary software processed trades and analyzed positions for the company. Dealer boards—electronic devices that allowed equity traders to hold several telephone conversations at once—were installed in early 1997.[15] Renaissance had a telephone system of 450 lines for its equity traders, with a Western-style trading floor with raised steel floors overlying high-bandwidth communications lines.

Most Western brokerage and trading houses import their own systems and procedures from the United States or Europe. In contrast, Russian banks prefer to keep their proprietary information technology closed to outsiders. Russia has a well-educated workforce that excels in technical products such as software. By keeping systems and data feeds proprietary, banks can keep outsiders from knowing secrets that they believe provide them with a competitive edge.[16]

Financial statements of listed firms typically are stated under both Russian accounting standards and international accounting standards (similar to U.S. generally accepted accounting principles). Russian accounting standards are claimed to provide more accurate accounting under inflation, or when asset valuation is ambiguous, as it is in an economy that still settles 40% of its industrial purchases through barter. Both Russian and Western banks use Russian accounting software packages, the two major packages provided by Diasoft and Program Bank.[17]

Early optimism ultimately gave way to incredulity, as investors found that markets lacking an accurate quality assessment function such as the highly regulated audit profession in the United States could not automatically generate correct valuations of assets. Indeed, without proper corporate audits, Moscow's Stock Exchange actually encouraged the misstatement of asset values. After four years in operation, the Exchange listed many companies that were overvaluing their output by a factor of two to three for barter transactions, and up to fivefold for sales made against promissory notes.[18] In the absence of true price information, it was impossible to determine which firms created value, and which destroyed it.

In contrast to more developed markets where settlement and clearing are instantaneous processes linked to price search, Russian back-office software "has to deal with a market in which completing a trade [often requires] sending a courier to *Surgut* to get the trade recorded in the company register."[19] Furthermore, equity traders require *at least* one other employee in the back office to register trades, obtain stamps and seals, and comply with mountains of government regulations.[20]

Russia's market-regulating authorities fully understand and acknowledge the difficulties trading and brokerage houses face in a market dominated by telephone trade. According to Skate Press and several Moscow brokerages, at least 60% of trades are completed over the telephone and not registered with regulatory bodies. Furthermore, much of this trade takes place "offshore," making trade tracking all the more difficult. This creates a major problem for both market makers and investors, as actual trading (market) prices often differ significantly from published (recorded) prices. As an example, for most of early August 1997, recorded trade volume for Gazprom averaged 100,000 shares traded per day. Actual trade volume, according to several Moscow-based brokers, was *at least* 20 times that amount.[21] Because settlement of trades (a paper-based system) takes place independently of price negotiation and discovery (automated on the computers of the stock exchanges), prices can be manipulated and published on the exchange without actual trades ever taking place.

Since 1996, Russia's equity market infrastructure has developed significantly, with rules for market participants created and implemented by the National Association of Securities Market Participants (NAUFOR). NAUFOR was created by major market participants to establish a regional and national trading system and develop market infrastructure. NAUFOR has grown to become a countrywide, self-regulating broker/dealer association with more than 400 members.[22]

Unfortunately, regulation of Russia's equity market still suffers from major abuses. These are exacerbated by poor monitoring and a settlement system which is not linked to the price discovery systems of the Moscow Stock Exchange. A recent article on Russian securities firms recounts the following tale. Johnny Manglani, an Indian tailor and amateur investor lost more than $100,000 on the Russian market. He says he is less bothered by the loss than the way his broker helped him lose it. Manglani's side of the story goes as follows. Late one night in early March 1998 Charles Shearer of the Moscow investment house Rinaco Plus called with bad news: Sberbank preferred stock, which Manglani had bought the previous year at $4.80 per share, was down to $1.70 and would shortly fall to $0.30. Manglani wanted to hold on, but claims that Shearer, who had not previously taken much interest in his trades, kept calling until he agreed to sell. Soon after, Sberbank preferred jumped to $2.15.[23]

This is just one of many broker abuses common in Russia. Insider trading is rampant. Laws exist, but are seldom enforced. Other widespread practices are

• *Price manipulation.*   Because the Moscow Stock Exchange does not handle settlement, 80% of trade in Russian shares happens outside the exchange, and investors are often left at the mercy of their broker to tell them how much a given stock really costs on a given day.

• *Favoring the house.*   Many of Russia's biggest houses do a lot of trading on their own account, known as the "proprietary book." When the traders want to get out of something, they tell their clients that it is a great buy.

• *Front-running.*   In a market as illiquid as Russia's, one big trade can send a stock's price soaring. A broker can first buy a little for the proprietary book, or for himself, then profit when the price rises on the client's purchase order. Brokers can also front-run on research reports.

• *Research flogging.*   In an up market, brokerages come out with glowing reports on companies in which they already have stakes. For example, the brokerage house Aton issued a report in September 1997 recommending the previously obscure Kazan Helicopter Factory. Aton analyst Nadeshda Golubeva noted that Aton took a "big stake" in the factory before even beginning research. Soon after Aton's report came out, the stock plunged, and by March 1998 was removed from the Russian Trading System.

Drawing the line between ethical and unethical behavior can be difficult in an emerging market such as Russia's. In a mature market such as the United States, when a bank's research department issues a buy recommendation on a formerly obscure company, clients can immediately purchase the shares through their brokers. In Russia, acquiring shares for such second-tier companies usually requires that someone physically travel to the company and buy the shares in cash from workers and other small shareholders, a process which can take weeks. Procurement can require brokers to drive long distances over dilapidated country roads, carrying millions of rubles along with a bodyguard or two. Moscow brokers need to start buying shares in advance so they will be available when the research report is published. In the United States this would be called front-running, but in Moscow, many fund managers are willing to pay a premium for this service.

Epilogue

On August 17, 1998, the Russian government defaulted on its own debt, ordered private borrowers to default on foreign loans, and abandoned its support for the ruble. The stock market, never liquid in the best of times, literally ground to a halt.

Many years earlier, Alexey, the main character in Dostoyevsky's book *The Gambler*, spoke for Russia when he explained:

We Russians do have great use for money, and so we are always very happy to come across such things as roulette, which can enable a man to become rich almost effortlessly within two hours.[24]

Russians were indeed very happy to have come across the invention of financial markets, which could enrich them just as effortlessly as roulette, without the incumbent risk. From 1994 to 1998 the Russian government raised around $45 billion from selling securities, while the Russian firms issuing these securities ran up debts of another $20 billion. During the same period, an estimated $60 billion left Russia as "flight capital," finding new homes in offshore accounts in the Grand Caymans and Bermuda.[25]

Many of the weaknesses in Moscow's Central Stock Exchange were symptoms of deeper faults that exposed Russia's worst inclinations. In the aftermath of the Russian privatization debacle, governments throughout Europe and Asia reconsidered the wisdom of open capital markets. Yet in Russia, it was not the concept of open capital markets that was to blame—it was their implementation through incomplete and flawed electronic trading systems. Three specific failings destroyed Russia's financial credibility:

1. De facto limitation of participation to a small circle of traders with inside information

2. Separation of price discovery and settlement operations, which allowed brokers wide latitude in manipulating posted market prices

3. Failure of listed firms to provide transparent information about the quality and profitability of their operations.

Had Moscow's Central Stock Exchange designed these problems out of their system prior to operation, the denouement might have been much different.

Notes

1. A. Shama, "Notes from Underground as Russia's Economy Booms," *Asian Wall Street Journal*, December 30, 1997. National income statistics are reported in *Asiaweek*, January 16, 1998, p. 51.

2. "Duma Debates on Privatization," *Kommersant*, No. 15, April 26, 1994, p. 37–38.

3. "Better to Buy Gazprom", *Kommersant*, No. 10, March 22, 1994, p. 32–34.

4. Ibid., p. 33.

5. Personal Interview with Mikhail Demin, Director, Fixed Income Trading, Your Financial Guarantor A/O, August 7, 1997, Moscow, Russia.

6. The gas industry was singularly notorious for restrictive voucher and share purchase measures. In a commentary on the gas industry's voucher program, *Kommersant*, a bimonthly Russian economic magazine, commented, "It seems as though no gas industry shares will be offered on the open market. Russia's gas industry has no desire to apportion ownership, not today, and not in the future."

7. "EDI Forum: Voucher Privatization Funds in the Russian Federation," World Bank Web Site, http://www.tomco.net/~edinp/fsu/funds.html

8. Ibid.

9. Roman Frydman, Katharina Pistor, and Andrezej Rapaczynski, "Investing in Insider-Dominated Firms: A Study of Voucher Privatization Funds in Russia," Oesterreichische Nationalbank Working Paper no. 21 (December 1995).

10. Ibid.

11. "Privatization of Voucher Investment Funds in Reflection: Most Important is Not Victory, but Participation", *Kommersant*, no. 5, February 15, 1994, p. 43–51.

12. *EDI Forum: "Ownership and Restructuring,"* World Bank Web Site, http://www.tomco.net/~edinp/fsu/ownres.html

13. Ibid.

14. *EDI Forum: "Ownership in Industry in Transition,"* World Bank Web Site, http://www.tomco.net/~edinp/fsu/inown.html

15. "VegaTech Seeks Market Serving Market-Makers," *Moscow Times*, June 17, 1997, p. III.

16. Ibid.

17. Ibid.

18. C. G. Gaddy, and B. W. Ickes, "Russia's Virtual Economy," *Foreign Affairs* (Sept./Oct. 1998) v.77(5), p. 53–67.

19. Ibid.

20. Personal Interview with Mikhail Demin, Director, Fixed Income Trading, Your Financial Guarantor A/O, August 7, 1997, Moscow, Russia.

21. Ibid.

22. Rinaco Plus Brokerage House Web Site, "Equity Index Methodology." http://win-www.fe.msk.ru/infomarket/rinacoplus/

23. M. Whitehouse, "Shortchanged on the Stock Exchange," *Russia Review*, May 8, 1998, reprinted from the Moscow Times.

24. F. Dostoyevsky, *The Gambler* (A. R. MacAndrew, translator) W.W. Norton & Company. Dostoyevsky, himself a compulsive gambler, wagered his own fortune on *The Gambler* manuscript. Under the pressure of a deadline from his publisher, who had won the rights to his entire prior work, Dostoyevsky dictated this book in less than a month to the star pupil of Russia's fist shorthand school (whom he subsequently married).

25. "The cash don't work," *Economist,* December 19, 1998, p. 120–112.

Electronic Securities Trading at the Bolsa de Comercio de Santiago

In our first century, we have become leaders in the stock market, with technological infrastructure that provides premier service to the customer. We have inherited a tradition of transparency, responsibility and efficiency that distinguishes us, placing us among the most important stock exchanges in the world.
—Bolsa de Comercio de Santiago 1993 *Annual Report*

1992 was an extraordinary year both for Chile and its largest and oldest stock exchange, the Bolsa de Comercio de Santiago (literally, Santiago's Commercial Stock Exchange). Nationally, Chile's economy grew at 10.4%, inflation was controlled at a reasonable (for Latin America) 12.7%, and unemployment was a low 4.4% at the end of 1992 among a population of 13 million people. In turn, during 1992 output grew 26.2%, and profits grew 7.5% for firms listed on the exchange. The Bolsa added 26 new firms, bringing its total number of listed firms to 232 at the end of 1992. The amount of transactions on the Bolsa grew 50.2% to over 17 quadrillion pesos (about US$40 billion) with much of that growth from fixed-income securities which represented 87.5% of all transactions (tables 8.1 and 8.2).

Yet challenges to the Bolsa's hegemony loomed. It faced stiff competition from the upstart Bolsa Electrónica, a completely electronic exchange started in 1989. The Bolsa Electrónica used a computer trading system very similar to the new electronic system developed for the Bolsa de Comercio. In just three years it had captured 30% of transactions in securities of listed companies, where virtually all of the companies listed on the Bolsa Electrónica were also listed on the Bolsa de Comercio. Thus the Bolsa Electrónica was cannibalizing transaction volume directly from the Bolsa de Comercio.

This trend worried Andres Araya, Manager of Trading Systems in the Information Systems Area of the Bolsa de Comercio, as well as Carlos Lauterbach, the system integrator who had designed the new electronic trading system to help the Bolsa de Comercio compete for business. The Bolsa's guiding policy was to fairly and transparently[1] provide access to and information about trading on the Bolsa. By any measure, the new system's implementation had been a success—it had been completed in 18 months without any disruption to trading, and it significantly improved the speed, reliability, and transparency of trading to the benefit of brokers using the Bolsa.

Success had fomented new demands by brokers. Many brokers resided in the exchange building, which possessed Ethernet network links providing much faster communications than existing 9600 baud lines. They were willing to pay the Bolsa considerably more for access to Ethernet links. But linking some brokers to fast

This case was prepared under a grant from the USC Center for International Business Education and Research by Associate Professor J. Christopher Westland.

Table 8.1
Comparative financial statements of the Bolsa de Comercio de Santiago, 1988 to 1992

Antecedentes financieros de Bolsa de Comercio
(cifras expresadas en miles de Pesos de Diciembre de 1992)

Cifras del balance	1988	1989	1990	1991	1992
Total activos	6.491.321	7.248.488	7.743.424	9.117.800	9.221.615
Patrimonio	6.117.247	6.884.207	7.376.320	8.104.786	8.704.312
Ingresos totales	3.844.115	4.782.492	4.686.644	5.992.788	4.963.813
Ingresos explotación	2.601.095	3.172.200	2.934.680	5.397.794	4.639.569
Utilidad operacional	1.237.862	1.586.766	1.092.680	3.269.669	2.110.790
Utilidad neta final	1.656.637	2.302.646	1.237.709	2.828.644	1.910.523
Utilidad neta final por acción	37.651	52.333	28.130	64.287	41.533
Indicadores financieros					
a) Liquidez corriente (veces)	6.3	8.8	6.8	3.6	5.9
b) Rentabilidad (%)					
Retorno sobre activos totales	25.5	31.8	16.0	31.0	20.7
Retorno sobre capital y reservas	37.1	50.3	20.2	53.6	28.1
c) Endeudamiento (%)					
Deuda total sobre patrimonio	6.1	5.3	5.0	12.0	5.9
d) Inversiones (%)					
Activo fijo sobre activo total	63.6	55.7	56.0	48.9	55.3

Table 8.2
Number of listed companies in the Bolsa de Comercio de Santiago, 1983 to 1992

Patrimonio bursátil y patrimonio contable de las sociedades inscritas en la Bolsa de Comercio de Santiago
(millones de pesos de diciembre de 1992)

AÑO	Numero de sociedades	Patrimonio bursatil (1)	Patrimonio contable (2)	Relacion bolsa libro
1983	211	1.174.594	3.019.487	0,39
1984	208	1.137.552	3.101.966	0,37
1985	215	1.230.340	3.947.378	0,39
1986	215	2.352.569	3.471.000	0,68
1987	211	2.891.979	4.147.209	0,70
1988	203	3.598.565	5.063.105	0,71
1989	213	4.800.921	6.138.065	0,78
1990	216	6.146.685	6.124.015	1,00
1991	223	11.895.632	6.857.661	1,73
1992	244	11.333.748	7.395.751	1,53

communications lines while leaving other brokers to trade on slower 9600 baud lines could create a caste system which would rob otherwise qualified brokers of business simply because of their location.

Even more divisive was the demand by brokers for the ability to "program trade"—to trade automatically relying on decisions made by software programs, using information gleaned from the Bolsa's electronic information feeds. Both problems presented significant challenges to the Bolsa's fairness policy, by allowing brokers who invested in information technology to "front-run" other traders, placing orders based on existing information faster through precedence in information processing speed.

Economic developments in Chile made these issues more pressing. The increase in the internationalization of the stock markets in Chile (in addition to domestic and internal perturbations) had significantly increased the volatility of stocks listed in the Bolsa de Comercio de Santiago. Market capitalization in 1994 was concentrated in 10 stocks (figure 8.1), and the IPSA (the stock price index of Bolsa de Comercio de Santiago) was experiencing significant ups and downs by that time. The market daily traded between 110 and 120 different stocks.

The issuance of American Depository Receipts (ADRs, i.e., deposits of money in the United States reflecting trading in the Chilean exchanges), which are actively traded in the United States, directed international attention toward the performance of Chilean shares. Traders increasingly represented the interests of large firms, pensions, and other institutions. The Bolsa served some 44 brokerage firms, in general representing large collective investing interests, especially Chile's huge and expanding pension funds. Velocity of trading increased, and decision making became more sophisticated. The growth of Chile's pension funds, which by law needed to invest in the Chilean economy, drove up share values, and further increased the market capitalization of stocks listed on the Bolsa.

This was a radical change from the Bolsa de Comercio of a decade earlier. The Bolsa had traditionally been dominated by small family traders with a managerial interest in the firms traded. Decision making was informal and "seat of the pants." Dramatic growth in the Chilean economy—particularly driven by exports of wood, copper, and financial and professional services—has fostered institutional interest in individual stocks and injected institutional capital into the market.

Fairness, in the sense that no trader could systematically gain an advantage over another trader by exploiting idiosyncrasies of the exchange mechanism, was particularly important in Chilean trading. Many of the traders traded on their own account, with family rather than institutional capital. Family traders would be less inclined to invest in information technology than institutions and brokers, and without the

LAS 10 "TOP" SEGUN PATRIMONIO BURSATIL
(13 / 05 / 94)

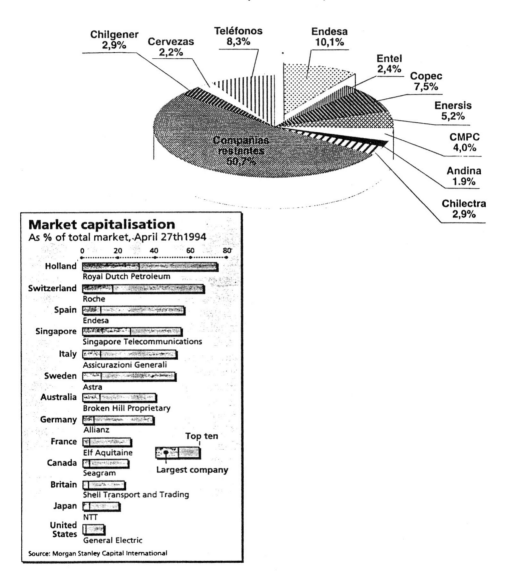

Figure 8.1
Market capitalization of largest firms as percentage of total market: Chile versus other markets

Bolsa's commitment to fairness, would be at a disadvantage. The Bolsa was legitimately concerned that this, in turn, might drive away their business.

So important was fairness to the Bolsa that they insisted on owning the PC terminals used by brokers, and tightly controlling the software residing on those PCs, assuring that no program trading was spirited onto the PC platforms. They recently sold their new computer trading system to the Cali exchange in Colombia, which supported trading in both Cali and Bogota. In order to assure fairness, trading in Cali was purposely delayed by a fraction of a second to equalize order posting delay originating from telephone-switching delays from Bogota 200 miles away.[2]

Markets Provided by the Bolsa de Comercio

The Bolsa de Comercio de Santiago provides markets for seven different classes of assets (table 8.3):

- Common stock (Mercado Accionario)
- Fixed-income securities (Mercado de Renta Fija)
- Commercial paper (Mercado de Intermediacion Financiera)
- Futures (Mercado de Futuros de IPSA, Mercado de Futuro de Dólar)
- Eurodollars (Mercado Monetario)
- Investment funds (Mercado de Cuotas de Fondos de Inversion)
- Gold (Mercado de Oro).

As with the exchanges in many smaller economies, a few large companies contributed a major part of the total market capitalization. The 10 largest Chilean companies contributed half of the Bolsa's capitalization. These included the major electric, telephone, petroleum, copper and beer suppliers (see figure 8.1).

The Bolsa provides specific market mechanisms directed toward specific types of market activity. It supports the following five market mechanisms for trading:

1. *Open outcry:* Open outcry is the traditional method for market trading in a "pit." This market is opened from 9:00 A.M. to 11:45 A.M. Monday through Friday. Here, for example, a trader enters the "stock" pit, shouts out a particular price to buy a number of shares, another trader shouts back acceptance of the price, constituting the consummation of a contract. The Bolsa de Comercio de Santiago is an auction market—i.e., a market in which buyers enter competitive bids and sellers enter competitive offers (asks) simultaneously—where the auctioneer in the pit determines the matching of bids and asks. In the Bolsa de Comercio, each of two pits (for two

Table 8.3
Transaction volumes in the Bolsa de Comercio de Santiago

Montos transados en la Bolsa de Comercio de Santiago—Promedio anual por Decenio 1930–1992
(*miles de pesos de diciembre de 1992*)

Periodo	Acciones	%	Intermediacion financiera	%	Renta fija	%	Monetarios	%	Futuros	%	CFI	%	Total
Decada 30	40.524.456	80	—	—	9.982.302	20	—	—	—	—	—	—	50.506.758
Decada 40	36.548.678	71	3.063.576	6	11.951.367	23	—	—	—	—	—	—	51.563.621
Decada 50	31.664.029	75	—	—	4.844.581	11	5.807.920	14	—	—	—	—	42.316.530
Decada 60	10.205.775	88	—	—	630.849	5	713.747	6	—	—	—	—	11.550.371
Decada 70	23.529.878	46	17.213.122	34	7.657.868	15	2.283.184	5	—	—	—	—	50.684.051
Decada 80	161.953.273	4	1.747.119.083	46	1.848.482.383	49	6.126.494	0	—	—	—	—	3.763.681.232
Decada 90	648.253.302	5	4.244.691.299	33	6.754.738.074	53	1.123.311.844	9	6.153.256	0	3.742.145	0	12.780.889.920

different groups of securities) is a four-meter circular open area (except for a central table with computer screen) surrounded by a one-meter-high wooden railing topped with green felt (thus the name for the trading area is *la sala de ruedas*, "the large room of circles/rings"). The auctioneer stands in the center of the pit, acknowledging and controlling the "outcries," and indicating when a transaction is complete. Scribes type an ongoing record of the pit proceedings into the computer to update the electronic record of trading. Matches are made at the judgment of the auctioneer, and are ostensibly based on time precedence for the crossing of the bid and ask prices. The market allows for market orders (i.e., orders to buy or sell a security at the best price possible after the order is presented to the trading crowd) and limit orders (i.e., orders to buy a security at a price no higher or to sell a security at a price no lower than the amount stated on the order). Trading activity in *la sala de ruedas* had, until 1992, been posted on a chalkboard; this was replaced by a large electronic display linked into the exchange's computer systems.

2. *Bulletin board:*   This auction system is used primarily for thinly traded stocks, where it may take several days for bids and asks to match. This was traditionally a chalkboard on which any listed company could post securities.

3. *Auction:*   This auction remains open for exactly five minutes, during which any collection of bids and asks can be posted. Matches are made based on best price, and time precedence is ignored.

4. *Direct order:*   This exchange allows person A to request to buy or sell directly from or to person B, but broadcasts the offer to see if there are others who would like to try to outbid either party.

5. *Electronic exchange:*   Bid and ask prices for given sized blocks of securities are posted to an electronic bulletin board. Matches are made based on time precedence, then best price whenever the bid and ask prices cross. Services on this exchange competed directly with those offered by the Bolsa Electrónica. The services offered by the Bolsa Electrónica were nearly identical to those offered by the electronic exchange on the Bolsa de Comercio, at roughly the same speeds.

Trading in options and other derivatives was planned. Because of disputes between the Bolsa and brokers over who should make the market (brokers did not want to provide the service) there was not yet a formal exchange. Several options were currently trading on the bulletin board—i.e., futures on the Chilean companies Endesa and CTC and on the Bolsa de Comercio's IPSA stock index.

The stock exchange was concerned about maintaining transparency of market activities. To this end, it supported a series of information dissemination activities to distribute information on a timely and accurate basis. The Bolsa published a series of informative brochures on various aspects of investing in the market, and on industries and firms represented in the market, including their Revista Tendencias Bursátiles (Market Trends Magazine). They issued a daily Boletín Bursátil, listing opening and closing prices, transaction volumes, and so forth, along with trimester and annual reports. This information was the basis for postings in daily newspapers.

As an integral part of their system to assure market transparency, the Bolsa provided a system of computers, microcomputer terminals (in brokers and Bolsa administrative offices) and television monitors which provide up-to-the-second information for investment decisions, drawing on the Bolsa's central databases. This terminal network provided information on price movements, price indices, income, historical and trend information on individual stocks, financial records, international price indices, interest and exchange rates, futures contracts, news, and other important information. Information from the Bolsa's central databases is communicated throughout the Bolsa and to banks, brokers, and governmental officials through a secure PBX (private branch exchange, a proprietary telephone system). In addition, the Fono Bolsa and Data Bolsa systems make price records from the Bolsa available through commercial telephone lines (through dial-up to a 700 number, which is the equivalent of a U.S. 900 number). Through this service, the Chilean telephone exchanges allowed the general populace access to the Bolsa's videotex services on televisions at home or the workplace; provided an automated *voice query* service for specific securities; and provided a "what if" capability through either voice or videotex to compute the value of an investor's specific portfolio. They also provided their Centro de Informatión Bursátil to handle voice queries on questions which investors could not answer through the other services.

The Electronic Trading System

Three years ago, electronic trading at the Bolsa de Comercio de Santiago was handled by an aging Wang system, which was responsible for reporting from, and, through intermediaries, posting transactions to the open outcry system. The new system was operational in January 1994, after 18 months of programming and testing by a team of four programmer/analysts under the direction of Dr. Carlos Lauterbach. Software was tested for six months prior to going on-line, by running simulations involving two to three days of actual transactions. These simulations compressed or expanded time to assure that the systems processing capacity was adequate to reliably handle worst-case scenarios. This gave the Bolsa de Comercio a credible challenge to stiff competition from the Bolsa Electrónica, the completely electronic exchange started in 1989. The Bolsa Electrónica and the Bolsa de Comercio provided very similar capabilities to traders.

To maintain its image of fairness, the Bolsa de Comercio rents out hardware and software services on the electronic exchange, forcing all transactions to be input through keyboards, and to be output through computer screens. The exchange mechanism is systematically leveled at the bottom—all clients have the same equipment and software, as well as the same communications line delays. This disallows "program trading"—i.e., the following of stock prices through electronic feeds, with posting of transactions by computer programs, expert systems, or artificial intelligence software which automatically looks for arbitrage or investment opportunities. Communications line delays are also tightly monitored, so that terminals, e.g., in the same building as the Bolsa, are not able to post their transactions more quickly than those further removed.

The electronic system captures trading that previously would have been handled through open outcry. By default, the open outcry system is fair—it is essentially self-regulating in this regard (though perhaps not efficient). It is the goal of the electronic exchange to capture that same image of fairness through sophisticated sets of trading policy implementations. The goal is to make the exchange systematically fair to all traders, and to avoid any features that would make the exchange systematically unfair—that is, reward some classes of traders at the expense of other classes of traders. For example, in the United States, issues of fairness have arisen concerning the National Association of Securities Dealers dealer-quote-driven NASDAQ system, which has traditionally exhibited wider bid-ask spreads than the competing order-driven New York Stock Exchange.

The Bolsa maintains a very sophisticated network for broadcast of market transactions and indicators through several services:

1. Continuous updates to Reuters news services through dedicated communications lines owned by Reuters

2. Dial-up modem services to personal computers

3. Videotex services to televisions at home or the workplace, provided by the Chilean telephone exchanges

4. An automated voice query service for specific securities

5. A "what if" capability through either voice or videotex to compute the value of a given portfolio

Technical Implementation of the Trading System

In both open outcry and electronic trading, the market provides a nexus for all offers and queries brought to the market. This presents the traders with a potential bottleneck. The electronic system relies on extremely fast on-line transaction processing (OLTP) by a Tandem Cyclone computer. In data servers (i.e., computers dedicated to "serving up" data records for update or reporting) such as the Tandem Cyclone, typically several CPUs (central processing units, the computing part of the computer, of which a desktop PC computer has only one) are required to achieve the desired processing performance. The Bolsa de Comercio de Santiago set as a benchmark that 95% of matchable transactions (i.e., where the bid and ask prices cross) could be completed on the Tandem within one second. In order to do this, the Tandem computer needed to be run at 40% of its peak load capabilities (a statistic established by the manufacturer Tandem Computers, Inc.). This required a Tandem computer with 6 CPUs to support 30,000 transactions per day (an average of 10 transactions per second) from 600 dedicated terminals in the offices of agents and brokers. In addition, the system needed to support the broadcast of stock market information (essentially a full-screen electronic ticker tape) through dial-up modem connections, and voice announcing provided through the equivalent of U.S. 900 numbers available through the telephone companies. Tandem processing was estimated to be linearly scalable[3] to about 300% of this performance, at a maximum configuration of 16 CPUs.

In traditional markets (including the open outcry market at the Bolsa de Comercio) this bottleneck is handled by breaking out trading by specific assets—i.e., certain stocks are traded only in one pit. This was tried in the electronic exchange. It failed to yield improvements in matching speed due to time clustering of trades in any given security or industry during the day, usually around the time of release of critical information such as financial reports.

The Matching Bottleneck

The Bolsa's greatest technical concern was the future scale-up that would be required if transaction growth continued to expand at 20–30% annually. This would outstrip the Tandem's processing capacity in around five years. Yet they knew that the New York Stock Exchange, using Tandem computers, was able to maintain similar performance standards, applying a more complex trading policy, for transaction volumes in the range of 1 million to 10 million transactions per day—30 to 350 times the current volume on the Bolsa de Comercio.

ECU and Software Decisions

The Tandem Cyclone was programmed in COBOL. In Chile, most programmers are COBOL programmers, since most work involves business transaction process (accounting systems),[4] and this places a distinct constraint on the nature of work that can be expected from them. To ease the labor problems associated with what was essentially a systems-level software task, Carlos Lauterbach developed the Event Control Utility (ECU) language to allow COBOL programmers to efficiently build the electronic trading system. ECU was programmed with:

1. A COBOL-like syntax to make programming easy for programmers with a majority of COBOL experience. In particular, event triggering was kept only in the kernel (interpreter)[5] and only screen designs and arithmetic functions were supported.

2. Small modules and efficient use of communications lines, since updating of software on dial-up clients in real time was often a consideration. When a remote user (e.g., from a brokerage office) dialed up to the exchange, he may not have been in communication for some time, and software updates may have occurred. The system needed to "sense" this, and immediately (in less than a second) update the software on the PC terminal. This could be done with small modules and a kernel. This update feature was another way of ensuring fairness by providing every user with identical software on his terminal.

3. Transaction processing and screen windows incorporated as an integral part of the syntax of the programming language. This required fewer lines and programmer decisions to be made to produce the trading system's program code.

With a varying set of around 600 terminals through which to process brokers' and agents' transactions, and open access to market information through dial-up modems to anyone with a telephone, the problem of software updates could become especially daunting. The users' software might be out of date, damaged, or missing. New users and terminals needed to gain access to software. In corporate situations, automatic downloads of software could be accomplished through dedicated communications lines at night, during off-business hours. Such downloads might take 30 minutes over dial-up lines, and could only be accomplished when the user dialed in. This would be an unacceptable delay for agents who needed to post transactions.

ECU solved this problem by breaking all of the client software (i.e., that residing on Intel-based PC terminals) into approximately 150 10,000-byte modules—small enough to download in approximately one second. A kernel resided on the client terminal, and on each logon of a terminal to the system, would determine if the client information was up to date and operational. If not, the necessary modules were downloaded from the Tandem.

The Bolsa electronic trading system's PC terminal kernel runs under Windows 3.1, coordinating the following client services:

1. Data delivery and formatting

2. Screen windows and information presentation

3. Algorithms for statistical analysis and reporting

4. Event triggers; these were purposely kept out of the ECU code, because COBOL programmers are not used to handling events,[6] only declarative code, e.g., for reading files, or writing reports.

In addition, terminals for the system could only be obtained from the Bolsa de Comercio. This insured that terminals were initially loaded with the kernel and a valid set of software modules. This provided an effective vehicle to level the playing field. The terminals provided from the Bolsa de Comercio locked out any possibility of program trading—offers needed to be entered from the keyboard, and transactions needed to be posted on the screen.

Security is maintained over the ability to post transactions by tracking specific terminals and where they are located, and insuring that both a password (i.e., an identification of the user) and the machine address (i.e., an identification of the computer and its location) were received by the Tandem server prior to accepting transactions. A tiered security system exists, managed by the Bolsa, which allows differing levels of security and different services for each individual and machine on the exchange network.

Splitting the Computational Workload

One of the most critical decisions in systems development for software spanning several machines is the scheme for splitting the workload between computers. The Bolsa had chosen to dedicate matching activities to the Tandem, broadcast activities (to Reuters, the Fono Bolsa, and other news reporting services) to the Sun, and transaction acquisition and real-time reporting to the PCs located in brokers' offices. Several factors are important in the Bolsa de Comercio system:

1. The constrained machine resource is the Tandem computer, which is the nexus for transaction matching. The Tandem should not be responsible for broadcasting

information on trades, volumes, and so forth. Broadcasts are required by the dial-up services offered over the telephone lines, as well as continuous updates to Reuters, and other news services.

2. The constrained resource for systems development is the programmers, who are skilled in COBOL programming, but know little of event triggering (e.g., posting an offer), or of software development for Intel PC client terminals.

3. The performance and reliability of the Intel PC client terminals may be uncertain, since they are in users' hands. Thus their responsibilities need to be limited to reporting status of offers and trades, and to input of transactions (offers or queries).

4. Cost issues were important. The six-CPU Tandem cost $1 million, depreciable over four years (mainly technological obsolescence). The client terminals were i286 or i386 PCs costing around $1,000 per terminal.

These constraints suggest that broadcast of information—such as that required by Reuters or the telephone voice and data broadcasts of market information—can be handled by neither the Tandem nor the terminals. For this reason, an intermediate tier of Sun workstations ($5,000 per terminal) was installed to handle two tasks: (1) format updates to the market for broadcast to the telephone companies and to news services such as Reuters, and (2) reliably format transactions coming from the client terminals for forwarding to the Tandem. The Sun workstations were wired to both the Tandem and to the client terminals in pairs to assure that if one Sun went down, another "hot standby" was ready to complete the transaction in less than one second (i.e., in "real time"). Each Sun workstation could handle transactions from around 100 terminals.

Computational performance targets:

1. 95% of matching transactions (on Tandem) complete in less than 1 second.

2. Sun batching and reporting introduces 200 milliseconds (.2 second) delay.

3. No PC software module greater than 10kbytes in size (which translates into less than 3 seconds download to update a PC terminal's software, done at time of logon).

The Tandem is mainly used as a data server, though some of the server programs (coded in COBOL) provide information search and formatting services. Since reliability, accuracy, security, and integrity are paramount to this function, the Tandem implements software and data mirroring.[7] Software and data mirroring are services that Tandem is famous for, and one of the reasons that they are the primary supplier of computers for stock exchanges and other mission critical applications where any downtime is unacceptable.

The majority of software and processing in the client terminals supports the graphical user interface, running under Windows. This is programmed in the ECU language, which is compiled (i.e., translated) into a very compact intermediate language (which can be quickly downloaded across 9600 baud communications lines if needed), and is interpreted (i.e., run) by the kernel.

The Sun workstations contain no custom code. They use packaged software for information broadcasting (where information is formatted by the Tandem), for managing the client terminals, for performing transactions for posting to the electronic exchange (on the Tandem), and for managing the multiple sessions running simultaneously. By not using custom code on the Sun workstations, and by performing only rudimentary services, well suited to a Tandem server on the Tandem, the job of updates, maintenance, extensions, and revisions to the system are kept mainly on the client terminals. And the client code is loaded to the Tandem, where it is automatically downloaded to each client whenever it logs on.

The Sun workstations

1. display amounts on the bulletin board in the *sala de ruedas* used for displaying transactions;

2. handle routing of transactions, storing and forwarding of transactions for integrity;

3. randomize the order of transactions in the queue to be forwarded to the Tandem for matching, and randomize the order of transactions in the similar queue to be broadcast to traders. This function is provided by the stock exchange to insure fairness in trading, and to thwart attempts at front-running.

The Sun workstations add a 200-millisecond per transaction delay (i.e., 20% of total 1-second target time for processing a transaction) due to storing and forwarding, but this is considered worthwhile, since during peak loading, the Tandem is freed for search and matching functions.

Challenges Facing the Bolsa

By the summer of 1994, Andres Araya and Carlos Lauterbach knew that they had to respond to brokers' requests for new services—no matter what the challenge to their traditional policies of fairness and transparency. The loss of trading to the Bolsa Electrónica had resulted in a loss of business revenue to the Bolsa de Comercio. Essentially the same electronic services were offered between the two exchanges, though the Bolsa Electrónica was asserted to have the edge on speed of matching, but lagged in closing the transaction and transferring the scrip. The pressing question was how to provide the requested services without alienating investors who were unwilling to invest in new technology, yet were an important component of the Bolsa's business.

This decision was intertwined with the Bolsa's need to quell the growth of the competing Bolsa Electrónica. If "technology investors" were likely to leave for the Bolsa Electrónica, then why bother to placate them with offerings that threatened to undermine the Bolsa de Comercios' traditional policies of fairness and transparency? This was not dissimilar to the U.S. debate between the merits of the totally electronic NASDAQ/SOES versus the hybrid NYSE system, which retained floor trading and specialists.

Communication line delays had recently been raised as a related issue. The Bolsa was considering providing Ethernet lines (i.e., with 10 million bits per second bandwidth) to brokers in the Bolsa's building for an additional charge. It also wanted to lay a high-speed fiber-optic line throughout Santiago which would be accessible for an additional charge. This would favor brokers and institutional investors (who could afford to pay the added charges) over the small investor. Their implementation would also open the Bolsa up to program trading, with sophisticated expert systems making trading decisions directly from the electronic feeds provided through these high-speed lines.

A somewhat different problem was engendered by the enormous growth of the Chilean economy, and the Chilean pension system, both of which had dramatically increased the volume of securities trading over the prior decade. Matching of orders was the major bottleneck in the Bolsa transaction processing. If both the volume of transactions increased with economic growth, *and* the speed of transaction arrival increased with innovations such as program trading, several questions needed to be answered:

1. How fast must transactions be processed on the Bolsa? (Is one second fast enough?)

2. What are the implications of significant matching delays?

3. What alternatives could be adopted to mitigate the impact of delay (e.g., only allowing manual input, no program trading)?

4. Traditional trading systems matched through open outcry, an approach which was adopted for many transactions in the exchange; how does this change the nature of trading?

It was these questions that Andres Araya and Carlos Lauterbach pondered as they designed the next version of the electronic trading system for the Bolsa de Comercio de Santiago.

Notes

1. *Transparency* of trading depends on the amount of information released about bids, asks, negotiation, parties trading, and so forth released through formal channels in the stock exchange.

2. Delays are not just introduced by the length of wire (or fiber), which given the speed of light would be negligible. Rather, switching delays and error correction (which may require resending information and transmitting signals in two directions for confirmation) introduce the most significant delays. Indeed, the modified version of Bolsa de Comercio's electronic trading system that was sold to the Cali exchange in Colombia had to support a large number of transactions from both Cali and from Bogota 200 miles to the northeast. To accommodate this, signals at Cali were artificially delayed to allow the Bogota signals to "catch up," insuring fairness in trading and diminishing the possibility of front-running.

3. "Linearly scalable" means, roughly, that if the Bolsa buys three Tandem CPUs, it will have a machine that processes roughly three times as many transactions in the same time interval.

4. As opposed to the U.S. experience, where aerospace has yielded markets with PL/1, Ada, FORTRAN programmers, and packaged software with C and Pascal programmers.

5. A "kernel" is a piece of software that is always running, and is responsible for scheduling, initiating, and running other pieces of software.

6. An "event" is something of significance to the Bolsa's system that happens at a specific point in time. For example, the posting of an order to buy or sell, the matching of an order, reporting of daily market transaction summaries, and so forth. In on-line transaction processing, almost all processing is triggered by an event.

7. "Mirroring" means that copies of the same data or program code are maintained in two places, managed by the same system. This is necessary for a mission-critical system, where information services cannot afford to be lost, as in the case of market transactions. It is a critical feature in providing fault-tolerant systems—i.e., systems which can recover quickly from faults, whether they be system or user induced.

9 Digital Storefronts

Through most of history, retailing has been a limited family or township affair. Traveling caravans would collect and trade goods in one place (e.g., along the Silk Road), and carry others' goods to another place for trade. Alternatively, towns would grow up around markets and fairs, where a few townspeople would work as traders and shopkeepers. Cities were small by modern standards, and most people were rural. Not until the 19th century, with the development of a network of post offices in rural America, did a new kind of retailing flourish: catalog retailing.

One entrepreneur recognized the potential of this network early on. Richard Sears was an agent of the Minneapolis and St. Louis Railway station in rural Minnesota. Sears's job as station agent left him considerable spare time, which he used to sell miscellaneous items to the local farmers. Cheap watches, which broke often, were one of his most successful products, mainly because they were sold "satisfaction guaranteed or your money back." To service his watches, Sears teamed with watch repairman Alvah C. Roebuck to form Sears, Roebuck and Co.

During this period, farmers in rural America had been forced to buy their goods from local general stores, which could more or less charge what they pleased. In 1891, for example, the wholesale price of a barrel of flour was $3.47 whereas the price at retail was at least $7—a 100% markup. Farmers formed protest movements, such as the Grange, in opposition to high prices and "profiteering by the middleman." Sears rode this populist theme, expanding its product line from watches to provide whatever the farmers needed. It used volume buying, railroads, and the post office to undercut prices at the general stores. Sears prospered by using transportation networks to overcome the monopoly the general stores held on location.

In 1900, America's rural population still outnumbered the urban population. By 1920, the situation was reversed. Chain stores in cities began eating into Sears' catalog business, and Sears was forced to retaliate by opening its own stores in cities. Retail stores at the turn of the century were unkempt affairs, with merchandise hanging from the ceiling and walls and in storage. Dry goods retailer Marshall Field in Chicago changed all that by recasting the retail store as a museum.[1] Both Sears and Field realized that consumers needed to be motivated to buy the products the store carried, and that attractive display and good advertising copy, either in a catalog or in the store window, was essential. Stores needed to take an active role in buyer decisions by feeding the consumer information about how products looked and what they could do for the consumer.

From the 1920s forward, retailing evolved rapidly, with a series of innovations that made consumers an integral part of the retail process. The Great Atlantic & Pacific Tea Co. (A&P) purchased and resold a wide range of grocery products directly to the consumer, bypassing distribution middlemen, using A&P-owned retail stores in the

1920s and 1930s. In the 1940s and 1950s, A&P and other grocery retailers introduced the grocery supermarket format across the United States, creating another revolution in retailing as consumers were willing to travel relatively long distances (up to 10 miles) to reach a large store that offered lower prices than the community grocery store. Rapid penetration of automobiles and the national highway system expansion in the United States provided the "technological infrastructure" to support this transition from community retail stores to more efficient large chain stores that offered consumers lower prices. The transportation infrastructure improvements between 1940 and 1960 made geographic distance less important to customers, enabling a new and more efficient form of retailing to replace the traditional community stores of the prior era.

Mass merchandise discount chains, such as Wal-Mart in the 1970s, extended this trend toward large discount retail stores that served a broad geographic market. The philosophy of Wal-Mart since the first stores opened has been to offer prices so low that people would drive for long distances to buy at Wal-Mart. By purchasing in volume, targeting a wide geographic customer base, and locating stores in low-cost areas, Wal-Mart was able to compete effectively with local retailers and gain the volume of sales needed to achieve profitability at low prices.

The growth of mail order catalogs, supermarkets, and mass merchandise chains was driven in each case by three forces: (1) declining costs of accessing a larger market that had prior retail formats, (2) providing customers with lower prices to achieve higher sales volumes in the new retailing format, and (3) providing customers with convenience in shopping by offering a wide range of products at a single location. A century after Sears, Roebuck's catalog debut and a half century after the emergence of supermarket chains, the world is undergoing an Internet retailing revolution with dramatic implications for the way retailers of the future will serve their customers. The same basic forces that drove the growth in previous revolutions in retailing are also driving the growth of this new Internet retailing format: declining importance of distance and larger potential market, increasing focus on providing attractive prices, and offering added convenience by offering more goods in one location (your home).

Although there will still be roles for the traditional retail store format as Internet retailing increases, we expect to see most of the growth in consumer retail sales shift to direct electronic sales channels over the next 10–20 years. Traditional formats will continue to provide the majority of retail sales to consumers during that time, but direct electronic marketing and sales channels will affect some industries more than others: In some industries, such as software sales or news distribution, Internet and other electronic distribution media could account for more than 50% of all retail transactions by 2010. Direct sales of software through mail order and Internet in

1998 are already larger than retail store sales, and Internet retailing represents the fastest-growing segment of the direct sales industry.

Internet sales to the consumer are still limited in scope today, with less than 0.1% of all retail sales to consumers being completed over the Internet in 1998. Even so, electronic commerce retail sales from 1996 to 1998 have increased at 10% per month, the same as the rate of growth as for Internet subscribers and usage worldwide. If this growth rate continues, sales via the Internet could reach more than 10% of U.S. retail sales ($60 million using 1998 data for total U.S. retail sales) by 2002. Globally, retail sales on the Web will constitute only a small portion of sales overall due to a combination of language and telecommunications infrastructure barriers to growth. However, even with a leveling off of Internet sales to consumers to less than 25% of the current rate of growth and with retail electronic commerce sales outside the United States reaching only half the sales revenues from the United States alone, global electronic commerce sales to consumers should reach at least $100 million by 2010. This estimate does not include wholesale transactions, which are expected to be as large as retail sales, providing an expected market for total electronic commerce transactions of more than $200 million by 2010.

Continued rapid growth in electronic direct sales to consumers is assured. However, direct electronic sales channels in 2010 are likely to look very different from the digital storefronts found on the Web today. With costs of information processing and transmission declining at 60% per year (which translates to price-performance doubling every 18 months), the digital retail sales infrastructure available in 10 years will be decidedly more cost-effective than the one we see today. Expect technological capabilities that are prohibitively expensive (e.g., high-quality video on demand and video conferencing) to become virtually free in the near future. Internet retailing based on the limited capabilities available in the late 1990s is a crude indicator of the potential future impact of electronic direct sales using improved information processing and transmission capabilities.

Digital Storefronts on the Web

One of the most visible aspects of electronic commerce is the digital storefront: the Web browser interface for advertising, display, and purchase of goods and services on the Web. Digital direct sales over the Internet existed prior to the emergence of the Web, but a text-based interface limited the medium's appeal for retail selling. Multimedia and user-friendly Web interfaces developed in the early 1990s allowed the creation of retail storefront analog offering a variety of products. Some products, such as software, could be sold *and* delivered using the Internet. Most products, however, were sold via the Internet and delivered using traditional services.

Products available via digital storefronts include books, music, flowers, consumer appliances, computer equipment and software, apparel and clothing accessories, lottery tickets, cellular phones and other electronic equipment, videos (some delivered via Internet), furniture, wine, antiques, pornography (of many types), houses, cars, toys, gifts, greeting cards (electronic or paper), and groceries. Digital retailers on the Web have the option of selling an almost infinite variety of goods, as shelf space on the Internet is not limited. The challenge for digital retailers is finding effective ways to offer goods and services to consumers via a user-friendly interface that minimizes search time. Because virtually any good or service can be sold on the Web, consumers are overwhelmed with potential choices and yet often still find it difficult to select a specific product among the wide range of potential choices offered.

Search engines (discussed in the next section) are one means for locating specific items among this wide variety of product offerings. Some retailers are also striving to become a "one-stop shop" for consumers that offers everything they might ever need within specific product categories at a low price. For example, Amazon.com offers consumers almost every book available in print with most sold at steep discounts relative to physical bookstore locations. Amazon's selection comprises virtually everything the publishing industry produces, and its pricing is as good as that of any bookstore on the Web or in the physical marketplace. A growing number of customers have begun to go immediately to *www.amazon.com* when they want to buy a book. Other book retailers are opening digital storefronts to compete with Amazon.com, but many customers are already comfortable with Amazon's interface, pricing, and selection and now see little need to shop at other on-line bookstores. Just as physical locations and store chains have been able to capture consumer loyalty and become the primary location for shopping, leading retailers on the Web today are working to create loyal customers of the future as digital retailing continues to grow in economic importance worldwide.

Digital malls on the Internet are also expanding, but it is unclear how important digital malls of multiple branded stores will be. A few large digital retailers offering a wide variety of products may emerge to dominate electronic commerce in the future because of the value to consumers of recognized branding and reputation in a fragmented and chaotic market. Alternatively, some form of consumer protection or rating agency may emerge on the Web as an independent verification of retailers' reliability and integrity, similar to the role of the independent inspectors in enabling the success of AUCNET[2] in the used-car auction market in Japan. In either case, reputation and some form of channel branding will likely be increasingly important for successful digital retailing to enable consumers to have confidence in this new innovation in direct sales.

Search Engines

Roughly one-third of World Wide Web transactions are directed toward search engines such as Yahoo, AltaVista and Web Crawler. Algorithms and business models are rapidly evolving in this arena. At stake is Web advertising space. The primary vehicle for advertising on the Web is the banner ad, with content linked to search keywords. Banner ads need to be placed where customers are looking (and with one-third of the hits on the Web, the search engines qualify as prime real estate). Banner content needs to be attractive to customers. Search engines—i.e., software that find and retrieve data—are uniquely positioned to customize banner advertisements to the individual, because customers provide them with information about their interests here and now—in the search keywords they choose.

Developments in search and indexing have congealed around the concept of an Internet *portal*, a type of search engine that provides an Internet gateway that leads you through to other destinations, such as a topic heading on a search engine's home page. A *hub* is a particular Web page in a central position from which everything radiates, like a popular search engine itself. A *home base* is a Web page that provides a comfortable starting point for forays out through a portal or hub. America Online has done an excellent job of positioning itself as a home base. All of these concepts center on the innovative usage of indexing.

Indexing has come a long way over man's history. Medieval scholars were expected to memorize everything teachers ever told them in school: Their memory provided their only index for written works. Medieval philosopher St. Thomas Aquinas even elevated memory to one of the four cardinal virtues, a view that prevailed until Aldus Manutius popularized the printed book nearly four centuries later. When bound manuscript pages supplanted the long manuscript roll, reference to original source books became much easier. By the 16th century, title pages, page numbers, and indexes typically accompanied books. As published works proliferated, indexing the content of expanding libraries became more challenging. American librarian Melvil Dewey developed the Dewey Decimal System for application in the Amherst College Library in 1873, and it grew to be the standard classification system for large collections. The explosion of information on the Web—information that is considerably more dynamic than that in a library—has demanded new tools for indexing and retrieval.

As traffic and information on the Web grows, Web searching becomes less precise, and more computationally intensive. There are limits to the usefulness of searching the entire Web, though new technologies are continually pushing back these limits. These limits were recognized in the 1950s in connection with full text information retrieval in libraries and news services.

The traditional performance measures for a search engine are precision and recall. If Web sites are divided between those relevant to a particular question and those not relevant, then *precision* deals with the proportion of documents that the search engine retrieves that are relevant to the question asked; *recall* involves the proportion of all relevant records on the Web that are retrieved.[3] Measuring precision and recall for a search engine involves computing average performance statistics over a number of queries.

In the 1980s, David Blair and Bill Maron[4] studied the retrieval performance of the then-industry-standard **IBM STAIRS** search engine on a textual database of several hundred thousand documents from a legal case involving San Francisco's Bay Area Rapid Transit system. As database size increased, the search engine tended not to increase the number of retrieved records proportionately. Users were most satisfied with a few records that the search engine could guarantee were relevant to their question (retrieval precision was maximized). However, fewer retrieved records meant that more relevant records were left unretrieved (recall was poor). Precision in their study exceeded 0.8, that is, more than 80% of retrieved records were relevant to queries. Recall, however, was generally less than 0.1; that is, less than 10% of the relevant records were retrieved from the database, a number that dropped to fractions of 1% for larger searches.

Blair and Maron surmised that users reached a *point of futility* in reading the retrieved records and would simply not read more than a small number. This comparative bias of search engines reaches its extreme in Web-based search, which sifts through hundreds of millions of records. Recall—the portion of relevant records on the Web that are actually retrieved—is likely to approach zero in the average search. This problem is compounded by the indirect approach used in Web search engines, which build large files of profile information on Web sites. This information is gathered by sending out WebBots (Web robots)—small, autonomous query programs that forage the Web for site information and return abstracts of site contents to add to the search engine database. Sophisticated indexing algorithms allow site information to be retrieved in near real time from the files. Unfortunately, the loss of information from abstracting and indexing further diminishes recall performance in Web-based search.

Various approaches have been engaged to improve the recall performance of Web-based searches. Most involve refinements in the search interface. Proper site design, though, can improve the odds of the site's being chosen for relevant queries. For instance, the Web designer can fill a site's home page with several hundred index words that are felt to capture the site's content. These can be written in background color and thus be invisible on the page (a method used extensively in adult sites). Search engines will then adopt the site's indexing as their own, providing a more accurate profile of the site.

Search engines can improve performance in one of two ways: by eliciting more information about the query, or by searching their files more accurately. In normal conversation, we gather more information through question and answer. Search engines employ a similar cycle of queries that allows users to narrow a search after reviewing the retrieved documents. For example, AltaVista allows successive retrievals to refine the set of keywords the user has chosen; Excite asks if the user would like "more documents like this"; and Yahoo imposes its encyclopedic index structure on Web documents. These approaches appeal to consumers as well. Lycos found that if the initial search was *too* accurate, users were not as satisfied as they were if there was some variance in the relevance of retrieved documents. Apparently consumers expect an element of serendipitous discovery in a Web search. Successive refinement of the search retains the serendipity without sacrificing accuracy of search.

Search engines can improve accuracy of search, and in particular increase recall, by narrowing the search domain, thus effectively reducing the number of documents searched. This approach is very effective and increasingly popular. Examples of sites with focused domains are:

1. *People and business finders:* Big Yellow, with names, addresses, and phone numbers for 16 million U.S. businesses; Four11 Internet white pages telephone directory; WhoWhere for e-mail addresses; and so forth.

2. *Discussions:* DejaNews tracks 10,000+ UseNet discussion groups.

3. *Private clubs:* CompuServe, America Online, ICQ.

4. *Reference:* Columbia University's ILTnet Virtual Reference Desk; Purdue University's Virtual Reference Desk; United States of America Reference Desk; Britannica Online; Rominger Legal Services On-Line Legal Research.

5. *Specialized pursuits:* Builder On-Line, for the home building industry; BuildNet, for architects, builders, contractors, suppliers, and manufacturers; College Net for information about location, tuition, enrollment, major subjects, and sports programs at various institutions; College Financial Aid for a database of 180,000+

scholarships and lenders; Collector's COIN UNIVERSE Web Site; and so forth down the alphabet.

6. *Internal site search:*   Good commercial Website design demands a search engine specific to the data in the site. Some, such as Microsoft's site, have data of interest to a broad spectrum of customers. Search engines and site maps make it attractive for customers to stay at the site or come back later.

Finally, the recall performance statistic can be improved by engaging several search engines in the same search through *search metaengines.* This has been taken to extremes in Copernic, which engages more than 120 search engines in pursuit of a query. Such metaengines can also provide comparison information that might otherwise be unavailable at any single site. For example, Excite's Jango, Buy-It-Online, and Computer ESP are search engines that are really intelligent agents or WebBots designed to act as a shopping assistant. You tell the program what product you want —books by a certain author, movies from a certain director, wine from a certain vintage—and the search engine surveys sites selling that kind of product. It retrieves information from all the sites and combines it into a single report. The results include prices, buying information, and product reviews. If you decide you want to buy, the search engine fills in your address and credit card information from a standard database that you set up. Metaengines must be careful, however, to adopt interfaces that do not overload the user with information. Successful sites have generally handled this well.

The Web as an Advertising and Marketing Channel

The statistics regarding electronic commerce retailing are in some ways misleading. Although less than 0.1% of total U.S. retail sales in 1996 were completed over the Internet, 75% of customers who shopped on the Internet went on to purchase their goods or services through traditional channels.[5] The main reason was that the Internet site lacked the processing capacity to complete the transaction. Thus, the most common use of the Internet in support of e-commerce was the presentation of product information, or in other words, advertising and promotion of products available.

The increasing availability of competitively priced digital storefront packages will enable more firms to offer complete implementation of transaction processing on Websites. This will remove one of the major barriers to completing transactions on the Web. In addition, advertising on the Web will continue to expand as Web and digital advertising technological capabilities continue to double in performance every 18 months. Digital advertising and promotion provide retailers and branded goods

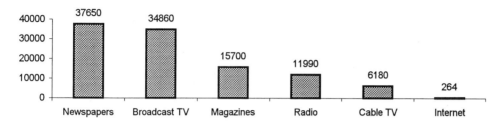

Figure 9.1
U.S. advertising revenues for various media—1996 $ millions
Sources: Veronis, Suhler Associates, Paul Kagan Associates, Jupiter Communications, and Morgan Stanley Research Report.

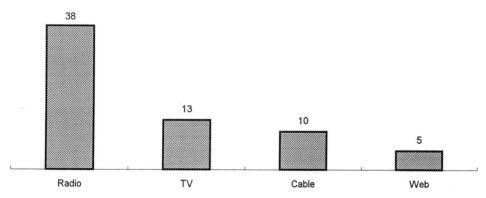

Figure 9.2
Years for new media to reach 50 million homes
Sources: McCann-Erickson, Paul Kagan Associates, and Morgan Stanley Technical Research.

manufacturers with the opportunity to reach selected consumers directly via this rapidly growing and unique communications, marketing, and sales channel. Leading Web advertisers in the late 1990s include three different types of firms: search engines (e.g., Yahoo!), news services (e.g., CNET or USAToday Online), and value-added ISPs (e.g., America Online).

According to a research report published by Morgan Stanley, advertising on the Web grew more than 50% per quarter during 1996 reaching approximately $250 million in revenues by the end of 1996.[6] Revenues from advertising on the Internet in 1996 were still quite small relative to those from other media (figure 9.1). However, the rapid growth of Web usage has enabled this new media to reach 50 million households in half the time required for TV and cable (figure 9.2). In 1996, three years after the first Web advertisement was launched, advertising revenues on the Web were larger than cable TV advertising revenues. Jupiter Communications projects that revenues from Web advertising will reach $5 billion by 2000, implying a rate of growth of more than 100% annually for this new media.[7] Forester Research projects similar growth, with almost 5% of the $100 billion advertising market shifting from newspapers and yellow pages (primarily) to Web advertising by 2000.

The growth in the Web as a medium has been unique in the sense that advertising has not been a major factor driving and funding its growth. In the past, revenues from advertising have been essential for providing the subsidies needed to achieve rapid expansion of a new medium in the market. With the Web, users directly pay for 99% of costs of equipment and content, including connection fees and subscription fees for some services. As advertising revenues on the Web expand, the percentage of total costs of services provided will shift from a user-fee model toward a more typical advertising-supported model for content access and distribution. This will further increase the relative attractiveness of the Internet for consumers, as advertising revenues increasingly subsidize or eliminate the costs of both access and content.

This growth projected for Web advertising is particularly impressive given the Web's limitations relative to TV and other broadcast media that dominate the advertising market. In general, all advertising has two primary purposes: building brands and direct marketing. Virtually all advertising media provide some level of each of these two capabilities, but the Web is interesting in that it has both characteristics of broadcast mass media and of direct response advertising (e.g., mail order catalogues). In this aspect, it is more like newspapers than TV, but the medium and response convenience are closer to TV than newspaper from the perspective of impact on consumers. The Web and future computer-based interactive multimedia channels represent a new form of advertising and marketing unlike any existing media (see table 9.1 and 9.2).

The Web is less effective for building brands than traditional broadcast media for two reasons: limited bandwidth and limited usage time. Until interactive multimedia services are commercialized to be able to provide video of similar quality to that of TV, interactive services such as the Web will not be able to provide the same emotional intensity and image building as can TV or cable advertising. In addition, Internet usage for the average U.S. consumer is projected to reach 28 hours per year by 2000, or less than 2% of the time consumers spend watching broadcast and cable TV (as shown in table 9.3). However, the Web is one of the fastest growing media in terms of usage per subscriber and total market penetration. Nielsen Media Research announced in late 1996 that TV viewing among the critical 18-to-34 year old demo-

Table 9.1
Shares of spending consumer communications media in 1995

Industry segment (not including user equipment, but including access or purchase costs)	Advertising spending (percent)	End-user spending (percent)
TV broadcasting	100	0
Radio broadcasting	100	0
Newspaper publishing	80	20
Magazine publishing	63	37
Interactive services (e.g., Internet)	1	99

Source: Veronis, Suhler & Associates, Wilkofsky Gruen Associates, Morgan Stanley Research Report.

Table 9.2
Estimated U.S. subscription fees versus advertising support for internet services

	Subscription revenues	Advertising revenues
1996	$120 million	$256 million
1997	$214 million	$1.1 billion
1998	$354 million	$2.2 billion
1999	$584 million	$3.6 billion
2000	$966 million	$5.0 billion

Source: Jupiter Communications, Morgan Stanley Research Report.

graphic group had declined owing to increasing usage of Internet services and other interactive computer activities (e.g., video games). Broadcasters, including NBC and Fox, responded to this news by threatening to sue Nielsen for providing inaccurate and unreliable statistics that could potentially force these networks to refund up to $100 million in advertising revenues because of this decline in viewer airtime. Supporting Nielsen's data is a recent survey by Coopers & Lybrand indicating that 58% of Internet users have reduced their TV viewing in order to spend more time on the Internet.

With Moore's law predicting double the computing power every 18 months for the same cost, it is only a matter of time before the Internet or other interactive computer media will be able to compete for viewer attention and emotions with our broadcast media of the 1990s. Even so, we do not expect the Internet to become a strong competitor with TV for creating brand awareness over the next five to ten years, with the exception of advertising among Web retailers and content providers, for whom Web advertising is highly effective for creating brand awareness and direct marketing to potential customers that are already using Web services.

Table 9.3
Hours per person per year using various U.S. media, 1990–2000E

Year	Broadcast TV	Cable TV	Radio	Recorded music	Newspaper	Consumer books	Consumer magazines	Home video	Movies in theaters	Video games	Internet/online
1990	1,120	350	1,135	235	175	95	90	42	12	12	1
1991	1,065	430	1,115	219	169	98	88	43	11	18	1
1992	1,073	437	1,150	233	172	100	85	46	11	19	2
1993	1,082	453	1,082	248	170	99	85	49	12	19	2
1994	1,091	469	1,102	294	169	102	84	52	12	22	3
1995	1,019	556	1,091	289	165	99	84	53	12	24	7
1996E	1,028	567	1,082	290	163	102	83	54	12	27	11
1997E	1,023	587	1,067	296	161	104	82	55	12	31	16
1998E	1,024	601	1,057	315	160	105	81	56	12	34	21
1999E	1,006	634	1,047	331	159	106	81	56	12	37	25
2000E	999	651	1,047	357	158	107	81	57	12	39	28

Source: Veronis, Suhler & Associates, Wilkofsky Gruen Associates, Morgan Stanley Research Report.

Table 9.4
Cost per response for a direct-mail advertiser and for a web advertiser

Response rate (%)	Direct mail cost per thousand homes (CPM)			
	$250	$500	$750	$1,000
30	$0.83	$1.67	$2.50	$ 3.33
25	$1.00	$2.00	$3.00	$ 4.00
20	$1.25	$2.50	$3.75	$ 5.00
15	$1.67	$3.33	$5.00	$ 6.67
10	$2.50	$5.00	$7.50	$10.00
Response rate (%)	Web ad cost per thousand viewers (CPM)			
	$10	$30	$60	$90
5	$0.20	$0.60	$1.20	$1.80
4	$0.25	$0.75	$1.50	$2.25
3	$0.33	$1.00	$2.00	$3.00
2	$0.50	$1.50	$3.00	$4.50
1	$1.00	$3.00	$6.00	$9.00

Note: Average response for direct mail marketing was approximately 17% in 1998 (*source:* Direct Marketing Association), with an average cost per thousand homes reached ranging from as low as $200 to more than $1,000, depending on size and quality of promotional materials mailed, including costs of printing, production, postage, and the like.

The most interesting opportunity driving most of the growth in Web advertising over the next five to ten years will be direct marketing to consumers. In this sense, Web advertising is similar to direct marketing advertising and selling via mail, telephone, or newspaper. Direct marketing advertising and sales are growing at 6–7% per year and represented more than $60 billion in sales revenues in 1995. Advertising costs as a percentage of sales for direct marketing media range from 9–10% (typical for direct mail or newspaper direct marketing advertising) to 15–19% (typical for telemarketing or TV-based direct marketing advertising), with cost per thousand homes reached averaging about $400–$1,000 for direct mail advertising.

One of the advantages of Web direct marketing is its much lower cost of reaching potential customers, translating into a lower acceptable response rate for achieving profitable operations. The cost for reaching a thousand potential buyers on the Web ranges between $10 and $80, in comparison to the $400–$1,000 cost typical for traditional direct mail sales. With costs more typical of traditional broadcast advertising per thousand impressions but with the added ability for consumers to respond immediately and enter into a purchase transaction on-line, the Web provides a unique direct marketing opportunity.

As shown in table 9.4, direct marketing via the Web can be economically attractive at response rates less than one-tenth of those typically required for traditional direct

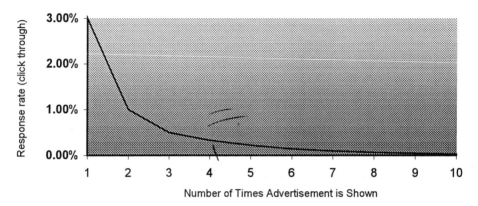

Figure 9.3
Response rate versus banner advertisement frequency
Source: DoubleClick.

marketing campaigns. Typical response (click-through) rates on the Web reported by I/PRO (a Web measurement company) are approximately 2.1%, although user response to ads declines dramatically as ad frequency increases (figure 9.3). In addition to providing lower cost per response, advertising on the Web can be more successfully targeted toward specific consumer attributes than traditional direct response or broadcast advertising. For example, Amazon.com pays to have its advertisements displayed on search engines whenever the word "book" is included in the list of words searched. Thus, cost of advertising as a percentage of sales could be significantly lower for a direct marketing retailer on the Web than for a direct marketing firm using traditional media. The potentially dramatic growth in Web advertising and direct marketing sales could make the rapid rise in sales for home shopping channels look insignificant by comparison. When compared with traditional direct marketing channels, the Internet presents the opportunity to reach large potential markets via direct sales to consumers at a cost that is an order of magnitude less than the cost of direct marketing via traditional distribution channels.

Although retailing on the Web can be viewed as either an advertising or direct marketing media alternative, the Web has effectively created an entirely new paradigm for connecting with the customer. In addition, the major software companies have committed themselves to creating a completely consistent experience for a user who wants everything to work like the Web. The Web and its search engines offer the promise of putting products and services at the service of customers. It frees the customer from the tyranny of marketing, advertising, and sales intermediaries who control information for the benefit of producers and channel intermediaries and to the disadvantage of consumers.

It is not possible to fully understand the Web's impact on the customer by simply looking at traditional marketing techniques. Electronic commerce on the Web re-engineers the customer's role in the producer-consumer relationship, which is why electronic commerce on the Web is like nothing you have seen before.

Customers Can Play an Active Part in the Production and Design Process

The traditional business model for marketing has been for a manufacturer or entrepôt (warehouse, retail store, etc.) to alert potential customers proactively to the existence of its product, build an image for it, describe the distribution channels through which it is available, and complete a sales transaction. The new business model evolving around the global Internet is fundamentally different in the essentially passive role played by the seller—the manufacturer or entrepôt. The product information is placed on a server with an address on the World Wide Web. Producers adopt an "incomplete production" model for inventory and design, which allows them to build to order highly customized products and services from standard parts. The customer is required to complete the production, by directing the way in which components are combined and potentially forcing the producer to reconsider its make-or-buy decisions.

Marketing's traditional role can narrowly focus on the interface created by marketing people and the customers while disregarding the channels that motivate this interface. In the *interactive electronic commerce model*, customer and seller interact organically: The customer has a crucial role to play in completing production.

Dell Computer provides a superb example of the new interactive electronic commerce model. In 1984, 19 year old Michael Dell began buying computers from a local store and upgrading their components to the personal order of customers. In cutting out inventory and making the customer part of the design and production process, Dell was establishing a business model to which he still adheres today. Dell says he didn't do well on his final exams that year, but it's easy to understand his distraction. His company, PCs Limited, was soon making more than $50,000 per month. Dell Computer reported in April 1998 that sales from its Internet site were increasing 20% per month and generating revenues in excess of $1 million per day. Today, Dell runs one of the largest computer companies in the world, with revenues of $7.8 billion for the 1997 fiscal year. Dell Computer employs more than 10,000 people worldwide and consistently outperforms the PC market as a whole by double and triple digits. Dell's ability to individualize design for each customer while maintaining negligible inventories of finished machines is a testament to the viability of the Internet retail model.

At www.dell.com, customers electronically design, price, and purchase computer systems and obtain on-line support. Dell's customers are not just consumers making low-value transactional purchases. They range from knowledgeable home users to small and large business users purchasing richly configured systems over the Internet, including high-end $30,000 servers. More than 225,000 customers per week currently visit Dell's Website. Dell's Internet model delivers both relationship and transactional benefits. Dell has created customized intranet sites for its largest corporate customers to simplify procurement and support processes. Business is leading the growth of the Internet, with more than 82% of all Fortune 500 companies already providing Internet access to employees, according to Forrester Research.[8] This suggests that the Internet is a medium with which most of Dell's customers—around 55% of whom are in business and government—are already familiar. While much of the industry is trying to retrofit a marketing and distribution channel designed for the industrial age, Dell is using the Internet to refine its direct model for the information age.

Internet Dynamics

Surveying the commercial sites in the early years of the Web—1995 to 1997—it might be easy to conclude that the Internet is just another advertising display medium or just another distribution channel, because Internet electronic commerce, currently hobbled by low bandwidth and poor security, limits users to accessing static Web content through imprecise search engines. In this environment, Internet retailing for most products currently lacks enough volume to argue for a compelling Internet business model.

However, increasing Internet penetration is making customer reach an extremely compelling reason to experiment with Internet e-commerce business models. Increasing bandwidth (doubling every nine months) is allowing new uses for the Internet, along with a new level of interactivity that will soon rival that of the door-to-door salesman, but with global reach and near-zero labor costs. This will make interactive selling techniques—question and answer, strong aftermarket technical support, follow-up sales support—available not just for big ticket items such as automobiles, but also for low-cost items like software and consumer electronics.

Customers are Targeted Differently

Most channels target a particular customer base, in one way or another, for strictly economic reasons: Marketing is a costly process. Thus vendors of larger items such as swimming pools or other home improvements can afford to send a sales representative to visit a customer. At the other extreme, a bag of flour can best be marketed through coupon advertisements. Specific products fit well with specific channels.

The seller can play an active role on the Internet using "push" technologies to target customers proactively, through automatic updates to screen savers and through targeted direct e-mail. The latter is derisively called *spam*, especially when uninvited by the recipient. Spam is widely loathed by Internet users, is filtered and discarded by some Internet service providers, and is even illegal in some places. However, direct e-mail marketing or information distribution to consumers can be highly effective, especially if such information is provided with the recipient's permission.

A new class of search engines, such as Alexa and Webturbo, that "suggest" links that might be of interest to someone looking at a particular Web page provide an alternative to targeted direct e-mail. These search engines provide separate windows that list links related to the user's browsing behavior. The suggestions are not obtrusive and may sometimes be useful. They do not provoke the negative reactions among recipients that spam or junk mail does. They instead follow the model of Catalina Marketing and other firms that produce equipment to print discount coupons for store goods automatically based on the items being rung up at the cash register: product promotion based on an individual's consumer behavior.

The reason is that these sites are likely to capture the consumer's attention long before a sale takes place. Consumers who are looking for a car, appliance, or other good would like to be able to rank the quality and performance of various models (in addition to obtaining a fairly complete listing of the purchase options available). Thus they are likely to look for quality assessment information—e.g., via *Consumer Reports*—before looking for a vendor. Banks and utilities naturally have long-term relationships with consumers, because they provide services that must exist from the start. For example, a consumer is unlikely to write a check to purchase a television without first having both electricity and a bank account.

Interactive Web Interfaces and Intelligent Agents Evolve to Serve Needs

In the near future, sufficient tools will exist to allow Web-based electronic commerce sites essentially to carry on a conversation with a customer. Combined with computer-aided design software to allow the customer to construct a given product for purchase and a massive database of the producer's product and industry knowledge, Web electronic commerce could be much more satisfying than retail or direct sales alternatives. An e-commerce browser could respond to customers' queries just as a salesman does. It could adjust arguments, change pitch, and provide information at customer's whim to better sell product. Retailing, in contrast, is constrained by the limited knowledge of its sale personnel, and direct mail is limited to an inherently static database.

Integration

In traditional commerce, the marketing function is distinct from inventory production and warehousing functions, a weakness because both out-of-stock and overstock situations are potentially costly. In e-commerce, inventory control is directly linked to the sales interface. Customers can receive accurate information on availability, shipping times, order status, and so forth, directly from the computer. For example, Amazon.com specifies the predicted order fill time (24 hours, 2–3 days, 1 week) for every book it lists. Where there are significant lead times in building to order, an e-commerce system can track building progress, keeping the customer accurately informed and maintaining a corporate image of efficiency and integrity.

In traditional commerce, the marketing function is distinct from warranty, help desk, and other aftermarket support functions, a weakness because the feedback acquired in aftermarket activities can be very beneficial for refining the marketing functions. With electronic commerce, all functions can be centralized on a single database, providing effective integration into the electronic commerce system.

Cisco Systems Inc. provides an exemplar for this concept. It has all but paved the information superhighway with its own routers. It also offers one of the superhighway's most outstanding e-commerce sites, and one of its most successful. Cisco processes more than $700 million per year through its e-commerce site. Its Commerce Agent lets customers enter profiles of themselves, configure products, and check on the status of their orders. Morgan Stanley[9] estimates that Cisco's system saves around $535 million per year—$270 million from product manual printing savings, $130 million from software distribution savings, $125 million from customer support savings, and over $10 million from recruitment savings. Its Web ordering and support system save it from handling around 250,000 phone calls per month.

Notes

1. In truth, museum displays of that day were just as jumbled as those of stores. Field's ideas had widespread influence, particularly through the museums of the University of Chicago, the university that Field cofounded with oilman John D. Rockefeller.

2. Konsynski, B., A. Warbelow, J. Kokuryo, AUCNET: TV Auction Network System, HBS Case 190001 (Field) 4/12/1996 15p. Lee, H. G., J. C. Westland, and S. Hong, Impacts of Electronic Marketplaces on Product Prices: An Empirical Study of the AUCNET Case, *International Journal of Electronic Commerce*, forthcoming 1999.

3. Library science has used measures of precision and recall since the 1920s. More recently, the trend has been to measure retrieval performance via the more widely accepted statistical measures: type I (i.e., not retreiving a relevant document) and type II (i.e., retreiving an irrelevant document) error. Precision and recall can be linearly mapped into type I and type II error, and thus contain equivalent information. The traditional terms are used here because Blair and Maron's study reported results in terms of precision and recall.

4. D. C. Blair and M. E. Maron, "An evaluation of retrieval effectiveness for a full text document-retrieval system," *Communications of the ACM*, 28(3), 1985, p. 289–299.

5. Survey on Electronic Commerce, *The Economist*, May 10, 1997. p. 4.

6. Roach, S., S. McCaughey, C. DePuy, The Internet Retailing Report, *Morgan Stanley*, May 28, 1997, Chapter 4, p. 2.

7. Jupiter Communications, 1999 Online Shopping Report, Internet Business Report p. 3 and Fig. 9.

8. Roach, S., S. McCaughey, C. DePuy, *The Internet Retailing Report*, Morgan Stanley, May 28, 1997, Chapter 1, p. 4.

9. Ibid., p. 3.

10 Secure Digital Payments

One challenge electronic commerce retailers face is providing payment mechanisms that consumers perceive as sufficiently secure and convenient to induce them to complete commercial transactions on-line. Many alternative ways have been proposed or are now in use for providing secure and convenient payment for Internet transactions, but none have anywhere near the acceptance that paper- and coin-based currency have today. For electronic commerce to grow beyond a small niche market, ordinary consumers will have to be persuaded to accept some form of digital payment mechanism as being as reliable and convenient to use as cash is today. To understand the potential for digital payments to replace cash as a medium of exchange for commercial transactions, it is helpful to understand how cash evolved as a payment medium and what that might mean for future development of currency for ordinary transactions into a digital medium of exchange.

The Origin and Development of Cash

Ten thousand years ago, in a world populated by nomadic hunter-gatherers, goods of any value were generally perishable. There was scarcely any trade and little need of cash. In fact, the acquisition of too many possessions could turn into a liability for people who might be called upon to travel long distances on foot and who had to be ready to migrate with little or no warning.

The assimilation of people into agricultural communities around 8000 B.C. encouraged planning, surplus production, and trade. Production limited to the needs of a particular family met most household needs. This soon gave way to surplus production and exchange as a means of satisfying household needs. Initially, trade was through barter.[1] However, as the number of goods produced began to increase, and as individuals and families became more selective in what they purchased, barter became increasingly cumbersome. Mechanisms of exchange arose to overcome inefficiency and excessive interactions among households in the quest to satisfy the need for household staple. Markets arose to decrease the "search costs" required to match consumers with producers. Figure 10.1 shows how markets could reduce to half the number of "search" contacts required to match producers and consumers where households specialized in a specific set of staples.

The first great markets arose with the agrarian settlements of the Middle East. Trade in agricultural surplus arose, without the benefit of cash, in the city of Sumer in the Middle East around 3500 B.C., initially as a part of a barter economy. Over time, the valuation of goods in terms of a "monetary" commodity, independent of their valuation in terms of other commodities, simplified market processes. Money then

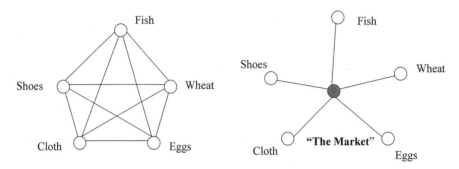

Figure 10.1
From barter to market

became a denominator (a numeraire) for determining the relative value of goods in an exchange, and for giving or receiving the excess in any unequal exchange.

In the case of the simple set of commodities shown in figure 10.1, the consumers of these commodities would be required to visit the producers in order to acquire a stock of each commodity (with the possibility of the producers not having any stock). Additional steps might be required if consumers acted also as traders by buying surplus quantities of one commodity to exchange for another desired commodity. The market saves considerable time and effort.

Markets emerged as a powerful vehicle for coordinating the activities of individual households. Any amount of surplus production assumes the risk that demand will fail to materialize to consume all of a household's excess production. Individuals who could see all of the production and marketing taking place in a locale could better judge the amount, content, and timing of their own production. Because households now had access to a larger population of consumers, they had more opportunities to sell all of their production within a reasonable time.

The needs of the Sumerian markets fostered early forms of writing (required to record transactions as well as accounts payable and receivable), with the appearance of cuneiform script, accounting, duplicate contracts, and established systems for negotiation, transaction completion, and transfer of property. These were further developed into accounting systems by the Phoenicians, the premier Mediterranean traders of the day, who needed to keep a record of goods on consignment aboard their ships.

Even with markets, consumers were subject to considerable amounts of unnecessary effort. A barter economy usually would require the purchase of quantities in excess of those needed in order to have something that other traders might find valuable in exchange for other goods. The whole process could become very complex. To simplify trading, "money" came into use.

Compact goods with a wide market and relatively high intrinsic value—for example, gems, salt, and hides—had been used as money in limited circles of trade dating from prehistory. Most of these early forms of money suffered from one or more shortcomings. Either they could not be divided into ever decreasing quantities (e.g., gemstones),[2] or impurities affecting quality and value could not be detected (e.g., precious metals), or they were perishable and would lose their value over time (e.g., foodstuffs). Currency or cash—the physical embodiment of money—only came into service during the first millennium B.C. in Lydia, an area now a part of Turkey. Gold, having a high intrinsic value, being divisible by either cutting or melting and being portable, seemed to have most of the characteristics of money, that is, a numeraire commodity. Only the question of purity was difficult. In the streams of a particular river in Turkey was found the black "touchstone": Rubbing pure gold against the touchstone left a specific discoloration that was distinguishable from the discoloration left by gold mixed with less-valuable metals. Because a technology existed for authenticating its worth, gold came into widespread use as a medium of exchange. Adoption of gold as a medium of exchange in the Greek city-states around 400 B.C. assured its widespread use and unique role in economic history.

Money eventually moved from being a medium of exchange to being a desirable commodity in itself. It became the basis for evaluating the wealth of individuals and households and was the basis of a science of economics. "Economics" came to be used in Greece to mean the management of a household. Aristotle's *Politics*[3] noted that the amount of household property which suffices for the good life is not unlimited, that there was a fixed bound, and this fixed stock was 'wealth.' Gold and silver became the universal measure of wealth. A "just price" was determined by what the seller was obligated to ask. "Usury" (the lending of money for interest, no matter how much) was discouraged; similarly, the unbounded accumulation of wealth was discouraged. Aristotle's *Politics* became the standard European textbook on economics during the Middle Ages.[4]

This image of an absolute wealth engendered the colonization of the world starting in the 15th century, beginning with the Spanish and Portuguese quests for El Dorado (the "guilded land"). Because gold was scarce, rulers fixated on the belief that wealth was limited, and that one country could gain only at the expense of another's loss. These ideas held sway from the 15th through the 18th centuries (and indeed are regularly revisited today). They were developed by a director of the East India Company, Sir Thomas Mun, who broached the idea of a "national economy." Mun's great contribution to Western thought was his assertion that a nation's "balance of trade" was favorable if its inflows of gold bullion exceeded its outflows.

The debate over the fate of the American colonies initiated a train of revisionist thinking culminating in Adam Smith's tome *The Wealth of Nations*, which discarded the importation of gold and silver as a basis for measuring the health of a national economy (though, in truth, a bullion or specie basis for wealth had already fallen into eclipse with the dramatic decline of Spain's economy after the British defeated the Spanish Armada). Smith argued for a vision of wealth based on ability to buy, ability to produce, and exchange mechanisms unfettered by national intervention. This seemed an appropriate vision of wealth for the 18th-century world that was moving away from conquest toward industrial growth in the Industrial Revolution.

Smith provided a framework that embraced the innovations of the Industrial Revolution. Division of labor and improvements in both technology and efficiency were demanded of the complex, precise production augered in during the Industrial Revolution. Rather than some intrinsic "just price" that measured the value of gold and other commodities, an "invisible hand" priced goods so as to clear a market of overproduction or too much demand. The invisible hand could flourish under the "perfect liberty" that accompanied a free and competitive economy. This fit well with ideas of democracy and equal opportunity in politics and social life.

Smith's perspective forced money into a more abstract role. The use of paper money (with no intrinsic value, but backed by the guarantees of a nation) became more widespread. Money was useful for valuing goods in exchange and for accounting for trade. It became useful through its active investment and expenditure, and it assumed a role as an accounting contrivance for the "economic" activities of individuals and states, with all the uncertainty incumbent in that role.

Smith's new perspective on money consigned the touchstone to oblivion and put the onus on mints to produce paper money of such delicate and intricate detail that it was virtually impossible to reproduce without assets comparable to those of the governmental treasury. Delicate, intricate art (enabled by advances in printing and papermaking technology) provided the new touchstone, one used by nations to establish the authenticity of a note.

In exchange for establishing a secure currency, governments were given the right of seigniorage of currency. Paper money could be viewed as a non-interest-bearing liability on the balance sheet of the national treasury, which earned interest on the corresponding assets backing the money. Governments recognized that large amounts of currency in circulation could provide substantial revenues.

By 1850, most economies in Europe and the Unites States employed more than half of their workforces in agriculture. In Smith's nomenclature, the farmer generated

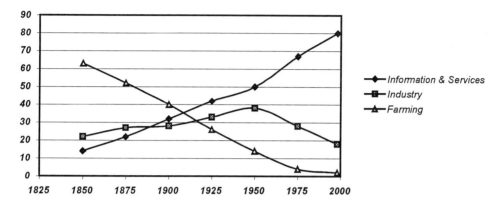

Figure 10.2
Employment in three sectors as a percentage of total U.S. workforce
Sources: U.S. Labor Statistics Bureau, OECD national statistics, and U.S. Commerce Department.

"wealth" through his production. Received wisdom was that workers in the factories needed to be fed, thus there would always be a role for the farmer.

This role has gradually withered away as we approach the end of the second millennium. Today fewer than 2% of the U.S. workforce is engaged in farming; the figure is even smaller if "hobby" farmers (tending less than 10 acres) are excluded. Less than a quarter of the workforce is engaged in industrial production, the other mainstay of the U.S. economy of 1850. The products of these sectors no longer generate sufficient demand to warrant employment levels anywhere near those of the 19th century. Smith's world was one of industrial products. In contrast, the end of the 20th century is marked by an unrelenting shift to intellectual products. The vast majority of national income in postindustrial societies is generated through services, information creation, and information distribution (figure 10.2).

The 20th century has witnessed the rise of variety of forms of cash and near cash. Credit cards, debit cards, stored-value cards, money orders and checks are just some of the cash and near-cash products readily available to consumers in the late 20th century. Governments, banks, and sometimes individuals or corporations have backed this incredibly diverse variety of payment methods. Authentication of payments is still very much a critical factor in payment, though it now takes on as many forms as there are means of payment.

Precipitous declines in computer prices over the past decade, coupled with increasing ease of use, global networks, and commodity software, have ushered in lucrative new markets for information. Databases, organizational learning, custom software, and internal communications all are firm assets and the new source of competitive power. They are capable of simultaneous multiple uses, and they are both inputs and outputs of business activities. Global networks have created complete markets for economic activities conducted over information networks. In an age of global links into nearly every computer system, the new basis of wealth has shifted from agricultural and industrial products to intellectual products. Job formation has shifted from the clerical-processing realm of the salaryman to the information creation and information management realm of postindustrial society.[5]

Where the basis of wealth is information, the old economic and accounting rules do not always apply. There may be increasing returns to scale for production; control of standards and networks may hold a more important source of competitive advantage than efficient production; human capital is a firm's primary productive resource, but one that can walk away at any moment. This raises serious questions for valuing business activity and assets, such as the issue of whether information assets should be capitalized on the firm's balance sheet. Electronic commerce needs to come to terms with all of the aspects of new information-based economies.

Electronic cash represents the most recent transformation of our concepts of wealth and money. Large U.S. retailers first used credit cards, which provided the root concepts behind most contemporary concepts in electronic cash, in the 1930s. Since that time, card variants, innovations, and extensions have provided some form or another of electronic cash (e-cash). Recent innovations in e-cash have claimed to provide unprecedented performance on a number of critical attributes of money: portability, divisibility, security, privacy, durability, and flexibility of use. Table 10.1 provides a synopsis of the attributes offered by various existing forms of e-cash.

Microtransactions

Several types of e-cash have been introduced with the express purpose of facilitating micropayments: for example, renting software by the hour, or downloading pictures for a few cents. With micropayments, customers can choose informational products such as pictures or software on the Web, yet not have to commit to a purchase or subscriptions. E-cash enables a low-cost niche between download of free Web content and transactions not large enough to warrant the administrative overhead of a credit card.

A large and egalitarian economy has been envisioned around micropayments. The idea is that anyone with news, software, or any other sort of informational product of value can become a publisher by charging a few cents per view. The economics are compelling: 100,000 downloads a day at 10 cents per download equals $10,000 per

Table 10.1
Performance of different forms of money on criteria considered desirable

	Cash	Near cash				
		Credit card	Debit card	Stored value	Hybrid	E-cash
Portability/ ease of use	Low (bulky, unsanitary)	Moderate (requires PIN authorization)	Moderate (requires PIN authorization)	High (especially for contactless)	Moderate requires PIN authorization)	Moderate (requires PIN authorization)
Divisibility	Limited[1]	Any level	Any level	Any level	Any level	Any level
Borrowing?	No	Yes	No (unused cash balance)	No (unused cash balance)	Yes	No (unused cash balance)
Security	Low to moderate	Moderate to high (up to credit limit)	Moderate (up to balance)	Moderate (up to balance)	Moderate (up to balance)	Moderate (up to balance)
Privacy	High	Low to moderate (central authorization)	Low to moderate (central authorization)	High	Low to moderate (central authori- zation)	High
Durability	Moderate	High	High	High	High	High
Transaction cost	Low	High (central authorization)	High (central authorization)	Low	High (central authorization)	Low
Flexibility	High	Moderate	Moderate	Low (currently only useful for transport)	Low to moderate (limited retailer subscription)	Low to Moderate (limited retailer subscription)

1. Portability and ease of use tend to decrease with increasing divisibility. Coins are bulky and thus many consumers refuse to carry more than a token amount on them. Lost sales on small purchases can be high for this reason. This has motivated the transport companies to issue stored value cards.

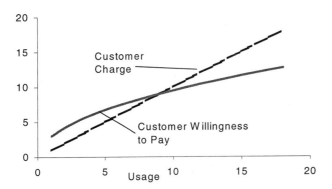

Figure 10.3
The fatal error in pay-per-use schemes

day. This can fund a cottage industry of information content providers and pack-agers. Chapter 12 describes cases, for example, Danni's Hard Drive, where content providers have done just that. However, this industry has been slow to develop.

It has been argued that the psychology of micropayments is wrong, because people intensely dislike being metered.[6] More importantly, consumers have grown used to the idea of free Web content. The same expectations have undermined pay-per-view television. Advertising that lowers subscription cost subsidizes magazines and news-papers sold on newsstands; it entirely subsidizes broadcast television.

Content providers are also unenthusiastic about micropayments. The main prob-lem with usage-based charges for information is that they artificially distort the underlying economics of electronic information supply and demand. Because a pay-per-use charge is typically linear (i.e., a fixed charge per minute, use, etc.), whereas the customer's marginal demand for usage may decline with additional use (satiation causes decreasing marginal returns to usage), pay-per-use schemes tend to overcharge regular customers and undercharge the casual user (see figure 10.3). Once informa-tion is on a Website, it costs the publisher nothing to have it read (i.e., marginal cost of usage is zero) and charging per view (i.e., marginal cost is greater than zero) seems mercenary, opening opportunities for competitors and predatory pricing.

Cygnus Support (described in more detail in chapter 12) has taken this discrepancy seriously and adopted an entirely different (and less distorted) perspective on Web economics: Drop the price to zero, and find other ways to extract payments from the product that are more in line with costs. Another solution would be to offer a number of payment schemes directed at different customers based on varying levels of usage.

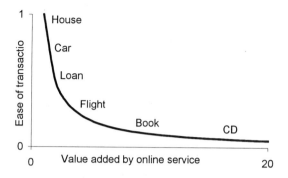

Figure 10.4
Products and ease of payment. O implies that simple payment methods are suitable; 1 implies the need for complex payment methods.
Sources: Microsoft and *The Economist*, May 10, 1997.

Payment mechanics aside, perhaps the biggest problem with micropayments is that traditional ways of paying for goods are satisfactory for most transactions. Any substitute has start-up and maintenance costs, for example, carrying an extra card, in addition to the associated frustrations of learning a new system. Indeed, with the addition of a secure interface to the major Web browsers and servers, credit cards have become the de facto standard for Internet electronic payment. The steady migration of business to the Internet is forcing centrally administered credit card companies to lower their minimum purchase requirements, further encroaching on the niche opened for micropayments. For a long time the minimum credit card purchase a credit card company would accept was $20, dropping to around $5 in 1997. The much touted advantage of "electronic purses"—that is, digital money such as Mondex without central authorization—is anonymity. But this carries its own risks. Because transactions are not confirmed through a central bank, hackers could conceivably counterfeit the script and churn out unlimited amounts of the digital currency, rendering it worthless. New e-cash products are proving harder to design than was originally thought.

It is not clear how large the markets will be that can be supported by micropayments. Microsoft produced figure 10.4, indicating where one might find niches for electronic payment on the Internet. Currently, the majority of electronic payments for products such as books and CDs are accomplished with credit cards.

Another perspective on micropayments is examined in the Mondex case study included in this chapter. Mondex, Octopus, Golden Harvest, and other stored-value cards tend to be useful where the alternative would be pocket change, which is not particularly portable. In these cases, convenience is more important than transaction costs in motivating their use.

The Resurgence of Barter

One of the most obvious ways that computers and networks have altered monetary bases for economic activities is by enabling new and efficient methods of barter. The reemergence of barter as a viable purchase method threatens taxation, customs, banking, and accounting conventions that underlie the functioning of most governments. For example in Russia, barter between industrial firms has reached 40% of total procurements. Of the corporations listed on the New York Stock Exchange, 65% are presently using some form of barter. Examples of specific transactions are General Motors' swap of locomotives for tea in Sri Lanka and PepsiCo's trade of syrup and technology for Russian vodka.[7] In the United States, nearly 400 independently operated barter exchanges represent a client base or network of more than 240,000 retailers, services, and manufacturers. Through the use of computers, exchanges can globally search for traders to match their needs.

Authentication of E-Commerce Payments

The descent of cash has been marked by successively more portable and less massive forms of cash. Digital payments represent the logical culmination of this evolution (at least on the portability/mass parameters). Digital cash is virtually weightless, bearing only the mass of the electrons that convey payment information, and can be ported to one place or another at the speed of light. This culmination represents yet another quantitative change so dramatic that its effect is qualitative.

Physical possession no longer provides a general basis for ownership of cash. Digital information can, in effect, be in multiple places at once. This qualitative change demands new mechanisms for authenticating the source and destination of payments. Authentication of digital payments relies on authenticating the identities of the payer and payee, typically through capture of private information—password, cryptographic key, fingerprint, iris scan—for each of the parties to a payment transaction. In addition, general controls must be implemented to prevent any particular individual from posing as some other individual in order to gain access to his or her assets.

Electronic payment schemes often retain physical vestiges reminiscent of earlier forms of cash, simply because consumers feel more comfortable holding something tangible. This physical vestige is typically the point most vulnerable to payment abuse. Indeed, where electronic media convey payment information at the speed of light, tangible, physical components—for example, cards, magnetic stripe readers, and so forth—present the exposed Achilles' heel of payment authentication.

Credit cards, for example, provide a link between an individual (with an identifying PIN) and a bank (with the individual's credit line and debit account balance). Using only electronic communications, a centrally administered payment system such as that used for credit card payments could theoretically identify an individual (e.g., through biometric identification), find his or her bank account records, and make a payment. Since physical possession of a credit card provides a surrogate identification for the individual (signatures occurring only after the sale, and kept locally at the retailer's), theft of the card essentially allows theft of the cardholder's identity.

Most credit card losses result from loss or theft of the physical card. Increasingly popular is the theft of card number and magnetic stripe information via handheld card readers, typically found in restaurants, where a waiter can swipe the card on the handheld reader while walking to the cashier. This information is later extracted from a hard disk on the handheld reader, electronically transmitted to another country, and used to manufacture a counterfeit credit card that can be put into circulation within hours of the theft. MasterCard and Visa International have reported similar figures on credit card fraud—more than 80% of credit card losses occur because of the misuse of the physical card.[8] Abuses from Internet theft or fraud of credit card information have been virtually nonexistent.

Payment authentication has had to reach new levels of sophistication and complexity to handle e-commerce. In the first two years of Web-based commerce, security was the oft-cited deterrent to wider commerce on the Internet. In answer, Web server and browser vendors quickly developed extensions to verify identities with passwords, electronic signatures, and Internet protocol (IP) addresses. Continual progress has been made in developing a more effective system of digital certification and authentication.[9]

Correspondingly, external threats from criminals and hackers have expanded significantly as larger segments of the population gain sophistication in computer usage. As digital assets and payment methods proliferate, so do the temptations that attract lawbreakers toward computer crime. These can best be understood in the context of a rational choice model of computer and network crime, which is depicted in figure 10.5.

Rational choice models of crime assume that individuals weigh choices and alternatives along the paths taken toward commiting a crime, though their choices may not always seem "rational" from the perspective of law-abiding citizens. The

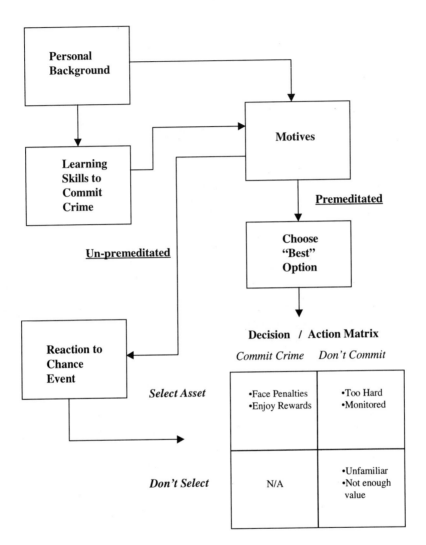

Figure 10.5
Rational choice schematic for computer and network crime

complexity of many computer crimes demands premeditation, problem solving, and perseverance. In this context an assumption of rational choice seems reasonable, and it can serve as a model for the larger framework needed for payment authentication.

Identification of Individuals

Passwords are the most commonly used deterrent to computer crime. Passwords appear in a number of differing contexts: as entry permit; as secret key that unlocks an encrypted message; as signature that identifies the author of a message; and so forth. In all cases, they serve one purpose: to uniquely identify an individual as having some type of authorization. Passwords assume that there is a system for authorization with procedures and a database of authorized individuals, that there is a system for approval (i.e., identifying whether an individual is in the database or not), and that approval errors—type I and type II—are limited. Passwords address only a small subset of the problems encountered in ensuring secure electronic commerce and secure digital payments. Several other components need to be actively controlled before any payment mechanism can be considered secure. The full set of components for a secure system can be understood in the context of the rational choice model of criminal behavior (see figure 10.5).

Authorization databases may either be maintained, verified, and located centrally —in which case security is centrally authorized, as is the case with most credit cards —or they may be maintained locally, in a card or other object physically located on the individual. The latter option offers the advantage of privacy, but is more difficult to administer. Approval involves a comparison of database information with personal information, such as a secret key. The "Mondex Electronic Cash in Hong Kong" case study included in this chapter considers some of the difficulties encountered in the decentralized authorization of payment. The case study "Access Security at McDonnell Douglas Aerospace Information Services" considers some of the difficulties encountered in managing a centralized authorization system.

Partly because they are the most common form of security applied to information assets, passwords are the most commonly breached controls. Passwords are particularly prone to subversion through social engineering, that is, tricking individuals into giving up passwords. Several methods are common. "Shoulder surfing" involves peering over the shoulder of a person as he enters his password (a technique that may be augmented with binoculars, listening devices for key tones, and so forth). Systems administrators may receive telephone calls from hackers posing as upset workers who have lost their passwords and ask them to be changed to another, which the hacker can then use to breach security. Workers can be threatened into giving up passwords, personal identification codes, key cards, and so forth. Passwords and keys provide poor protection in the face of these threats.

Technology offers biometric systems that offer much greater accuracy, and much less threat of being breached, than passwords. Although they still face the normal social and legal resistance incurred by any new technology, they are appearing more often in monitoring and control systems. Biometric systems use unique human characteristics or behaviors to distinguish among people. The first biometric identification systems were based on the fingerprint. Various police departments in the United States since the 1920s have kept fingerprint files of criminals. Biometric systems now span the spectrum from voiceprints, signature analysis, hand geometry, and keystroke dynamics to retinal scan, iris scan, hand and wrist veins, and facial recognition. Biometric systems have become more accurate, reliable, and affordable, but still give too many false negatives to be widely accepted by consumers (or banks interested in promoting their payment schemes).

Of all currently available biometric systems, iris imaging probably has the edge in accuracy and ease of application, but it is considerably more expensive than fingerprint recognition. Iris-imaging technology is likely to be combined with a digital certificate and a coded database image of a person's iris in its applications to digital payments. The technology was developed by Leonard Flom and Aran Safir, two ophthalmologists who now work for IriScan in the United States. In the 1980s, they proved that the iris's complex patterns provide a more precise means of identification than the relatively simple loops and whorls of a fingerprint. The human iris has some 260 independent variables compared to fingerprints' roughly 35. The iris pattern can be read from a distance of up to 10 meters. The iris and its unique pattern do not change as a person ages, unlike fingerprints and other biometrics. For this reason, the unintrusive technology of iris-scanning systems offers high recognition accuracy.

Low technology solutions should not be overlooked, however, since they may be even more effective in identifying individuals than sophisticated biometrics. For example, credit cards with photographs of their owners provide very effective identification of individuals. The Royal Bank of Scotland, which introduced photocards several years ago, claimed that photographs cut credit card fraud by 85%. In considering the implementation of any of these technologies, banks and other payment authorities may face a delicate public relations dilemma: whether to accept moderate levels of fraud, rather than invest in costly new technology or risk alienating their customers with additional security precautions.

Privacy

Privacy is security over information that people consider to be uniquely their property. The protection of personal privacy has become one of the most controversial aspects of computer security. The primary impetus for concern is the growth of information on the World Wide Web, and the ease of use and thoroughness of search engines for accessing that information. In the United States, there has been strong resistance to any governmental interference in access to Internet information. The U.S. government has reserved the right to access Internet transactions, and in doing so has long argued for maintaining an export ban on strong cryptography. In another arena, the U.S. Communications Decency Act, passed in conjunction with the U.S. Telecommunications Act of 1996, specifies certain restrictions on material that may be accessed through the Internet (focusing largely on pornographic material) and in certain situations making strong encryption a criminal offence.[10]

A number of European laws implemented over the past two decades address the ever increasing scope of databases of personal information and the threats to individual privacy arising from potential abuse of personal data. These laws in general have built upon the basic laws protecting privacy implemented in Bavaria in the late 1970s. Perhaps the most clearly articulated and comprehensive set of privacy standards are reflected in the U.K. Data Protection Act of 1984, perhaps one of the most far-reaching and well-conceived laws protecting privacy of personal records. (Similar laws have been enacted in Germany and elsewhere in Europe.)

The act provides individuals with a number of safeguards against abuse of personal information contained in databases. Individuals are able to apply for a copy of all data stored on computer that relates to them. They can also insist on that information's being corrected if it is wrong or out of date. The act provides for compensation for financial loss or physical injury that occurs as a result of data that is inaccurate, lost, destroyed, or disclosed without authority. Liability under this act is criminal. The following principles guide the act:

• Data can be obtained only by lawful means and with the data subject's knowledge or consent.

• A data collector may collect only data relevant to its purposes, and such data must be kept up to date, accurate, and complete.

• At the time of collection, the purposes to which the data will be applied must be disclosed to the data subject, and the data may not be used for purposes beyond this.

• The collector may not disclose the data to outsiders without the consent of the data subject, unless the law otherwise requires it.

• Data collectors must take reasonable precautions against loss, destruction, or unauthorized use, modification, or disclosure.

• The data subject should be able to determine the whereabouts, use, and purpose of personal data relating to him or her.

• The data subject has the right to inspect any data concerning him or her as well as the right to challenge the accuracy of such data and have errors rectified or erased by the collector.

• The data collector, under the edicts of the act, is accountable to the data subject in complying with the above principles.

Courts throughout the world seem to lean toward protection of privacy over commercial interests, though there is still much legal ground to traverse. Computer-related privacy issues are unlikely to be resolved in the courts in the near future.

Controls

Controls on crime are implemented in specific processes that limit damage from adverse events or prevent them altogether. Controls can be classified by point in time of application with respect to commission of the crime, point of application, breadth of application, objective of the controls applied, nature of the crime, or type of response.

The rational choice framework, presented in figure 10.5, favors a sequential rather than a layered control strategy. A sequential strategy attempts to influence criminal decision making at several points in the sequence leading up to a computer crime. In contrast, layered strategies and firewalls (closely monitored gateways through which all transactions entering a particular system are channeled) can be enhanced through the rational choice model's role for social engineering. Monitoring individuals with motives to commit crimes (e.g., ex-employees with a potential revenge motive) or making it difficult to learn the skills required to break into the system can provide perimeter controls. Physically isolating particular computers, data, or production software narrows the window of opportunity for a breach. Encryption and password controls can deter specific breach-of-control events.

The risk from threats arising external to an organization may be smaller than that from internal threats posed by employees and ex-employees, but it is also less foreseeable and thus less controllable. For this reason, much of an organization's control effort may be directed toward the monitoring and control of external attacks. (For an example, see the case study "Access Security at McDonnell Douglus Aerospace

Information Services" included in this chapter.) Of great concern to governments is an attack by a foreign government or group or domestic terrorists. They hold the potential to harm military operations as well as to disrupt banking and finance, create power outages, interrupt transportation nodes, and crash entire communications networks. "The Department of Defense is a prime target for even individual hackers who want to test their skills. They see the Department of Defense as the big banana, the final exam, the ultimate challenge to test their skills," commented Michael Vatis, the chief of the National Infrastructure Protection Center (NIPC) of the FBI, created in February 1998.[11]

The major avenue of attack from external sources is the Internet; the Internet may also be the greatest source of computer value and the most compelling reason for computer use. Approximately 100 million users in 70 countries link their computers through 27,000 Internet networks. According to Vincent Cerf, president of the Internet Society, a company with one computer stands a 1 in 1,540 chance of a hacker break-in per year based on 1994 statistics.[12] This says nothing about the magnitude of loss, or how quickly these statistics are changing given the exponential growth of Internet connections.

Given the enormous scale of this external threat, underreporting of crime may is likely more prevalent for computer and network crime than for traditional crimes. Donn Parker, an authority on computer crime, has commented that reliable statistics do not exist because the majority of computer crimes go unreported even if the victim detects them. Of the cases that make it to court, less than 3% of the accused ever face time in prison.[13] The number of crimes that actually occur but are not recorded by the police has been called "the dark figure."

The ephemerality of computer data amplifies computer and network crime's dark figure. This creates four problems for the control of computer and network crime. First, to provide enough evidence to prosecute, firms usually have to reveal weaknesses in their computer security systems, weaknesses that may not be easy to rectify, thus advertising their problems to other criminals.

Second, it is often easier for a firm to cut costs by eliminating the computer security group rather than to stop potential losses from crooks. If there are no systems for detection of computer crime, then no manager or lawyer has to face the chagrin (let alone political disadvantage) of a loss.

Third, gathering evidence about a computer or network crime requires expertise that is often difficult to acquire in the corporation and that often does not exist in police forces or district attorneys' offices. There may simply be no one available to construct a case.

Finally, even if a case can be constructed, the technical evidence is often too abstract or complex for juries to understand. Jury sympathies are often not with the victim, since most information crimes do not result in bodily harm, nor is the asset physically lost to the victim. Because computer-based evidence can be modified without an audit trail of the modifications, crucial evidence may be inadmissible, or at best subject to doubt. Prosecutors therefore find it difficult to prove guilt beyond a reasonable doubt and are not likely to take the case to trial at all.

Because of the ephemerality of computer data, the immediate response upon evidence of a computer or network crime is much like that for a burglary. The investigators should

- freeze the scene of the crime,

- document what has happened, and

- preserve the documentation (e.g., do not reconstruct a file without first copying it in its damaged state).

Strict rules govern the admissibility of evidence in court. These are designed to ensure fairness and to guard against tampering or misrepresentation. Computer evidence and records must be gathered and documented with great care, especially because of the volatile and manipulable nature of computer media. Note that there has been a tendency to exclude as evidence computer-resident data in recent years, extending even to videotapes, which may be recorded and modified on computers.

The victimized corporation is often in a better position to deal with a crime than law enforcement. Although initially it may be reluctant to take action because it wishes to protect its reputation or does not feel it has a strong case, if a company has its own experienced investigators, they can assemble a case—interview employees, assemble phone and audit trail records—more effectively than law enforcement officials. Once law officers are involved, they are required to abide by an inflexible set of rules that can significantly slow the progress of a case.

Corporations are used to prosecuting civil cases. Standards are much higher for a criminal case, and ignorance of privacy laws and so forth can leave the evidence open to attack in court. Law enforcement officers are used to this greater burden of proof. Many computer cases in criminal court are concluded based not on what the perpetrator did or what the evidence is, but whether it was obtained legally and whether it is admissible. Once you have collected evidence incorrectly, you cannot go back and do it correctly. Because of the technical complexity of much of the evidence, law enforcement may often call in computer security consultants to collect evidence.

Table 10.2
Steps in prosecuting a computer crime

Step	Potential outcome that may terminate the case at that step
Crime committed	Not detected
Reported	Not investigated
Investigation	Unsolved
Arrest	Released without prosecution
Booking	Released without prosecution
Preliminary appearance in court	Charges dopped or dismissed
Bail or detention	
Adjudication	Arbitration, settlement out of court
Arraignment	Charges dismissed
Trial	Acquittal
Sentencing	Appeal
Sentencing	Probation
Sentencing	Prison, fine

Because of the complexities of investigating computer crime, law enforcement is often very selective in choosing cases and committing resources and will demand serious commitment from the victim. There is also a great deal of legal uncertainty in computer and network crime. Many laws have not been tested, and few companies want to break new legal ground.

Unfortunately for the control of computer and network crime, effective, deterrent penalties are difficult to formulate because of the low probability of prosecution. Expected reward from computer crime is immediate. Expected penalties are low and made lower by discounting over time, recognizing the long and tortuous route to detection and prosecution of computer crime. Table 10.2 shows how, at each step in the chain of actions required to bring a computer crime from commission to eventual punishment in the court system, a certain number of cases cease to be pursued.

The concepts of guilt and shame cultures introduced by Ruth Benedict[14] may provide suggestions for control, given the level of underreporting inherent in computer crime statistics. Shame cultures, according to Benedict, favor close monitoring of behavior to ensure conformity to social norms. They tend to place a low value on individualism, to monitor individual behavior tightly, especially by conducting activities in groups, and to use shame in front of the group as a behavioral sanction. Guilt cultures, on the other hand, depend on early and intense indoctrination into social norms, work ethic, and mission of the organization.

Parallels may be drawn to the narrower world of a corporation's information assets. Employees and ex-employees are potentially the easiest group to monitor and control. Shame controls would monitor and log keystrokes on personal computers, maintain video cameras everywhere, and regularly subject employees to tempered interrogation. In contrast, guilt controls would attempt to create a workforce with *esprit de corps* combined with a distinct respect for the firm and its managers. Such a corporate culture can be perpetuated by careful hiring and promotion, by clearly stated corporate mission and project agendas, and by recognizing contributions to the company. A 1990 study by Kerbo and Inoue[15] showed that a shame culture exerts less control over white-collar crime than a guilt culture.

Encryption and Password Controls

Secure electronic commerce and digital payment are made possible by advances in one particular class of controls: encryption and password controls,[16] which scramble information assets while they are in transit through networks such as the Internet, making them difficult for criminals to steal or sabotage. The variety of transactions protected by encryption is broad: electronic mail is gradually replacing conventional paper mail; electronic data interchange is rapidly replacing paper documentation for ordering and billing; electronic commerce channels are finally being refined and made operational. Unencrypted electronic transactions are relatively easy to intercept and scan for interesting keywords. Even with secure databases, unencrypted transactions to and from the database can leave corporate data open to surveillance, which can be accomplished easily, routinely, automatically, and undetectably on a grand scale. International cablegrams are already scanned this way on a large scale by intelligence organizations, by organized crime, and by drug traffickers. Because of the vulnerability of electronic transactions, encryption has become an important control over networked computer systems risk. The following sections provide a brief overview of encryption controls.

Single-Key Cryptosystems

Encryption systems follow a simple set of principles in their design. Assume that I want to send you a message and do not want anyone but you to read it. I "encrypt" or "encipher" the message, scrambling the information content so that it is unreadable to anyone except you, the intended recipient. I supply a "key" or password to encrypt the message, and you have to use the same key to decipher or "decrypt" it. This sort of system is called a single-key encryption system. Single-key systems are the simplest way to secure messages. They are also the least secure encryption approach.

Conventional cryptosystems such as the U.S. Federal Data Encryption Standard (DES) use a single key for both encryption and decryption. DES encryption is the only encryption that the U.S. government allows to be implemented in software transferred outside of the United States (including free software that may be downloaded from the Internet). Even good software that uses DES in the correct modes of operation has problems. Standard DES uses a 56-bit key, which may be easily broken by exhaustive key searches.

The primary weakness in a single-key system is that the key must be transmitted via secure channels so that both parties can know it. If you already have a secure channel for transmitting information, then you do not need encryption. In practice, the key is sent over an unsecured but different communication channel.

Public Key Cryptosystems and Digital Signatures

Security can be greatly improved by the use of public-key cryptosystems. In such systems, the sender and the receiver of a message have two related, complementary keys, a publicly revealed key and a private key (which is kept secret). Each key unlocks the code that the other key makes.

An individual's public and private keys are generated simultaneously using a mathematical algorithm. Messages encrypted with one key (the public key) can be decrypted only with the other key (the private or secret key). Public keys can be known to anyone. In fact it is best for public keys to be widely disseminated (e.g., via the recipient's Web page). Private keys must be kept as that individual's own personal secret.

To transmit a secure message, the sender encrypts her message with the public key of the intended recipient. The recipient decrypts that message with her own secret key. Indeed, the only key that will decrypt the message is the private key which was generated with the public key used to originally encrypt that message.

When public key cryptography is used to digitally sign a message, this process is turned on its head. The sender "signs" the message with her private key—that is, in this case the message is encrypted with the private rather than the public key. The recipient can then validate the signature by applying the sender's public key to the message—that is, decrypting the message with a key that is widely known to belong to the sender. Ideally, this public key will have been downloaded from the sender's Web site, or from some other public forum. If the public key successfully decrypts the message, it must have been signed with the corresponding private key.

Public key encryption and decryption are slower than equivalently secure private key algorithms, often thousands of times slower. Slow speed of operation can be a major deterrent to public key encryption in retail transactions. For this reason, public and private key algorithms are often used in conjunction; for example, Phil Zimmermann's widely used Pretty Good Privacy encryption uses a combined public key/ private key algorithm to enhance its response time.

It is not possible to discover the private key from knowing the public key. Thus the public key can be published and widely disseminated across (unsecured) communications networks. This protocol provides security without the need for the same kind of secure channels that a single key cryptosystem requires.

A public-key system provides several advantages that make it the choice for digital cash and electronic commerce systems across the World Wide Web. Anyone can use a recipient's public key to encrypt a message to that person; that recipient then uses its private key to decrypt that message. No one but the recipient can decrypt it, because no one else has access to that private key. Not even the person who encrypted the message can decrypt it.

Public-key cryptosystems also provide message authentication, in which the sender's private key can be used to encrypt a message, thereby "signing" it digitally. (The private key is unique like a signature, in that no one else can easily reproduce this information.) The recipient or anyone else can check this digital signature by using the sender's public key to decrypt it. Signing authenticates that the sender was the true originator of the message, and that the message has not been subsequently altered by anyone else. The electronic signature is actually an improvement over hand signatures in commerce, because forgery of a signature is infeasible, and the sender cannot later disavow his or her signature.

A sender can combine signatures and encryption to provide both privacy and authentication by first signing a message with his or her own private key, then encrypting the signed message with recipient's public key. The recipient reverses these steps by first decrypting the message with his or her own private key, then checking the enclosed signature with the sender's public key.

In most systems, sender and recipient do not explicitly perform these steps; they are done automatically by the encryption software. The only real drawback to public-key encryption systems is that since public-key encryption algorithms are much more complex than single-key encryption algorithms, they are also significantly slower.

Key Rings

Keys are kept in individual "key certificates" that include the key owner's user identification (the person's name), a time stamp of when the key pair (the public key and its corresponding private key) was generated, and the actual key material. Pubilc-key certificates contain the public-key material, whereas private-key certificates contain the corresponding (secret) private-key material. Each private key is also encrypted with its own password, in case it gets stolen. A key file, or "key ring" contains one or more of these key certificates. Public key rings contain public key certificates, and private key rings contain private key certificates. These rings are the principal method of storing and managing public and private keys. Rather than keep individual keys in separate key files, they are collected in key rings to facilitate the automatic lookup of keys either by key identification or by individual's name. Each user keeps his or her own pair of key rings.

Certifying Authorities

Rather than being protected from exposure, public keys are widely disseminated. However, it is important to protect public keys from being tampered with, to make sure that a public key really belongs to whom it appears to belong to. This may be the most vulnerable aspect of a public-key system. We illustrate here how a public key system might be abused.

Suppose you wanted to send a private message to individual A. You download A's public key certificate from an anonymous FTP site. You encrypt your message transaction to A with this downloaded public key and send it to him through Internet e-mail header. Unfortunately, unbeknownst to you or A, another individual, C, has altered A's information on the FTP site and generated a public key of his own with A's name attached to it. He covertly substitutes his bogus key in place of A's real public key. You unwittingly use this bogus key belonging to C instead of A's public key. All looks normal to you, because this bogus key has A's name on it. Now C can decipher the message intended for A because he has the matching private key (which his encryption program created at the same time that its key generation routine generated his bogus public key—the one that has A's name attached to it). He may even reencrypt the deciphered message with A's real public key and send it along to A so that no one suspects any wrongdoing. Furthermore, he can even make apparently valid signatures from A with this private key because everyone will use the bogus public key (the one that C created) to check A's signatures.

The only way to prevent this sort of masquerade is to stop anyone from tampering with public keys. If you obtained A's public key directly from A, this is not a problem. However, personally authenticating identities is impractical for large volumes of commercial transactions, or even for long distance personal communications. An alternative is to get A's public key from a mutual trusted friend D who knows he has a good copy of A's public key. D could sign A's public key, vouching for its integrity.

This requires that you have a known good copy of D's public key to check D's signature. D can also provide A with a signed copy of your public key, thus serving as an "introducer" between you and A. A widely trusted person or institution can specialize in providing this service of introducing users to each other by vouching, via its own signature, for their public key certificates. This trusted source is called a *certifying authority.*

A trusted centralized key server or certifying authority is especially appropriate for large, impersonal, centrally controlled corporate or government institutions. Some institutional environments use hierarchies of certifying authorities. A logical choice for a certifying authority is a large, trustworthy and wealthy institution. The U.S. Postal Service has actively sought to be the primary U.S. certifying authority for digital payments. Banks and governmental units such as the Treasury Department could also credibly provide the services of a certifying authority.

With the growth of digital cash, banking and financial institutions are increasingly entering into the business of being certifying authorities. These institutions are issuing *digital certificates,* the electronic counterpart to drivers' licenses, passports, and the like in cyberspace. These digital certificates provide a reliable tool for verifying that people are who they say they are, a crucial matter for commerce on open networks like the Web. In practice, digital certificates are just an embellishment on public key signatures discussed earlier in this chapter. With digital signatures, the sender generates public and private keys, then "signs" (i.e., encrypts) with the private key and broadcasts the public key. With digital certificates, a certifying authority (rather than the individual) generates the public and private keys at the request of an individual contracting for the services of the certifying authority. Both keys are retained on the certifying authority's database, under the certifying authority's control. The private key is given to the individual as a "signature." The public key becomes a "digital certificate" that verifies that the sender (i.e., the individual with that particular private key) is who they say they are, providing a digital counterpart to an ID card such as a passport or driver's license. A vendor asking for verification of a particular electronic transaction asks the certifying authority for the "digital certificate" (i.e., public key), which the certifying authority vouches is truly identified with a particular individual. In Internet-based transactions, digital identification takes place invisibly through software built into the browser, and via icon clicks. The U.S. company Verisign uses a relatively standard approach that offers several classes of security. A class 1 certificate verifies only e-mail addresses, by e-mailing a personal information number that the user must enter into the registration. A class 2 certificate provides to Websites, on demand, the holder's real name, which Verisign has confirmed by checking name, address, U.S. social security number, and other information against a credit bureau database. A class 3 certificate is available to companies; corporate employees go to a Verisign office and present photo identification.

Certificates (provided to consumers) augment the security of passwords (which identify consumers by what they know). Certificates are the digital equivalent of a driver's license or employee badge. Possessing a driver's license authorizes an individual to drive; possessing an employee badge authorizes an individual to occupy and use company property; possessing a digital certificate authorizes an individual to access information resources.

Internet certificates appear in Secure Socket Layer (SSL) protocol, which requires a server to present its digital certificate to the client as part of the SSL handshake. Single-user logon via a browser/client is a local operation, but browsers, once logged on, are required to present their certificates to servers they access during a session. Certificates also play a central role in secure e-mail over S/MIME.

Automated Cancellation

Additional control can be exerted through automated cancellation of message transactions after an elapsed period of time. This type of control is used in the Kerberos security system. Automatic cancellation ensures that there is a limited window of opportunity for any computer abuse. Since a delay is associated with many types of computer abuse (because criminals may need several attempts to breach security), one that does not exist with the legitimate processing of the transaction, automated cancellation can effectively thwart much abuse.

Automated cancellation is particularly useful where computers communicate with each other without human intervention. Such communication is common in electronic data interchange and in Internet transactions where the average message is sent through 10 to 15 different machines in traveling from sender to receiver. When machines are communicating, cancellation can occur after only a few seconds, significantly lowering the probability that human or computer intervention can steal or corrupt the message transaction.

Firewalls

The security of Internet transactions remains a central concern for e-commerce. Two commonly employed security measures are *electronic certificates*, which allow Internet users to accurately identify the host and client in a transaction, and *firewalls*, which serve as gatekeepers to restrict access to resources.

Firewalls act as buffers between the internal network and the global Internet that prevent illegitimate access (though not necessarily with 100% effectiveness). There are two main types of Internet firewalls: packet-level filters and application-level gateways. As its name suggests, *packet-level filtering* provides the capability to monitor each Internet (TCP/IP) packet, and examines addresses and port numbers of those seeking network access to ensure that the traffic is authorized. *Application-level gateways* masquerade as surrogate as machines for all of the machines on the network for incoming and outgoing Internet traffic. Packet-level filtering is commonly implemented and is often augmented by application-level gateway monitoring.

Notes

1. Barter is still common worldwide. It is estimated that 40% of Russia's business is transacted through barter.

2. Shortcomings in divisibility plague even modern currency. Coca Cola has estimated that 20–25% of its vending machine sales are lost because a customer's pocket change does not match that required by the machine for purchase. E. K. Clemons, D. C. Croson, and B. W. Weber, "Reengineering Money: The Mondex Stored Value Card and Beyond, *International Journal of Electronic Commerce*, 1(2), Winter 1996–97, p. 5–31.

3. Aristotle, *Politics* (translated by Benjamin Jowett), The Internet Classics Archive, *http://classics.mit.edu// Aristotle/politics.html*, part VIII.

4. D. J. Boorstin, *The discoverers*, New York: H. N. Abrams, 1991, p. 652–657.

5. Alvin Toffler, *Powershift: Knowledge, wealth, and violence at the edge of the 21st century*, New York: Bantam Books, 1990.

6. Andrew Odlyzko of AT&T, in his article "Tragic Loss or Good Riddance" (October 16, 1996 available on-line: *ftp://elib.zib.de/netlib/att/math/odlyzko/tragic.loss.long.ps*), describes an experiment by AT&T to test customers' receptiveness to metered local telephone calling as a substitute for the flat fee in effect then. Metered service was set at $5 per month for 50 free calls, after which calls were metered at 5 cents each. Flat rate was $7.50 for unlimited calls. AT&T found that 50% of customers where were making well under the 50 calls still preferred to stay with flat rates.

7. A. Nucifora, "Businesses Buying into Age-Old Barter System," Austin *Business Journal*, May 5, 1997 (available on-line: http://cgi.amcity.com/austin/stories/050597/smallb5.html).

8. Reported in separate seminars by MasterCard and Visa International at the IT Security Management Seminar, June 17–18, 1998, jointly presented by the Hong Kong Police and Hong Kong University of Science & Technology.

9. In particular, the U.S. government supports the development of both a domestic and global uniform commercial legal framework that will recognize, facilitate, and enforce electronic transactions worldwide. Internationally, the U.S. government is working with the United Nations Commission on International Trade Law (UNCITRAL), which has completed work on a model law that supports the commercial use of international contracts in electronic commerce. The government is also encouraging the work of the International Chamber of Commerce, which has issued model commercial code guidelines.

10. US citizens can purchase and use products with the strongest encryption available on the market without providing the government with any extraordinary access to encrypted information. U.S. law prohibits domestic companies from exporting products with strong security features—i.e., any algorithm using a key longer than 40 bits (the more bits, the stronger the encryption). The 40-bit limit was set in 1992, which today is easy to break. At the time of writing, U.S. products utilizing the 20-year-old 56-bit Data Encryption Standard are prohibited from export, yet products using 128 bit keys are available outside the United States from non-U.S. vendors.

11. P. Connole, FBI unit reports 'substantial' cyber attacks, *ZDNet Anchordesk*, June 11, 1998 (available on-line: http://www.zdnet.com/anchordesk/).

12. With many computers, the risk increases rapidly. Taking Mr. Cerf's estimates literally, the probability of a security breach each year is $1 - \left(\frac{1539}{1540}\right)^n$ for n computers—this is roughly $n \times \frac{1}{1540}$ up to about 500 computers, and levels off to a certainty of at least one breach per year after a few thousand computers.

13. This figure has appeared in a number of Parker's works, including D. B. Parker, *Managers' Guide to Computer Security* (Reston, Virginia: Reston Publishing 1981). Donn Parker explained in a personal communication with one of the authors (Westland) that most experts considered this a credible estimate, but lacked data to support their opinion. For lack of other evidence, the figure is often cited.

14. R. Benedict, *Patterns of Culture* (Boston: Houghton Mifflin, 1989; first printing 1934).

15. H. R. Kerbo and M. Inoue, Japanese Social Structure and White Collar Crime: Recruit Cosmos and Beyond, *Deviant Behavior* 11, 2 (April–June 1990): p. 139–154.

16. For the purpose of this book, password and encryption controls will be considered equivalent, despite differences in their implementation from a technical perspective. Both require that the accessor possess a secret word (a "key" in the case of encryption) used to gain admittance to assets and access to information. This password is a way of identifying the accessor, as well as ensuring that the accessor indeed does have authorization for access. A straightforward password verification compares the unaltered password with a database of authorized passwords, allowing access if it finds a match. Encryption processes the password (or "key") through a mathematical algorithm to determine its validity; it may also compare it to a database of authorized passwords. And various combinations and refinements of these procedures can be built into an encryption system. We have relied on the documentation to Phil Zimmermann's Pretty Good Privacy software package in preparing this section. The most recent update of Pretty Good Privacy, along with FAQ's and reports on new developments (legal and technical) can be obtained is available on the PGP Web page (http://www.ifi.uio.no/~staalesc/PGP/).

Mondex Electronic Cash in Hong Kong

Cash is a generic term for coins, banknotes, and checks, which constitute the most liquid class of assets. All the coins in Hong Kong are minted by a company owned by the Hong Kong Monetary Authority. Banknotes are issued by three major banks in Hong Kong—The Hong Kong and Shanghai Banking Corporation (Hong Kong Bank), Standard Chartered Bank, and The Bank of China. This peculiarity of Hong Kong carried over from British colonial rule in the 19th century where the official medium of payment was uncoined silver, or *bullion* (as opposed to *specie*, the term for coined silver or gold). Consequently the colonial government never established a mint. Because of the inconvenience of carrying bullion, Japanese and local banks operating in Hong Kong began issuing their own banknotes, which proved more portable and convenient. In Hong Kong, banks continue to print all of the bank-notes, long after bullion has ceased to serve as a medium of payment. Today, payments in cash comprise 80% of all transactions in Hong Kong and 70% of total money spent.

The major advantages of using cash, including coins, checks, and banknotes, are anonymity, divisibility, and usability anywhere. (In addition, cash should possess characteristics of portability, ease of use, time shifting, security, privacy, durability, and flexibility.) Coins are unsanitary, heavy, and bulky, features detracting from their portability. Banknotes provide a solution, but with their own disadvantages. One may have money in the bank, but must go to the bank in order to get the banknotes in hand. This is both expensive and risky—money has to be printed and then circulated, a time during which it can be stolen or forged. These weaknesses have been a primary reason for introduction of alternative forms of money.

Cash substitutes are closely monitored and controlled by the Monetary Authority, which is also responsible for maintaining Hong Kong's U.S. dollar peg. A currency board arrangement redeems banknotes against the U.S. dollar at a fixed rate of about HK$7.8 to US$1. Cash substitutes that might store value and be used to purchase goods in multiple currencies present potential long-run challenges to this system. The Monetary Authority is also concerned with the seigniorage of legal tender. Banknotes may be viewed as non-interest-bearing liabilities on the balance sheet of the Exchange Fund. The fund earns interest on the corresponding U.S. dollar assets backing the banknotes. To the extent that cash substitutes may reduce the use of banknotes, this profit would be reduced, again presenting potential long-run challenges to this system.

In addition to cash, consumer payment relies increasingly on several card-based products that are used as retail substitutes for cash. A magnetic stripe card has a strip of magnetic tape (basically audio recording tape) attached to a paper core printed

This case was prepared by J. Christopher Westland.

with graphics and sealed inside clear plastic. The magnetic stripe is divided laterally into three tracks, each of which has been designed for differing applications. Credit and debit cards are specific types of magnetic stripe value access cards that can initiate transfers from one store of value (e.g., a bank account) to another store of value (e.g., a retailer's bank account).

Diners Club issued the first credit card in Hong Kong in 1959. Since then, the number has grown to 5 million credit cards in a population of 6.4 million people. The average resident has two credit cards, though only 20–30% of cardholders ever use their cards for payment at all. Credit card purchases account for 5% of all transactions (22% in terms of value). Drawing cash advances on credit cards is not common (Banking World 1996).

Credit cards offer the major advantage of deferred payment. But credit cards have limitations also. Customers' credit limits cannot be exceeded, sometimes resulting in lost sales. Credit card transactions involve multiple parties, resulting in considerable overhead costs, time, and infrastructure investment. Because of such transaction costs, more merchants are refusing to accept credit cards for low-value transactions, or alternatively, are passing the cost of authorizing and accounting directly to the customer as a credit card surcharge of between 3% and 5%.

Debit cards are mainly magnetic stripe cards that enable the cardholder's account to be debited immediately after the transaction is finished. Debit card transactions may involve fund transfer or withdrawal transactions at automated teller machines (ATMs). As a result of credit card surcharges, they are increasingly being used for retail purchases (called electronic fund transfers at the point of sale, or EPSs). Most debit cards in Hong Kong may serve either purpose.

Visa Cash is representative of a hybrid application of magnetic stripe card technology that has characteristics of credit, debit, and stored-value cards. Visa currently has issued 200,000 disposable HK$200 stored-value cards and logged 250,000 transactions, an average of 2,500 weekly, with the average charge between HK$5 and HK$10. The card is accepted at most of the approximately 2,500 ATMs in Hong Kong.

Mondex Electronic Cash

Electronic cash (e-cash) means different things to different people. Though there have been over 50 market introductions of e-cash around the world since the beginning of the decade (at substantial cost for each introduction), no one form of e-cash has predominated. Mondex has the most mature e-cash product; it is in use in approximately fifteen markets in 1998. It is implemented as a hybrid debit card, electronic purse, and Internet payment scheme, and thus subsumes the three major markets intended for e-cash in general. Functional depth and maturity make Mondex e-cash a suitable representative for generic e-cash. Mondex's e-cash format is widely accepted by the finance and computer science communities as a standard for e-cash. Mondex's product is considered an archetype for e-cash implementation.[1]

Mondex reported from test marketing that customers were using their e-cash to replace approximately 9% of physical cash transactions. This figure was questioned by Clemons, Croson, and Weber (1997), who noted that the claimed usage was an order of magnitude greater than first-year rates of consumer adoption for electronic home banking or debit card use in the United States. They also pointed out confounding factors in the Mondex statistics—(1) usage was self-reported, subjecting it to faulty memory and "halo" effects, and (2) the trial was subsidized (i.e., the service was deliberately underpriced), which inflated demand for the service, assuming that the subsidies achieved their intended purpose.

A Mondex card must be physically in contact with the card reading/writing device, just as is required of a debit card, except the magnetic stripe has been replaced by an ISO 7816–compliant microcomputer chip. The chip memory is loaded with value, to be used in future payment for goods or services at retailers or service outlets that participate. Money is secured through a password, and transactions are logged on the card. Two cardholders can transfer cash between their cards over a telephone line. Otherwise, operation and features are similar to traditional debit cards. An e-cash transaction starts by placing the e-cash card into a card reader. Several steps ensure that the transferred value reaches the correct destination and that fraud does not take place:

1. *Registration:* Information from the customer's card is validated against the merchant's database and vice versa.

2. *Value Transfer:* The merchant's terminal requests payment of a certain amount and transmits a digital signature with the request. Both cards check the authenticity of each other's message.

3. The customer's card checks the digital signature and, if satisfied, sends the amount, with its own digital signature attached. At this point, the value is deducted from the total value on the customer's card.

4. The merchant's terminal checks the digital signature and, if satisfied, sends acknowledgment, again with a digital signature.

5. Only after the amount has been deducted from the customer's card is value transferred to the merchant. This prevents the possibility of duplication or unauthorized creation of value.

On July 3, 1995, the first Mondex electronic cash payment was made by Bridget Marshall, a 22-year-old Royal Mail worker who bought a copy of the local newspaper. By late 1996, Mondex had already been pilot tested in the United Kingdom (13,000 cardholders in Swindon, 13,000 cardholders on two university campuses, 5,000 cardholders in office environments), Canada (900 cardholders), San Francisco (900 cardholders), and New Zealand (800 cardholders), though customer and merchant statistics were only available for the limited Byte and Swindon pilots (Ives and Earl 1997).

Mondex's Hong Kong pilot was launched on October 17, 1996. This has been the largest global pilot of an e-cash product to date. It is also the first trial outside a North American or Commonwealth environment, which significantly differentiates the pilot from prior studies, which is significant given that e-cash technologies are often justified in terms of their global reach.

Hong Kong offers a promising environment for e-cash. It has one of the highest penetrations of communications and computer technologies in the world, and the market potential for e-cash is large. HK$370 billion (US$50 billion) is spent by Hong Kong people annually in the retail market. 80% of all transactions are by cash payments, which account for almost 70% of the total money actually spent (Apple Daily Newspaper, 1997). Hong Kong's macroeconomics are sound, with Hong Kong's currency pegged at HK$7.75 to US$1 during the period. This insured that consumer perception concerning inflation and retail price stability, which could have altered customer preferences for cash or credit purchasing, did not influence buying behavior during the time of our survey.

The pilot was restricted to the Cityplaza and Kornhill Plaza shopping centers in Taikoo Shing and the New Town Plaza in Shatin. Customers of the banks who lived or worked near the shopping areas were invited to apply for Mondex cards, and more than 400 merchants in the malls had signed up to accept Mondex for payments. New Town Plaza, one of the busiest shopping centers and traffic interchanges in the New Territories in Hong Kong, also provided an excellent venue for the study of e-cash because of its large number of varied retail outlets.

Mondex heavily subsidized the pilot. During the pilot launch, all services and equipment were given free to cardholders and the merchants. Customers were offered a basic Mondex package consisting of a card and a balance reader free of charge and reductions on purchase of Mondex wallets. Sponsoring banks Hong Kong Bank and Hang Seng Bank promised that the actual charges to merchants after the launch would be lower than the rate levied by the existing electronic payment system, a debit system—0.75% of the purchase amount. One goal of the pilot launch was to provide information required to set the ultimate pricing structure of Mondex, and to establish

Table 10.3
E-cash and purchase amount

Amount (HK dollars)	Percentage of total e-cash use
<$100	58
$100 to $199	19
$200 to $499	4
$500 to $999	8
<$1,000	11

a pattern of card use and the capability of the supporting technology. The effect of these subsidies on the results of the survey, if any, would tend to bias retailer and customer behavior toward greater acceptance of the card.

By April 1997 in Hong Kong, more than 45,000 customers had applied for the Mondex card and around 420 merchants had also signed up to accept Mondex for payments (383 were actually using Mondex at the time of our survey). Mondex reported that the average usage in Hong Kong at that time was about HK$65, and 77% of the customers purchased goods under $200 with the Mondex card. According to Mondex, the average terminal withdrawal was HK$300, reflecting that the early usage was still at the low-value end (see table 10.3). Thus far the two primary e-cash products in Hong Kong, Prime Visa Cash and Mondex, together have penetrated less than 1% of the market, leaving considerable room for growth.

The Hong Kong Market for E-Cash

Mondex reported that 45% of its card transactions in Hong Kong were between about HK$11.50 and HK$60. E-cash tended to be most popular for fast-food restaurants. For high-value purchases like furniture and jewelry, credit cards and debit cards (EPSs) were typically the only payment methods used (*Mondex Magazine*, September 1996).

Mondex introduced their product into a market that had considerable experience with sophisticated electronic payment methods.

There are particular cost and operational advantages to the Mondex format of e-cash. Card level administration of transactions offers a significant cost advantage over centrally administered credit and debit cards—both overhead costs and risks. Most debit/credit card transactions involve at least five parties—purchaser and bank, merchant and bank, and the settlement agency. It is this separate settlement function which leads to overhead costs and is difficult to cost justify for small transactions.

Risks are also involved as banks extend credit to purchasers in the use of a credit card. The lower level of security of debit/credit cards also introduces risks to the banks as well as the merchants. Mondex e-cash is prepaid—customers download cash onto the card prior to payment. Money value stored in the card is non-interest-bearing, and banks profit from the float.

In addition, very small transactions—such as those required by many products sold over the Internet—are manageable with Mondex e-cash because the marginal cost of a transaction is extremely small. Mondex originally intended their e-cash product to be primarily a replacement for small cash purchases.[2] In March 1997, AT&T and Mondex jointly launched chip-to-chip payments on the Internet in the United States. This is integrated with AT&T Secure Buy Service. The Internet Open Trading Protocols will also be implemented, in coordination with AT&T and Hewlett-Packard.

Hong Kong's 6.4 million residents are connected to the Internet through around 50 Internet service providers, with one of the highest penetration rates of computer and communications technology in the world. Internet service providers are now charging US$0.01 and less per access for pictures, sound, and other intellectual property. Because Mondex security is implemented at the chip level, overhead costs associated with the central accounting systems of traditional credit cards do not exist. This means that Mondex transactions charges of fractions of one cent become viable. Currently, around 45% of smart card transactions in Hong Kong are between about US$1.50 and US$7.50—too small to be economically feasible on a centralized credit card system.

Though there is not one precise substitute for the services offered by Mondex e-cash, there are several competing payment technologies in Hong Kong which may substitute for Mondex e-cash in particular situations. At least for particular classes of transactions, these can be perceived as substitutes for Mondex-based payments. By providing viable substitutes they possibly diminish the acceptance of Mondex's e-cash offering.

Contact-based cards:

• *Prime Visa Cash Card:*   a reloadable multifunctional card combining credit, debit and stored-value card functions.

• *The Hong Kong Jockey Club Card:*   a multipurpose card that can process Jockey Club transactions, provide access to Jockey Club premises, as well as deduct payments for purchases from any one of the club's facilities. Like the Mondex card, it serves the purpose of electronic purse, but just for the Club's facilities.

• *Golden Harvest Movie Card:* This card functions as electronic purse and electronic coupon for the purchase of cinema tickets.

Contactless cards:

• *The Hospital Authority Patient Card:* The Patient Card issued by the Hospital Authority (the umbrella organization which manages 92% of the hospitals in Hong Kong) uses an optical memory to store information on the lifetime medical care of a patient.

• *The Creative Star Octopus Card:* developed by the Creative Star, a company formed by the Mass Transit Railway Corporation, Kowloon Canton Railway Corporation, Kowloon Motor Bus, Hong Kong and Yaumatei Ferry Company Ltd., and the City Bus. The customer can use the Octopus for travelling on the entire transportation network provided by the above companies. The idea is to minimize the use of coins, which brings about very high handling costs, and facilitate the common usage of payment methods among all the different modes of transportation.

Mondex's main competitor is Prime Visa Cash, which is the only general purpose e-cash card competing with Mondex. Prime Visa Cash currently has issued 200,000 cards and logged 250,000 transactions, an average of 2,500 weekly with the average charge between HK$5 and HK$10. In comparison to Mondex, the acceptance of Prime Visa Cash is very low. Prime Visa Card has the backing of Jetco, the region's largest automated teller machine network, with 47 member banks and 1,300 ATMs in Hong Kong and Macau, a number that is important in a community that deals in cash and that expects to find an ATM on every block. Both groups are talking with the manufacturers of the terminals and telephones to encourage them to develop devices to support their payment systems.

Mondex is a new product developed to be a true cash substitute. But existing payment methods in the market, including credit cards, EPSs and other on-line payment methods also can substitute for cash. Mondex theoretically has a cost advantage over electronic on-line payment systems—payment by credit cards is relatively costly for low-value transactions, and this cost is transferred to merchants and users. Consequently merchants and customers should prefer Mondex to other on-line payment methods for low-value transactions. Since Mondex stores value, the potential loss of interest and the risk of theft will not justify the use of Mondex for high-value transactions. Opportunities for Mondex seem to be higher at the low-value end, where the threat of substitute is lower. Profits tend to be thinner at this end of the market, and must be made up through high volumes.

Mondex's greatest threat of substitution is from cash, though much of this threat may derive from habit and conservative biases. Customers see cash as costless,[3] whereas use of Mondex may involve annual fees and purchase of accessory devices such as balance reader, electronic wallet, Mondex phone set, and so forth. These additional costs must be compensated by additional value added in using Mondex. Wide—probably global—applicability is very important to promote the product and change customers' payment habits.

Different payment methods possess advantages and limitations of their own. The major advantages of using cash, including coins, checks, and banknotes are that it is anonymous, divisible, and usable anywhere—from the street hawkers to the upscale merchants. Mondex is more anonymous (though it is not clear that customers fully understand or trust this to be the case), and more divisible than coins (with their discrete denominations), but is not as usable, because of the need for card-reading machines. This is particularly important in an economy in which most transactions are in currency and many merchants small and peripatetic. The survey revealed that over 90% of merchants saw cash as the most popular payment method. There is no involvement of a third party in cash transactions, which are more efficient anyway and take less time for each transaction than other payment methods.

Mondex's e-cash also corrects some of the significant defects of cash. Cash can be unsanitary and bulky. Fraud involving banknotes and coins can take place through the use of adequate forgeries produced with relatively inexpensive technology. If a forgery of the Mondex chip or the cryptography is not perfect, it will fail. Users are theoretically assured a level of privacy similar to that in currency-based transactions because Mondex does not track the movement of e-cash after it is issued to consumers. Many sales are lost because of mismatch between the desire to purchase a product and the means (i.e., particular currency denominations) to do so—in the case of Coca Cola, as much as 25% of vending machine sales may be lost because consumers cannot find the correct change. Mismatches are obviated by e-cash.

The necessity to get banknotes led to ATMs. ATMs provide immediate access to cash for customers with a debit card. This has reduced significantly the costs of having the customer physically visit the bank. ATM technology is expected to become less attractive with the introduction of cheaper and more adaptable cash withdrawal technologies such as telephones connected to desktop computers. An ATM costs US$25,000 to acquire and about the same cost each year to maintain. ATMs are threatened by facilities which would require a telephone and computer costing around US$2,000 (though where customers already own these items, their marginal cost is zero).

Credit cards offer the major advantage of deferred payment. Customers need only to pay back the card-issuing company within a certain defined time period to avoid interest charges. Growth of the credit market in Hong Kong has not slowed. On average 44% of all the transactions in our survey were by credit card payment, while cash payment constituted 50% of purchases. The high usage of credit cards may be due to the fact that the two areas are main shopping malls where many high-value items are sold. The increasing utilization of credit cards explains why the Hong Kong retail market continued to expand at a rapid rate in the midst of a retail slump in 1995. By one estimate, it would take at least five to ten years for the credit card market in Hong Kong to become saturated (Clemens, Croson, and Weber 1996–97).

A survey was conducted on Mondex e-cash usage in Hong Kong

1. to determine whether people are using Mondex and if so, who, when, and what type of purchases people are using it for, and

2. to assess the satisfaction of merchants with Mondex and what they think about the future of Mondex in Hong Kong.

Hong Kong's Mondex subscribers provided a representative sample of both potential Mondex adopters *and* non-adopters because

1. Mondex services were subsidized (essentially provided free of charge during the pilot), and

2. shopping centers' management coerced stores in their malls to adopt Mondex at the start of the pilot, assuring nearly 100% of the established stores in the malls accepted Mondex.

The detailed business lines of retailers accepting Mondex are listed in table 10.4.

The survey also revealed in detail how merchants ranked the utility of Mondex's e-cash, as shown in table 10.5. It is interesting to note the marginal percentages for each rank. There was a bias toward either giving a particular payment method a 1st or 2nd ranking, or otherwise refusing to rank a method (which shows as a "not applicable" on the chart). Though this is unlikely to bias the comparative preference for each payment method, it is consistent with the high level of ambivalence noted in merchants' responses to other questions. To further explore retailer preferences, the following hypothesis was tested against the sample data:

H_0:   Median{Preference for e-cash} $\geq$ Median{Preference for payment method i}

versus

H_a: Median{Preference for e-cash} $<$ Median{Preference for payment method i}

Table 10.4
Merchant lines of business

Business line	Sites
Beauty	19
Books and stationery	10
Department/convenience store	7
Drug store	9
Entertainment	26
Fashion	86
Food and restaurant	36
Gift shop	11
Household	50
Kid's apparel	13
Oil stations	5
Others	11
Personal care	14
Photo finishing and video products	7
Shoes and leather goods	38
Sports	9
Supermarket	2
Telecommunications	8
Travel and transport	6
Watches and jewelry	16
Total	*383*

Table 10.5
Survey response

Merchants' assessment of the ranking of frequency of use of alternative payment	Percentage of merchants who report each payment alternative as ranking 1st through 4th					
	Cash	Credit card	EPS	Mondex	VisaCash	*Total*
1	**53**	**44**	2	0	0	*99*
2	**39**	**27**	**11**	19	0	*96*
3	8	5	**35**	**35**	4	*87*
4	0	5	4	**46**	8	*63*
NA	0	19	48	0	88	*155*
Total	*100*	*100*	*100*	*100*	*100*	*500*

Table 10.6
Results of hypothesis test

Payment method i	P-value	Decision
Cash	P = 0.5000	Fail to reject Ho
Credit card	P = 0.3851	Fail to reject Ho
Debit card	P = 0.2807	Fail to reject Ho
Hybrid card	P = 0.7778	Fail to reject Ho

In other words, the hypothesis test attempts to determine whether the preference for e-cash is at least as high as the preference for payment method i, where payment method i is either cash, debit card, credit card or a hybrid card. Two-sided Mann-Whitney U tests[5] were applied to test $\mathbf{H}_0$ at significance level $\alpha = .05$. Table 10.6 shows the results obtained. Though the data are unable to reject e-cash's superiority over other forms of payment, the p-values from the Mann-Whitney U test are not particularly convincing.

First- and second-order stochastic dominance of e-cash over other forms of payment was also investigated. A payment method is stochastically dominant over another if an arbitrary customer receives greater utility from it over all possible outcomes (in this case the merchant reported preference-ranking choices of consumers). *First-order stochastic dominance* applies to all increasing utility functions (presumably the consumers' utility increases with an increase in any form of cash or near cash). A payment method that is preferred with cumulative probability distribution $G(U)$ over all utility levels $U \in \{U_i\}$ will stochastically dominate a payment method that is preferred with cumulative probability distribution $F(U)$ over all utility levels $U \in \{U_i\}$ if $G(U) \leq F(U)$ for all $U \in \{U_i\}$ and $G(U) < F(U)$ for at least one $U \in \{U_i\}$.[6] Figure 10.6 shows the first-order stochastic dominance curves for the five payment methods in the study.

This sheds some light on the equivocal results returned from the Mann-Whitney U test. E-cash dominates the apparently lackluster offering of a hybrid card (as implemented in VisaCash), but is clearly dominated by traditional cash. But e-cash neither dominates nor is dominated by credit cards and debit cards. E-cash preferences cross these two payment methods and confound the results of testing.

Equivocal preference orderings are often the result of the failure to incorporate risk aversion into the preference model. Fortunately, it is possible to reassess the preference ordering under an assumption that customers are risk averse. An assumption of risk aversion is especially appropriate when investigating new technologies such as e-cash. There are likely to be extreme differences, either between socioeconomic

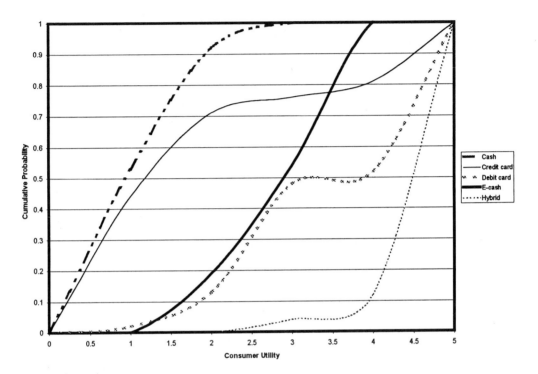

Figure 10.6
First-order stochastic dominance in consumer payment methods

groups or between age groups, in willingness to accept risk associated with adopting any new technology.[7]

To check whether this is the case with Mondex's e-cash, merchants were asked to assess the usage of e-cash by age and occupation. The primary users were office workers in various age groups as shown in table 10.7. Clearly, there are significant age-related biases in the adoption of e-cash, as well as a bias arising from the fact that Mondex is most often used by office workers (who are likely to be regular computer users). Thus e-cash usage should be correlated with differing tolerances for bearing technology risk. Younger professionals will tend to be more tolerant of a new technology and its associated risks. In addition, Mondex's own studies have found that e-cash tends to be used for smaller purchases than competing products such as credit cards. The tendency to limit e-cash transactions to small purchases may be at least partially influenced by technology-risk-averse behavior.

Table 10.7
Age and e-cash usage

Age group	Percentage of total e-cash usage
<20	12
21–30	65
31–40	23
>40	0

Assume, then, that cash, near cash, and e-cash users have an aversion to technology—that they see new technology a risky, and prefer to avoid this risk. Then *second-order stochastic dominance* may be used to assess the risk-adjusted preference for the new technology of e-cash. Second-order stochastic dominance assumes upward-sloping utility functions that increase at a decreasing rate (i.e., utility is nondecreasing and strictly concave, which implies that individuals are risk averse). E-cash with cumulative distribution function (c.d.f.) F(•) will second-order stochastically dominate another payment method with c.d.f. G(•) for all risk-averse consumers if

$$\int_{-\infty}^{U_i} [G(U) - F(U)] \, dU \geq 0$$

for all utility levels $U_i \in \{U_i\}$, where $G(U) \neq F(U)$ for at least one $U \in \{U_i\}$. Figure 10.7 shows the second-order stochastic dominance curves for e-cash versus each of the other four payment methods in the study.

Once the preference ordering is adjusted for technology adoption risk, we obtain a clear preference ordering:

• Cash and credit cards are preferred to *e-cash*.

• E-cash is preferred to *debit cards* and *hybrids*.

The survey results provide insight into the risk-adjusted ordering of payment methods obtained in figure 10.7. The survey found that the main benefits that customers receive from credit cards but not from e-cash are

• credit,

• convenience, and

• bonus points and other promotional awards from the issuers.

They also noted that many times credit cards were used out of habit as the first card pulled out of a wallet or purse (reflective of high customer switching costs. E-cash could not offer the same benefits as credit cards because

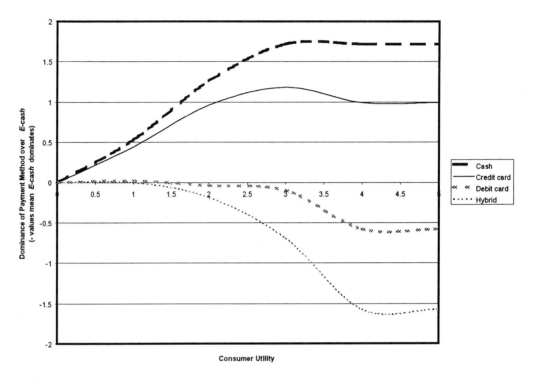

Figure 10.7
Second-order stochastic dominance of consumer payment methods versus e-cash

• e-cash cards need a separate machine to reload value, which customers find inconvenient; and

• customers find limited applicability and have to think of where they can use e-cash before making a purchase.

There were similar reasons stated for the preference for cash, which was considered to be convenient, fast, and a long-standing habit for payments (again reflecting high customer switching costs).

The Future of Mondex

Mondex's Hong Kong rollout suggests that Mondex's card-based, decentralized e-cash is unlikely to compete well against cash and credit cards for three reasons:

1. *Switching costs:* Merchants and customers have already invested in equipment and learning associated with cash and credit cards. E-cash as implemented by Mondex seems to provide insufficient additional utility to overcome these switching costs associated with new equipment and learning (particularly memorizing another password). Switching costs are likely to be even more difficult to overcome once Mondex has removed its subsidies.

2. *Technology risk:* E-cash was best received and most often used by younger office workers. In Hong Kong, this group contains inveterate adopters of new technology, who keep the electronics and telecommunications industries healthy with habitual purchases of the newest electronic accessories.

3. *Insufficient market differentiation:* E-cash failed to differentiate itself significantly from a debit card, and thus generated insufficient utility to overcome switching costs. Oddly, because of the "card" format, e-cash was perceived to be closer to the near-cash magnetic stripe cards than to coins, banknotes, or checks.

These results are significant, because Mondex's e-cash format is widely accepted by the finance and computer science communities as an archetype for e-cash implementation. Indeed, they indicate that there may not be a real niche in the marketplace for something called e-cash.

Merchants in particular were pessimistic about the future of e-cash, with 81% of those surveyed claiming it was disadvantageous for them to use e-cash. The most frequently-mentioned disadvantages were:

1. Merchants needed to clear one more machine at night;

2. E-cash was time consuming, requiring more procedures per transaction than credit or debit cards;

3. Customers often forget their security password.

Despite heavy subsidies from Mondex and Hong Kong Bank, only 23% of the merchants indicated a desire to continue using Mondex, and only 35% felt that customers would increase their use of e-cash. Merchants indicated that some customers had terminated their cards even though use of the card was free during the pilot test. The survey revealed that over 90% of merchants saw cash as the most popular payment method. Cash demands no involvement from third parties and takes less time.

The survey found that only 31% of merchants felt they had realized benefits by reducing their handling of coins, one of the primary motivations touted by Mondex for using their service. Indeed, the Hong Kong light rail and bus companies have met this objective much more successfully with their contactless Octopus card.

("Contactless" implies that input/output is accomplished through a microscopic antenna rather than a physical plug.) The Octopus is one of a variety of stored-value/debit/credit card hybrids that have been introduced to support vertical markets such as mass transit, cinema, and medical care. Its objective is to minimize the use of coins. Handling coins is a significant expense for light rail and bus companies, plus their use retards the speed with which people can be loaded or unloaded. There is no way of identifying the cardholder for these cards (e.g., like a password or thumbprint), so they are only appropriate for storing small values. They do point the way toward a new generation of user-friendly cards. The Octopus is not available for retail purchases and thus is not directly comparable to the other cards.

Niche cards, such as the Octopus card, the similar Golden Harvest Cinema card, or the Hospital Authority Patient card are better at substituting for cash than Mondex e-cash. These cards are secured by only maintaining limited balances for specific vertical markets, and can offer special services like the patient medical history maintained on the Hospital Authority Patient card.

The emergence of vertical market cash substitutes is perhaps not surprising. In a world where most products are progressing toward customization to a focused cross-section of consumers, the creation of a one-size-fits-all surrogate for traditional cash seems ill-informed and recidivist. Hong Kong merchants and consumers seem to have recognized this already and have voted against e-cash with their well-heeled feet.

Notes

1. Many of the e-cash offerings, e.g., DigiCash's, are focused only on Internet payments, which automatically restricts their use to the fraction of a percent of consumers who purchase on-line. Even among Internet products, surveys indicate a preference for credit cards.

2. The Internet market for Mondex is potentially more promising than that for Cybercash.

3. In fact it is not, due to seigniorage, policing of counterfeit currency, and various other ongoing costs.

4. This figure differs significantly from the 44% of transactions at the Mondex pilot mall shops. This is because mall shops tend to offer relatively high markup goods, often designed for impulse purchases, which are an ideal use for credit cards. But outside of malls, where customers may buy new or secondhand appliances, cars, furniture, and so forth, transactions between individuals, craftsmen, small shopkeepers and vendors are commonly made in cash. Cash payments may hide sources of wealth and income, but also reflect small business's resistance to acquiring equipment, services, and bank accounts.

5. Revealed preferences will only be unique up to a rank ordering (see, e.g., Samuelson 1996 for the seminal work on integrability and revealed preferences). Thus hypothesis testing must be nonparametric. Several nonparametric testing methods are appropriate, among which the most commonly used are the paired sign test, Wilcoxon signed rank test, and the Mann-Whitney U test. The Mann-Whitney U test has the best small-sample characteristics and was therefore applied to this data.

6. Throughout, $F(\bullet)$ is used to denote the cumulative probability distribution of preferences (utilities) for e-cash (Mondex), and $G(\bullet)$ is used to denote the cumulative probability distribution of preferences (utili-

ties) for competing payment methods. Lower case $f(\bullet)$ and $g(\bullet)$ denote the corresponding mass functions. Thus $f(U)$ is the probability that an individual chosen randomly from the population will find e-cash to be of utility U; since this is a mass function, $f(U)$ may be equivalently viewed as the proportion of the population who find e-cash of utility U.

7. Second-order dominance is consistent with revealed preference and thus may be used in the analysis to assess preferences when consumers are averse to technology-adoption risk associated with e-cash. Risk aversion measures such as the Markowitz risk premium and the Pratt-Arrow measures of risk aversion require expected utility measurements that are not consistent with the revealed preferences elicited by the survey.

References

Apple Daily Newspaper, February 19, 1997 (with Chinese subtitles).

Cards reveal prospects for Strong Growth in next decade. *Banking World Hong Kong*, June 1996.

Chaum, D., and I. Schaumuller-Bichl. *Smart Card 2000: The Future of IC Cards*. Elsevier Science Publishers B.V., 1989.

Clemons, E. K., D. C. Croson, and B. W. Weber. Reengineering money: The Mondex stored value card and beyond, *International Journal of Electronic Commerce*, 1(2), Winter 1996–97.

Ives, B., and M. Earl. *Mondex International: Reengineering Money*, London Business School Case Study CRIM CS97/2, 1997.

Mondex Magazine, September 1996.

Mondex Website (*http://www.mondex.com*).

Murphy, P. A. Smart cards begin first major U.S. test, *Stores*, July 1996, pp. 76–78.

Samuelson, P. A. *Collected Scientific Papers of Paul A. Samuelson*, vol. 1 (J. Stiglitz, ed.), Cambridge: MIT Press, 1966.

Simmel, G. *The Philosophy of Money* (T. Bottomore and D. Frisby, trans.), London: Routledge, 1990.

Vogelstein, F. Regulating electronic cash. *Institutional Investor*, April 1995, p. 23.

Westland, J. C., M. Kwok, J. Shu, T, Kwok, and H. Ho. Electronic Cash in Hong Kong, *Electronic Markets*, 7(2), 1997.

Appendix: Interview with Ms. Manjoosh Joshi, Manager, Project Mondex of Hong Kong Bank, May 1, 1997

Marketing Strategies

1. *What are the targeted market size and segments like by location, demography, lifestyle, application, or transaction amount in Hong Kong?*

The market that we target is anywhere that you can spend cash, i.e., it is intended to be an alternative to cash. It is not intended to be in competition with or replace credit cards. The intention is to provide an alternative for payment, and the card should therefore be complementary to credit cards. Currently, cash payment accounts for 80–90% of total payments in Hong Kong. Worldwide, cash payment accounts for 65–90%. The market for electronic cash is therefore huge. Past figures in ATM usage also substantiate this.

Both high and low value ends are targeted. However, early usage was limited to low-valued items because people usually use cash for such items.

For the next step, vending machines, car-parks, minibuses, and other transport-type applications would also be targeted, apart from merchant stores. We are now waiting for confirmation from the Transport Department for minibuses and will be seeing this happen soon. The Post Office has also signed an agreement with Mondex on April 1 this year, and the Tai Koo Shing Branch is using it right now.

2. *What are the marketing strategies in terms of pricing, promotion, product, and place?*

In terms of pricing, the card is free of charge for both customers and merchants during the pilot.

In terms of promotion, the two most important ones are to raise the awareness of the public and educate the users. Earlier on, people confused Mondex with credit cards. We tried to clear up the confusion by carrying out exhibitions, posters, etc. We also opened up two shops that can give people a chance to come in contact with Mondex and feel it. We also stressed convenience in using the card and had promotional discounts for using it.

3. *What makes you think there are opportunities for marketing the card in Hong Kong? What benefits can the merchants derive from accepting Mondex for payment? What are the critical success factors for the implementation and penetration of the Mondex card?*

Mondex can provide a lot of advantages for both merchants and customers:

· It offers merchants cost saving in cash handling, e.g., transportation, security, staff involved in counting money, etc. Currently the cost of handling cash in Hong Kong is about 4–7 billion. The cost saving for merchants is very big.

· It increases efficiency and enhances turnover, which in turn brings in more business.

· It is clean compared with money.

· For stores which do not accept credit cards but cash only, Mondex would be a good alternative.

The critical success factor is the right balance of merchants in terms of trade mix to ensure wide applicability. Wide applicability may bring about wide acceptance of the card by customers, which somehow has a chicken-and-egg relationship.

4. What is your plan or target penetration for consumers and merchants (in terms of number) in one year or five years? What will be the expected product life cycle?

It is difficult to forecast because it all depends on customer acceptance. You can see from the previous experience in implementing ATM and credit cards, it took a long time for people to accept and widely use them in the early stage. But once people got familiar with them, they grew tremendously.

5. What are the major difficulties in marketing Mondex in Hong Kong? What difficulties do you anticipate in the national pilot and how are you going to tackle them?

The initial hurdle is to educate people and change the payment habit of consumers. Mondex should be easily acceptable as it is convenient and user-friendly. You can find that the acceptability is in fact increasing. There should be no major marketing barrier because Hong Kong people are willing to accept new things.

Costs and Benefits

6. What are the main reasons for Hong Kong Bank to run Mondex?

Mondex is a new product developed to improve banking services. Customers are demanding more convenience from banks. They want control over their accounts at all times. We have the enabling technology and can use it to find business opportunities. Mondex is a first step for remote banking advantages which enable greater convenience for merchants and customers to access their own funds in the bank. We are moving towards technology, such as the use of PCs and telephone banking. The impact can be very long term.

In the short term, Mondex adds a new payment service to customers. It offers customers and merchants more convenience. Through Mondex, we market the concept of banking at any time and anywhere. It can reduce cash-handling costs and can reduce ATM queues and then the number of ATMs. The overall cost saving to the community is big. It also fosters remote banking opportunities.

7. What will be the major source of revenue for Mondex—fees or charges on merchants or consumers?

Merchants require a separate machine to settle transactions with Mondex and this requires a terminal fee. During the pilot, it is free of charge. However, we expect the fees or charges on merchants will be an income source in the long run. But the charges will be different from that of the credit card.

8. Would running Mondex lead to any negative effect on the existing products and services provided by Hong Kong Bank?

No. Mondex is targeting a different market. It is at the forefront of electronic cash and is intended to provide an additional alternative to the public for payment. The problem of competition, say between credit card products and Mondex, does not exist.

Competition and Threats

9. *Who are the main competitors, both current and potential?*

Cash. Although people think Mondex is good, they may not use it. It is difficult to change the habits of customers. Cash is still the dominating payment method, accounting for 80%–90% of total transactions in Hong Kong, and so the major competitor is still cash.

10. *Do you think Mondex is in direct competition with various credit or debit cards in the market or do you think Mondex is targeting a new niche of the market? How do you differentiate yourself especially with the reloadable Prime Visa Cash?*

People always think that Mondex card is in competition with Prime Visa Cash or credit cards. In fact, it is not. We think that having other cash cards like Prime Visa Cash is beneficial because this can raise consumer awareness for the product. It can produce a win-win situation for both Mondex and other cash cards. Besides, the market is so big. regarding credit cards, Mondex is not intended to compete with them either because it is a separate market. As I have said above, Mondex is at the forefront of electronic cash.

Concerning the differences with Prime Visa Cash, it records single cash transactions and needs a third party to do the clearance. It has both disposable and reloadable types. On the other hand, Mondex replicates cash features and provides additional benefits. It does not record single cash transactions. It can handle card-to-card transfer and does not require a third party to do the clearance, i.e., merchants need not record every transaction and send back to banks. It allows remote access and transfer by telephones. It has only reloadable ones. One more point is that we serve our existing customers only because customers need to have an account with us first before we issue them a Mondex card.

11. *Is the threat of entry high? Who would be the new entrants and how can you deter them?*

The threat of entry is low because the barrier is high.

Mondex enjoys significant first-mover advantage as the technology for Mondex is more advanced and several years ahead. Further, the same kind of technology is being used worldwide and is patented. Only members would be able to get this technology. It is difficult for competitors to enter the market and compete with Mondex because it would be hard to find a better technology. Taking Visa Cash as an example, they altogether have to use four different technologies in different parts of the world.

Future Development and Opportunities

12. Is there any plan to develop various versions of the Mondex Card, say with respect to stored-value limit, functions, appearance, etc.?

Not initially. We will keep our products simple in the initial stages and get people familiar with the concept first. When the product becomes more widely accepted, we will respond to customers' feedback and improve the product based on their needs.

Mondex cards are designed to be multicurrency but the card in Hong Kong is not yet at this stage because it needs reciprocal arrangement.

For dollar amount, right now the maximum limit is HK$3,000. We may increase it if necessary. However, there must be a balance between security and usage. Again, it all depends on customer feedback. We still do not find people use Mondex for high-value purchases at this stage.

As Mondex requires a separate terminal machine now, we may develop one machine that can combine Mondex, credit cards, etc. in future.

Access Security at McDonnell Douglas Aerospace Information Services

Marcus Wegner was a highwayman. Only the highways he traversed were electronic, not concrete. His highways had signposts, bridges, and gateways. They had turnpikes and intersections. His current haunt—an intersection (one of many) where electronic freight mingled and crossed.

After weeks of scarching through back doors, trap doors, and gateways on the Milnet computer network, he found the entryway he sought—into the computers of McDonnell Douglas. McDonnell Douglas's weapons secrets, personnel files, research, and commercial aircraft designs were open to his scrutiny. As design plans for the MD-12 (MD's newest commercial airliner) downloaded by his side, Wegner relaxed and lit another cigarette.

Halfway around the globe, Tom Thompson, Security Manager for McDonnell Douglas Aerospace Information Services (MDAIS) in Long Beach, California, pondered the difficulties in securing MDAIS's systems. His chore was increasingly hampered by unfettered growth of networked workstations and microcomputers within the company. Thompson suspected these harbored a growing underground "sneaker network" of stolen software, data, and proprietary secrets, along with the odd computer virus. He suspected that both networks and diskettes left McDonnell Douglas's (MD's) computers open to intrusion. Now events seemed to bear out his suspicions.

Dave Komendat, Principal Specialist for International Security Operations, had just contacted Thompson about a report received from Army Intelligence. An unidentified hacker had made several attempts to access military files on McDonnell Douglas's aircraft through a convolution of telephone lines, computer bulletin boards, and corporate data systems. The common thread in all of these access attempts was the use, at one or more points, of the Milnet military communications network. Milnet was actually two networks—one that was relatively insecure, and used extensively for research, often for military R&D; and the other secured and intended only for military use. Komendat believed that the hacker was able to access either side, although the Army could not be sure until it further perused access logs and other audit trails. The hacker had used a number of clever ruses to infiltrate military systems without leaving a trail. The Army assured Komendat, though, that these systems were secure, and that all of the hacker's attempts had been thwarted. Komendat was not so sure. Despite its scrutiny, the Army was unable to track accurately the source of the telephone calls through the hacker's telephone connections, computer commands, retransmissions and automated log-in attempts across U.S. military computing sites.

This case was prepared by J. Christopher Westland.

All this worried Thompson. Although he felt that MDAIS's mainframe data was secure, he was unsure of the microcomputer network and another R&D network connecting several clusters of VAX minicomputers. Because these networks did not support critical "production" systems—i.e., systems that handled commercial transactions, whose accuracy, privacy, security, audit trails, and transaction integrity needed to be insured—they were allowed a certain degree of unmanaged growth. This was beneficial for two reasons—(1) it allowed hardware and networks to alter quickly in support of new projects, often by retrofitting existing standalone microcomputers; and (2) it promoted a laissez-faire spirit toward collaboration and communication that favored creativity and productivity.

Unfortunately, the data needed by users of microcomputer networks frequently resided on the secured, mission-critical, "production" side of the mainframes. It was only a matter of time before microcomputer users requested access. That meant providing gateways to the mainframe, and a new layer of security at the gateway. Thompson was concerned with security beyond the gateway, over which he had little control. An impostor might easily gain access to authorized log-in IDs and passwords in the microcomputer network, leaving him free to prowl through supposedly secure databases.

Some gateways were opened to appease programmers, programmers who might not even work for MDAIS and who in any case were suspected of placing back doors and trap doors in production programs to palliate their own software maintenance chores. Data security became more complex by the day.

Hackers invoked several ploys to gain access. *Shoulder surfing* let hackers gather information (e.g., passwords) by looking over another user's shoulder. *Worms* and *viruses* could be used to capture and return information, as well as for damage or illicit access. *Logic bombs*—programs that perform an unauthorized act when a specified system condition occurs—could be used to cover a hacker's trail and make prosecution difficult. *Leakage* through disclosure of proprietary or confidential information could compromise information assets. *Dumpster diving*—the search of trash from corporations—was a major source of sensitive information. Thompson had heard of one California bank where a trash collector had figured out the bank's system from paper waste and transferred $1 million into his own account without detection (for a while). *Zapping* used utility programs to override system controls. *Piggybacking* onto another's computer account without authorization (often because a user failed to log off) was a common problem at MDAIS. Adding confusion to these and many other options was the *salami technique* where theft of information or resources was hidden in a large group of activities, such as skimming rounding errors from interest calculations. Thompson liked to summarize violators' *modi operandi* with "the seven Es":

- *Embezzlement:* the unauthorized (usually undetectable) appropriation of company data.
- *Eavesdropping:* the invasion of privacy.
- *Espionage:* the theft of R&D and other corporate information assets.
- *Enmity:* revenge of disgruntled employees, through time bombs, sabotage, etc.
- *Extortion:* the use of time bombs, sabotage, and so forth, with the objective of personal gain.
- *Error:* the most common abuse.
- *Ego:* committing abuse for enjoyment or prestige, the hacker's motivation.

MDAIS Background

MDAIS was founded in St. Louis as a separate division of McDonnell Douglas called McAuto in 1969. MDAIS consolidated under one management team the diverse and widespread data processing operations of MD Aerospace. For several years MDAIS resources were dedicated solely to McDonnell Douglas information processing. In 1973 MDAIS successfully launched their first major commercial venture, "CUADATA," a credit union back-office processing support system. This was followed in 1976 by a second successful commercial venture, the "UNIGRAPHICS" commercial computer-aided design/computer-aided manufacturing (CAD/CAM) system. MDAIS essentially offered internal expertise on a "time-shared" basis for use by outside firms. Prior to the advent of powerful low-cost microcomputers, time-sharing was a popular option for purchase of discrete chunks of computing time, without a substantial and permanent investment in capacity.

By 1981, MDAIS's various time-sharing initiatives were consolidated under the Timenet and Telecheck programs. In that year, MDAIS consolidated its operations on a 1.1 million square foot campus in St. Louis. Yet operational problems were also surfacing by that time. Capital and operational costs had outpaced revenues. What is more important, MDAIS started losing commercial contracts for nonpeak batch processing (in the evening and early morning) as demand shifted toward on-line transaction processing (OLTP) during daylight hours. This exacerbated management's incentive to cut nonessential costs—among which they included information systems security.

Between 1984 and 1991, the peak hour processing needs of MD forced MDAIS to divest itself of many of its commercial ventures. At the same time operations were split between St. Louis, Missouri, and Long Beach, California. The divestiture made securing MD's information assets significantly easier, since control systems did not have to track a large and shifting body of external users. Yet the same period saw the rapid growth of VAX minicomputer networks and networks of workstations—especially in the engineering design and development area. These networks installed numerous gateways to other networks outside of MDAIS. They also had numerous dial-up ports, which provided valuable telecommuting and access capabilities to engineers and management. Although critical on-line transaction processing resided on a tightly controlled mainframe, most of the valuable R&D resided on unsecured networks.

MDAIS increasingly received its transaction revenue from sources outside of MD. In the 1970s MDAIS was a time-sharing company—they sold raw computer time, counting on customers to supply their own software, data, processing procedures and standards, and error control. Although they were one of the most efficient and reliable providers of mainframe computer processing, they lacked a portfolio of software packages and services to sell, and were ill-prepared to assume the comprehensive range of facilities' management services increasingly being offered by their competition. What was worse, their customers were increasingly skeptical of MDAIS's ability to run a secure operation when only the hardware aspect of processing was under their management. Many customers made proprietary and sensitive processes, trade secrets, and market data available to MDAIS. They might be less likely to procure processing time were these to be subject to unfettered access by competitors and hackers. In contrast, facilities' management/systems integrators such as EDS and Arthur Andersen could assure a "closed shop" by tightly controlling which software accessed whose databases, and tightly managing the disposition of media and resident data.

By 1992 MDAIS presided over a far-flung empire of mainframe computers, VAX minicomputers, and networked microcomputers. Eight satellite operations completed the system (Florida Space Center; Houston; Macon, Gary; Toronto; Tulsa; Salt Lake City; Columbus, Ohio; San Diego) which handled mainly administrative and accounting processing. Engineering R&D computing tended to take place on the VAX network, and Secure DOD work took place at special centers facetiously called "black holes."

The MDAIS operation processed around 15 million transactions per day in 1992, and around 4 billion transactions annually. Systems tuning and load balancing between various machines was performed on a continuous basis. Over 8 trillion bytes of data were retained in 250,000 volumes of tape storage, most of which could be accessed within 15 seconds via tape silos and similar automated mounting systems.

Continual load balancing, tuning, and refinement of machine hardware and software and operating procedures made the MDAIS computers some of the most efficient among any computer service provider. Outside reviews benchmarked capacity utilization higher than virtually any other comparable installation.

This traffic became increasingly expensive to service. Networked microcomputers were offering as much as 100-to-1 improvements in price performance over mainframes. But they were unreliable compared to proprietary mainframes, and provided few services to ensure data integrity. Yet cost pressures were increasing demand for dedicated minicomputers and workstations. Ad hoc networks were popping up to support data and software transfer around these networks, and these were seen by MDAIS management as real sources of security and data integrity problems.

The growth of transaction traffic in the 1970s and 1980s was not unlike the parallel growth of traffic in neighboring Los Angeles—with similar problems arising in both the computer and highway networks. Healthy investments in infrastructure had allowed both MDAIS and Los Angeles to keep up (barely) with the demands of traffic, especially during peak hours. But policing both networks became more difficult, and risky or shortsighted decisions were made in the face of tight budgets. Thompson felt it was only a matter of time before the computer equivalents of carjackings, drive-by shootings, and unsafe vehicles got out of hand.

Of even more concern to MDAIS was the growing threat from hackers, industrial spies, and disgruntled employees. Microcomputer viruses were being detected at a rate of around six per day in 1992, less than 10 years after the concept of a computer virus was first proposed by Fred Cohen at the University of Southern California. Computer hacking was at an all-time high, with the vast majority of intrusions no doubt going unnoticed. Damages could potentially be in the billions. MDAIS was very likely being hurt by the potential for security breaches, although no one could be sure.

Thompson had been with MD since 1968. In the early 1980s, Thompson left MDAIS and traveled to Oregon to become a gentleman farmer. Several years of farming had left him yearning for the structure and routine of industry, and he had returned to assume responsibility for implementation of ACF-2, a popular mainframe security package. ACF-2 operated by defining computer assets as "objects" to be accessed only by "authorized individuals." Authorization was granted on a "need-to-know" basis. In theory this provided adequate security where virtually all sensitive information resided on the mainframe. In practice, it was often difficult to determine who needed to know what concerning sensitive R&D information—needs would often evolve as R&D progressed. Thus "need-to-know" was interpreted laxly. This presented the corporation with significant exposure to loss of corporate secrets, with consequent loss of competitive position and potential patent rights.

Thompson estimated that roughly 20% of MDAIS's information technology investments were in hardware, 30% in proprietary software, and the remaining 50% in the corporation's databases, of which engineering R&D data constituted the largest share. Proprietary software investments reflected mainly costs of intellectual effort associated with development and maintenance. Data costs were largely acquisition costs, which tended to be labor intensive. Given the relative proportions of MDAIS's investments, security tended to focus most intensely on databases and other data assets. This was in sharp contrast to security programs initiated in the 1970s, which attempted to ensure that machine time was used efficiently and solely for corporate affairs.

There was increased concern over maintenance to proprietary software. Although investment in proprietary software was substantial, it was doubtful that much of it would find widespread application outside MDAIS. But this same software could access, alter, and copy data with impunity; neither ACF-2 nor corporate authorization schemes were equipped to deal with this possibility. Thompson thought that control could be enhanced by tightly monitoring programmers' access to production software.

Maintenance costs on MDAIS's software ran an annual 10% of installed cost. Around 75% of this reflected the addition or refinement of features to ensure data integrity and accuracy. An internal study revealed that approximately 50% of maintenance expenditures were incurred reading old code, trying to figure out what tasks it performed. Since the average seven-year-old system contained around 50% "dead code," this work was often tedious and unrewarding. Given the economics of software maintenance, Thompson felt that any security measures must be transparent to maintenance programmers and could not impede their already tedious task. Programmers who perceived their efforts being seriously hampered by security could bring unpleasant politics to bear on Thompson and his staff. To this end, mainframe systems were dichotomized into "production" and "test" sides. Maintenance programmers were allowed access to copies of "production" software modules and databases on a prophylactic "test" side. Since their use and modification might be substantial, this seemed an appropriate way to sequester sensitive production data.

Dave Komendat glanced over Thompson's shoulder at the maze of data scrolling forth on the screen. Four hours of searching activity logs had left them exhausted and irritable. But now they had him—the hacker who had eluded them over the past week. This is what they saw:

```
>Telnet Milnet

Welcome to McDonnell Douglas Aerospace Information Services.
Please enter your user ID.

>login: Cracker

>Password?: Tom

Incorrect login, try again

>login: Cracker

>Password?: Dick

Incorrect login, try again

>login: Cracker

>Password?: Harry

Incorrect login; session disconnected
```

And the hacker had made 183 similar attempts from the same Milnet gateway over the past week, under different log-in ID's, but using similar passwords from a list of around 100 names. Except that the last four attempts had proven successful!

"Check the current activity log," suggested Komandat.

Thompson pecked at the keyboard.... "He's in the system right now!"

"Can you shut him down?"

"I think so. He's going after design specs for the MD-12 flight control electronics." Thompson rapped on the keyboard. "There. That puts the entire database off limits until we can get a positive ID."

Marcus Wegner's repose was interrupted by the unexpected silencing of his printer. For reasons unknown, it had failed to complete the printout of MD-12 plans. He had seen the data on his screen only half an hour earlier, but had been unable to download, let alone print. Fortunately, months of knocking at electronic doors had inured him to these little glitches. He had other routes into McDonnell Douglas's networks.

MDAIS's Strategy for Mainframe Security

In 1968, all mainframe access security tasks were consolidated under Tom Thompson, Director of Information Protection. Thompson transferred into the position from an operator's position in the corporate data processing area. The purpose of the group was to implement management policy.

In 1977, when the Foreign Corrupt Practices Act was passed, MD executives raised new concerns about the accuracy and security of financial information. Computer security programs were expanded at that time to deal with local police, as well as military security personnel. Audit coordination, with user guidance and training, gained new emphasis. During this period, the International Information Security Foundation, Telecommunications Security Council, and National Research Council Security Systems Study Committee were formed, further emphasizing the concern of management over security and control of information assets.

Access was controlled using ACF-2, and an associated "lock and key" conceptual framework that specifically allowed access links based on (1) individuals, and (2) objects. *Individuals* were employees and outside users of MD's information systems (see figure 10.8). In its simplest rendition, MDAIS perceived its security problem to be one of ensuring that individuals were allowed access to objects only when explicitly authorized. This was equivalent to partitioning the company's assets into rooms, and issuing keys to access only those rooms that individuals actually needed access to as a part of their jobs. Each of the three components required extensive interpretation before this scheme could be implemented in practice.

The precise definition of an *object* was left open, to ensure flexibility in a rapidly evolving computing environment. Major classes of objects that had been defined in past use were (1) central processing units (real and virtual); (2) software modules; (3) databases and files; (4) individual data fields on databases and files; (5) networks; (6) network gateways; (7) general ledger accounts (for charging P.O.s); and (8) individual users' computer time accounts.

Each object was assumed to be useful (valuable) to some individual—otherwise MDAIS, would divest itself of the object. Individuals could be employees of MDAIS; more often they were not. Since the majority of MDAIS's business was time-sharing, the majority of their information technology assets (software, data, and transactions) could be considered to be held on consignment. Identification of the full population of individuals who might desire access to a given object was a crucial but vexing endeavor; the identifications that existed were generally considered to be incomplete.

Individuals needed to be categorized into authorized users, potential violators of access security, and nonaccessors. There was an inherent bias in all authorization schemes to delineate the authorized accessors, while ignoring the potential for unauthorized access. The risk was that there existed users who would try to circumvent information access controls. There might be diverse motivations for circumventing control—the price of authorized access was unaffordable; competition or survival of

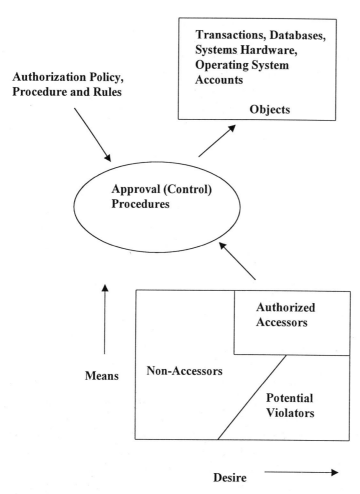

Figure 10.8
Access security schematic

the unauthorized might depend upon gaining access; or successful circumvention might be touted as a sign of cleverness or just good fun. The latter case was an increasing concern. Thompson suspected the growth of a computer underground. Recent spectacular cases of intrusion had been reported and profiled in books such as Cliff Stoll's *The Cuckoo's Egg*[1]; these accounts had been especially embarrassing for the firms and individuals mentioned in them. But Thompson surmised that reported offenses were only the tip of the iceberg—these were the foolish hackers ... the ones who had been caught.

Compared to hackers, it seemed relatively easy to identify other classes of unauthorized users. These violators could be assumed to have some type of identifiable link to the information asset—either they were competitors, or employees, or consumer groups with an agenda which included the information asset. Employees and ex-employees presented the greatest threat. A recent survey[2] found that around 30% of all employees were honest; another 40% would under the right conditions, be compromised; and the final 30% of employees fully expected to exploit the corporation when it suited their needs.

But hackers—they were irrational and unpredictable. Their motivation for access could range from "catch-me-if-you-can" playfulness to theft and vandalism. And they could manifest themselves either through personal access attempts or through impersonal artifices—automated viruses, worms, or Trojan horse software. Identifying them was difficult enough; foiling them was nearly impossible.

Thompson attempted to gain a more complete identification of unauthorized users. But it was common for users and management to disregard Thompson's entreaties. They claimed there was no evidence of unauthorized access, thus it was not a problem that demanded investment of resources. Ignoring, of course, that lack of evidence may have been due more to systems that failed to detect unauthorized access than to the nonexistence of violators. Industry periodicals documented evidence that, across the industry, abuse of computer assets was growing rapidly. In 1992 the total cost in lost work, vandalized assets, and stolen data in the United States alone was estimated to be around $50 billion per year (though for obvious reasons this number was considered highly speculative).

Authorization consisted of two components—the authorization scheme and the approval process. The authorization scheme was a part of management policy that determined how ownership, access, and use of assets under the firm's jurisdiction were distributed. *Approval* was the actual process of granting authorization at the event/incident level. As much as possible, Thompson wanted to see the approval process automated. Automated approval was less expensive in the long run, and could be vigilant 24 hours a day, 7 days a week. Unfortunately, automation was rigid, inflexible, and lacked the intuitiveness of human intervention that was often crucial to identifying and apprehending a perpetrator.

Owing to the nature of its business and service structure, many of MDAIS's information assets (objects) were provided on consignment from their customers, rather than belonging to MD outright. Authorization policies were loosely based on a "need-to-know" dictum for data, and "contractual payment" for machines and software. Unfortunately, this dictum was often difficult to interpret in practice because of uncertainty about end user needs.

A prime example appeared in the joint development agreement reached with Taiwan Aerospace Corporation, the newly formed Taiwanese national firm committed to codeveloping the MD-12 commercial airliner. MDAIS retained the MD-12 engineering specification, prototype, and R&D files for MD as a part of their subsidiary relationship. It was impossible to determine exactly what files would ultimately be needed by engineers on either side, since MD-12 specifications were still evolving. Thus the Taiwanese firm was essentially given unrestricted access to MD-12 specifications, even in areas in which no subcontracting was being performed by them. McDonnell Douglas felt that it may have unnecessarily divulged hundreds of millions of dollars of proprietary R&D that could be used in the design of competing airliners. Thompson was determined not to let this happen in the future. But how to restrict access more accurately without limiting the usefulness of the data?

The Information Highway

Thompson had read somewhere that the most effective way to secure a home was to build it in a neighborhood distant from any highway. This, it seemed, had proven effective where armed guards, gated communities, increased policing, or other enforcement had failed. Thompson was concerned that MDAIS's mainframe security under ACF-2 was sort of a gated community, serving the firm's geriatric legacy systems, close to all the major highways. Unfortunately, much of the valuable new data and software resided on microcomputers. Microcomputer networks were MDAIS's vibrant but dangerous urban neighborhoods, highways running through; some gentrified, some decaying; steps for some on the way to a better neighborhood. There was no central planner for these streets—ad hoc and chaotic, signposts conflicting, laws undocumented or ignored—they carried their traffic with efficient anarchy. No doubt the gated community was more secure; but it never seemed to satisfy the young, creative, and productive community vital to MD.

Unlike crimes against property, once a computer crime was committed, it became very difficult to gather evidence or prosecute. Thompson knew that computer crime left very little evidence after the fact. The best evidence could be found in paper audit trails, computer memory, computer backup media, and computer logs. But there was almost never any physical evidence

Dave Komendat contended that the best immediate response upon evidence of a computer crime was much like police response after a burglary:

· Freeze the scene of the crime.

· Document what happened.

· Preserve the documentation—e.g., do not reconstruct a file without first copying it in its damaged state.

Furthermore, preparing the legal case should be handled by

· calling in and cooperating with local law enforcement officers, recognizing that they might lack expertise in systems;

· recognizing the difficulties in presenting computer related evidence to a jury; and

· recognizing that U.S. attorneys or district attorneys would rather prosecute a mail fraud or wire fraud case, because of difficulties in presenting the computer aspects of crime to a jury.

One of the greatest problems in prosecuting computer crimes was posed by the strict rules governing the admissibility of evidence in court. These were designed to ensure fairness, and to guard against tampering or misrepresentation. But the volatile and manipulable nature of computer media made many computer counterparts to traditional evidence inadmissible—e.g., documents, photos, and recently video. Computer evidence and records had to be gathered and documented with great care.

Both Komendat and Thompson believed that the victimized corporation was often in a better position to deal with a crime than law enforcement. They might be reluctant because they wished to protect their reputation or did not feel they had a strong case. But if a company had its own experienced investigators they could assemble a case—interview employees, assemble phone and audit trail records—better than law enforcement officials. Thompson knew that once law enforcement was brought in, they were required to play by Miranda rules, which could significantly slow the progress of a case.

Komendat knew that corporate evidence gathering might be at risk because firms were used to prosecuting civil cases rather than criminal cases. Standards were much higher in a criminal case, and ignorance of privacy laws and so forth could leave the evidence open to attack in court. Law enforcement officers were used to this greater burden of proof. And Komendat knew that many computer crime cases were disposed of not based on what the perpetrator did or what the evidence was, but whether it was gotten legally and whether it was admissible.

Komendat was also aware that once you had collected evidence incorrectly, you could not go back and redo it correctly. Because of the complexities of investigating computer crime, district attorneys were very selective in choosing cases and assigning resources. They would demand commitment from the victim. Given the legal uncertainty in computer crime, no one wanted to break new legal ground.

"He's in the microcomputer network?"

"We've left it open to keep him on the line while the phone company runs a trace," returned Komandat. "CAD/CAM swapped the MD-12 specifications and bill of material with 256 duplicates of a Cessna T-37 "Tweety Bird" trainer ... only the fuselage was kept. There are enough bogus schematic files in that MD-12 directory to keep him downloading for another hour," observed Komendat. He handed Thompson a printout of the hacker's latest attempts to exploit cracks in their security.

Thompson saw a stream of telephone numbers and log-on ID's with Komendat's notations carefully penciled into the margins. Sure enough, Komandat had woven together a credible trace of accesses, attempts, retransmissions, and routings. The final links to the hacker were almost complete.

The phone rang. Following his cursory affirmation, Komendat place the receiver back on its cradle. "We've got him! His line was traced to an apartment in Paris. The police are on their way to make the arrest."

Komendat reflected on the printouts. "You know what?... He's not even paying for his own telephone calls. He entered Tymnet through one of our subcontractors who's picking up the overseas charge, and then got into our database as an authorized user, Bill Davis, in Tulsa's engineering department. He's in there right now. Looks like he's scanning blueprints for the electronics of the MD-12."

"You mean the 'Tweety Bird,'" corrected Thompson.

Across the Atlantic, Marcus Wegner was ecstatic. He had never seen so much information before. Yes, modern commercial aircraft *were* complex, but the MD-12 must have had three times as many parts as any aircraft design he had ever seen.

But Marcus worried that he would not be able to download the schematics to disk in time. It was noon. The Gambini brothers would arrive to pick up the schematics at any minute. He knew they would pay him well for his work. He knew they did not like to be kept waiting. If they weren't satisfied, he could end up with broken kneecaps ... with any luck.

The computer completed its download just as Wegner heard a knocking at his door. "What luck," he thought to himself as rose to meet his guests.

Notes

1. Stoll, C. (1990). *The Cuckoo's Egg*, New York: Pocket Books.
2. Krivda, C. D. (1992). Breaking and Entering, Midrange Systems, May 26, 1992.

11 Logistics and Service Opportunities and Issues

Logistics professionals have been engaged in a battle for more than half a century to gain respect for their profession. Analogies such as "Dry as toast" and "sexy as oatmeal" as well as comments like "a necessary evil" have been used to described their field. While everything else has been reengineered to the last degree, logistics has been in exile from the corporate boardroom. However, it would appear that the tide is turning as businesses are realizing that logistics costs often represent their single highest operating expenditure and can account for as much as 10–35% of a company's gross sales (see table 11.1). Statistics are not available for information distributors such as Connexion, the third-party service for distribution of software. It is likely that distribution costs of these entities, though, are less than 1% of product cost.

Logistics costs consume on average 10%–15% of GDP in developed economies, and when aftermarket services are included, this figure may grow to as much as 25% of total GDP. This number has steadily declined over the past two decades as transportation companies have exploited innovative synergies, as well as information technology, to lower their costs. Logistics costs are contributed by a number of different operations; table 11.2 provides a representative breakdown for Australian companies in the 1980s. Packing and inventory costs have dropped dramatically over the past decade, leaving transport as the primary cost in the late 1990s. The United States alone spent nearly $800 billion on logistics costs in 1996, representing slightly more than 10% of the 1996 GDP.

The role of electronic commerce in redefining logistics and service is an important factor to consider when evaluating ways that new processes and systems can be used to improve customer satisfaction, reduce costs, and increase control. Improvements in logistics efficiencies and changing cost structures are also important to understand as critical factors for enabling the development and expansion of the global marketspace.

Electronic commerce depends on efficient logistics to deliver goods physically to the consumer. The cost of providing this delivery has been declining rapidly over the past decade. The percentage of U.S. GDP spent on logistics has declined from 14.7% in 1980 to 10.5% in 1997; similar figures can be presented for other developed economies. Express delivery services companies are now able to offer overnight delivery of small packages for mail order and Internet retailers for less than US$3 per package delivered to any U.S. residential addresses. In addition, since most of the cost involved in delivery is in getting the package delivered locally, the cost of logistics is virtually the same for a package delivered across town versus a package delivered thousands of miles away in a distant city. This shift in logistics cost for residential delivery of goods makes the cost of selling goods over the Internet almost

Table 11.1
Transport costs for some U.S. industries in 1982

Industry	Inbound and outbound costs as a percentage of product costs
Stone, clay, and glass	27
Petroleum products	24
Lumber and wood	18
Chemicals	14
Food	13
Furniture and fixtures	12
Paper and allied products	11
Fabricated metal products	8
Textile mill products	8
Machinery	5
Apparel	4
Publishing	4
Leather and leather products	3

Source: Anderson, 1983.

Table 11.2
Logistics costs for Australian companies in 1985

Source	Logitisics cost as a percentage of sales
Transportation	2.7
Receiving and dispatch	1.0
Warehousing	2.2
Packaging	3.2
Inventory	7.2
Order processing	2.0
Administration	2.8
Total logistics	*21.1*

Source: P. Gilmour, *Operations management in Australia*, Melbourne, Australia: Longman Cheshire, 1991.

location independent for many goods and services (although there may be added costs for some international transactions). Even for international shipments, the costs of local transportation and delivery costs can often exceed the costs involved in shipping goods across the ocean to a distant foreign country.

The declining costs of logistics have fostered growth in both Internet retailing and in specialized mail order retailing. At the same time, information technology and electronic commerce have played an important role in enabling the goods transportation industry to reduce costs and improve services dramatically. For example, onboard computer systems, such as those being investigated by Consolidated Freightways in the case included in this chapter, have become essential tools of business for transportation providers today. However, as the Consolidated Freightways case illustrates, the path to achieving these savings is filled with many areas of uncertainty and risk for those firms pioneering in the use of electronic commerce tools and technologies. Today, most transportation providers have the ability to track product shipments electronically from the time of pickup to final delivery, and many allow their customers to link into their on-line databases to be able to verify the location and expected delivery time for any package.

Trucking constitutes by far the largest single component of logistics costs in the United States, with motor carriers (trucking firms) accounting for nearly half of this $800 billion expense for the economy in 1996. Transportation costs have declined rapidly in the United States since deregulation in 1980. Reduced logistics costs, both for transport and because of reductions in warehousing and inventory costs, have contributed significantly to the ongoing economic upswing and one of the longest business expansions in U.S. history. Some industry experts believe that it will be possible to further reduce total logistics costs in the United States to below 9% of the GDP within the next five years by using improved supply chain management practices and by leveraging investments in information systems and electronic commerce applications.

Competitive Advantage Using Logistics and Information Technology

Companies that have used software and electronic commerce tools to choreograph the movement of inbound and outbound goods are literally dancing all the way to the bank and making their customers applaud. U.S. Department of Commerce figures indicate that nearly 60% of all Fortune 500 companies' logistics costs are spent on transporting goods from manufacturers to distribution centers or retailers. These transportation figures are then translated into between 2% and 8% of a company's sales, so that even reducing this by 1% for a multibillion dollar organization adds up to substantial savings. Pamida Inc., an $800 million general merchandise retailer based in Omaha, Nebraska, sliced millions of dollars from its logistics costs by using transportation management and tracking software that improved its ability to negotiate with suppliers and track deliveries on-line. The time taken to pay off this enterprise was a mere 90 days and has enabled the company to replenish its stores more quickly. Rolm and Haas, a $4 billion manufacturer of chemicals and plastics based in Philadelphia, experienced savings after installing a transportation optimization and tracking application that paid for itself in less than one year by giving the company vital information that could be used to negotiate more advantageous contracts with shippers.

Transportation has historically been treated as a commodity and as such, relegated to a low priority below, for example, IT segments like sales force automation and financial systems. "It was never seen as an area where you could improve customer service or eliminate costs or put together programs that improved delivery or fill rates," noted Gregory Owens, Managing Partner at Andersen Consulting's logistics strategy practice.[1] However that traditional pattern of thought is changing given several recent developments—the general growth of companies (and corresponding transportation budgets), an increase in customer demands, and innovative practices with supply chain pioneers such as Wal-Mart—so that transportation management is now being seen as a vital business strategy. In a November 1997 survey by Kynveld Peat Marwick Goerdeler (KPMG) and the University of Tennessee, 33% of the 360 logistics professionals surveyed said they reported to the CEO or equivalent, compared to 21% just a year before. With this new adjustment in status level comes demanding choices, and one is whether to either reengineer or to outsource transportation. Outsourcing, notes Steve Gold, partner in charge of KPMG's national logistics practice, has become more popular, with almost 40% of the survey respondents planning to rely more heavily on third-party providers in in the future.

However, both Pamida and Rolm perceive transportation an area where they can gain competitive advantage. They would therefore rather control the process themselves. Kelly Abney, Vice President of logistics at Pamida, would like to see the company be the premiere retailer for rural America. To keep 148 stores stocked with general merchandise presents a formidable challenge. Merchandise has to be shipped along a national network comprised of thousands of vendors, three distribution centers, one return center, one bulk center and one national return center to stores located anywhere from the Midwest to the Rocky Mountains. Until 1995, this process was handled manually, which involved poring over atlases and sorting through seas of paperwork and purchase orders in an attempt to find routes that would result in the fewest empty trailers and less-than-full truckloads.

Outsourced Logistics in the Supply Chain

One way that firms have been able to save money on both transportation and warehousing is by outsourcing their logistics process to leading services providers. They are then able to manage the flow of goods through information links by means of logistics services outsourcing. For example, General Motors (GM) now has a warehouse of components owned and operated by Federal Express (FedEx). A buffer stock of components is available for delivery to any GM production site overnight from this warehouse by simply placing an electronic order with the on-line FedEx inventory management system. Thus one single FedEx outsourced warehouse in Memphis, Tennessee, is able to store backup inventory of components needed for all GM sites nationwide and enables GM factories to operate using just-in-time delivery of components with no inventory buffer.

Similarly, PC Connection has outsourced its U.S. product delivery operations to Airborne Express. This mail order company operates its sales offices from New Hampshire (which has no state sales tax), but the products are physically inventoried in a warehouse owned by Airborne Express in Ohio. Airborne takes care of picking up all products from vendors, storing the inventory in its warehouse, and delivering products to consumers at their home or office. PC Connection uses an electronic on-line connection to Airborne to schedule shipments from the Ohio warehouse location after selling the product to consumers either through its Internet store, from mail order catalog sales, or from telephone sales in response to its many computer magazine advertisements. For telephone or Internet sales, customers can place orders as late as 2 A.M. (Eastern U.S. time zone) and receive delivery by 10 A.M. the next morning at their home or office. The total cost of product pickup, warehousing, and delivery for PC Connection is less than US$3 for most products that can be delivered in a standard-sized overnight shipment envelope. Thus this outsourced logistics relationship enables PC Connection to deliver products to consumer at very low cost while offering the customer more convenient delivery service than would be provided by a local retail store.

Parsons Technology along with other software vendors, has completely eliminated the physical logistics process for delivery of its products to consumers. Customers purchasing software on-line can simply download the product as soon as they buy it. This eliminates sales costs for delivery and enables customers to have almost instant fulfillment of their orders without having to go to a physical store location to pick up their product. In addition, the Web has enabled Parsons and other software companies to develop new marketing techniques that take advantage of the instant and zero-marginal-cost delivery mechanism available via the Internet. The cost advantages available for low-cost and fast delivery of software from companies such as PC Connection and Parsons Technology either on-line or via low-cost overnight transportation providers have dramatically reduced software sales in retail stores.

Outsourced Logistics and Electronic Commerce for Physical Goods

Could the same pressures apply for sales and distribution of physical goods that cannot be delivered on-line? Some on-line retailers are betting that a new model of selling and delivery of goods will replace the existing retail store format, with many goods and services delivered directly to consumers by firms such as FedEx or Airborne Express. One such example is Netgrocer Inc., which offers for sale more than 4,000 grocery products for home delivery anywhere in the United States via its online Web site. By outsourcing delivery to a transportation provider at a very attractive negotiated rate, Netgrocer is able to deliver any product order for $2.99 (orders less than $50) or $4.99 (orders over $50). By centralizing all inventories at one warehouse location, the company is able to minimize rental, storage, and operating costs of its grocery store operations.

With no retail store rents or operating costs, Netgrocer is able to offer prices that are very competitive with local supermarkets while providing home delivery of the products at minimal cost within two or three days at most. To date, only about .1% of American households order groceries on-line. But *Progressive Grocer* magazine forecasts that the so-called consumer-direct model will account for 10–15% of the industry within 10 years. The opportunity is huge, with the US$300 billion domestic market for groceries larger than the combined markets for books and music, two popular electronic commerce categories. Consumers invariably rate going to the supermarket as one of their least favorite chores. If the Internet brings back the home delivery model, which was popular before the rise of supermarkets, some experts predict that on-line grocers would skim off the most profitable shoppers. The convenience of home delivery and Internet shopping could become the most significant threat to established grocery product retailing since the emergence of the supermarket innovation earlier this century.

The Consumer Direct Cooperative (CDC) predicts that within a decade, the consumer-direct channel (Internet and telephone orders) will generate $85 billion in sales and capture 8–12% of the market share for grocery products and other market services.[2] CDC estimates that more than 15% of American households in 2007 will be consumer-direct customers. Many consumers appear to be flexible on the question of delivery and limited product selection and are willing to share purchase information so long as there is something tangible in return for that disclosure. Common operating aspects of a profitable consumer-direct model are an efficient and fast order method, low customer acquisition and service costs, and simplified high-volume fulfillment operations. Strategies for order methods include having customers place their orders electronically, as labor-intensive options such as phone orders can be more than 30 times as expensive as receiving orders via on-line sales channels. In addition, consumers can customize their interface and shopping lists via electronic on-line shopping, increasing convenience and customer loyalty to a single on-line products provider.

Geographic Information Services and Logistics

New information challenges within logistics include looking at geographical information systems (GISs); Sears was able to reduce its four-hour delivery time to two hours while still maintaining a service level of 97% by working with a vendor of GISs to install onboard computer systems in their delivery fleet (similar to the onboard computer systems described in the Consolidated Freightways case, but using the latest equipment available in 1996). Sears has also consolidated its routing and dispatch centers from 46 to 22. By developing optimal routing systems for home delivery, Sears was able to reduce costs and improve service levels dramatically. In addition, by using GIS technology and digitizing the warehouse and delivery processes, Sears saved more than US$6 million per year.

Rapid advances in GIS technologies are enabling dramatic savings in local delivery and storage costs. As these costs decline by more than 50% in some cases, home delivery can become less expensive than maintaining an expensive retail location for many goods. Since local delivery is the largest portion of transportation expense for many goods, information technology is enabling transportation providers to become active participants in the move toward the new location-independent marketspace.

The Internet and the Future of Logistics

Some companies express concern about the Internet's current technical limitations. Those who conduct EDI transactions over VANs (Value-Added Networks) have the confidence and experience that important information will arrive at its destination, on schedule, intact. If any problems do arise, a single network service provider is accountable and responsible for resolving them. Companies expecting this level of service worry that the Internet offers no such guarantees. Because it is a public network that connects many smaller, interconnected networks and service providers, no single entity is responsible for ensuring that a message leaves one point and arrives, intact, at another. And because companies have a need to transmit confidential information, they want assurance that it remains secure.

Companies are taking different approaches to address the Internet's current technical limitations. Some use the Internet to purchase lower-value, indirect materials while keeping their higher-value, direct material purchases over VANs. Some rely on extranets, or "virtual private networks," that limit access to a certain prequalified set of businesses and their partners. It is common in industry, for protection of privacy and ensuring the security of Internet transactions, to use encryption products and firewalls. Other companies await a resolution of current export limitations on encryption software before they plan to increase their Internet business.

The automotive industry's ANX (automobile network exchange) is an example of an extranet that will provide automotive trading partners with a single, secure network for electronic commerce and data transfer. The industry has created a management structure and business rules to ensure that the network meets the performance, reliability, and security requirements the industry has put forward. The ANX overseer, Bellcore, has direct operations and management responsibilities over the network. Participating Internet service providers and network exchange points have been certified and will operate according to the terms of the ANX. A common set of business practices, including "acceptable use" policies and common network level security methods, are additional conditions of participation in the ANX.

Businesses will pursue alternatives most suitable for their immediate business requirements. For some, standard off-the-shelf solutions running over the public Internet are satisfactory. For others, customized solutions—along with explicit rules and operating procedures—may be the answer. As the Internet's performance and reliability improves over time, and as predictable legal frameworks emerge, the growth of business-to-business electronic commerce will accelerate.

Notes

1. http://www.ac.com/news/1996-7 archives/

2. Victor J. Orler and David H. Friedman, Consumer-direct: Here to stay, *Progressive Grocer*, January 1998, p. 51.

Consolidated Freightways: The On-Board Computer Project

Phil Seeley, Vice President of MIS at Consolidated Freightways (CF), was evaluating his alternatives in implementing the On-Board Computer (OBC) project, which was in final testing at the Cincinnati pilot location. The objectives of the OBC were to provide the terminal with an active, intelligent link to the trucks which would enable the dispatcher to more actively and accurately manage the entire trucking fleet. The OBC system represented a major investment that would require changes in operations throughout the company. Senior executives and field managers were excited about its potential to reduce costs and improve service, providing the company with a significant advantage in the highly competitive less-than-truckload (LTL) trucking industry. The pilot was designed to test the OBC's technical viability, employee acceptance, and projected economic benefits.

In September 1990, the pilot seemed to be working well technically, and the employees seemed to accept the system relatively well. However, its projected economic benefits had not yet been demonstrated. To realize the full potential of the new system required changing individual work patterns, which proved more difficult than expected. Unfortunately, the pilot was running about nine months behind schedule. Because development of the system had taken longer than expected, full testing of the system had not started until August. Phil was anxious to finish the pilot test and get on with the project implementation and rollout. However, some key issues remained to be resolved.

Phil was considering whether to deploy the existing OBC system immediately or delay the rollout to modify the system to reduce costs and increase flexibility. As a secondary issue, Phil wondered if CF should license the OBC system to competitors to help cover the costs of development. If licensed, how should fees be charged to provide maximum benefits through balancing competitive advantage benefits versus potential royalty income?

The Less-Than-Truckload Shipping Industry

The LTL shipping industry transported shipments too large for UPS or the postal service but not large enough to justify a full trailer load. LTL shipments cost more per pound than full-load shipments and were generally carried by different trucking companies. Regional overnight trucking companies transported LTL shipments of less than 500 miles and were generally considered a different market from the long-

This case was prepared by Theodore H. Clark under the supervision of Professor James L. McKenney.
© 1990 by the President and Fellows of Harvard College.
Harvard Business School case 9-191-069.

Table 11.3
Market shares of top three LTL carriers—1988

	Long-haul shipment (over 500 miles)	All LTL shipments
Consolidated Freightways	16.9%	9.3%
Yellow Freight	19.2	9.2
Roadway	16.0	8.0

Note: Total shares based on revenues for all subsidiaries; Roadway excludes Viking, which was acquired in 1989.

haul LTL market of shipments transported more than 500 miles. Until 1980, the industry was regulated and prices were high and service was inconsistent.

The industry gradually consolidated after deregulation, and price competition became intense. By 1988, the top three carriers controlled 52.1% of the $8.7 billion long-haul LTL market, and 26.5% of the $19.6 billion total LTL market. (See table 11.3.) Operating margins were generally less than 5% of revenues, and price competition had become relatively intense since deregulation. Average discounts from the standard list prices were 35% to 40%, with different carriers' prices for the same customer shipment varying by as much as 15% of list price. The industry standard list prices, modified versions of the tariffs in place before deregulation, were based on weight, volume, and distance, and were revised annually to reflect changes in the industry cost structure (e.g., fuel prices). Customers were generally quite price-sensitive as most considered freight a commodity, but they also required reliable and timely service. This requirement limited the number of carriers a single customer was willing to deal with, especially for long-haul shipments. In addition, volume discounts and negotiated rate agreements offered after deregulation encouraged customers to aggregate shipments with a few carriers.

The LTL logistics system was a series of pickup, sort and load, move, and delivery steps (shown in figure 11.1 as a flow diagram). Drivers picked up freight from the customer in local terminal trucks, and then shipped it to a consolidation center. At customer pickup, drivers loaded shipments flat on the bed of the trailer rather than stacking it. This saved the driver time, which was generally more limiting than trailer space for determining pickup capacity. The consolidation center unloaded the freight from multiple terminals and sorted and loaded it into fully stacked, "high and tight" trailers for delivery to each destination consolidation center. After arrival, the freight was unloaded and packed onto other trailers for each destination terminal, where the freight was again unloaded and packed onto separate trailers for each local delivery route.

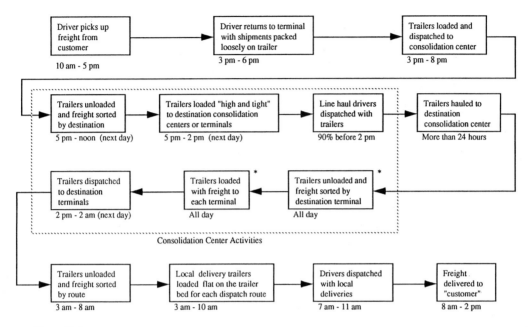

Figure 11.1
LTL logistics flow diagram

Larger carriers were able to take advantage of economies of scale by eliminating one or more steps in this process. For example, the origination terminal could load a full trailer of freight for a single destination terminal. Bypassing one step in the transportation chain reduced the costs of handling freight. In addition, less handling resulted in fewer lost or damaged shipments, thereby reducing claims costs and improving customer service. Finally, larger carriers were able to provide faster delivery times on long-haul routes, with more frequent departures. Smaller carriers often delayed shipments to balance loads in order to transport only full trailers to destination centers.

Shipment volume varied during the week, especially for the local terminal operation. Delivery volume on Monday would generally be twice the level of volume on Wednesday through Friday. The long-haul system operated seven days per week; therefore, a lot of freight arrived at the consolidation center over the weekend, when the weekday-only local delivery operations were closed. Pickup volume tended to be heavier later in the week, when customers tried to get shipments out before the weekend. It was also quite heavy the last few days of the month and at the end of the quarter. This imbalance in volume by day and by time of month made scheduling a

Table 11.4
Consolidated Freightways financial summary ($ millions)

	1989	1988
Revenues	3,670	2,689
CF Motor Freight	1,997	1,836
Con-Way Transportation Services	558	464
Emery Worldwide	1,205	389
Operating income (loss)	51	162
CF Motor Freight	108	119
Con-Way Transportation Services	40	33
Emery Worldwide	(97)	10

Note: Emery Worldwide was acquired during 1988.

challenge. Most LTL carriers managed delivery capacity with a mixture of full-time "regular" drivers and part-time "casual" drivers.

Customers in the industry were concentrated, with 20% of the customers providing more than half of total industry revenues. These large customers had a lot of negotiating power with carriers, and contracted with at least two carriers. Price was the primary criterion for carrier selection. Although poor service, such as lost or delayed shipments, could lose customers, most were not willing to pay more for excellent service. However, the expanded use of just-in-time (JIT) inventory systems had increased the willingness of some customers to pay premiums for faster, more reliable service.

Company Background

Consolidated Freightways, Inc. offered a diversified mix of transportation services, specializing in the movement of commercial and industrial freight shipments worldwide. Major subsidiaries included: Consolidated Freightways Motor Freight (CFMF), the company's long-haul LTL carrier and largest subsidiary; Con-Way Transportation Services (CTS), local and regional LTL carriers; and Emery Air Freight, acquired in 1988 and merged with the existing CF Air Freight business. (See table 11.4.) CFMF was unionized, while most of the CTS carriers were nonunion companies. The company's heritage and primary business was long-haul LTL trucking. While the OBC project was developed for both the CFMF and CTS subsidiaries, the primary beneficiary of the system was the larger and more complex long-haul subsidiary.

Consolidated Freightways reacted to deregulation and increased competition by focusing on improving service in an effort to become the best LTL carrier in the business. During the 1980s, service improved dramatically as the company demonstrated a willingness to invest capital and time toward this objective. The CFMF mission statement clearly outlined the company's commitment to service:

CF Motor Freight intends to distinguish itself as the premier long-haul carrier in North America. The Company will achieve this position by embracing a no-compromise philosophy of customer orientation throughout the organization. Evidence of our success will be in the development of an unquestioned marketplace perception of CF Motor Freight as the preferred service company with which to do business.

In some instances, CFMF demonstrated a strong enough difference in performance to overcome a premium price compared with that of other carriers, especially for companies using JIT inventory systems. For example, CFMF was able to provide faster and more reliable delivery service than other carriers to support Buick's conversion to a JIT system. This enabled CFMF to capture most of Buick's business in one plant and to become a preferred supplier of transportation for all plants. This strong service-based relationship with Buick was in spite of larger discounts offered by aggressive competitors.

Other large customers valued the superior service CFMF provided, but most were unwilling to pay more than 1% differential in pricing for this service. Ford awarded CFMF its Transportation Excellence Award for 1989, but still split shipments among multiple carriers, with price a primary criterion for selection. Over time, CFMF expected the number of customers willing to pay for better service to increase, but recognized that the market in 1990 was still very price sensitive. Thus, CFMF still had to match prices offered by major competitors to avoid losing a large portion of the market.

In 1990, CFMF had more than 3,000 tractors for the line-haul operations and more than 5,000 tractors for local freight distribution at the almost 700 local distribution centers. The line-haul route network linked the 30 consolidation centers nationwide and provided multiple paths over which freight could travel, depending on road conditions and daily distribution of trailers and destinations. (See figure 11.2.) Of the more than 26,000 trailers in the CFMF system, almost 90% were 28-foot doubles that were carried in tandem for line-haul or as a single trailer for local delivery. This dual use of the 28-foot trailers simplified operations and sometimes reduced handling requirements between consolidation centers and terminals. At the local terminals, drivers had their own tractors, which they drove every day, but line-haul drivers were not assigned to a single tractor.

CFMF Information Services

CFMF had a long history of investing in information systems and automation to improve service and reduce costs. From an early adoption of bar codes, increasingly

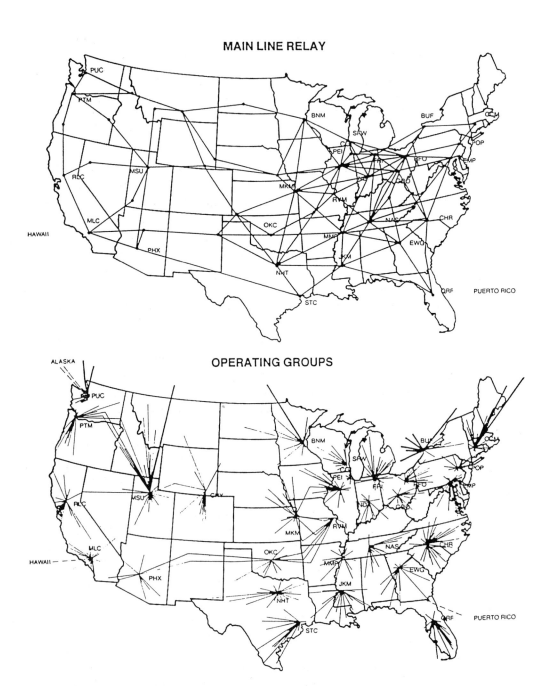

Figure 11.2
CFMF distribution network

sophisticated information systems had enabled CFMF to reduce shipping time and lost packages. This investment also reduced operating costs, more than offsetting the additional cost of the information systems. During the 1980s, senior management adopted a vision of becoming a paperless trucking company, whereby all paper not legally required would be replaced by electronic information.

CFMF was one of the first LTL carriers to use bar codes to identify packages and shipping labels. Drivers applied bar code tags to all shipments at pickup. These shipment bar codes were encoded with the "PRO number" recorded on each customer's shipping bill. All terminals and consolidation centers were linked in a single database that tracked shipments by these PRO numbers. This system allowed tracking of shipments from the origination terminal to the destination terminal, reducing lost or delayed shipments as well as handling costs. In addition, customers were able to link with the CFMF database and determine the status of their shipments. This on-line information service was valued by many users and served as an example of CFMF's commitment to superior service. This information system also enabled automated invoicing based on the shipping information entered into the system by clerks in the terminal office. Finally, the information in the system on each shipment and customer enabled CFMF management to track overall profitability by customer and by type of shipment, which was helpful in making pricing decisions in a very competitive market.

During 1990, the company began pilot testing an optical scanning system that scanned all shipment records and replaced decentralized paper files with an on-line centralized database. It was a major step toward realizing the paperless office vision and would provide a significant improvement in responsiveness to customer inquiries. Under the paper-based system, responding to a customer inquiry about a past shipment could take a week or more, as records were stored in each terminal and were often difficult to access. Shippers often needed a copy of the signed delivery receipt form to prove that their customer had received the shipment and that payment was due for products delivered. With the electronic on-line system, customer would be able to link directly with the database and access their own historical shipping files, saving time for the customer and cost for CFMF. This systems would supplement the on-line service already developed for shipments in transit.

Although CFMF was willing to invest in technology to improve service levels, cost control was still important. Major investments had to be economically justified. For example, the company investigated using cellular phones for the sales force and drivers to increase service levels and access to the customer. They proved to be a valuable tool for the sales force, as the benefits of increased sales force productivity more than offset the costs. However, for the drivers, the costs were too large, given the potential benefits, and alternative tools to leverage driver productivity were investigated, such as terminal voice-mail systems and the OBC project.

Developing and Testing the On-Board Computer

The idea of placing a computer in the truck that would communicate directly to the dispatcher was initially tested in 1985, but years of testing and development were required to produce an operational pilot, due to the harshness of the environment and the complexity of the system requirements. A number of feasibility questions needed to be addressed before any serious design could be proposed. One key issue was whether the drivers could effectively learn to use the system, or would be willing to do so. The ability of a computer to withstand the harsh environment of the truck cab was also unknown. Finally, the capabilities required or possible in a truck-based computer had to be determined.

Early testing of prototypes indicated that truck drivers could learn to use a simple computer input device, such as a wand or a hand-held numerical keypad, but resisted using a standard "QWERTY" keyboard to interface with the computer. In these tests, hardware reliability proved to be a serious problem in the harsh truck environment. Not until 1987 was hardware available that provided capabilities needed in the OBC and that could withstand the truck environment. Unfortunately, none of the products then on the market could provide the complete functionality needed in a single system. In addition, the user interfaces on existing systems were not sufficiently simple for use by CFMF's drivers. For example, one vendor offered acceptable functionality in an integrated system, but offered only a "QWERTY" keyboard interface and was unwilling to modify the system software to support a simpler interface.

In late 1987, discussions with IBM about the OBC concept led to a proposal to develop a system integrating the best components from multiple vendors to provide a solution tailored to CFMF's specifications. The system would combine digital radio communications with location tracking and mapping systems from two separate vendors (to improve reliability and redundancy) and would use a terminal with built-in function keys and a numeric keypad. The host controller for the dispatcher would be an IBM PS/2–based system for communications and location of all trucks on an electronic mapping system. After lengthy discussions and careful review of the economic justification for the new system, the CF Board approved the IBM proposal to build a production version of the OBC and test the system in a pilot location. The $4 million development project was begun in late 1989, with pilot testing projected to begin in January 1990.

Table 11.5
OBC system Phase One projected economics

Installation costs		Number of terminals = 118
Hardware and software	$ 9,290,000	Number of trucks = 1,882
Training	1,297,000	Recurring costs $1,029,000/yr.
Total	$10,587,000	Projected savings $13,560,115/yr

Projected cash flow ($ thousands)

	Initial investment	Year 1	Year 2	Year 3	Year 4	Year 5	Year 6	Year 7
Expenses	3,539	4,932	5,528	1,106	1,122	1,188	1,205	1,275
Savings	0	6,780	14,034	14,526	15,034	15,561	16,105	16,669
Net cash flow	(3,539)	1,848	8,506	13,420	13,912	14,373	14,900	15,394

Note: Investment spread over first two years, and only 50% of projected annual savings realized in initial year. Both cost and savings increased for expected increases due to inflation.

Economic Benefits of the System

The projected savings possible with deployment of the OBC would provide a payback on all development and implementation costs of slightly more than one year, with most of the savings in reduced labor costs. (See table 11.5.) Based on a study completed in the Los Angles (LA) division, the projected benefits of the OBC Phase One deployment would exceed $13 million per year. (See table 11.6.) More than half of the savings were in reduced driver hours, with dispatch and clerical labor reductions each providing about 20% of the total savings. Though impressive, these savings did not include any of the potential strategic benefits the system would also provide in terms of better customer responsiveness. In addition, the information provided by the system could be used to improve operations in the consolidation centers and for headquarters planning. The OBC was designed as a system to support local pickup and delivery operations, and the cost justification was based solely on improving productivity in the local terminal operations.

The OBC team selected the LA division to evaluate the proposed system's benefits in order to allow involvement of all terminal managers and district managers in a single division. In an extensive and iterative Delphi interview process, the management group developed both a consensus and an excitement about the system's benefits. Terminal managers and dispatchers estimated the benefits the proposed system would provide in their operations, with justifications provided for projected savings in each area of operations. These estimates were complied by the OBC team and average responses and extreme cases were discussed with all the participants in a joint

Table 11.6
Projected benefits of OBC Phase One implementation

	Savings projected in LA division evaluation		Savings projected for Phase One implementation		Wage rates and cost per mile		Projected daily savings
Driver hours	9.5%	---	1411.5 hs/day	×	$20.98/hr	=	$29,613
Dispatcher hours	39.8%		509.6 hs/day		$21.41/hr		$10,908
Clerical hours	4.1 hrs/terminal		488.5 hs/day		$17,32/hr		$8,461
Mileage per day	4.7 miles/truck		8845 miles/day		$0.57/mile		$5,042

Total daily savings = $54,024

Total annual savings = daily savings * 251 days = $13,560,115

follow-up meeting, leading to a consensus on potential savings. The projected savings estimated by the terminal managers and dispatchers were then reduced by the LA division manager to ensure that the projections given were realistic. Even so, the savings were sufficient to justify the entire cost of deploying the OBC system throughout the LA division with just the first year's savings.

Developing the System

Integrating the separate components of the OBC into a single system proved much more difficult than originally expected by either CF or IBM. Hardware integration proceeded fairly smoothly, despite some changes in equipment offerings by vendors, but integrating the software systems developed by different groups proved to be quite difficult. Individually, all of the component systems worked. However, major problems emerged when they were combined into an integrated system. Part of the challenge in coordinating the systems was the lack of coordination among design teams. There were six different teams in geographically separate locations working on different parts of the system software, and the coordination between development groups was often weak. Significant portions of code had to be modified, which delayed the pilot test by nine months from the planned schedule.

In anticipation of starting the pilot tests, the hardware was installed in the trucks in early 1990. The magnitude of the software integration problem was not fully appreciated at that time, but installing the hardware prior to software completion did facilitate driver acceptance once the pilot test was implemented. By the time the system was ready to become operational, truckers had mostly overcome annoyance with the intruding terminal in their personal space and were curious about how the system would work. As one manager observed, "If you live with a rattlesnake in a cage beside you long enough, you come to believe it is harmless." Many of the truckers resisted the new system initially, but were generally accepting of it by the time full-scale pilot testing had begun in August.

The OBC Pilot Test

The purposes of the pilot were to test system reliability and technical performance, to determine training requirements and challenges, and to evaluate the potential economic benefits. Cincinnati was chosen as a test site location because it had three CFMF terminals and one CTS terminal that could share the radio antennas and systems. A moderately small city with several terminals was needed, with each terminal large enough to justify an OBC dispatch system to coordinate trucks. Cincinnati was small enough to be affordable as a pilot test, but large enough to have the required attributes.

By September 1990, the early results of the pilot testing indicated that technical problems were minimal, but more training and operational changes were needed to realize the projected benefits. Startup costs in terms of driver and dispatcher learning time were larger than expected, and savings were not yet evident. Most participants believed that the savings would eventually offset the cost, but virtually everyone involved believed that the savings in labor would come from someone else's functional area.

Although the full pilot did not begin until August 1990, testing of hardware in the trucks and installation of the dispatch automation system was completed in early 1990. Some minor problems were detected and corrected, but no major problems were uncovered in six months of testing the hardware in actual truck operation conditions. The dispatch system, without the map or truck communications subsystems, was installed and tested to simplify the transition to the full-scale pilot test once the software modifications were completed. By September, the dispatchers had been trained on the system and used key elements of it for more than six months.

In general, driver acceptance was good; however, some had a difficult time adapting to the new system. One driver said, "I've never yet been able to get that dumb computer to work right. I'm probably doing something wrong, but I just can't seem to figure this thing out." Several also felt that the system was taking away their independence. As one driver said, "I'm just like a PFC (in the army) now, I just do what I'm told." However, some drivers preferred the OBC to the prior system. With more information and less calling in, the drivers were "left alone to do our job, with less need to report in to dispatcher."

Unfortunately, the dispatchers in the pilot test seemed to have difficulty changing work patterns to use the new system effectively. One dispatcher said he basically did everything on paper first and then entered the information into the computer, because the paper systems provided more information and a better picture of the overall operation. For this dispatcher, the computer was more a burden than a tool to leverage his time. When asked how the system could eventually help him on the job, he responded, "I have no idea." Another dispatcher used the system as a effective tool, but still mostly replaced his normal paper planning by using the computer in a similar mode. The OBC project team was concerned that the dispatchers were not expanding their management role enough to realize the system's potential benefits. The dispatchers, who had a key pivotal role in changing the terminal operations to utilize the OBC capabilities, were not learning to adapt to the new job requirements as quickly or easily as expected.

Operational Implications of the On-Board Computer

The OBC would reduce costs and improve service by enabling singificant improvements in the operation of the terminal dispatch systems. Realizing the potential savings would require significant changes in the dispatch job requirements, as well as changes in other areas. Simply deploying the computer as a replacement for manual methods would not provide the expected benefits. As one manager stated, this would be simply "replacing a 5 cent pencil with a $5,000.00 machine." The most significant change with the OBC system would be in the dispatcher and terminal manager responsibilities, though the system would also have significant impact on both drivers and clerical workers. In addition, faster availability of information offered significant benefits for consolidation center planning, but would require additional changes in operations.

Changing the Dispatch Management Function

Dispatching under the existing system was a skilled management position, requiring a good knowledge of the local streets and geography in order to effectively assign deliveries and pickups to routes. Dispatchers also had to understand the capabilities and preferences of individual drivers in order to effectively plan and assign routes each day. In figure 11.3, a flow diagram shows how the system operated manually before OBC installation.

Before the OBC, dispatchers would start coding and sorting shipments by delivery route at about 4 o'clock in the morning. There was no single standard for assigning shipments to routes, with some dispatchers using physical pigeonholes and others a paper system to list shipments by route. Most terminals had several designated route areas, and multiple trucks would cover a single area, especially on Mondays and

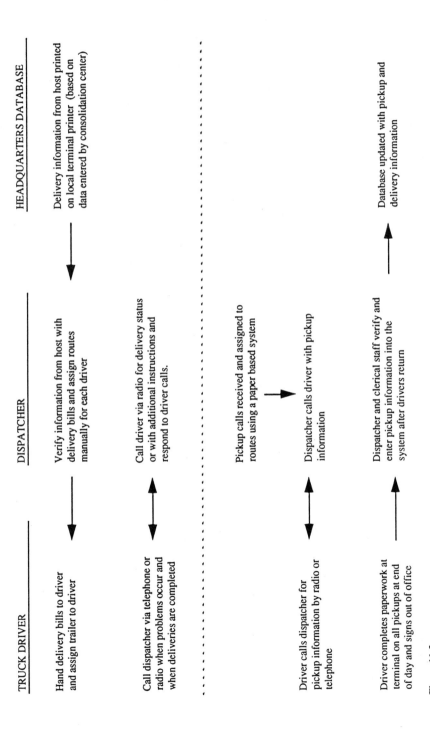

Figure 11.3
Information flow before the OBC

Tuesdays when delivery volume was highest. Once shipments were geographically divided into route areas, the dispatcher separated deliveries into individual truck routes. This assignment was often based as much on the capabilities and needs of the drivers on duty as on geographic proximity of deliveries within a single area.

A second dispatcher generally relieved the first dispatcher in the early afternoon, handling pickup requests and driver coordination for the remainder of the day. The pickup dispatcher was assisted by the entire office in taking pickup calls, but was responsible for assigning all pickups and ensuring that no pickups were missed. Because a single missed pickup was a serious error that could damage customer relationships, careful organization and follow-up was needed for pickup dispatching.

The dispatchers often worked long days of 10 hours or more, and few were able to function at an optimal level. The level of complexity and speed of decisions made *coping* a challenge and optimizing or maximizing virtually impossible. Most of the dispatchers' time was spent on the radio or the telephone receiving pickup requests or communicating with drivers. In a real sense, the dispatcher needed to be an "expert" with a large internal database of geographic and interpersonal knowledge to be able to coordinate both pickup and delivery operations.

The OBC and associated dispatch automation system freed the dispatcher of the need to know the geography and street names, as this information was already in the system. The information flows between dispatchers, drivers, and the host mainframe system are shown in figure 11.4. Much of the delivery and pickup route planning could be automated, eliminating all of the sorting step in the delivery dispatch process and facilitating individual driver route assignments. Pickups could also be planned better as more information was available on truck location and status. When necessary, pickup assignments could be dynamically changed to balance loads better and reduce unnecessary overlap of truck routes. Using the OBC system as a preprogrammed "expert assistant" would free the dispatchers to spend more time on the interpersonal aspects of the job and more effectively manage the drivers.

The skills needed to be effective in the dispatch function would change, with street familiarity no longer necessary and better planning and managerial skills necessary. In addition, pickup dispatching could be centralized in a metropolitan area, replacing the afternoon dispatcher in each terminal with a single dispatcher supported by clerical staff to answer telephones and log calls into the system. Most large cities had multiple CFMF terminals, and consolidation of pickup dispatching into a single location for the city could significantly reduce dispatch labor hours. The time required for the morning dispatcher to plan delivery routes would also be reduced, enabling him or her to spend more time managing the drivers. The delivery planning could not be

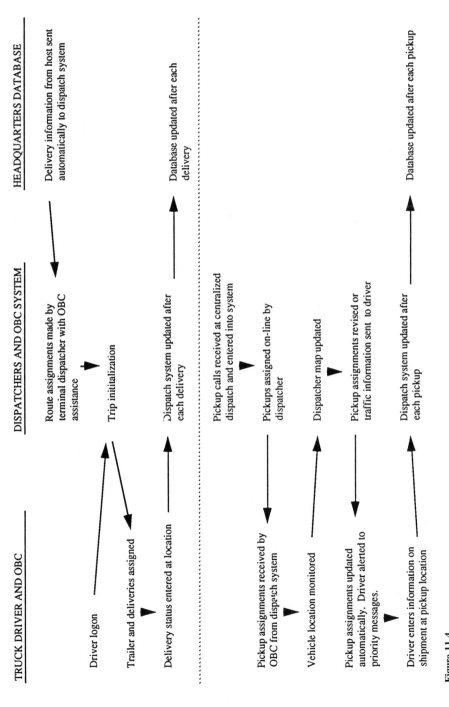

Figure 11.4
Information flow using the OBC

centralized, because the system did not have enough information on driver abilities or freight characteristics to be able to effectively plan delivery routings completely. However, it could serve as an effective tool for the morning dispatcher. With the elimination of the evening dispatcher position through centralized pickup dispatching, the terminal manager would have to be responsible for some of the tasks formerly performed by the evening dispatcher. However, the terminal manager would be able to shift some tasks to the morning dispatch manager, who would have more time available with the OBC performing some of the planning functions automatically.

Changing the Driver's Role

The OBC's most significant impact on drivers would be the replacement of frequent contact with a human dispatcher with almost exclusive interaction with a computer terminal. The driver would also have more tasks to perform with each pickup and delivery, as data would have to be entered into the system throughout the day. However, paperwork that drivers normally completed at the end of the day in the terminal would be eliminated. Thus, the net time reduction or increase due to the system data entry was likely to be minimal. The real time savings came from better dispatch planning that would reduce unproductive time for the driver. In addition, the drivers would save time by not having to call in for pickups or instructions that could automatically be transmitted to the computer. The managers in the LA division estimated that the net impact of these changes would result in a 9.5% reduction in total driver hours.

Although the system did provide more information for the driver and dispatcher faster and more reliably than the voice radio system, some drivers expressed concern that they lost some independence and were forced to rely more on the system than on their own judgment. As one driver said: "It's hard to argue with a computer. If it tells you to do something dumb, you can't say no." However, some dispatchers liked the fact that truckers were less able to debate instructions given over the computer.

With the OBC, the drivers became the primary data entry point in the system and provided real-time updates of the status of all shipments, both pickups and deliveries. This information was useful in planning in the consolidation centers and would enable dispatchers to have better information to dynamically manage truck schedules and routing. In addition, dispatchers or terminal managers could provide more accurate information to customers on when shipments would be picked up or delivered. While this timely information could be useful in managing the trucks and terminal, some managers worried that "we could simply be turning union truckers into very expensive data entry clerks."

Changing the Role of Clerical Support

With drivers performing the initial data entry function, office clerks would no longer need to enter shipment information in the evening. Under the pre-OBC system, several clerks worked until 8 or 9 P.M., entering all the outbound shipment information into the computer. Direct links between on-line systems would also reduce data entry requirements. At the same time, the new dispatch system would make it easier for secretaries, clerks, or terminal managers to receive pickup calls and input the customer information directly into the system. Thus, the office staff would become assistant dispatchers, relieving the dispatcher of much of the initial contact role with the customer. With the centralization of the pickup dispatch function, some clerical staff would be assigned to support the centralized operation. Although this change would add new responsibilities and positions, total clerical hours would be reduced.

Improved Information for Consolidation Centers

A potentially important strategic benefit of the OBC system was the ability to provide the consolidation centers with earlier information about shipments, including destinations. Although the OBC system was justified on costs, the vision was based as much on improving information flows as on cost reduction. With access to outbound shipment information as soon as the driver completed each pickup, the consolidation centers could better plan direct shipments to destination terminals and reduce freight handling. Direct shipments, in which a trailer was completely loaded with freight to a single destination terminal, were planned based on experience and late information from terminals on outbound shipments. Direct shipment was only economical when the trailer could be at least 80% to 90% loaded at the origination consolidation center. With the OBC, the consolidation center would have earlier and more accurate information on shipments to each destination terminal so that loads could be more effectively planned to minimize handling and cost. Given the time-critical nature of these operations, having information available a few hours earlier could be a significant advantage. Of course, having the information available would provide little benefit for CFMF if the consolidation centers were not able to use it. Thus, operational change requirements would extend beyond the terminal to other areas of the company for the full benefits of the OBC to be realized.

Next Steps for the On-Board Computer

After the pilot test was successfully completed, Phil planned to expand the OBC system to the rest of the company, with a phased implementation over a five-year period. The first phase would deploy the OBC systems only in the most economically attractive terminals having more than 20 trucks in a single city in order to leverage the investment in centralized radio equipment and antennas. The planned Phase One locations included 150 of the larger terminals, with almost 2,000 tractors to be equipped with the OBC system. Later phases would expand the OBC system or some scaled-down version to most of the other locations in the company. The system developed by IBM and tested in the pilot was designed as a production system to be rolled out in the implementation phase with minimal modification. However, given the initial results of the pilot testing, Phil was evaluating the best approach for implementing the Phase One rollout.

The pilot test demonstrated that the OBC system worked technically and that drivers could learn to use the system. However, gaining the expected cost savings would take time. Dispatchers would have to change the way were using the system, and gaining the savings in the dispatch labor costs would require centralization of pickup dispatching for multiple terminals. The first phase of the pilot was with only one terminal in the city; therefore, no dispatch hours savings would be possible until the system was expanded to the other pilot locations in the city. In addition, eliminating one-half of a clerical person was unlikely to be possible in a single terminal implementation, but in a citywide pilot test, some labor cost savings could be realized. Although the pilot test had not yet demonstrated savings, field management remained convinced that the system would provide large savings once fully deployed.

The cost of the OBC system used in the pilot was close to $6,000 per truck-mounted unit. In production volumes, Phil expected the cost to be between $3,500 and $4,000 per unit. While this cost was higher than the $3,060 projected initially and shown in table 11.5, modifications to the system being considered could reduce the cost by $300 or more per unit. The cost of these truck-mounted units represented approximately 70% of the total equipment cost for the Phase One rollout. In addition to higher equipment costs, more training appeared to be needed than was initially projected, especially for the dispatchers. Even with the higher cost of training and equipment, the economics of the system were still very attractive, assuming the projected savings could be realized.

Beyond the cost savings potential, Phil believed that the OBC was a strategic system that would allow CFMF to provide better service to customers. With a goal of being the quality and price leader in the industry, the OBC implementation might be justified based on service improvements alone. Combining the OBC and the optical scanning and storage system for shipment records would allow CFMF to move much closer to the paperless company ideal. This combination could provide a significant competitive advantage over the rest of the industry. Delaying implementation of the OBC for further testing or development could reduce CFMF's competitive advantage by allowing competitors such as Yellow Freight and Roadway time to develop similar systems. At the same time, Phil did not want to invest too early in emerging technology and be stuck with high-cost systems if competitors were able to purchase much less expensive commercial systems several years later.

12 Successful E-Commerce

Listen to the technology; find out what it's telling you.
—Carver Mead, Physicist, California Institute of Technology Physics of Computation Lab

We close our book with a collection of short cases that demonstrate how e-commerce is changing our perceptions of markets, organizational hierarchies, jobs, and wealth. These are success stories involving e-commerce that we feel, in one way or another, point the way toward future business models. Of course, prediction is by its very nature hazardous: You are almost certain never to be right. Nevertheless, we have tried to present what we feel are significant innovations in electronic commerce and a brief explanation of why these innovations work or do not work, along with why we feel that they are important.

E-commerce success stories tend not to come from the traditional commercial giants of the physical world. More often they are stories about outsiders who knew almost nothing about the markets they chose to enter. Jeff Bezos, founder of the highly successful Amazon.com Internet bookstore, is a prime example: a financial analyst who had no previous experience in selling books. These novices succeeded because they understand the Internet and how to harness its potential. Internet e-commerce sites that transpose catalog to screen or render yet another virtual mall are usually e-commerce failures. Success requires rethinking what the Web is about. Our examples of companies that have successfully used the Web to improve their business performance are intended to help the individual understand the many possibilities available to tap into this expanding information-enabled revolution for business-to-business and business-to-consumer transactions.

Redefining the Marginal Cost/Marginal Revenue Equation

Cygnus Support

Michael Tiemann, founder of Cygnus Support, a developer of programming tools, received his inspiration from MIT programmer Richard Stallman, a staunch opponent of strict legal protection (i.e., patents, copyrights) for computer software. Cygnus gained market share by giving its software away for nothing, with no restrictions on its reproduction. Cygnus charges $300 per hour to tailor its existing programs to a customer's specific needs—a fee that Sun Microsystems, Adobe, Hitachi, and others have been happy to pay. Precisely because Cygnus's competitors are protective of their source code, companies find these rival products much more difficult to custom tailor. This, combined with a thorough knowledge of the complexities of its own products, gives Cygnus a sustainable competitive edge.

Cygnus reserves the right to include any of the modifications it makes for customers in its free products. Thus it continually lets customers complete their production process, by specifying the requirements for new and useful innovations. Cygnus evolves a more valuable product, which expands demand, and so forth. This is Cygnus's incomplete production model, in which the customer indirectly pays Cygnus by helping it develop their product. This is feasible only where information exchange is high in both directions.

Cygnus brings to market a new marketing and production paradigm. The base product is given away free (no cash changes hands); the client "pays" with innovative requirements specifications; Cygnus, for a fee, implements the requirements, and Cygnus generates future "consulting" fees by reserving the option to keep its product competitive—that is, maintain or gain market share—by incorporating innovations suggested by others. The innovations ensure an expanding market and the consulting fees ensure a steady cash flow.

McAfee Software

John McAfee built a prosperous business out of giving software away along with predictions of disaster at the hands of computer viruses. In the early 1990s, McAfee Associates began distributing antiviral software on computer bulletin boards (the predecessors to modern FTP sites) no questions asked, without shareware's honor system. McAfee would then make its money by collecting license fees from corporations scrupulous about their software ownership. The people who download software from public sites usually have technical jobs. McAfee used them as agents to get the software onto a corporate system, then billed the organization for site licensing their software.

To do this effectively, the programs had to be self-sufficient, requiring little support from McAfee. They also had to meet the needs of the technical staff, since these individuals would ultimately recommend the acquisition of a site license. McAfee has since merged with Network General, PGP, and Helix to create Network Associates. With maturity has come a more prosaic pricing policy, and McAfee's antiviral software now sells mostly in the under $100-per-user range.

Turnkey E-Commerce and Site Management

General Electric's Trading Process Network (TPN) Website now does $1 billion worth of business a year with about 1,400 suppliers, single-handedly exceeding all retail electronic commerce. In the first year of business, GE reported that it had cut the length of the bidding process in GE's lighting division to less than half, from 21 days to 10. Because requesting vendor bids is easy, purchasing staff approach more suppliers. The increased competition has lowered the cost of goods by 5–20%. Previously, it had been too much trouble and too time-consuming to include foreign suppliers. But after implementation of TPN, foreign orders accounted for 15% of the total.

GE's Web-based TPN service provides three functions:

- *Auctions:* For a fee, buyer companies can participate in the auction provided at this site.

- *Electronic ordering and purchase settlement:* Buyers can browse an electronic catalog of goods and services and generate electronic purchase orders. Some provision is made for use of digital cash.

- *Web page production:* GE Information Services can create Websites for customers based on a few forms that state the customer's Web presentation preferences.

Prior to establishing TPN, GE was the world's largest provider of EDI services, which gives it excellent credibility in electronic commerce. Among Fortune 1000 companies, 95% use EDI in some way, and this use grew 50% in 1997. TPN improves on EDI by providing an alternative to EDI's proprietary networks and static parts lists. In combination with various umbrella sites for industry firms such as Industry.net, the flexibility offered by TPN is dramatically altering the relationships between suppliers and customers.

One of GE's vendors, Hartford Computer Group, has quintupled its business since signing onto TPN. Whereas originally it was selling to just one part of GE, after adopting TPN it found it was getting requests for bids from divisions of GE with which it had never dealt. Another vendor, 20-employee Drabik Tool, reports greater control over production because TPN lets it establish precise delivery dates rather than the nondescript "RUSH" that often accompanied faxed orders. Drabnik was able to access TPN with an existing PC and an AOL account.

General Electric has provided a portfolio of secure, easy-to-use products to set up an e-commerce site quickly. GE set up this Website in 1994 for its vendors to make bids on GE electronics components contracts through a user-friendly EDI. It has since broadened into a secure public on-line commerce network linking suppliers and buyers and even provides a suite of tools for conducting interactive auctions on-line. GE's focus is naturally on industrial commodities like plastic parts, chemicals, packaging, and electronics.

Digital Storefronts

PG Music

PG Music's Band-in-a-Box was the brainchild of physician Peter Gannon at the suggestion of his brother, Juno Award–winning jazz guitarist Oliver Gannon. Gannon developed a set of sophisticated software engines to read music from digital piano keyboards, improvise solos, provide a highly flexible jazz rhythm section to back up solos, record music in musical instrument digital interface (MIDI) files, and print out sheet music. He then moved from software engineer to recording producer, approaching top artists in classical, blues, gospel, and modern jazz piano to record their music. The focus of all this effort was nothing less than the automation of piano teaching. This goal was especially important given the difficulty that most of his customers had locating good teachers for styles such as blues and gospel.

Gannon has since branched into guitar, with a library of his brother's performances, as well as bluegrass and other ensemble styles. Pieces are selected and arranged to provide an encyclopedia of the techniques and styles of the jazz masters. The computer interface delivers the music as notes on a piano keyboard or guitar fretboard, as sheet music, and as the musical sound itself. Music can be paused and stepped through either note by note or chord by chord for learning. The product has also found use as a quick and inexpensive way to generate a piano score from a song for the theater.

Because all of his products are information based—software, MIDI files, music style files, manuals, and so forth—they should, in theory, be delivered over the Internet. Increasingly his customers agree (particularly international customers) and prefer to download PG Music products from its Website.

Gannon's primary interest was in his products, and thus he has invested little in electronic commerce software. The site simply accepts credit card numbers from a Web-based form that is filled out by a customer, then authorizes a third-party ISP to make a file available to the customer for several days to download. No passwords or key codes are used. Customer satisfaction has been high, with comments like, "It's great to buy and download off the Internet. Every one should do it!"

Persian Kitty and Danni's Hard Drive[1]

"I would bet that between 80% and 90% of all [e-commerce] on the Internet is conducted at adult sites," said Tony, the owner of a site called Planet Hornywood (he asked that his last name not be used). There are approximately 10,000 adult sites generating about $1 billion in revenue per year, mostly through electronic credit card transactions. Erotic content accounted for sales of $52 million on the Internet in 1997—one-tenth of all retail business on the Web (though some estimates run to three times that amount or even more, as in the above quote from Tony).[2] This puts adult business behind sales of computer products and travel, but with the telephone videoconferencing segment of that business increasingly migrating to the Internet, these figures could rapidly change.[3]

Not all of the adult surfing is done during leisure time. A study of 185 companies by consulting firm Digital Detective Services found that a quarter of the companies' workers visited pornographic Websites. Media Metrix, a Web traffic analysis company, reports that 19% of users at work visit smut sites (compared with 69% for news or information sites).[4] A Nielsen Media Research study claimed that staffers at IBM, AT&T, and Apple Computer made 13,000 workplace visits to the *Penthouse* magazine Website during a single month.[5]

Two of the most profitable adult Websites have been Persian Kitty and Danni's Hard Drive. Danni Ashe got the idea for her site during a vacation in the Bahamas. During her break, she studied up on HTML and read Nicholas Negroponte's *Being Digital.* Two weeks later she had built her first adult Website: Danni's Hard Drive. The first day Danni's Hard Drive went on-line, it received 70,000 hits. Since then, Ashe's hobby has grown into a $2.5 million-a-year business. Some 80% of the site's revenue comes from the site's 18,000 subscriptions and the rest from fan club sales for Danni Ashe and for several other models.

Danni attracts customers to her site by advertising through banner ads on Persian Kitty—dubbed the Yahoo! of porn sites. Its on-line directory links to 1,400 adult Websites and receives hundreds of thousands of hits a day. It also grosses $80,000 a month for the housewife and mother of two who runs the site from her suburban home. Webmistress Persian Kitty, an accountant by trade, started the site in October 1995, carrying over her name from her CompuServe moniker. Persian Kitty is indexing what is arguably the most active and lucrative area of e-commerce on the Internet. While most corporate home pages tabulate monthly hits in the thousands, top adult sites regularly garner more than one million hits per day. That puts them well ahead, in fact, of such corporate sites as General Electric or Boeing. Of more immediate relevance, porn site visitors are more likely to spend money on the spot.

Operators say adult sites that get 10,000 hits per day usually gross about $3,000 per month. Midsize sites attracting 50,000 hits daily bring in roughly $20,000 in revenue monthly. Large sites, with multimillion daily hits, can bring in more than $1 million per month. The field is split between pay sites charging a monthly membership fee, such as Danni's Hard Drive, and free sites, such as Persian Kitty, which are supported by banner ads from the former. Free sites became popular in early 1996, when

Intertain Inc. and Amateur Hardcore—two well-financed pay sites—arrived, sold passwords, and started promoting with banner ads on adult pages scattered around the Web. Suddenly, running a free sex site became lucrative. Another site, XPics, raised its banner ad rates from $1,500 per month to $4,500 in only three months, and stopped flat-rate pricing while moving to a two-cents-per-click-through scheme. With 250,000 visits per day at XPics' free sites, the click-through pricing pays nicely.[6]

Another Network[7]

You *can* buck the Internet with your own proprietary network, and win (for a while at least). America Online (AOL) has developed a strong brand name having successfully made AOL synonymous with "being on-line" and "the Internet": "My family is finally on the Internet, we got AOL."

What is more interesting is how AOL has accomplished this. AOL has routinely chalked up the worst reliability rate of any major provider of Internet service. It misled customers so flagrantly that it had been sued by 44 states. It had been sued three times in less than three years over billing problems and access glitches. It had been caught making unethical use of its members' names, only to back down in the face of customer outrage. Nevertheless, AOL has become the leading on-line service provider in America. It does this through three interlinked strategies.

First, AOL makes it easy to subscribe to its service (and nearly impossible to unsubscribe), thus gaining as much market share as possible. Other ISPs concentrate on content or interface quality. AOL focuses on making it effortless to sign up for its service. In the early years, whenever AOL Chairman and CEO Steve Case had the choice between improving customer service or sending out more sign-up disks, he chose the disks. As in magazines and TV, controlling the distribution network is more important than providing the best content. It is better to have many unsatisfied customers than a few happy ones.

Second, AOL markets to technologically unsophisticated consumers. It targets people who would be afraid and confused to switch once they finally got on-line, delivering to them simple, everyday services that fit their lifestyle and are easy to understand. This in itself can be a difficult objective to communicate to the technical crews that set up and maintain ISPs. Too often, technical staffs interpret "better" as "more" or even "more complex."

By meeting these first two objectives, AOL is able to achieve its third objective: to lock in customers. Technologically unsophisticated consumers would put up with almost anything—poor reliability, bad service, higher prices—rather than go through the pain of starting over again. Subscription termination requires users to seek out a telephone number buried several levels deep in the fine print of AOL's menu system, then to endure an extended wait on the telephone while a harried clerk tries to talk them out of terminating their subscription.

Through these strategies, AOL has developed a strong brand name. AOL strives to be a distribution channel to consumers, just as TV and magazines are now, except that the AOL model is highly leveraged. There is no real cost to add another user. Marketing costs have fallen from $6.67 per user per month to $3.31 per user per month in one year with the addition of about four million new users per year. In 1998, traffic was doubling on AOL every 100 days. AOL e-commerce in 2002 is projected at $500 million, with the average AOL user on-line for 50 minutes per day.

From Hobby to Business[8]

In Ogden, North Carolina, Bill Burnett's business venture—the Internet Telescope Exchange (ITE)—brought in $80,000 in revenue in 1997, after its first year in operation. Burnett turned a hobby into a business when he established ITE at the beginning of 1997, selling Russian-made telescopes, binoculars, and night vision equipment on the Internet. ITE is only a sideline to Burnett's main business, Coastal Environmental Services Co., but has experienced growth outpacing his core business.

Burnett's interest in astronomy dated back to when he was 15, growing up in Kenilworth, New Jersey. A major comet piqued his interest, so he ordered lenses from a catalog and put them together with a length of stovepipe to create an 80 mm refractor telescope. "I was totally amazed that it worked," he said. He put aside that hobby when he went off to Rutgers University to study microbiology. That led to a career in evaluating water quality problems and suggesting solutions, punctuated by teaching stints.

Burnett and his wife moved to southeastern North Carolina in 1975, where he worked for an engineering firm as an environmental planner before leaving in 1990 to start Coastal Environmental. The company performs environmental checks on property, helps implement cleanups, and also specializes in inspecting underground oil tanks.

Burnett's long-standing interest in astronomy led him to buy a Russian-made telescope from a Canadian supplier. He was so happy with the quality of the instrument and its relatively modest price that he began purchasing and reselling the telescopes himself. Burnett runs ITE out of the same 1,200-square-foot building that houses Coastal Environmental. Some of the products are shipped to Ogden to be reshipped to ITE's customers, but others are shipped directly from factories. Burnett buys only when he has orders and with no sales floor, there is no need to keep a costly inventory. The site advertises only on the Websites of astronomy magazines.

Burnett's Website was designed by his teenaged son and also offers a free listing of used equipment. That generates traffic and helps his customers sell their used goods as they buy from him. With customers from Japan, Chile, Spain, and Canada, the little building in Ogden has become an international marketplace. Burnett's site gets from 150 to 400 visitors a day and has been doubling revenues annually. Burnett commented that through the global reach of the Internet he is regularly uncovering new clusters of individuals who are interested in amateur astronomy, and who are potential customers.

Information Retailers

Amazon.com

Jeff Bezos, founder of Amazon.com, was a financial analyst unfamiliar with the book business. When he was first scouting around for retail sectors in which to work, he considered music, but decided against it. The book industry had thousands of publishers and millions of titles. The recorded music industry, in contrast, had only about 25,000 titles at any one time (small enough for retail outlets) and was controlled by just a few labels. He was afraid that these companies would stifle any serious on-line competitor (a valid concern, as it turned out).

Amazon touts over 2.5 million titles—yet it keeps only about 400 in stock. Most of the others it orders from the nearby warehouse of Ingram Book, one of America's largest book distributors, whose proximity was the main reason for Amazon's decision to set up in Seattle. One of Amazon's most important services is to provide information about books free of charge in the form of reviews, customer feedback, and discussion. Much of this comes from its customers, who write reviews on books for Amazon. The site is heavily linked, with its own internal search engine to suggest other books by the same author, related titles, and so forth. These services contribute to Amazon.com's customer loyalty. It also keeps its prices low, an advantage of not having to finance store inventories.

Microsoft Expedia

Some of Microsoft's ventures are major businesses by almost anyone else's measure. One such venture, Expedia, covers a lot of territory, from reserving hotel rooms and rental cars to purchasing airline tickets. As with other Microsoft products, the interface is friendly, with bright and bold icons and colors and engaging content. Content includes personalized e-mail messages about low-cost flights to favorite destinations and a digest of news stories that might affect your travel plans. Also included are links to weather sites, a currency converter, an adventure magazine, and forums where users can share travel tips.

Expedia is completely funded by advertising sponsors, through banner-thumbnails (the equivalent of Internet billboards), its yellow pages directory, and the percentage it takes from bookings made on the site. It is free to the consumer and, after only a few months of operation, is generating $3 million per month. Still, on-line sales make up less than 1% of total airline ticket sales, mainly because airlines are prohibited by law from offering on-line bookers, or anyone else for that matter, a price advantage. Sales (and revenue) may expand in the future with promotions such as those offered by Southwest Airlines. Southwest offers bonus frequent-flyer miles for customers who book flights on-line, avoiding the travel agent's commissions. Travel agents, though, may yet have the last word.

Reintermediation[9]: Travel Agents' Revenge

Travel agents are supposed to be major casualties of disintermediation from sites such as Expedia. In addition, airlines have been cutting travel agents' commissions steadily over the past few years. Internet retailing gives airlines the chance to cut out intermediaries altogether. In an interesting challenge to the power of the airlines, Priceline.com was founded by Jay Walker, a former Monopoly world champion and founder, in 1993, of Walker Digital, the "intellectual property laboratory" that owns the U.S. patient on Priceline.com.[10] Priceline.com is based on a simple idea – a buyer-driven e-commerce system that collects buyer demand in the form of conditional purchase offers and presents that demand to sellers. The sellers then decide whether or not to accept the offers, each of which is guaranteed with a credit card. Unlike participants in an auction, Priceline.com buyers do not compete with each other for items; each purchase offer is "shopped" individually by Priceline.com to sellers.

Priceline.com provides an efficient method for filling some of the 500,000 seats that fly empty every day. They can discreetly accept offers for seats at bargain rates without resorting to publicly announced sales Priceline.com makes its money two ways. On airline tickets and hotel rooms, it collects "the spread": the difference between the buyer's offer and the seller's price. For instance, it might find a $245 airline ticket to fill a $250 purchase offer and pocket the $5. On each car or truck deal it arranges, it collects a $25 fee from the buyer and a $75 fee from the seller. Mortgage sales will also involve a flat fee.

Two challenges are presented from the airline's point of view. First, Priceline could lower travelers' perceptions of the value of a ticket, encouraging them to buy only at a discount. Second, the airline seat business could cease to be a traditional supply-and-demand market. Priceline inverts the existing power relationship: The customer is telling the airline what he will pay. It shifts power to the consumer, who knows not just the list price that an airline is offering publicly, but the price it is willing to take rather than see a seat go empty. Priceline provides a demand revelation system that accumulates a schedule of marginal prices that customers are willing to pay.

Some of the airlines' resistance also arises from decades of investment in customer profiles. Accurately predicting consumer behavior with the objective of selling each seat incrementally at the highest possible price at the latest time is the key to airline profitability. But under this system, an average of 30% of seats on an airline go empty, which amounts to around 500,000 seats a year. Each additional sale of a seat at any price is marginal profit.

Jeff Walker plans to expand his business model into other markets, such as automobiles and home mortgages, but only after the model has proven itself in airlines.

Where Multimedia Fails

Virtual Vineyards has found effective solutions to one of the great shortcomings of the multimedia computer interface—the computer monitor's inability to convey taste and smell. Virtual Vineyards helps buyers make olfactory and gustatory choices, such as when to serve red or white wine, or whether to buy California or French Champagne. Food browsers will find such items as smoked salmon, caviar, organic maple syrup, rack of lamb, Belgian chocolates, and mango cilantro chutney. Sensory information is communicated through the computer monitor by providing "tasting charts." The site's tasting charts provide profiles of foods and wines on five to ten different dimensions with detailed explanations of oenological terms such as "oak" and "tannin."

Personalizing the Retail Cyberstore

Despite the potential convenience of shopping at home, many people are discouraged from Internet retail sites by their lack of personal interaction. Vendors are getting better at remedying this shortcoming of Web retailing through a particular type of intelligent agent—usually written as browser-resident Java or ActiveX code—that carries on a limited conversation with shoppers, answering questions and providing product information in real time. Examples of such intelligent agents are sold by @Once Express, Webline Communications, Contact Dynamics Inc., and Face Time.

These products are designed to appear to the customer as an Internet chat room—such as those offered by Mirabilis's ICQ or AOL's Instant Messenger—with the other side of the conversation picked up by an automated WebBot. Potential exists to provide "avatars," for example, personalized images of the intelligent agent, with even greater enhancement of the illusion of personal interaction. These systems can be operated much more cheaply than toll-free telephone numbers, because they work at flat Internet rates and require less employee time.

Initially, Web-retailing benefits were based on the economies of running a global, virtual shop, with low inventory and wide selection. However, with increasing competition, sites are beginning to differentiate themselves from the pack by improving the Internet shopping experience. Two-thirds of shoppers who get as far as putting items in a virtual "shopping cart" abandon the process before checking out.[11] Only one or two abandoned carts in a chain store would start to make management fidgety.

Simple Auctions with Real-Time Price Quotes

ONSALE[12] sells refurbished and out-of-style everything by auction on the Internet. Its test sales show that almost anything can be sold, including unused time-share condominium vacation weeks, foreclosed homes, last-minute cruise ship cabin vacancies, as well as the more common computers and peripherals. ONSALE expects to dominate the auction market for five reasons:

1. First-mover advantage
2. Established brand identity
3. Economies of scale
4. Greater diversity of product
5. Extensive partnership relationships, including Yahoo Computers and AOL Shopping Channel.

Of more interest is the reporting of real-time price quotes for ONSALE auctions in process. Yahoo Computers' Website provides real-time updates on the results of ONSALE auctions, somewhat like stock quotes—for example, "What is the current value for a PalmPilot III?"

ONSALE's buyers tend to be loyal, with 74% being repeat buyers. The company describes its buyers as an "addicted audience who feel they are 'winning' rather than 'buying'," and as "omnivores" who will buy anything we feed them. The average buyer bids 7.4 times and makes 2.7 buys per quarter, according to ONSALE.[13] ONSALE takes title to 45% of the merchandise it resells. With thin margins, it runs a risk of bloated inventory problems if the current buying frenzy ever slows down. ONSALE gives the user two auction formats: English (where the highest bidders win the available inventory at their actual bid price) and Dutch (where the highest bidders win the available inventory at the lowest successful bidder's price). This has been successful in selling items as large as an IBM mainframe (if you must ask, for $12,250, in a transaction conducted entirely over the Internet).

Double-Auction Markets for Securities

Discount brokerages such as Charles Schwab and Accutrade have taken their proprietary networks to the Web, with bright graphics and well-thought-out designs. E*Trade is a relatively new entrant to the brokerage market, having started operations in February 1996 and offering only Web-based trading services to customers. Assets worth $111 billion were managed on-line in 1997 through brokers such as E*Trade, and the volume of business on-line is doubling about once a year.[14] Electronic sites let investors get advice and market information from many sources other than full-service brokers.

Facing thin margins and stiff competition, electronic brokerage sites cut costs on the majority of trades by making markets outside of the exchanges. They may do this through third-party brokerages, such as Bernard Madoff of New York, whose volume in New York Stock Exchange–listed securities is around 10% of the exchange's volume. Or they may make their own markets, thus saving the exchange's commission.

Competition is intense. There are now more than 70 on-line brokerages in the United States, and many more in Europe and other parts of the world. In 1997, Credit Suisse First Boston estimated that the number of Americans investing on-line doubled to 3.3 million, accounting for one-fifth of all retail securities trades—around 26 million trades. Internet trading thrives because it is cheap. E*Trade offers US$19.95 trades (versus around U.S.$60 minimum for discount brokerages). Other firms have dropped the price of a trade as low as US$5 for simple stock transactions.[15]

The payments proffered by stockbrokers to send business to their firms—called "payment for order flow"—have been a primary source of revenue for electronic stock brokerages. However, new rules imposed by the U.S. Securities and Exchange Commission in response to alleged abuses by NASDAQ market makers have lowered the profits that market makers can earn on the bid-ask spread. In 1996, market makers were paying around US$10 per trade; by 1998 that figure had dropped to US$3 per trade.

In response, E*Trade is moving upmarket by providing research and financial services such as bill payments. Research provision pits it against traditional full-service brokerages; bill payment pits it against retail Internet banks such as Security First Network Bank (see chapter 3). Banks, in turn, may enter the fray by offering discount brokerage services to their regular customers. This is likely to pose a much bigger threat to E*Trade and other Internet brokerages. Retail banks have no established brokering business to lose, and are already ahead in offering retail banking services and bill payment.

Infrastructure

Microsoft[16]

Bill Gates, CEO of Microsoft, may not have successfully predicted every major trend in personal computing over the past decade, but he has certainly been adept a profiting from them and maintaining Microsoft's dominant position in a dynamic, complex, and turbulent product market. Our point in including Microsoft in this list is to emphasize the importance of being big in an industry where marginal costs are near zero and marginal revenues are positive. Microsoft is the 800-pound gorilla among the desktop operating system providers. Other gorillas are Intel and Cisco Systems, who, alongside Microsoft, enjoy a "winner take all" scenario characterized by increasing returns as market share increases and long periods of competitive advantage. Also, they use their dominant position to develop related businesses with existing companies.

All of these gorillas use the Internet to buy, sell, distribute, and maintain products and services and are realizing significant cost savings and increased sales opportunities. The benefits can only increase as the network of businesses conducting electronic commerce grows. Cisco, Dell, and General Electric were responsible for about $3 billion in Internet commerce in 1997 and should their current projections prove accurate, these three companies alone will conduct more than $17 billion in Internet commerce by the year 2001 or 2002.

Design Assistance

National Semiconductor has not bent over backwards to produce an attractive Web page: It is strictly business. It does provide an intelligently indexed and organized catalog with a wealth of information on how to use its integrated circuits, why it has chosen specific designs, and where engineers can find applications. When you consider that the major cost of engineering a new product is likely to be search and research, National Semiconductor's wealth of design and product information can demand the loyalty of electrical engineers who recommend purchases to their employers.

Supply Chain Management

Japan Airlines (JAL) has faced several years of forced cost reductions. To stay within its initial target of 6 billion yen a year that the airline spends on in-flight consumables (waste bags, plastic cups, and the like), the airline has turned away from the host of high-price suppliers located in Tokyo and Yokohama, closest to JAL's operation center at Haneda airport, and to the company Website. The airline now hopes to attract the attention of more competitive suppliers elsewhere in the world. The procurements department's Web pages list items—along with full specifications, photographs, and engineering drawings—on which it wants foreign suppliers to bid. The Website even provides on-screen application forms so that would-be suppliers can submit their quotes electronically. Initially 15 of the carrier's most urgently needed items were put up for Internet tender.

Consumer Durables

Auto-By-Tel

Auto-By-Tel has sold automobiles over the Internet to more than 1 million customers through 2,700 U.S. auto dealers. Customers can visit the site to research model and price information, specify where they are located in the United States via a postal ZIP code, and then arrange to pay for and pick up the car at the closest dealer. The dealer contacts the customer in 24 hours or less with a price quote that the customer can take or leave. Financing is available at competitive rates, and the terms and details are delivered with the price quote. The dealer prepares financing and licensing paperwork prior to the customer's arriving at the dealership. Approximate time in the dealers is less than one hour. Dealers are able to quote a single price with the understanding that information-empowered buyers already know the vehicle they want to buy and what they want to pay for it through the research resources available on Auto-By-Tel's Website, as well as traditional consumer information magazines, like *Consumer Reports*.

Auto-By-Tel also offers used cars available at its 2,700 associated dealers. Vehicle listings are accompanied by a digital photo of the vehicle, and the report from a stringent 135-point certification quality check. Auto-By-Tel offers used car customers a 72-hour money-back guarantee, and a 3 month/3,000 mile warranty. Customers report prices up to 10% lower than their best face-to-face haggling efforts could achieve, without having to visit a dealership until payment and pickup. It costs a dealer only about $25 to respond to an Auto-By-Tel lead, instead of hundreds of dollars to advertise and sell a car through a dealer visit and negotiation.

Manheim Auctions

Manheim Auctions is a division of Cox Enterprises Inc., which provides a proprietary auction network for trading in used automobiles. The auction itself is limited to dealers, so Manheim does not save customers from showroom haggling as does Auto-By-Tel. But Manheim does bring the Web to the used automobile supply chain, the network of automakers, banks, leasing companies, rental companies, and users of fleet vehicles that buy and sell millions of vehicles annually. Like Amazon.com, Manheim claims a huge inventory (U.S.$ 20 billion in value) that is less a physical goods inventory than simply a list of available vehicles. Manheim handles the difficult job of quality assurance and administrative and title work, which is where much of the value added by its service is generated. The site has expanded to include live video and is funded by dealer subscription.

The Font of Future Wealth

Each of these cases demonstrates an aspect of the rich, expanding, and chaotic mélange of innovations that have been fostered by the growth of e-commerce and the Internet. E-commerce can take, and has taken, a variety of routes to realize success. Commercial success, though, increasingly requires an understanding of the unique character of global networks and information technology.

Successful companies recognize that the realm of competition has shifted. Late-20th-century commerce has been marked by a move from the economics of physical scarcity to an economics based on information content and processing. The emergence of information and services as primary generators of wealth in the developed world suggests that traditional concepts of wealth, rooted in the trade of tangible goods, are unlikely to apply in the new world order.

The growth of global electronic commerce has spawned new models of firm economic activity. Innovations continue, offering an opulent but treacherous blend of business challenges and opportunities. Global electronic commerce is not just creating new avenues to become wealthy, but redefining what wealth means in the first place. Stock markets regularly value firms that produce no tangible product at all—for example, Microsoft, Yahoo, and Excite—at multiples of the value of larger firms making tangible products. For example, Microsoft's 22,000 employees run a firm that is valued at around four times the value of General Motors, a firm with 647,000 employees.[17] Microsoft's wealth is measured in information and expertise, not in concrete, glass, and steel. The shift to information-based wealth is a qualitative change. The world is still sorting out how to measure and manage this change.

Jeff Bezos of Amazon.com observed that "there are quantitative changes so profound that they become qualitative." Evolution can occur so quickly that it represents, in effect, a revolution. Information technology, by increasing the speed and efficiency of commercial activity in retailing, supply and distribution channels, and other parts of business, has brought about a widespread qualitative restructuring of global industry. It has revolutionized our fundamental perspective on wealth, on value, and on expertise.

The technologies of electronic commerce contribute value in many innovative and subtle ways to the world's economies. This contribution is uneven. Automation has bequeathed more to purely informational industries such as banking and information services than to raw materials such as oil and steel. It has shifted the old balance of power in directions that, only a decade ago, we had no idea existed. The potential exists to create new societies of winners (and losers) in the revolution toward global, information-based economies. The spoils of revolution will go to those who can understand and use the information technologies of electronic commerce.

Notes

1. R. Barrett, "Porn Pays Big Time Online," *Inter@ctive Week Online*, October 29, 1997. http://www.zdnet.com/intweek/

2. Forrester Research, in Survey of Electronic Commerce, *Economist*, May 10, 1997.

3. "An Adult Affair," *Economist,* January 4, 1997.

4. M. Seminerio, Porn sites remain hot in the workplace, ZDNet, October 31, 1997, http://www.zdnet.co.uk/news/news1/ns-3100.html

5. Ibid.

6. Cybersex: an adult affair, Economist, January 4, 1997, p. 53–55.

7. J. Berst, "The AOL Lesson: How to Get Ahead by Mistreating Customers," ZDNet, June 8, 1998 (http://www.zdnet.com).

8. J. Cantwell, *The Morning Star* (Wilmington, North Carolina), March 30, 1998, Business section, p. 1.

9. Reported in Kevin Jones, "You've Got a Ticket to Ride," *Inter@ctive Week Online*, June 1, 1998. http://www.zdnet.com/intweek/

10. D. Noonan, The priceline.com is Right, at http://www.thestandard.com.

11. Forrester Research, in Survey of Electronic Commerce, *Economist*, May 10, 1997.

12. Hambrecht & Quist Investment Conference, April 27, 1998. http://www.etrade.com

13. Hambrecht & Quist Investment Conference, April 27, 1998, http://www.etrade.com

14. Forrester Research, in Survey of Electronic Commerce, *Economist*, May 10, 1997.

15. "The Lap-top Trader," *Economist*, October 17, 1998, p. 66.

16. T. Kippola, G. Moore, and P. Johnson, " 'Gorillas' Trump Kings and Princes," presented at the Third Annual Informed Investors Silicon Valley Technology Forum, April 27, 1998; excerpted from "The Gorilla Game: An Investor's Guide to Picking Winners in High Technology" (http://www.gorillagame.com).

17. This is a conservative estimate based on Microsoft's proxy statement of November 14, 1997, stating that there were 1,212,567,717 shares of shares of common stock outstanding on September 12, 1997, at which time market valuation was about $140 per share. General Motors' 1997 10-K filing lists 678,564,579 shares of common stock outstanding on February 28, 1998, which the market valued at about $60 per share.

Appendix: Internet Timeline[1]

A brief history of the Internet is provided to help readers understand how electronic commerce capabilities have evolved over the past 30–35 years and the speed at which capabilities have evolved over the past 5–10 years.

1961
Packet-switching theory described in Leonard Kleinrock, MIT: "Information Flow in Large Communication Nets," *RLE Quarterly Progress Report*, July 1961.

1966
ARPANET (original name for the Internet) plan presented in Larry Roberts and T. Merrill, MIT: "Towards a Cooperative Network of Time-Shared Computers," Fall AFIPS Conf., Oct. 1966.

1968
Packet-switching network proposed to the Advanced Research Projects Agency (ARPA).

1969
ARPANET commissioned by U.S. Department of Defense for research into networking:

Node 1:   University of California at Los Angeles

Node 2:   Stanford Research Institute

Node 3:   University of California at Santa Barbara

Node 4:   University of Utah

First node-to-node message sent between UCLA and SRI (October).
University of Michigan, Michigan State and Wayne State University establish X.25-based Merit network for students, faculty, alumni (:sw1:).

1970
ARPANET hosts start using Network Control Protocol (NCP).

1971
ARPANET expands to 15 nodes (23 hosts): UCLA, SRI, UCSB, University of Utah, BBN, MIT, RAND, SDC, Harvard, Lincoln Lab, Stanford, UIU(C), CWRU, CMU, NASA/Ames.
Ray Tomlinson of BBN invents e-mail program to send messages across a distributed network. The original program was derived from two others: an intramachine e-mail program (SNDMSG) and an experimental file transfer program (CPYNET).

1972

Ray Tomlinson (BBN) writes basic e-mail message send and read software (March). Larry Roberts writes first e-mail utility to list, selectively read, file, forward, and respond to messages (July).
Telnet specification for remote terminal access.

1973

First international connections to the ARPANET: University College of London (England) and Royal Radar Establishment (Norway).
Bob Metcalfe's Harvard Ph.D. dissertation outlines idea for Ethernet.
File Transfer Protocol specification for use of Internet to transfer data.

1974

Vint Cerf and Bob Kahn publish "A Protocol for Packet Network Intercommunication," which specifies in detail the design of a Transmission Control Protocol (TCP).
V. G. Cerf and R. E. Kahn, "A protocol for packet network interconnection," *IEEE Trans. Comm. Tech.*, vol. COM-22, V 5, p. 627–641, May 1974.
BBN opens Telenet, the first public packet data service (a commercial version of ARPANET).

1979

USENET established using UUCP between Duke and UNC by Tom Truscott, Jim Ellis, and Steve Bellovin. All original groups were under net.* hierarchy.

1981

BITNET, the "Because It's Time NETwork"

• Started as a cooperative network at the City University of New York, with the first connection to Yale.

• Provides electronic mail and listserv servers to distribute information, as well as file transfers.

Minitel, the only profitable videotex service, is deployed across France by France Telecom.

1982

DCA and ARPA establish the Transmission Control Protocol (TCP) and Internet Protocol (IP), as the protocol suite, commonly known as TCP/IP, for ARPANET, which generates the first definition of an "internet" as a connected set of networks, specifically those using TCP/IP, and "Internet" as connected TCP/IP internets.

1983

ARPANET split into ARPANET and MILNET; the latter becomes integrated with the Defense Data Network created the previous year.

Desktop workstations come into being, many with Berkeley UNIX, which includes IP networking software.

1984

Domain Name System (DNS) introduced.

Number of hosts breaks 1,000.

1985

Symbolics.com is assigned on 15 March to become the first registered domain. Other firsts: cmu.edu, purdue.edu, rice.edu, ucla.edu (April); css.gov (June); mitre.org, .uk.

1986

NSFNET created (backbone speed of 56 kbps) and establishes five supercomputing centers to provide high-computing power for all (JVNC@Princeton, PSC@Pittsburgh, SDSC@UCSD, NCSA@UIUC, Theory Center@Cornell).

USENET name change; moderated newsgroups changed in 1987.

1987

NSF signs a cooperative agreement to manage the NSFNET backbone with University of Michigan spin-off Merit Network, Inc.

Number of hosts breaks 10,000.

1988

2 November—Internet worm burrows through the Net, affecting around 6,000 of the 60,000 hosts on the Internet.

CERT (Computer Emergency Response Team) formed by ARPA in response to the needs exhibited during the Morris worm incident. The worm is the only advisory issued this year.

NSFNET backbone upgraded to T1 (1.544 Mbps).

Internet Relay Chat (IRC) developed by Jarkko Oikarinen.

1989

Number of hosts breaks 100,000.

First relays between a commercial electronic mail carrier and the Internet: MCI Mail through the Corporation for the National Research Initiative (CNRI), and Compuserve through Ohio State University.

1990

ARPANET ceases to exist, leaving the Internet.

Archie released by Peter Deutsch, Alan Emtage, and Bill Heelan at McGill.
world.std.com becomes the first commercial provider of Internet dial-up access.

1991

Wide Area Information Servers (WAISs), invented by Brewster Kahle, released by Thinking Machines Corporation.
Gopher released by Paul Lindner and Mark P. McCahill from the University of Minnesota.
World-Wide Web (WWW) released by CERN; Tim Berners-Lee, developer.
PGP (Pretty Good Privacy) released by Philip Zimmerman.
NSFNET backbone upgraded to T3 (44.736 Mbps).
NSFNET traffic passes 1 trillion bytes/month and 10 billion packets/month.

1992

Internet Society (ISOC) is chartered.
Number of hosts breaks 1,000,000.
First MBONE audio multicast (March) and video multicast (November).
Veronica, a gopherspace search tool, is released by University of Nevada.
The term "surfing the Internet" is coined by Jean Armour Polly.

1993

InterNIC created by NSF to provide specific Internet services:

- directory and database services (AT&T)
- registration services (Network Solutions Inc.)
- information services (General Atomics/CERFnet)

U.S. White House comes on-line (http://www.whitehouse.gov/):

- President Bill Clinton: president@whitehouse.gov
- Vice-President Al Gore: vice-president@whitehouse.gov

Internet Talk Radio begins broadcasting.
Businesses and media really take notice of the Internet.
Mosaic takes the Internet by storm; WWW proliferates at a 341,634% annual growth rate of service traffic. Gopher's growth is 997%.

1994

Communities begin to be wired up directly to the Internet (Lexington and Cambridge, MA).
U.S. Senate and House provide information servers.

Shopping malls arrive on the Internet.

Vladimir Levin of St. Petersburg, Russia, is the first publicly known Internet bank robber, stealing millions of dollars from Citibank between June and August.

Arizona law firm of Canter & Siegel "spams" (the colloquial term for bulk e-mailing of junk e-mail) the Internet with e-mail advertising green card lottery services; Net citizens flame back.

NSFNET traffic passes 10 trillion bytes/month.

WWW edges out Telnet to become second most popular service on the Net (behind ftp-data) based on percent of packets and bytes traffic distribution on NSFNET.

Radio stations start rockin' (rebroadcasting) round the clock on the Net: WXYC at University of North Carolina, WJHK at University of Kansas-Lawrence, KUGS at Western Washington University.

1995

The new NSFNET is born as NSF establishes the very high speed Backbone Network Service (vBNS) linking supercomputing centers: NCAR, NCSA, SDSC, CTC, PSC.

Hong Kong police disconnect all but one of the colony's Internet providers in search of a hacker; 10,000 people are left without Net access.

Radio HK, the first commercial 24-hour, Internet-only radio station, starts broadcasting.

WWW surpasses ftp-data in March as the service with greatest traffic on NSFNet based on packet count, and in April based on byte count.

Traditional on-line dial-up systems (Compuserve, America Online, Prodigy) begin to provide Internet access.

A number of Net-related companies go public, with Netscape leading the pack with the third-largest-ever NASDAQ IPO share value (9 August).

Security First Network Bank, the first cyberbank, opens up for business (see *SFNB* case study in chapter 2).

Registration of domain names, up until now subsidized by NSF, is no longer free. Beginning 14 September, a $50 annual fee is imposed. NSF continues to pay for .edu registration, and on an interim basis for .gov.

The first official Internet wiretap was successful in helping the Secret Service and Drug Enforcement Agency (DEA) apprehend three individuals illegally manufacturing and selling cell phone cloning equipment and electronic devices.

1996

Internet phones catch the attention of U.S. telecommunication companies, who ask Congress to ban the technology (which has been around for years).

Various U.S. government sites are hacked into and their content changed, including those of the CIA, Department of Justice, and Air Force.

The Internet Ad Hoc Committee announces plans to add seven new generic Top Level Domains (gTLD): .firm, .store, .web, .arts, .rec, .info, .nom. The IAHC plan also calls for a competing group of domain registrars worldwide.

A malicious cancelbot is released on USENET, wiping out more than 25,000 messages. The WWW browser war, fought primarily between Netscape and Microsoft, rushes in a new age in software development, whereby new releases are made quarterly with the help of Internet users eager to test upcoming (beta) versions. Restrictions on Internet use around the world (*Source:* Human Rights Watch):

- *China:* requires users and ISPs to register with the police.

- *Germany:* cuts off access to some newsgroups carried on Compuserve.

- *Saudi Arabia:* confines Internet access to universities and hospitals.

- *Singapore:* requires political and religious content providers to register with the state.

- *New Zealand:* classifies computer disks as "publications" that can be censored and seized

1997

The American Registry for Internet Numbers (ARIN) is established to handle administration and registration of IP numbers for the geographical areas currently handled by Network Solutions (InterNIC), starting March 1998.

U.S. Justice Department sues Microsoft for restraint of trade over issue of bundling browser with Windows 95 version released in 1997 and in planned Windows 98 software releases in future.

1998

Electronic postal stamps become a reality, with the U.S. Postal Service allowing stamps to be purchased and downloaded for printing from the Web.

America Online projects first profitable quarter in its history.

Internet growth rate globally begins to slow from its prior rate of 10% growth per month, suggesting that the technology and adoption of the standard by consumers worldwide may finally be heading toward maturity after four years of rapid and un-interrupted growth.

Note

1. *Source*: Hobbes' Internet Timeline (©1998 Robert H. Zakon), *http://www.isoc.org/zakon/Internet/history/HIT.html*

References

Abernathy, F. H., J. T. Dunlop, J. H. Hammond, and D. Weil. (1995). The information-integrated channel: A study of the US apparel industry in transition. *Brookings Papers on Economic Activity: Micro Economics*. Martin Neil Baily, Peter C. Reiss, and Clifford Winston, eds. Washington, DC: Brookings.

Bakos, J. (1991). Information links and electronic marketplaces: The role of interorganizational information systems in vertical markets. *Journal of Management Information Systems*, 8(2): p. 31–52.

Barrett, S., and B. Konsynski. (1982). Inter-organization information sharing systems. *Management Information Systems Quarterly*, Fall, p. 93–105.

Beniger, J. R. (1990). *The control revolution*. Cambridge: Harvard University Press.

Berst, J. The AOL lesson: How to get ahead by mistreating customers. ZDNet: June 8, 1998 (http://www.zdnet.com).

Boorstin, D. J. (1991). *The discoverers*. New York: H. N. Abrams.

Cards reveal prospects for strong growth in next decade. (1996). *Banking World Hong Kong*, June, p. 3.

Cash, J. I., and B. R. Konsynski (1985). IS redraws competitive boundaries. *Harvard Business Review*, March–April, p. 35.

Clark, D. (1996). Nearly every horse in race for home banking solutions. *American Banker*, p. 161–164.

Clark, T. H. (1997). *Security First Network Bank: The world's first Internet bank*. Case Study no. 9-39605, Hong Kong University of Science and Technology, Hong Kong.

Clark, T. H. (1996). *Global Electronics Manufacturing (HK) Ltd*. Case Study no. 9-39603, Hong Kong University of Science and Technology, Hong Kong.

Clark, T. H. (1994). Linking the grocery channel: Technological innovation, organizational transformation, and channel performance. Ph.D. diss. Harvard Business School, Boston, MA.

Clark, T. H., D. C. Croson, J. L. McKenney, and R. L. Nolan. (1994). *H. E. Butt Grocery Company: A Leader in ECR Implementation*. Case no. 9-195-125, Harvard Business School, Boston, MA.

Clark, T. H., and J. H. Hammond. (1997). Reengineering channel reordering processes to improve total supply-chain performance. *Journal of Production and Operations Management*, Fall.

Clark, T. H., and H. G. Lee. (1997). EDI-enabled channel transformation: Extending business process redesign beyond the firm. *International Journal of Electronic Commerce*, Fall: p. 7–21.

Clark, T. H., and P. Lovelock. (1996). *Andersen Consulting: The Asia Intranet opportunity*. Case study no. 9-39604, Hong Kong University of Science and Technology, Hong Kong.

Clark, T. H., and J. L. McKenney, (1995). *Procter & Gamble: Improving consumer value through process design*. Case no. 9-195-126, Harvard Business School, Boston, MA.

Clark, T. H., and J. L. McKenney. (1990). Consolidated Freightways: The On-Board Computer Project. Case no. 9-191-069, Harvard Business School, Boston, MA.

Clark, T. H., and D. B. Stoddard. (1996). Interorganizational business process redesign: Merging technological and process innovation. *Journal of Management Information Systems*, Fall: p. 9–28.

Clark, T. H., and John J. Sviokla. (1996). *China Internet corporation*. Case no. 9-396299, Harvard Business School, Boston, MA.

Clemons, E. K., D. C. Croson, and B. W. Weber. (1996–97) Reengineering money: The Mondex stored value card and beyond. Proceedings of 29th Annual Hawaii International Conference on System Sciences Vol. IV, p. 254–261.

Clemons, E. K., S. P. Reddi, and M. Row. (1993). The impact of information technology on the organization of economic activities: The "move to the middle" hypothesis. *Journal of Management Information Systems* 10(2): p. 9–35.

Clemons, E. K., and M. C. Row. (1992). Information power, and control of the distribution channel: Preliminary results of a field study in the consumer packaged goods industry. *Proceedings of the Thirteenth International Conference on Information Systems*, Dec. 13–16, 1992, p. 21–30.

Concise Columbia Encyclopedia. (1991). New York: Columbia University Press.

Conklin, J. E. (1989). *Criminology*. New York: Macmillan.

Cooke, S. (1995). Carry on swindling. *Euromoney*, 319 (November): p. 24.

David, Paul. (1990). The dynamo and the computer: An historical perspective on the modern productivity paradox. *American Economic Review*, 80(2): p. 355–361.

de Sola Pool, Ithiel. (1983). Technologies of freedom. Cambridge, MA: Belknap.

de Sola Pool, Ithiel. (1983). Forecasting the telephone: a retrospective technology assessment, Ablex: Norwood, NJ.

Direct Marketing Association (http://www.the-dma.org), New York, NY.

DoubleClick (http://www.doubleclick.com), New York, NY.

Downes, J., and J. E. Goodman. (1991). *Dictionary of finance and investment terms*. New York: Barrons.

Eccles, R. G. and R. L. Nolan. (1993). A framework for the design of the emerging global organizational structure. In Bradley, S., Hausman, J., and Nolan, R. eds., *Globalization, Technology, and Competition*, ed. Boston: Harvard Business School Press, p. 57–80.

Feeney, F. (1986). Robbers as decision-makers. In D. B. Cornish and R. V. Clarke (eds.), *The reasoning criminal: Rational choice perspectives and offending*. New York: Springer-Verlag, p. 53–71.

Forrester Research (http://www.forrester.com).

Fulk, J., and G. DeSanctis. (1995). Electronic communication and changing organizational forms. *Organization Science*, 6(4): p. 337–349.

Gilmour, P. (1991). *Operations management in Australia*. Melbourne: Longman Cheshire.

Glaser, D. (1974). The classification of offenses and offenders. In D. Glaser (ed.), *Handbook of criminology*, p. 45–85. Chicago: Rand McNally.

Gurbaxani, V., and S. Whang. (1991). The impacts of information systems on organizations and markets. *Communications of the ACM*, 34(1): p. 59–73.

Gwennap, Linley. (1996). Birth of a chip. *BYTE*, December, p. 163–187.

Hammond, J. H. (1993). Quick response in retail/manufacturing channels. In Bradley, S., Hausman, J., and Nolan, R. (eds.), *Globalization, Technology, and Competition*. Boston: Harvard Business School Press, p. 185–214.

Hammond, J. H. (1991). Coordination as the basis for quick response: A case for "Virtual" integration in supply networks. Working paper, Harvard Business School, Boston, MA.

Harowitz, S. L. (1994). Building security into cyberspace. *Security Management*, 38(6): p. 50–58.

Harris L. H. (1991). *Liquidity, fairness, and trading rules*. New York: New York University Monograph.

Hildreth, S. S. (1988). *The A to Z of Wall Street*. New York: Longman.

Hogan, K. (1994). The human hack. *Forbes* (ASAP Supplement, August 29), p. 128.

I/PRO (http://www.ipro.com), San Francisco, CA.

Interactive Media Services (http://www.netmedia.com), Palo Alto, CA.

Itami, H. (1987). *Mobilizing invisible assets*. Cambridge: Harvard University Press.

Ives, B., and M. Earl. (1997). *Mondex International: Reengineering money*. Case study no. CRIM CS97/2, London Business School.

Jackson, K. M., J. Hruska, and D. B. Parker (eds.). (1992). *Computer security reference book*. Boca Raton. FL: CRC.

Jupiter Communications, LLC (http://www.jup.com), New York, NY.

Keen, P. G. W. (1992). Get a handle on IT. *Modern Office Technology*, 37(6): p. 14–18.

Keen, P. G. W. (1986). *Competing in time*. Cambridge, MA: Ballinger Company.

Kluepfel, H. M. (1995). A recipe for hacker heartburn. *Security Management*, 39(1): p. 40–44.

Knoke, W. K. (1996). *Bold new world.* New York: Kodansha.

Kochen, Manfred (ed.). (1989). *The small world.* Norwood, NJ: Ablex Publishing.

Kokuryo, J. (1992). *The impact of the retailing industry's EDI-based quick response systems on vendor logistics operations.* Ph.D. diss., Harvard Business School, Boston, MA.

Kotler, P. (1986). Prosumers: A new type of consumer. *Futurist* 20(5): p. 24–28.

Kurt Salmon Associates. (1993). *Efficient consumer response: Enhancing consumer value in the grocery industry.* Washington, DC: Food Marketing Institute.

Lee, H. G. (1996). Electronic brokerage and electronic auction: The impact of IT on market structures. *Proceedings of 29th Hawaii International Conference on System Science,* Maui, Hawaii, January, p. 397–406.

Lee, H. G., and T. H. Clark. (1997). Market process reengineering through electronic market systems: Opportunities and challenges. *Journal of Management Information Systems,* 13(3): p. 113–136.

Lee, H. G., and T. H. Clark. (1996). Impacts of electronic marketplace on transactions cost and market structure. *International Journal of Electronic Commerce,* Fall, p. 127–149.

Lehn, K., and R. Kamphuis (eds.). (1993). *Modernizing US securities regulation.* Homewood, IL: Irwin.

Lovelock, P., and Clark, T. H. (1997). *Financial Times Syndication Services: Making money on the Web.* Case study no. 9-39711, Hong Kong University of Science and Technology, Hong Kong.

Lucas, H. C. Jr., and J. Baroudi. (1994). The Role of information technology in organization design. *Journal of Management Information Systems,* 10(4): p. 9–23.

Malone, T., J. Yates, and R. Benjamin. (1987). Electronic markets and electronic hierarchies. *Communications of the ACM,* 30(6): p. 484–497.

Malone, T. W., and J. F. Rockart. (1993). How will information technology reshape organizations? Computers as coordination technology. In Bradley, S., Hausman, J., and Nolan, R. eds., *Globalization, Technology, and Competition,* Boston: Harvard Business School Press.

Mansell, Robin. (1994). Strategic issues in telecommunications: Unbundling the information infrastructure. *Telecommunications Policy,* 18(8): p. 588–600.

Meeker, M. (1997). *The internet advertising report.* New York: Harper Business, HarperCollins Publishers.

Meeker, Mary, and Sharon Pearson. (1997). Morgan Stanley U.S. Investment Research: Internet Retail. Morgan Stanley, May 28, p. 2-2, 2-6.

Menkus, B. (1991). "Hackers": Know the adversary. *Computers & Security,* 10(5): p. 405–409.

Metcalfe, B. (1996). "Godless far left" takes correct stand on 1996 Decency Act. *InfoWorld,* 18(16): p. 60.

Mondex Magazine, September 1996. Mondex (http://www.mondex.com).

Moore, Gordon. The continuing silicon technology evolution inside the PC platform. Intel archives (http://developer.intel.com/solutions/archive/issue2/feature.htm).

Meeker, M., C. DePuy, and S. McCuen, (eds.). (1996). *The Internet Report.* Morgan Stanley Technology Research Report, New York, NY.

Muller, E. J. (1994). Faster, faster, I need it now! *Distribution,* 93(2): p. 30–36.

Neumann, P. G. (1994). Risks of passwords. *Communications of the ACM,* 37(4): p. 126.

Noam, Eli, and Ithiel de Sola Pool. (1990). *Technologies without boundaries: On telecommunications in a global age.* Cambridge: Harvard University Press.

Ongetta, S. (1995). Hackers: An enemy to know better. *Computer Fraud & Security Bulletin* (May): p. 8–9.

Parker, D. B., B. N. Baker, and S. Swope. (1990). *Ethical conflicts in information and computer science, technology, and business.* Wellesley, MA: QED Information.

Phlips, L. (1988). *The economics of imperfect information.* Cambridge: Cambridge University Press.

Pickering, J. M., and J. L. King. (1995). "Hardwiring weak ties: Interorganizational computer-mediated communication, occupational communities, and organizational change." *Organization Science,* 6(4): p. 479–486.

Productivity: Lost in cyberspace. (1997). *Economist*, September 13, p. 80.

Rayport, J. F., and J. J. Sviokla. (1995). *Exploiting the virtual value chain*. Boston: Harvard Business Review.

Rayport, J. F., and J. J . Sviokla. (1994). *Managing in the marketspace*. Boston: Harvard Business Review.

Riggins, F. J., C. H. Kriebel, and T. Mukhopadhyay. (1994). The growth of interorganizational systems in the presence of network externalities. *Management Science*, 40(8): p. 984–998.

Riggins, F. J., and T. Mukhopadhyay. (1994). Interdependent benefits from interorganizational systems: Opportunities for business partner reengineering. *Journal of Management Information Systems*, 11(2): p. 37–57.

Rockart, J. F. and J. E. Short. (1991). The networked organization and the management of interdependence. In Michael S. Scott Morton (ed.), *The corporation of the 1990s*. New York: Oxford University Press, p. 189–219.

Roush, W. (1995). Hackers: Taking a byte out of computer crime. *Technology Review*, 98(3): p. 32–40.

Scott Morton, M. S. (1992). The effects of information technology on management and organizations. In Kochan and Useem (eds.), *Transforming Organizations*. New York: Oxford University Press, p. 132–151.

Senge, P. M., and J. D. Sterman. (1992). Systems thinking and organizational learning: Acting locally and thinking globally in the organization of the future. In Kochan and Useem (eds.), *Transforming Organizations*. New York: Oxford University Press, p. 35–49.

Short, J. E., and N. Venkatraman. (1991). Beyond business process redesign: Refining Baxter's business network. *Sloan Management Review*, Fall, p. 7–21.

Sobel, R. (1975). N.Y.S.E.: *A history of the New York Stock Exchange*. New York: Weybright and Talley.

Stern, L. W., A. I. El-Ansary, and J. R. Brown. (1989). *Management in marketing channels*. Englewood Cliffs, NJ: Prentice-Hall.

Teweles, R. J., E. S. Bradley, and T. M. Teweles. (1992). *The stock market*. New York: Wiley.

Toffler, Alvin. (1990). *Powershift: Knowledge, wealth, and violence at the edge of the 21st century*. New York: Bantam Books.

Tushman, M., and G. Nadler. (1978). Information processing as an integrative concept in organizational design. *Academy of Management Review*, 1: p. 613–624.

U.S. Government Census Bureau (http://www.census.gov), Washington, DC.

Venkatraman, N. (1994). IT-enabled business transformation from automation to business scope redefinition. *Sloan Management Review*, Winter, p. 73–88.

Violino, B. (1993). Hackers for hire. *Information Week* 430 (21 June): p. 48–9, 52, 54, 56.

Weinhaus, Carol L., and Anthony G. Oettinger. (1988). *Behind the telephone debates*. Norwood, NJ: Ablex Publishing Corporation.

Weiss, K. (1991). The Outs and Ins of Computer Access Control, Computing Canada, v17n23, Nov. 7, p. 42.

Westland, J. Christopher. (1998). Customer and merchant acceptance of electronic cash: Evidence from Mondex in Hong Kong. *International Journal of Electronic Commerce* 2(4): p. 5–26.

Westland, J. Christopher. (1998). Some conditions for cost efficiency in hypermedia. *Information Processing and Management:* 32(4). p. 309–323.

Westland, J. Christopher. (1998). The Moscow Stock Exchange and the Shanghai Stock Exchange: Electronic markets for voucher driven and state managed privatization of state owned enterprises. In Banerjee, Hackney, Dhillon, and Jain (eds.), *Business information technology management: Closing the international divide*. Delhi: Haranand, p. 357–394.

Westland, J. Christopher. (1998). Topic specific market concentration in the information services industry: Evidence from the DIALOG group of databases. *Information society* 6: p. 127–138.

Westland, J. Christopher. (1996). A rational choice model of computer network security. *Journal of Electronic Commerce*: p. 109–126.

Westland, J. Christopher. (1994). Bayesian alternatives to neural computing. IEEE *Transactions on Systems, Man and Cybernetics*, January 1995 25(1): p. 59–67.

Westland, J. Christopher. (1993). Cinema theory, video games, and multimedia production. In Reisman (ed.), *Multimedia computing: Preparing for the 21st century*. Middletown, PA: Idea Group Publishing. p. 433–457.

Westland, J. Christopher. (1993). Reporting strategies for "events" accounting. *Journal of Information Systems*, Spring 1992, 6(1): p. 32–46.

Westland, J. Christopher. (1992). Collaboration and productivity in information systems research. *The Information Society* 7(1): p. 33–50.

Westland, J. Christopher. (1992). Congestion and network externalities in the short run pricing of information systems services. *Management Science*, 38(6): p. 992–1099.

Westland, J. Christopher. (1992). Economic incentives for database normalization. *Information Processing and Management*, 28(5): p. 647–662.

Westland, J. Christopher. (1992). The marginal analysis of investments in information technology. In Mahmood, M., Banker, R., and Kauffman, R. (eds.), *Strategic and economic impacts of information technology investment: Perspectives on organizational growth and competitive advantage*, p. 55–81. Middletown, PA: Idea Group Publishing.

Westland, J. Christopher. (1991). Scaling up output volumes predicted by information systems prototypes. *Association for Computing Machinery/TODS*, 15(3): p. 341–358.

Westland, J. Christopher. (1990). Economic constraints in hypertext. *Journal of the American Society for Information Science*, 42(3): p. 178–184.

Westland, J. Christopher. (1989). A net benefits approach to measuring retrieval performance. *Information Processing and Management*, 25(5): p. 579–581.

Westland, J. Christopher, with Grace Au. (1997). A comparison of shopping experiences in three competing digital retailing interfaces. *International Journal of Electronic Commerce*: 2(2). p. 57–69.

Westland, J. Christopher, with M. Kwok, J. Shu, T. Kwok, and H. Ho. (1997). Electronic cash in Hong Kong. *Electronic Markets*, 7(2): p. 3.

Westland, J. Christopher, with S. M. So. (1997). Automation of China's securities markets. *Electronic Markets*, 7(2): p. 3.

Williamson, O. E. (1985). *The economic institution of capitalism: Firms, markets, relational contracting*. New York: Free Press.

Williamson, O. E. (1983). *Markets and hieerarchies*. New York: Free Press.

Wilson, J. Q., and R. J. Herrnstein. (1985). *Crime and human nature*. New York: Simon and Schuster.

Zipf, G. K. (1949). *Human behavior and the principle of least effort*. New York: Hafner, 1965.

Index

ADSL. *See* Asymmetric Digital Subscriber Line
AHSC. *See* American Hospital Supply Corporation
AMEX. *See* American Stock Exchange
AOL. *See* America Online
ARPANET. *See* Advanced Research Projects Agency Network
ATM. *See* Automatic teller machine
AT&T, 238, 274, 285–290, 490, 498, 561, 578
AUCNET, 346, 462
Abernathy, F. H., 581
Accutrade, 382, 568
ActiveX, 566
Adobe, 557
Advanced Research Projects Agency Network (ARPANET), 234, 287, 575–577
AltaVista, 449, 451
Amazon.com, 3, 4, 557, 564, 565
America Online (AOL), 278, 279, 288, 300, 368, 372, 380, 449, 451, 453, 562, 572, 580, 599
American Hospital Supply Corporation (AHSC), 21
American Stock Exchange (AMEX), 395
Andersen Consulting, 27–30, 32, 39, 43–50, 581
Andreessen, M., 232, 275
Anet, 28, 33, 34, 50
Aquinas, St. Thomas, 449
Aristotle, 25, 350, 467, 490
Asia Online, 278–298, 322, 338
Asymmetric Digital Subscriber Line (ADSL), 225–227, 231
Auctions, 1, 4, 6, 9, 343–349, 353–365, 387–391, 402, 420, 433, 435, 448, 462, 559, 565–583
Auto-by-Tel, 10, 570, 749
Automatic Teller Machine (ATM), 94–97, 246, 412, 494, 499, 510
Automation, 1, 3, 5–7, 23, 29, 42, 54, 66, 367, 392–394, 405, 407, 409, 415, 422, 525, 532, 541, 547, 550, 560, 572, 584, 585

BITNET. *See* Because It's Time NETwork
BPR. *See* Business Process Reengineering
Baily, N., 581
Baker, B. M., 583
Bakos, J., 581
Bandwidth, 6, 11, 31, 50, 71, 222–228, 231, 233, 259, 304, 318, 327, 341, 355, 385, 454, 460
Barnes & Noble, 9
Baroudi, J., 583
Barrett, S., 581
Bauer, E., 4
Because It's Time NETwork (BITNET), 576
Beer Game, 146, 150, 151, 155
Bellcore, 227, 536
Bell Laboratories, 27

Beniger, R. J., 69, 581
Benjamin, R., 365, 583
Berners Lee, T., 232
Berst, J., 572, 581
Bezos, J., 3, 62, 557, 564, 572
Blair, D., 450
Bolsa de Comercio de Santiago, 347, 396, 430–438, 443
Boorstin, D. J., 490, 581
Bradley, E. S., 69, 582–584
Breaking Bulk, 18, 19
Brown, J. R., 584
Business Process Reengineering (BPR), 2, 28, 48, 141, 152, 205, 254–256, 352, 509, 581–584

CAO. *See* Computer-Assisted Ordering
CDC. *See* Consumer Direct Cooperative
CD-ROM, 224
CERNET, 242, 249, 251, 253, 304
CIC. *See* China Internet Corporation
CM. *See* Category Management
CRP. *See* Continuous Replenishment
CSMA/CD. *See* Collision Sense Multiple Access with Collision Detection
CSRC. *See* China Securities Regulatory Commission, 401, 409
Calahan, E. A., 385
Cash, 3, 17, 59, 88, 91, 100, 116, 141, 238, 246, 264, 286, 292, 368, 399, 402, 408, 412, 425, 427, 461, 465, 469, 470, 474, 477, 486, 488, 493–513, 545, 558, 584
Cash, J. I., 581
Category Management (CM), 157, 170–173, 179, 188, 192–195, 216–218
Channel automation, 5, 54
Channel intermediaries, 6, 16–19, 21, 350, 459
Chile, 347, 429–432, 439, 564
China Internet Corporation (CIC), 279, 299–314, 581
China Securities Regulatory Commission (CSRC), 401, 409
China's Golden Projects, 235, 239–249, 252–257, 304, 305
ChinaNet, 249, 250–252, 304, 305
Cisco Systems Inc., 462
Clark, D., 581
Clark, T. H., 27, 71, 91, 121, 157, 190, 193, 197, 235, 281, 299, 315, 537, 581, 583
Clemons, E. K., 356, 364, 365, 490, 495, 509, 581
Collision Sense Multiple Access with Collision Detection (CSMA/CD), 230
Compaq, 10, 13, 257
CompuServe, 249, 278, 300, 329, 368, 372, 380, 451, 561, 579
Computer-Assisted Ordering (CAO), 165, 177, 188

Conklin, J. E., 582
Consolidated Freightways, 531, 535, 537, 538, 540, 581
Consumer Direct Cooperative (CDC), 534
Continuous Replenishment (CRP), 157, 167–170, 174–190, 194, 202–206, 214–220, 279
Cooke, S., 315, 582
Copernic, 452
Croson, D.C., 157, 365, 490, 495, 501, 509, 581
Cryptosystems, 484–486
Cyberbanks, 95, 579
Cyberspace, 25, 54, 59, 71, 79, 82, 297, 488, 582, 584
Cygnus Support, 472, 557

DEC, 273
DNS. *See* Domain name system
DOT. *See* Designated Order Turnaround
DSD. *See* Direct Store Delivery
David, Paul, 582
DePuy, C., 463, 583
DeSanctis, G., 582
De Sola Pool, Ithiel, 53, 57, 69, 582, 583
Dell Computers, 9
Dell, Michael, 459
Designated Order Turnaround (DOT), 386, 392
Digital money, 473
Digital Payments, 7, 465–491, 495–527
Digital Railroads, 12
Digital Storefronts, 6, 7, 445–463, 560
Digital transmission, 224–226
Direct-Mail, 14, 62, 164, 457, 462
Direct Store Delivery (DSD), 159, 162, 167, 170, 173, 190, 191
Disintermediation, 22, 565
Domain name system (DNS), 82, 577
Downes, J., 582
Dunlop, J. T., 581
Dutch Auctions, 364, 365
Dutch Flower Industry, 355, 356, 365

ECR. *See* Efficient Consumer Response
EDI. *See* Electronic Data Interchange
ENIAC. *See* Electronic Numerical Integrator and Computer
Earl, M., 509, 582
eBay, 4
Eccles, R. G., 582
Edison, Thomas, 6, 10, 385
Efficient Consumer Response (ECR), 141, 157, 160, 167, 187–191, 194, 195, 198, 216, 218, 581
El-Ansary, A. I., 584
Electronic Auctions, 6, 344–348, 351–355, 363–365, 583

Electronic Banks, 15, 92, 95, 246
Electronic Cash (e-cash), 17, 265, 286, 402, 412, 465, 470–474, 477, 486, 493–509, 559, 584
Electronic Data Interchange (EDI), 6, 21, 59, 60, 70, 136, 175–180, 182–185, 194, 202–206, 245, 274, 279, 286, 351, 359, 394, 426, 535, 559, 581
Electronic Financial Markets, 6
Electronic Mail (e-mail), 1, 3, 62, 64, 80, 137, 162, 178, 249, 274–276, 291, 301–303, 307, 315, 323, 325, 334, 370, 451, 461, 487, 565, 575–579
Electronic Numerical Integrator and Computer (ENIAC), 11
Electronic payments, 15, 473, 474, 496, 497
Encryption, 232, 479, 480, 484–487, 490, 536
English Auctions, 345
Enhanced fax, 274
Ethernet, 230, 347, 396, 429, 443, 576
E*Trade Securities, Inc., 367–383, 405, 568, 569
Expedia, 564, 565

FMI. *See* Food Marketing Institute
FT. *See* Financial Times
FTP. *See* File Transfer Protocol
Feeney, F., 582
Fidelity Investments, 371
File Transfer Protocol (FTP), 82, 86, 87, 137, 276, 325, 487, 558
Financial Times (FT), 60, 71–89
Financing, 17, 387, 570
Firewalls, 278, 489
Food Marketing Institute (FMI), 160
Forbes, 70, 369, 582
Forrester Research, 8, 25, 284, 373, 460, 572, 582
Fortune, 2, 281, 460, 531, 559
Fraud, 248, 413, 415, 475, 478, 495, 500, 526, 583
Frequency Spectrum, 222
Fulk, J., 582
Fungibles, 257

GDP. *See* Gross Domestic Product
GISs. *See* Geographical Information Systems
Gates, Bill, 352, 569
General Motors, 53, 274, 474, 533, 572, 573
Geographical Information Systems (GISs), 535
Gilmour, P., 530, 582
Glaser, D., 582
Global Electronics Manufacturing (GEM), 61, 121–125, 127–139
Globex, 347
Gold Exchange, 385
Golden Projects, 239, 241–246, 248, 252, 255–257, 304, 305
Goodman, J. E., 582
Gopher, 232, 276, 325, 578

Gross Domestic Product (GDP), 5, 7, 9, 11–13, 54, 66–68, 260, 399, 400, 415, 418, 529, 531
Groupware, 38, 274
Grove, Andy, 1
Gurbaxani, V., 582
Gwennap, L., 582

HARNET. *See* Hongkong Academic and Research NETwork
HEB. *See* H. E. Butt
HEPL. *See* High Energy Physics Lab
HKIGS. *See* Hong Kong Internet and Gateway Services
HKUST. *See* Hong Kong University of Science and Technology
HTML. *See* Hypertext Markup Language
HTTP. *See* Hypertext Transfer Protocol
Hammer, Michael, 353
Hammond, J. H., 581, 582
Harowitz, S. L., 582
Harris, L. H., 582
Hayes-compatible, 225
H. E. Butt (HEB), 161–194
Hierarchy, 17, 33, 53, 65, 170, 180, 256, 312, 355, 365, 488, 557, 576, 583
High Energy Physics Lab (HEPL), 304
Hildreth, S. S., 582
Hitachi, 557
Hogan, K., 582
Hongkong Academic and Research NETwork (HARNET), 287
Hong Kong Internet and Gateway Services (HKIGS), 315, 318, 323, 338
Hong Kong SuperNet, 287, 315, 317–329, 333, 337, 339
Hongkong Telecom, 281, 287, 294, 296, 297, 305, 320, 321, 327–329, 338
Hong Kong University of Science and Technology (HKUST), 315, 317, 318, 320, 321, 324, 336, 338, 339
Hruska, J., 582
Hypertext Markup Language (HTML), 233, 561
Hypertext Transfer Protocol (HTTP), 79, 233, 579, 581, 583

IAHC. *See* Internet ad hoc committee
IBM Corporation, 25, 63, 219
IEEE. *See* Institute of Electrical and Electronics Engineers
ILTnet, 451
IOSs. *See* Interorganizational systems
ISDN. *See* Integrated Services Digital Network
ISPs. *See* Internet Service Providers
IT. *See* Information Technology

ITE. *See* Internet Telescope Exchange
Industrial Revolution, 14, 64, 468
Information Technology (IT), 9–13, 41, 42, 45, 66, 69, 88, 138, 144–146, 151–153, 155, 222, 230, 237, 246, 253, 255, 256, 281, 282, 289, 355, 356, 361–364, 490, 532, 582, 583
Ingram Book, 564
Institute of Electrical and Electronics Engineers (IEEE), 52, 70, 365, 576, 585
Integrated Services Digital Network (ISDN), 224–227, 285
Intel, 1, 10, 11, 13, 64, 258, 336, 393, 437, 441, 583, 569
InterNIC. *See* Network Solutions
Internet ad hoc committee (IAHC), 580
Internet Service Providers (ISPs), 278, 282, 284, 288, 291, 295, 301, 315–318, 321, 325, 327, 329, 338, 560
Internet Telescope Exchange (ITE), 563, 564
Internet timeline, 275, 580
Interorganizational systems (IOSs), 144, 146, 152–154
Interorganizational applications, 144, 152, 177, 181, 205, 581–584
Intranet, 27, 28, 32, 38, 40, 41, 43, 46, 47, 49, 50, 52, 88, 155, 277, 278, 283, 460, 581
Intuit, 4, 19, 20, 23, 24, 28, 94, 96, 98, 119, 525
Inventory, 1, 4, 10, 15, 42, 45, 59, 130–139, 145–152, 159, 165–169, 174–176, 179, 182, 185–195, 200–204, 217, 352, 360, 387, 390, 462, 499, 529–533, 540, 564–568, 571
IriScan, 478
Ives, B., 582, 509

JAL. *See* Japan Airlines
JIT. *See* Just-in-time
Jackson, K. M., 582
Jango, 452
Japan Airlines (JAL), 570
Java, 566
Just-in-time (JIT), 141, 540, 541

KPMG. *See* Kynveld Peat Marwick Goerdeler
Kamphuis, R., 583
Keen, P. G. W., 582
Key certificates, 486–488
King, J. L., 583
Kluepfel, H. M., 582
Knoke, W. K., 70, 583
Knowledge Exchange, 29, 33, 38–40
Kochen, Manfred, 5, 53, 583
Kokuryo, J., 462, 583
Konsynski, B., 462, 581
Kotler, P., 583

Kriebel, C. H., 584
Kynveld Peat Marwick Goerdeler (KPMG), 532

LANs. *See* Local Area Networks
Latency, 301, 346, 348
Lee, H. G., 462, 581, 583
Lehn, K., 583
Local Area Networks (LANs), 28–44, 253, 335, 442
Logistics, 1, 7, 9, 47, 55, 122, 143, 166–169, 175, 180–187, 190–192, 202, 214, 219, 356, 358–364, 529–535, 538, 583
Lotus, 32, 33, 37, 44, 277
Lovelock, P., 27, 71, 235, 581, 583
Lucas, H. C., 583
Lycos, 451

MC. *See* Multinational Corporation
MDAIS. *See* McDonnell Douglas Aerospace Information Services
MEI. *See* Ministry of Electronic Industries
MIPS. *See* Million Instructions Per Second
Madoff, B. L., 384
Malone, T. W., 69, 355, 365, 583
Manheim Auctions, 571
Mansell, R., 583
Market Information, 15, 17, 253, 352, 399, 409, 414, 438–441, 568
Marketspace, 54, 55, 60, 61, 69, 529, 535
Maron, Bill, 450, 463
Marshall Field, 23, 351, 445
McAfee, John, 558
McCuen, S., 583
McDonnell Douglas Aerospace Information Services (MDAIS), 273, 515–520, 522, 525
McKenney, J. L., 157, 197, 537
Meeker, M., 583
Menkus, B., 583
Mentis Corp., 14
Metcalfe, B., 576, 583
Microsoft, 4, 34, 64, 94, 96, 119, 277–279, 289, 393, 452, 473, 564, 569, 572, 573, 580
Milgram, Stanley, 53, 69
Million Instructions Per Second (MIPS), 64
Ministry of Electronic Industries (MEI), 238, 239, 240, 246, 304, 305
Minitel, 1, 576
Modems, 44, 78, 98, 223–230, 285, 308, 309, 318, 327–329, 350, 362, 368, 380, 383, 405, 437–439
Mondex, 473, 477, 490, 493–513, 581–584
Moore, Gordon, 221, 573, 583
Mosaic, 232, 275, 578
Moscow Stock Exchange, 396, 417, 422–426, 584
Mukhopadhyay, T., 155, 584

Muller, E. J., 583
Multinational Corporation (MC), 31, 257, 269, 283, 304

NASDAQ. *See* National Association of Securities Dealers Automated Quotation
NAUFOR. *See* National Association of Securities Market Participants
NIPC. *See* National Infrastructure Protection Center
NSCC. *See* National Securities Clearing Corporation
NSF. *See* National Science Foundation
NYSE. *See* New York Stock Exchange
Nabisco, 60, 70
Nadler, G., 584
National Association of Securities Dealers Automated Quotation (NASDAQ), 367, 389–396, 422, 437, 568, 579
National Association of Securities Market Participants (NAUFOR), 423, 424
National Infrastructure Protection Center (NIPC), 481
National Science Foundation (NSF), 316, 577–579
National Securities Clearing Corporation (NSCC), 395
Negotiation, 7, 15–17, 21, 54, 55, 123, 128, 132, 161, 179–183, 199, 200, 217, 255, 313, 339, 341, 386, 393, 423, 444, 466, 532, 538, 540, 571
Netgrocer, 534
Netscape, 232, 275, 277, 289, 579, 580
Network Solutions (InterNIC), 578, 580
Neumann, P. G., 583
New York Stock Exchange (NYSE), 367, 368, 381, 385, 386, 388–397, 443, 584
Noam, E., 583
Nolan R. L., 157, 581–583

OFTA. *See* Office of Telecommunications Authority
ONSALE, 347, 567, 568
OSB. *See* Ordering, Shipping, and Billing System
OTC. *See* Over-the-counter
Octopus, 473, 499, 507, 508
Office of Telecommunications Authority (OFTA), 295, 327, 328
Ongetta, S., 583
Ordering, Shipping, and Billing System (OSB), 205–208, 210
Oettinger, A. G., 56, 584
Over-the-counter (OTC), 368, 369, 381, 393–395, 403
Ownership, 15, 99, 100, 127–131, 235, 240, 295, 389, 395, 401, 414, 418–421, 426, 474, 524, 558

PC Connection, 19
PC Warehouse, 19
P&G. *See* Procter & Gamble Worldwide
PNETS. *See* Public Non-exclusive
    Telecommunication Service
POS. *See* Point-of-sale
PRC. *See* People's Republic of China
PT&T. *See* Philippines Telephone and Telegraph
Packet Switching, 9, 11, 226, 232, 267, 275, 302
PalmPilot, 567
Parker, D. B., 491, 582, 583
Parsons Technology, 533, 534
Passwords, 80, 82, 84, 408, 411, 440, 477–480, 484,
    487–491, 495, 507, 516, 521, 560, 562, 583
Pearson, S., 583
Pearson Group, 75, 86
People's Republic of China (PRC), 46, 237, 400
Persian Kitty, 560, 561
Petrazzini, B., 235
PG Music, 560
Philippines Telephone and Telegraph (PT&T),
    259–261, 269–271
Phlips, L., 583
Pickering, J. M., 583
Point-of-sale (POS), 141–145, 162–165, 183, 184,
    188–192, 474
Porter, Michael, 145, 155
Post-Industrial Revolution, 5, 9, 10
Priceline.com, 4, 565, 573
Procter & Gamble Worldwide (P&G), 145, 174,
    175, 197–207, 214–220, 279
Public Non-exclusive Telecommunication Service
    (PNETS), 305, 327, 328

QR. *See* Quick Response
Quick Response (QR), 141

RMB. *See* Renminbi
Rayport, J. F., 54, 69, 584
Reengineering. *See* Business Process Reengineering
Renminbi (RMB), 401, 403, 405–407, 409, 410
Remapping, 5, 12, 55, 56
Reuters, 305, 347, 406, 437, 440, 441
Riggins, F. J., 584
Risk Bearing, 15, 17
Rockart, J. F., 69, 583, 584
Roush, W., 584
Row, M. C., 173, 581

SCM. *See* Supply Chain Management
SFNB. *See* Security First Network Bank
SIAC. *See* Securities Industry Automation
    Corporation
SKU. *See* Stock Keeping Unit

SOE. *See* State-owned Enterprise
SQL, 278
SSE. *See* Shanghai Stock Exchange
SSL. *See* Secure Socket Layer
SSRC. *See* Sino Service Research Center
STAQ. *See* Securities Trading Automatic
    Quotation System
Schematic, 7, 136, 245, 287, 290, 294, 320, 321, 327,
    440, 472–478, 495, 520–524, 527, 562
Schwab, Charles, 4, 367, 371–374, 382, 386, 568
Scott Morton, M. S., 584
Sealed-bid, 345
Search Engines, 4, 63, 82, 276, 283, 353, 448–453,
    458–461, 479, 564
Sears, Roebuck & Co., 445, 446
Secure Socket Layer (SSL), 489
Security First Network Bank (SFNB), 60, 61, 91–
    94, 97–102, 108–110, 113, 116–120
Securities Industry Automation Corporation
    (SIAC), 395
Securities Trading Automatic Quotation System
    (STAQ), 403, 404, 406
Segmentation, 91, 116, 120–123, 144, 159, 195, 201,
    283–288, 368–378, 382, 447, 455, 475, 509, 532,
    561
Semiconductor, 129, 569, 570
Senge, P. M., 69, 584
Shanghai Stock Exchange (SSE), 399, 404
Shopper.com, 4
Short, J. E., 584
Sino Service Research Center (SSRC), 317, 318,
    320
Small world phenomenon, 5, 53
Smith, Adam, 350, 468
Sobel, R., 397, 584
Space-time, 5, 55, 171
State-owned Enterprise (SOE), 255, 301, 400–402,
    404, 419
Sterman, J. D., 69, 584
Stern, L. W., 584
Stock Keeping Unit (SKU), 166, 167, 176, 203,
    204, 217
Stoddard, D. B., 581
Sun Microsystems, 422, 557
SuperDOT, 392
SuperNet, 285, 287, 290, 291, 315–339, 341
Supply Chain Management (SCM), 141, 145
Supply channels, 15, 55
Sviokla, J. J., 69, 91, 235, 299, 581, 584
Swope, S., 583

T-Bonds (Treasury Bonds), 395, 400–403
TCP/IP. *See* Transmission Control Protocol and
    Internet Protocol

TPN. *See* Trading Process Network
Telecom. *See* Telecommunications
Telecommuting, 229, 518
Telecommunications (Telecom), 6, 13, 21, 27, 31,
    40–58, 221–223, 231–270, 282, 288, 287, 294–
    308, 311, 318–321, 327–329, 335, 338–418, 447,
    479, 502, 507, 522, 579, 576, 583
Telnet, 325, 521, 576, 579
Tesla, N., 10
Teweles, R. J., 584
Teweles, T. M., 584
Timeline. *See* Internet Timeline, 275, 580
Touchstone, 467, 468
Trading Process Network (TPN), 558, 559
Transaction processing, 4, 44, 48, 64, 274, 276, 278,
    300, 396, 438–444, 452, 517
Transmission Control Protocol and Internet
    Protocol (TCP/IP), 231, 278, 490, 576
Travel Agents, 22, 23, 350, 351, 565
TurboTax, 19, 20, 23, 24
Turnkey, 341, 381, 558
Tushman, M., 584

UCLA. *See* University of California at Los Angeles
UCSB. *See* University of California at Santa
    Barbara
U.K. Data Protection Act (1884), 479
UNIX, 277, 577
URLs. *See* Unified Resource Locators
U.S. Communications Decency Act, 479
U.S. Federal Data Encryption Standard (DES),
    485
U.S. Telecommunications Act (1986), 479
USENET, 232, 325, 451, 577, 580
Unbundling, 284, 583
Unencrypted, 484
Unified Resource Locators (URLs), 233
University of California at Los Angeles (UCLA),
    234, 575
University of California at Santa Barbara (UCSB),
    234, 575

VANs. *See* Value Added Networks
Value Added Networks (VANs), 274, 535, 536
Value Chains, 145
Venkatraman, N., 584
Verisign, 488, 489
Vickery, 345
Violino, B., 584
Virtual Vault, 98, 117
Virtual Vineyards, 566

WAIS. *See* Wide Area Information Server
WWW. *See* World Wide Web

Wal-Mart, 4, 17, 21, 145, 157–163, 174, 187, 191,
    201, 446
Wall Street Journal, 73, 93, 305, 369, 379, 382, 391,
    397, 426, 582
Web-based e-commerce, 14, 63, 66, 450, 461
WebBots (Web Robots), 450, 452
Weber, B. W., reference, 365, 490, 495, 501, 509
Web Hosting, 283–286, 297
WebTurbo, 461
Weil, D., 581
Weinhaus, C. L., 56, 584
Weiss, K., 584
Westinghouse, George, 10
Westland, J. C., 70, 491, 493, 509, 516, 584, 585
Whang, S., 582
Wide Area Information Server (WAIS), 276
Williamson, O. E., 585
Wilson, J. Q., 585
World brain, 5, 53
World Wide Web (WWW), 3, 6, 16, 20, 24, 58, 81,
    88, 97, 113, 232, 278, 283–286, 300–304, 311,
    332, 380, 449, 459, 479, 486, 540, 578–580

Xiaoping, Deng, 237, 399
Xinhua, 301–303, 305, 308, 312–314

Yahoo, 449–453, 561, 567, 572
Yates, J., 365, 583

ZDNet, 491, 572, 581
Zipf, G. K., 585